Marinated Beef Tenderloin, page 241, on plate with Fall Vegetables, page 260; Sugar Snap Peas With Bell Peppers, page 255; Pecan Praline Cheesecake, page 269; Cranberry Jezebel Sauce, page 250

Meet the
Southern Living®
Foods Staff

E ach day dozens of dishes go through our Test Kitchens, where they are evaluated on taste, appearance, practicality, and ease of preparation. On these pages, we invite you to match the names and faces of the people who test, photograph, and write about our favorites (left to right unless otherwise noted).

SANDRA J. THOMAS, *Administrative Assistant;*
SUSAN DOSIER, *Executive Editor;*
PAM LOLLEY, *Editorial Assistant*

(sitting) SCOTT JONES, ANDRIA SCOTT HURST, *Foods Editors;*
(standing) SHIRLEY HARRINGTON, *Associate Foods Editor;*
DONNA FLORIO, *Senior Writer*

Assistant Foods Editors: (sitting) KATE NICHOLSON,
SHANNON SLITER SATTERWHITE, KIM SUNÉE;
(standing) JOY E. ZACHARIA, CYNTHIA ANN BRISCOE, VICKI POELLNITZ

LYDA H. JONES, *Test Kitchens Director;*
REBECCA KRACKE GORDON, ANGELA SELLERS, VIE WARSHAW, JAMES SCHEND, *Test Kitchens Staff;*
MARY ALLEN PERRY, *Recipe Development Director;* LAURA MARTIN, VANESSA A. MCNEIL, *Test Kitchens Staff*

Photographers and Photostylists:
BUFFY HARGETT, BETH DREILING,
MARY MARGARET CHAMBLISS, CARI SOUTH

Photographers and Photostylist:
(sitting) CHARLES WALTON IV; (standing) WILLIAM DICKEY,
CINDY MANNING BARR, RALPH ANDERSON

3

Chocolate Velvet "Pound" Cake with ice cream and Chocolate Ganache, pages 286–287

Southern Living®

2003 ANNUAL RECIPES

Oxmoor House®

ISBN: 0-8487-2744-4
ISSN: 0272-2003

Printed in the United States of America
First printing 2003

To order additional publications, call 1-800-765-6400.

Congratulations!

As a buyer of *Southern Living 2003 Annual
Recipes,* you have exclusive access to the
Southern Living® Web site on America Online.
Simply go to **www.southernliving.com.**
   When prompted, log on with this Web site
access code: **SLAR5498**
   Effective until December 31, 2004

Southern Living®
Executive Editor: Susan Dosier
Senior Writer: Donna Florio
Foods Editors: Andria Scott Hurst, Scott Jones
Associate Foods Editor: Shirley Harrington
Assistant Foods Editors: Cynthia Ann Briscoe, Kate Nicholson,
   Vicki Poellnitz, Shannon Sliter Satterwhite, Kim Sunée,
   Joy E. Zacharia
Test Kitchens Director: Lyda H. Jones
Recipe Development Director: Mary Allen Perry
Test Kitchens Staff: Rebecca Kracke Gordon, Laura Martin,
   Vanessa A. McNeil, James Schend, Angela Sellers,
   Vie Warshaw
Administrative Assistant: Sandra Thomas
Photography and Color Quality Director: Kenner Patton
Copy Chief: Dawn Cannon
Senior Foods Photographer: Charles Walton IV
Photographers: Tina Cornett, William Dickey, Beth Dreiling
Senior Photo Stylists: Cindy Manning Barr, Buffy Hargett
Photo Stylist: Rose Nguyen
Assistant Photo Stylists: Lisa Powell, Cari South
Photo Librarian: Tracy Duncan
Photo Assistant: Catherine Carr
Production Manager: Katie Terrell Morrow
Production Coordinator: Jamie Barnhart
Production Assistant: Allison Brooke Wilson

Oxmoor House, Inc.
Editor-in-Chief: Nancy Fitzpatrick Wyatt
Executive Editor: Susan Carlisle Payne
Art Director: Cynthia R. Cooper
Copy Chief: Allison Long Lowery

Southern Living® *2003 Annual Recipes*
Editors: Susan Hernandez Ray, Catherine Ritter Scholl
Copy Editor: Donna Baldone
Editorial Assistants: Megan Graves Kassebaum, Terri Laschober
Director of Production: Phillip Lee
Books Production Managers: Theresa L. Beste, Larry Hunter
Production Assistant: Faye Porter Bonner

Contributors
Designer: Carol O. Loria
Indexer: Mary Ann Laurens
Editorial Consultant: Jean Wickstrom Liles

Cover: Chocolate Velvet Cake with Cream Cheese-Butter Pecan
Frosting, page 288

Contents

Our Year at
Southern Living®

Dear Friends,

What an exciting year for our staff! We awarded our second $100,000 grand prize at *Southern Living* Cook-Off 2003. To learn about this year's winners, check out the special section on page 321 and then enjoy the full coverage of the cook-off in the January 2004 issue of the magazine. The entries just keep getting better, and we love hearing from you. We've just decided to add a new category next year: "Healthy and Good for You." (For complete rules and entry forms, visit **www.southernlivingcookoff.com** or call 1-866-587-3353.) Just think, YOU could be receiving that check for $100,000 next year. Start testing those winners now!

One of the most enjoyable experiences of this year was taking a look back. This volume of *Southern Living® Annual Recipes* marks the 25th year of capturing the great recipes of the magazine in a book format. Not surprisingly, the idea for *Annual Recipes* came from you, our readers. You told us you didn't want to cut up your magazines, and you were the ones who suggested the solution. Once more, our readers hold the key to our success, and we thank you.

"One of the most enjoyable experiences of this year was taking a look back."

As a special token of recognition in this year's book, we asked current and past members of our staff who had worked here at least 12 years to submit their favorite recipes from the last 25 years in several categories. Then, we set about the arduous (right!) task of taste testing these recipes to see if they had, indeed, stood the test of time. I can't wait for you to revisit these favorites in your own home. The recipes begin on page 310, and they're just as good now as the first time they appeared in the magazines. Now, I'll caution you . . . our staff still has a sweet tooth. And I'll match our cake recipes against anyone, anywhere.

It was good for me to see the evolution in our thoughts about quick and easy recipes as we sampled our favorite recipes from the last 25 years. Our taste standards are as high today as they ever were—and we seem to subject quick and easy recipes to special scrutiny. These recipes must taste just as good as those made from scratch—even though we may use shortcuts or convenience products. Now, as in the past, taste is the final test for every recipe in our kitchens.

With that, I wish you more time in your kitchen and the good fortune of family and friends with which to enjoy it. May your kitchen be a place of joy!

Warmly,

Susan Dosier

Executive Editor

Best Recipes of 2003

Members of our Foods staff gather almost every day to taste-test recipes and rate them based on taste, overall appeal, ease of preparation, and even cost. Here we share this year's highest rated recipes.

Ham-and-Greens Pot Pie With Cornbread Crust and Pimiento-Cheese Corn Sticks (page 20) Frozen vegetables are the speedy secret to this pot pie. The corn sticks add a delicious touch to this Southern specialty.

Honey-Pecan Dressing (page 28) Drizzle a fruit salad with this heavenly combination of honey and pecans.

Sally Lunn Bread (page 27) Use this slightly sweet bread for a tomato sandwich, French toast, or as the base for croutons.

Make-Ahead Pork Dumplings (page 64) This Asian dish makes a bunch and is so versatile that you can make them ahead and freeze them.

Chicken-Fried Steak (page 72) Your family will love every crispy bite of our version of this Texas specialty. We rated it among our Top 5 "Ultimate Southern Recipes" in 25 years (page 311).

Apple-Raisin Relish (page 83) Savor this sweet-tart relish over pound cake or alongside slices of salty ham.

Lemon Icebox Pie Filling (page 104) Fresh lemon juice and grated lemon rind mingle to make a zesty filling for icebox cake. Variations for lime and orange filling give you tangy options for a citrusy treat.

Lime Icebox Pie Cake (page 104) Choose any of the three colorful and citrusy fillings mentioned above to create an old-fashioned cake topped with Whipped Cream Frosting (page 105).

Orange Chiffon Cake With Orange Icebox Pie Filling (page 105) Scrumptious Orange Buttercream Frosting (page 105) tops this citrusy layered cake. Prepare the option baked in 13- x 9-inch pans to feed a crowd.

Shrimp Burgers (page 110) A South Carolina twist on the crab cake is a great way to enjoy a distinct regional favorite.

Skillet Cornbread (page 112) Crumble this tender cornbread into buttermilk and eat it with a spoon for a taste of the South.

Hot-Water Cornbread (page 112) This old-fashioned cornbread, pan-fried in small rounds, has a crisp and buttery crust with a tender inside. It was selected as one of our Top 5 "Family Favorites" in 25 years (page 313).

Molasses-Coffee Glazed Ham (page 119) The sweet flavors of jam and molasses combine with coffee, Dijon mustard, and cider vinegar for a simply divine finish for ham.

Molasses-Coffee Glazed Turkey Breast (page 119) Make this crowd-pleasing turkey, a variation on the ham recipe mentioned above, the centerpiece of a celebration buffet.

Classic Mint Julep (page 129) Using fresh mint leaves and stirring up each serving to order are the keys to this cool Kentucky beverage.

Peach-Rosemary Jam (page 134) This sparkling gold-colored spread is so divine that everyone will think you've been jellying all day instead of the 45 minutes that it actually takes.

Best Pinto Beans (page 159) Take advantage of summer's plentiful harvest and use fresh pinto beans to make this family favorite seasoned with ham hock and spicy tomatoes.

Smoky Barbecue Brisket (page 160) Weeknight meals have never been so delicious—and easy—with this slow-cooked, melt-in-your-mouth brisket.

Mediterranean Wrap (page 168) Cream cheese, spinach, avocado, feta, and basil create a healthy—and tasty—sandwich roll that's great for picnics.

Lemon Sorbet (page171) Lemons give this icy summer treat a burst of citrusy flavor.

Our Best Southern Fried Chicken (page 178) The secret to this classic dish is in the oil—we added a little bacon drippings to the oil for a tasty crunch. In fact, we found this recipe so delicious that we rated it as one of our Top 5 "Ultimate Southern Recipes" in 25 years (page 310).

Baby Blue Salad (page 178) The Balsamic Vinaigrette and Sweet-and-Spicy Pecans put this salad in a category of its own. We honored it as one of our Top 5 "Family Favorites" in 25 years (page 313).

Blueberry Cheesecake (page 182) You'll never guess that this *Southern Living* classic underwent a nutrition makeover. This lightened version is as rich and creamy as the original.

Traditional Brisket (page 188) Scrumptious Brisket Rub, Brisket Mopping Sauce, and Brisket Red Sauce pack a spicy punch in this slow-smoked Texas specialty.

Jalapeño-Pecan-Mustard Butter (page 205) Creole mustard and jalapeño peppers spice up this fall spread for all sorts of savory breads as well as grilled fish and chicken.

Basil Pesto (page 208) Fresh basil pureed with generous amounts of garlic, Parmesan cheese, pine nuts, and olive oil makes a buttery blend you can serve in a variety of ways. You can even freeze it for use year-round.

Basil-Garlic Butter (page 208) So simple, but so spectacular, this spread tops bread, potatoes, or just about anything absolutely deliciously.

Lemon-Basil Mayonnaise (page 208) You may never settle for plain mayonnaise again after you taste this zesty concoction. Use it as a substitute anywhere you typically use the traditional spread.

Curried Acorn Squash-and-Apple Soup (page 221) You can taste fall in every bite of this soup, which gets its rich flavor and silky texture from acorn squash, apples, baking potatoes, and a host of spices.

The Best Ever Caramel Sauce (page 216) We're sure you'll agree that this sauce created from butter, whipping cream, and brown sugar is about the best you've ever tasted.

Buttery Herb-Cheese Muffins (page 232) Melted butter and garlic-and-herb spreadable cheese enrich the flavor of these delectable little muffins.

Potato-Caramelized Onion Buns (page 234) Sweet onions add a delicious flavor to this potato bread that's perfect for hamburgers or other sandwiches.

Dried Cherry-Walnut Sweet Rolls (page 235) Frozen roll dough is the base for this sweet treat that's sprinkled with dried cherries and walnuts.

Apricot-Orange Sweet Rolls (page 235) Dried apricots and fresh orange juice highlight these delicious little breads that are topped with a powdered sugar drizzle.

Quick Whipping Cream Biscuits (page 238) It takes less than 30 minutes to make these rich, butter-flavored biscuits.

Fig-Walnut Pudding (page 244) The soft challah bread in this pudding just soaks up the flavor of the Rum Sauce made with whipping cream and flavored with orange rind.

Chocolate Bread Pudding With Custard Sauce (page 244) Executive Chef Vagn Nielson shares this decadent dessert crowned with a custard sauce.

Apricot-Cream Cheese Pastries (page 245) These delicious bite-size rugalach will be the star of any party.

Cinnamon Rolls (page 247) These sweet yeast rolls are drizzled with icing and filled with cinnamon flavor.

Spicy-Sweet Smoked Turkey Breast (page 250) Sweet pepper sauce and six hours in the smoker are the secret to this holiday main dish.

Cranberry Jezebel Sauce (page 250) Serve this versatile sauce with the holiday turkey or as an appetizer poured over cream cheese.

After-the-Dance Pralines (page 251) This beloved New Orleans confection boasts just three simple ingredients.

Easy Yeast Rolls (page 256) Foods Editor Andria Scott Hurst shares her mother's delicious roll recipe.

Chocolate Velvet Cake Batter; Chocolate-Mint Cake; Vanilla Buttercream Frosting; Chocolate Ganache; Chocolate Velvet "Pound" Cake; Chocolate Velvet Cake With Vanilla Buttercream Frosting; Chocolate-Bourbon-Pecan Cake; White Chocolate-Almond Cake; Chocolate-Peppermint Candy Cupcakes; Turtle Cake; Chocolate Velvet Cake With Cream Cheese-Butter Pecan Frosting; Chocolate-Praline Pecan Cake; Mississippi Mud Cake; Chocolate-Cream Cheese Coffee Cake (pages 286-288). One easy-to-make and incredibly delicious velvety-rich cake batter is the basis for these moist and scrumptious cakes. This single recipe is paired with our favorite frostings and toppings for some of the best Christmas cakes ever.

For our other favorite recipes, check out our two bonus chapters, Top 25 Recipes in 25 Years, beginning on page 310, and Southern Living® 2003 Cook-Off Winners, *beginning on page 322.*

Taste of the South

We renew our commitment to classic Southern fare in this monthly column that is one of our most-read features. Here are highlights from this year.

Sally Lunn Bread (page 27) Many old Southern cookbooks contain the recipe for this sweet batter bread, but this one rivals them all.

Southwest Fried Oysters (page 45) Few finger foods compare to these fabulous fried oysters, which are soaked in buttermilk and enveloped in a crispy, seasoned crust.

Skillet Pineapple Upside-Down Cake (page 65) Its ease and simple flavors keep this old-fashioned skillet cake a favorite.

Basic Deviled Eggs (page 88) No potluck gathering in the South would be complete without a dozen or two of these yellow and white treasures.

Classic Mint Julep (page 129) The smooth flavor of bourbon is the essence of this Kentucky hallmark.

She-Crab Soup (page 137) This creamy Carolina classic will have you clamoring for more.

Fried Green Tomatoes (page 173) Fry a crusty batch of firm, green tomatoes and serve them hot out of the skillet for a crowd-pleasing favorite.

Frogmore Stew (page 181) Boil up some shrimp, corn, sausage, and potatoes to create this regional, take-your-shoes-off-and-relax kind of dish.

Traditional Brisket (page 188) A Texas favorite, this slow-smoked cut of beef has all the fixings for some great barbecue—a great rub, a juicy mopping sauce, and a tangy sauce on the side.

Southern Turnip Greens and Ham Hocks (page 220) Turnip greens purists will love this version that gets its great flavor from long simmering.

Oysters Rockefeller (page 272) A wealth of bright green herbs provides the true taste to this timeless favorite that originated in New Orleans.

Quick & Easy

We understand the need for simple recipes that taste great because we're all so busy. That's why readers love this column—and so does our staff!

■ It's easy to add something green and nutritious to your supper with these easy-to-make salads and dressings (page 28).

■ These colorful side dishes showcase simple spring veggies (page 66).

■ Noodles go Mexican, Italian, and all-American in these speedy one-dish meals served in a bowl (page 123).

■ Try a few tasty Southern sides that are big on flavor—and convenience (page 135).

■ Looking for some main dishes your family will love? Try these updated ground beef recipes (page 172).

■ A Southern vegetable dinner was never so easy. You can whip up the veggies while the Baked Macaroni and Cheese bubbles in the oven (page 184).

■ Three skillet pork chop recipes help you get a hearty supper on the table in a hurry (page 205).

■ Guests will think you've spent hours cooking this casual creamed chicken dish that's served in little biscuit bowls made from refrigerated biscuit dough (page 222).

■ Create your own pizzas at home faster than you can order take out by using premade pizza crusts and a variety of fresh toppings (page 235).

Living Light

*Each month we focus on different foods and timely concepts
to help you make healthy choices for your family.*

❤ Indulge in your favorite down-home dishes with these light-ened Southern classics (page 24).

❤ Enjoy a creamy spaghetti and meatballs supper with a salad, bread, and dessert to round out the meal (page 34).

❤ These Asian-inspired recipes will fill your kitchen with mouthwatering aromas (page 64).

❤ Flavor-packed jarred sauces make getting a healthy dinner on the table a snap (page 96).

❤ Try these zesty Mexican recipes that are full of spicy, colorful ingredients (page 128).

❤ A busy mom and cookbook author shares her secrets for healthy weeknight meals that your family will love (page 146).

❤ It's easy to get your 5-a-day with these satisfying meat-free dishes (page 174).

❤ Satisfy your burger craving with a Mediterranean variation, and round out the meal with two deliciously cool side dishes (page 183).

❤ Look no further than your supermarket's freezer section for produce that helps you create garden-fresh vegetables any season (page 193).

❤ Enjoy the scrumptious flavor of fried foods without the fat by oven frying (page 212).

❤ Vegetarians and meat lovers alike will enjoy this hearty meal that's perfect anytime you want to impress family or friends (page 236).

❤ Cooking for a crowd has never been so easy as with these scrumptious, make-ahead recipes that call for easy-to-find ingredients (page 290).

Top-Rated Menus

*We like to create new menus using our most memorable recipes from past years.
We retest and update each one in terms of can sizes, cooking trends, and techniques.*

■ Whip up a tasty morning meal and tell your friends to **Come By for Brunch**. Start the day off right with a Brie-and-Sausage Breakfast Casserole, Spiced Apples, and Pecan Crescent Twists. Toast your guests with a Mulled Cranberry Drink (page 36).

■ Extend **A Sweet Invitation** to celebrate the gift of friendship over two of our all-time best desserts that make a great dessert party. A rich buttermilk glaze makes our Best Carrot Sheet Cake a super-moist treat. Fresh Key lime juice is the secret to Key Lime Cheesecake With Strawberry Sauce (page 55).

■ **Down-Home Flavor** is what you get with our tried-and-true diner-style dishes. Crushed saltine crackers form a crispy crust on Chicken-Fried Steak, a true Texas specialty. Mashed potatoes and a lettuce wedge salad complete this comfort meal (page 72).

■ Serve an **Italian Supper Tonight.** The base of our hearty lasagna is purchased pasta sauce and frozen meatballs. A

Roasted Onion Salad topped with Parmesan Crisps makes the perfect accompaniment with this menu that's sure to be popular with family or friends (page 142).

■ Invite friends for a **Harvest Breakfast** that embraces the flavors of fall. Your guests will love the hearty combination of Balsamic Pork Chops With Apples and Cornbread Waffles. Or, if you prefer an egg dish, try our version of an oven-baked omelet. Round out the meal with juice, coffee, and sweet rolls (pages 204-205).

■ **Entertain with Ease** over a jazzed-up chicken and rice menu with Glazed Roasted Chicken and Sweet Onion Risotto. Complete the meal with a slice of tangy Lemon Chess Pie (page 217).

■ **Make a Party Around These Appetizers** that include a tasty Cranberry-Cheese Box, Baby Hot Browns, Pork Tenderloin with Mustard Sauce, and Quick Whipping Cream Biscuits (page 238).

January

New Year's Potluck Southern Style

In Charleston, it's Hoppin' John.
In Dallas, it's chili. Whatever your traditions,
you'll love these regional specialties.

A New Year's Menu From South Carolina

Serves 8

Michelle's Baked Ham   Michelle's Black-Eyed Peas

Esau's Collard Greens   Esau's Hoppin' John

Bob's Squab (see box on facing page for recipe)

Cheese grits   Cornbread

The seeds of this story were planted when several members of our staff began discussing which food they fixed for New Year's Day to bring luck and prosperity in the coming year. Surprisingly, there was not one universal New Year's dish—the choices varied depending on where each of us had grown up.

Friends Cook in South Carolina

On a trip to Charleston, South Carolina, Executive Editor Susan Dosier was still pondering New Year's food when she tasted the fabulous collard greens Esau Graham makes at the Charleston Grill in the Charleston Place Hotel. After raptly listening to Esau explain how he cooks the greens and his other favorite foods, Susan asked him about New Year's Day observances. He told her that his family makes Hoppin' John (a mixture of rice and peas cooked in a flavorful broth) with cornbread and collard greens. However, the Grahams use field peas, also called cow peas, in the Hoppin' John. "I don't know who came up with using black-eyed

peas," Esau said. "Black-eyed peas are not the real McCoy."

Esau's colleague, sous-chef Michelle Weaver, was raised in North Alabama. Her tastes, Susan discovered, played to a different tune. Her family's New Year's meal generally includes a baked ham with black-eyed peas, rice, cheese grits, and collard greens served on the side.

Which recipes were the best? Executive chef and boss Bob Waggoner volunteered his home kitchen to allow each chef to cook selected New Year's Day specialties. Borrowing from his training in France, Bob decided to make a simple yet succulent pan-seared squab. Esau made his signature Hoppin' John, collard greens, and cornbread. Michelle cooked her ham and black-eyed peas. The air in the kitchen crackled with friendly competition and old-fashioned regional pride.

Our Test Kitchens proclaimed each of these recipes a winner. We hope you'll try them and decide which version brings you the best of luck and prosperity.

MICHELLE'S BAKED HAM

chef recipe • family favorite

MAKES 16 SERVINGS

Prep: 5 min., Bake: 3 hrs., Stand: 15 min.

- 1 (10-pound) smoked ham
- 1 (13-ounce) jar orange marmalade
- ¼ cup stone-ground mustard
- 1 tablespoon chopped fresh thyme

WRAP ham in aluminum foil, and place in a lightly greased 13- x 9-inch pan; bake at 300° for 2 hours.
REMOVE ham from oven, and unwrap. Remove skin and excess fat from ham. Score fat on ham in a diamond pattern.
STIR together marmalade and remaining ingredients in a small bowl. Spoon glaze over ham, and bake 1 hour, basting every 15 minutes or until a meat thermometer inserted into the thickest portion registers 140°. Let stand 15 minutes before slicing.

MICHELLE'S BLACK-EYED PEAS

chef recipe

MAKES 6 TO 8 SERVINGS

Prep: 15 min., Stand: 1 hr., Cook: 2 hrs.

Michelle makes her peas separately and serves them on a bed of rice or simply on the side.

- 1 (16-ounce) package dried black-eyed peas
- 3 cups low-sodium chicken broth
- 2 cups water
- 2 (8-ounce) smoked ham hocks
- 1 large onion, chopped
- 1 celery rib, chopped
- 2 medium carrots, diced
- 1 small jalapeño pepper, seeded and diced
- 1 teaspoon salt
- 1 teaspoon pepper

PLACE peas in a Dutch oven; add water to cover 2 inches above peas. Bring to a boil; boil 1 minute. Cover, remove from heat; let stand 1 hour. Drain; set aside.
BRING broth, 2 cups water, and ham hocks to a boil in the Dutch oven over medium-high heat. Cover, reduce heat, and cook 1 hour.

ADD peas, onion, and remaining ingredients; cook, covered, 45 minutes to 1 hour or until peas are tender, stirring occasionally.

ESAU'S COLLARD GREENS

chef recipe

MAKES 10 TO 12 SERVINGS

Prep: 10 min.; Cook: 2 hrs., 20 min.

At the restaurant, Esau takes almost two days to make the stock and cook these greens. He adapted this recipe for busy home cooks. For tips on preparing greens, see "From Our Kitchen" on page 30.

- 1 pound hickory-smoked bacon, finely chopped
- 3 medium-size sweet onions, finely chopped
- 8 garlic cloves, finely chopped
- 4 (32-ounce) containers chicken broth
- 5 pounds fresh collard greens, washed, trimmed, and cut into strips
- 1 pound smoked ham, chopped, or 1 ham bone with meat
- ½ cup red wine vinegar
- 1 tablespoon Old Bay seasoning
- 2 teaspoons celery seeds
- 4 teaspoons sugar
- 1 teaspoon pepper
- ½ teaspoon salt
- Garnish: duck cracklings or pork rinds

COOK bacon in a 9-quart stockpot 10 to 12 minutes or until semicrisp. Add onions, and sauté 5 minutes; add garlic, and sauté 1 minute.

STIR in broth, greens, and next 7 ingredients. Cook, uncovered, over medium heat 2 hours or until greens are tender. Garnish, if desired.

NOTE: Esau occasionally adds beer or dark ale to the recipe near the end of cooking and simmers until the extra liquid is reduced.

ESAU'S HOPPIN' JOHN

chef recipe

MAKES 6 TO 8 SERVINGS

Prep: 35 min.; Stand: 1 hr.; Cook: 3 hrs., 10 min.

Esau stirs in a dark, thick stock right after the rice goes in. Because it takes hours to make that stock, we used chicken broth and still got great results.

- 1 (16-ounce) package dried field peas or black-eyed peas
- 3 garlic cloves, peeled
- 3 bay leaves
- 2 sprigs fresh rosemary
- 2 to 3 sprigs fresh thyme
- 6 ounces fatback*
- 2 (8-ounce) smoked ham hocks
- 1 cup finely chopped medium-size sweet onion
- 2 garlic cloves, minced
- 10 cups water, divided
- 2 cups uncooked short-grain rice
- 3 teaspoons kosher salt, divided
- 1 teaspoon pepper
- Chicken broth

PLACE field peas in a Dutch oven; add water to cover 2 inches above peas. Bring to a boil, and boil 1 minute. Cover, remove from heat, and let stand 1 hour. Drain peas, and set aside.

PLACE peeled garlic cloves and next 3 ingredients in the center of a large coffee filter; bring sides up, and tie with kitchen twine. Set garlic-and-herb bag aside.

SAUTÉ fatback in Dutch oven over medium-low heat 10 minutes or until crisp. Remove fatback, reserving drippings in Dutch oven, and discard.

ADD ham hocks to Dutch oven, and cook 5 minutes or until skin becomes crispy and lean portion of the ham hock is tender. (Use the tines of a fork to test tenderness.)

ADD onion and minced garlic; sauté 2 minutes. Add 6 cups water. Bring to a boil, reduce heat to medium, and cook, uncovered, 1½ hours.

BRING remaining 4 cups water to a boil in a saucepan; stir in rice and 2 teaspoons salt. Cover, reduce heat, and simmer 20 minutes or until liquid is absorbed. Set rice aside.

ADD field peas, garlic-and-herb bag, remaining 1 teaspoon salt, and pepper to ham hock mixture in Dutch oven. Bring to a boil over medium-high heat. Reduce heat, and simmer, stirring occasionally, 45 minutes. Remove and discard garlic-and-herb bag.

STIR cooked rice into field pea mixture; simmer 5 minutes or until heated through, adding broth, if necessary.

*Substitute salt pork, if desired.

NOTE: Esau uses a short-grain rice. You can substitute 4 cups of cooked long-grain rice, prepared according to directions, but it will have a different texture.

Bob's Squab

To prepare squab (you can use Cornish hens), tie legs with twine; tuck wings in. Coat with a thin layer of butter; sprinkle with salt and pepper. Brown 2 to 3 minutes on all sides over medium-high heat in an ovenproof skillet. Transfer skillet to oven; roast at 400° for 30 to 40 minutes or until meat thermometer registers 180°. Garnish with fresh thyme leaves.

A Texas Football Buffet

Serves 6 to 8

Gorditas With Turkey Mole

Chili Con Carne

Buzz's Pot of Beans

Tortilla chips, salsa, guacamole, margaritas

Texas Sheet Cake

It's New Year's Day in Texas

When we sent out an e-mail asking many of our Texas colleagues what they ate on New Year's Day, the answers were varied—from barbecue ribs and brisket to jalapeño-spiked cornbread. The one constant for this region, however, was pinto beans. Beans are woven into the fabric of a Southern New Year's meal as sure as "sweet" is a part of "tea." So when Dallasite Dotty Griffith agreed to host a New Year's Day football gathering for us, we had a hunch that beans, especially pintos, might be on the menu.

As the dining editor and restaurant critic for *The Dallas Morning News,* Dotty is a nationally recognized food journalist, and she knows Texas food like a cowboy knows his steers. In fact, many food lovers credit Dotty with defining what Texas home cooking truly is in her many cookbooks and news articles.

Because it was New Year's Day, Dotty added black-eyed peas to her brother Buzz's Pot of Beans along with the recipe's traditional pinto beans, black beans, and red kidney beans. Although some of her Texas "purist" guests teased her about adding the not-so-Texas black-eyed peas, Buzz's Pot of Beans was delectable served on the side or stirred into the Chili Con Carne. Texas Sheet Cake made a crowd-pleasing end to the meal. It's easily served straight from the pan or sliced on a buffet during halftime.

GORDITAS WITH TURKEY MOLE

MAKES 12 SERVINGS

Prep: 40 min., Stand: 30 min., Cook: 4 min. per batch

A gordita is a thick pancake made of masa; the edges are pinched up to hold a meat or bean filling and toppings. Dotty usually layers refried beans onto her gorditas; when we tested in our kitchens, we used mashed beans from Buzz's Pot of Beans. Either yields great results. Dotty also stirs leftover turkey into her mole topping. Better yet, she doesn't spend hours making her mole. She starts with a canned product as a base and spiffs it up.

2 cups masa harina
1¼ cups chicken broth
¼ cup vegetable shortening
½ cup plus 1 tablespoon all-purpose flour
½ teaspoon salt
1 teaspoon baking powder
Vegetable oil
1 cup refried beans or 1 cup drained and mashed Buzz's Pot of Beans
Turkey Mole
Toppings: 1 (15-ounce) can black beans, rinsed and drained (optional); shredded lettuce; chopped tomato; sour cream
Garnishes: lime wedges, cilantro sprigs

STIR together masa harina and broth in a large mixing bowl. Cover and let stand 30 minutes. Add shortening, flour, salt, and baking powder; beat at medium speed with an electric mixer until smooth.

DIVIDE dough into 12 golf-size balls. Arrange on wax paper, and cover with damp towels. Pat each ball of dough into a 3-inch circle. (Lightly oil fingers to keep mixture from sticking.) Pinch edges of circles to form a ridge, and press a well into each center to hold toppings. Cover with a damp towel to prevent dough from drying.

POUR oil to a depth of ¼ inch into a large skillet; heat to 350°. Fry gorditas, in batches, 2 minutes on each side, or until golden brown. Drain gorditas on paper towels.

DOLLOP each gordita with 2 tablespoons refried beans; spoon 1 tablespoon Turkey Mole over beans on each gordita. (Reserve extra beans and mole for other uses.) Top gorditas with desired toppings, and garnish, if desired.

TIP: Fill a squirt bottle with sour cream. Squeeze onto top of gordita.

NOTE: Masa harina is corn flour used to make corn tortillas. It can be found in the ethnic foods section of larger grocery stores.

Turkey Mole:

MAKES 6½ CUPS

Prep: 20 min., Cook: 15 min.

1 (8¼-ounce to 9¼-ounce) can mole sauce
1 (10-ounce) can enchilada sauce
4 cups chicken broth
1 tablespoon creamy peanut butter
2 (1-ounce) unsweetened dark chocolate baking squares
1½ pounds cooked turkey, shredded (about 5 cups)
½ teaspoon salt

STIR together mole and enchilada sauces in a medium saucepan, and add chicken broth. Bring mixture to a boil; reduce heat, and simmer 5 minutes.

STIR in peanut butter and chocolate until melted and smooth. Stir in turkey and salt; cook until thoroughly heated.

NOTE: Turkey Mole may also be spooned into taco shells or rolled into tortillas. Canned mole sauce may be found in the Mexican foods section of large supermarkets.

CHILI CON CARNE

MAKES 6 TO 8 SERVINGS
Prep: 10 min.; Cook: 1 hr., 45 min.

People in Texas don't take much to having beans in their chili. If they do, they add them separately. That's exactly what guests at Dotty's party did with Buzz's Pot of Beans. If you can't find coarsely ground beef in your supermarket, a regular grind works fine.

- **3 pounds coarsely ground beef**
- **4 garlic cloves, minced**
- **7 tablespoons chili powder, divided**
- **1 tablespoon ground cumin**
- **1 (8-ounce) can tomato sauce**
- **2 cups water**
- **3 tablespoons masa harina**
- **1 teaspoon salt**
- **1 teaspoon ground red pepper**
- **1 tablespoon paprika (optional)**
- **Garnishes: shredded Cheddar cheese, chopped green onions, chopped tomatoes, shredded lettuce**

COOK ground beef, in batches, in a large skillet over medium-high heat about 5 minutes, stirring until meat crumbles and is no longer pink. Drain well.
ADD garlic, reduce heat to medium, and sauté 2 minutes until tender. Add 6 tablespoons chili powder and 1 tablespoon cumin, stirring to coat meat evenly. Add tomato sauce and 2 cups water. Bring to a boil; cover, reduce heat, and simmer 1 hour. Stir 1 tablespoon masa at a time into meat mixture, allowing chili to thicken between additions to desired consistency.
COOK, uncovered, 20 more minutes. Stir in salt, red pepper, and, if desired, paprika. Stir in remaining 1 tablespoon chili powder 5 minutes before serving, and garnish, if desired.

BUZZ'S POT OF BEANS

MAKES 12 SERVINGS
Prep: 15 min., Soak: 8 hrs., Cook: 3 hrs.

To incorporate black-eyed peas into this dish, reduce black beans and kidney beans to ¼ pound each; add ½ pound dried black-eyed peas.

- **1 pound dried pinto beans**
- **½ pound dried black beans**
- **½ pound dried red kidney beans**
- **14 cups water**
- **6 cups chopped onion, divided**
- **10 whole garlic cloves**
- **3 bacon slices, cut into 1-inch pieces**
- **3 chicken bouillon cubes**
- **3 tablespoons chili powder**
- **1 tablespoon salt**
- **2 teaspoons ground black pepper**
- **½ to 1 teaspoon ground red pepper**

COMBINE beans and water to cover 3 inches in a large Dutch oven; soak 8 hours. Drain.
COMBINE beans, 14 cups water, 4 cups chopped onion, garlic, and next 6 ingredients. Bring to a boil over high heat. Reduce heat, cover, and simmer, stirring occasionally, 1 hour. Add remaining 2 cups chopped onion, and cook, covered, 2 hours or until beans are tender, adding more water, as needed.

Regional Reading

The recipes in this menu are adapted from Dotty's books: *The Texas Holiday Cookbook* (Gulf Publishing Company, Houston) and her recent release, *The Contemporary Cowboy Cookbook: Recipes From the Wild West to Wall Street* (Lone Star Books, Houston).

TEXAS SHEET CAKE

family favorite

MAKES 12 TO 15 SERVINGS
Prep: 10 min., Cook: 15 min., Bake: 20 min.

Make the icing 5 minutes before taking the cake out of the oven, and spread it on the hot cake.

- **2 cups sugar**
- **2 cups all-purpose flour**
- **½ cup butter or margarine**
- **½ cup shortening**
- **¼ cup unsweetened cocoa**
- **1 cup water**
- **½ cup buttermilk**
- **2 large eggs, lightly beaten**
- **1 teaspoon baking soda**
- **1 teaspoon vanilla extract**
- **Chocolate Icing**

SIFT together sugar and flour in a large bowl; set aside.
COMBINE butter and next 3 ingredients in a medium saucepan over medium-high heat. Bring to a boil, stirring constantly, until butter and shortening melt. Remove from heat, and pour over sugar mixture, stirring until dissolved. Cool slightly.
STIR in buttermilk and next 3 ingredients. Pour into a greased and lightly floured 15- x 10-inch jellyroll pan.
BAKE at 400° for 20 minutes. (Cake will have a fudgelike texture.) Spread hot cake with Chocolate Icing.

Chocolate Icing:

MAKES ABOUT 4 CUPS
Prep: 5 min., Cook: 10 min.

- **½ cup butter or margarine**
- **¼ cup unsweetened cocoa**
- **⅓ cup milk**
- **1 (16-ounce) package powdered sugar**
- **1 teaspoon vanilla extract**
- **1 cup chopped pecans**

COMBINE butter, cocoa, and milk in a medium saucepan. Cook over low heat 5 minutes or until butter melts. Bring to a boil over medium heat.
REMOVE from heat; stir in sugar, vanilla, and pecans. Beat at medium speed with an electric mixer until mixture is smooth and sugar dissolves.

Pot Pies & Cobblers Made Simple

You've got to try these hearty main dishes and desserts. Convenience never tasted so good.

Comfort foods are always in style, and an all-time favorite is the good ol' pot pie. Making it from scratch, however, takes time. Enter Recipe Development Director Mary Allen Perry (think of her as your personal culinary superhero). She's taken labor-intensive crusts and replaced them with a variety of batters that are quickly stirred together and poured over a hearty mixture of meat and vegetables for the ultimate in ease and Southern flavor. Mary Allen has even perfected a method for dessert cobblers.

These mouthwatering recipes have been further streamlined using items such as frozen vegetables, leftover barbecue, canned cherries, and apple pie filling. To round out your meal, try our suggestions for tasty salads and dressings in this month's Quick & Easy column (page 28).

Cook's Notes

- To ensure even cooking, fillings should be hot before crust batters are added.
- All the fillings can be made ahead. Simply reheat, and add crust batters.
- Feel free to mix-and-match these crust batters and fillings, or try them with your favorite pot pie-filling recipe.
- Seasoning blends may be convenient to use, but salt content between brands can vary dramatically. Choose a blend that best suits your needs. For our Ham-and-Greens Pot Pie, we used salt-free blends.

HAM-AND-GREENS POT PIE WITH CORNBREAD CRUST

MAKES 8 TO 10 SERVINGS

Prep: 10 min., Cook: 25 min., Bake: 25 min.

Pimiento-Cheese Corn Sticks add a deliciously decorative touch to this satisfying Southern entrée.

- 4 cups chopped cooked ham
- 2 tablespoons vegetable oil
- 3 tablespoons all-purpose flour
- 3 cups chicken broth
- 1 (16-ounce) package frozen seasoning blend
- 1 (16-ounce) package frozen chopped collard greens
- 1 (16-ounce) can black-eyed peas, rinsed and drained
- ½ teaspoon dried crushed red pepper
- Cornbread Crust Batter
- Pimiento-Cheese Corn Sticks (optional)

SAUTÉ ham in hot oil in a Dutch oven over medium-high heat 5 minutes or until lightly browned. Add flour, and cook, stirring constantly, 1 minute. Gradually add chicken broth, and cook, stirring constantly, 3 minutes or until broth begins to thicken.

BRING mixture to a boil, and add seasoning blend and collard greens; return to a boil, and cook, stirring often, 15 minutes.

STIR in black-eyed peas and crushed red pepper; spoon hot mixture into a lightly greased 13- x 9-inch baking dish. Pour Cornbread Crust Batter evenly over hot filling mixture.

BAKE at 425° for 20 to 25 minutes or until cornbread is golden brown and set. Top with Pimiento-Cheese Corn Sticks, if desired.

NOTE: For testing purposes only, we used McKenzie's Seasoning Blend.

Cornbread Crust Batter:

MAKES 1 (13- X 9-INCH) CRUST

Prep: 5 min.

- 1½ cups white cornmeal mix
- ½ cup all-purpose flour
- 1 teaspoon sugar
- 2 large eggs, lightly beaten
- 1½ cups buttermilk

COMBINE first 3 ingredients in a large bowl, and make a well in the center of mixture.

ADD eggs and buttermilk to cornmeal mixture, stirring just until moistened.

Pimiento-Cheese Corn Sticks:

MAKES ABOUT 5 DOZEN

Prep: 10 min., Bake: 8 min.

PREPARE Cornbread Crust Batter as directed above, adding 1 cup (4 ounces) shredded Cheddar cheese and 1 (7-ounce) jar drained, diced pimiento.

HEAT oven to 450°, and place cast-iron miniature corn stick pans in oven; heat 5 minutes or until hot. Remove pans from oven, and coat pans with vegetable cooking spray. Spoon batter into hot pans.

BAKE at 450° for 8 minutes or until golden brown. Remove from pans immediately.

BARBECUE POT PIE WITH CHEESE GRITS CRUST

MAKES 8 TO 10 SERVINGS

Prep: 20 min., Cook: 9 min., Bake: 25 min.

Mary Allen suggests using a thick barbecue sauce. "Thin sauces don't work as well with this recipe," she warns. If you don't have time to make barbecued pork from scratch, purchase shredded pork from your favorite restaurant.

- **1 large sweet onion, diced**
- **1 tablespoon vegetable oil**
- **2 tablespoons all-purpose flour**
- **1½ cups thick barbecue sauce**
- **1½ cups beef broth**
- **1 pound shredded barbecued pork***
- **Cheese Grits Crust Batter**

SAUTÉ onion in hot oil in a large skillet over medium-high heat 5 minutes or until golden brown. Stir in flour, and cook, stirring constantly, 1 minute. Gradually stir in barbecue sauce and beef broth; cook, stirring constantly, 3 minutes or until mixture begins to thicken.

STIR in pork, and bring to a boil. Remove from heat, and spoon mixture into a lightly greased 13- x 9-inch baking dish.

SPOON Cheese Grits Crust Batter evenly over hot barbecue mixture.

BAKE at 425° for 20 to 25 minutes or until golden brown and set.

*Substitute 1 pound shredded beef for pork, if desired.

Cheese Grits Crust Batter:

MAKES 1 (13- X 9-INCH) CRUST

Prep: 9 min., Cook: 7 min.

- **2 cups water**
- **2 cups milk**
- **1 cup quick-cooking grits**
- **2 cups (8 ounces) shredded sharp Cheddar cheese**
- **¾ teaspoon salt**
- **½ teaspoon seasoned pepper**
- **2 large eggs, lightly beaten**

BRING water and milk to a boil in a large saucepan; add grits, and cook, stirring often, 5 minutes or until thickened. Stir in cheese, salt, and pepper, and remove from heat.

STIR about one-fourth of grits mixture gradually into beaten eggs, and add to remaining grits mixture, stirring constantly.

BARBECUE POT PIE WITH MASHED POTATO CRUST: Prepare 1 (22-ounce) package frozen mashed potatoes according to package directions. Stir in ½ (8-ounce) package softened cream cheese until melted. Spoon hot potato mixture evenly over hot barbecue mixture; sprinkle with 1 cup shredded Cheddar cheese. Bake at 425° for 15 minutes.

APPLE-GINGERBREAD COBBLER

MAKES 8 SERVINGS

Prep: 15 min., Cook: 5 min., Bake: 35 min.

Using a packaged gingerbread mix, this easy-to-make cobbler is ready for the oven in 15 minutes.

- **1 (14-ounce) package gingerbread mix, divided**
- **¾ cup water**
- **¼ cup firmly packed light brown sugar**
- **½ cup butter, divided**
- **½ cup chopped pecans**
- **2 (21-ounce) cans apple pie filling**
- **Vanilla ice cream**

STIR together 2 cups gingerbread mix and ¾ cup water until smooth; set mixture aside.

STIR together remaining gingerbread mix and brown sugar; cut in ¼ cup butter until mixture is crumbly. Stir in pecans; set aside.

COMBINE apple pie filling and remaining ¼ cup butter in a large saucepan, and cook, stirring often, 5 minutes over medium heat or until thoroughly heated. Spoon hot apple mixture evenly into a lightly greased 11- x 7-inch baking dish. Spoon gingerbread mixture evenly over hot apple mixture; sprinkle with pecan mixture.

BAKE at 375° for 30 to 35 minutes or until set. Serve cobbler with vanilla ice cream.

DOUBLE-CHERRY CHEESECAKE COBBLER

MAKES 8 SERVINGS

Prep: 15 min., Cook: 5 min., Bake: 30 min., Stand: 15 min.

- **1 (8-ounce) package cream cheese, softened**
- **⅓ cup sugar**
- **⅓ cup all-purpose flour**
- **1 large egg**
- **1 teaspoon vanilla extract**
- **¼ teaspoon almond extract**
- **1 (15-ounce) can dark sweet cherries, drained**
- **1 (21-ounce) can cherry pie filling**
- **¼ cup butter, melted and divided**
- **20 vanilla wafers, crushed**

BEAT cream cheese, sugar, and flour at low speed with an electric mixer; add egg and extracts, beating until smooth. Set aside.

STIR together cherries, cherry pie filling, and 2 tablespoons melted butter in a large saucepan, and cook over medium heat, stirring often, 5 minutes or until thoroughly heated. Spoon hot cherry mixture into a lightly greased 9-inch deep-dish pieplate. Spoon cream cheese mixture evenly over hot cherries.

COMBINE crushed vanilla wafers and remaining 2 tablespoons melted butter. Sprinkle vanilla wafer mixture evenly over cream cheese mixture.

BAKE at 350° for 30 minutes or until golden brown and set. Let stand 15 minutes before serving.

Simple Family Suppers

These strategies turn dinnertime stress into fast, delicious, and nutritious meals.

Like many moms, Melina Cohen's enduring quandary is serving a healthy and tasty meal after a busy workday. She and husband Steve, of Potomac, Maryland, stay in perpetual motion. "I know what I should feed my family, but we're so busy that we just grab anything," Melina admits.

The Cohens told Assistant Foods Editor Joy Zacharia that spaghetti and meatballs and Mexican food were favorites, so she created a couple of superfast casseroles that can be paired with prewashed salad greens and bottled vinaigrette. Joy brought the Cohen children, Christopher and Maria, into the kitchen and asked them to help prepare the meal. The outcome: two kids excited about what they were tasting (well, sort of). At least they were willing to try everything.

Nutrition Makeover

▪ Melina and Joy toured a local supermarket together, and Joy introduced Melina to unfamiliar fruits and vegetables, whole grains, beans, and high-fiber cereals. Melina's challenge: choosing a new food every trip to the market.

▪ Joy snooped around the Cohens' kitchen, paying close attention to pantry, fridge, and freezer foods. Their challenge: buying (and eating) fewer processed snack foods and selecting more fresh fruit, dried fruit, low-sugar cereals, and fresh or frozen veggies. Eating breakfast every day is also a goal.

EASY MEXICAN LASAGNA

family favorite

MAKES 6 TO 8 SERVINGS

Prep: 15 min., Cook: 20 min., Bake: 40 min.

This simple and delicious one-dish supper calls for almost no preparation (especially if you buy precooked, cut-up chicken).

- 3 cups chopped cooked chicken breast
- 1 (15-ounce) can black beans, rinsed and drained
- ⅔ cup canned diced tomatoes and green chiles
- 1 teaspoon garlic powder
- 1 teaspoon ground cumin
- ½ teaspoon pepper
- 1 (10¾-ounce) can fat-free cream of chicken soup
- 1 (10¾-ounce) can fat-free cream of mushroom soup
- 1 (10-ounce) can enchilada sauce
- Vegetable cooking spray
- 9 (6-inch) corn tortillas
- 1 cup (4 ounces) low-fat shredded Cheddar cheese
- 1 cup (4 ounces) shredded Monterey Jack cheese
- Toppings: shredded lettuce, nonfat sour cream, mild chunky salsa

COOK first 6 ingredients in a saucepan over medium heat 10 minutes or until thoroughly heated.

STIR together chicken and mushroom soups and enchilada sauce in a saucepan; cook, stirring often, 10 minutes or until thoroughly heated.

SPOON one-third of sauce into a 13- x 9-inch baking dish coated with cooking spray; top with 3 tortillas. Spoon half of chicken mixture and one-third of sauce over tortillas; sprinkle with half of Cheddar cheese. Top with 3 tortillas; repeat layers once with remaining chicken, sauce, Cheddar cheese, and tortillas, ending with tortillas. Sprinkle with Monterey Jack cheese.

BAKE at 350° for 30 to 40 minutes or until bubbly. Serve with desired toppings.

Calories 358 (29% from fat); Fat 11.6g (sat 4.5g, mono 2.1g, poly 1.3g); Protein 30g; Carb 34g; Fiber 3.7g; Chol 64mg; Iron 1.8mg; Sodium 1,332mg*

*To lower sodium, choose reduced-sodium soups, canned tomato products, and cheeses.

LINGUINE WITH MEAT SAUCE CASSEROLE

family favorite

MAKES 8 SERVINGS

Prep: 5 min., Cook: 35 min., Bake: 30 min., Stand: 5 min.

We adapted this rich and creamy entrée from a 2001 *Southern Living* dish.

- 1 pound extra-lean ground beef
- 1 teaspoon bottled minced garlic
- Vegetable cooking spray
- 1 (28-ounce) can crushed tomatoes
- 1 (8-ounce) can tomato sauce
- 1 (6-ounce) can tomato paste
- 2 teaspoons sugar
- ½ teaspoon salt
- 8 ounces uncooked whole wheat linguine*
- 1 (16-ounce) container nonfat sour cream
- 1 (8-ounce) package fat-free cream cheese, softened
- 1 bunch green onions, chopped
- 1½ cups (6 ounces) shredded low-fat mozzarella cheese

COOK beef and garlic in a Dutch oven coated with cooking spray, stirring until beef crumbles and is no longer pink. Drain; pat dry with paper towels. Return beef mixture to Dutch oven.

STIR in tomatoes and next 4 ingredients; simmer 30 minutes. Set meat sauce aside.

COOK pasta according to package directions, omitting salt and oil; drain. Place pasta in a 13- x 9-inch baking dish coated with cooking spray.

STIR together sour cream, cream cheese, and green onions. Spread over linguine. Top with meat sauce.

BAKE at 350° for 20 to 25 minutes or until thoroughly heated. Sprinkle with mozzarella cheese, and bake 5 more minutes or until cheese melts. Let stand 5 minutes.

Calories 398 (30% from fat); Fat 13g (sat 7.4g, mono 1.9g, poly 0.6g); Protein 26g; Carb 42g; Fiber 3g; Chol 45mg; Iron 2.8mg; Sodium 874mg**; Calc 339mg

*Substitute regular linguine, if desired.

**To lower sodium, omit the salt, and use reduced-sodium canned tomato products.

The Follow-Up

Since Joy's visit to the Cohen home, Melina reports several positive changes.

■ She's adopted supper short-cuts, such as placing meats along with marinades in zip-top plastic bags and freezing them for later use. Then, she simply thaws the meat in the marinade in the refrigerator, and when she arrives home, it's ready to go on the grill or under the broiler.

■ "We eat at home a lot more. That way I control the menu and portion sizes. Plus, I can enforce my rule of fruits or vegetables at every meal," Melina says.

■ She eats breakfast every day. "I knew it was important, but now I'm doing it, and I have so much more energy."

■ Melina shops more from the produce aisle. A good rule of thumb is to choose most groceries from the perimeter of the supermarket (which includes the produce, dairy, meat, and deli sections).

What's for Supper?

Simmered Beef Tips

Sirloin, cut into pieces by the butcher and packaged under the label beef tips, is a great choice for weeknight suppers. It's a lean cut that shrinks little during cooking, so you get full value for your money. Here, we give you two clever ways to use beef tips. You can prep each recipe in about 20 minutes, then walk away for an hour or so while slow simmering tenderizes the beef.

FESTIVE CAJUN PEPPER STEAK

MAKES 4 TO 6 SERVINGS

Prep: 20 min.; Cook: 1 hr., 20 min.

1½ pounds sirloin beef tips
1 teaspoon salt-free Cajun
    seasoning
1 tablespoon vegetable oil
1 medium-size green bell pepper,
    chopped
1 onion, chopped
3 garlic cloves, minced
1 (14½-ounce) can beef broth
1 (14½-ounce) can diced tomatoes,
    undrained
2 teaspoons Worcestershire sauce
1 teaspoon white wine vinegar
½ teaspoon dried basil
¼ teaspoon salt
⅛ teaspoon pepper
1 (22-ounce) package frozen
    mashed potatoes
2 tablespoons cornstarch
2 tablespoons cold water

SPRINKLE beef tips with 1 teaspoon Cajun seasoning.

COOK beef in hot oil in a large skillet over medium-high heat 10 minutes or until browned. Add bell pepper, onion, and garlic; sauté 3 minutes. Stir in broth and next 6 ingredients. Bring to a boil; reduce heat, cover, and simmer 1 hour or until meat is tender.

COOK frozen mashed potatoes according to package directions.

STIR together cornstarch and water until smooth; stir into meat mixture. Bring to a boil; cook, stirring constantly, 2 minutes or until thickened. Serve over mashed potatoes.

KAREN MARTIS
MERRILLVILLE, INDIANA

BEEF STROGANOFF

MAKES 4 SERVINGS

Prep: 20 min.; Cook: 1 hr., 10 min.

Serve steamed broccoli, tossed with melted butter and lemon pepper, with this hearty main dish.

1½ pounds sirloin beef tips
½ teaspoon salt
½ teaspoon pepper
3 tablespoons vegetable oil
2 medium-size sweet onions, diced
2 (8-ounce) packages fresh
    mushrooms, sliced
2 cups beef broth
2 tablespoons tomato paste
1 teaspoon Dijon mustard
1 (16-ounce) package egg noodles
½ cup sherry
2 tablespoons all-purpose flour
1 (8-ounce) container sour cream
2 tablespoons chopped fresh
    parsley (optional)

SPRINKLE beef tips evenly with salt and pepper.

COOK beef in hot oil in a large skillet over medium-high heat; add onions and mushrooms, and sauté 3 to 5 minutes or until tender.

STIR broth, tomato paste, and mustard into beef mixture. Cover, reduce heat to low, and cook 1 hour or until beef is tender.

COOK noodles according to package directions; drain.

COMBINE sherry and flour; stir into beef mixture, and cook, stirring constantly, until thickened. Stir in sour cream. Serve over hot egg noodles; sprinkle with parsley, if desired.

WALTER C. LUND, SR.
MIAMI, FLORIDA

Southern Gone Light

Some may argue that truly Southern recipes can't be lightened without giving up their rich flavor. It's true some can't, but these featured here definitely can. We're betting our versions of these classics will become family favorites at your house. And as an added bonus, most of them are ready in 35 minutes or less.

BANANA PUDDING

family favorite

MAKES 10 SERVINGS

Prep: 25 min., Cook: 8 min., Bake: 25 min., Cool: 30 min.

Friends and family will love this lighter rendition of Banana Pudding.

- ⅓ cup all-purpose flour
- Dash of salt
- 2½ cups 1% low-fat milk
- 1 (14-ounce) can fat-free sweetened condensed milk
- 2 egg yolks
- 2 teaspoons vanilla extract
- 3 cups sliced ripe banana
- 45 reduced-fat vanilla wafers
- 4 egg whites
- ¼ cup sugar

COMBINE flour and salt in a medium saucepan. Gradually stir in milks and yolks, and cook over medium heat, stirring constantly, 8 minutes or until thickened. Remove from heat; stir in vanilla.

ARRANGE 1 cup banana slices in a 2-quart baking dish. Spoon one-third pudding mixture over bananas; top with 15 vanilla wafers. Repeat layers once; top with remaining bananas and pudding. Arrange remaining 15 wafers around inside edge of dish. Gently push wafers into pudding.

BEAT egg whites at high speed with an electric mixer until foamy. Add sugar,

1 tablespoon at a time, beating until stiff peaks form and sugar dissolves (2 to 4 minutes). Spread meringue over pudding, sealing to edge of dish.

BAKE at 325° for 25 minutes or until golden. Let cool at least 30 minutes.

Per serving: Calories 359 (10% from fat); Fat 2.9g (sat 1g, mono 0.9g, poly 0.2g); Protein 7.9g; Carb 49.5g; Fiber 0.1g; Chol 51mg; Iron 0.4mg; Sodium 155mg; Calc 161mg

SWEET POTATO CASSEROLE

MAKES 6 SERVINGS

Prep: 15 min., Bake: 30 min.

- 3 medium-size sweet potatoes*
- ½ cup firmly packed dark brown sugar
- 1 cup fat-free evaporated milk
- ¼ cup butter or margarine, melted
- ¼ cup egg substitute
- 3 tablespoons all-purpose flour
- ½ teaspoon pumpkin pie spice
- ¼ teaspoon salt
- Vegetable cooking spray
- Garnish: 2 tablespoons diced pecans

MICROWAVE potatoes 1 inch apart on paper towels at HIGH 12 minutes or until done, turning and rearranging after 5 minutes; cool, peel, and mash.

STIR together potatoes and next 7 ingredients; spoon into a shallow 2-quart casserole coated with cooking spray.

BAKE at 350° for 30 minutes or until a knife inserted in center comes out clean. Garnish, if desired.

*Substitute 2 (14½-ounce) cans mashed sweet potatoes, if desired.

Per serving: Calories 286 (31% from fat); Fat 9.8g (sat 5g, mono 3.3g, poly 0.8g); Protein 6.1g; Carb 44.6g; Fiber 2.5g; Chol 22mg; Iron 1.4mg; Sodium 257mg; Calc 164mg

BUTTERMILK BISCUITS

fast fixin's • family favorite

MAKES 16 BISCUITS

Prep: 10 min., Bake: 15 min.

- 2 cups all-purpose flour
- 2 teaspoons baking powder
- ¼ teaspoon baking soda
- ¼ teaspoon salt
- ¼ cup butter or margarine
- 1 cup nonfat buttermilk

COMBINE flour, baking powder, baking soda, and salt in a large bowl.

CUT butter into flour mixture with a fork or pastry blender until crumbly; add buttermilk, stirring just until dry ingredients are moistened.

TURN dough out onto a lightly floured surface; knead 2 or 3 times.

PAT or roll to ½-inch thickness; cut with a 1½-inch round cutter, and place on a baking sheet.

BAKE at 400° for 15 minutes or until biscuits are golden.

Per biscuit: Calories 83 (33% from fat); Fat 3.1g (sat 1.9g, mono 0.8g, poly 0.2g); Protein 2.1g; Carb 11.8g; Fiber 0.4g; Chol 8mg; Iron 0.7mg; Sodium 135mg; Calc 43mg

FRIED PORK CHOPS WITH CREAM GRAVY

fast fixin's

MAKES 8 SERVINGS

Prep: 5 min., Cook: 25 min.

- 1 cup all-purpose flour
- 1 teaspoon Cajun seasoning
- ¼ teaspoon garlic powder
- ¼ teaspoon pepper
- 8 (4-ounce) boneless center-cut pork chops
- 1 cup nonfat buttermilk
- Vegetable cooking spray
- 3 tablespoons vegetable oil
- 1 cup fat-free milk
- ¼ teaspoon salt
- Garnish: coarse ground pepper

RESERVE 2 tablespoons flour; set aside. Place remaining flour in a shallow dish.

COMBINE Cajun seasoning, garlic powder, and pepper. Rub pork chops evenly on both sides with seasoning mixture.

DIP pork in buttermilk; dredge in flour. Lightly coat both sides of pork with cooking spray.

COOK pork, in batches, in hot oil in a large heavy skillet over medium-high heat 5 minutes on each side or until golden brown. Drain on paper towels.

ADD reserved 2 tablespoons flour to pan drippings in skillet; stir in milk and salt, and cook, stirring constantly, until thickened and bubbly. Serve immediately with pork. Garnish, if desired.

Per chop: Calories 267 (42% from fat); Fat 12.3g (sat 3.7g, mono 4.9g, poly 2.6g); Protein 26.2g; Carb 11.2g; Fiber 0.3g; Chol 69mg; Iron 1.5mg; Sodium 250mg; Calc 63mg

CHICKEN AND DUMPLINGS

fast fixin's • family favorite

MAKES 6 SERVINGS

Prep: 15 min., Cook: 15 min.

- 3 celery ribs, sliced
- 2 carrots, sliced
- Vegetable cooking spray
- 3 (14½-ounce) cans low-sodium fat-free chicken broth
- ½ teaspoon poultry seasoning
- ½ teaspoon pepper
- 1⅔ cups reduced-fat baking mix
- ⅔ cup fat-free milk
- 3 cups chopped cooked chicken

SAUTÉ celery and carrots in a large Dutch oven coated with cooking spray over medium-high heat 6 minutes or until tender. Stir in broth, poultry seasoning, and pepper; bring to a boil.

STIR together baking mix and milk until blended.

TURN dough out onto a heavily floured surface; roll or pat dough to ⅛-inch thickness. Cut into 3- x 2-inch strips.

DROP strips, 1 at a time, into boiling broth; stir in chicken. Cover, reduce heat, and simmer, stirring occasionally, 8 minutes.

Per serving: Calories 276 (21% from fat); Fat 6.5g (sat 1.6g, mono 2.7g, poly 1.7g); Protein 20.7g; Carb 27.2g; Fiber 1.1g; Chol 51mg; Iron 1.2mg; Sodium 476mg; Calc 65mg

Better Snacking

Three square meals a day—with never an extra bite in between—was once the golden rule for a healthy diet. Nowadays, though, there's a better approach. While not eating between meals can result in low blood sugar (which leaves you famished and lethargic), snacking actually increases energy levels and boosts metabolism as it helps curb hunger pangs. Plus, you won't inhale your next meal and wind up feeling uncomfortably full.

The challenge today is finding healthy snacks—especially in the South with our down-home cooking. Try these easy and nutritious treats. Cranberry-Cinnamon Granola Bars and Lemon-Blueberry Muffins are ideal for taking to work or on a road trip—and kids love them. And because they're so quick to stir up, the cook will love them, too.

Snacking Smart

Just as we should hydrate ourselves throughout the day, we also need to nourish our bodies. Here are some guidelines for healthful snacking.

■ Plan your day to make snacking a conscious activity, and have some healthful snacks on hand.

■ Choose snacks from several different food groups, limiting those high in fat and sugar.

■ Eat snacks well ahead of your next meal so you won't spoil your appetite. Snack only when you're hungry.

■ Brush your teeth between meals and snacks to prevent constant munching. A minty fresh feeling can help suppress the desire to eat.

For more information on healthful snacking, visit the American Dietetic Association at **www.eatright.org**

YOGURT-FRUIT SMOOTHIE

fast fixin's

MAKES 5 CUPS

Prep: 5 min.

This quick and easy smoothie is the perfect breakfast to drink on your way to work or for children on the way to school. It's also a great source of calcium. Blend in other fruits for a variety of flavors.

- 2 cups fat-free milk
- 1 (8-ounce) container vanilla low-fat yogurt
- ½ cup thawed pineapple-orange juice concentrate
- 2 cups frozen strawberries
- 1 banana, coarsely chopped

PROCESS all ingredients in a blender until smooth, stopping to scrape down sides. Serve immediately.

Per 1 cup: Calories 183 (4% from fat); Fat 0.8g (sat 0.5g, mono 0.2g, poly 0.07g); Protein 6.5g; Carb 37g; Fiber 2.2g; Chol 4mg; Iron 1mg; Sodium 93mg; Calc 227mg

CHUNKY BLACK BEAN SALSA

fast fixin's • make ahead

MAKES 6 CUPS

Prep: 15 min.

Salsa is a low-calorie, naturally fat-free snack.

- 3 tomatoes, seeded and chopped
- 1 (15-ounce) can black beans, rinsed and drained
- 1 jalapeño pepper, seeded and diced
- ½ small sweet onion, chopped
- ¼ cup chopped fresh cilantro
- ½ teaspoon grated lime rind
- 3 tablespoons fresh lime juice
- ½ teaspoon salt
- ½ teaspoon ground pepper
- Baked tortilla chips

COMBINE first 9 ingredients in a bowl. Cover and chill until ready to serve. Serve with baked tortilla chips.

Per ½ cup (not including tortilla chips): Calories 21 (5% from fat); Fat 0.14g (sat 0.02, mono 0.02, poly 0.04); Protein 1g; Carb 5g; Fiber 1.4g; Chol 0mg; Iron 0.5mg; Sodium 182mg; Calc 9.6mg

CREAMY VEGETABLE DIP

fast fixin's • make ahead

MAKES ABOUT 1½ CUPS

Prep: 10 min.

- 1 (8-ounce) package fat-free cream cheese, softened
- 2 tablespoons fat-free milk
- 2 tablespoons freshly grated Parmesan cheese
- 4 teaspoons Ranch-style dressing mix
- ¼ cup chopped red bell pepper
- 1 green onion, chopped (about 2 tablespoons)
- Assorted fresh vegetables

BEAT cream cheese and milk at medium speed with an electric mixer until creamy; add cheese and dressing mix, beating until blended. Stir in bell pepper and green onions. Cover and chill until ready to serve. Serve with assorted fresh vegetables.

Per ¼ cup (not including vegetables): Calories 62 (17% from fat); Fat 1.2g (sat 0.7g, mono 0.13g, poly 0.03g); Protein 6.3g; Carb 4.3g; Fiber 0.21g; Chol 5mg; Iron 0mg; Sodium 406mg; Calc 104mg

CRANBERRY-CINNAMON GRANOLA BARS

fast fixin's • make ahead

MAKES 9 BARS

Prep: 10 min., Bake: 15 min., Cool: 5 min.

Granola is a good source of soluble fiber, which can lower the risk of coronary heart disease.

> 2 cups low-fat granola cereal
> ¼ cup firmly packed brown sugar
> ¼ cup sweetened dried cranberries
> 1 large egg, lightly beaten
> 1 teaspoon vanilla extract
> ½ teaspoon ground cinnamon
> Vegetable cooking spray

COMBINE first 6 ingredients, and press mixture evenly into an 8-inch square pan coated with cooking spray.

BAKE at 350° for 15 minutes or until golden. Cool in pan on a wire rack 5 minutes, and cut into bars. Store in an airtight container.

NOTE: For testing purposes only, we used Kellogg's Low-Fat Granola without Raisins.

Calories 139 (14% from fat); Fat 2g (sat 0.6g, mono 0.2g, poly 0.08g); Protein 3g; Carb 27g; Fiber 2g; Chol 24mg; Iron 1mg; Sodium 32mg; Calc 19mg

LEMON-BLUEBERRY MUFFINS

MAKES 1 DOZEN

Prep: 10 min., Bake: 25 min.

> 1¾ cups all-purpose flour
> 2 teaspoons baking powder
> ¼ teaspoon salt
> 1 cup fresh or frozen blueberries, thawed and drained
> ¾ cup fat-free milk
> ½ cup sugar
> ¼ cup vegetable oil
> 2 teaspoons grated lemon rind
> 1 teaspoon vanilla extract
> 2 egg whites
> Vegetable cooking spray

COMBINE first 3 ingredients in a large mixing bowl; add blueberries, and gently toss to coat. Make a well in center of mixture.

STIR together milk, sugar, and next 3 ingredients; add to dry ingredients, stirring just until moistened.

BEAT egg whites at medium speed with an electric mixer 1 minute or until soft peaks form; fold into batter. Spoon batter into muffin pans coated with cooking spray, filling two-thirds full.

BAKE at 350° for 20 to 25 minutes or until done.

Calories 151 (30% from fat); Fat 5g (sat 0.4g, mono 2.7g, poly 1.4g); Protein 3g; Carb 24g; Fiber 1g; Chol 0.3mg; Iron 0.8mg; Sodium 133mg; Calc 50mg

Affordable Chicken

When you're looking for a bargain, check out bone-in chicken. Whether you buy the whole bird and cut it up yourself or just pick up your favorite pieces, it's the best deal for family meals. Remove the skin and bones from regular breasts for a supper that's a fraction of the cost of the boneless, skinless breasts sold in stores.

CHICKEN AND ARTICHOKES

MAKES 4 SERVINGS

Prep: 25 min., Cook: 28 min., Bake: 15 min.

> 4 bone-in chicken breast halves
> 9 tablespoons butter or margarine, divided
> 1 cup sliced fresh mushrooms
> ½ small onion, diced
> 1 garlic clove, minced
> ¼ cup dry white wine*
> ¼ cup all-purpose flour
> 1½ cups milk
> 2 (14-ounce) cans artichoke heart quarters, drained and chopped
> ¼ cup grated Parmesan cheese
> ½ teaspoon salt
> ¼ teaspoon pepper
> 1 teaspoon chopped fresh parsley

REMOVE and discard skin and bones from chicken breasts. Cut chicken breasts into strips, and set aside.

MELT 3 tablespoons butter in a large non-stick skillet over medium heat; add mushrooms and onion, and sauté 6 minutes. Add garlic, and sauté 2 minutes. Remove mushroom mixture from skillet.

MELT 2 tablespoons butter in the same skillet over medium heat; add chicken strips, and cook 10 minutes or until chicken is tender. Stir in wine, and cook 5 minutes. Return mushroom mixture to skillet, stirring well. Remove skillet from heat.

MELT remaining 4 tablespoons butter in a small saucepan. Whisk in flour until blended and smooth. Gradually whisk in milk, and cook, whisking constantly, 5 minutes or until mixture thickens. Stir in artichokes and next 3 ingredients.

SPOON chicken mixture into an 11- x 7-inch baking dish; top evenly with artichoke mixture.

BAKE at 300° for 15 minutes or until bubbly. Sprinkle with parsley.

*Substitute chicken broth for white wine, if desired.

WINE-GLAZED CHICKEN

MAKES 4 SERVINGS

Prep: 10 min., Cook: 35 min.

> 1 teaspoon salt
> ½ teaspoon ground nutmeg
> 8 chicken legs
> ¼ cup butter or margarine
> 1⅓ cups dry white wine*
> 1 cup sliced fresh mushrooms
> 1 red bell pepper, thinly sliced
> 3 green onions, chopped
> 2 tablespoons chicken broth
> 4 teaspoons cornstarch
> Hot cooked rice
> Garnish: chopped flat-leaf parsley

SPRINKLE salt and ground nutmeg over chicken.

MELT butter in a medium skillet over medium heat; add chicken. Cook, turning often, 10 minutes or until chicken is golden.

STIR in wine, mushrooms, bell pepper, and green onions; bring to a boil over medium heat. Reduce heat to medium-low; cover and simmer 20 minutes or until chicken is done. Remove chicken from skillet; keep warm.

WHISK together broth and cornstarch until smooth; add to drippings in skillet. Cook over medium heat, stirring constantly, 1 minute or until thickened. Serve drumsticks over rice; spoon glaze over chicken. Garnish, if desired.

*Substitute sparkling white grape juice for white wine, if desired.

ELLIE WELLS
LAKELAND, FLORIDA

CHICKEN STRIPS WITH HONEY SAUCE

fast fixin's

MAKES 4 SERVINGS

Prep: 15 min., Stand: 5 min., Broil: 10 min.

Purchase sesame seeds from a health food store or from the Middle Eastern area of a grocery store, where they're much less expensive.

4 bone-in chicken breast halves
1 large egg
1 tablespoon cornstarch
2 teaspoons soy sauce
½ cup sesame seeds
¼ cup fine, dry breadcrumbs
½ teaspoon garlic powder
3 tablespoons butter or margarine, melted
½ cup Dijon mustard
¼ cup honey
¼ to ½ teaspoon hot sauce

REMOVE and discard skin and bones from chicken. Cut chicken into strips.
WHISK together next 3 ingredients in a bowl; add chicken strips, coating well.
LET chicken mixture stand 5 minutes.
COMBINE sesame seeds, breadcrumbs, and garlic powder in a large zip-top plastic bag. Add chicken, seal bag, and shake to coat.
PLACE on a lightly greased baking sheet; drizzle with butter.
BROIL 5½ inches from heat 5 minutes on each side or until golden.
STIR together mustard, honey, and hot sauce. Serve with chicken strips.

CHARLOTTE BRYANT
GREENSBURG, KENTUCKY

Taste of the South

A Sweet Little Bread

Some of our Foods staff had never heard of Sally Lunn Bread when Executive Editor Susan Dosier proposed it for this column. But after trying it, the group was sold on the slightly sweet flavor, nice shape, and ease of this yeast bread from the colonial South. They also offered suggestions for additional ways to use this top-rated recipe: in a luscious tomato sandwich, for French toast, or as the base for croutons. Our Recipe Development Director Mary Allen Perry says, "Sally Lunn Bread is like grits—the flavor complements everything."

This recipe starts with an easy-to-make yeast batter. Eggs offer the yellow color and rich taste. Baking in a Bundt or tube cakepan lends the signature shape. And the bread is sturdy enough to serve with supper and sop up gravy.

Where does this versatile food get its name? We don't really know who Sally Lunn was. Some sources contend that she was a woman who sold bread in England. Other historians say the name may have come from the French words "soleil" (which means sun) and "lune" (which means moon). The bread has a top as golden as the sun and a bottom as pale as the moon. Some food historians believe that the Jamestown colonists made this bread to remind them of their home in England. The recipe shows up in old Southern cookbooks from that time period and beyond.

Whatever its origin, you can make this sweet treat today to enjoy its light, buttery goodness. When you do, smile and raise your cup to Sally Lunn.

SALLY LUNN BREAD

MAKES 12 TO 16 SERVINGS

Prep: 10 min.; Stand: 2 hrs., 5 min.;
Cook: 5 min.; Bake: 40 min.

2 (¼-ounce) envelopes active dry yeast
½ cup warm water (100° to 110°)
1½ cups milk
¾ cup sugar
½ cup butter or margarine
1 teaspoon salt
2 large eggs
5 cups all-purpose flour
Blackberry Butter (optional)

COMBINE yeast and ½ cup warm water in a 1-cup measuring cup; let stand 5 minutes.
HEAT milk and next 3 ingredients in a medium saucepan over medium heat, stirring until butter melts. Cool to 100° to 110°.
BEAT yeast mixture, milk mixture, and eggs at medium speed with an electric mixer until blended. Gradually add flour, beating at lowest speed until blended. (Mixture will be a very sticky, soft dough.)
COVER and let rise in a warm place (85°), free from drafts, 1 hour or until dough is doubled in bulk.
STIR dough down; cover dough, and let rise in a warm place (85°), free from drafts, 30 minutes or until dough is doubled in bulk.
STIR dough down, and spoon into a well-greased, 10-inch Bundt pan or tube pan. Cover and let rise in a warm place (85°), free from drafts, 20 to 30 minutes or until dough is doubled in bulk.
BAKE at 350° for 35 to 40 minutes or until golden brown and a wooden pick inserted into center of bread comes out clean. Remove from pan immediately. Serve bread with Blackberry Butter, honey, molasses, or jelly, if desired.

BLACKBERRY BUTTER: Stir 2 to 3 tablespoons seedless blackberry jam into ½ cup softened butter.

Side Salads in a Flash

These dressings will keep in the refrigerator up to a week. Pair them with our pot pie recipes beginning on page 20.

ROASTED RED BELL PEPPER DRESSING

fast fixin's

MAKES ABOUT 2 CUPS

Prep: 5 min.

- 1 (7-ounce) jar roasted red bell peppers, drained
- 2 large garlic cloves, chopped
- 1 cup nonfat yogurt
- 1 teaspoon salt

PULSE all ingredients in a blender 5 or 6 times or until smooth.

CUCUMBER SALAD WITH ROASTED RED BELL PEPPER DRESSING: Combine gourmet salad greens, diced cucumber, and sliced red onion; serve with Roasted Red Bell Pepper Dressing.

SWEET-AND-SOUR DRESSING

fast fixin's

MAKES ABOUT 1 CUP

Prep: 5 min.

- ⅓ cup sugar
- 2½ tablespoons white vinegar
- 1 tablespoon diced onion
- ¼ teaspoon salt
- ¼ teaspoon garlic salt
- ⅛ teaspoon pepper
- ½ cup vegetable oil

PULSE first 6 ingredients in a blender 2 or 3 times or until smooth. With blender running, pour oil through food chute in a slow, steady stream; process until smooth.

RED LEAF LETTUCE SALAD WITH SWEET-AND-SOUR DRESSING: Combine 1 bunch red leaf lettuce, torn; 1 cup frozen peas, thawed; 1 cup shredded mozzarella cheese; ½ cup toasted slivered almonds; and 6 bacon slices, cooked and crumbled. Toss with Sweet-and-Sour Dressing just before serving.

MARTHA BRADFORD
JOHNSON CITY, TENNESSEE

HONEY-PECAN DRESSING

fast fixin's

MAKES 2½ CUPS

Prep: 5 min.

- 3 tablespoons sugar
- 1 tablespoon chopped sweet onion
- ½ teaspoon dry mustard
- ¼ teaspoon salt
- ½ cup honey
- ¼ cup red wine vinegar
- 1 cup vegetable oil
- 1 cup chopped pecans, toasted

PULSE first 6 ingredients in a blender 2 or 3 times until blended. With blender running, pour oil through food chute in a slow, steady stream; process until smooth. Stir in pecans.

FRUIT SALAD WITH HONEY-PECAN DRESSING: Arrange fresh orange and grapefruit sections, sliced avocado, and sliced strawberries over Bibb lettuce leaves; drizzle with dressing.

RASPBERRY SALAD DRESSING

fast fixin's

MAKES ABOUT 2 CUPS

Prep: 5 min.

- 1 (10-ounce) jar seedless raspberry fruit spread or preserves
- ½ cup seasoned rice wine vinegar
- ¼ cup olive oil

MICROWAVE raspberry spread in a microwave-safe bowl at LOW (30% power) 1 minute or until melted. Whisk in vinegar and olive oil until blended; cool. Serve at room temperature.

ROMAINE SALAD WITH RASPBERRY DRESSING: Combine 1 head romaine lettuce, torn; 1 small red onion, sliced; 1 cup crumbled feta cheese; ½ cup chopped toasted pecans; and 4 bacon slices, cooked and crumbled. Serve with Raspberry Salad Dressing.

CHRIS FENOGLIO
CROWLEY, TEXAS

Sunny-side Up Dinner Ideas

Breakfast remains the meal that's welcome around the clock. So tonight, serve one of these morning staples that's filling enough for the dinnertime shift.

CHEESY SHRIMP-AND-GRITS CASSEROLE

MAKES 10 TO 12 SERVINGS

Prep: 10 min., Cook: 25 min., Bake: 45 min.

- 4 cups chicken broth
- ½ teaspoon salt
- 1 cup uncooked regular grits
- 1 cup (4 ounces) shredded sharp Cheddar cheese, divided
- 1 cup (4 ounces) shredded Monterey Jack cheese with peppers
- 2 tablespoons butter or margarine
- 6 green onions, chopped
- 1 green bell pepper, chopped
- 1 garlic clove, minced
- 1 pound small fresh shrimp, peeled and cooked
- 1 (10-ounce) can diced tomatoes and green chiles, drained
- ¼ teaspoon salt
- ¼ teaspoon pepper

BRING 4 cups chicken broth and ½ teaspoon salt to a boil in a large saucepan;

stir in grits. Cover, reduce heat, and simmer 20 minutes.

STIR together grits, ¾ cup Cheddar cheese, and Monterey Jack cheese.

MELT butter in a large skillet over medium heat; add green onions, bell pepper, and garlic, and sauté 5 minutes or until tender.

STIR together green onion mixture, grits mixture, shrimp, and next 3 ingredients. Pour into a lightly greased 2-quart baking dish. Sprinkle top with remaining ¼ cup shredded Cheddar cheese.

BAKE at 350° for 30 to 45 minutes.

JAN BECK
CHARLOTTE, NORTH CAROLINA

LEVEE CAMP GRIDDLE CAKES

fast fixin's

MAKES 12 PANCAKES OR 42 APPETIZER-SIZE PANCAKES

Prep: 10 min., Cook: 5 min. per batch

Brenda Cason-Brown tells us that the name for this recipe comes from the old levee camps in Greenville, Mississippi, where the cakes were a popular dish with the workers. She serves these as appetizers at an evening meal along with slices of country ham or pork sausage.

- 1 cup white cornmeal
- 1 cup all-purpose flour
- 1 teaspoon baking soda
- ½ teaspoon salt
- ½ teaspoon baking powder
- 1 cup buttermilk
- ½ cup sour cream
- 1 large egg, lightly beaten
- Honey or maple syrup

COMBINE cornmeal and next 4 ingredients in a large bowl.

COMBINE buttermilk, sour cream, and egg; add to dry ingredients, stirring just until moistened.

POUR about 3 tablespoons batter for each cake onto a hot, lightly greased griddle. Cook pancakes 3 minutes or until tops are covered with bubbles and edges look cooked; turn and cook 2 minutes. (Cakes should be golden brown.) Serve with honey or maple syrup.

BRENDA CASON-BROWN
SHREVEPORT, LOUISIANA

ITALIAN BRUNCH CASSEROLE

make ahead

MAKES 8 SERVINGS

Prep: 20 min., Cook: 10 min., Chill: 8 hrs., Bake: 1 hr.

- 1 (8-ounce) package sweet Italian sausage
- 8 green onions, sliced (1 cup)
- 2 zucchini, diced (about 3 cups)
- 1 teaspoon salt
- ½ teaspoon pepper
- 1 (7-ounce) jar roasted red bell peppers, drained and chopped
- 1 (16-ounce) Italian bread loaf, cut into 1-inch cubes (about 8 cups)
- 2 cups (8 ounces) shredded sharp Cheddar cheese
- 6 large eggs
- 1½ cups milk

REMOVE and discard casings from sausage. Cook sausage in a large skillet, stirring until sausage crumbles and is no longer pink; drain.

ADD green onions and next 3 ingredients to skillet. Sauté 4 minutes or until vegetables are tender. Stir in roasted bell peppers. Drain and cool.

SPREAD 4 cups bread cubes in a lightly greased 13- x 9-inch baking dish. Top with half each of sausage mixture and cheese. Repeat with remaining bread, sausage, and cheese.

WHISK together eggs and milk. Pour mixture over bread. Cover and chill 8 hours.

BAKE, covered, at 325° for 1 hour or until bubbly and hot.

MARY LOU COOK
WELCHES, OREGON

Cozy Soups and Stews

If there's one thing that will get you through cold, gray days, it's a hearty soup or stew. These body-warming recipes are sure to keep the winter blues at bay. What's more, they're so easy to make, you'll be in high spirits all season.

BRUNSWICK STEW

MAKES 8 TO 10 SERVINGS

Prep: 5 min., Cook: 30 min.

- 3 cups chicken broth
- 2 cups chopped cooked chicken
- 1 (24-ounce) container barbecued shredded pork
- 1 (16-ounce) package frozen vegetable gumbo mixture
- 1 (10-ounce) package frozen corn
- ½ (10-ounce) package frozen petite lima beans
- ½ cup ketchup

BRING all ingredients to a boil in a Dutch oven over medium-high heat, stirring often. Cover, reduce heat to low, and simmer, stirring occasionally, 25 minutes or until thoroughly heated.

BILL STRANGE
SPRINGVILLE, ALABAMA

BAKED POTATO SOUP

MAKES ABOUT 12 CUPS

Prep: 30 min., Cook: 30 min.

To microwave potatoes, prick them several times with a fork. Cook 1 inch apart on paper towels at HIGH 14 minutes or until done, turning after 5 minutes. Cool.

- 5 large baking potatoes, baked
- ¼ cup butter or margarine
- 1 medium onion, chopped
- ⅓ cup all-purpose flour
- 1 quart half-and-half
- 3 cups milk
- 1 teaspoon salt
- ⅛ teaspoon ground white pepper
- 2 cups (8 ounces) shredded Cheddar cheese
- 8 bacon slices, cooked and crumbled

PEEL potatoes; coarsely mash with a fork.

MELT butter in a Dutch oven over medium heat; add onion, and sauté until tender. Add flour, stirring until smooth.

STIR in potatoes, half-and-half, and next 3 ingredients; cook over low heat until thoroughly heated. Top each serving with cheese and bacon.

INA STONE
BIRMINGHAM, ALABAMA

from our kitchen

New Year's Ease

■ **Squeaky clean collard greens**—While some of our readers have suggested taking fresh greens for a spin in the washing machine to get rid of those annoying bits of sand and grit, we'd like to suggest a different tack. While working on the New Year's Day story on page 16, Esau Graham shared his method.

First, Esau breaks the bunches of collard greens apart. He removes any tough stalk from the center of the leaves and stacks the leaves one on top of the other. Then he rolls them up, cigar style. Next, he cuts the roll into 1-inch slices, yielding a chiffonade, or strips, of greens. Finally, he washes the strips under cold running water.

"This way, sand can't hide in nooks and crannies of the greens," Esau explains. Now the grit-free greens are ready for cooking—and your washing machine is available for your clothes.

■ **Flavor for Hoppin' John**—We also loved Esau's quick tip for a simple bouquet garni that's used on page 17. Esau uses a coffee filter, rather than cheesecloth, to bundle herbs and garlic. The edges of the coffee filter are gathered up, tied with kitchen twine, and then the bundle is dropped into the cooking liquid to infuse it with flavor. The garlic-and-herb bag is easy to remove; just pull it out by the string.

■ **Quick-soak method for dry beans**—Many of our New Year's dishes call for dried beans or field peas. While the traditional method of cooking beans requires an overnight or 8-hour soak in water at room temperature, you can also get great results with this shortcut (it takes just over an hour): Place the beans in a large pot; add water 2 inches above the beans, and bring to a boil. Cover, remove from heat, and let stand 1 hour. Drain the beans, and continue cooking according to the recipe or package directions.

■ Steel-cut oats have wonderful texture and full flavor, but these coarse oats require at least 30 minutes of cooking time. To save time, make a large pot of oatmeal while you're cooking Sunday dinner. Divide it evenly into five plastic containers. Add your favorite toppings to each—honey, raisins, brown sugar, butter; seal and refrigerate them. Now you have a week's supply of good-for-you breakfasts. All you have to do is heat and eat.

■ Make 2003 the year for family dinners. It's a lofty goal, but try these tips out for starters: Rotate places at the table—the person at the head leads the discussion. Acknowledge someone's accomplishment by serving his or her meal on a special plate. Let each family member select the dinner music once a week. Plan the meals together, and decide who helps with each part.

Big Pots of Chili

January is the prime time for stirring up a pot of homemade chili. Bush Beans of Knoxville conducted a chili survey and found a delicious assortment of flavors. While many chili recipes contain the basic tomatoes, meat, and beans, the ingredients in the pots sometimes vary depending on the region.

Texas chili often has chunks of beef and hot chile peppers, without tomatoes and beans. It's usually served with tortillas or crackers and beans on the side. (See our recipes for the chili and beans on page 19.)

White chili is becoming known in most areas as a healthier alternative to the traditional red. It contains white beans (such as great Northern), turkey or chicken, cumin, chicken broth, and lime juice.

Cincinnati chili is seasoned with cardamom, chocolate, cloves, coffee, and cinnamon. It's most often served over spaghetti and topped with kidney beans, onion, and shredded cheese.

Whatever your favorite, put on a big pot of chili, and call your friends for dinner tonight. For more information visit **www.bushbeans.com**

Frost-Kissed Artichokes

This time of year you may notice brownish spots on the leaves of artichokes. The industry calls these "bronze tipped" or "frost kissed." They aren't very pretty, and in some cases the winter prices might be a little higher. Still, they have a sweeter, nuttier flavor than unblemished ones. The discoloration is caused by the frost that forms on the artichokes on cold winter nights. The brown disappears when the artichoke is cooked, and it turns an even green. When you see those frost-kissed, bronze-tipped artichokes, buy several; you'll be glad you did.

February

Southwestern Supper

This San Antonio couple shares their best recipes for hearty, authentic Mexican food.

Spring comes early to South Texas, and folks all over the region take advantage of the mild weather and insect-free nights to get out of the house and entertain. Jim and Andrea Peyton love this time of year so much, they decided to build an outdoor kitchen and dining area.

When out-of-town friends ask Jim where to find the best food in San Antonio, he simply replies, "My house." For more than 20 years, Jim has devoted himself to the study of Mexican cooking. As a result, he enjoys nothing more than preparing authentic south-of-the-border food—in his trademark casual style—for family and friends.

"I love a good ole Mexican *parrillada* (pah-ree-yah-dah), which means a barbecue party," says Jim. "This laid-back way of entertaining offers a selection of broiled or grilled meats and fish all chopped up and served on platters with items such as tortillas, guacamole, rice, beans, and salsas. Everything is prepared ahead and presented family style, so there's plenty of time to relax and mingle with your guests," he said.

Jim was kind enough to share a few of his favorite recipes, all of which received high marks from our staff. For more of Jim's wonderful dishes, see "Mexican Sides" on facing page.

MEXICAN-GRILLED SHRIMP WITH SMOKY SWEET SAUCE

MAKES 4 SERVINGS

Prep: 20 min., Cook: 7 min., Grill: 6 min.

If you use wooden skewers for this recipe, soak them in water for at least an hour to keep them from burning.

- 2 pounds unpeeled, large fresh shrimp
- 20 (12-inch) skewers
- ½ cup firmly packed dark brown sugar
- 6 garlic cloves, pressed
- 1 canned chipotle pepper in adobo sauce, minced
- 1 tablespoon adobo sauce
- 2 tablespoons rum
- 2 tablespoons water
- ¼ teaspoon salt
- 1 tablespoon tamarind paste
- 1 tablespoon olive oil
- Smoky Sweet Sauce

PEEL shrimp, leaving tails on; devein, if desired.

THREAD 4 shrimp onto each skewer. Set aside.

COOK brown sugar in a small heavy saucepan over low heat until melted. Add garlic and next 6 ingredients. Cook 5 minutes or until tamarind paste melts. Remove from heat.

BRUSH shrimp with olive oil. Grill, without grill lid, over medium-high heat (350° to 400°) for 4 to 6 minutes or until shrimp turn pink, turning once, and basting with tamarind glaze. Serve with Smoky Sweet Sauce.

NOTE: Tamarind is a tree-growing fruit. Its long pods contain a sweet-and-sour pulp from which a paste is made. Look for tamarind paste in the Mexican or Asian section of your grocery store.

Smoky Sweet Sauce:

MAKES ABOUT 1¾ CUPS

Prep: 8 min., Cook: 6 min.

- 1 cup low-sodium fat-free chicken broth
- ½ cup chopped refrigerated mango slices
- ¼ cup loosely packed chopped fresh cilantro
- 2 teaspoons adobo sauce
- ¾ teaspoon salt
- ⅓ cup whipping cream
- 2½ tablespoons butter

PROCESS first 5 ingredients in a blender 1 minute. Pour mixture into a saucepan, and bring to a boil over medium-high heat. Add cream, and cook, whisking often, 6 minutes or until slightly thick. Remove from heat, and whisk in butter until melted.

ORPHAN'S RICE

MAKES 6 TO 8 SERVINGS

Prep: 10 min., Cook: 30 min., Stand: 10 min.

The name of this dish comes from the Spanish name, which loosely translated means "feast for orphans." The original recipe used white rice and saffron; we used packaged yellow rice to streamline.

- 1 tablespoon butter
- ¾ cup pecan halves
- ½ cup slivered almonds
- ⅓ cup pine nuts
- ½ small onion, minced
- 1 garlic clove, minced
- 2 tablespoons vegetable oil
- 1 (10-ounce) package yellow rice
- 3 cups low-sodium chicken broth
- 2 bacon slices, cooked and crumbled
- ¼ cup finely chopped ham
- 1 tablespoon minced fresh parsley

MELT butter in a skillet over medium heat. Add pecan halves, almonds, and pine nuts, and sauté, stirring often, 3 minutes or until almonds are light golden brown.

SAUTÉ onion and garlic in hot oil in a large saucepan over medium-high heat 5 minutes or until tender. Add rice, and sauté, stirring constantly, 1 minute. Add broth, and cook rice 18 minutes. Remove from heat.

STIR in nuts, bacon, ham, and parsley. Cover and let stand 10 minutes.

NOTE: Jim likes to use three different nuts for this recipe; however, feel free to use all the same variety.

DRUNKEN SAUCE

fast fixin's

MAKES ABOUT 1½ CUPS

Prep: 10 min., Cook: 7 min., Cool: 5 min.

This Mexican barbecue sauce is often served with slow-roasted, shredded beef or lamb.

- **6 medium-size fresh tomatillos, husks removed**
- **3 pasilla chiles, stemmed, seeded, and chopped***
- **1 garlic clove, minced**
- **¼ cup flat beer**
- **1 tablespoon vegetable oil**
- **½ tablespoon red or rice wine vinegar**
- **½ teaspoon dried oregano**
- **½ teaspoon salt**
- **1 tablespoon (1 ounce) finely crumbled feta cheese****

COMBINE tomatillos, chiles, and water to cover in a saucepan. Bring mixture to a boil.

REDUCE heat, and cook, covered, 5 to 7 minutes or until tender. Drain. Allow to cool for 5 minutes.

PULSE tomatillo mixture, garlic, and next 5 ingredients 3 or 4 times in a blender until chopped. Stir in cheese.

*Substitute 1 large dried ancho chile for pasilla chiles, if desired.

**Substitute cotija cheese for feta, if desired. Look for cotija cheese in Latin markets.

Mexican Sides

If the story on the facing page whetted your appetite for real Mexican cuisine, here are more offerings to satisfy your craving. Cooking expert Jim Peyton has studied Mexican food for more than 20 years, and he builds his meals on straightforward, flavorful recipes perfectly paired with broiled and grilled meat. Include these tasty selections at your next gathering.

SALSA SALPICÓN

fast fixin's • make ahead

MAKES ABOUT 1 CUP

Prep: 10 min., Chill: 4 hrs.

"Salpicón" means "something chopped up." For an authentic flavor boost, Jim prefers to use ½ habanero pepper, chopped, in place of the jalapeño pepper.

- **5 radishes, grated**
- **1 small red onion, finely chopped**
- **1 small jalapeño pepper, seeded and minced**
- **2 tablespoons finely chopped fresh cilantro**
- **¼ cup orange juice**
- **1½ tablespoons fresh lime juice**
- **¼ teaspoon salt**

COMBINE all ingredients in a bowl. Cover and chill at least 4 hours.

PORK RIND SOUP

MAKES 6 SERVINGS

Prep: 20 min., Broil: 5 min., Cook: 25 min.

This takes the classic Southern snack to a sublime new level. Look for pork rinds in the snack section of your grocery store. *(pictured on page 39)*

- **1 (3-ounce) package pork rinds**
- **4 medium tomatoes, halved**
- **1 tablespoon butter**
- **1 large onion, chopped**
- **2 teaspoons bottled minced roasted garlic**
- **1 canned chipotle pepper**
- **6 cups low-sodium fat-free chicken broth**
- **¼ cup loosely packed fresh cilantro, finely chopped**
- **1 cup whipping cream**
- **¼ teaspoon salt**
- **¼ teaspoon pepper**
- **Garnishes: sour cream, ancho chile powder**

PROCESS pork rinds in a food processor until thoroughly ground; set aside.

PLACE tomato halves, cut sides down, on an aluminum foil-lined baking sheet.

BROIL 10 inches from heat 5 minutes or until tomatoes look blistered. Set aside.

MELT butter in a medium skillet over medium heat; add onion, and sauté 5 minutes or until tender.

PROCESS tomatoes, onion, garlic, and chipotle pepper in a food processor or blender about 45 seconds or until smooth. Pour through a wire-mesh strainer into a saucepan, using the back of a spoon to squeeze out liquid.

WHISK in ground pork rinds, broth, and next 4 ingredients; bring to a boil. Reduce heat, and simmer 15 minutes. Ladle soup into 6 bowls. Garnish, if desired.

Light Spaghetti Supper

Italian Family Feast
Serves 6

Spinach-Red Pepper Crostini

Mixed green salad with
Creamy Gorgonzola Dressing

White Spaghetti and Meatballs

Orange Cream Pie

SPINACH-RED PEPPER CROSTINI

fast fixin's

MAKES 26 CROSTINI

Prep: 15 min., Bake: 10 min.

We adapted this recipe from one sent by Hilda Hamilton. The spinach mixture can be prepared a day ahead.

- 1 (8-ounce) French baguette, cut diagonally into ¼-inch-thick slices
- 1 (10-ounce) package frozen chopped spinach, thawed
- ½ cup shredded Parmesan cheese
- ¼ cup walnuts, toasted*
- 3 tablespoons fat-free mayonnaise
- 2 tablespoons fat-free milk
- 1 large garlic clove
- ¼ teaspoon salt
- ¼ teaspoon pepper
- 1 (7-ounce) jar roasted peppers, drained and cut into thin strips

BAKE bread slices on a baking sheet at 375° for 5 minutes. Set aside.
DRAIN spinach well, pressing between paper towels.

PROCESS spinach, Parmesan cheese, and next 6 ingredients in a food processor until mixture is smooth. Spread spinach mixture evenly over bread slices.
BAKE at 375° for 5 minutes. Top evenly with pepper strips. Serve immediately.

HILDA HAMILTON
KNOXVILLE, TENNESSEE

Per slice: Calories 40 (29% from fat); Fat 1.4g (sat 0.4g, mono 0.3g, poly 0.5g); Protein 1.9g; Carb 5.5g; Fiber 0.4g; Chol 1.1mg; Iron 0.4mg; Sodium 143mg; Calc 35mg

*Substitute ¼ cup pecans, if desired.

NOTE: To toast walnuts, spread on a baking sheet, and bake at 350°, stirring occasionally, 5 to 10 minutes.

CREAMY GORGONZOLA DRESSING

fast fixin's • make ahead

MAKES 2 CUPS DRESSING

Prep: 10 min.

Pair this dressing with mixed greens, sliced pears, and strawberries to create a perfect salty-sweet salad.

- ½ (15-ounce) container part-skim ricotta cheese*
- ¾ cup fat-free buttermilk
- 3 ounces Gorgonzola cheese, crumbled*
- 3 tablespoons rice wine vinegar
- 1 teaspoon Worcestershire sauce
- 1 small garlic clove, minced
- ½ teaspoon freshly ground pepper

PROCESS all ingredients in a food processor or blender until smooth, stopping to scrape down sides. Chill until ready to serve.

Per 2 tablespoons: Calories 43 (55% from fat)**; Fat 2.7g (sat 1.7g, mono 0.3g, poly 0g); Protein 3g; Carb 2g; Fiber 0g; Chol 10mg; Iron 0.1mg; Sodium 85mg; Calc 83mg

*Substitute low-fat cottage cheese for the part-skim ricotta cheese, and blue cheese for the Gorgonzola cheese, if desired.

**Serving this dressing with mixed salad greens topped with sliced pears and strawberries will reduce the total percentage of fat per serving.

WHITE SPAGHETTI AND MEATBALLS

MAKES 6 SERVINGS

Prep: 30 min., Chill: 20 min., Bake: 13 min., Cook: 45 min.

This may seem like a long list of ingredients, but don't be intimidated—you probably have most of them on hand already.

- 1½ pounds skinned and boned chicken breast halves, cut into chunks
- 1 large garlic clove
- 1 large egg
- 10 saltine crackers, finely crushed
- 1 teaspoon Italian seasoning
- Vegetable cooking spray
- 1 (8-ounce) package sliced fresh mushrooms
- ⅛ teaspoon ground nutmeg
- 1 teaspoon olive oil
- 1 large garlic clove, minced
- 2 tablespoons all-purpose flour
- ½ cup dry white wine
- 3 cups fat-free, reduced-sodium chicken broth
- 1 (8-ounce) package ⅓-less-fat cream cheese
- ¼ teaspoon ground red pepper
- ¼ cup chopped fresh Italian parsley
- 1 (8-ounce) package spaghetti

PROCESS chicken and garlic clove in a food processor until ground.
STIR together chicken mixture, egg, and next 2 ingredients in a large bowl. Cover and chill 20 minutes.
SHAPE mixture into 1-inch balls. Place a rack coated with cooking spray in an aluminum foil-lined broiler pan. Arrange meatballs on rack; lightly spray meatballs with cooking spray.
BAKE at 375° for 13 minutes or until golden and thoroughly cooked.
SAUTÉ mushrooms and nutmeg in hot oil in a Dutch oven over medium-high heat 8 to 10 minutes or until mushrooms are tender. Add minced garlic; sauté 1 minute. Sprinkle with flour, and cook, stirring constantly, 1 minute. Add wine, stirring to loosen browned particles from bottom of pan. Whisk in broth.
BRING to a boil; reduce heat, and simmer, stirring occasionally, 15 minutes.

Add cream cheese, whisking until smooth and sauce is thickened.
ADD meatballs, red pepper, and parsley to sauce; simmer 10 minutes. Meanwhile, cook pasta according to package directions omitting salt and oil; drain. Serve sauce with meatballs over pasta.

Calories 431 (24% from fat); Fat 11.2g (sat 5.2g, mono 3.5g, poly 1.1g); Protein 40g; Carb 39g; Fiber 1.7g; Chol 122mg; Iron 3.8mg; Sodium 629mg; Calc 78mg

ORANGE CREAM PIE

make ahead • freezable

MAKES 8 SERVINGS

Prep: 10 min., Freeze: 8 hrs.

For neat servings, run a knife under hot water for 1 minute before slicing.

- **4 cups (1 quart) sugar-free, fat-free ice cream, softened**
- **1 (11-ounce) can mandarin oranges, drained**
- **1 (6-ounce) reduced-fat graham cracker crust**
- **Orange Glaze (optional)**
- **Garnish: orange rind curls**

BEAT softened ice cream and mandarin oranges at medium speed with an electric mixer until blended. Spoon into piecrust. Cover and freeze 8 hours or until firm. Serve with Orange Glaze, if desired. Garnish, if desired.

Calories (pie without glaze) 154 (21% from fat); Fat 3.5g (sat 0.5g, mono 0g, poly 0g); Protein 2.5g; Carb 28g; Fiber 0g; Chol 0mg; Iron 0.5mg; Sodium 112mg; Calc 40mg

Calories (with glaze) 250 (12% from fat); Fat 3.5g (sat 0.5g, mono 0g, poly 0g); Protein 2.5g; Carb 51g; Fiber 0.1g; Chol 0mg; Iron 0.5mg; Sodium 112mg; Calc 40mg

Orange Glaze:

MAKES 1 CUP

Prep: 5 min., Cook: 7 min., Chill: 2 hrs.

- **⅔ cup sugar**
- **¼ cup water**
- **3 tablespoons orange liqueur**
- **1 tablespoon grated orange rind**
- **2½ tablespoons light corn syrup**

BRING all ingredients to a boil in a small saucepan, stirring constantly; boil 2 minutes.
COVER glaze, and chill 2 hours.

Fresh Flavor With Dried Herbs

Good news: Dried herbs lend an earthy and delicious quality to many dishes, and they're right in your spice cabinet or pantry. Enjoy these flavorful dishes.

HUNGARIAN BEEF STEW

MAKES 8 SERVINGS

Prep: 25 min.; Cook: 2 hrs., 20 min.

- **5 small onions**
- **2 pounds beef stew meat**
- **⅓ cup all-purpose flour**
- **2 tablespoons vegetable oil**
- **2 garlic cloves, minced**
- **1 (10¾-ounce) can tomato soup, undiluted**
- **1¾ cups water, divided**
- **2 bay leaves**
- **1 tablespoon dried parsley flakes**
- **1½ teaspoons dried thyme**
- **2 teaspoons salt**
- **½ teaspoon pepper**
- **3 large baking potatoes, peeled and cut into 1-inch pieces**
- **1 pound carrots, peeled and sliced**
- **4 celery ribs, sliced**
- **1 pound egg noodles, cooked**

PEEL onions, and set 4 aside. Chop remaining onion.
DREDGE beef in flour. Brown in hot vegetable oil in a Dutch oven over medium-high heat. Add chopped onion and garlic; sauté until onion is tender. Stir in soup, 1 cup water, and next 5 ingredients. Cover, reduce heat to low, and simmer 1 hour.
ADD whole onions, potato, carrot, celery, and remaining ¾ cup water. Bring to a boil; reduce heat, and simmer 1 hour or until beef is tender. Discard bay leaves. Serve stew over hot cooked egg noodles.

NAOMI MAYER
TAYLORS, SOUTH CAROLINA

SALAD NIÇOISE

MAKES 8 SERVINGS

Prep: 20 min., Cook: 18 min., Chill: 30 min.

- **2 pounds unpeeled small red potatoes**
- **1½ pounds fresh green beans**
- **Herb Dressing**
- **2 heads romaine lettuce**
- **6 (3-ounce) packages albacore tuna, flaked**
- **1 (2-ounce) can anchovy fillets, drained (optional)**
- **5 hard-cooked eggs, quartered**
- **5 plum tomatoes, cut into wedges, or 1 (8-ounce) container grape tomatoes**
- **1 cup sliced ripe olives**

COOK potatoes in boiling water to cover 15 minutes or until tender; drain. Cool slightly; cut into slices. Set aside.
COOK green beans in boiling water to cover 3 minutes; drain. Plunge into ice water to stop the cooking process.
TOSS together potato slices, green beans, and ½ cup Herb Dressing in a large bowl. Chill at least 30 minutes.
TEAR 1 head romaine lettuce into bite-size pieces. Line a platter with leaves of remaining lettuce. Arrange potato mixture over lettuce. Top with torn lettuce pieces. Mound tuna in center of greens. Arrange anchovies around tuna, if desired. Place eggs and tomato wedges on salad. Sprinkle with sliced olives. Serve with remaining Herb Dressing.

Herb Dressing:

MAKES 1½ CUPS

Prep: 10 min.

- **1 cup olive oil**
- **½ cup red wine vinegar**
- **¼ cup drained capers**
- **2 green onions, chopped**
- **2 teaspoons dried basil**
- **2 teaspoons dried marjoram**
- **2 teaspoons dried oregano**
- **2 teaspoons dried thyme**
- **½ teaspoon dry mustard**
- **½ teaspoon salt**
- **½ teaspoon freshly ground pepper**

WHISK together all ingredients.

SHERRON GOLDSTEIN
BIRMINGHAM, ALABAMA

Come By for Brunch

When the usual eggs and bacon just won't do, treat weekend guests to a delicious brunch that starts the day off right. Parmesan, Brie, and fresh sage give our Brie-and-Sausage Breakfast Casserole high flavor appeal. You can even make homemade sweet rolls with a little help from refrigerated crescent rolls.

BRIE-AND-SAUSAGE BREAKFAST CASSEROLE

make ahead

MAKES 8 TO 10 SERVINGS

Prep: 20 min., Chill: 8 hrs., Bake: 50 min. Stand: 10 min. *(pictured on facing page)*

1 (8-ounce) round Brie*
1 pound ground hot pork sausage
6 white bread slices
1 cup grated Parmesan cheese
7 large eggs, divided
3 cups whipping cream, divided
2 cups fat-free milk
1 tablespoon chopped fresh or
   1 teaspoon dried rubbed sage
1 teaspoon seasoned salt
1 teaspoon dry mustard
Garnish: chopped green onions

TRIM and discard rind from top of Brie. Cut cheese into cubes; set aside.
COOK sausage in a large skillet over medium-high heat, stirring until it crumbles and is no longer pink; drain well.
CUT crusts from bread slices, and place crusts evenly in a lightly greased 13- x 9-inch baking dish. Layer evenly with bread slices, sausage, Brie, and grated Parmesan cheese.
WHISK together 5 eggs, 2 cups whipping cream, and next 4 ingredients; pour evenly over cheeses. Cover and chill 8 hours.
WHISK together remaining 2 eggs and 1 cup whipping cream; pour evenly over chilled mixture.
BAKE at 350° for 50 minutes or until set. Let stand 10 minutes before serving. Garnish, if desired.

*Substitute 2 cups (8 ounces) shredded Swiss cheese for Brie, if desired.

PECAN CRESCENT TWISTS

fast fixin's

MAKES 8 SERVINGS

Prep: 15 min., Bake: 12 min. *(pictured on facing page)*

2 (8-ounce) cans refrigerated
   crescent rolls
3 tablespoons butter or margarine,
   melted and divided
½ cup chopped pecans
¼ cup granulated sugar
1 teaspoon ground cinnamon
⅛ teaspoon ground nutmeg
½ cup powdered sugar
2½ teaspoons maple syrup or milk

UNROLL crescent rolls, and separate each can into 2 rectangles, pressing perforations to seal. Brush evenly with 2 tablespoons melted butter.
STIR together chopped pecans and next 3 ingredients; sprinkle 3 tablespoons pecan mixture onto each rectangle, pressing in gently.
ROLL up, starting at 1 long side, and twist. Cut 6 shallow ½-inch-long diagonal slits in each roll.
SHAPE rolls into rings, pressing ends together; place on a lightly greased baking sheet. Brush rings evenly with remaining 1 tablespoon butter.
BAKE at 375° for 12 minutes or until rings are golden.
STIR together powdered sugar and maple syrup until smooth; drizzle over warm rings. Cut rings in half, and serve.

SPICED APPLES

fast fixin's

MAKES 8 SERVINGS

Prep: 10 min., Cook: 20 min *(pictured on facing page)*

½ cup butter or margarine
8 large Granny Smith apples,
   peeled, cored, and sliced
1½ cups sugar
1½ teaspoons ground cinnamon
½ teaspoon ground nutmeg

MELT butter in a large skillet over medium-high heat; add apples and remaining ingredients. Sauté 15 to 20 minutes or until apples are tender.

MULLED CRANBERRY DRINK

fast fixin's

MAKES 10 CUPS

Prep: 5 min., Cook: 10 min. *(pictured on facing page)*

1 (48-ounce) bottle cranberry juice
   drink
3 cups apple juice
3 cups orange juice
½ cup maple syrup
1½ teaspoons ground cinnamon
¾ teaspoon ground cloves
¾ teaspoon ground nutmeg
1 orange, sliced
Garnishes: whole cinnamon sticks,
   orange slices

BRING first 7 ingredients to a boil in a Dutch oven. Add orange slices just before serving. Garnish, if desired.

Brie-and-Sausage Breakfast Casserole, Spiced Apples, Pecan Crescent Twists, and Mulled Cranberry Drink, facing page

Lemon-Thyme Roasted Chicken, page 44

Fig-Balsamic Roasted Pork Loin, page 45

Sweetheart Jamwiches, facing page

Sweet Treats

Cupid's arrow found the heart of Jan Moon, formerly of our Test Kitchens, when she shared these darling desserts with our staff. The idea came from Editor John Floyd as he strolled through Charleston, South Carolina, last year and noticed the displays at Charleston Chocolates. He suggested we make our own sweets and package them in candy boxes.

These goodies are created from items you have on hand—refrigerated piecrusts, crisp rice cereal, marshmallows, jam, and more. Try them, and you'll find that enticing your sweetie has never been so easy.

SWEETHEART JAMWICHES

MAKES 23 TARTS

Prep: 45 min., Bake: 8 min.
(pictured on facing page)

- 1 (15-ounce) package refrigerated piecrusts
- 1 egg white, lightly beaten
- 2 tablespoons granulated sugar
- 1 (3-ounce) package cream cheese, softened
- ¼ cup powdered sugar
- 2 tablespoons butter, softened
- ½ teaspoon almond extract
- ½ (10-ounce) jar seedless raspberry preserves or strawberry jam
- ½ cup white chocolate morsels
- 1 tablespoon butter
- Red sparkling sugar (optional)

UNFOLD piecrusts on a lightly floured surface, and roll to press out fold lines. Cut with a 2-inch heart-shaped cookie cutter. Reroll remaining dough, and repeat procedure. (There should be a total of 46 pastry hearts.) Brush 1 side of each pastry heart with egg white, and sprinkle evenly with granulated sugar. Place pastry hearts on 2 ungreased baking sheets.

BAKE at 400° for 7 to 8 minutes or until lightly browned. Remove hearts to wire racks, and cool.

STIR together cream cheese, powdered sugar, 2 tablespoons butter, and almond extract until blended.

SPREAD cream cheese mixture evenly on unsugared sides of half the hearts; spread about ½ teaspoon preserves over mixture. Top with remaining hearts, unsugared sides down.

MICROWAVE white chocolate morsels and 1 tablespoon butter in a glass bowl at HIGH 1 minute or until melted. Stir until smooth. Place mixture in a small zip-top freezer bag; seal bag. Snip a tiny hole in 1 corner of bag, and drizzle over tarts. Cool completely; sprinkle with red sparkling sugar, if desired. Place in candy boxes, if desired.

MINI TIRAMISÙ ÉCLAIRS

MAKES 24 ÉCLAIRS

Prep: 35 min.

- ⅓ cup hot water
- 2 teaspoons instant coffee granules
- 2 tablespoons granulated sugar
- 2 (3-ounce) packages ladyfingers, split
- 1 (8-ounce) package mascarpone cheese*
- 1½ cups powdered sugar, divided
- 2 tablespoons chocolate syrup
- ½ cup semisweet chocolate morsels
- 1 tablespoon butter
- 1 tablespoon whipping cream

STIR together first 3 ingredients until sugar is dissolved; set aside 2 tablespoons mixture. Brush cut sides of ladyfingers evenly with remaining coffee mixture.

STIR together mascarpone cheese, ½ cup powdered sugar, and chocolate syrup until blended. Spoon or pipe mascarpone cheese mixture evenly onto 24 cut sides of ladyfinger halves; top with remaining ladyfinger halves, cut sides down.

MICROWAVE chocolate morsels, butter, and cream at HIGH 30 seconds or until melted, stirring twice. Place chocolate mixture in a small zip-top freezer bag; seal bag. Snip a tiny hole in 1 corner of bag, and drizzle over éclairs. Let stand until firm.

STIR together reserved coffee mixture and remaining 1 cup powdered sugar, stirring until blended. Place coffee-powdered sugar mixture in a small zip-top freezer bag; seal bag. Snip a tiny hole in 1 corner of bag.

DRIZZLE éclairs evenly with coffee-powdered sugar mixture. Place on a serving platter, cake stand, or in candy boxes, if desired.

*Substitute 1 (8-ounce) package cream cheese, softened, for mascarpone, if desired.

CRISPY CHOCOLATE HEARTS

fast fixin's • make ahead

MAKES 15 HEARTS

Prep: 30 min., Stand: 1 hr.

- 1 (12-ounce) package semisweet chocolate morsels*
- ½ cup smooth peanut butter
- 2 cups crisp rice cereal
- 1½ cups peanuts
- 1½ cups miniature marshmallows
- 2 (2-ounce) chocolate bark coating squares, melted
- White nonpareils (optional)

MICROWAVE chocolate morsels in a large glass bowl at HIGH 2 minutes or until melted, stirring chocolate every 30 seconds.

STIR in peanut butter, stirring until well blended.

STIR in cereal, peanuts, and marshmallows. Line a 13- x 9-inch pan with aluminum foil. Lightly grease foil. Press mixture into foil-lined pan. Drizzle with chocolate. Sprinkle with white nonpareils, if desired.

LET stand 1 hour or until firm; cut with a 3-inch heart-shaped cookie cutter to make hearts. Store in an airtight container or place in a candy box, if desired.

*Substitute 6 (2-ounce) almond bark coating squares for chocolate morsels, if desired.

NOTE: White nonpareils (tiny decorative beads) are available in cake decorating shops and large supermarkets.

JUDY FRAZER
SYLACAUGA, ALABAMA

CHOCOLATE-ALMOND HEARTS

fast fixin's • make ahead

MAKES 2½ DOZEN HEARTS

Prep: 20 min.

Blanched almonds are pretty white nuts with no brown skin coating. You can buy them at the supermarket.

- ½ cup whole blanched almonds, toasted
- 1 (2-ounce) chocolate bark coating square, melted

DIP almonds halfway in melted chocolate, pointed ends down. Lay 2 almonds side by side, pointed ends down and touching, on wax paper, forming a heart shape. Let stand until firm.

What's for Supper?

Good Taste in a Hurry

Teresa Stokes is one busy lady. She homeschools her three boys—Will, Andrew, and Jackson—as well as chauffeurs them to soccer, basketball, art, and Boy Scouts. Yet she always manages to serve a great meal to her family. Here Teresa gladly shares some of her tried-and-true recipes with us. Her Fruit Salad provides a refreshing cool complement to the Speedy Chicken Stew.

SPEEDY CHICKEN STEW

fast fixin's

MAKES 6 SERVINGS

Prep: 8 min., Cook: 30 min.

- 2 (14-ounce) cans chicken broth
- 2 chicken bouillon cubes
- 1 (20-ounce) package frozen creamed corn
- 1 (10-ounce) package frozen baby lima beans
- 1 large baking potato, peeled and diced
- 1 small jalapeño pepper, seeded and minced (optional)
- ½ large sweet onion, diced
- ⅛ teaspoon ground red pepper
- ¼ teaspoon dried thyme
- 3 cups chopped cooked chicken
- 1 (14½-ounce) can seasoned diced tomatoes with garlic, basil, and oregano
- 1 (6-ounce) can tomato paste

COMBINE first 9 ingredients in a Dutch oven. Bring to a boil over medium-high heat, stirring often. Reduce heat, and simmer 15 to 20 minutes or until potato and lima beans are tender. Stir in chicken, diced tomatoes, and tomato paste; simmer 10 more minutes.

FRUIT SALAD

fast fixin's • make ahead

MAKES 6 SERVINGS

Prep: 5 min.

- 1 (11-ounce) can mandarin oranges, drained
- 1 (20-ounce) can pineapple chunks, drained
- 1 cup seedless green grapes
- 3 bananas, sliced
- ⅔ cup vanilla yogurt
- 2 tablespoons orange marmalade
- ¼ teaspoon ground ginger

COMBINE mandarin oranges, pineapple chunks, grapes, and banana.
STIR together yogurt, orange marmalade, and ground ginger, and toss with fruit mixture.
CHILL salad until ready to serve.

CHEDDAR-NUT BREAD

fast fixin's

MAKES 12 LARGE MUFFINS

Prep: 10 min., Bake: 15 min.

- 3¾ cups all-purpose baking mix
- 1½ cups (6 ounces) shredded Cheddar cheese
- 1 large egg
- 1 (12-ounce) can evaporated milk
- ½ cup chopped pecans, toasted

COMBINE baking mix and cheese in a large bowl; make a well in center of mixture. Stir together egg and milk; add to dry ingredients, stirring just until moistened. Stir in toasted pecans, and spoon into greased muffin pans, filling two-thirds full.
BAKE at 375° for 12 to 15 minutes.

PEANUT BUTTER-KISS COOKIES

fast fixin's • family favorite

MAKES 3 DOZEN COOKIES

Prep: 10 min., Bake: 11 min.

- 1 (14-ounce) can sweetened condensed milk
- ¾ cup smooth peanut butter
- 2 cups all-purpose baking mix
- 1 teaspoon vanilla extract
- ¼ cup sugar
- 1 (13-ounce) package milk chocolate kisses, unwrapped

BEAT condensed milk and peanut butter at medium speed with an electric mixer until creamy. Add baking mix and vanilla, beating at low speed just until blended.
SHAPE dough into 1-inch balls; roll in sugar. Place on lightly greased baking sheets.
BAKE at 350° for 11 minutes. Remove from oven, and immediately place a chocolate kiss in center of each cookie. Remove cookies to wire racks to cool.

Bravo for Brownies

If you want a quick bar cookie, it's brownies to the rescue—but add some pizzazz, please. Stir a palmful of sweet ingredients into a brownie mix to create Banana-Split Brownies, or add peanuts and peanut butter for Elephant Stomp Brownies. If you have time to spare, pull out all the stops and showcase Beverly Nesbit's recipe for Caramel-Pecan Filled Brownies.

BANANA-SPLIT BROWNIES

MAKES 1 DOZEN

Prep: 10 min., Bake: 45 min.

- 1 (17.6-ounce) package chocolate double-fudge brownie mix
- ½ cup dried cherries
- ¼ cup water
- 1 medium banana, sliced
- 1 teaspoon vanilla extract
- ½ cup sliced almonds, toasted (optional)
- Toppings: ice cream, hot fudge and caramel sauces, toasted flaked coconut, grated milk chocolate, chopped pecans, candy-coated chocolate pieces, whipped cream, maraschino cherries with stems

PREPARE brownie mix according to package directions, following cakelike instructions.
MICROWAVE cherries and ¼ cup water at HIGH 1½ minutes. Drain and cool.
Stir cherries, banana, vanilla, and, if desired, almonds into batter.
POUR batter into a lightly greased 8-inch square pan.
BAKE at 350° for 40 to 45 minutes. Cool and cut brownies into squares. Serve with desired toppings.

NOTE: For testing purposes only, we used Duncan Hines Chocolate Lover's Double Fudge Brownie Mix.

EMMA THOMAS
ROME, GEORGIA

ELEPHANT STOMP BROWNIES

MAKES 2 DOZEN

Prep: 20 min., Bake: 50 min.

- 1 cup quick-cooking oats
- 1 cup all-purpose flour, divided
- 1¼ cups butter or margarine, softened and divided
- ¼ cup plus 2 tablespoons firmly packed brown sugar
- ½ cup smooth peanut butter
- 5 large eggs, divided
- ¼ cup salted Spanish peanuts (optional)
- 2 cups granulated sugar
- ¾ cup unsweetened cocoa

COMBINE oats and ½ cup flour in a medium bowl.
BEAT ¼ cup butter at medium speed with an electric mixer until creamy; gradually add brown sugar and peanut butter, beating well. Add 1 egg, beating just until blended. Add oat mixture, stirring until blended.
REMOVE ¼ cup peanut butter mixture, and reserve.
ADD peanuts to remaining peanut butter mixture, if desired. Press evenly into a lightly greased 13- x 9-inch pan.
BAKE at 350° for 10 minutes; cool crust.
BEAT remaining 1 cup butter at medium speed with an electric mixer until creamy; gradually add granulated sugar, beating well. Add remaining 4 eggs, 1 at a time, beating just until blended. Stir in cocoa and remaining ½ cup flour. Spread batter over crust, and sprinkle with reserved peanut butter mixture.
BAKE at 350° for 35 minutes or to desired degree of doneness. Cool and cut brownies into 2-inch squares.

KITCHEN EXPRESS: Prepare crust as directed. Substitute 1 (19-ounce) package brownie mix for batter; prepare according to package directions. Spread over crust, and proceed with recipe as directed.

CAROL NOBLE
BURGAW, NORTH CAROLINA

CARAMEL-PECAN FILLED BROWNIES

MAKES 3½ DOZEN

Prep: 35 min., Bake: 25 min., Chill: 40 min.

- 3 large eggs
- 1½ cups butter or margarine, melted and divided
- 1¾ cups granulated sugar
- ½ teaspoon salt
- 1 teaspoon vanilla extract
- 1 cup all-purpose flour
- 1 cup unsweetened cocoa, divided
- 1 (14-ounce) package caramels, unwrapped
- 1 cup milk, divided
- 3 cups chopped pecans, toasted
- 10 large marshmallows or 1 cup miniature marshmallows
- 1 (16-ounce) package powdered sugar, sifted

WHISK together eggs, 1 cup butter, granulated sugar, salt, and vanilla in a large bowl. Add flour and ½ cup cocoa, blending well. Spread into a greased 13- x 9-inch pan.
BAKE at 350° for 20 to 25 minutes or until a wooden pick inserted in center comes out clean. Cool.
MICROWAVE caramels and ⅔ cup milk in a large glass bowl at HIGH 3 minutes or until melted and combined. Stir in pecans, and spread evenly over brownies. Chill 20 minutes or until set.
COOK marshmallows and remaining ½ cup butter, ½ cup cocoa, and ⅓ cup milk in a saucepan over medium heat, stirring constantly until mixture is smooth and thoroughly heated. Remove from heat.
BEAT marshmallow mixture and powdered sugar with an electric mixer until smooth. Spread evenly over caramel mixture. Chill 20 minutes or until set. Cut brownies into 1½- x 2-inch pieces.

BEVERLY NESBIT
WINSTON-SALEM, NORTH CAROLINA

Ready, Set, Roast

Follow our recipes and tips for juicy entrées every time.

For former Assistant Foods Editor Cybil B. Talley, her mom's roasted chicken tops her list of ultimate comfort foods. After liberally seasoning a plump bird, Cybil's mom would pop it in the oven and set off to tackle other tasks. That's the beauty of roasting. For little effort in the kitchen, you are rewarded with entrées that appeal to everyone. Leftover meat will work overtime in sandwiches, salads, or casseroles.

Dry-heat roasting allows the juices in meat to rise to the surface and caramelize. Remember that roasting chickens are generally juicier and more flavorful than broiler-fryers. Tender cuts of meat work best—if in doubt, ask your butcher which to choose.

LEMON-THYME ROASTED CHICKEN

family favorite

MAKES 4 SERVINGS

Prep: 20 min.; Bake: 1 hr., 30 min.; Stand: 10 min.; Cook: 5 min.

We start off at a high temperature to first brown the skin and lock in juices and taste. Reducing the heat ensures that the bird cooks evenly. (*pictured on page 38*)

- 1 lemon, halved
- ½ medium onion
- 1 (5-pound) whole roasting chicken
- ¼ cup butter or margarine, softened
- 3 garlic cloves, minced
- 2 teaspoons chopped fresh thyme
- 1 teaspoon coarse-grain salt
- 1 teaspoon coarsely ground pepper
- 1 cup chicken broth
- ½ cup dry white wine
- 2 tablespoons all-purpose flour

PLACE 1 lemon half and onion half into chicken cavity. Squeeze remaining lemon half into chicken cavity.

STIR together butter, garlic, and thyme. Starting at neck cavity, loosen skin from breast and drumsticks by inserting fingers and gently pushing between skin and meat. (Do not totally detach skin.) Rub half of butter mixture evenly under skin.

TIE ends of legs together with string; tuck wingtips under. Spread remaining half of butter mixture over chicken. Sprinkle evenly with salt and pepper. Place chicken, breast side up, on a lightly greased rack in a lightly greased shallow roasting pan.

BAKE at 450° for 30 minutes.

REDUCE heat to 400°, and bake 55 to 60 minutes or until a meat thermometer inserted into thigh registers 180°.

COVER loosely with aluminum foil to prevent excessive browning, if necessary. Remove to a serving platter, reserving drippings in pan. Cover with foil, and let stand 10 minutes before slicing.

ADD 1 cup chicken broth to reserved drippings in pan, stirring to loosen browned bits from bottom of pan.

WHISK together pan drippings mixture, wine, and flour in a small saucepan. Cook, stirring often, over medium heat 5 minutes or until thickened. Serve with chicken.

CHIPOTLE ROASTED CHICKEN: Substitute 1 canned chipotle pepper, chopped, and ¼ cup adobo sauce from can for garlic cloves and chopped fresh thyme. Sprinkle chicken with 1 teaspoon ground cumin and 1 teaspoon each salt and pepper. Proceed as directed.

BARBARA A. BROWN
ATLANTA, GEORGIA

CURRIED LEG OF LAMB WITH CUCUMBER-YOGURT SAUCE

MAKES 6 TO 8 SERVINGS

Prep: 20 min.; Chill: 8 hrs.; Bake: 1 hr., 50 min.; Stand: 15 min.

Serve leftover slices of lamb in warm pita rounds with lettuce and sliced red onions.

- 2 cups plain yogurt
- ¼ cup chopped fresh cilantro
- 4 garlic cloves, minced
- 3 jalapeño peppers, seeded and minced
- 2 tablespoons curry powder
- 1 tablespoon minced fresh ginger
- 1½ teaspoons ground coriander
- 1½ teaspoons salt
- 1 (5- to 6-pound) leg of lamb, boned
- Cucumber-Yogurt Sauce

PROCESS first 8 ingredients in a food processor or blender until smooth, stopping to scrape down sides. Place lamb in a large shallow dish or zip-top freezer bag. Pour yogurt mixture over lamb. Cover or seal, and chill 8 hours, turning occasionally.

REMOVE lamb from marinade, discarding marinade. Place lamb on a rack in a roasting pan.

BAKE at 425° for 25 minutes; reduce temperature to 350°, and bake 1 hour and 25 minutes or until a meat thermometer inserted into thickest portion registers 145°. Remove from oven, and let stand 15 minutes or until a meat thermometer registers 150° (medium-rare). Serve with Cucumber-Yogurt Sauce.

Cucumber-Yogurt Sauce:

MAKES 2½ CUPS

Prep: 10 min.

- 1½ cups plain yogurt
- 1 cucumber, peeled, seeded, and chopped
- 3 tablespoons chopped fresh cilantro
- 1 tablespoon lemon juice
- ½ teaspoon salt
- ¼ teaspoon ground cumin

STIR together all ingredients. Cover and chill sauce.

FIG-BALSAMIC ROASTED PORK LOIN

MAKES 8 TO 10 SERVINGS

Prep: 45 min.; Bake: 1 hr., 30 min.; Stand: 15 min.; Cook: 18 min.

Purchase a pork loin roast, not a rolled pork loin roast (which has two loins tied together). Don't trim away the entire fat cap on top of the loin; this layer prevents the meat from drying out. *(pictured on page 39)*

- ½ pound ground pork sausage
- 1¾ cups herb-seasoned stuffing mix
- 1 large ripe Bartlett pear, peeled and chopped
- ½ red bell pepper, finely chopped
- ⅓ cup chopped dried figs
- ½ cup hot chicken broth
- 1 tablespoon minced fresh thyme
- 1 (4-pound) boneless pork loin roast
- 1 teaspoon salt
- 1 to 2 tablespoons cracked pepper
- 1 (11.5-ounce) jar fig preserves
- 1 cup Madeira wine
- 2 tablespoons balsamic vinegar
- ¼ cup butter or margarine
- ¼ cup all-purpose flour
- Garnishes: dried figs, Bartlett pear slices, fresh parsley sprigs

COOK sausage in a skillet over medium-high heat, stirring often, 4 to 5 minutes or until it crumbles and is no longer pink. Drain well. Stir together sausage, stuffing mix, and next 5 ingredients.
BUTTERFLY pork loin roast by making a lengthwise cut down center of 1 flat side, cutting to within ½ inch of the bottom. (Do not cut all the way through roast.) Open roast, forming a rectangle, and place between 2 sheets of heavy-duty plastic wrap. Flatten to ½-inch thickness using a meat mallet or rolling pin. Sprinkle roast evenly with salt and pepper. Spoon sausage mixture evenly over roast, leaving a ½-inch border. Roll up roast, and tie with string at 1½-inch intervals. Place roast, seam side down, in a greased shallow roasting pan.
BAKE at 375° for 55 to 60 minutes or until a meat thermometer inserted into thickest portion registers 145°. Remove roast from pan; reserve drippings. Return roast to pan.

STIR together fig preserves, Madeira, and balsamic vinegar. Spoon half of preserves mixture evenly over roast.
BAKE at 375° for 20 to 30 more minutes or until meat thermometer registers 160°. Let stand 15 minutes before slicing.
MELT butter in a medium saucepan; whisk in flour until smooth. Cook, whisking constantly, 3 minutes. Whisk in reserved pan drippings and remaining fig preserves mixture, and cook over medium-high heat 5 minutes. Serve sauce with roast; garnish, if desired.

Tips for Pork Loin

Pounding the pork loin with the flat, smooth side of a meat mallet to ½-inch thickness produces an even surface and allows for easier rolling of the stuffed meat.

Leave a ½-inch border on the edge of the meat to prevent stuffing from spilling out. The stuffing will expand as you roll it.

Using butcher's twine, tie the roast at 1½-inch intervals. Find twine on the cooking utensils aisle of grocery stores.

Taste of the South

Fabulous Fried Oysters

Oysters are a true Southern delicacy. While purists prefer them raw, they can also be cooked in a variety of ways. Some recipes pair them with rich cream sauces and fancy ingredients. But one of the most down-home ways to enjoy oysters is deep-fried.

Whether you enjoy oysters with tartar sauce, cocktail sauce, salsa, or a squeeze of fresh lemon, you can't go wrong with this recipe.

SOUTHWEST FRIED OYSTERS

chef recipe

MAKES 4 TO 6 SERVINGS

Prep: 20 min., Chill: 2 hrs., Fry: 3 min. per batch

- 2 pints fresh select oysters, drained
- 2 cups buttermilk
- 1 cup all-purpose flour
- ½ cup yellow cornmeal
- 1 tablespoon paprika
- 1½ teaspoons chili powder
- 1½ teaspoons ground red pepper
- 1½ teaspoons garlic powder
- 1½ teaspoons dried oregano
- ½ teaspoon dry mustard
- ½ teaspoon salt
- ½ teaspoon ground black pepper
- Vegetable oil

COMBINE oysters and buttermilk in a large shallow dish or zip-top freezer bag. Cover or seal and chill at least 2 hours. Drain oysters well.
COMBINE flour, cornmeal, and next 8 ingredients. Dredge oysters in flour mixture, shaking off excess.
POUR oil to a depth of 1 inch into a Dutch oven; heat to 370°. Fry oysters, in batches, 3 minutes or until golden. Drain on paper towels. Serve immediately.

KEVIN WILLIAMSON
CHEF/OWNER, *RANCH 616*
AUSTIN, TEXAS

Living in the Kitchen

Make this space your favorite room in the house. Follow these tips for success, and try our quick-and-easy recipes.

Kitchens—we spend a lot of time in them, not only preparing daily meals, but also entertaining and just plain hanging out. Because kitchens are our new living rooms, they should be functional as well as enjoyable. So, let's have some fun in them.

In that spirit, the Foods and Homes editors of *Southern Living* have joined forces to fill an existing kitchen with great decorating ideas, food tips, and organizing solutions to make your life easier. Julia and Dit Rutland's kitchen was in need of an update. With a young daughter, Emily, they needed solutions that made sense for a busy family. By looking at one family's lifestyle, we've suggested recipes for an entire day. Also, we've created distinct meal zones that make breakfast and supper simpler. And as always, we'll lead the way in adding a dash of style to your true "living room," which is sure to be a hit with family and friends.

breakfast

Start the morning off right with timesaving ideas to make the most important meal of the day the least stressful to prepare.

Few moments in a family's schedule require more juggling than breakfast. We streamlined the Rutlands' kitchen by grouping the coffeemaker, toaster, cups, and breakfast items. (See "Smart Idea for Storage" at right.)

MOCHA LATTE SYRUP

fast fixin's • make ahead

MAKES 1¼ CUPS

Prep: 5 min., Cook: 1 min.

COMBINE ¾ cup sugar, ⅓ cup unsweetened cocoa, 4 tablespoons instant espresso, and ½ teaspoon ground cinnamon in a medium saucepan. Whisk in ½ cup water, and bring to a boil over medium heat. Boil 1 minute, stirring often. Remove from heat; stir in 2 tablespoons vanilla extract. Refrigerate up to 2 weeks.

Mocha Latte Beverage:

MAKES 1 SERVING

SPOON 1 tablespoon Mocha Latte Syrup into a coffee cup; stir in ¾ cup hot milk.

HONEY-NUT SPREAD

fast fixin's • make ahead

MAKES 1¼ CUPS

Prep: 10 min.

PROCESS ½ cup walnuts or pecans, toasted, in a food processor until coarsely ground. Add 1 cup butter, softened, and ½ cup honey; pulse 5 or 6 times or until blended. Cover and chill until ready to serve. Let stand at room temperature 5 minutes before serving. Serve with bagels or toast.

BARBARA SHERRER
BAY CITY, TEXAS

BANANA BREAKFAST SMOOTHIE

fast fixin's

MAKES 4 SERVINGS (ABOUT 5 CUPS)

Prep: 5 min.

Reader Erma Jackson's original recipe calls for orange juice concentrate and 1 cup sliced strawberries, but it's equally delicious with lemonade and fresh blueberries.

- **6 tablespoons frozen lemonade or orange juice concentrate, unthawed and undiluted**
- **2 ripe bananas**
- **1 cup fresh blueberries or strawberries**
- **2 cups milk**
- **1 tablespoon honey**
- **1 teaspoon vanilla extract**
- **8 ice cubes**

PROCESS all ingredients in a blender, stopping to scrape down sides. Pour mixture into tall glasses.

ERMA JACKSON
HUNTSVILLE, ALABAMA

Smart Idea for Storage

Island—When breakfast is done, the Rutlands can conveniently store items such as the toaster oven and blender on their island's shelves. There's even a space devoted to daughter Emily, so she can play while her parents prepare meals.

Kitchen islands come in a variety of prices, styles, and construction. Inexpensive ones are sold at discount stores and unfinished-furniture outlets. You can add wheels to one, so it can be rolled away when not in use.

The Rutlands picked an island not just for storage, but so the cook could have another work surface. Theirs has a wooden top that's great for chopping and other food preparation.

MAPLE-BANANA SYRUP

fast fixin's

MAKES ½ CUP

Prep: 5 min., Cook: 5 min.

MELT 1 tablespoon butter in a skillet over medium heat; add 3 bananas, sliced, and sauté 5 minutes. Add ½ cup maple syrup, and cook, stirring constantly, 3 minutes or until heated. Serve over waffles or pancakes; garnish with ⅓ cup pecans, toasted and chopped, if desired.

NORA HENSHAW
OKEMAH, OKLAHOMA

all day long

Behind every efficient kitchen is a great pantry. It's not the size that matters, but how it's organized.

We've established the pantry as its own separate meal zone to get the Rutland family through the day. Along with tips and suggestions to help you, we offer recipes that combine commonly found pantry items.

FRUITY SNACK MIX

fast fixin's • make ahead

MAKES 5 QUARTS

Prep: 5 min.

    1 (17-ounce) box O-shaped
        sweetened oat-and-wheat bran
        cereal
    1 (6-ounce) package banana chips
    1 (21.3-ounce) package candy-
        coated chocolate pieces
    1 (10-ounce) package miniature
        pretzels
    1 (7-ounce) package dried mixed fruit*

COMBINE all ingredients. Store in an airtight container.

NOTE: For testing purposes only, we used Cracklin' Oat Bran cereal and Snyder's pretzels.

***Substitute** 1 (12-ounce) package raisins for dried mixed fruit, if desired.

BUTTERSCOTCH-CHOCOLATE BROWNIES

family favorite

MAKES 2 DOZEN

Prep: 10 min., Cook: 5 min., Bake: 30 min.

    2 cups all-purpose flour
    2 teaspoons baking powder
    ¾ cup butter
    1 (16-ounce) package light brown
        sugar
    2 large eggs
    ¼ teaspoon salt
    1 teaspoon vanilla extract
    1 cup chopped pecans
    1 (6-ounce) package semisweet
        chocolate morsels

SIFT together flour and baking powder. **MELT** butter in a 10-inch ovenproof skillet over low heat. Stir in brown sugar until dissolved.
REMOVE from heat; add flour mixture, stirring until smooth. Stir in eggs, salt, and vanilla until blended. Add pecans and chocolate morsels, stirring until chocolate melts.
BAKE brownies in skillet at 350° for 30 minutes.

NOTE: Pour batter into a lightly greased 13- x 9-inch pan, if desired. Bake as directed.

RALEIGH HUSSUNG
NASHVILLE, TENNESSEE

EASY SOUTHWEST SALAD

fast fixin's

MAKES 6 TO 8 SERVINGS

Prep: 10 min.

STIR together ¾ cup buttermilk Ranch salad dressing and ½ cup chunky salsa. Toss together 1 head romaine lettuce, torn, and salad dressing mixture; sprinkle with 1 cup crushed tortilla chips.

Must-Have Pantry Checklist

☐ **Canned soups:** cream of mushroom, cream of chicken, cream of celery, tomato, chicken broth, beef broth

☐ **Soup mix:** dry onion soup mix

☐ **Canned tomatoes:** diced tomatoes, diced tomatoes and green chiles, Italian-style diced tomatoes, crushed tomatoes, stewed tomatoes, tomato paste

☐ **Canned vegetables:** whole and sliced mushrooms, artichoke hearts, asparagus, beets, olives, chiles

☐ **Canned beans and peas:** great Northern beans, kidney beans, black beans, black-eyed peas, chickpeas

☐ **Canned meat:** tuna, salmon, crabmeat

☐ **Rice:** long-grain rice, instant rice, quick-cooking rice, long-grain and wild rice mix, Arborio rice, yellow rice

☐ **Pastas:** elbow macaroni, fettuccine, spaghetti, rotini, penne, ziti, bow tie

☐ **Sauces:** pasta sauce, spaghetti sauce, pizza sauce

☐ **Milks:** sweetened condensed milk, evaporated milk

☐ **Baking items:** flour, granulated sugar, brown sugar, powdered sugar

☐ **Aluminum foil, plastic wrap, zip-top plastic bags**

Remember to check the dates on all canned goods (discard cans that are more than one year old).

Be sure to check the dates on baking powder and baking soda. If their dates have expired, so has their ability to leaven properly.

Santa Fe Chicken and Dressing

family favorite

MAKES 4 TO 6 SERVINGS

Prep: 15 min., Bake: 30 min.

  3 cups cornbread stuffing mix
  2 cups chopped cooked chicken
  1 (4.5-ounce) can chopped green
    chiles, drained
  ½ (7-ounce) jar roasted red bell
    peppers, drained and chopped
  2 teaspoons ground coriander
  1 (10¾-ounce) can cream of
    mushroom soup, undiluted
  1 (8¾-ounce) can cream-style corn
  1 cup sour cream
  2 teaspoons ground cumin
  1 cup (4 ounces) shredded Monterey
    Jack cheese
    Tortilla chips (optional)
    Pico de gallo or chunky salsa
    (optional)

STIR together first 5 ingredients in a large bowl; stir in soup and next 3 ingredients. Spread in a lightly greased 2-quart shallow baking dish.

BAKE, covered, at 350° for 25 minutes or until thoroughly heated. Uncover and sprinkle evenly with cheese; bake 5 more minutes or until cheese melts. Serve with tortilla chips and pico de gallo or chunky salsa, if desired.

Weeknight Italian Pasta

fast fixin's

MAKES 4 SERVINGS

Prep: 10 min., Cook: 10 min.

COOK 8 ounces angel hair pasta according to package directions; drain. Sauté 1 pint grape tomatoes, 3 minced garlic cloves, 1 tablespoon Italian seasoning, 2 tablespoons balsamic vinegar, and ½ teaspoon salt in ¼ cup hot olive oil in a skillet 3 minutes. Serve over hot pasta; top with Parmesan cheese.

Storage

Thoughtful organization ideas keep kitchen activities streamlined. Plus, they're easy to incorporate.

Spices

The logical choice for these items in the kitchen is an upper cabinet that is close to the cooktop. We found a small stair-stepped shelf that allows the rows of spices to be easily identified, especially if they're in alphabetical order.

Drawers

You probably have one or more handy little dividers in your kitchen drawer already. Don't let them go to waste; organize your drawers by task. For example, keep flatware and serving utensils close to the dishwasher or heat-proof spatulas and whisks near your cooktop. Never store knives loose in a drawer. For more information on knives, see "From Our Kitchen" on page 50.

Pots and Pans

Use pullout drawers to store your pots and pans so that they don't get lost or overlooked. Many kitchens are equipped with such drawers, but if yours isn't, don't fret—they're easy to add.

If your kitchen doesn't have pullout drawers, you can add them in one of two ways. Attach them with drawer slides to the top of your existing shelves (which often limits the amount of storage space you have), or remove your existing shelves, and add new ones with side-mounted slides.

To prevent pots from shifting when the drawers open, we lined the Rutlands' shelves with sheets of vinyl flooring, which were painted to match the kitchen floorcloth. Separate stacked pots and pans with inexpensive dishtowels to keep them nick free.

---

night shift

After a long day at work or school, make dinner a no-fuss meal with these easy recipes.

Supper is an important time for the family. However, we also know that between busy work schedules and activities for the kids, you need simple suggestions for getting dinner on the table in a hurry.

These family favorites cover everything from main dishes to sides. What's more, the recipes use a variety of appliances, such as the oven, cooktop, and microwave, so you're never waiting for a burner to become available. Enjoy a delicious meal with minimal effort.

Easy Italian Bread

fast fixin's

MAKES 12 SERVINGS

Prep: 10 min., Bake: 20 min.

DIVIDE 1 (32-ounce) package frozen bread dough loaves, thawed, into 3 equal portions. Roll each portion into a 6½-inch circle, and place on a lightly greased baking sheet. Brush each portion with 2 tablespoons olive oil, and sprinkle with 2 teaspoons Italian seasoning, ½ teaspoon garlic powder, and ¼ cup shredded Parmesan cheese. Bake at 375° for 10 minutes. Prick several times with a fork. Bake 10 more minutes or until golden. Cool slightly on baking sheet. Cut each round into 4 wedges.

CHICKEN-AND-SAUSAGE SKILLET SUPPER

MAKES 6 SERVINGS

Prep: 15 min., Cook: 45 min.

- 1 (16-ounce) package Cajun sausage, sliced
- 1 medium onion, chopped
- 1 medium-size green bell pepper, chopped
- 1 tablespoon vegetable oil
- 2 garlic cloves, chopped
- 1 (14-ounce) can low-sodium chicken broth
- 2 cups shredded cooked chicken
- 1 cup uncooked long-grain rice
- 1½ teaspoons Cajun seasoning
- 2 (10-ounce) cans diced tomatoes and green chiles, undrained
- ⅓ cup chopped fresh parsley

SAUTÉ sausage, onion, and bell pepper in hot oil in a large nonstick skillet over medium heat 10 minutes or until vegetables are tender. Add garlic, and cook, stirring constantly, 30 seconds.
ADD broth and chicken; bring to a boil. Stir in rice and Cajun seasoning; reduce heat to low, cover, and cook, stirring occasionally, 25 minutes. Stir in diced tomatoes and green chiles; cook, uncovered, 10 minutes, stirring occasionally. Remove from heat, and stir in parsley.

KATHAN DEARMAN
NEW ORLEANS, LOUISIANA

BARBECUE CHICKEN PIZZA

fast fixin's

MAKES 4 SERVINGS

Prep: 5 min., Stand: 15 min., Bake: 15 min.

- 2 cups chopped cooked chicken
- ¾ cup barbecue sauce
- 1 (14-ounce) package prebaked Italian pizza crust
- 1 cup (4 ounces) shredded mozzarella cheese
- ¼ medium-size red onion, thinly sliced
- 2 green onions, chopped

COMBINE chicken and barbecue sauce; let stand 15 minutes.

PLACE pizza crust on a baking sheet.
SPREAD chicken mixture over pizza crust. Top with cheese and remaining ingredients. Bake at 450° for 15 minutes or until cheese melts.

NOTE: For testing purposes only, we used Boboli Original Italian Pizza Crust.

DAVID LEE WALLACE
APOPKA, FLORIDA

APRICOT-STUFFED PORK CHOPS

MAKES 5 SERVINGS

Prep: 25 min., Bake: 20 min., Cook: 5 min.

- 10 dried apricot halves (about ⅓ cup)
- ¼ cup chopped pecans
- 1 garlic clove
- 2 teaspoons chopped fresh or 1 teaspoon dried thyme
- 2 tablespoons molasses, divided
- ¼ teaspoon salt
- ¼ teaspoon pepper
- 5 (¾-inch-thick) boneless pork chops
- ¾ cup chicken broth
- ½ cup whipping cream
- 2 teaspoons all-purpose flour

PULSE first 4 ingredients, 1 tablespoon molasses, ¼ teaspoon salt, and ¼ teaspoon pepper in a food processor 5 or 6 times until finely chopped. (Mixture may be chopped by hand, if desired.)
TRIM excess fat from each pork chop, and cut a slit in 1 side of each chop to form a pocket. Spoon apricot mixture evenly into each pocket. Pinch edges to seal; secure with wooden picks, if necessary.
BRUSH chops with remaining 1 tablespoon molasses. Place on a rack in a lightly greased broiler pan. Bake at 350° for 15 to 20 minutes or until done. (Pork chops should be slightly pink inside; do not overcook.)
REMOVE wooden picks, if necessary, and place chops on a serving platter; keep warm. Add chicken broth to pan; place pan over medium-high heat, stirring to loosen browned bits from bottom.
STIR together whipping cream and flour until smooth. Stir into broth, and cook 3 minutes or until slightly thickened. Serve over chops.

JULIA RUTLAND
BIRMINGHAM, ALABAMA

EASY BROCCOLI CASSEROLE

fast fixin's • family favorite

MAKES 8 SERVINGS

Prep: 20 min.

- 2 (16-ounce) packages frozen broccoli florets, thawed
- ¼ cup low-sodium chicken broth
- 1 (10¾-ounce) can low-sodium cream of mushroom soup, undiluted
- 1 (7-ounce) jar roasted red bell peppers, drained and chopped
- ¼ cup (1 ounce) shredded sharp Cheddar cheese
- ¼ cup light mayonnaise
- 1½ teaspoons lemon juice
- 1 teaspoon garlic powder
- ½ teaspoon pepper
- 2 tablespoons Italian-seasoned breadcrumbs

COMBINE broccoli and broth in a lightly greased 2-quart baking dish.
COMBINE cream of mushroom soup and next 6 ingredients in a medium bowl; stir well. Spoon over broccoli.
COVER with heavy-duty plastic wrap, and microwave at HIGH 4 to 5 minutes. Sprinkle with breadcrumbs. Rotate dish, and microwave at HIGH 4 to 5 minutes.

BLACK-EYED PEAS

fast fixin's • family favorite

MAKES 4 SERVINGS

Prep: 15 min., Stand: 5 min.

- 2 (15.8-ounce) cans black-eyed peas, drained
- 6 bacon slices, cooked and crumbled
- 1 (14-ounce) can chicken broth
- 1 medium onion, chopped
- 1 garlic clove, finely chopped
- 1 bay leaf
- ¼ teaspoon hot sauce
- ¼ teaspoon salt
- ¼ teaspoon pepper

STIR together all ingredients in a 2-quart glass dish, mixing well. Cover dish with heavy-duty plastic wrap. Microwave at MEDIUM (50% power) 10 minutes; stir well. Let stand, covered, 5 minutes. Discard bay leaf.

from our kitchen

What About Convection Cooking?

Convection ovens have fans that circulate hot air around food, cooking it about 25% faster than conventional ovens. You save time and energy with this method. Plus, there's the added bonus that food loses less moisture and retains most of its nutrients. Several companies combine convection and conventional options in the same unit.

No special equipment is required, but it helps to know which pans to choose. For best results with convection cooking, consider the following.

■ It's best to use shallow, uncovered casserole dishes (no more than 2 inches deep) and baking pans with sides no higher than an inch or so, such as baking sheets and jellyroll pans.

■ Deep roasting pans, oven roasting bags, and covered casserole dishes keep the heat from circulating around the food and block the efficiency of convection cooking.

■ Avoid using aluminum foil tents that blow off by the force of circulating air. Switch to the conventional cooking method when using these.

Most manufacturers suggest the following guidelines for converting cooking times and temperatures for a convection oven. Make adjustments as necessary.

■ Reduce the temperature by 25 degrees, and bake for the same time specified in the recipe.

■ You could also keep the oven temperature the same and bake for 5 to 10 minutes less.

■ After you bake the first cake and roast a chicken and vegetables, you will know exactly what works best with your oven.

Cutlery

With the right knife in your hand, every cooking experience will be better. Buy the best ones you can afford. Cheap cutlery doesn't hold a sharp edge, blades bend easily, and handles break quickly. Good-quality individual knives range in price from $30 to $60; sets range from $199 to $499.

Look for those with full tangs, which means you can see the metal of the blade extending all the way to the end of the handle. Each knife should feel well balanced in your hand. The handle can be wood, plastic, rubber, or metal, but it should be firmly attached with several rivets.

The Basics

These include a chef's knife, paring knife, utility knife, and serrated knife. They will take you through most food preparation. The main thing is to select the right knife for the job and for your cooking style. You may need only one.

■ **Chef's knife**—a large tapered blade, about 8 inches long, used for chopping, slicing, dicing, and mincing.

■ **Paring knife**—similar to a chef's knife with a tapered blade about 3 to 4 inches long, used for peeling and slicing fruits and vegetables.

■ **Utility knife**—a larger version of a paring knife, used for slicing meats and large vegetables.

■ **Serrated or scalloped-edge knife**—wonderful for cutting foods with tough skins or crusts such as tomatoes, roasts, ham, and breads.

Specialty Cutlery

Don't be pressured into buying pieces you won't use. If you're an adventurous cook, you may want to invest in a large set, but make sure it includes the knives you really want. Or you can simply design your own set. Here are some specialty knives you might want to know about.

■ **Bird's beak parer**—great for working with round fruits and vegetables. Its small size makes it easy to handle and a good tool for creating garnishes.

■ **Santoku (Japanese cook's knife)**—makes fast work of large amounts of chopping, and the wide blade is a helpful scoop.

■ **Baby chef's knife**—has an extra wide blade with just the right curve to allow for good rocking motion when chopping and slicing. The Messermeister cutlery catalog calls this one a "paring knife with attitude."

■ **Cheese knife**—allows air between the food and the blade's surface so the cheese doesn't stick to it for a clean cut. The forked tip lets you lift and serve the sliced pieces.

Handle With Care

Protect your investment with proper care and storage. Keep knives in a slotted wooden block or a special drawer insert with slots for the blades. You'll further protect the blades if you slide them into the block cutting-edge up. Knives get dull and nicked if they're stored loose in drawers with other kitchen gadgets or utensils. You may choose to attach a magnetic bar on a wall for storage, but be sure it's in a safe zone.

Tips and Tidbits

For those of you who don't like to touch raw meat and poultry with your bare hands, try this tip. Use powder-free latex disposable gloves, available at drugstores. Keep a box in a kitchen drawer, and you'll discover you can use them for many other tasks, such as handling hot peppers.

March

Eggs Benedict Goes Southern

Here's the classic, but be sure to try the regional twists.

Eggs Benedict is a lavish dish. Open-faced English muffins layered with Canadian bacon, poached eggs, and rich Hollandaise sauce make a showstopping brunch when paired with seasonal fruit. Though it's hard to imagine how it can get much better, we've added some fresh ideas to this tried-and-true classic.

Lyda Jones, our Test Kitchens Director, is passionate about these richly flavored delights. She developed the regional variations, merging traditional Southern ingredients with a variety of bread bases. We thought the popular Lowcountry dish shrimp and grits couldn't be improved. Yet Robert Stehling of Hominy Grill in Charleston put a delicious twist on this recipe using fried grits squares, asparagus spears, and a creamy shrimp sauce.

All the versions received high ratings, but it was the Country Ham Eggs Benedict that captured Assistant Foods Editor Cynthia Ann Briscoe's Kentucky heart. The recipe was also inspired by a Charleston restaurant—The Baker's Café. How can you go wrong with tender cornbread pancakes, fried ham, and eggs all smothered in a Swiss Cheese Sauce?

You'll find these recipes may take a little extra time, but they are worth the effort. Some variations offer make-ahead tips so you can get a head start before company comes. Don't let the thought of poaching eggs scare you. We've included instructions (see instructions on facing page) as well as tips in "From Our Kitchen" on page 70 so you can poach to perfection every time.

TRADITIONAL EGGS BENEDICT

family favorite

MAKES 2 SERVINGS

Prep: 25 min., Cook: 10 min.
(pictured on page 73)

- 8 (½-ounce) Canadian bacon slices
- Vegetable cooking spray
- 2 English muffins, split and toasted
- 4 large eggs, poached
- Hollandaise Sauce
- Coarsely ground pepper
- Paprika

COOK bacon in a skillet coated with cooking spray over medium heat until thoroughly heated, turning once. Drain on paper towels.

PLACE 2 bacon slices on each muffin half. Top each with a poached egg, and drizzle evenly with Hollandaise Sauce. Sprinkle with pepper and paprika; serve immediately.

Hollandaise Sauce:

MAKES 1½ CUPS

Prep: 5 min., Cook: 10 min.

- 4 large egg yolks
- 2 tablespoons fresh lemon juice
- 1 cup butter, melted
- ¼ teaspoon salt

WHISK yolks in top of a double boiler; gradually whisk in lemon juice. Place over hot water (do not boil). Add butter, ⅓ cup at a time, whisking until smooth; whisk in salt. Cook, whisking constantly, 10 minutes or until thickened and a thermometer registers 160°. Serve immediately.

COUNTRY HAM EGGS BENEDICT

MAKES 8 SERVINGS

Prep: 35 min., Cook: 20 min.

- 1 (12-ounce) package thinly sliced country ham
- 1 cup yellow cornmeal
- ½ cup all-purpose flour
- 2 teaspoons baking powder
- 1 teaspoon sugar
- ¼ teaspoon salt
- 2 large eggs, lightly beaten
- ¾ cup buttermilk
- 1 (8.75-ounce) can cream-style corn
- 2 tablespoons vegetable oil
- 8 large eggs, poached
- Swiss Cheese Sauce

BROWN country ham in a large skillet over medium-high heat. Remove ham from skillet, and keep warm.

STIR together cornmeal and next 4 ingredients in a large bowl; make a well in center of mixture. Stir together 2 beaten eggs, buttermilk, cream-style corn, and vegetable oil; add to dry ingredients, stirring just until moistened.

POUR about ¼ cup batter for each pancake onto a hot, lightly greased nonstick skillet. Cook pancakes until tops are covered with bubbles and edges look cooked; turn and cook other side.

TOP each pancake with a poached egg, ham, and warm Swiss Cheese Sauce.

Swiss Cheese Sauce:

MAKES 2 CUPS

Prep: 10 min., Cook: 10 min.

- 2 tablespoons butter
- 2 tablespoons all-purpose flour
- 2 cups milk
- 1 cup (4 ounces) shredded Swiss cheese
- ½ teaspoon salt
- ¼ teaspoon pepper

MELT butter in a heavy saucepan over low heat; whisk in flour until smooth. Cook, whisking constantly, 1 minute. Gradually whisk in 2 cups milk; cook over medium heat, whisking constantly until mixture is thickened and bubbly.

ADD shredded Swiss cheese, salt, and pepper, stirring until cheese melts.

SOUTHWEST EGGS BENEDICT

MAKES 8 SERVINGS

Prep: 30 min., Fry: 4 min. per batch

Corn tortillas can be fried 2 hours ahead.

- 8 (5-inch) corn tortillas
- ¼ cup vegetable oil
- 8 large eggs, poached
- Chipotle Hollandaise Sauce
- 1 cup (4 ounces) shredded Monterey Jack cheese with peppers
- 1 cup salsa
- Garnish: chopped fresh cilantro

FRY corn tortillas in hot oil in a medium skillet 1 to 2 minutes on each side or until crisp.

TOP each with a poached egg, Chipotle Hollandaise Sauce, shredded cheese, and salsa. Serve immediately. Garnish, if desired.

Chipotle Hollandaise Sauce:

MAKES 1¼ CUPS

Prep: 10 min.

- ⅓ cup egg substitute
- ¼ teaspoon salt
- ¼ teaspoon pepper
- 1 cup butter, melted and cooled
- 1 tablespoon minced fresh cilantro
- 4 teaspoons pureed chipotle peppers in adobo sauce
- 2 tablespoons fresh lime juice

PROCESS egg substitute, salt, and pepper in a blender on high 1 minute. Reduce to low speed; with blender running, pour melted butter through food chute in a slow, steady stream.

ADD minced cilantro, pureed chipotle peppers, and lime juice; process until smooth.

NOTE: Chipotle peppers in adobo sauce may be found in the international food section of your supermarket or in Latin grocery stores.

SHRIMP-AND-GRITS EGGS BENEDICT

chef recipe

MAKES 8 SERVINGS

Prep: 45 min., Cook: 30 min., Chill: 8 hrs.

Start on this recipe a day ahead—the grits cakes need to chill 8 hours.

- 5 cups water
- ½ teaspoon salt
- 1 cup uncooked quick-cooking grits
- ½ teaspoon pepper
- ¾ cup freshly grated Parmesan cheese
- 1 pound fresh asparagus
- ⅓ cup all-purpose flour
- 1 tablespoon butter or margarine
- 1 tablespoon vegetable oil
- 8 large eggs, poached
- Creamy Shrimp Sauce
- Garnish: freshly grated Parmesan cheese

BRING 5 cups water and salt to a boil in a medium saucepan; gradually stir in grits. Cook over medium heat 8 minutes or until thickened. Whisk in pepper and ¾ cup Parmesan cheese; spoon into a lightly greased 11- x 7-inch baking dish. Cover and chill 8 hours.

SNAP off tough ends of asparagus. Combine asparagus and water to cover in a saucepan. Bring to a boil, and cook 5 minutes or until crisp-tender. Drain and plunge asparagus into ice water to stop the cooking process.

CUT grits into 8 (3- x 3-inch) squares. Lightly dredge in flour. Melt butter with oil in a large nonstick skillet over medium-low heat. Cook grits squares, in batches, 3 to 4 minutes on each side or until golden. Top each square with asparagus, a poached egg, and Creamy Shrimp Sauce. Serve immediately. Garnish, if desired.

Creamy Shrimp Sauce:

MAKES 2¼ CUPS

Prep: 15 min., Stand: 30 min., Cook: 10 min.

- 1 pound unpeeled, medium-size fresh shrimp
- 2½ tablespoons butter, divided
- 1 small shallot, sliced
- 1 (14.5-ounce) can chicken broth
- 1½ tablespoons all-purpose flour
- 1 cup whipping cream
- 2 tablespoons sherry

PEEL shrimp, reserving shells; devein, if desired.

MELT 1 tablespoon butter in a 3½-quart saucepan over medium heat.

ADD shrimp, and cook 5 minutes or just until shrimp turn pink. Chop shrimp, and set aside.

ADD shrimp shells, shallot, and chicken broth to saucepan; bring to a boil. Remove from heat, cover, and let stand 30 minutes. Pour broth mixture through a wire-mesh strainer into a bowl, discarding shells and shallot.

MELT remaining 1½ tablespoons butter in saucepan over medium heat. Whisk in flour. Cook, whisking constantly, 1 minute. Gradually whisk in broth mixture. Bring to a boil; boil 1 minute or until slightly thickened. Add cream; reduce heat to low. Add chopped shrimp and sherry; stir until thoroughly heated.

ROBERT STEHLING
HOMINY GRILL
CHARLESTON, SOUTH CAROLINA

Poached Eggs

Add water to a depth of 3 inches in a large saucepan. Bring to a boil; reduce heat, and maintain at a light simmer. Add ½ teaspoon white vinegar. Break eggs and slip into water, 1 at a time, as close as possible to surface of water. Simmer 3 to 5 minutes or to desired degree of doneness. Remove with a slotted spoon. Trim edges, if desired.

Salad for Supper

Make a complete meal in no time with these satisfying recipes.

A day featuring big colorful salads at our taste-testing table is a good day indeed. We're sure these fantastic recipes will satisfy your desire for a salad.

ITALIAN BREAD SALAD

MAKES 4 SERVINGS

Prep: 30 min., Bake: 15 min., Stand: 15 min.

For an Italian sublike flavor, substitute 1 cup thinly sliced salami, such as Genoa, for 2 cups ham. *(pictured on page 74)*

- 4 cups cubed French bread
- 6 tablespoons olive oil
- 3 tablespoons red wine vinegar
- 2 garlic cloves, minced
- 1 teaspoon dried oregano
- 1 teaspoon salt
- ¾ teaspoon freshly ground black pepper
- ⅛ to ¼ teaspoon dried crushed red pepper
- 1 large head romaine lettuce, chopped
- 4 to 5 large plum tomatoes, chopped
- 2 cups chopped smoked ham
- 1 (8-ounce) package fresh mozzarella cheese, cubed
- 3 green onions, chopped

PLACE bread cubes on a baking sheet. Bake at 325° for 15 minutes or until lightly browned. Set aside. Whisk together olive oil and next 6 ingredients.
RESERVE 1 cup bread cubes. Scatter remaining cubes on a serving platter. Top with lettuce and next 3 ingredients. Drizzle with dressing; toss. Let stand 15 minutes before serving. Sprinkle with reserved bread cubes and green onions.

ELEANOR M. GIBSON
LATROBE, PENNSYLVANIA

BLACK BEAN AND BLACK-EYED PEA SALAD

fast fixin's • vegetarian

MAKES 6 SERVINGS

Prep: 20 min., Chill: 30 min.

Reader Marion Hall uses only black beans in her version; we added black-eyed peas for Southern flavor. You can top this salad with grilled or deli rotisserie chicken, leftover steak strips, or canned albacore tuna for a meaty main dish. Serve with Blue Cheese Bread, if desired. *(pictured on page 75)*

- 1 teaspoon grated lime rind
- ½ cup fresh lime juice (about 4 limes)
- ¼ cup olive oil
- 1 teaspoon brown sugar
- 1 teaspoon chili powder
- ½ teaspoon ground cumin
- ½ to 1 teaspoon salt
- 1 (15-ounce) can black beans, rinsed and drained
- 1 (15.5-ounce) can black-eyed peas, rinsed and drained
- 1½ cups frozen whole kernel corn, thawed
- ½ small green bell pepper, chopped
- ⅓ cup chopped fresh cilantro
- Romaine lettuce
- 2 large avocados, sliced
- Garnishes: lime wedges, fresh cilantro sprigs

WHISK together first 7 ingredients in a large bowl. Add black beans and next 4 ingredients, tossing to coat. Cover and chill 30 minutes.
SERVE over lettuce; arrange avocado slices around salad. Garnish, if desired.

MARION HALL
KNOXVILLE, TENNESSEE

BLUE CHEESE BREAD

fast fixin's

MAKES 8 SERVINGS

Prep: 8 min., Bake: 7 min.

- 1 (12-ounce) crusty French bread loaf
- ½ cup butter, softened
- 1 (4-ounce) package crumbled blue cheese

CUT bread loaf at ¾-inch intervals, cutting to, but not through, bottom of loaf.
STIR together butter and cheese; spread evenly on both sides of each bread slice. Wrap loaf in aluminum foil, and place on a baking sheet.
BAKE at 375° for 7 minutes or until toasted.

JOYCE T. LONG
ANNAPOLIS, MARYLAND

SWEET PEANUT-CHICKEN SALAD

fast fixin's

MAKES 4 TO 6 SERVINGS

Prep: 30 min.

- 1 (8-ounce) can crushed pineapple, drained
- ¾ cup mayonnaise
- 1 teaspoon grated lime rind
- 1 tablespoon fresh lime juice
- 1½ teaspoons lite soy sauce
- ½ teaspoon pepper
- 2 cups coarsely chopped cooked chicken
- 1 small Granny Smith apple, chopped
- ½ cup chopped salted peanuts
- 1 head green leaf lettuce
- 1 fresh pineapple, peeled, cored, and cut into 1-inch pieces
- 2 oranges, cut into wedges
- 2 kiwifruit, peeled and sliced
- 2 cups red or green seedless grapes
- 2 tablespoons chopped salted peanuts

STIR together first 6 ingredients in a bowl. Stir in chicken, apple, and ½ cup peanuts.
ARRANGE lettuce leaves on a large platter. Spoon chicken mixture in center of platter, and arrange pineapple and remaining fruit around platter. Sprinkle with 2 tablespoons chopped peanuts.

A Sweet Invitation

As spring approaches, the promise of warmer, brighter weather ahead makes us eager to get together with folks. This month, get a jump on your entertaining, and extend an invitation for dessert and coffee to your friends. Our luscious delicacies will easily lure them out of hibernation. Both are easy to assemble and bake, but do plan to make Key Lime Cheesecake With Strawberry Sauce one day ahead.

KEY LIME CHEESECAKE WITH STRAWBERRY SAUCE

make ahead

MAKES 10 TO 12 SERVINGS

Prep: 20 min.; Bake: 1 hr., 13 min.; Stand: 15 min.; Chill: 8 hrs.

Fresh Key lime juice makes this authentic, but use bottled juice if fresh limes aren't available. Look for the juice at your grocery store, or order it from Key West Key Lime Shoppe at 1-800-376-0806. (*pictured on page 80*)

- 2 cups graham cracker crumbs
- ¼ cup sugar
- ½ cup butter or margarine, melted
- 3 (8-ounce) packages cream cheese, softened
- 1¼ cups sugar
- 3 large eggs
- 1 (8-ounce) container sour cream
- 1½ teaspoons grated lime rind
- ½ cup Key lime juice
- Garnishes: strawberry halves, lime slices, lime zest
- Strawberry Sauce

STIR together first 3 ingredients, and firmly press on bottom and 1 inch up sides of a greased 9-inch springform pan.
BAKE at 350° for 8 minutes; cool.
BEAT cream cheese at medium speed with an electric mixer until fluffy, and gradually add 1¼ cups sugar, beating until blended. Add eggs, 1 at a time, beating well after each addition. Stir in sour cream, lime rind, and juice. Pour batter into crust.
BAKE at 325° for 1 hour and 5 minutes; turn oven off. Partially open oven door; let stand in oven 15 minutes. Remove from oven, and immediately run a knife around edge of pan, releasing sides.
COOL completely in pan on a wire rack; cover and chill 8 hours. Garnish, if desired, and serve with Strawberry Sauce.

Strawberry Sauce:

MAKES 1 CUP

Prep: 5 min.

- 1¼ cups fresh strawberries
- ¼ cup sugar
- 1½ teaspoons grated lime rind

PROCESS all ingredients in a food processor until smooth, stopping to scrape down sides.

BEST CARROT SHEET CAKE

family favorite

MAKES 10 TO 12 SERVINGS

Prep: 25 min., Bake: 43 min.

A rich buttermilk glaze makes this treat super-moist and delicious.

- 2 cups all-purpose flour
- 2 teaspoons baking soda
- 2 teaspoons ground cinnamon
- ½ teaspoon salt
- 3 large eggs
- 2 cups sugar
- ¾ cup vegetable oil
- ¾ cup buttermilk
- 2 teaspoons vanilla extract
- 2 cups grated carrots (about 3 large carrots)
- 1 (8-ounce) can crushed pineapple, drained
- 1 (3½-ounce) can sweetened flaked coconut
- 1 cup chopped pecans or walnuts
- Buttermilk Glaze
- Cream Cheese Frosting

STIR together first 4 ingredients.
BEAT eggs and next 4 ingredients at medium speed with an electric mixer until batter is smooth. Add flour mixture, beating at low speed until blended. Fold in carrots and next 3 ingredients. Pour batter into a greased and floured 13- x 9-inch pan.
BAKE at 350° for 30 minutes; cover pan loosely with aluminum foil to prevent excessive browning, and bake 13 more minutes or until a wooden pick inserted in center comes out clean. Drizzle Buttermilk Glaze evenly over cake; cool completely in pan. Spread Cream Cheese Frosting evenly over cake.

Buttermilk Glaze:

MAKES 1½ CUPS

Prep: 5 min., Cook: 10 min.

- 1 cup sugar
- 1½ teaspoons baking soda
- ½ cup butter or margarine
- ½ cup buttermilk
- 1 tablespoon light corn syrup
- 1 teaspoon vanilla extract

BRING sugar, baking soda, butter, buttermilk, and corn syrup to a boil in a Dutch oven over medium-high heat. Boil, stirring often, 4 minutes or until mixture is golden brown. Remove from heat, and stir in vanilla.

Cream Cheese Frosting:

MAKES 4 CUPS

Prep: 5 min.

- ½ cup butter or margarine, softened
- 1 (8-ounce) package cream cheese, softened
- 1 (3-ounce) package cream cheese, softened
- 1 (16-ounce) package powdered sugar
- 1½ teaspoons vanilla extract

BEAT butter and cream cheese at medium speed with an electric mixer until creamy.
ADD powdered sugar and vanilla; beat at high speed 10 seconds or until smooth.

Flavor in a Flash

From the cooktop to the table, sautéing shortens your time in the kitchen.

Sautéing is one of Associate Foods Editor Shirley Harrington's favorite techniques—it's energetic, cooks supper in less than 30 minutes, and lends itself to creative flavor combinations. The term "sauté" means to quickly cook food in a small amount of fat in a hot pan, and the technique is surprisingly easy. If you've cooked onions in oil or butter to put in a casserole, you've got sauté experience.

This method is frequently used to cook chopped vegetables, but it also applies to cooking thin, tender cuts of meat and seafood such as boneless pork chops, chicken breasts, or fish fillets. When the directions say to sauté onions, for example, we want you to stir constantly while cooking. When preparing meat, the food is usually turned once.

Shirley sautés frequently—for herself and for company, and definitely for the sheer fun of hearing that first sizzle as the food goes into the hot oil. When sautéing, watch and listen for cooking clues that tell you when to move to the next step. (See the box on facing page for an explanation of these prompts.) After you finish a meat or seafood sauté, you can make a great sauce from the browned bits in the skillet. Just add a liquid, such as wine or broth, to loosen the bits—this is called deglazing the pan. Then boil briefly to reduce, or thicken, the sauce.

Great sautés start with a great skillet, so turn to "From Our Kitchen" on page 70 for hints on the perfect pan. Then follow our step-by-step directions to get the hang of this terrific timesaving cooking technique.

STEAKS WITH CARAMEL-BRANDY SAUCE

fast fixin's

MAKES 4 SERVINGS

Prep: 5 min., Cook: 10 min.

This recipe cooks the steaks to medium-rare doneness. Lower the temperature and increase cook time for more well-done steaks. *(pictured on page 77)*

- 4 (6-ounce) beef tenderloin fillets
- 1 teaspoon salt
- 1 teaspoon pepper
- 3 tablespoons butter, divided
- 3 tablespoons brandy
- 1 tablespoon light brown sugar
- ¼ cup whipping cream
- Garnish: fresh chives

SPRINKLE steaks evenly with salt and pepper.

MELT 1 tablespoon butter in a medium skillet over medium-high heat.

ADD steaks, and cook 3 minutes on each side or to desired degree of doneness. Remove steaks from skillet; keep warm.

ADD brandy to skillet, stirring to loosen particles from bottom of skillet. Add remaining 2 tablespoons butter and sugar, and cook, stirring constantly, until sugar dissolves and browns.

REMOVE skillet from heat; whisk in cream until blended. Return to heat, and bring to a boil; cook, stirring constantly, 1 minute or until thickened. Serve immediately over steaks. Garnish, if desired.

THOMAS AVANT
DERIDDER, LOUISIANA

SPICY CATFISH WITH VEGETABLES AND BASIL CREAM

MAKES 4 SERVINGS

Prep: 25 min., Cook: 25 min.

This recipe, developed by Laura Martin of our Test Kitchens, shows the versatility and creativity of sautéing. *(pictured on page 76)*

- 3 tablespoons butter, divided
- 1 (16-ounce) package frozen whole kernel corn, thawed
- 1 medium onion, chopped
- 1 medium-size green bell pepper, chopped
- 1 medium-size red bell pepper, chopped
- ¾ teaspoon salt
- ¾ teaspoon pepper
- ½ cup all-purpose flour
- ¼ cup yellow cornmeal
- 1 tablespoon Creole seasoning
- 4 (6- to 8-ounce) catfish fillets
- ⅓ cup buttermilk
- 1 tablespoon vegetable oil
- ½ cup whipping cream
- 2 tablespoons chopped fresh basil
- Garnish: fresh basil sprigs

MELT 2 tablespoons butter in a large skillet over medium-high heat. Add corn, onion, and peppers; sauté 6 to 8 minutes or until tender. Stir in salt and pepper; spoon vegetables onto serving dish, and keep warm.

COMBINE flour, cornmeal, and Creole seasoning in a large shallow dish. Dip fillets in buttermilk, and dredge in flour mixture.

MELT remaining 1 tablespoon butter with oil in skillet over medium-high heat. Cook fillets, in batches, 2 to 3 minutes on each side or until golden. Remove and arrange over vegetables.

ADD cream to skillet, stirring to loosen particles from bottom of skillet. Add chopped basil, and cook, stirring often, 1 to 2 minutes or until thickened. Serve sauce with fillets and vegetables. Garnish, if desired.

CHICKEN SAUTÉ WITH ARTICHOKES AND MUSHROOMS

MAKES 4 SERVINGS

Prep: 20 min., Cook: 25 min.

Pound chicken breasts from end to end to an even thickness for cooking. Thinly pounded breasts cook faster and sometimes require a larger skillet. When you finish this sauce by adding butter and capers, remove the skillet from the heat. If left on the heat, the butter melts, separating and thinning the sauce.

- 1 (6-ounce) jar marinated artichoke hearts
- 4 skinned and boned chicken breast halves
- ¼ cup all-purpose flour
- 1 teaspoon seasoned salt
- ¼ teaspoon pepper
- 5 tablespoons butter, divided
- 12 fresh cremini or button mushrooms, halved
- ⅓ cup dry white wine
- ¼ cup chicken broth
- 2 tablespoons capers, drained

DRAIN artichokes, reserving 2 tablespoons marinade; set artichoke hearts and reserved marinade aside.

PLACE chicken between 2 sheets of heavy-duty plastic wrap; flatten to ½-inch thickness, using a meat mallet or rolling pin. Combine flour, salt, and pepper in a shallow dish; dredge chicken in flour mixture, and set aside.

MELT 3 tablespoons butter in a large skillet over medium-high heat; add mushrooms, and sauté 5 minutes. Push mushrooms to one side of pan, and melt 1 tablespoon butter in pan; add chicken. Cook chicken 5 to 6 minutes on each side. Remove chicken from pan.

ADD wine to skillet, and cook over medium-high heat, stirring to loosen particles from bottom of skillet. Add chicken broth, artichokes, and reserved artichoke marinade to skillet, and cook 3 minutes or until liquid is reduced by half.

REMOVE skillet from heat; add remaining 1 tablespoon butter and capers, stirring often until smooth. Serve sauce over chicken.

MARIE RIZZIO
TRAVERSE CITY, MICHIGAN

Six Steps to Sauté Success

1. Get Off to a Hot Start—To sauté in a small amount of fat means about ⅛ inch of fat. Butter adds great flavor, but it has a low smoke point, meaning it burns quickly. So when the milk solids (the white foam you see) just start to brown, add the food. Don't substitute margarine for butter; because margarine contains water, it will steam the food rather than fry it. A great solution is to use vegetable oil and butter for heat control plus flavor. Vegetable and canola oils have high smoke points and can withstand high cooking temperatures. Olive oils labeled "virgin" or "pure" also hold up to heat. Extra-virgin olive oil tends to burn quickly. When the oil in a hot pan shimmers, it's time to add the food.

2. Take Your Time—When food is added, the skillet and oil temperatures fall. Add ingredients gradually, so you hear a constant sizzling sound. We've all seen pros using some fancy wrist action to flip the food in the skillet without using a utensil. It's dramatic; however, the skillet cools when taken off the heat, and the food cools when tossed in the air.

3. Beautifully Browned—For a crispy, browned crust, lightly dust meat or fish with flour, breadcrumbs, or cornmeal just before adding to the hot skillet. To sauté without breading, pat juicy meats,

poultry, or seafood dry with paper towels (excess liquid will cause the oil to pop). Season with salt, pepper, or spices before cooking.

4. Hear the Sizzle—Add the first piece of fish or meat, pretty side down (skin side up on fish) with the thickest portion in first. You'll hear a fast sizzle that will slow as the temperature drops. Bubbles of oil or butter will form all around the food. As the temperature rises, the sizzle increases. Add the next fillet (leave 1 inch of space around each—a crowded skillet steams rather than crisps). Expect splatters on the cooktop when the temperature is correct.

5. Time to Turn—When the fillets look done around the top of the sides, it's time to turn. Give the pan a shake. Food should release and slide when it's ready to turn. Flip it with tongs or a spatula, and continue to cook until done. Then remove it from the skillet. If the food doesn't release easily, you skimped on the oil or the pan wasn't hot enough.

6. Capture All the Flavor—Add a liquid such as whipping cream, wine, or broth to the hot skillet to loosen the browned bits of coating from the bottom of the skillet. For a stronger flavor, boil the added liquid until the volume reduces by half. Add delicate herbs just before serving for fullest flavor.

Quiche for Every Taste

Serve up this gorgeous salad alongside any of these creative quiches for your next supper club gathering or Saturday brunch.

When it was Beth Gundersen and Lou Lacey's turn to host supper club, friends were welcomed with a fabulous spread. A scrumptious array of quiches and a colorful, crunchy salad covered the kitchen counter.

The quiches are all prepared in the same fashion, but each has its own delicious personality. You can choose just one for a family brunch or lunch. Or do as Beth and Lou did and share several quiche options with dinner guests.

LOADED VEGGIE SALAD

fast fixin's

MAKES 6 TO 8 SERVINGS

Prep: 15 min.

    2 (7-ounce) packages mixed salad
        greens
    2 large avocados, chopped
    1 large cucumber, peeled and sliced
    ½ (10-ounce) package shredded
        carrots
    ¾ cup sweetened dried cranberries
    ½ cup sliced almonds, toasted
    1 pint grape tomatoes, halved
    1 (4-ounce) package crumbled feta
        cheese with basil and herbs
    Kosher salt to taste
    Freshly ground pepper to taste
    1 (0.7-ounce) package Italian
        dressing mix
    ½ cup vegetable oil
    ¼ cup balsamic vinegar
    2 tablespoons tomato chutney
    Croutons (optional)

COMBINE first 8 ingredients in a large bowl. Sprinkle with salt and pepper.
WHISK together dressing mix and next 3 ingredients. Drizzle over salad, tossing to coat. Top with croutons, if desired.

NOTE: For testing purposes only, we used Good Seasons Italian Dressing Mix.

LOU LACEY
BIRMINGHAM, ALABAMA

CHICKEN-OLIVE-CHEDDAR QUICHE

MAKES 6 SERVINGS

Prep: 15 min., Cook: 5 min., Bake: 53 min.,
Stand: 10 min.

    ½ (15-ounce) package refrigerated
        piecrusts
    2 cups chopped grilled chicken
    1 (8-ounce) can sliced mushrooms,
        drained
    2 to 3 green onions, chopped
    2 tablespoons sliced black olives
    1 garlic clove, minced
    2 tablespoons chopped fresh or
        1 teaspoon dried basil
    ¼ teaspoon ground red pepper
    Vegetable cooking spray
    1 cup (4 ounces) shredded Cheddar
        cheese
    1 cup half-and-half
    4 large eggs
    ¼ teaspoon black pepper

UNFOLD piecrust, and place on a lightly floured surface. Roll out to ⅛-inch thickness. Carefully place piecrust in a 9-inch pieplate. Fold edges under, and crimp.
BAKE on lowest oven rack at 400° for 8 minutes. Cool.
SAUTÉ chicken and next 6 ingredients in a skillet coated with cooking spray over medium-high heat 5 minutes. Spoon mixture into prepared crust. Sprinkle with cheese.
WHISK together half-and-half, eggs, and ¼ teaspoon black pepper. Pour over chicken mixture.
BAKE at 400° on lowest oven rack for 45 minutes or until set. Let stand 10 minutes.

BETH GUNDERSEN
BIRMINGHAM, ALABAMA

SALMON-AND-DILL QUICHE

MAKES 6 SERVINGS

Prep: 15 min., Bake: 48 min., Stand: 10 min.

    ½ (15-ounce) package refrigerated
        piecrusts
    1 (3-ounce) package cream cheese,
        softened
    1 cup half-and-half
    3 large eggs
    ¼ teaspoon salt
    ¼ to ½ teaspoon black pepper
    ⅛ teaspoon ground red pepper
    1 (4-ounce) package smoked
        salmon, chopped
    2 tablespoons minced red onion
    1 tablespoon chopped fresh dill or
        1 teaspoon dried dillweed
    1 tablespoon capers, chopped

UNFOLD piecrust, and place on a lightly floured surface. Roll out to ⅛-inch thickness. Carefully place in a 9-inch pieplate. Fold edges under, and crimp.
BAKE on lowest oven rack at 400° for 8 minutes. Cool.
WHISK together cream cheese and half-and-half until smooth. Add eggs and next 3 ingredients, whisking until smooth. Stir in salmon and next 3 ingredients. Pour into prepared crust.
BAKE on lowest oven rack at 400° for 35 to 40 minutes or until set. Let stand 10 minutes.

BETH GUNDERSEN
BIRMINGHAM, ALABAMA

CRABMEAT-PARMESAN QUICHE

MAKES 6 SERVINGS

Prep: 15 min., Bake: 48 min., Cook: 4 min., Stand: 15 min.

Old Bay seasoning and lemon rind highlight the sweet, succulent crabmeat in this rich dish.

½ (15-ounce) package refrigerated
　piecrusts
3 to 4 green onions,
　chopped
2 teaspoons olive oil
2 (6-ounce) cans lump crabmeat,
　rinsed and drained
1 teaspoon grated lemon rind
½ teaspoon Old Bay seasoning
⅛ teaspoon ground red pepper
1 cup half-and-half
3 large eggs
¼ teaspoon salt
¼ teaspoon black pepper
1 (5-ounce) package shredded
　Parmesan cheese

UNFOLD piecrust, and place on a lightly floured surface. Roll out to ⅛-inch thickness. Carefully place piecrust in a 9-inch pieplate; fold edges under, and crimp.
BAKE on lowest oven rack at 400° for 8 minutes. Cool.
SAUTÉ chopped green onions in hot oil in a large skillet over medium-high heat 2 minutes.
STIR in crabmeat and next 3 ingredients; sauté 2 minutes.
WHISK together half-and-half and next 3 ingredients in a large bowl; stir in cheese and crabmeat mixture. Pour into prepared crust.
BAKE on lowest oven rack at 400° for 35 to 40 minutes or until set. Let stand 15 minutes.

BETH GUNDERSEN
BIRMINGHAM, ALABAMA

MUSHROOM-SPINACH-SWISS QUICHE

vegetarian

MAKES 6 SERVINGS

Prep: 20 min., Bake: 48 min., Cook: 15 min., Stand: 10 min.

½ (15-ounce) package refrigerated
　piecrusts
1 tablespoon butter or margarine
1 (8-ounce) package fresh
　mushrooms, chopped
1 roasted red bell pepper,
　chopped
2 tablespoons port wine or
　apple juice
1 cup half-and-half
3 large eggs
½ teaspoon Italian seasoning
½ teaspoon salt
¼ to ½ teaspoon black pepper
⅛ teaspoon ground red pepper
1 cup chopped fresh spinach
1 (5-ounce) package shredded Swiss
　cheese

UNFOLD piecrust, and place on a lightly floured surface. Roll out to ⅛-inch thickness. Carefully place in a 9-inch pieplate. Fold edges under, and crimp.
BAKE on lowest oven rack at 400° for 8 minutes. Cool.
MELT butter in a large skillet over medium-high heat. Add mushrooms and bell pepper; sauté 7 to 10 minutes or until tender. Stir in port; cook, stirring often, until liquid is absorbed.
WHISK together half-and-half and next 5 ingredients in a large bowl. Stir in mushroom mixture, spinach, and cheese. Pour into prepared crust.
BAKE on lowest oven rack at 400° for 40 minutes or until set. Let stand 10 minutes.

BETH GUNDERSEN
BIRMINGHAM, ALABAMA

Oatmeal Cookies

Try this wonderful cookie recipe for a wholesome, crisp-yet-chewy snack. Serve these with glasses of milk for a hearty after-school treat, or tuck a pair into a lunchbox. That way, there will be one for eating, one for sharing, and two to bring a smile.

GIANT OATMEAL-SPICE COOKIES

family favorite

MAKES ABOUT 2½ DOZEN

Prep: 20 min., Bake: 14 min. per batch

1½ cups all-purpose flour
1 teaspoon ground cinnamon
½ teaspoon salt
½ teaspoon baking soda
½ teaspoon ground ginger
¼ teaspoon ground allspice
⅛ teaspoon ground cloves
1 cup butter or margarine, softened
1 (16-ounce) package dark brown
　sugar
2 large eggs
1 teaspoon vanilla extract
3 cups quick-cooking oats
1 cup chopped pecans, toasted
½ cup raisins (optional)

STIR together first 7 ingredients.
BEAT butter and sugar at medium speed with an electric mixer until fluffy. Add eggs and vanilla, beating until blended. Gradually add flour mixture, beating at low speed until blended.
STIR in oats, chopped pecans, and if desired, raisins.
DROP dough by ¼ cupfuls onto lightly greased baking sheets; lightly press down dough.
BAKE, in batches, at 350° for 12 to 14 minutes. (Cookies should not be brown around the edges, and centers will not look quite done.) Cool slightly on baking sheets. Remove to wire racks; cool completely.

ANNE H. YOUNG
DURHAM, NORTH CAROLINA

Appetizers Anytime

Nibble on these munchies at your next gathering.

If the thought of entertaining friends sends you scrambling for appetizer ideas, you're on the right page. Our readers' top-notch starters give the standard chip-and-dip the boot. Take Crispy Moroccan Triangles, for example. Instead of using pita or tortilla chips, Marilou Robinson dusts wonton wrappers with a tantalizing spice mixture. A creamy dip, such as Black-Eyed Pea Hummus, makes these extra-crisp snacks almost addictive.

CRISPY MOROCCAN TRIANGLES

fast fixin's

MAKES 40 TRIANGLES

Prep: 10 min., Bake: 8 min.

To get a smooth, even coating of spices, use a fine wire-mesh strainer to sprinkle mixture on wontons. You can find the wrappers in the produce section of your supermarket nearest the specialty items.

- 20 wonton wrappers
- 1 teaspoon ground cinnamon
- ½ teaspoon ground cumin
- ¼ teaspoon ground ginger
- ¼ teaspoon ground turmeric
- ¼ teaspoon ground coriander
- ¼ teaspoon salt
- Vegetable cooking spray

CUT wonton wrappers in half diagonally, and arrange on 2 lightly greased baking sheets.
STIR together cinnamon and next 5 ingredients.
COAT wonton wrappers with cooking spray, and sprinkle evenly with cinnamon mixture.

BAKE at 375° for 8 minutes or until golden and crisp.

MARILOU ROBINSON
PORTLAND, OREGON

BLACK-EYED PEA HUMMUS

fast fixin's • make ahead

MAKES 2 CUPS

Prep: 10 min., Chill: 1 hr.

- 1 (15-ounce) can black-eyed peas, rinsed and drained
- 2 tablespoons tahini
- 2 tablespoons olive oil
- ¼ cup fresh lemon juice
- 2 garlic cloves
- ½ teaspoon salt
- ¼ teaspoon ground cumin
- ½ teaspoon freshly ground black pepper
- ⅛ teaspoon ground red pepper
- 3 tablespoons water
- Olive oil (optional)
- Chopped fresh parsley (optional)

PROCESS first 9 ingredients in a food processor until blended, stopping to scrape down sides. Gradually add 3 tablespoons water until desired consistency.
COVER and chill 1 hour. Drizzle with olive oil, if desired, and sprinkle with chopped parsley, if desired.

HUMMUS: Substitute 1 (15-ounce) can chickpeas, rinsed and drained, for black-eyed peas. Proceed with recipe as directed.

PORK PICADILLO EMPANADAS

make ahead • freezable

MAKES 16 EMPANADAS

Prep: 20 min., Cook: 12 min., Chill: 8 hrs.,
Bake: 20 min., Cool: 5 min.

These Caribbean-inspired pastries may be made in advance. Freeze baked pastries, and reheat at 350° for 15 minutes the day of the party.

- ¾ pound ground pork
- ½ jalapeño pepper, seeded and minced
- 1 teaspoon chili powder
- 1 teaspoon ground cumin
- ¾ teaspoon ground cinnamon
- ¼ teaspoon salt
- ¼ cup golden raisins
- 2 cups chipotle salsa, divided
- 2 tablespoons fresh lime juice
- 3 tablespoons chopped almonds, toasted
- 3½ tablespoons sour cream
- 1 (16.3-ounce) can refrigerated buttermilk biscuits
- 1 large egg, lightly beaten

BROWN pork in a large nonstick skillet over medium-high heat 8 to 10 minutes or until meat crumbles and is no longer pink; drain. Add jalapeño pepper and next 4 ingredients; cook, stirring occasionally, 2 minutes.
STIR in raisins, ½ cup salsa, and lime juice. Remove from heat, and stir in almonds and sour cream. Cool.
SEPARATE dough into 8 biscuits. Separate each biscuit in half to make 16 rounds. Roll each round on a lightly floured surface to a 4-inch circle.
SPOON pork mixture evenly in center of each dough circle. Fold dough over filling, pressing edges with a fork to seal. Cover with plastic wrap, and chill up to 8 hours.
PLACE empanadas on lightly greased baking sheets. Brush evenly with egg.
BAKE at 350° for 15 to 20 minutes or until golden. Cool 5 minutes on baking sheets. Serve with remaining 1½ cups chipotle salsa.

NOTE: For testing purposes only, we used Pillsbury Grands buttermilk biscuits.

GLORIA BRADLEY
NAPERVILLE, ILLINOIS

SPICY CHEESE-WALNUT WAFERS

make ahead

MAKES 80 CRACKERS

Prep: 20 min., Chill: 8 hrs., Bake: 15 min.
per batch

- 2 (4-ounce) packages crumbled blue cheese
- ½ (8-ounce) package cream cheese, softened
- ½ cup butter, softened
- 1½ cups all-purpose flour
- ¼ teaspoon salt
- 1 teaspoon to 1½ teaspoons ground red pepper
- 1 cup finely chopped walnuts
- 2 egg yolks, lightly beaten

BEAT first 3 ingredients at medium speed with an electric mixer until blended; add flour and remaining ingredients, beating until blended.

SHAPE dough into 2 (10-inch) logs. Wrap in plastic wrap; chill 8 hours.

CUT cold dough into ¼-inch slices; place on ungreased baking sheets.

BAKE in batches at 350° for 12 to 15 minutes or until lightly browned. Remove to wire racks to cool. Store in an airtight container up to 1 week.

LINDA NORMAN
SOUTHLAKE, TENNESSEE

Two New Takes on Quesadillas

We have Southwestern cuisine to thank for the easy-to-prepare quesadilla. So it's no surprise these flour tortilla-and-cheese "sandwiches" are usually filled with south-of-the-border ingredients. These recipes, however, borrow well-known flavor combinations from other cuisines. We think you'll love the new direction.

GREEK QUESADILLAS

vegetarian

MAKES 4 SERVINGS

Prep: 15 min., Cook: 23 min.

Don't let the long list of ingredients scare you away. Most of them are as close as your pantry. You can substitute spinach, sun-dried tomato, or chile flour tortillas for a different flavor.

- 1 small onion, chopped
- 1 teaspoon olive oil
- 2 garlic cloves, minced
- 1 (7-ounce) package fresh baby spinach*
- 1 (4-ounce) package crumbled feta cheese
- 1 (3-ounce) package cream cheese, softened
- ½ cup ricotta cheese
- 1 teaspoon fresh lemon juice
- ¼ teaspoon ground cumin
- ¼ teaspoon salt
- ¼ teaspoon freshly ground pepper
- ⅛ teaspoon ground nutmeg
- 4 (8-inch) flour tortillas
- Vegetable cooking spray
- Chunky salsa (optional)

SAUTÉ onion in hot oil in a large non-stick skillet over medium-high heat 6 minutes or until tender. Add garlic, and sauté 1 minute; add spinach, and sauté 3 to 4 minutes or until spinach is slightly wilted. Drain mixture on paper towels; cool slightly. Wipe skillet clean, and set aside.

STIR together feta cheese and next 7 ingredients until blended. Gently stir in spinach mixture.

SPOON mixture evenly onto half of each tortilla. Fold tortilla in half, pressing gently to seal.

HEAT skillet coated with cooking spray over medium-high heat. Add quesadillas, in 2 batches, and cook 2 to 3 minutes on each side or until quesadillas are lightly browned. Serve with chunky salsa, if desired.

*Substitute 1 (10-ounce) package frozen chopped spinach, thawed, if desired. Drain spinach well, and press between paper towels.

DIANE HALFERTY
CORPUS CHRISTI, TEXAS

APPLE PIE 'N' CHEDDAR QUESADILLAS

MAKES 6 SERVINGS

Prep: 20 min., Cook: 18 min.

- 2 (12-ounce) packages frozen baked apples with cinnamon
- 4 tablespoons light brown sugar, divided
- ½ teaspoon apple pie spice, divided
- ½ teaspoon vanilla extract
- 6 (8-inch) flour tortillas
- 2 cups (8 ounces) shredded Cheddar cheese
- 3 tablespoons butter or margarine, melted
- Vegetable cooking spray
- ½ cup chopped pecans, toasted
- Vanilla ice cream (optional)

MICROWAVE apples according to package directions.

STIR together apples, 3 tablespoons brown sugar, and ¼ teaspoon apple pie spice in a medium bowl until well blended. Pour mixture through a wire mesh strainer into a small bowl, reserving sauce. Stir vanilla into sauce, and keep warm.

SPOON apple mixture evenly onto half of each tortilla; top with cheese. Fold in half, pressing gently to seal. Stir together butter, remaining 1 tablespoon brown sugar, and remaining ¼ teaspoon apple pie spice. Brush butter mixture on both sides of quesadillas.

HEAT a large nonstick skillet coated with cooking spray over medium-high heat. Add quesadillas, in 3 batches, and cook 2 to 3 minutes on each side or until lightly browned and Cheddar cheese begins to melt.

DRIZZLE with reserved sauce, and sprinkle with pecans. Serve with ice cream, if desired.

NOTE: For testing purposes only, we used Stouffer's Harvest Apples for frozen baked apples with cinnamon.

SHANNON CHAMBLISS
BIRMINGHAM, ALABAMA

Serve Up Italian Tonight

Few things go together like the convenience and value of ground beef and Italian seasonings.

We've pulled together delicious, easy-to-make reader recipes that include everything from a spaghetti sauce to pizza to stuffed peppers.

"My teenage boys love Stuffed Green Peppers," says reader Paula Biehler of Austin, Texas. Kids will also love the Cheesy Ground Beef Pizza. It's easy to put together with refrigerated pizza crust.

SICILIAN SPAGHETTI SAUCE

family favorite

MAKES 4 TO 6 SERVINGS

Prep: 20 min.; Cook: 2 hrs., 40 min.

- ½ pound mild Italian sausage
- ½ pound lean ground beef
- 1 large onion, chopped
- 2 garlic cloves, minced
- 4 (8-ounce) cans tomato sauce
- 1 (6-ounce) can Italian-style tomato paste
- 3 cups water
- ¼ cup sugar
- 1 to 1½ teaspoons salt
- 1 teaspoon dried parsley
- 1 teaspoon dried basil
- ¼ to ½ teaspoon ground red pepper
- 1 cup sliced fresh mushrooms
- Hot cooked linguine
- Shredded Parmesan cheese
- Breadsticks (optional)

REMOVE casings from sausage, and discard. Cook sausage and ground beef in a large skillet or Dutch oven over medium heat 6 minutes, stirring until meat crumbles. Add onion and garlic, and sauté 4 minutes or until beef and sausage are no longer pink. Drain and set aside. Wipe skillet clean.

COMBINE tomato sauce and next 7 ingredients in skillet or Dutch oven; cook, stirring occasionally, 1 hour. Add sausage mixture and mushrooms. Cook, stirring occasionally, 1 hour and 30 minutes or until mixture thickens. Serve over linguine; sprinkle with cheese. Serve with breadsticks, if desired.

SUE THARP
LOUISVILLE, KENTUCKY

STUFFED GREEN PEPPERS

family favorite

MAKES 6 SERVINGS

Prep: 10 min., Cook: 19 min., Bake: 15 min.

- 6 medium-size green or red bell peppers
- 1 pound lean ground beef
- 1 medium onion, chopped
- 2 garlic cloves, minced
- 1 (15-ounce) can Italian-style tomato sauce
- ¼ teaspoon dried crushed red pepper
- ½ teaspoon salt
- ½ teaspoon pepper
- ½ cup Italian breadcrumbs
- ½ cup shredded Parmesan cheese

CUT off tops of bell peppers, reserving tops. Remove seeds and membranes. Cook peppers 4 minutes in boiling salted water to cover; drain and set aside. Remove stems from pepper tops, and discard. Chop pepper tops, and set aside.

COOK beef in a skillet over medium heat 6 minutes, stirring until beef crumbles.

Add reserved chopped bell pepper, onion, and garlic, and sauté 4 minutes or until beef is no longer pink. Drain.

STIR in tomato sauce and next 3 ingredients; cook, stirring often, 5 minutes or until mixture thickens.

SPOON mixture evenly into bell pepper cups; place in an aluminum foil-lined 11- x 7-inch baking dish.

COMBINE breadcrumbs and cheese; sprinkle over peppers.

BAKE at 350° for 15 minutes or until golden brown.

PAULA BIEHLER
AUSTIN, TEXAS

CHEESY GROUND BEEF PIZZA

family favorite

MAKES 4 SERVINGS

Prep: 20 min., Cook: 9 min., Bake: 15 min.

- 1 pound lean ground beef
- 1 small green or red bell pepper, cut into thin strips
- 1 small onion, thinly sliced and separated into rings
- ¾ teaspoon salt
- ½ teaspoon pepper
- ½ (24-ounce) package refrigerated pizza crusts
- 2 teaspoons vegetable oil
- 1 cup pizza sauce
- 1 (8-ounce) package shredded mozzarella cheese

COOK beef in a large skillet over medium heat 6 minutes, stirring until meat crumbles. Add bell pepper and next 3 ingredients; sauté 3 minutes or until beef is no longer pink. Remove from heat; drain and pat dry with paper towels.

PLACE pizza crust on a baking sheet; brush with oil.

BAKE crust at 450° for 5 minutes.

SPREAD pizza sauce on crust; top with beef mixture. Sprinkle with cheese.

BAKE at 450° for 10 minutes or until cheese melts.

NOTE: For testing purposes only, we used Mama Mary's refrigerated pizza crust.

AGNES L. STONE
OCALA, FLORIDA

Chicken Dinner Winners

From soup to pasta, these easy recipes are ready in less than an hour.

What's one hour worth? We all find out when we turn our clocks ahead. With these two chicken recipes, stay on schedule when it comes time to "spring forward." They can be on the table in less than an hour. Add a salad and speedy breadsticks seasoned to match the flavor of the chicken recipe, and it's time for supper.

MEXICAN CHICKEN SOUP

MAKES 11 CUPS

Prep: 15 min., Cook: 25 min.

- 1 small onion, chopped
- 1 green bell pepper, chopped
- 1 tablespoon vegetable oil
- 2 (32-ounce) containers chicken broth
- 1 (15-ounce) can black beans, rinsed and drained
- 1 (15-ounce) can kidney beans, rinsed and drained
- 1 (14½-ounce) can diced tomatoes
- 3 cups chopped cooked chicken
- 1 cup frozen whole kernel corn
- 1 teaspoon pepper
- ½ teaspoon salt
- ½ teaspoon ground cumin
- 2 tablespoons chopped fresh cilantro
- 2 tablespoons fresh lime juice
- Garnishes: lime slices, tortilla chips, sour cream, fresh cilantro

SAUTÉ onion and bell pepper in hot oil in a large Dutch oven over medium-high heat 5 minutes. Stir in chicken broth and next 8 ingredients, and bring to a boil. Reduce heat, and simmer, stirring occasionally, 20 minutes. Remove from heat; stir in 2 tablespoons cilantro and lime juice. Garnish, if desired.

MEDITERRANEAN CHICKEN AND PASTA

MAKES 4 SERVINGS

Prep: 20 min., Cook: 20 min.

This broth-based sauce is a nice change from a heavy cream-based pasta sauce.

- 8 ounces penne pasta
- 4 skinned and boned chicken breast halves (about 1½ pounds)
- 2 tablespoons olive oil
- 1 (8-ounce) package fresh mushrooms, sliced
- 3 garlic cloves, minced
- ½ cup chopped dried tomatoes in oil, drained
- ½ cup chicken broth
- ½ cup dry white wine
- 1 teaspoon dried basil
- ½ cup chopped fresh parsley
- 1 tablespoon butter or margarine
- ½ cup grated Parmesan cheese

COOK pasta according to package directions; drain.
CUT chicken into 1-inch pieces. Cook in hot oil in a large skillet over high heat 8 minutes or until browned. Remove from skillet.

SAUTÉ mushrooms in skillet for 4 minutes. Add garlic; sauté 1 minute. Add tomatoes, broth, wine, and basil. Bring to a boil; return chicken to skillet, and cover. Cook over low heat 4 minutes or until chicken is tender.
ADD cooked pasta, parsley, and butter to chicken mixture, tossing to combine. Cook 2 minutes or until thoroughly heated. Sprinkle with cheese, and serve immediately.

MIRIAM BAROGA
FIRCREST, WASHINGTON

SOUTHWESTERN KNOTS

fast fixin's

MAKES 12 SERVINGS

Prep: 5 min., Bake: 15 min.

- 2½ tablespoons butter or margarine, melted
- ¼ teaspoon chili powder
- ¼ teaspoon ground cumin
- 1 (11-ounce) can refrigerated breadsticks

STIR together melted butter, chili powder, and cumin until blended.
UNROLL breadsticks. Separate each dough portion. Loosely tie each portion into a knot, and place, 1 inch apart, on an ungreased baking sheet. Brush evenly with butter mixture.
BAKE at 350° for 15 minutes or until breadsticks are golden.

ITALIAN BREAD KNOTS: Substitute ¼ teaspoon Italian seasoning for chili powder and cumin. Sprinkle with 1 tablespoon Parmesan cheese. Proceed with recipe as directed.

CAJUN BREAD KNOTS: Substitute ½ teaspoon Cajun seasoning for chili powder and cumin. Add ¼ teaspoon dried thyme, if desired. Proceed with recipe as directed.

NOTE: For testing purposes only, we used Colonel Paul's Cajun Seasoning.

Great Tastes Go Healthy

Yeow Chang of Memphis knows a lot about great Asian dishes. "My mom has been my inspiration," he says. "She gave me my own clay pot when I was little, and I've been cooking ever since."

Yeow is particular about certain things when preparing Asian dishes. "I cook with high heat and use lots of vegetables with small amounts of meat." Adopt this strategy, prepare these recipes, and learn how good healthy can taste.

MAKE-AHEAD PORK DUMPLINGS

freezeable • make ahead

MAKES 116 DUMPLINGS

Prep: 2 hrs., Cook: 25 min.

This recipe makes a bunch, so ask a friend to help you assemble the dumplings; then freeze some for later. Our Test Kitchens Director created the dipping sauce to accompany them.

- 1½ pounds lean boneless pork loin chops, cut into chunks
- 1 (12-ounce) package 50%-less-fat ground pork sausage
- 1½ teaspoons salt
- 15 water chestnuts, finely chopped
- 1 to 2 tablespoons minced fresh ginger
- ½ cup cornstarch
- 2 teaspoons lite soy sauce
- ½ cup fat-free reduced-sodium chicken broth
- 4 tablespoons sugar
- 1 teaspoon teriyaki sauce
- 1 teaspoon dark sesame oil
- ¼ cup chopped fresh parsley
- 4 green onions, diced
- 2 (16-ounce) packages wonton skins
- Oyster sauce (optional)
- Thai chili sauce (optional)
- Ginger Dipping Sauce (optional)

PROCESS pork loin in a food processor until finely chopped.

COMBINE pork loin, pork sausage, and next 11 ingredients.

CUT corners from wonton skins to form circles. Drop 1 teaspoon mixture onto middle of each skin. Gather up sides, letting dough pleat naturally. Lightly squeeze middle while tapping bottom on a flat surface so it will stand upright.

ARRANGE dumplings in a bamboo steam basket over boiling water. Cover and steam 20 to 25 minutes. Serve with sauces, if desired.

Calories per dumpling 40 (17% from fat); Fat 0.8g (sat 0.2g, mono 0.3g, poly 0.2g); Protein 2.5g; Carb 6g; Fiber 0.2g; Chol 6mg; Iron 0.4mg; Sodium 101mg; Calc 7mg

NOTE: To freeze, arrange dumplings on a baking sheet; freeze 2 hours. Place in zip-top freezer bags; label and freeze up to 3 months. To cook from frozen state, steam for 22 to 25 minutes.

Ginger Dipping Sauce:

MAKES ⅓ CUP (ABOUT 5 SERVINGS)

Prep: 10 min., Cook: 1 min.

- 1 garlic clove, minced
- 1 tablespoon minced fresh ginger
- 1 teaspoon dark sesame oil
- 2 tablespoons lite soy sauce
- 1 tablespoon rice wine vinegar
- 2 teaspoons teriyaki sauce
- 1 green onion, minced

SAUTÉ garlic and ginger in hot oil 1 minute; remove from heat. Whisk in remaining ingredients.

Calories 17 (50% from fat); Fat 0.9g (sat 0.1g, mono 0.4g, poly 0.4g); Protein 0.7g; Carb 1.4g; Fiber 0.1g; Chol 0mg; Iron 0.1mg; Sodium 335mg; Calc 4mg

BABY SPINACH WITH PINE NUTS

fast fixin's

MAKES 4 SERVINGS

Prep: 5 min., Cook: 5 min.

- 2 (7-ounce) packages baby spinach
- 2 garlic cloves, minced
- 1 teaspoon olive oil
- ¼ teaspoon salt
- ¼ teaspoon pepper
- 2 tablespoons pine nuts, toasted*

SAUTÉ spinach and garlic in hot oil in a large nonstick skillet over medium-high heat 5 minutes or until spinach wilts. Stir in salt and pepper; sprinkle with pine nuts. Serve immediately.

Calories 51 (62% from fat); Fat 3.5g (sat 0.5g, mono 1.6g, poly 1.1g); Protein 2.6g; Carb 3.7g; Fiber 2g; Chol 0mg; Iron 1.2mg; Sodium 275mg; Calc 62mg

*****Substitute 2 tablespoons chopped toasted pecans or toasted sliced almonds, if desired.

BEEF WITH GINGER

MAKES 4 SERVINGS

Prep: 25 min., Cook: 10 min.

Chilling the beef in the freezer for 5 minutes makes it easier to cut into very thin slices.

- 1 pound sirloin steak, chilled
- ¼ teaspoon salt
- ½ teaspoon pepper
- 2 tablespoons grated fresh ginger
- 2 teaspoons vegetable oil
- ½ teaspoon minced garlic
- 2 teaspoons lite soy sauce
- ½ cup fat-free reduced-sodium beef broth
- 2 teaspoons cornstarch
- 6 green onions, cut diagonally into 1-inch pieces
- ½ teaspoon dried crushed red pepper (optional)
- 4 cups hot cooked long-grain rice

CUT steak diagonally across the grain into very thin slices. Sprinkle with salt and pepper.

SAUTÉ ginger in hot oil in a large non-stick skillet over high heat 2 minutes or until tan-colored. Add minced garlic, and sauté 30 seconds. Add beef; cook 2 minutes, stirring constantly. Stir in soy sauce.

STIR together beef broth and cornstarch until smooth. Drizzle over beef mixture. Cook, stirring constantly, 1 minute or until thickened. Add green onions, and, if desired, dried crushed red pepper; cook 1 minute. Serve immediately over hot cooked rice.

Calories 309 (28% from fat); Fat 9.6g (sat 2.9g, mono 4.2g, poly 1g); Protein 26g; Carb 27g; Fiber 1.5g; Chol 62mg; Iron 3.1mg; Sodium 399mg; Calc 18mg

FLUFFY WHITE RICE

fast fixin's

MAKES 4 SERVINGS

Prep: 5 min., Cook: 15 min., Stand: 10 min.

Rinsing the rice reduces its starchiness, making a fluffy, not sticky, product.

- **1 cup uncooked long-grain rice**
- **1½ cups water**
- **1 teaspoon vegetable oil**

PLACE rice in a large bowl. Rinse with water 3 or 4 times or until water is no longer cloudy. Drain.

BRING rice, 1½ cups water, and oil to a boil in a heavy saucepan. Cover, reduce heat, and simmer 15 minutes or until done.

REMOVE from heat, and let stand 10 minutes. Fluff with a fork.

Calories 196 (7% from fat); Fat 1.6g (sat 0.2g, mono 0.8g, poly 0.5g); Protein 3.8g; Carb 40g; Fiber 0.6g; Chol 0mg; Iron 1.7mg; Sodium 1.4mg; Calc 14mg

SPINACH EGG DROP SOUP

fast fixin's

MAKES 6 CUPS

Prep: 5 min., Cook: 5 min., Stand: 1 min.

For extra texture, flavor, and color, add sliced fresh shiitake or button mushrooms and thinly sliced red bell pepper. Sprinkle into empty bowls; ladle soup into bowls.

- **6 cups fat-free reduced-sodium chicken broth**
- **1 large egg, lightly beaten**
- **1 tablespoon soy sauce**
- **½ teaspoon sugar**
- **2 green onions, chopped**
- **2 cups fresh spinach**

BRING broth to a boil; reduce heat to a simmer. Slowly add egg, stirring constantly, until egg forms lacy strands. Immediately remove from heat. Let stand 1 minute. Stir in soy sauce, sugar, and green onions. Place spinach in bowls; ladle soup over spinach. Serve immediately.

Per 1 cup: Calories 50 (43% from fat); Fat 2.4g (sat 1g, mono 0.3g, poly 0.1g); Protein 4.7g; Carb 2.8g; Fiber 0.5g; Chol 39mg; Iron 0.3mg; Sodium 297mg; Calc 30mg

Taste of the South

Turn Dessert Upside Down

Assistant Foods Editor Cynthia Ann Briscoe's sweet memories of Pineapple Upside-Down Cake go back to childhood. She counted herself lucky if she was able to retrieve a portion of the softened pineapple that stuck to the bottom of the skillet. These morsels only increased her anticipation for the time when a real slice would come accompanied with a dollop of sweetened cream.

This Southern delight is noted for being baked in a cast-iron skillet. Our Test Kitchens' skillets got a workout as we tested recipes in search of the all-time best. The cake that wowed us came from *My Mother's Southern Desserts* by James and Martha Pearl Villas. If you're short on time, check out our express version that uses a cake mix.

SKILLET PINEAPPLE UPSIDE-DOWN CAKE

family favorite

MAKES 8 TO 10 SERVINGS

Prep: 20 min., Bake: 50 min., Cool: 30 min.

Use a cast-iron skillet that measures 9 inches across the bottom to be sure the cake doesn't overflow. We used light brown sugar, but you can use whichever type you have on hand.

- **¼ cup butter**
- **⅔ cup firmly packed light or dark brown sugar**
- **1 (20-ounce) can pineapple slices, undrained**
- **9 maraschino cherries**
- **2 large eggs, separated**
- **¾ cup granulated sugar**
- **¾ cup all-purpose flour**
- **⅛ teaspoon salt**
- **½ teaspoon baking powder**
- **Whipped cream or vanilla ice cream (optional)**

MELT butter in a 9-inch cast-iron skillet. Spread brown sugar evenly over bottom of skillet. Drain pineapple, reserving ¼ cup juice; set juice aside. Arrange pineapple slices in a single layer over brown sugar mixture, and place a cherry in center of each pineapple ring; set skillet aside.

BEAT egg yolks at medium speed with an electric mixer until thick and lemon-colored; gradually add granulated sugar, beating well.

HEAT reserved pineapple juice in a small saucepan over low heat. Gradually add juice mixture to the yolk mixture, beating until blended.

COMBINE all-purpose flour, salt, and baking powder; add dry ingredients to the yolk mixture, beating at low speed with electric mixer until blended.

BEAT egg whites until stiff peaks form; fold egg whites into batter. Spoon batter evenly over pineapple slices.

BAKE at 325° for 45 to 50 minutes. Cool cake in skillet 30 minutes; invert cake onto a serving plate. Serve warm or cold with whipped cream or ice cream, if desired.

ADAPTED FROM
MY MOTHER'S SOUTHERN DESSERTS
BY JAMES AND MARTHA PEARL VILLAS
(William Morrow and Company, Inc., 1998)

EXPRESS PINEAPPLE UPSIDE-DOWN CAKE: Follow original recipe directions for first 4 ingredients. Substitute 1 (9-ounce) package golden yellow cake mix for next 5 ingredients. Prepare mix according to package directions, substituting ½ cup pineapple juice for ½ cup water. Spoon batter over prepared pineapple slices as directed. Bake at 350° for 20 to 25 minutes or until a wooden pick inserted in center comes out clean.

NOTE: For testing purposes only, we used Jiffy Golden Yellow Cake Mix.

Mardi Gras Celebration

Mobilian Martha Rutledge adds Gulf Coast flavor to her Mardi Gras recipes. Citrus-Marinated Shrimp With Louis Sauce and Croissant Bread Pudding are both surefire crowd-pleasers.

CITRUS-MARINATED SHRIMP WITH LOUIS SAUCE

MAKES 10 TO 12 APPETIZER SERVINGS

Prep: 35 min., Cook: 5 min., Chill: 25 min.

   2 lemons, halved
   2 limes, halved
   ½ orange, halved
   1 tablespoon dried crushed red
      pepper
   4 pounds unpeeled, large fresh
      shrimp
   2 cups fresh orange juice
   2 cups grapefruit juice
   2 cups pineapple juice
   ½ cup fresh lemon juice
   ½ cup fresh lime juice
   1 lemon, sliced
   1 orange, sliced
   1 lime, sliced
   1 grapefruit, sliced
   1 teaspoon dried crushed red
      pepper
   Lettuce leaves
   Louis Sauce
   Garnish: citrus fruit slices

COMBINE lemon halves, next 3 ingredients, and salted water to cover in a Dutch oven. Bring to a boil; add shrimp, and cook 2 to 3 minutes or just until shrimp turn pink.
PLUNGE shrimp into ice water to stop the cooking process; drain.
PEEL shrimp, leaving tails on. Devein, if desired.
COMBINE orange juice and next 9 ingredients in a large shallow dish or zip-top freezer bag. Add shrimp, cover or seal, and chill 25 minutes. Drain off liquid. Serve shrimp over lettuce leaves with Louis Sauce. Garnish, if desired.

Louis Sauce:

MAKES 3 CUPS

Prep: 10 min.

This sauce can be prepared a day ahead.

   1 (12-ounce) jar chili sauce
   2 cups mayonnaise
   2 tablespoons grated onion
   2 tablespoons grated lemon rind
   3 tablespoons fresh lemon juice
   1 tablespoon prepared horseradish
   1½ teaspoons Greek seasoning
   1½ teaspoons Worcestershire
      sauce
   ¼ teaspoon ground red pepper
   ½ teaspoon hot sauce
   Garnish: lemon zest

STIR together first 10 ingredients. Cover and chill until ready to serve. Garnish, if desired.

CROISSANT BREAD PUDDING

MAKES 6 TO 8 SERVINGS

Prep: 30 min., Cook: 2 min., Stand: 10 min., Chill: 1 hr., Bake: 1 hr.

   9 large croissants
   ¼ cup bourbon
   ⅓ cup golden raisins
   8 large eggs
   1½ cups sugar
   3 cups heavy cream
   2 tablespoons vanilla extract
   ⅛ teaspoon salt
   Bourbon Sauce

SLICE croissants in half lengthwise; tear bottom halves of croissants into small pieces.
HEAT bourbon in a small saucepan over low heat; stir in raisins. Remove from heat, and let stand 10 minutes.
LAYER croissant pieces evenly in a lightly greased 13- x 9-inch baking dish. Sprinkle with golden raisins. Place croissant tops, crust sides up, over mixture.
WHISK together eggs and sugar. Whisk in cream, vanilla, and salt. Slowly pour mixture over croissant tops; press bread to absorb liquid. Cover; chill 1 hour.
PLACE dish into a larger pan. Pour hot water into larger pan, filling half full.

BAKE at 350° for 45 minutes or until set. Cover with aluminum foil, and bake 15 more minutes. Remove from oven, and remove dish from water pan. Serve warm with Bourbon Sauce.

Bourbon Sauce:

MAKES 1½ CUPS

Prep: 15 min.

   2 teaspoons cornstarch
   2 tablespoons water
   1 cup whipping cream
   ¼ cup sugar
   2 tablespoons bourbon

STIR together cornstarch and 2 tablespoons water.
BRING cream and sugar to a boil in a heavy saucepan.
REDUCE heat to low, and whisk in cornstarch mixture until cream mixture thickens. Remove from heat, and stir in bourbon.

Quick & Easy

Spring Vegetables

Perk up asparagus or broccoli with sesame seeds and easy dressings. Or try these carrots or green beans, both with a tangy new attitude.

GREEN BEANS WITH LEMON

fast fixin's

MAKES 6 TO 8 SERVINGS

Prep: 10 min., Cook: 12 min.

   2 quarts water
   1 teaspoon salt
   2 pounds tiny fresh green beans
   ¼ cup butter or margarine
   2 tablespoons grated lemon rind
   1 tablespoon fresh lemon juice
   1 teaspoon pepper

BRING 2 quarts water to a boil in a Dutch oven; add salt and beans. Cook 7 to 8 minutes; drain. Plunge into ice water to stop the cooking process; drain.

MELT butter in Dutch oven over medium heat; add beans, and sauté 2 minutes. Add lemon rind, and sauté bean mixture 1 minute. Stir in lemon juice and pepper. Serve immediately.

SESAME BROCCOLI

fast fixin's

MAKES 2 TO 3 SERVINGS

Prep: 10 min., Cook: 12 min.

- **1 pound fresh broccoli**
- **1 tablespoon sugar**
- **1 tablespoon soy sauce**
- **1 tablespoon vegetable oil**
- **2 teaspoons white vinegar**
- **2 teaspoons sesame seeds, toasted**

CUT broccoli into spears; arrange in a steamer basket over boiling water. Cover and steam 5 minutes or until crisp-tender. Place on a serving platter.

STIR together sugar and next 3 ingredients in a saucepan over medium heat. Cook, stirring often, until sugar dissolves and mixture is thoroughly heated. Drizzle over broccoli; sprinkle with sesame seeds.

RHONDA BUHAGIAR
ARRINGTON, TENNESSEE

CARROT RELISH

make ahead

MAKES 2½ CUPS

Prep: 15 min., Cook: 18 min.

- **1 pound fresh carrots, diced**
- **¼ cup chopped green bell pepper**
- **2 tablespoons chopped onion**
- **1 (2-ounce) jar diced pimiento, drained**
- **¼ cup sugar**
- **¼ cup white vinegar**
- **1 tablespoon all-purpose flour**
- **3 tablespoons honey**
- **¼ teaspoon salt**
- **¼ teaspoon ground red pepper**
- **¼ teaspoon dry mustard**
- **¼ teaspoon celery salt**

COOK carrots in boiling water to cover in a medium saucepan 8 to 10 minutes or until tender; drain carrots, and return to saucepan.

STIR in bell pepper and remaining ingredients; bring to a boil over medium heat, stirring constantly. Reduce heat, and simmer, stirring occasionally, 3 minutes. Serve warm or cold.

SHERRIE YARBRO
CLARKSBURG, TENNESSEE

CHILLED SESAME ASPARAGUS

fast fixin's • make ahead

MAKES 4 TO 6 SERVINGS

Prep: 5 min., Cook: 5 min., Chill: 2 hrs.

- **1½ to 2 pounds fresh asparagus, trimmed**
- **2 tablespoons plus 2 teaspoons dark sesame oil**
- **1 tablespoon plus 1 teaspoon rice vinegar**
- **1 tablespoon plus 1 teaspoon soy sauce**
- **1 teaspoon sugar**
- **1 tablespoon sesame seeds, toasted**

COOK asparagus in boiling water about 4 to 5 minutes or until crisp-tender. Plunge asparagus into ice water to stop the cooking process; drain, cover, and chill 2 hours.

WHISK together dark sesame oil and next 3 ingredients. Chill 2 hours. Arrange asparagus on a serving dish; spoon dressing over top. Sprinkle with sesame seeds.

ELIZABETH T. CLARKE
BURLINGTON, NORTH CAROLINA

Southern Gravies

You can have gravy whether you've roasted a large piece of meat or not. Complete your next meal with one of these rich variations. Pour on extra flavor with these basic recipes.

SAUSAGE GRAVY

fast fixin's • family favorite

MAKES 2 CUPS

Prep: 15 min., Cook: 10 min.

Serve over buttermilk biscuits or grits.

- **½ pound ground pork sausage**
- **¼ cup all-purpose flour**
- **2⅓ cups milk**
- **½ teaspoon salt**
- **½ teaspoon pepper**

COOK sausage in a large skillet over medium heat, stirring until it crumbles and is no longer pink. Remove sausage, and drain on paper towels, reserving 1 tablespoon drippings in skillet.

WHISK flour into hot drippings until smooth; cook, whisking constantly, 1 minute. Gradually whisk in milk, and cook, whisking constantly, 5 to 7 minutes or until thickened. Stir in sausage, salt, and pepper.

SAWMILL GRAVY

fast fixin's

MAKES 3¾ CUPS

Prep: 15 min., Cook: 10 min.

- **½ pound ground pork sausage**
- **¼ cup butter or margarine**
- **⅓ cup all-purpose flour**
- **3¼ cups milk**
- **½ teaspoon salt**
- **½ teaspoon pepper**
- **⅛ teaspoon dried Italian seasoning**

COOK sausage in a large skillet over medium heat, stirring until it crumbles and is no longer pink. Remove sausage, and drain on paper towels, reserving 1 tablespoon drippings in skillet.

MELT butter with drippings in skillet over low heat. Whisk in flour until smooth. Cook, whisking constantly, 1 minute. Gradually whisk in milk, and cook, whisking constantly, over medium heat until thickened and bubbly.

STIR in sausage, salt, pepper, and Italian seasoning.

CARYN NABORS
GADSDEN, ALABAMA

MEAT GRAVY

MAKES 2 CUPS

Prep: 5 min., Cook: 40 min.

- 1 medium onion, halved and sliced
- 2 celery ribs, sliced
- 2 tablespoons vegetable oil
- 1 (10½-ounce) can beef consommé, undiluted
- 1¼ cups water, divided
- 1 beef bouillon cube
- 2 tablespoons cornstarch
- ¼ teaspoon browning-and-seasoning sauce

SAUTÉ onion and celery in hot oil in a medium saucepan over medium-high heat 10 minutes; stir in consommé, 1 cup water, and bouillon cube. Bring to a boil; cover, reduce heat, and simmer 25 minutes or until onion is tender.
STIR together cornstarch, remaining ¼ cup water, and seasoning sauce until smooth.
ADD cornstarch mixture to consommé mixture. Bring to a boil over medium heat, stirring constantly; boil, stirring constantly, 1 minute.

NOTE: For testing purposes only, we used Kitchen Bouquet for browning-and-seasoning sauce.

CHARLOTTE BRYANT
GREENSBURG, KENTUCKY

CREAM GRAVY

fast fixin's

MAKES ¾ CUP

Prep: 5 min., Cook: 5 min.

If you have drippings from fried chicken or other meat, you can substitute those for the butter.

- 1 cup milk
- 1 (¼-inch-thick) onion slice
- 1 fresh parsley sprig
- 2 tablespoons butter or margarine
- 2 tablespoons all-purpose flour
- 2 tablespoons whipping cream
- ⅛ teaspoon salt
- ⅛ teaspoon ground white pepper
- Dash of ground nutmeg

BRING first 3 ingredients to a boil, and remove from heat. Pour milk mixture through a wire-mesh strainer into a small bowl, reserving the hot milk and discarding solids.
MELT butter in a skillet over low heat; whisk in flour until smooth. Cook, whisking constantly, 1 minute. Gradually whisk in reserved hot milk and cook, whisking constantly, over medium heat, until thickened and bubbly. Whisk in whipping cream and remaining ingredients.

GREG FERNALD
KINGWOOD, TEXAS

Double-Duty Sides

Who says side dishes have to be either a veggie or starch? These recipes bring both together—and they're quick too. Easy to prepare and full of flavor, they pair perfectly with chicken, beef, or pork. By combining the usually separate sides, you might find picky eaters enjoying one of them for the first time.

GREEN BEAN RISOTTO

MAKES 6 TO 8 SERVINGS

Prep: 15 min., Cook: 40 min.

- 1 pound fresh green beans
- 1 (32-ounce) container low-sodium chicken broth, divided
- ¼ cup butter or margarine
- 1 red onion, coarsely chopped
- 2 garlic cloves, pressed
- 1 cup uncooked Arborio rice
- 1 cup dry white wine or chicken broth
- 1 teaspoon chopped fresh thyme
- ½ teaspoon pepper
- 1 cup shredded Parmesan cheese

TRIM beans, and cut into bite-size pieces. Bring beans and ¼ cup broth to a boil in a Dutch oven over medium-high heat; cook 10 minutes or until crisp-tender. Remove beans with a slotted spoon, and set aside.
BRING remaining broth to a simmer in a saucepan (do not boil), keeping warm over low heat.
ADD butter, chopped onion, and garlic to broth in Dutch oven; cook 3 minutes. Add rice and white wine, and cook, stirring constantly, 5 minutes or until liquid is absorbed. Reduce heat to medium.
ADD 1 cup simmering broth to rice mixture in Dutch oven, and cook, stirring often, until liquid is absorbed. Repeat procedure with remaining broth, 1 cup at a time. (Cooking time is about 15 to 20 minutes.)
STIR in beans, thyme, pepper, and Parmesan cheese; serve immediately.

ASPARAGUS RISOTTO: Substitute 1 pound fresh asparagus for green beans. Proceed as directed.

LINDA DUSSZIV
HOUSTON, TEXAS

SPICY TOMATO MACARONI AND CHEESE

fast fixin's

MAKES 6 SERVINGS

Prep: 15 min., Cook: 15 min.

To tame the spiciness, switch to regular prepared cheese product and milder diced tomatoes and green chiles.

- 8 ounces uncooked penne pasta
- ¼ cup butter or margarine
- ½ medium-size sweet onion, chopped
- 1 (8-ounce) loaf Mexican-style pasteurized prepared cheese product, cubed
- 1 (8-ounce) container sour cream
- 1 (10-ounce) can diced tomatoes and green chiles, drained

COOK pasta according to package directions, draining well.
MELT butter in a large skillet over medium heat; add onion, and sauté 3 to 5 minutes or until tender.
ADD cheese, and cook, stirring constantly, 5 minutes or until cheese melts. Stir in sour cream, blending well. Stir in

tomatoes and green chiles and pasta; cook, stirring constantly, 5 minutes or until thoroughly heated.

ROSEMARY JOHNSON
IRONDALE, ALABAMA

EASY SQUASH-AND-CORN CASSEROLE

family favorite

MAKES 6 TO 8 SERVINGS

Prep: 15 min., Cook: 10 min., Bake: 50 min., Stand: 10 min.

- 1 (12-ounce) package frozen corn soufflé
- 2 tablespoons butter or margarine
- ½ small sweet onion, chopped
- 1 pound yellow squash, sliced
- 1 cup (4 ounces) shredded sharp Cheddar cheese
- ¾ cup soft breadcrumbs
- 2 tablespoons chopped fresh parsley
- 1 large egg, lightly beaten
- ½ teaspoon garlic salt
- ¼ teaspoon pepper

THAW corn soufflé according to package directions, and set aside.
MELT butter in a skillet over medium-high heat; add onion, and sauté 5 minutes or until tender. Add squash, and sauté 5 minutes.
STIR together corn soufflé, squash mixture, cheese, and remaining ingredients. Spoon mixture into a lightly greased 8-inch square baking dish.
BAKE at 350° for 50 minutes or until set. Let stand 10 minutes before serving.

Reuben Revival

Generous layers of corned beef, Swiss cheese, and sauerkraut nestled between rye bread make up the Reuben sandwich, a classic deli staple. Some of our readers have combined these ingredients into family-friendly recipes.

SOUTHERN REUBEN MELTS

fast fixin's

MAKES 4 SERVINGS

Prep: 15 min., Bake: 15 min.

- 1 cup mayonnaise
- ¼ cup ketchup
- 1 to 2 tablespoons sweet pickle relish
- ⅛ teaspoon ground red pepper
- 3 cups coleslaw mix
- 8 rye bread slices
- 1 (6-ounce) package Swiss cheese slices
- 12 ounces thinly sliced ham
- Butter-flavored cooking spray

STIR together first 4 ingredients.
STIR together coleslaw mix and ½ cup mayonnaise mixture.
SPREAD 1 tablespoon mayonnaise mixture evenly on 1 side of each bread slice; top 4 slices evenly with cheese, ham, and coleslaw mixture. Top with remaining bread slices.
PLACE sandwiches on a baking sheet coated with butter-flavored cooking spray.
COAT bottom of another baking sheet with cooking spray, and place, coated-side down, on sandwiches.
BAKE at 375° for 10 to 15 minutes or until bread is golden and cheese melts.

JENNIFER DANIELSON
CALLAWAY, MARYLAND

CHICKEN REUBEN CASSEROLE

MAKES 4 SERVINGS

Prep: 10 min., Bake: 35 min.

- 4 skinned and boned chicken breast halves
- ½ teaspoon salt
- ¼ teaspoon pepper
- 1 (14.5-ounce) can sauerkraut, drained
- 8 deli corned beef slices
- 8 (1-ounce) Swiss cheese slices
- 1½ cups Thousand Island dressing
- 1 cup soft rye breadcrumbs
- 2 tablespoons butter or margarine, melted
- 1 tablespoon chopped fresh parsley

SPRINKLE chicken with salt and pepper; place in a lightly greased 13- x 9-inch baking dish.
LAYER chicken evenly with sauerkraut, corned beef, and Swiss cheese. Pour dressing over top.
COMBINE breadcrumbs, butter, and parsley; sprinkle over casserole.
BAKE casserole at 350° for 35 minutes or until golden and bubbly.

HELEN CHITTERLING
WILMOT FLAT, NEW HAMPSHIRE

REUBEN PIZZA

fast fixin's

MAKES 8 SLICES

Prep: 10 min., Bake: 20 min.

- 1 (14-ounce) package prebaked Italian pizza crust
- ½ cup Thousand Island dressing
- 12 ounces thinly sliced corned beef*
- 1½ cups sauerkraut, drained
- 1½ to 2 cups shredded Swiss cheese
- 1 teaspoon caraway seeds
- Chopped dill pickles (optional)

PLACE pizza crust on a baking sheet.
SPREAD dressing evenly over pizza crust; top evenly with corned beef slices and sauerkraut.
SPRINKLE pizza evenly with shredded Swiss cheese and 1 teaspoon caraway seeds.
BAKE pizza at 450° for 20 minutes or until cheese melts. Top with pickles, if desired, and serve immediately.

*Substitute deli ham for corned beef, if desired.

NOTE: For testing purposes only, we used a Boboli pizza crust.

KEVIN BROUGHTON
MADISON, MISSISSIPPI

from our kitchen

Step 1: Pour water to a depth of 3 inches in a large saucepan. Bring to a boil; reduce heat, and maintain at a light simmer.
Step 2: Add ½ teaspoon white vinegar. Break eggs and slip into water, 1 at a time, close to the surface of the water. Simmer 3 to 5 minutes or to desired degree of doneness.
Step 3: Remove eggs with a slotted spoon. Trim edges, if desired.

Sauté Pans and Skillets

Southern Living Associate Foods Editor Shirley Harrington's story on sautéing, on pages 56-57, is terrific. The quick-cooking method and great recipes started a big discussion during taste testing about the difference between a skillet and a sauté pan. Here are the official definitions.

A sauté pan is a straight-sided frying pan that allows food to be flipped and tossed with less spattering. The sides are usually about 3 inches high; the pan can measure from 6 to 14 inches wide. It's perfect for quickly frying food in very little oil. A sauté pan generally has a long handle on one side and comes with a lid.

A skillet has sides that flare outward. It's shallow with sloped sides that prevent steam from forming in the pan. It's great for scrambling, searing, and shallow frying.

However, don't feel limited by the title of the pan. Most of our recipes can be done in either one. Call it a skillet or a sauté pan, but as long as it gets the job done, all is well.

Let your cooking style guide your selection of pots and pans. If you're avoiding fats, a nonstick pan is a good choice because you can pan-fry with just a little cooking spray. Be sure you buy a high-quality nonstick pan. Plan to spend $40 to $60 for an excellent pan that you'll use for years. (Those $25 bargain sets are no bargain at all: They're too thin, heat is not evenly distributed, and the coating wears off.)

If nonstick is not your choice, just remember to buy the best quality pan you can afford. It will give years of good service regardless of your cooking method.

There's a renewed interest today in copper cookware. Belgique now offers Gourmet Copper for cooks who want exceptional cookware at a reasonable price. Copper heats and cools quickly and evenly. Look for copper with a stainless steel interior and a hefty feel. Belgique's eight-piece set, which includes a 7-inch pan and a 9½-inch pan, costs about $200.

You'll need to clean copper pots and pans in hot, soapy water as soon after use as possible. Rinse and dry cookware thoroughly with a soft cloth to prevent spotting. Don't use oven cleaners or steel wool on copper (nylon scrubbing pads work fine). Wash cookware by hand, never in the dishwasher. Remove tarnish or dark spots with a good copper cleaner recommended by the manufacturer.

Tips and Tidbits

■ Store minced fresh garlic in a jar with olive oil, covered with a tight-fitting lid. Remove roasted garlic cloves from the bulb, and store them in olive oil too. Refrigerate for up to four weeks.

■ Keep peeled potatoes submerged in ice-cold water to prevent them from turning brown. You can store them in the refrigerator in a large bowl covered with plastic wrap—it's the air that discolors them.

Down-Home Flavor

You'll love every bite of these tried-and true diner-style dishes.

Family Favorites Supper

Serves 4

Chicken-Fried Steak

Three-Cheese Mashed Potato
Casserole

Iceberg Lettuce Wedges With
Blue Cheese Dressing

Iced tea

CHICKEN-FRIED STEAK

family favorite

MAKES 4 SERVINGS

Prep: 15 min., Cook: 18 min.

This ranked as one of our Top 5 winners in the Ulti-mate Southern category in Our Top 25 Recipes in 25 Years. See the special section at the end of the book for more about our favorite recipes in 25 years.

- ¼ teaspoon salt
- ¼ teaspoon pepper
- 4 (4-ounce) cubed steaks
- 38 saltine crackers, crushed (about 1 sleeve)
- 1¼ cups all-purpose flour, divided
- 2 teaspoons salt, divided
- 1½ teaspoons ground black pepper, divided
- ½ teaspoon ground red pepper
- ½ teaspoon baking powder
- 4¾ cups milk, divided
- 2 large eggs
- 1 cup peanut oil

SPRINKLE ¼ teaspoon salt and ¼ tea-spoon pepper evenly over steaks.

COMBINE crackers, 1 cup flour, 1 tea-spoon salt, ½ teaspoon black pepper, red pepper, and baking powder. Whisk together ¾ cup milk and eggs. Dredge steaks in cracker mixture; dip in milk mix-ture, and dredge again in cracker mixture.
POUR oil into a 12-inch skillet; heat to 360°. (Do not use a nonstick skillet.) Fry steaks 2 to 3 minutes or until golden. Turn and fry 2 to 3 minutes or until golden. Remove steaks to a wire rack in a jellyroll pan. Keep steaks warm in a 225° oven. Carefully drain hot oil, reserving cooked bits and 1 tablespoon drippings in skillet.
WHISK together remaining 4 cups milk, ¼ cup flour, 1 teaspoon salt, and 1 tea-spoon black pepper. Add to reserved drippings in skillet; cook, whisking con-stantly, over medium-high heat, 10 to 12 minutes or until thickened. Serve over steaks and mashed potatoes.

THREE-CHEESE MASHED POTATO CASSEROLE

family favorite • make ahead

MAKES 4 SERVINGS

Prep: 35 min., Cook: 15 min., Bake: 20 min.

- 4 large potatoes, peeled and cubed*
- 1 cup sour cream
- 1 (3-ounce) package cream cheese, softened
- ¼ cup butter or margarine, softened
- ⅔ cup milk
- ½ cup (2 ounces) shredded Cheddar cheese
- ½ cup (2 ounces) shredded Muenster cheese
- 1½ teaspoons salt
- ½ teaspoon pepper

COOK potatoes in boiling water to cover 15 minutes or until tender. Drain.

BEAT potatoes and next 3 ingredients at medium speed with an electric mixer until mixture is smooth. Stir in milk and remaining ingredients. Spoon mixture into a lightly greased 2-quart baking dish. (Cover and chill 8 hours, if desired; let stand at room temperature 30 min-utes before baking.)
BAKE, uncovered, at 400° for 15 to 20 minutes or until thoroughly heated.

*Substitute frozen mashed potatoes, if desired. Prepare potatoes according to package directions for 4 servings. Pro-ceed with recipe as directed. For testing purposes only, we used Ore Ida Mashed Potatoes.

ICEBERG LETTUCE WEDGES WITH BLUE CHEESE DRESSING

fast fixin's

MAKES 4 SERVINGS

Prep: 20 min.

- Blue Cheese Dressing
- 1 medium head iceberg lettuce, cut into 4 wedges
- 6 to 8 bacon slices, cooked and crumbled
- ½ cup shredded Parmesan cheese
- ¼ cup chopped fresh chives

POUR Blue Cheese Dressing over lettuce wedges. Combine bacon, cheese, and chives; sprinkle over dressing.

Blue Cheese Dressing:

MAKES ABOUT 2½ CUPS

Prep: 5 min.

- 1 cup mayonnaise
- 1 (8-ounce) container sour cream
- 1 (4-ounce) package crumbled blue cheese
- ¼ teaspoon salt
- 1 tablespoon Worcestershire sauce
- 1 teaspoon lemon juice

STIR together all ingredients. Cover and chill until ready to serve.

NOTE: To lighten recipe, substitute turkey bacon, reduced-fat mayonnaise, and reduced-fat sour cream.

Traditional Eggs Benedict, page 52

Italian Bread Salad, page 54

Black Bean and Black-Eyed Pea
Salad, page 54

Potato Salad With Cucumbers
and Tomatoes, page 92

Spicy Catfish With Vegetables and Basil Cream, page 56

Steaks With Caramel-Brandy Sauce , page 56

Creamy Ham Casserole, page 83

Creole Jambalaya, page 83

Buttered Rum Pound Cake With
Bananas Foster Sauce, page 94

79

Tropical Rum Trifle, page 85

Melt-in-Your-Mouth Muffins

It's the time for blooming azaleas, chirping birds, and spring gatherings, and these irresistible muffins—served fresh from the oven—are a great addition to your breakfast or brunch menu. For a fun display, stack colorful plates on top of oversize coffee mugs to form a tiered stand. But don't limit these treats to indoors; take them camping or on road trips too. Choose one, or try all the different flavor combinations our readers have to offer.

BROCCOLI CORNBREAD MUFFINS

MAKES 2 DOZEN MINI MUFFINS

Prep: 10 min., Bake: 20 min., Stand: 3 min.

- 1 (8½-ounce) package corn muffin mix
- 1 (10-ounce) package frozen chopped broccoli, thawed
- 1 cup (4 ounces) shredded Cheddar cheese
- 1 small onion, chopped
- 2 large eggs
- ½ cup butter or margarine, melted

COMBINE first 4 ingredients in a large bowl; make a well in center of mixture.
STIR together eggs and butter, blending well; add to broccoli mixture, stirring just until dry ingredients are moistened. Spoon into lightly greased mini muffin pans, filling three-fourths full.
BAKE at 325° for 15 to 20 minutes or until golden. Let stand 2 to 3 minutes before removing from pans.

KIMBERLY MASLANKA
LAUREL, MISSISSIPPI

HAM-AND-CHEDDAR MUFFINS

MAKES 12 (3-INCH) MUFFINS

Prep: 15 min., Cook: 5 min., Bake: 18 min., Stand: 3 min.

- 3 tablespoons butter or margarine
- 1 medium-size sweet onion, finely chopped
- 1½ cups all-purpose baking mix
- 2 cups (8 ounces) shredded Cheddar cheese, divided
- ½ cup milk
- 1 large egg
- 1 cup finely chopped cooked ham
- Poppy seeds (optional)

MELT butter in a skillet over medium-high heat; add onion, and sauté 3 to 5 minutes or until tender. Set aside.
COMBINE baking mix and half of cheese in a large bowl; make a well in center of mixture.
STIR together milk and egg, blending well; add to cheese mixture, stirring until moistened. Stir in onion and ham.
SPOON mixture into lightly greased muffin pans, filling two-thirds full. Sprinkle batter with remaining 1 cup cheese. Sprinkle with poppy seeds, if desired.
BAKE at 425° for 18 minutes or until golden. Let stand 2 to 3 minutes before removing from pans.

NOTE: Substitute mini muffin pans for regular pans, if desired. Bake at 425° for 14 minutes or until golden. Makes 2½ dozen mini muffins.

REDUCED-FAT HAM-AND-CHEDDAR MUFFINS: Substitute low-fat baking mix, fat-free or low-fat shredded Cheddar cheese, and fat-free milk. Reduce butter to 1 tablespoon; proceed with recipe as directed.

HAM-AND-SWISS MUFFINS: Substitute shredded Swiss cheese for Cheddar; whisk in 2 tablespoons Dijon mustard with milk and egg. Proceed with recipe as directed.

SAUSAGE-AND-CHEESE MUFFINS: Substitute 1 cup hot or mild ground pork sausage, cooked and crumbled, for chopped ham. Proceed with recipe as directed.

CHICKEN-AND-GREEN CHILE MUFFINS: Substitute 1 cup finely chopped cooked chicken for ham and 2 cups shredded Mexican four-cheese blend for Cheddar; add 1 (4.5-ounce) can chopped green chiles. Proceed with recipe as directed.

SHARON BUCHANAN
HUMBOLDT, TENNESSEE

SESAME-CHEESE MUFFINS

MAKES 8 (3-INCH) MUFFINS

Prep: 10 min., Cook: 3 min., Bake: 20 min.

- 1 tablespoon butter
- 1 small sweet onion, finely chopped
- 1½ cups all-purpose baking mix
- 1 cup (4 ounces) shredded sharp Cheddar cheese, divided*
- 1 large egg
- ½ cup milk
- 1 teaspoon sesame seeds, toasted
- 2 tablespoons butter or margarine, melted

MELT 1 tablespoon butter in a small skillet over medium-high heat. Add onion, and sauté 2 minutes or until tender; set aside.
COMBINE baking mix and half of cheese in a large bowl; make a well in center of mixture.
STIR together onion, egg, and milk, blending well; add to cheese mixture, stirring just until dry ingredients are moistened.
SPOON into lightly greased muffin pans, filling two-thirds full. Sprinkle evenly with remaining cheese and sesame seeds; drizzle with 2 tablespoons butter.
BAKE at 400° for 15 to 20 minutes or until golden.

NOTE: Substitute mini muffin pans for regular pans, if desired. Bake at 400° for 12 to 14 minutes or until golden. Makes 1½ dozen mini muffins.

*Substitute 1 cup (4 ounces) shredded Monterey Jack cheese with peppers for Cheddar cheese, if desired.

DONNA HARMON
SEWANEE, TENNESSEE

Start With a Ham

Bake it for the big weekend meal,
and turn the leftovers into weeknight suppers
that taste like special occasions.

The first time that former Assistant Foods Editor Cybil B. Talley ventured to prepare a ham, she ended up buying a mega-size orb with not a clue as to how much she needed, how long to bake it, or how to carve it. If your experiences have been similar to Cybil's, we're here to ease your mind about tackling this cut of meat. Let us help you prepare a ham that's stellar enough for an Easter buffet and so good left over that you won't mind savoring it again in our weeknight dinner ideas.

Simple Mathematics
Wondering how much to buy? Plan to purchase a ham large enough to serve for both dinner and multiple meals later. Say you want to serve eight people for Easter supper. Allotting two to three servings per pound for a bone-in ham, you'll need to buy a 7- to 9-pound ham. After you make a few sandwiches, you'll still have enough to prepare any of these recipes. You can even opt to create your own specialty by tossing some ham into a pasta or green salad.

Which To Buy
Overall, we find the taste and texture of a bone-in ham to be the best. Besides, you've got prime real estate underneath all that goodness—the ham bone. Save this premium ingredient for your next pot of beans, greens, or soup.

You'll find half hams cut into shank and butt portions. Though pricier, the butt portion offers more meat because there's not as much bone as in the shank. Also available are spiral-sliced hams, which may be easier to serve, but you'll pay for this added convenience. You can substitute a reduced-sodium ham in our recipes if you're watching your sodium count.

To Cook or Not?
The label on a ham tells you whether it's ready to eat or should be cooked. We recommend that you bake a fully cooked ham at 325° for 15 to 20 minutes per pound or until it reaches an internal temperature of 140°. Even though it technically doesn't require additional cooking, reheating it thoroughly maximizes its yumminess. Uncooked hams should be baked at 325° for 18 to 22 minutes per pound or until a meat thermometer registers 160°.

How To Store It
If you don't plan on using the remaining meat within four to five days, slice or cube it, then wrap tightly in heavy-duty plastic wrap. Freeze it in an airtight container up to two months, but don't store it any longer because its texture and flavor change. Cybil likes to package it in small, manageable portions so she wastes less.

Carving Clues

Carving the ham is a cinch. A sharp carving knife, a meat fork, and these simple instructions are all you need for the job. Hold the knife perpendicular to the bone. Cut full slices just until you feel the knife touching the bone. Then, place your knife at a 90-degree angle to the slices, parallel to the bone, and cut to release the slices. Once all the meat has been cut from this side, turn the ham over, and repeat the procedure.

PINEAPPLE-GLAZED HAM
family favorite

MAKES 14 TO 18 SERVINGS

Prep: 35 min.; Cook: 30 min.;
Bake: 2 hrs., 30 min.; Stand: 15 min.

Brown sugar and Dijon mustard give this ham the right balance of sweetness and saltiness.

- 4 cups pineapple juice
- 1 (1-inch) piece fresh ginger, peeled and sliced
- 4 garlic cloves, pressed
- 1 (7- to 9-pound) bone-in smoked fully cooked ham
- 12 to 16 whole cloves
- ¼ cup Dijon mustard
- 1 cup firmly packed light brown sugar
- 1 (20-ounce) can pineapple slices in juice, drained
- 10 maraschino cherries, halved

STIR together first 3 ingredients in a saucepan; bring to a boil. Reduce heat to medium-low, and simmer 25 minutes or until liquid is reduced by half. Pour mixture through a wire-mesh strainer into a bowl, discarding solids.

REMOVE skin and excess fat from ham. Make ¼-inch-deep cuts in a diamond design, and insert cloves at 1-inch intervals.

PLACE ham in an aluminum foil-lined roasting pan. Spread Dijon mustard evenly over ham. Pat brown sugar on top of mustard. Pour pineapple juice mixture into pan.

ARRANGE pineapple and cherries evenly over mustard layer on ham; secure with wooden picks.

BAKE at 325° for 1 hour. Shield with aluminum foil after 1 hour to prevent excess browning, and bake 1 to 1½ hours or until a meat thermometer inserted into thickest portion registers 140°, basting every 30 minutes with pan juices. Let stand 15 minutes before slicing.

REMOVE from pan, reserving drippings. Cover ham, and chill, if desired. Chill reserved drippings.

REMOVE and discard fat from drippings. Bring drippings to a boil in a small saucepan. Serve warm with ham.

ANNETTE B. CHANCE
CAPE CHARLES, VIRGINIA

APPLE-RAISIN RELISH

make ahead

MAKES 4 CUPS

Prep: 20 min., Cook: 25 min.

Reader Dottie B. Miller suggests serving this sweet-tart relish over pound cake, but we love it alongside slices of pleasantly salty ham. You can substitute pecans for almonds if you prefer.

**2 cups sugar
1 cup chopped dried apricots
1 cup golden raisins
½ cup slivered almonds, toasted
¼ cup white vinegar
2 tablespoons grated orange rind
4 Granny Smith apples, peeled and
chopped**

BRING all ingredients to a boil in a large saucepan, stirring constantly. Reduce heat to low, and simmer, stirring often, 20 to 25 minutes, until apples are tender and mixture has thickened.

DOTTIE B. MILLER
JONESBOROUGH, TENNESSEE

HAM-BROCCOLI POT PIE

MAKES 6 SERVINGS

Prep: 20 min., Bake: 35 min.

**1 (10-ounce) package frozen
chopped broccoli, thawed
1 (11-ounce) can sweet whole
kernel corn, drained
1 (10¾-ounce) can cream of
mushroom soup, undiluted
2 cups diced cooked ham
2 cups (8 ounces) shredded colby-
Jack cheese blend
1 (8-ounce) container sour
cream
½ teaspoon pepper
½ teaspoon dry mustard
½ (15-ounce) package refrigerated
piecrusts**

ARRANGE chopped broccoli in a lightly greased 11- x 7-inch baking dish.
STIR together corn and next 6 ingredients. Spoon over broccoli.
UNFOLD piecrust; pat or roll into an 11- x 7-inch rectangle, and place over ham mixture. Crimp edges, and cut 4 slits for steam to escape.
BAKE at 400° for 30 to 35 minutes or until golden.

CINDY ENFINGER
OKEECHOBEE, FLORIDA

CREOLE JAMBALAYA

family favorite

MAKES 8 SERVINGS

Prep: 25 min., Cook: 1 hr. *(pictured on page 78)*

**2 tablespoons butter or margarine
1 large onion, chopped
1 green bell pepper, chopped
8 green onions, chopped
2 celery ribs, chopped
3 cups cubed cooked ham (1 pound)
1 pound Cajun-flavored or smoked
sausage, sliced
1 (8-ounce) can tomato sauce
½ teaspoon salt
½ teaspoon ground black pepper
¼ teaspoon ground red pepper
5 cups cooked rice
Garnishes: fresh parsley sprig,
chopped fresh parsley**

MELT butter in a large skillet over medium heat. Add onion and next 3 ingredients; sauté until tender. Add ham, sausage, and next 4 ingredients. Cook, stirring occasionally, 20 minutes.
STIR in rice; cover, and cook, stirring occasionally, 30 minutes over low heat. Garnish, if desired.

PAT RUSH BENIGNO
VICKSBURG, MISSISSIPPI

CREAMY HAM CASSEROLE

MAKES 6 SERVINGS

Prep: 25 min., Cook: 15 min., Bake: 45 min.
(pictured on page 78)

**1 medium cauliflower
4 tablespoons butter or margarine
⅓ cup all-purpose flour
1 cup milk
1 cup (4 ounces) shredded Cheddar
cheese
½ cup sour cream
2 cups cubed cooked ham
1 (3-ounce) can sliced mushrooms,
drained
1 cup soft breadcrumbs
1 tablespoon cold butter or margarine**

CUT cauliflower into florets (about 3 cups). Cook in boiling salted water to cover 10 to 12 minutes or until tender; drain and set aside.
MELT 4 tablespoons butter in a medium saucepan over medium-high heat. Whisk in flour until smooth. Gradually add milk, whisking constantly, until mixture begins to thicken.
ADD Cheddar cheese and sour cream, stirring until cheese melts. (Do not boil.)
STIR cauliflower, ham, and mushrooms into cheese sauce; pour into a 2-quart baking dish.
SPRINKLE breadcrumbs evenly over casserole. Cut 1 tablespoon butter into pieces, and sprinkle evenly over the breadcrumbs.
BAKE casserole, uncovered, at 350° for 45 minutes.

EUGENE F. HARRISON
MANASSAS, VIRGINIA

One Great Sandwich

The prospect of a terrific sandwich for a quick lunch or satisfying midnight snack immediately comes to mind whenever we serve ham. It's a pretty simple recipe. Other than lettuce and tomato, no major embellishments are needed. In fact, a survey from the National Pork Board confirms that two slices of white bread, a slather of mayo or mustard, and a sliver of cheese are the fixings of choice for most Americans. For a special touch, pan-fry thin pieces of ham just until golden and crispy around the edges.

Trifles With a Twist

Make these luscious layered desserts in almost any dish you have on hand.

Intimidated by the thought of making a trifle? Chill out—trifles are really easy. Find a glass salad bowl, wine goblets, or just a big ol' mixing bowl, and give these layered desserts a try.

Lorraine Schumacher of Glendale, Missouri, stepped out of the box—or trifle dish, as the case may be—with a clever makeover that she calls Jumbleberry Trifle. The classic version of the dessert combines sherry-soaked pound cake with cooked custard and fruit. Lorraine created her version by layering bite-size pound cake sandwiches with a two-ingredient, no-cook custard and a sauce prepared from frozen fruits.

Inspired by Lorraine's creativity, Test Kitchens professional Laura Martin and Associate Foods Editor Shirley Harrington were off and layering. They combined rum-soaked pound cake with tropical fruits and strawberries with sugared biscuits. The results were wonderful. For chocolate lovers, reader Sara Nichols offers a recipe combining brownies with white chocolate pudding. No matter which trifle you make, be sure to chill it well—this allows the flavors to blend.

JUMBLEBERRY TRIFLE

make ahead

MAKES 8 SERVINGS

Prep: 45 min., Chill: 50 min.

1 (10-ounce) package frozen
    unsweetened raspberries, thawed
1 (18-ounce) jar seedless blackberry
    jam or preserves, divided
1 (10.75-ounce) frozen pound cake,
    thawed
2 tablespoons cream sherry
1½ cups whipping cream
1 (10-ounce) jar lemon curd
Garnishes: whipped cream, fresh
    raspberries and blackberries,
    fresh mint sprigs, lemon rind
    strips

STIR together raspberries and 1 cup jam. Press mixture through a wire-mesh strainer into a bowl; discard seeds. Cover sauce, and chill 20 minutes.

CUT pound cake into ¼-inch-thick slices. Spread remaining jam on 1 side of half of slices; top with remaining slices. Cut sandwiches into ½-inch cubes; drizzle with sherry, and set aside.

BEAT whipping cream and lemon curd at low speed with an electric mixer until blended. Gradually increase mixer speed, beating until medium peaks form. Cover and chill 30 minutes.

SPOON 1 tablespoon berry sauce into 8 large wine glasses; top with about ¼ cup each of cake cubes and lemon curd mixture. Repeat layers once, ending with berry sauce. Serve immediately, or chill until ready to serve. Garnish, if desired.

LORRAINE SCHUMACHER
GLENDALE, MISSOURI

STRAWBERRY-SUGAR BISCUIT TRIFLE

family favorite • make ahead

MAKES 10 TO 12 SERVINGS

Prep: 35 min., Chill: 4 hrs.

When prepping for this recipe, make the custard first; then bake the biscuits, and prepare the fruit.

Sugar Biscuits
6 tablespoons orange liqueur or
    orange juice, divided
2½ pounds strawberries, halved
Trifle Custard
1½ cups whipping cream
¼ cup plus 2 tablespoons powdered
    sugar
Garnishes: strawberries, mint
    leaves

CUT Sugar Biscuits in half; brush cut sides evenly with 5 tablespoons orange liqueur.

LINE bottom of a 4-quart bowl or trifle bowl with eight Sugar Biscuit halves.

ARRANGE strawberry halves around lower edge of bowl. Spoon one-third of Trifle Custard evenly over Sugar Biscuit halves; top with one-third of remaining strawberry halves. Repeat layers twice, ending with strawberry layer. Drizzle remaining orange liqueur evenly over top. Cover and chill 3 to 4 hours.

BEAT whipping cream until foamy; gradually add powdered sugar, beating until soft peaks form. Spread over trifle; serve immediately. Garnish, if desired.

Trifle Custard:

MAKES 4 CUPS

Prep: 5 min., Cook: 8 min., Chill: 2 hrs.

1 cup sugar
⅓ cup cornstarch
6 egg yolks
2 cups milk
1¾ cups half-and-half
1 teaspoon vanilla extract

WHISK together all ingredients in a heavy saucepan. Bring to a boil over medium heat, whisking constantly; boil, whisking constantly, 1 minute or until thickened. Remove from heat. Place pan in ice water; whisk occasionally until cool. Chill completely, about 2 hours.

Sugar Biscuits:

MAKES 12 BISCUITS

Prep: 10 min., Bake: 20 min.

1 (12-count) package frozen buttermilk biscuits
2 tablespoons whipping cream
1 tablespoon sugar
¼ teaspoon ground cinnamon

BRUSH tops of frozen biscuits with whipping cream; sprinkle evenly with sugar and ground cinnamon. Place biscuits on a lightly greased baking sheet. Bake at 350° for 20 minutes. Cool.

TROPICAL RUM TRIFLE

make ahead

MAKES 10 TO 12 SERVINGS

Prep: 45 min.; Chill: 1 hr., 50 min.

Make the Coconut Cream Custard first; while it's chilling, prepare the remaining ingredients. *(pictured on page 80)*

2 mangoes, peeled and cut into ½-inch cubes*
1 (20-ounce) can pineapple chunks in syrup, undrained
⅓ cup coconut-flavored rum
1 (10.75-ounce) frozen pound cake, thawed and thinly sliced
2 bananas, sliced
Coconut Cream Custard
1⅓ cups sweetened flaked coconut, toasted
⅔ cup chopped macadamia nuts, toasted
1 cup whipping cream
¼ cup powdered sugar
¼ teaspoon vanilla extract
Garnishes: mango, star fruit, toasted coconut, toasted macadamia nuts

STIR together first 3 ingredients in a bowl. Cover and chill 20 minutes.
REMOVE fruit from bowl with a slotted spoon, reserving syrup mixture.
BRUSH pound cake slices with syrup mixture. Arrange half of slices in bottom of a 4-quart bowl or trifle bowl. Top with half each of mango mixture, banana slices, Coconut Cream Custard, coconut, and macadamia nuts. Repeat layers.

BEAT whipping cream until foamy; gradually add sugar, beating until soft peaks form. Add vanilla; beat until blended. Spread evenly over top of trifle. Cover and chill 1½ hours. Garnish, if desired.

NOTE: For testing purposes only, we used Malibu Caribbean Rum With Coconut Flavor.

*Substitute 1 (24-ounce) jar refrigerated mango, drained and cut into ½-inch cubes, if desired.

Coconut Cream Custard:

MAKES 4 CUPS

Prep: 10 min., Cook: 3 min., Chill: 1 hr.

1 cup sugar
⅓ cup cornstarch
2 cups milk
1 (14-ounce) can coconut milk
6 egg yolks

WHISK together all ingredients in a heavy saucepan. Bring to a boil over medium heat, whisking constantly; boil, whisking constantly, 1 minute or until thickened. Remove from heat. Place pan in ice water; whisk custard occasionally until cool.
COVER and chill 1 hour.

Which Dish?

Trifle recipes traditionally prepared in a large bowl can be assembled in individual serving glasses. Look under the recipe title for the number of servings; you'll need about that many glasses. For example, if the recipe makes 12 servings, you'll need 12 glasses.

BROWNIE TRIFLE

family favorite • make ahead

MAKES 15 SERVINGS

Prep: 1 hr., 20 min.; Chill: 2 hrs.

For a change, assemble this trifle in a 3-quart bowl. Measure the size of your bowl with water; it should hold at least 12 cups. Assemble the brownie pieces, marshmallow mixture, pudding, and caramel topping in several layers when using a deep bowl.

2 (21-ounce) packages chewy fudge brownie mix
1 (8-ounce) package cream cheese, softened
1 (7-ounce) jar marshmallow cream
2 (8-ounce) containers frozen whipped topping, thawed and divided
3 cups fat-free milk
2 (3.3-ounce) packages white chocolate instant pudding mix
1 (12¼-ounce) jar caramel topping

PREPARE each brownie mix according to package directions for chewy brownies in a 13- x 9-inch pan. Cool; break into large pieces.
BEAT cream cheese at medium speed with an electric mixer until creamy; beat in marshmallow cream. Stir in 1 container of whipped topping; set mixture aside.
STIR together milk and white chocolate pudding mix, stirring until thickened. Stir in remaining container of whipped topping.
CRUMBLE half of brownie pieces in an even layer in a 13- x 9-inch baking dish. Pour cream cheese mixture evenly over brownies; drizzle evenly with caramel topping. Pour pudding evenly over caramel topping; crumble remaining brownie pieces over top. Cover and chill 2 hours.

NOTE: For testing purposes only, we used Duncan Hines Chewy Fudge Brownie Mix and Smucker's Caramel Topping.

SARA L. NICHOLS
EAST BEND, NORTH CAROLINA

Italian Tonight

Step inside this Sarasota, Florida, kitchen, which is full of ideas and irresistible recipes.

Little Gabriella Hazan, looking every bit the Italian version of Shirley Temple, climbs confidently onto a kitchen chair and begins to stir the pot of risotto on the burner. She's only 4, but she takes cooking in stride. Her father, Giuliano, close at her side, whispers encouragement in Italian, undaunted by the notion of a young helper. His cookbook *Every Night Italian* promises easy recipes for fresh, healthy food, and Gabriella beautifully illustrates the point. "One of *my* first duties was to stir the risotto, so this continues the tradition," says Giuliano, son of international cookbook author Marcella Hazan.

His approach to cooking—few ingredients, simple directions, quick results, and impressive taste—gives us recipes such as Chicken With Green Olives, Lamb Shanks Braised With Tomatoes, Zucchini Sautéed With Fresh Mint, Mixed Fruit Marinated With Kirsch, and Risotto With Shrimp and Asparagus. No shortcuts, no skimping on quality though. "Something doesn't have to have 15 ingredients to be good," says Giuliano. "My recipes are still guided by the principles I grew up with, but making them doesn't have to be difficult."

Off to Italy

For cooks who want to learn Giuliano's methods, the author and his wife, Lael, lead food-filled pilgrimages to the 15th-century Villa Giona, near Verona, Italy, each spring and summer. Students explore the flavors of the countryside, then return to the villa. Granted, the ingredients are the very best—but Giuliano, a new Southerner who now lives in Sarasota, thinks you'll do equally well locating what you need for his recipes. "Amazing markets are cropping up in larger cities, and farmers markets are all around," he says.

The Kitchen Design

Back home, Giuliano's kitchen lends itself to social cooking and to efficiency. He and Lael designed the room with those goals in mind, using the concept of integrated space. Visually the kitchen, rimmed with a boomerang-curved bar, is a seamless extension of the living and dining rooms. Still it stands apart in small but important ways.

For one thing, the flooring changes from bamboo in the other areas to easy-on-the-feet cork in the food prep area. "It's so much springier," says Giuliano, stepping from one section to the other. Indeed, one feels like cotton, the other sturdy stone.

That's just the beginning of this thinking man/cooking man's kitchen, all so sensible and doable.

MIXED FRUIT MARINATED WITH KIRSCH

chef recipe • make ahead

MAKES 4 TO 6 SERVINGS

Prep: 15 min., Chill: 2 hrs.

- **2 ripe mangoes, peeled and chopped**
- **1 pound fresh strawberries, halved or quartered**
- **2 kiwifruit, peeled, halved lengthwise, and sliced**
- **2 tablespoons sugar**
- **⅓ cup orange juice**
- **2 tablespoons kirsch or other fruit brandy**
- **2 teaspoons grated lemon rind**

PLACE first 3 ingredients in a shallow serving bowl.

GENTLY stir in sugar and remaining ingredients. Cover and chill for at least 2 hours or overnight, if desired.

RISOTTO WITH SHRIMP AND ASPARAGUS

chef recipe

MAKES 4 TO 6 SERVINGS

Prep: 20 min., Cook: 40 min.

- **½ pound unpeeled, medium-size fresh shrimp**
- **6½ cups water**
- **½ teaspoon salt**
- **½ pound fresh asparagus, cut into 1-inch pieces**
- **1 small onion, diced**
- **2 tablespoons olive oil**
- **1½ cups Arborio rice**
- **1 teaspoon salt**
- **½ teaspoon pepper**

PEEL shrimp, and devein, if desired. Set aside.

BRING 6½ cups water and ½ teaspoon salt to a boil in a 3½-quart saucepan. Add asparagus pieces, and cook 4 minutes. Remove asparagus with a slotted spoon, and set aside, reserving broth in pan over low heat to keep warm.

SAUTÉ diced onion in hot oil in a large Dutch oven over medium heat 6 minutes or until tender and golden.

ADD 1½ cups rice, and cook, stirring constantly, 2 minutes. Reduce heat to medium; add 1 cup reserved hot asparagus broth. Cook, stirring constantly, until liquid is absorbed.

REPEAT procedure with remaining hot broth, ½ cup at a time (cooking time is about 20 minutes). Add shrimp and asparagus pieces, and cook, stirring constantly, 3 minutes or just until shrimp turn pink. Remove from heat; stir in salt and pepper. Serve immediately.

By the Book

We adapted these recipes from Giuliano's *Every Night Italian* (Scribner, 2000), available in most bookstores. Visit **www.giulianohazan.com** for more recipes and future plans.

Zucchini Sautéed With Fresh Mint

chef recipe

MAKES 4 TO 6 SERVINGS

Prep: 10 min., Cook: 11 min.

- 1½ pounds small zucchini
- 2 garlic cloves, finely chopped
- 2 tablespoons olive oil
- 1 tablespoon finely chopped fresh Italian parsley
- 1 teaspoon chopped fresh mint leaves
- 1 tablespoon shredded fresh basil leaves
- ½ teaspoon salt
- ½ teaspoon pepper

CUT zucchini lengthwise in half, and cut into ¼-inch-thick wedges about 1½ inches long.

SAUTÉ garlic in hot oil in a skillet over medium-high heat until lightly browned; stir in parsley, and cook about 30 seconds. Add zucchini, cook, stirring occasionally, 8 to 10 minutes or until tender.

STIR in 1 teaspoon chopped mint leaves and remaining ingredients; cook 30 seconds or until thoroughly heated. Remove from heat, and serve immediately.

Chicken With Green Olives

chef recipe

MAKES 4 TO 6 SERVINGS

Prep: 25 min., Cook: 1 hr.

- 5 anchovy fillets
- 1½ cups (8 ounces) green olives, slivered and divided
- 3 pounds chicken legs, thighs, and wings
- ½ teaspoon salt
- ½ teaspoon pepper
- 2 tablespoons olive oil
- 4 garlic cloves, peeled and crushed
- ½ cup dry white wine
- 3 tablespoons red wine vinegar
- 2 tablespoons water
- 3 tablespoons lemon juice
- 3 tablespoons finely chopped fresh Italian parsley

PROCESS anchovy fillets and ¾ cup green olives in a food processor until

chopped, stopping to scrape down sides; set aside.

SPRINKLE chicken with salt and pepper. Brown chicken on all sides in hot oil in a large skillet over medium-high heat. Remove chicken, reserving 2 teaspoons drippings in skillet; add garlic, and sauté 1 minute. Add white wine and vinegar; cook 2 minutes, stirring to loosen browned particles. Stir in anchovy mixture and 2 tablespoons water.

RETURN chicken to skillet, turning to coat pieces in sauce.

COOK, covered, over medium-low heat 45 minutes or until chicken is tender. (Stir in additional water, if needed.)

ADD 3 tablespoons lemon juice, Italian parsley, and remaining ¾ cup green olives; cook 1 to 2 more minutes. Serve immediately.

Lamb Shanks Braised With Tomatoes

chef recipe

MAKES 4 TO 6 SERVINGS

Prep: 15 min.; Cook: 1 hr., 30 min.

Giuliano's recipe calls for lamb shoulder, but we found shanks were more readily available.

- 3 pounds bone-in lamb shanks, cut into 1- to 1½-inch-thick slices
- 1 teaspoon salt
- 1 teaspoon pepper
- 2 tablespoons olive oil
- ½ cup dry white wine
- 1 teaspoon chopped fresh rosemary leaves
- 3 garlic cloves, finely chopped
- 1 (28-ounce) can whole peeled tomatoes, coarsely chopped
- 2 bay leaves

SPRINKLE lamb with salt and pepper. Brown lamb on all sides in hot oil in a skillet over medium-high heat. Stir in wine, rosemary, and garlic; cook 3 minutes. Add tomatoes and bay leaves.

COVER, reduce heat, and simmer 1 to 1½ hours, turning lamb every 15 to 20 minutes or until tender.

REMOVE lamb to a serving platter. Discard bay leaves, and serve lamb with sauce from pan.

More Kitchen Tips From Giuliano

"I have a drawer just for lids," says Giuliano, knowing how we all grapple with the lid-losing syndrome. Other features and advice include the following.

- Pots and pans reside beneath the six-burner cooktop for handy access.
- A vegetable sink, located in the middle of the kitchen, offers quick washing while cooking; a large, nondivided sink works for final cleanup.
- A custom-made glass vent hood provides ventilation for the cooktop without disrupting the view.
- Monorail lighting, a new generation of track lighting, curves a single row of lights along the perimeter of the kitchen.
- Countertops and a backsplash of 1½-inch-thick granite are thinner than the double bullnose edge some designers favor. The reason: to accommodate Giuliano's clamp-on pasta maker. By the way, he never chops on the granite.
- Panels for the dishwasher and refrigerator match the maple and bird's-eye maple in the cabinets, creating a smooth visual transition.
- Star lights, tiny recessed bulbs scattered on the ceiling, provide an even light for the workspace.
- An appliance garage, using corner space on the counter, features a sliding panel to hide the coffeepot, toaster, etc.

Taste of the South

Deviled Eggs

No covered-dish dinner in the South is complete without those cheery little yellow-and-white ovals known as deviled eggs. Take a couple of dozen to a gathering, and they'll disappear as fast as Vienna sausages before a flock of seagulls. Deviled eggs are such a part of our culture that we still give plates designed to hold them as wedding gifts.

Our staff likes them prepared almost any way, but all agree that a modest amount of mayonnaise (no runny fillings for us), a touch of mustard, and a little sweet pickle are requirements. Simply hard-cook the eggs, slice them in half lengthwise, and gently scoop out the yolks. Put the yolks in a bowl with the above-mentioned ingredients (see recipe for proportions), mix well, and spoon them back into the whites.

This basic formula is the foundation for some creative additions, among them bacon, shrimp, chives, crabmeat, and pimiento. Whether or not to dust with paprika before serving is a purely personal decision.

Jill Conner Browne, author of *The Sweet Potato Queens' Book of Love,* is so well known for her love of deviled eggs that fans often bring them to her book signings. "It's the combination of taste and textures," she says, that inspires her devotion. "I like to put the whole thing in my mouth—I don't like to bite it. I guess that's just a personal thing, kind of like how you eat your Oreos."

The Jackson, Mississippi, native prefers her deviled eggs basic, with only sweet pickles added to the yolk-mayo-mustard combo. Being the Sweet Potato Queen, boss of all the other Queens, Jill naturally possesses an egg plate. And not just any pressed-glass discount store version. "I own a Gail Pittman egg plate," she says regally. She offers a last word on the importance of deviled eggs in Southern society. "If they invented a special plate for it, that says it all right there."

BASIC DEVILED EGGS

family favorite • make ahead

MAKES 6 SERVINGS

Prep: 20 min., Cook: 5 min., Stand: 15 min.

If you're feeding more than three people (or Jill Conner Browne), you'll likely need to double this recipe.

6 large eggs
2 tablespoons mayonnaise
1½ tablespoons sweet pickle relish
1 teaspoon prepared mustard
⅛ teaspoon salt
Dash of pepper
Garnish: paprika

PLACE eggs in a single layer in a saucepan; add water to a depth of 3 inches. Bring to a boil; cover, remove from heat, and let stand 15 minutes.
DRAIN immediately, and fill the pan with cold water and ice. Tap each egg firmly on the counter until cracks form all over the shell. Peel under cold running water.
SLICE eggs in half lengthwise, and carefully remove yolks. Mash yolks with mayonnaise. Add relish, mustard, salt, and pepper; stir well. Spoon yolk mixture into egg whites. Garnish, if desired.

The Deal on Peeling

Opinions vary widely on the easiest way to peel eggs and keep those pesky shells from sticking, but Assistant Foods Editor Kate Nicholson swears by this method.

Remove cooked eggs from heat, and pour off the water. Add about 1 inch of cold water and several ice cubes to the saucepan (it's okay if the insides of the eggs are still warm). Cover the pot, and shake vigorously so that the eggs crack all over. Peel under cold running water, starting at the large end—the air pocket will give you something to grip.

Cook's Corner

Receive 50 recipes by ordering these free pamphlets.

To fill her resource files, Assistant Foods Editor Vicki Poellnitz has been gathering brochures full of hints and recipes. Egg Beaters, Perdue Farms Incorporated, The Catfish Institute, and The Almond Board of California all offer free brochures—with a total of 50 recipes among them. To receive yours, follow the simple ordering instructions.

RECIPES MADE HEALTHY & DELICIOUS from Egg Beaters contains useful nutritional information concerning cholesterol, fat, and calories. Directions for use when baking and cooking answer all your questions about substitutions. There are great instructions for scrambling in a skillet and even for hard cooking (think hard-cooked egg) for use in egg salad. The 21 recipes provided cover a wide range of uses. Send your request to Egg Beaters, P.O. Box 6130, Douglas, AZ 85655-6130.

SIMPLY PERDUE—SIMPLIFYING FAMILY MEALTIME offers 19 delightful recipes. These quick recipes average 25 minutes kitchen time. The pamphlet is arranged with three or four recipes covering two pages with a grocery list to make shopping easy. A 55-cent coupon is included. Several other brochures from Perdue are available too. Check out all of them, and place your order at **www.perdue.com** or call 1-800-473-7383.

FROM POND TO PLATE by The Catfish Institute is full of information about U.S. farm-raised catfish, along with storage and handling guidelines covering refrigeration, freezing, and thawing, and what to look for when purchasing fresh catfish.

Great recipes from The Mr. Food Kitchen are yours if you send a self-addressed, stamped, business-size envelope to The Catfish Institute, c/o Fleishman Hillard, 2405 Grand Blvd., Kansas City, MO 64108. The Catfish Institute's Web site is **www.catfishinstitute.com**

WHAT'S ALL THE TALK ABOUT CALIFORNIA ALMONDS? is a booklet full of nutritional advice concerning beneficial vitamin E, protein, and vital minerals. Tidbits for toasting, storage, and purchasing almonds prove helpful in the kitchen. There are six recipes as well as other ideas for adding almonds to foods. Attached are a cute magnet and a bookmark. You can order a brochure by e-mail at staff@almondboard.com or by sending a postcard to Almond Board of California, 1150 Ninth Street, Suite 1500, Modesto, CA 95354.

Fresh, Fruity Lemonades

When we decided to take a fresh approach to this favorite sweet-tart elixir, one look at some readers' recipes made it clear that you aren't just sipping plain lemonade.

Jazz up these jewel-toned sippers with ice cubes made from the same liquid. Fill ice trays with any lemonade recipe, and freeze until firm. Before freezing, tuck a maraschino cherry or your favorite fruit into each section to add a splash of color.

RASPBERRY LEMONADE

fast fixin's • make ahead

MAKES ABOUT 6 CUPS

Prep: 10 min.

- 1 (14-ounce) package frozen raspberries, thawed
- 1 (16-ounce) jar maraschino cherries without stems
- 1¼ cups sugar
- ¾ cup fresh lemon juice (about 5 lemons)
- ¼ cup fresh lime juice (about 1 large lime)
- 3 cups water

PROCESS first 5 ingredients in a blender until smooth, stopping to scrape down sides. Pour fruit mixture through a wire-mesh strainer into a pitcher, discarding solids. Stir in 3 cups water. Serve over ice.

BLACKBERRY LEMONADE: Substitute 1 (14-ounce) package frozen blackberries, thawed, for frozen raspberries. Proceed as directed. Makes 6 cups.

CHERRY-BERRY LEMONADE: Substitute 1 (16-ounce) package frozen mixed berries, thawed, for frozen raspberries. Proceed as directed, using 2 cups water. Makes 5 cups.

CHERRY-BERRY LEMONADE POPS: Pour Cherry-Berry Lemonade evenly into 14 (4-ounce) plastic pop molds. Insert plastic pop sticks, and freeze 4 hours or until firm. Makes 14 pops.

BETTY LAURY
MONTGOMERY, ALABAMA

KIWI-LEMONADE SPRITZER

fast fixin's

MAKES 5 CUPS

Prep: 10 min.

- 4 kiwifruit, peeled
- 1 (12-ounce) can frozen lemonade concentrate, thawed and undiluted
- 3 cups lemon-lime soft drink, chilled

CUT kiwifruit into chunks. Process fruit chunks and lemonade concentrate in a food processor until smooth, stopping to scrape down sides.
POUR mixture through a wire-mesh strainer into a pitcher, discarding solids. Stir in lemon-lime soft drink just before serving.

STRAWBERRY-KIWI-LEMONADE SPRITZER: Process 2 cups fresh strawberries; 4 kiwifruit, peeled and cut into chunks; and 1 (12-ounce) can frozen lemonade concentrate, undiluted and thawed, in a food processor until smooth, stopping to scrape down sides. Proceed as directed. Makes 7 cups.

TRACEY BILODEAU
TAUNTON, MASSACHUSETTS

FRESH MINT-CITRUS SIPPER

fast fixin's

MAKES 8 CUPS

Prep: 15 min., Cook: 5 min.

This refreshing drink starts out with a simple syrup. You can store the syrup in an airtight container in the refrigerator up to two weeks.

- 1½ cups fresh lemon juice
- 1 cup fresh lime juice
- 1 cup fresh orange juice
- Fresh Mint Sugar Syrup
- 1 (25-ounce) bottle lemon-flavored sparkling water, chilled (about 3 cups)

COMBINE first 4 ingredients in a large pitcher, stirring well. Stir in sparkling water just before serving. Serve over ice.

Fresh Mint Sugar Syrup:

MAKES 2 CUPS

Prep: 5 min., Cook: 5 min.

- 2 cups sugar
- 1 cup water
- 1 cup loosely packed fresh mint leaves

BRING all ingredients to a boil in a saucepan, stirring until sugar dissolves; boil 1 minute. Remove from heat; cool.
POUR mixture through a wire-mesh strainer into a pitcher, discarding mint.

FRESH MINT-CITRUS SIPPER BY THE GLASS: Combine 3 tablespoons Fresh Mint Sugar Syrup; 2 tablespoons each fresh lemon, lime, and orange juice; and ¾ cup lemon-flavored sparkling water, chilled; stir mixture well.

BLT Goes Big Time

Try our fresh variations, from tortilla wraps to salads.

Bacon, lettuce, and tomato is an inspired combination. The clean, fresh taste of tomato tempers the deep saltiness of crisp-chewy bacon, while a lettuce leaf adds cool crunch. Try these versions of this toothsome threesome.

SOUTHWEST BLT WRAP

fast fixin's

MAKES 6 SERVINGS

Prep: 10 min.

- ½ cup salsa
- ⅓ cup frozen corn, thawed
- 6 (8-inch) flour tortillas
- 18 bacon slices, cooked and chopped
- ½ head iceberg lettuce, chopped
- Avocado-Lime Sauce

STIR together salsa and corn. Set aside.
TOP 1 side of each tortilla evenly with bacon, lettuce, and corn salsa. Drizzle with Avocado-Lime Sauce. Roll up, and, if desired, secure with wooden picks.

Avocado-Lime Sauce:

MAKES 1½ CUPS

Prep: 5 min.

- 1 avocado, mashed
- 4 teaspoons fresh lime juice
- ½ cup mayonnaise
- 1 teaspoon chopped fresh cilantro
- Salt to taste
- Garnish: fresh cilantro

STIR together first 5 ingredients in a small bowl. Cover and chill until ready to serve. Garnish, if desired.

KIM CUMMINS
BIRMINGHAM, ALABAMA

ITALIAN BLT BREAD SALAD

make ahead

MAKES 6 TO 8 SERVINGS

Prep: 10 min., Bake: 5 min., Chill: 1 hr.,
Stand: 20 min.

- 1 (8-ounce) Italian or French bread loaf, cut into 1-inch pieces*
- ½ pound fresh mozzarella, cut into ½-inch pieces
- 1 cup olive oil-and-balsamic vinegar dressing
- ½ cup kalamata olives, pitted and halved
- 1 pint grape tomatoes, halved
- 2 green onions, sliced
- 2 tablespoons chopped fresh basil
- 1 tablespoon chopped fresh thyme
- ¼ teaspoon pepper
- 3 cups chopped romaine lettuce
- 10 bacon slices, cooked and crumbled

PLACE bread on a baking sheet, and bake at 400° for 5 minutes or until lightly toasted.
COMBINE mozzarella and dressing in a shallow dish or zip-top plastic bag; cover or seal, and chill 1 hour.
TOSS together bread, olives, next 5 ingredients, and mozzarella mixture. Let stand 20 minutes. Serve over lettuce, and sprinkle with crumbled bacon.

*Substitute 8 cups cubed and lightly toasted cornbread, if desired.

KAREN GALLOWAY
CHARLESTON, SOUTH CAROLINA

CARAMELIZED ONION BLT

fast fixin's

MAKES 4 SERVINGS

Prep: 15 min.

- 2 medium tomatoes
- ½ cup mayonnaise
- 1 tablespoon chopped fresh basil
- 8 sourdough bread slices, toasted
- 12 bacon slices, cooked
- 4 Swiss cheese slices
- Caramelized Onions
- Salt and pepper to taste
- 4 lettuce leaves

CUT each tomato into 4 slices.
STIR together mayonnaise and basil; spread on 1 side of each bread slice. Top 4 bread slices with 3 bacon slices, 2 tomato slices, and cheese. Top evenly with Caramelized Onions; sprinkle with salt and pepper. Top with lettuce leaves and remaining bread slices.

Caramelized Onions:

MAKES 1½ CUPS

Prep: 5 min., Cook: 20 min.

- 2 tablespoons butter
- 1 tablespoon bacon drippings
- 2 small sweet onions, sliced
- ⅛ teaspoon salt
- ⅛ teaspoon freshly ground pepper

MELT butter with bacon drippings in a skillet over medium-high heat. Add onions, salt, and pepper; sauté 15 to 20 minutes or until golden brown.

BARBARA VAUGHN
CHARLESTON, SOUTH CAROLINA

Bacon Bites

Cook a lot of bacon the easy way—in the oven. Place it on the rack of a roasting pan, and bake at 400° for 20 to 25 minutes or until crisp. This leaves you free to prep the other ingredients.

Spectacular Shrimp

In the South, we love shrimp any way it's served. It offers lots of delicious possibilities.

CRISPY SHRIMP BUNDLES WITH CHIVE BUTTER SAUCE

MAKES 4 SERVINGS

Prep: 1 hr., Cook: 12 min., Chill: 1 hr., Bake: 20 min.

- ½ pound unpeeled, medium-size fresh shrimp
- 1 leek
- 2 tablespoons butter or margarine
- ½ onion, diced
- 2 garlic cloves, minced
- ½ cup wild rice mix, cooked
- 2 tablespoons chopped fresh chives
- ½ teaspoon salt
- ½ teaspoon pepper
- 8 phyllo pastry sheets
- Melted butter or margarine
- Chive Butter Sauce

PEEL shrimp, and devein, if desired; coarsely chop, and set aside.

CUT white end from leek, and cut into thin slices, reserving top for another use.

MELT butter in a large skillet over medium-high heat; add leek, onion, and garlic, and sauté 5 minutes or until onion is tender. Add shrimp; cook 3 to 5 minutes or until shrimp turn pink. Remove from heat; let cool. Combine shrimp mixture, wild rice, and next 3 ingredients in a large bowl. Cover and chill at least 1 hour.

UNFOLD phyllo on a lightly floured surface. Stack 4 phyllo sheets, brushing with melted butter between sheets. Cut into 4 squares. Repeat with remaining phyllo sheets and butter.

SPOON 2 tablespoons filling in center of each square. Bring corners of pastry together, pinching seams, to resemble a bundle. Tie each with an aluminum foil strip to secure. Place on a baking sheet.

BAKE at 350° for 15 to 20 minutes or until golden. Remove and discard foil strips. Serve with Chive Butter Sauce.

Chive Butter Sauce:

MAKES ¾ CUP

Prep: 5 min., Cook: 5 min.

- 1 cup dry white wine
- 3 tablespoons lemon juice
- 1 shallot, diced
- 1 teaspoon black peppercorns
- ¼ teaspoon salt
- ¼ cup whipping cream
- ½ cup butter or margarine, cut up
- 2 tablespoons chopped fresh chives

BRING first 4 ingredients to a boil in a large saucepan; reduce heat, and simmer 2 to 3 minutes or until liquid is reduced to ⅓ cup.

STIR in salt and cream; cook 2 minutes, stirring constantly. Whisk in butter until sauce thickens.

POUR mixture through a wire-mesh strainer into a bowl; stir in chives. Serve immediately.

ARTICHOKE-SHRIMP CHOWDER

MAKES ABOUT 4 QUARTS

Prep: 30 min., Bake: 1 hr., Cook: 40 min.

- ⅔ cup sifted all-purpose flour
- 2 pounds unpeeled, medium-size fresh shrimp
- 3 (14-ounce) cans quartered artichoke hearts
- 6½ cups chicken broth
- 8 green onions, chopped
- 1 tablespoon Creole seasoning
- 1½ teaspoons ground white pepper
- 1 teaspoon dried thyme
- ½ cup butter or margarine
- 1 quart whipping cream

BAKE flour in a shallow pan at 350°, stirring occasionally, 1 hour. Set aside.

PEEL shrimp, and devein, if desired; set aside.

DRAIN artichokes, reserving 1½ cups liquid. Bring artichokes, 1½ cups liquid, broth, and next 4 ingredients to a boil. Reduce heat, and simmer 30 minutes.

MELT butter in a small saucepan over medium heat; whisk in flour, and cook, whisking constantly, 1 minute. Whisk flour mixture into broth mixture. Whisk in cream; bring to a boil over medium heat. Add shrimp; cook 3 to 5 minutes or until pink.

DEBORAH TOUCHY
HOUSTON, TEXAS

What's for Supper?

Try Stir-Fry Tonight

SESAME-VEGETABLE LO MEIN

MAKES 4 SERVINGS

Prep: 25 min., Cook: 15 min.

- 1 (7-ounce) package vermicelli
- 3 tablespoons dark sesame oil, divided
- 2 cups fresh sugar snap peas or snow pea pods
- 2 cups broccoli florets
- 1 large red bell pepper, cut into strips
- 2 carrots, shredded
- 4 green onions, diagonally sliced
- 2 garlic cloves, pressed
- 1 teaspoon grated fresh ginger
- ¼ teaspoon dried crushed red pepper
- ¼ cup soy sauce
- 1 tablespoon water
- 1 tablespoon toasted sesame seeds (optional)

PREPARE pasta according to package directions.

HEAT 2 tablespoons oil in a wok or large skillet over medium-high heat 1 minute or until hot. Add peas and next 7 ingredients, and stir-fry 5 to 7 minutes or until crisp-tender.

STIR in soy sauce and 1 tablespoon water; add pasta, tossing until thoroughly heated. Remove from heat, and toss with remaining 1 tablespoon oil and, if desired, 1 tablespoon sesame seeds. Serve immediately.

SHERYL DAVIDSON
MERIDIAN, MISSISSIPPI

SWEET-AND-SOUR PORK STIR-FRY

MAKES 4 TO 6 SERVINGS

Prep: 30 min., Cook: 16 min.

1½ pounds pork tenderloin, cubed
¼ cup cornstarch
3 tablespoons dark sesame oil, divided
1 (20-ounce) can pineapple tidbits
2 tablespoons lite soy sauce
1 red bell pepper, chopped
1 green bell pepper, chopped
4 green onions, chopped
½ cup hoisin sauce
1 tablespoon Asian garlic-chili sauce
Hot cooked rice
1 tablespoon sesame seeds, toasted

DREDGE pork in cornstarch.
HEAT 2 tablespoons oil in a wok or large skillet over medium-high heat; stir-fry pork in batches, 3 minutes or until browned. Remove pork from skillet; set aside.
DRAIN pineapple, reserving ¼ cup juice. Add reserved juice and soy sauce to skillet, stirring to loosen browned particles.
ADD remaining 1 tablespoon sesame oil to skillet; stir-fry pineapple, bell peppers, and green onions 5 minutes or until peppers are tender.
STIR together hoisin sauce and garlic-chili sauce; add to skillet. Add pork, and stir-fry 5 minutes. Serve over rice. Sprinkle with sesame seeds.

NOTE: For testing purposes only, we used A Taste of Thai Garlic Chili Pepper Sauce.

Hot Tips for Stir-Fry

■ Heat a wok or large skillet until a few beads of water dropped in the pan sizzle and evaporate immediately.
■ "Ring" the wok with oil drizzled near the top edge of the wok or skillet, allowing it to run down the sides. This gives the pan a smooth surface with minimal oil.

Reunions

Gather for Great Food

The Franklin Forest neighborhood of McLean, Virginia, has been a tight-knit group since the 1940s. Neighbors who have moved away often come back to join the gatherings that take place every year, bringing a dish to share with their old friends. Here are a few favorites from the annual event.

FROLICKERS BAKED BEANS

family favorite

MAKES 15 SERVINGS

Prep: 25 min., Cook: 5 min., Bake: 3 hrs.

The neighbors refer to themselves as the Franklin Forest Frolickers. These beans have been baked in the "official" pot for many years.

10 bacon slices
4 (28-ounce) cans baked beans
5 green bell peppers, cut into 1-inch pieces
3 large onions, chopped
2 cups ketchup
½ cup firmly packed brown sugar
2 tablespoons prepared mustard
1 tablespoon white vinegar

COOK bacon in a large skillet until crisp; reserve 2 tablespoons drippings. Crumble bacon.
STIR together bacon, bacon drippings, beans, and next 5 ingredients in a roasting pan.
BAKE, covered, at 350° for 3 hours. Stir in vinegar.

POTATO SALAD WITH CUCUMBERS AND TOMATOES

MAKES 10 TO 12 SERVINGS

Prep: 25 min., Cook: 30 min. *(pictured on page 75)*

5 pounds potatoes
⅔ cup olive oil
½ cup red wine vinegar
1½ teaspoons salt
1 teaspoon pepper
¼ cup chopped fresh basil
1 cucumber, peeled, seeded, and chopped
2 pints grape or cherry tomatoes
1 large yellow tomato, diced
Garnish: fresh basil sprig

COOK potatoes in boiling salted water to cover 30 minutes or until tender; drain. Cool potatoes slightly, and cut into 1-inch cubes.
STIR together oil and next 3 ingredients in a large bowl; stir in basil. Add potatoes, cucumber, and tomatoes, tossing to coat. Garnish, if desired.

ANGELA LEWIS
MCLEAN, VIRGINIA

MINI CRAB CAKES AND DIJON SAUCE

MAKES 25 CRAB CAKES

Prep: 30 min., Cook: 20 min., Chill: 30 min.

2 tablespoons butter or margarine
1 small onion, minced
3 celery ribs, diced
1 teaspoon paprika
1 pound fresh lump crabmeat, drained
2 tablespoons minced fresh parsley
1 teaspoon minced fresh thyme
¼ teaspoon salt
¼ teaspoon pepper
1½ cups soft breadcrumbs
2 large eggs, lightly beaten
¼ cup vegetable oil
Dijon Sauce

MELT butter in a large skillet over medium heat; add onion, and sauté 3 minutes. Stir in celery and paprika. Cover and cook over low heat 5 minutes, and cool.

STIR together crabmeat, onion mixture, parsley, and next 3 ingredients. Stir in breadcrumbs and eggs.

SHAPE crabmeat mixture into 25 (1½-inch) patties. Place on a baking sheet, and chill 30 minutes.

COOK crabcakes, in batches, in hot oil in a large skillet over medium-high heat 3 minutes on each side or until golden; drain on paper towels. Serve with Dijon Sauce.

Dijon Sauce:

MAKES 1¼ CUPS

Prep: 5 min.

- 1 (8-ounce) container sour cream
- 3 tablespoons Dijon mustard
- 1 tablespoon white wine vinegar
- 1 teaspoon sugar
- ¼ teaspoon salt
- ⅛ teaspoon pepper

WHISK together all ingredients.

JOAN ANTHONY
MCLEAN, VIRGINIA

Strawberries and Dips

There's nothing tastier than ripe strawberries. They're yummy dipped in powdered sugar, but combining them with flavored dips kicks them up a level.

STRAWBERRIES WITH BROWN SUGAR-AND-SOUR CREAM DIP

make ahead

MAKES 1½ CUPS DIP

Prep: 5 min., Chill: 24 hrs.

- 1 (16-ounce) container sour cream
- ⅓ cup maple syrup
- 3 tablespoons dark brown sugar
- Garnishes: sliced strawberries, fresh mint sprig, orange slices
- Fresh whole strawberries

THICKEN sour cream (see "Make a Great Dip" below).

DISCARD liquid in bowl, and whisk together thickened sour cream, maple syrup, and dark brown sugar until blended. Garnish, if desired. Serve with strawberries.

STRAWBERRIES WITH VANILLA PUDDING DIP

make ahead

MAKES 2 CUPS DIP

Prep: 10 min., Chill: 2 hrs.

- 1 (3.4-ounce) package French vanilla instant pudding mix
- 1 cup milk
- 1 (8-ounce) container sour cream
- 1 teaspoon vanilla extract
- ¼ to ½ teaspoon almond extract
- Garnish: sliced whole strawberry
- Fresh whole strawberries

WHISK together pudding and milk until blended. Stir in next 3 ingredients; cover and chill 2 hours. Garnish, if desired. Serve with strawberries.

STRAWBERRIES WITH MINT YOGURT DIP

make ahead

MAKES 2 CUPS DIP

Prep: 10 min., Chill: 24 hrs.

Low-fat or fat-free yogurt may be used, but be sure to choose a brand that does not have gelatin as an ingredient. This does not make a good strained yogurt.

- 1 quart vanilla yogurt
- 1 tablespoon minced fresh mint
- ¼ teaspoon grated lemon rind
- 2 to 3 tablespoons honey
- Garnish: fresh mint sprig
- Fresh whole strawberries

THICKEN yogurt (see box at right).

DISCARD liquid in bowl, and whisk together thickened yogurt, mint, lemon rind, and honey until blended. Garnish, if desired. Serve with strawberries.

STRAWBERRIES WITH FLUFFY CREAM CHEESE DIP

fast fixin's

MAKES 3 CUPS DIP

Prep: 10 min.

- 1 (8-ounce) package cream cheese, softened
- 2 cups powdered sugar
- 2 teaspoons vanilla extract
- 1 cup whipped cream
- Fresh whole strawberries

BEAT cream cheese, powdered sugar, and vanilla at medium speed with an electric mixer until fluffy. Fold in whipped cream; serve with berries.

CITRUS-CREAM CHEESE DIP: Add 1 tablespoon grated lime, lemon, or orange rind with cream cheese mixture. Proceed with recipe as directed.

ORANGE-FLAVORED CREAM CHEESE DIP: Add ¼ cup orange liqueur with cream cheese mixture. Proceed with recipe as directed.

ORANGE MARMALADE-CREAM CHEESE DIP: Add ½ cup orange marmalade with cream cheese mixture. Proceed with recipe as directed.

Make a Great Dip

Yogurt and sour cream have a thicker consistency when excess liquid is removed. This procedure takes 24 hours, but it yields perfect results for dipping fresh fruit.
1. Line a fine wire-mesh strainer with a coffee filter, and place over a bowl.
2. Spoon yogurt or sour cream into coffee filter. Cover with plastic wrap, and chill at least 24 hours. Yogurt or sour cream can be chilled up to 72 hours. It gets thicker the longer it chills. Discard liquid in bowl.

Favorite Pound Cakes

Show up with a homemade pound cake, and you've got a friend for life. It's one of those desserts that says Southern hospitality. The sturdy texture ensures they travel well and freeze nicely, making them just right for giving.

We chose a couple of our readers' favorite pound cake recipes, including our editor's favorite. For our tips on baking a perfect pound cake, see "From Our Kitchen" on page 102, or visit our Web site at **www.SouthernLiving.com**

BUTTERED RUM POUND CAKE WITH BANANAS FOSTER SAUCE

MAKES 1 (10-INCH) CAKE

Prep: 30 min.; Bake: 1 hr., 30 min.;
Cool: 15 min.; Stand: 4 hrs.

(pictured on page 79)

- **1 cup butter, softened**
- **2½ cups sugar**
- **6 large eggs, separated**
- **3 cups all-purpose flour**
- **¼ teaspoon baking soda**
- **1 (8-ounce) container sour cream**
- **1 teaspoon vanilla extract**
- **1 teaspoon lemon extract**
- **½ cup sugar**
- **Buttered Rum Glaze**
- **Bananas Foster Sauce**
- **Vanilla ice cream**

BEAT butter at medium speed with a heavy-duty mixer until creamy. Add 2½ cups sugar, beating 4 to 5 minutes or until fluffy. Add egg yolks, 1 at a time, beating just until yellow disappears.
COMBINE flour and baking soda; add to butter mixture alternately with sour cream, beginning and ending with flour mixture. Stir in flavorings.
BEAT egg whites until foamy; gradually add ½ cup sugar, 1 tablespoon at a time, beating until stiff peaks form. Fold into batter.
POUR batter into a greased and floured 10-inch tube pan.

BAKE at 325° for 1½ hours or until a long wooden pick inserted in center comes out clean. Cool in pan 10 to 15 minutes; remove from pan, and place on a serving plate. While warm, prick cake surface at 1-inch intervals with a wooden pick; pour warm Buttered Rum Glaze over cake. Let stand 4 hours or overnight before serving. Serve with Bananas Foster Sauce and vanilla ice cream.

LEMON POUND CAKE: Add 2 tablespoons grated lemon rind to batter. Proceed with cake recipe as directed. Omit Buttered Rum Glaze; do not serve with sauce.

Buttered Rum Glaze:

MAKES ABOUT 1¼ CUPS
Prep: 2 min., Cook: 5 min.

- **6 tablespoons butter**
- **3 tablespoons light rum**
- **¾ cup sugar**
- **3 tablespoons water**
- **½ cup chopped pecans, toasted**

COMBINE first 4 ingredients in a small saucepan; bring to a boil. Boil, stirring constantly, 3 minutes. Remove from heat, and stir in pecans.

Bananas Foster Sauce:

MAKES 8 SERVINGS
Prep: 5 min., Cook: 8 min.

- **½ cup firmly packed brown sugar**
- **¼ cup butter or margarine, melted**
- **¼ teaspoon ground cinnamon**
- **⅓ cup banana liqueur**
- **4 bananas, peeled and sliced**
- **⅓ cup light rum**

COMBINE first 4 ingredients in a large skillet; cook over medium heat, stirring constantly, until bubbly. Add bananas, and cook 2 to 3 minutes or until thoroughly heated. Remove from heat.
HEAT rum in a small saucepan over medium heat (do not boil). Quickly pour rum over banana mixture, and immediately ignite with a long match just above the liquid mixture to light the fumes (not the liquid itself). Let flames die down; serve immediately with Buttered Rum Pound Cake.

RED VELVET CUPCAKES

MAKES 3½ DOZEN CUPCAKES

Prep: 45 min., Bake: 30 min.

- **1 cup shortening**
- **½ cup butter, softened**
- **3 cups sugar**
- **6 large eggs**
- **2 teaspoons vanilla extract**
- **1 (1-ounce) bottle red food coloring**
- **3 cups all-purpose flour**
- **2 tablespoons unsweetened cocoa**
- **1 teaspoon salt**
- **1 cup milk**
- **Chunky Cherry Icing**

BEAT first 3 ingredients at medium speed with an electric mixer until fluffy. Add eggs, 1 at a time, beating just until yellow disappears. Stir in vanilla and food coloring until blended.
COMBINE flour, cocoa, and salt. Add to shortening mixture alternately with milk, beginning and ending with flour mixture, beating just until blended. Spoon batter into greased and floured muffin pans, or line with lightly greased cupcake liners, filling two-thirds full.
BAKE at 325° for 30 minutes or until a wooden pick inserted in center comes out clean. Remove from pans, and cool completely on a wire rack. Spread evenly with Chunky Cherry Icing.

Chunky Cherry Icing:

MAKES ABOUT 6 CUPS
Prep: 15 min.

- **1 (8-ounce) package cream cheese, softened**
- **½ cup butter, softened**
- **6 cups powdered sugar**
- **1 cup maraschino cherries, drained and chopped**
- **1 cup chopped pecans, toasted**
- **1 cup sweetened flaked coconut**

BEAT cream cheese and butter at medium speed with an electric mixer until smooth and creamy. Add powdered sugar, beating until blended. Stir in cherries, chopped pecans, and coconut.

JEAN H. GOAD
SALEM, VIRGINIA

Food in the Fast Lane

Join us for a behind-the-scenes look at a hot young NASCAR driver who loves to cook.

NASCAR Winston Cup driver Jimmie Johnson makes a living going fast—very fast. But even the best have to slow down sometime. "Cooking, especially outdoors, really helps me relax. I can drop my race face and do something normal," he says.

During a race weekend, cooking duties fall squarely on Mary Whitesell, chef for the No. 24 and 48 teams. Mary cooks enough food to feed more than 50 active and very hungry crew members throughout the day (and often into the night).

CHICKEN-VEGETABLE KABOBS

chef recipe

MAKES 4 SERVINGS

Prep: 15 min., Chill: 2 hrs., Soak: 30 min., Grill: 20 min.

Serve these with a side of rice and your favorite salad for a complete meal.

- **4 skinned and boned chicken breast halves**
- **¼ cup dry white wine**
- **⅓ cup orange juice**
- **2 tablespoons olive oil**
- **2 tablespoons soy sauce**
- **2 tablespoons Worcestershire sauce**
- **1 teaspoon ground ginger**
- **1 teaspoon garlic powder**
- **8 (8-inch) wooden or metal skewers**
- **8 cherry tomatoes**
- **8 large mushrooms**
- **1 green bell pepper, cut into 1-inch pieces**

CUT chicken into 2- x 1-inch strips.
WHISK together ¼ cup white wine, orange juice, olive oil, and next 4 ingredients, reserving ¼ cup for basting. Pour remaining marinade into a shallow dish or large zip-top freezer bag; add chicken. Cover or seal, and chill 2 hours, turning chicken occasionally.
SOAK wooden skewers in water for 30 minutes to prevent burning.
REMOVE chicken from marinade, discarding marinade.
THREAD chicken and vegetables onto 8 (8-inch) skewers.
GRILL chicken, covered with grill lid, over medium-high heat (350° to 400°) 15 to 20 minutes or until done, turning occasionally and basting with reserved marinade.

MARY WHITESELL
CHEF, *TEAM LOWE'S RACING*

GUACAMOLE

fast fixin's

MAKES 4 CUPS

Prep: 10 min.

Jimmie's dad, Gary, is known throughout NASCAR for his unbeatable guacamole.

- **5 ripe avocados**
- **½ to ¾ cup reduced-fat sour cream**
- **¼ cup chopped fresh cilantro**
- **3 tablespoons fresh lime juice**
- **2 tablespoons Italian dressing**
- **½ teaspoon garlic salt**
- **¼ teaspoon hot sauce**
- **Tortilla chips**

CUT avocados in half. Scoop pulp into a bowl; mash with a potato masher or fork just until slightly chunky. Stir in sour cream and next 5 ingredients. Serve with tortilla chips.

NOTE: For testing purposes only, we used Cholula Hot Sauce.

GARY JOHNSON
MOORESVILLE, NORTH CAROLINA

SOUTHWEST FLANK STEAK WITH SALSA

MAKES 4 TO 6 SERVINGS

Prep: 5 min., Chill: 4 hrs., Grill: 16 min.

- **2 tablespoons fajita seasoning**
- **½ teaspoon dry mustard**
- **1 teaspoon pepper**
- **2 tablespoons olive oil**
- **1 (1½-pound) package flank steak (½ inch thick)**
- **Salsa**

COMBINE first 3 ingredients. Rub olive oil evenly over flank steak; sprinkle with seasoning blend. Cover and chill at least 4 hours.
GRILL, covered with grill lid, over medium-high heat (350° to 400°) 7 to 8 minutes on each side or to desired degree of doneness. Cut steak diagonally across grain into thin strips. Serve with Salsa.

Salsa:

MAKES 1¾ CUPS

Prep: 5 min.

- **4 to 5 plum tomatoes, quartered and seeded**
- **2 garlic cloves, chopped**
- **1 small jalapeño pepper, seeded and sliced**
- **3 tablespoons lime juice**
- **½ teaspoon salt**
- **½ teaspoon pepper**
- **¼ cup fresh chopped cilantro**

PROCESS first 6 ingredients in a blender or food processor until smooth, stopping to scrape down sides. Stir in cilantro. Cover and chill until ready to serve.

GARY JOHNSON
MOORESVILLE, NORTH CAROLINA

Saucy Starts

Get a head start on tonight's supper with store-bought pasta sauce, salsa, or other flavor-packed jarred products.

Putting supper on the table quickly is a top priority for most of us—especially on weeknights. That's why we're sharing reduced-calorie entrées that deliver a ton of flavor with a helping hand from products in a jar. We think you'll be proud to serve these delightful dishes during the week or on special occasions.

Quick Supper Ideas

■ For a kicked-up sandwich spread, stir a little basil or dried tomato pesto into light or fat-free mayonnaise. Pesto is also great whisked into vinegar and a touch of olive oil to make a tangy salad dressing or marinade for chicken or pork.

■ For a really quick meal, cook lean ground beef or low-fat spicy sausage; drain. Stir in a jar of pasta sauce (pick any flavor you like). Add a splash of red wine; simmer until heated through. Serve over pasta. Sprinkle with shredded Parmesan or Romano cheese.

CREAMY CHIPOTLE MANICOTTI

MAKES 4 SERVINGS

Prep: 30 min., Bake: 30 min., Stand: 10 min.

This calcium-rich recipe (almost 800mg per serving) makes four very hearty portions. For a lighter meal, enjoy one stuffed shell alongside steamed green beans and a colorful salad drizzled with vinaigrette. To reduce the recipe's total fat, use fat-free ricotta cheese and mozzarella cheese, and use ½ cup Monterey Jack cheese with peppers instead of 1 cup.

 8 manicotti shells
 1 (15-ounce) container part-skim
   ricotta cheese
 2 green onions, chopped
 2 tablespoons chopped fresh
   cilantro
 1 cup (4 ounces) shredded part-skim
   mozzarella cheese
 ¼ cup egg substitute
 Vegetable cooking spray
 2 cups chipotle salsa, divided*
 1 cup (4 ounces) shredded Monterey
   Jack cheese with peppers

COOK pasta according to package directions, omitting salt and oil. Rinse with cold water; drain and set aside.
STIR together ricotta cheese and next 4 ingredients.
COAT an 11- x 7-inch baking dish with cooking spray, and pour ½ cup salsa in dish. Spoon cheese mixture evenly into shells, and arrange in dish. Pour remaining salsa over shells.
BAKE at 350° for 20 minutes. Sprinkle with Monterey Jack cheese. Bake 10

more minutes or until thoroughly heated and cheese melts. Let stand 10 minutes before serving.

NOTE: For testing purposes only, we used D.L. Jardine's Holy Chipotle Salsa.

*Substitute 1 or 2 canned chipotle peppers in adobo sauce stirred into 2 cups regular mild salsa for chipotle salsa, if desired. Canned chipotle peppers may be found in the Mexican section of the supermarket. Store remaining peppers in a zip-top plastic bag in the refrigerator up to 2 weeks or in the freezer up to 2 months.

Calories 507 (42% from fat); Fat 23g (sat 14g, mono 6.7g, poly 1.3g); Protein 35g; Carb 40g; Fiber 4.8g; Chol 74mg; Iron 2.6mg; Sodium 1,277mg; Calc 794mg

SIRLOIN IN VODKA SAUCE

MAKES 6 SERVINGS

Prep: 25 min., Cook: 10 min.

To balance your meal and to reduce the total percentage of fat, serve with crisp-tender green beans or a colorful veggie medley.

 1½ pounds boneless sirloin steak,
    trimmed and cut into
    1-inch pieces
 2 tablespoons all-purpose flour
 ¼ teaspoon salt
 ½ teaspoon pepper
 2 bacon slices, diced
 1 large sweet onion, diced
 1 (8-ounce) package fresh
   mushrooms, quartered
 3 garlic cloves, pressed
 1 cup vodka pasta sauce
 ½ cup fat-free sodium-reduced beef
   broth
 1 (8-ounce) container fat-free sour
   cream
 Hot cooked rice or egg noodles

PLACE first 4 ingredients in a large zip-top freezer bag, and shake to coat.
COOK bacon in a Dutch oven over medium-high heat until crisp. Add beef, and cook 1 to 2 minutes on each side or until lightly browned. Remove beef mixture from pan, and set aside.
ADD onion, mushrooms, and garlic; sauté over medium-high heat 5 minutes. Stir in beef mixture, vodka sauce, and broth;

bring to a boil. Remove from heat, and stir in sour cream. Serve over hot cooked rice or egg noodles.

NOTE: For testing purposes only, we used Emeril's Vodka Pasta Sauce.

Calories 297 (40% from fat); Fat 13.2g (sat 4.9g); Protein 27g; Carb 17g; Fiber 1.9g; Chol 75mg; Iron 3.2mg; Sodium 427mg; Calc 87mg

SHRIMP WITH ROASTED RED PEPPER CREAM

fast fixin's

MAKES 6 SERVINGS

Prep: 15 min., Cook: 8 min.

- 1 (7-ounce) package vermicelli
- 1 (12-ounce) jar roasted red bell peppers, drained
- 1 (8-ounce) package ⅓-less-fat cream cheese, softened
- ½ cup low-sodium, fat-free chicken broth
- 3 garlic cloves, chopped
- ½ teaspoon ground red pepper
- 2 pounds cooked, peeled large shrimp
- ¼ cup chopped fresh basil
- Garnish: fresh basil sprig

PREPARE pasta according to package directions, omitting salt and oil. Keep pasta warm.
PROCESS red bell peppers and next 4 ingredients in a blender or food processor until smooth, scraping down sides. Pour mixture into a large skillet.
COOK over medium heat 5 minutes, stirring often, until thoroughly heated. Add shrimp, and cook, stirring occasionally, 2 to 3 minutes or until thoroughly heated. Remove from heat. Serve over hot cooked pasta. Sprinkle with chopped basil. Garnish, if desired.

NOTE: For testing purposes only, we used Alessi Sweet Pimento Italian Style Fire Roasted Peppers.

CARLY DRUDA
CLEARWATER, FLORIDA

Calories 353 (18% from fat); Fat 6.8g (sat 2.8g, mono 0.4g, poly 1.2g); Protein 40.2g; Carb 30g; Fiber 1.5g; Chol 243mg; Iron 5mg; Sodium 530mg; Calc 123mg

SWEET-AND-SOUR CHICKEN AND RICE

MAKES 8 SERVINGS

Prep: 20 min., Cook: 1 hr.

Skinned and boned chicken thighs contain a little more fat than breast meat, but they're nutritious and hold on to lots of flavor and moisture.

- ½ teaspoon salt
- ½ teaspoon pepper
- 2 pounds skinned and boned chicken thighs
- Vegetable cooking spray
- 1 small onion, diced
- 1 medium-size red bell pepper, chopped
- 2 garlic cloves, minced
- 1 cup uncooked long-grain rice
- 1 cup sweet-and-sour dressing
- 1 cup low-sodium, fat-free chicken broth
- 2 green onions, chopped

SPRINKLE salt and pepper evenly over chicken thighs.
BROWN chicken in a Dutch oven coated with cooking spray over medium-high heat 2 to 3 minutes on each side or until browned. Remove chicken from pan, and set aside.
ADD onion, bell pepper, and garlic to Dutch oven coated with cooking spray; sauté 5 minutes.
ADD rice; sauté 2 minutes or until rice is opaque. Stir in dressing and broth. Add chicken pieces; bring to a boil.
COVER, reduce heat, and simmer 45 minutes or until liquid is absorbed and chicken is done. Sprinkle with green onions.

NOTE: For testing purposes only, we used Old Dutch Sweet & Sour Dressing.

Calories 289 (16% from fat); Fat 5g (sat 1.3g, mono 1.4g, poly 1.2g); Protein 25g; Carb 35g; Fiber 1.2g; Chol 95mg; Iron 2.4mg; Sodium 739mg; Calc 31mg

ITALIAN-STYLE MEAT AND POTATOES

MAKES 8 SERVINGS

Prep: 30 min., Bake: 35 min.

This hearty casserole starts with frozen mashed potatoes and a jar of pasta sauce.

- 1 pound extra-lean ground beef
- 1 large onion, chopped
- ¼ teaspoon salt
- ½ teaspoon pepper
- Vegetable cooking spray
- 1 (26-ounce) jar sundried tomato and sweet basil pasta sauce
- 1 (22-ounce) package frozen mashed potatoes
- 1 (16-ounce) jar Parmesan and mozzarella cheese sauce
- 1 cup (4 ounces) shredded part-skim mozzarella cheese

COOK first 4 ingredients in a large skillet coated with cooking spray, stirring until beef crumbles and is no longer pink. Drain well, and pat dry with paper towels.
STIR together beef mixture and pasta sauce. Spoon into a 13- x 9-inch baking dish coated with cooking spray.
PREPARE potatoes according to package directions, using fat-free milk. Stir together mashed potatoes and cheese sauce. Spread over beef mixture.
BAKE at 350° for 30 minutes. Sprinkle with cheese, and bake 5 more minutes or until cheese melts.

NOTE: For testing purposes only, we used Ragu Sundried Tomato & Sweet Basil sauce and Ragu Cheese Creations Parmesan & Mozzarella sauce.

Calories 316 (38% from fat); Fat 13g (sat 6.3g, mono 3.1g, poly 0.2g); Protein 18.7g; Carb 31g; Fiber 2.7g; Chol 50mg; Iron 1.5mg; Sodium 1,023mg; Calc 202mg

Culinary Adventures With Friends

Foods Editor Andria Scott Hurst loves to cook for friends. She served this menu at a successful gathering. She has more recipe ideas than she has time to make, but she dreams about the possibilities.

Company Supper

Serves 6

Grilled Lamb Chops With Chipotle and Cilantro Oils

Onion Risotto

Asparagus, Roasted Beet, and Goat Cheese Salad

Ginger Pound Cake   Ice cream

GRILLED LAMB CHOPS WITH CHIPOTLE AND CILANTRO OILS

chef recipe

MAKES 8 SERVINGS

Prep: 45 min., Chill: 2 hrs., Soak: 30 min., Grill: 16 min.

- **1 cup loosely packed fresh cilantro**
- **½ cup canola oil**
- **8 garlic cloves**
- **4 shallots**
- **2 jalapeño peppers, seeded**
- **16 (2-inch-thick) lamb loin chops**
- **Hickory wood chips**
- **2 tablespoons kosher salt**
- **2 tablespoons cracked pepper**
- **Chipotle Oil**
- **Cilantro Oil**

PROCESS cilantro and next 4 ingredients in a blender or food processor until smooth, stopping to scrape down sides.
PLACE chops in a large shallow dish or zip-top freezer bags. Pour oil mixture over chops. Cover or seal, and chill 2 hours, turning occasionally.
SOAK wood chips in water 30 minutes.
REMOVE chops from marinade, discard marinade. Sprinkle with salt and pepper.
PREPARE a fire by piling charcoal and wood chips in grill. Place food rack on grill. Arrange chops on rack, and grill, covered with grill lid, over high heat (400° to 500°) 6 to 8 minutes on each side or until desired degree of doneness. Drizzle with Chipotle and Cilantro Oils.

Chipotle Oil:

MAKES ½ CUP

Prep: 5 min.

- **2 tablespoons chipotle peppers in adobo sauce**
- **½ cup olive oil**
- **½ teaspoon kosher salt**

PROCESS all ingredients in a blender or food processor until smooth.

Cilantro Oil:

MAKES ½ CUP

Prep: 5 min.

- **½ cup loosely packed fresh cilantro**
- **½ cup olive oil**
- **1 tablespoon fresh lime juice**
- **½ teaspoon kosher salt**

PROCESS all ingredients in a blender or food processor until smooth.

KENT RATHBUN
ABACUS RESTAURANT, DALLAS

ONION RISOTTO

MAKES 6 SERVINGS

Prep: 10 min., Cook: 45 min.

- **3 large sweet onions, chopped**
- **2 garlic cloves, pressed**
- **1 teaspoon salt**
- **2 tablespoons olive oil**
- **1 (16-ounce) package Arborio rice**
- **8 cups chicken broth, warmed**
- **1 cup dry white wine**
- **½ cup shredded Parmesan cheese**
- **2 tablespoons butter or margarine**

SAUTÉ first 3 ingredients in hot oil in a Dutch oven over medium-high heat until tender.
ADD rice, stirring constantly, 2 minutes. Reduce heat to medium; add 1 cup broth. Stir until liquid is absorbed.
REPEAT procedure with remaining broth, 1 cup at a time. (Cooking time for rice mixture is about 30 minutes.)
ADD wine; cook, stirring gently, until liquid is absorbed. Stir in cheese and butter. Serve immediately.

ASPARAGUS, ROASTED BEET, AND GOAT CHEESE SALAD

MAKES 6 SERVINGS

Prep: 15 min., Bake: 45 min., Cook: 2 min.

- **18 small red beets (about 6 pounds)**
- **1 cup olive oil**
- **⅓ cup red wine vinegar**
- **½ teaspoon salt, divided**
- **½ teaspoon freshly ground pepper, divided**
- **60 small fresh asparagus spears**
- **1 (11-ounce) goat cheese log**
- **1 tablespoon chopped fresh chives**
- **Cracked pepper (optional)**
- **Chopped fresh chives (optional)**
- **Gourmet salad greens (optional)**

ARRANGE beets in a single layer on a lightly greased baking sheet; bake at 425° for 40 to 45 minutes or until tender, stirring every 15 minutes. Cool beets completely.
WHISK together oil, vinegar, ¼ teaspoon salt, and ¼ teaspoon ground pepper in a small bowl.

PEEL beets, and cut into wedges. Toss together beets, ½ cup vinaigrette, and remaining ¼ teaspoon salt and ¼ teaspoon ground pepper; set aside.

SNAP off tough ends of asparagus; discard ends. Cook asparagus in boiling water to cover 1 to 2 minutes or until crisp-tender. Plunge into ice water to stop the cooking process; drain. Combine asparagus and ½ cup vinaigrette.

CUT cheese into 6 equal slices. Place 1 cheese slice in a 3-inch round cutter; sprinkle with ½ teaspoon chives. Press chives into cheese; remove cutter. Repeat procedure with remaining cheese and 2½ teaspoons chives.

ARRANGE asparagus over cheese. Surround with beets, and drizzle with remaining vinaigrette. Sprinkle with cracked pepper and chives, if desired; serve with salad greens, if desired.

GINGER POUND CAKE

MAKES 1 (10-INCH) CAKE

Prep: 25 min.; Stand: 15 min.;
Bake: 1 hr., 25 min.; Cool: 10 min.

- ¾ cup milk
- 1 (2.7-ounce) jar crystallized ginger, finely minced
- 2 cups butter or margarine, softened
- 3 cups sugar
- 6 large eggs
- 4 cups all-purpose flour
- 1 teaspoon vanilla extract
- Vanilla ice cream

COOK milk and ginger in a saucepan over medium heat until thoroughly heated (do not boil). Remove from heat, and let stand 10 to 15 minutes.

BEAT butter at medium speed with an electric mixer until creamy; gradually add sugar, beating 5 to 7 minutes. Add eggs, 1 at a time, beating after each addition just until yellow disappears.

ADD flour to butter mixture alternately with milk mixture, beginning and ending with flour. Beat at low speed just until blended after each addition. Stir in vanilla. Pour batter into a greased and floured 10-inch tube pan.

BAKE at 325° for 1 hour and 25 minutes or until a wooden pick inserted in center

comes out clean. Cool in pan on a wire rack 10 minutes. Remove from pan, and cool completely on wire rack. Serve with vanilla ice cream.

Crave Carrots

Will Rogers once said, "Some guy invented vitamin A out of a carrot. I'll bet he can't invent a good meal out of one." If you feel the same, we've gathered some reader recipes that are sure to change your mind about these flavorful orange roots.

While testing these recipes, our Test Kitchens' staff discovered an important fact: Unless carrots are to be pureed for soup, they are best cooked over medium heat just until they are tender.

Look for firm, smooth carrots that have a deep orange color, avoiding those with cracks. Carrots are best stored in a plastic bag in the vegetable bin of your refrigerator. Keep them away from apples, which impart a bitter flavor.

If your fresh-cut carrots begin to look lifeless, revive them in a bowl of ice water. One pound of carrots equals about 3 cups chopped or sliced or about 2½ cups shredded.

SCALLOPED CARROTS

MAKES 6 SERVINGS

Prep: 30 min., Cook: 12 min., Bake: 25 min.

- 4 cups sliced carrots (about 11)
- 4 bacon slices, chopped
- 1 medium onion, chopped
- 1 (10¾-ounce) can cream of mushroom soup, undiluted
- 1 cup (4 ounces) shredded sharp Cheddar cheese
- ½ teaspoon pepper
- 2 cups herb-seasoned stuffing mix
- ¼ cup butter or margarine, melted

COOK carrots in boiling water to cover in a large saucepan 10 to 12 minutes or until tender. Drain and set aside.

COOK bacon in a large saucepan until crisp; remove bacon, and drain on paper towels, reserving 2 tablespoons drippings in pan.

SAUTÉ chopped onion in hot drippings 5 minutes or until tender. Stir in bacon, soup, Cheddar cheese, and pepper until cheese melts; stir in carrots. Spoon mixture into a lightly greased 11- x 7-inch baking dish.

STIR together stuffing mix and melted butter, and spoon evenly over carrot mixture.

BAKE at 350° for 25 minutes.

EILEEN R. MACUTCHAN
CLEARWATER, FLORIDA

CARROT-AND-DILL SALAD

make ahead

MAKES 6 TO 8 SERVINGS

Prep: 20 min., Cook: 12 min., Chill: 2 hrs.

- 2 (10-ounce) packages French-cut cooking carrots*
- ⅓ cup olive oil
- ¼ cup red wine vinegar
- 2 tablespoons lemon juice
- 2 tablespoons chopped fresh or 2 teaspoons dried dill
- 1 shallot, minced
- 1 garlic clove, minced
- 1 teaspoon salt
- ½ teaspoon pepper
- Garnish: fresh dill sprig

COOK carrots in boiling water to cover in a medium saucepan 10 to 12 minutes or until tender. Plunge carrots into ice water to stop the cooking process, and drain.

WHISK together oil and next 7 ingredients in a medium bowl. Add carrots, and toss gently to coat. Cover and chill 2 hours. Garnish, if desired.

*Substitute 2 pounds carrots, cut into 2- x ¼-inch strips, if desired.

DOROTHY J. CALLAWAY
COOLIDGE, GEORGIA

Make-Ahead Magic

Senior Writer Donna Florio thinks she first encountered stratas around 1978. These make-ahead dishes were popular among her friends who were just learning to entertain. As with so many stylish ideas—like hip-hugger pants, say—stratas are making a comeback. The basic egg-milk-bread formula lends itself to a variety of flavors and styles. So try one of these recipes for your next get-together. Older guests will find stratas comfortingly familiar, while younger ones will think you're a trendsetter. Either way, they'll know you're a great cook.

ENGLISH MUFFIN BREAKFAST STRATA

family favorite • make ahead

MAKES 8 SERVINGS

Prep: 20 min., Chill: 8 hrs., Bake: 40 min., Stand: 10 min.

Serve this with fruit for a tasty breakfast.

- **1 (16-ounce) package ground pork sausage**
- **1 (12-ounce) package English muffins, split and buttered**
- **1 (10-ounce) block sharp Cheddar cheese, shredded**
- **1 (8-ounce) block mozzarella cheese, shredded**
- **8 large eggs**
- **1½ cups sour cream**
- **1 (4-ounce) can chopped green chiles, drained**

COOK sausage in a skillet, stirring until it crumbles and is no longer pink; drain on paper towels, and set aside.
CUT muffin halves into quarters, and arrange in an even layer in a lightly greased 13- x 9-inch baking dish.
SPRINKLE half each of sausage, Cheddar cheese, and mozzarella cheese evenly over muffins.
WHISK together eggs, sour cream, and chiles in a large bowl; pour evenly over sausage and cheeses. Top with remaining sausage and cheeses. Cover and chill 8 hours.
BAKE at 350° for 40 minutes. Let stand 10 minutes before serving.

MARY JANE APPLEGATE
LEON, IOWA

TURKEY-CHEDDAR-BROCCOLI STRATA

make ahead

MAKES 7 SERVINGS

Prep: 20 min., Chill: 8 hrs., Bake: 30 min., Stand: 10 min.

We liked this dish just as Gladys Ulip submitted it, then added broccoli for color. You can make it in a 13- x 9-inch dish—just adjust the baking time to 45 minutes.

- **1 tablespoon butter, softened**
- **½ (12-ounce) package French bread loaves, cubed**
- **2 cups chopped cooked turkey**
- **1 (10-ounce) package frozen broccoli florets, thawed and chopped (optional)**
- **½ cup diced celery**
- **2 cups (8 ounces) shredded sharp Cheddar cheese**
- **6 large eggs, lightly beaten**
- **2 cups milk**
- **3 tablespoons all-purpose flour**
- **1 teaspoon salt**
- **1 teaspoon curry powder**
- **1 teaspoon dry mustard**
- **1 teaspoon Worcestershire sauce**
- **½ teaspoon pepper**

GREASE bottom and sides of 7 (10-ounce) custard cups with butter.
LAYER half each of bread cubes, turkey, broccoli, if desired, celery, and Cheddar cheese in custard cups; repeat layers, ending with Cheddar cheese.
WHISK together eggs and remaining 7 ingredients in a large bowl; pour evenly over cheese, pressing down lightly to absorb liquid. Cover and chill 8 hours. Bake at 350° for 30 minutes or until golden. Let stand 10 minutes.

GLADYS ULIP
SEATTLE, WASHINGTON

TOMATO-BACON STRATA

make ahead

MAKES 6 SERVINGS

Prep: 20 min., Cook: 10 min., Chill: 4 hrs., Bake: 45 min.

- **6 bacon slices**
- **½ small onion, chopped**
- **12 very thin white bread slices**
- **4 to 6 plum tomatoes, sliced**
- **1 teaspoon salt, divided**
- **½ teaspoon pepper**
- **¼ teaspoon dried basil**
- **6 Swiss cheese slices**
- **4 large eggs**
- **1½ cups milk**
- **⅓ cup shredded Parmesan cheese**

COOK bacon in a large skillet until crisp; remove bacon, and drain on paper towels, reserving 1 tablespoon drippings in skillet. Crumble bacon; set aside.
ADD onion to hot drippings in skillet, and sauté 5 minutes or until tender.
CUT crusts from bread slices, and reserve for another use. Arrange 6 bread slices in an even layer in a greased 11- x 7-inch baking dish; top with

An Extra Helping

Cornbread-Chili Strata

MAKES 4 TO 6 SERVINGS

Prep: 10 min., Broil: 5 min., Chill: 4 hrs., Bake: 40 min.

Cut 1 (8-inch) square cornbread into 9 equal portions; split each portion in half horizontally. Place squares, cut sides up, on a baking sheet; broil 5 minutes or until slightly crusty. Place half of cornbread squares in an even layer in an 11- x 7-inch baking dish. Stir together 1 (25-ounce) can beef chili with beans and 1 (7-ounce) jar tomatillo salsa; spread mixture over cornbread. Sprinkle 1 cup shredded Cheddar cheese over chili mixture; top with remaining cornbread, and sprinkle with ½ cup shredded Cheddar cheese. Cover and chill at least 4 hours. Bake at 350° for 40 minutes or until bubbly.

tomato slices, and sprinkle with ½ teaspoon salt, pepper, and basil.

SPRINKLE bacon and onion evenly over tomatoes; top with Swiss cheese slices and remaining bread slices.

WHISK together eggs, milk, and remaining ½ teaspoon salt. Pour evenly over bread. Cover and chill at least 4 hours.

BAKE at 350° for 40 minutes or just until set. Top with Parmesan cheese, and bake 5 more minutes or until cheese melts.

NOTE: For testing purposes only, we used Pepperidge Farm Very Thin Sliced White Bread.

Crispy, Crunchy, and Nutty

Looking for a really easy way to add texture and flavor to your recipes? Try nuts. Dredging meats and fish in finely chopped nuts will give them crispier coatings. From pecans to almonds, any type will do. Mix and match in these nutty recipes.

CRISPY CATFISH

family favorite

MAKES 4 SERVINGS

Prep: 20 min., Chill: 8 hrs., Fry: 6 min. per batch

    4 (6-ounce) catfish fillets
    Milk
    2 teaspoons hot sauce
    2 teaspoons salt, divided
    1 large egg
    ¾ cup all-purpose flour
    1 teaspoon ground red pepper
    1 teaspoon ground black pepper
    1 cup pecans, finely chopped
    Vegetable oil
    Garnish: lemon wedges
    Pecan Tartar Sauce (recipe at right)

COMBINE catfish and milk to cover in a shallow dish; add hot sauce. Cover and chill 8 hours, turning occasionally.

REMOVE catfish from milk mixture, reserving mixture; sprinkle catfish evenly with ½ teaspoon salt, and set aside.

WHISK egg into milk mixture until blended.

COMBINE flour, ground peppers, and remaining 1½ teaspoons salt. Dredge catfish in flour mixture, shaking off excess; dip in egg mixture, and coat with chopped pecans.

POUR oil to a depth of 2 inches into a Dutch oven; heat to 360°. Fry catfish 3 minutes on each side or until fish flakes with a fork. Drain on paper towels. Place on a serving platter; garnish, if desired. Serve with Pecan Tartar Sauce.

PECAN TARTAR SAUCE

fast fixin's • make ahead

MAKES ABOUT 1 CUP

Prep: 15 min., Chill: 1 hr.

You can substitute other nuts in this tasty sauce. Use it for dipping, or spread it on a sandwich.

    ½ cup light or regular sour cream
    ½ cup light or regular mayonnaise
    2 tablespoons chopped pecans, toasted
    2 tablespoons chopped fresh parsley
    ¼ teaspoon grated lemon rind
    1 tablespoon fresh lemon juice
    1 teaspoon paprika
    2 teaspoons capers, drained and chopped (optional)

STIR together first 7 ingredients and, if desired, capers. Cover and chill at least 1 hour.

AGNES L. MIXON
OCALA, FLORIDA

MIXED GREENS WITH SEASONED ALMONDS AND TANGY BALSAMIC VINAIGRETTE

fast fixin's

MAKES 6 TO 8 SERVINGS

Prep: 10 min.

A 1-ounce envelope of Ranch dressing mix is used to season the almonds and vinaigrette. Toss half of the mix with the almonds, and use the remaining half in the vinaigrette.

    8 cups mixed salad greens
    2 large Golden Delicious apples, sliced
    2 carrots, shredded
    1 large tomato, diced
    ½ red onion, thinly sliced
    Seasoned Almonds
    Tangy Balsamic Vinaigrette

TOSS together first 5 ingredients. Sprinkle salad with Seasoned Almonds before serving. Serve with Tangy Balsamic Vinaigrette dressing.

Seasoned Almonds:

MAKES 1½ CUPS

Prep: 5 min., Cook: 3 min.

    2 tablespoons butter or margarine
    1½ cups sliced almonds
    2 tablespoons Ranch dressing mix

MELT butter in a skillet over medium-high heat. Add almonds; sauté 2 to 3 minutes or until toasted. Remove nuts from skillet; toss with dressing mix to coat. Store in an airtight container.

Tangy Balsamic Vinaigrette:

MAKES ¾ CUP

Prep: 5 min.

    ½ cup olive oil
    ¼ cup white balsamic vinegar
    2 tablespoons Ranch dressing mix
    1 tablespoon sugar
    ¼ teaspoon salt
    ¼ teaspoon pepper

WHISK together all ingredients until well combined.

from our kitchen

Pound Cake Primer

We get many requests for tips on how to make great cakes like the ones on page 94. Here are a few tips that ensure success.

■ Start with the right ingredients. Don't substitute self-rising flour for all-purpose flour. If you want to substitute cake flour for all-purpose flour, use 1 cup plus 2 tablespoons cake flour in place of 1 cup all-purpose flour.

■ To measure flour, spoon it into a dry measuring cup, and level with a knife. (Don't scoop the measuring cup into the flour or pack the flour.)

■ Use butter or margarine containing more than 70% fat. Soft butter spreads and reduced-fat or tub margarines contain too much water and do not work well in baked goods.

■ Spoon batter evenly into a 10-inch tube pan greased with solid shortening and coated with flour. Place the pan in the center of the oven, and bake as directed. (A temperature that is too low causes the cake to fall.) When placed on a rack too low in the oven, the crust browns too much on the bottom.

■ Keep the oven door closed until minimum baking time has elapsed. Test the cake for doneness with a cake tester or wooden pick. Insert it into the center of the cake; it should come out with no batter or crumbs clinging to it.

■ Cool the cake in the pan on a wire rack 10 to 15 minutes. Removing it too soon may cause dampness and sinking in the center.

■ Store the cake in an airtight container up to three days. You may also wrap it with plastic wrap and aluminum foil, and refrigerate up to one week or freeze up to two months. Thaw the cake without unwrapping for best results.

Is It Overdone?

An instant-read thermometer is your best friend when you're checking meat for doneness. Refer to our recipes for suggested internal temperature of meat and poultry. But be aware that the meat continues to cook once removed from the heat source, causing the internal temperature to rise further. If rare to medium rare is your desired degree of doneness, you may want to remove the meat from the heat when the temperature is 5 degrees less than directed. The residual heat will continue to "cook" the meat, and it will be just right when you're ready to serve it.

Italian Flavors

Southern Living Favorites

Icebox Cakes

Enjoy the flavors of old-fashioned pies in these delightful new desserts.

Who can resist the pleasure of dreamy icebox pies? As a salute to these cool classics, we created great cakes incorporating the best feature of these pies—the filling. These recipes offer mix-and-match fillings and layers that can be baked in a variety of shapes and sizes. Lime Icebox Pie Cake, for example, can also be made with lemon or orange filling. And if you want to bake Orange Chiffon Cake in 13- x 9-inch pans to serve a crowd, simply adjust the baking times as directed in the recipe. So make a sweet, citrusy memory for your family and friends. Some may not be old enough to remember icebox pies, but they certainly won't forget these fabulous cakes.

LEMON ICEBOX PIE FILLING

MAKES ABOUT 3 CUPS

Prep: 5 min., Cook: 8 min., Chill: 10 min.

- ¾ cup milk
- ¼ cup cornstarch
- 1 (14-ounce) can sweetened condensed milk
- 3 large eggs
- ½ cup fresh lemon juice
- 3 drops yellow liquid food coloring (optional)
- 3 tablespoons butter
- 1 tablespoon grated lemon rind

WHISK together ¾ cup milk and ¼ cup cornstarch in a 3-quart heavy saucepan, whisking until cornstarch dissolves.
WHISK in sweetened condensed milk and eggs until blended; whisk in lemon juice and, if desired, food coloring. Bring to a boil over medium heat, whisking constantly. (Mixture will begin to thicken when lemon juice is first added, and then become thin again during first few minutes of cooking. It will thicken quickly as it comes to a boil.)
BOIL 1 minute, whisking constantly, or until mixture thickens. Remove from heat; whisk in butter and lemon rind until smooth. Pour filling into a bowl; place bowl in a larger bowl filled with ice. Stir regularly until cold (about 10 minutes).

LIME ICEBOX PIE FILLING: Substitute ½ cup fresh lime juice for lemon juice, 1 drop green liquid food coloring and 1 drop yellow liquid food coloring for the 3 drops yellow liquid food coloring (optional), and 1 tablespoon grated lime rind for lemon rind.

ORANGE ICEBOX PIE FILLING: Substitute ½ cup thawed frozen orange juice concentrate for fresh lemon juice, 2 drops red liquid food coloring and 4 drops yellow liquid food coloring for 3 drops yellow liquid food coloring, and 1 tablespoon fresh grated orange rind for lemon rind.

Three Fabulous Fillings

One of the best attributes of these cakes is the flexibility to use the lemon, lime, or orange fillings interchangeably. All of the flavors are delicious. To prevent the fillings from tasting chalky, Recipe Development Director Mary Allen Perry recommends dissolving the cornstarch in the milk before adding the sweetened condensed milk.

LIME ICEBOX PIE CAKE

freezable • make ahead

MAKES 12 TO 16 SERVINGS

Prep: 45 min., Bake: 25 min., Cool: 10 min., Chill: 8 hrs. *(pictured on page 116)*

- ½ cup butter or margarine, softened
- ½ cup shortening
- 2 cups sugar
- ⅔ cup water
- ⅔ cup milk
- 3 cups all-purpose flour
- 1 tablespoon baking powder
- ½ teaspoon salt
- 1 tablespoon vanilla extract
- 6 large egg whites
- Lime Icebox Pie Filling (recipe at left)
- Whipped Cream Frosting

BEAT butter and shortening at medium speed with an electric mixer until fluffy; gradually add sugar, beating well.
COMBINE water and milk. Stir together flour, baking powder, and salt; add to butter mixture alternately with milk mixture, beginning and ending with flour mixture. Stir in vanilla.
BEAT egg whites at medium speed with an electric mixer until stiff peaks form; fold into batter. Spoon batter evenly into 2 greased and floured 13- x 9-inch baking pans.
BAKE at 350° for 20 to 25 minutes or until a wooden pick inserted in center comes out clean. Cool in pans on wire racks for 10 minutes; remove from pans, and cool completely on wire racks.
CUT each cake layer in half lengthwise, creating 4 narrow rectangular layers. Spread Lime Icebox Pie Filling evenly between layers. Cover cake securely with plastic wrap, and chill 8 hours. Gently turn assembled cake onto its side so layers of cake and filling run

vertically. (Cake may be frozen up to 1 month; thaw overnight in refrigerator, and proceed with recipe as directed.)

SPREAD Whipped Cream Frosting evenly on top and sides of cake. Serve immediately, or chill up to 3 hours.

NOTE: Cake batter can be baked in 3 (9-inch) round cakepans for 20 minutes or until a wooden pick inserted in center comes out clean or in 3 (10-inch) round cakepans for 18 minutes or until a wooden pick inserted in center comes out clean.

Whipped Cream Frosting:

MAKES 4 CUPS

Prep: 5 min.

- **2 cups whipping cream**
- **⅓ cup powdered sugar**

BEAT whipping cream at medium speed with an electric mixer until foamy; gradually add powdered sugar, beating until stiff peaks form. Use immediately.

ORANGE CHIFFON CAKE WITH ORANGE ICEBOX PIE FILLING

freezable • make ahead

MAKES 12 TO 16 SERVINGS

Prep: 45 min., Bake: 20 min., Cool: 10 min., Chill: 4 hrs. *(pictured on page 116)*

- **2½ cups sifted cake flour**
- **1 tablespoon baking powder**
- **1 teaspoon salt**
- **1⅓ cups sugar**
- **½ cup vegetable oil**
- **5 large eggs, separated**
- **¾ cup orange juice**
- **3 tablespoons grated orange rind**
- **½ teaspoon cream of tartar**
- **Orange Icebox Pie Filling (recipe on facing page)**
- **Orange Buttercream Frosting**

COMBINE first 4 ingredients in a mixing bowl. Make a well in center of flour mixture; add vegetable oil, egg yolks, and orange juice. Beat at medium-high speed with an electric mixer 3 to 4 minutes or until smooth. Stir in orange rind.

BEAT egg whites and cream of tartar at medium-high speed with an electric mixer until stiff peaks form. Gently fold egg mixture into flour mixture. Spoon batter evenly into 3 greased and floured 9-inch round cakepans.

BAKE at 350° for 18 to 20 minutes or until a wooden pick inserted in center comes out clean. Cool in pans on wire racks 10 minutes; remove from pans, and cool layers completely on wire racks.

SPREAD Orange Icebox Pie Filling evenly between layers and on top of cake. Cover cake, and chill at least 4 hours.

SPREAD Orange Buttercream Frosting evenly around sides of cake. (Cake may be completely assembled and frozen up to 1 month.)

NOTE: Cake batter can be baked in 3 (10-inch) round cakepans or 2 (13- x 9-inch) baking pans for 15 minutes or until a wooden pick inserted in center comes out clean.

Orange Buttercream Frosting:

MAKES ABOUT 2½ CUPS

Prep: 10 min.

- **½ cup butter, softened**
- **1 (16-ounce) package powdered sugar, divided**
- **⅓ cup milk**
- **2 tablespoons grated orange rind**

BEAT butter at medium speed with an electric mixer until creamy; gradually add 1 cup powdered sugar, beating at low speed until blended.

ADD milk, beating until blended. Gradually add remaining powdered sugar, beating until blended. Stir in grated orange rind.

LEMON BUTTERCREAM FROSTING: Substitute 2 tablespoons grated lemon rind for orange rind.

LIME BUTTERCREAM FROSTING: Substitute 2 tablespoons grated lime rind for orange rind.

Freezing Tips

Once the filling is spread between the layers, these unfrosted cakes can be frozen up to a month. Thaw overnight in the refrigerator, and proceed with the recipe as directed. (In the case of the Orange Chiffon Cake With Orange Icebox Pie Filling, the entire cake can be frozen, buttercream frosting and all.)

Barbecue Sides

What you eat with barbecue is as important as the meat itself. Complete your perfect 'cue experience with coleslaw, hearty baked beans, and something sweet.

CREAMY SWEET COLESLAW

make ahead

MAKES 8 SERVINGS

Prep: 20 min., Chill: 1 hr.

- **1 medium cabbage, shredded***
- **1½ cups mayonnaise**
- **¾ cup sweet salad cube pickles**
- **⅓ cup sugar**
- **⅓ cup prepared mustard**
- **1 tablespoon celery seeds**
- **2 tablespoons cider vinegar**
- **1½ teaspoons salt**
- **⅛ teaspoon pepper**

STIR together all ingredients in a large bowl. Cover and chill 1 hour.

*Substitute 8 cups coleslaw mix, found in the produce section of the supermarket, if desired.

FREEZER SLAW

fast fixin's • freezeable

MAKES ABOUT 6 CUPS

Prep: 30 min.

1½ cups sugar
1 cup cider vinegar
3 (10-ounce) packages shredded angel hair cabbage slaw
1 large carrot, shredded
1 small green bell pepper, diced
1 teaspoon celery salt
1 teaspoon mustard seeds

BRING sugar and vinegar to a boil in a small saucepan, stirring until sugar dissolves; cool.
COMBINE cabbage, carrot, and remaining 3 ingredients. Pour vinegar mixture over cabbage mixture, tossing to coat. Seal in a zip-top freezer bag or an airtight container; freeze up to 3 months. Thaw in refrigerator before serving.

BLUEBERRY-PECAN COBBLER

MAKES 4 SERVINGS

Prep: 15 min., Cook: 15 min., Bake: 20 min.

4 pints fresh or frozen blueberries
1½ cups sugar
½ cup all-purpose flour
⅓ cup water
2 tablespoons lemon juice
1 teaspoon vanilla extract
½ teaspoon ground cinnamon
1 (15-ounce) package refrigerated piecrusts, divided
½ cup chopped pecans
Vanilla ice cream (optional)

BRING first 7 ingredients to a boil in a saucepan over medium heat; stir until sugar melts. Reduce heat to low; cook, stirring occasionally, 10 minutes.
SPOON half of blueberry mixture into a lightly greased 8-inch square pan. Roll 1 piecrust to ⅛-inch thickness on a lightly floured surface; cut into an 8-inch square. Place over blueberry mixture; sprinkle with pecans.

BAKE at 450° for 10 minutes. Spoon remaining blueberry mixture over baked piecrust.
ROLL remaining piecrust to ⅛-inch thickness, and cut into 1-inch strips. Arrange strips in lattice design over blueberry mixture.
PLACE pan on a baking sheet on middle oven rack. Bake at 450° for 10 minutes or until golden. Serve with vanilla ice cream, if desired.

COCONUT CREAM PIE

make ahead

MAKES 1 (9-INCH) PIE

Prep: 25 min., Bake: 8 min., Chill: 2 hrs.

Cream of coconut is near the margarita mixes.

1⅔ cups graham cracker crumbs
¼ cup sugar
⅓ cup butter or margarine, melted
1 (8-ounce) package cream cheese, softened
1 cup cream of coconut
1 (3.4-ounce) package cheesecake instant pudding mix
1 (6-ounce) package frozen sweetened flaked coconut, thawed
1 (8-ounce) container frozen whipped topping, thawed
1 cup whipping cream

STIR together first 3 ingredients; press mixture evenly in bottom and up sides of a 9-inch pieplate.
BAKE at 350° for 8 minutes; remove to a wire rack, and cool completely.
BEAT cream cheese and cream of coconut at medium speed with an electric mixer until smooth. Add pudding mix, beating until blended.
STIR in coconut; fold in whipped topping. Spread cream cheese mixture evenly into prepared crust; cover and chill 2 hours or until set.
BEAT cream with an electric mixer until soft peaks form; spread over top of pie.

NOTE: For testing purposes only, we used Jell-O Instant Pudding Cheesecake Flavor.

SORGHUM BAKED BEANS

family favorite

MAKES 4 TO 6 SERVINGS

Prep: 10 min., Cook: 4 min., Bake: 45 min.

4 bacon slices
1 (28-ounce) can pork and beans, drained
1 small onion, diced
¼ cup firmly packed brown sugar
¼ cup sorghum
¼ cup ketchup
1 teaspoon Worcestershire sauce
½ teaspoon dry mustard

COOK bacon in a large skillet over medium-high heat 3 to 4 minutes.
STIR together pork and beans and remaining ingredients in a lightly greased 1-quart baking dish. Top mixture with bacon.
BAKE at 350° for 45 minutes.

THREE-BEAN BAKE

MAKES 6 SERVINGS

Prep: 15 min., Cook: 10 min., Bake: 55 min.

This is a favorite of our editor, John Floyd.

½ pound ground chuck
6 bacon slices, chopped
1 small onion, chopped
1 (15¼-ounce) can lima beans, drained and rinsed
1 (15-ounce) can kidney beans, drained and rinsed
1 (15-ounce) can pork and beans, undrained
½ cup firmly packed brown sugar
½ cup ketchup
½ cup barbecue sauce
1 teaspoon dry mustard

COOK first 3 ingredients in a large skillet, stirring until beef crumbles and is no longer pink; drain and return mixture to skillet.
STIR in lima beans and remaining ingredients. Pour into a lightly greased 1½-quart baking dish. Bake at 400° for 45 to 55 minutes.

K.C. BAKED BEANS

MAKES 6 TO 8 SERVINGS

Prep: 20 min., Bake: 1 hr.

2 (15-ounce) cans pork and beans, drained
1 Granny Smith apple, peeled and chopped
1 medium onion, chopped
¾ cup barbecue sauce
½ cup firmly packed light brown sugar
¼ cup golden raisins
1 teaspoon ground cumin
½ teaspoon ground red pepper
3 bacon slices, halved

STIR together first 8 ingredients in a lightly greased 2-quart baking dish; top evenly with bacon.
BAKE at 350° for 1 hour.

NOTE: For testing purposes only, we used K.C. Masterpiece Original Barbecue Sauce.

Our Favorite Chicken Casseroles

These aren't just any casseroles— they're some of the best we've published from readers. Beyond fabulous flavor, what makes these recipes stand out? They cut preparation time by using convenience products such as seasoning mix, quick-cooking rice blend, and jarred picante sauce. Save even more time by purchasing deli-roasted chicken for each casserole. A roasted whole chicken generally yields about 3 cups chopped chicken. We've also included make-ahead freezing directions for one of the dishes.

LESLIE'S FAVORITE CHICKEN-AND-WILD RICE CASSEROLE

freezable • make ahead

MAKES 6 TO 8 SERVINGS

Prep: 30 min., Cook: 10 min., Bake: 35 min.

This Southern Living classic is from 2000.

2 (6.2-ounce) packages fast-cooking long-grain and wild rice mix
¼ cup butter or margarine
2 medium onions, chopped
4 celery ribs, chopped
2 (8-ounce) cans sliced water chestnuts, drained
5 cups chopped cooked chicken
4 cups (16 ounces) shredded Cheddar cheese, divided
2 (10¾-ounce) cans cream of mushroom soup, undiluted
1 (16-ounce) container sour cream
1 cup milk
½ teaspoon salt
½ teaspoon pepper
½ cup soft breadcrumbs

PREPARE rice mix according to package directions; set aside.
MELT butter in a large skillet over medium heat; add onions, celery, and water chestnuts. Sauté 10 minutes or until tender.
STIR in rice, chicken, 3 cups cheese, soup, and next 4 ingredients.
SPOON mixture into a lightly greased 15- x 10-inch baking dish or a 4-quart casserole. Top with breadcrumbs.
BAKE at 350° for 30 minutes. Sprinkle with remaining 1 cup cheese; bake 5 more minutes.

TO MAKE AHEAD: Freeze unbaked casserole up to 1 month, if desired. (Do not sprinkle with cheese before freezing.) Let stand at room temperature 1 hour. Bake, covered, at 350° for 30 minutes. Uncover casserole, and bake 55 more minutes. Sprinkle with 1 cup cheese, and bake 5 more minutes.

NOTE: Casserole can also be baked at 350° in 2 (11- x 7-inch) baking dishes for 25 minutes. Sprinkle each with

½ cup of the remaining cheese; bake 5 more minutes.

LESLIE FLEMISTER
DUNWOODY, GEORGIA

HEARTY TEX-MEX SQUASH-CHICKEN CASSEROLE

family favorite

MAKES 6 TO 8 SERVINGS

Prep: 35 min., Cook: 6 min., Bake: 35 min.

If you're watching your fat intake, use reduced-fat soup, sour cream, and cheese.

1 (10-ounce) package frozen chopped spinach, thawed
3 medium-size yellow squash, thinly sliced
1 large red or green bell pepper, cut into ½-inch pieces
1 small yellow onion, thinly sliced
2 tablespoons peanut oil
3 cups shredded cooked chicken or turkey
12 (6-inch) corn tortillas, cut into 1-inch pieces
1 (10¾-ounce) can cream of celery soup, undiluted
1 (8-ounce) container sour cream
1 (8-ounce) jar picante sauce
1 (4.5-ounce) can chopped green chiles, undrained
1 (1.4-ounce) envelope fajita seasoning
2 cups (8 ounces) shredded sharp Cheddar cheese, divided

DRAIN spinach well, pressing between paper towels; set aside.
SAUTÉ squash, bell pepper, and onion in hot oil in a large skillet over medium-high heat 6 minutes or until tender. Remove from heat.
STIR in spinach, chicken, next 6 ingredients, and 1½ cups cheese. Spoon into a lightly greased 13- x 9-inch baking dish.
BAKE at 350° for 30 minutes. Sprinkle with remaining ½ cup cheese, and bake 5 more minutes.

CATHERINE BOETTNER
CHARLESTON, TENNESSEE

Savory Shortbreads

When you see the word "short" in the name of a food, expect a buttery, tender-crisp pastry—a melt-in-your-mouth experience. Although different cheeses, herbs, and nuts make each unique, these shortbreads (created by Recipe Development Director Mary Allen Perry) would be perfect served together at a spring luncheon or tea. And because they freeze beautifully, you'll have these scrumptious delights on hand for unexpected company or to enjoy with a cup of tea and favorite book. See the box below, left for helpful hints on making perfect shortbread.

Tips for Preparation and Storage

■ We recommend shredding your own cheese for these recipes; it's stickier and blends much better than preshredded cheese.
■ All of these doughs (unbaked and wrapped in plastic wrap) can be frozen in an airtight container or in zip-top freezer bags up to 3 months. Be sure to let dough thaw overnight in the refrigerator; then cut and bake as directed.
■ Once baked, these shortbreads can be frozen in an airtight container or in zip-top freezer bags up to 1 month.
■ When cutting chilled dough logs, rotate about a quarter turn after every few slices to preserve the rounded shape of the log.
■ Vary the round, wedge, or strip shapes with any of these doughs.
■ These recipes call for baking the shortbread until lightly browned (golden). Baking to a darker golden brown produces a nuttier flavor in the shortbread, particularly with those recipes that include Cheddar or Parmesan cheese.

PESTO SHORTBREAD

freezable • make ahead

MAKES 14 DOZEN

Prep: 20 min., Chill: 8 hrs., Bake: 18 min.

You can have Parmesan cheese shredded in the deli of your local grocery store. Unless you have a paddle attachment, we don't recommend using your mixer when stirring in the flour.

> 1 cup butter, softened
> 1 (8-ounce) block Parmesan cheese, shredded
> 3 garlic cloves, pressed
> ½ cup pine nuts, finely chopped and toasted
> 1 tablespoon chopped fresh basil
> ¼ teaspoon ground red pepper
> 2 cups all-purpose flour
> ½ cup whole pine nuts

BEAT butter and Parmesan cheese at medium speed with an electric mixer until blended. Add garlic and next 3 ingredients, beating just until blended. Gradually stir in flour with a spoon (mixture will become crumbly); stir until mixture is blended and smooth (about 2 to 3 minutes). Or instead of stirring the dough with a spoon after adding flour, you can gently press mixture together with hands, and work until blended and smooth.
SHAPE dough into 8 (7-inch-long) logs. Wrap each log in plastic wrap, and chill 8 hours.
CUT logs into ⅓-inch-thick slices, and place on lightly greased baking sheets. Press 1 whole pine nut into the center of each dough slice.
BAKE at 350° for 15 to 18 minutes or until lightly browned. Remove shortbread to wire racks, and let cool.

JALAPEÑO-PECAN SHORTBREAD: Substitute 1 (8-ounce) block Monterey Jack cheese with jalapeño peppers, shredded, for 1 (8-ounce) block Parmesan cheese, shredded; and 1 cup finely chopped, toasted pecans for ½ cup finely chopped, toasted pine nuts. Omit garlic and basil, and proceed with recipe as directed to make dough. Shape dough into 4 (7-inch-long) logs, and proceed as directed. Cut chilled logs into ¼-inch-thick slices, and place on lightly greased baking sheets. Substitute 2½ cups pecan halves (about 65 to 75 halves) for ½ cup pine nuts, pressing 1 pecan half into center of each slice. Bake as directed. Makes about 9 dozen.

CAJUN-BENNÉ SEED SHORTBREAD: Substitute 1 (8-ounce) block sharp Cheddar cheese, shredded, for 1 (8-ounce) block Parmesan cheese, shredded; and ½ cup toasted sesame seeds for ½ cup chopped, toasted pine nuts. Omit garlic and basil, and add 2 tablespoons Cajun seasoning. Proceed with recipe as directed to make dough. Shape dough into 4 (5-inch-long) logs, and proceed with recipe as directed. Cut chilled logs into ¼-inch-thick slices, and place on lightly greased baking sheets. Omit whole pine nuts. Bake as directed. Makes about 6½ dozen.

NOTE: For testing purposes only, we used McCormick Gourmet Blend Cajun Seasoning for Cajun seasoning. (We recommend this seasoning because others may be too salty for this recipe.) Benné seeds are the Lowcountry name for sesame seeds.

BLUE CHEESE-WALNUT SHORTBREAD: Substitute 4 ounces crumbled blue cheese and 4 ounces shredded white Cheddar cheese for 1 (8-ounce) block Parmesan cheese, shredded; and 1 cup finely chopped, toasted walnuts for ½ cup finely chopped, toasted pine nuts. Omit garlic and basil, and add 3 tablespoons dried chives. Proceed with recipe as directed to make dough; divide dough into 6 equal portions, shaping each portion into a ball. Flatten each ball on a lightly floured surface, and roll into a 6-inch circle. Place each circle on a sheet of wax paper; wrap in plastic wrap, and chill 8 hours. (Dough circles may be stacked with a sheet of wax paper between them, placed on a plate or cardboard before wrapping with plastic wrap and chilling.) Press edges of each chilled circle with the tines of a fork, and prick tops, forming a decorative pattern in dough. Cut each circle into 8 wedges, and place on lightly greased baking sheets. Omit whole pine nuts. Bake as directed. Makes 4 dozen wedges.

HERBED-FETA CHEESE SHORTBREAD:
Substitute 2 (4-ounce) packages crumbled feta cheese with basil and tomato for 1 (8-ounce) block Parmesan cheese, shredded. Omit ½ cup chopped, toasted pine nuts, garlic, and basil. Proceed with recipe as directed to make dough. Roll dough into a 12- x 10-inch rectangle on a lightly floured piece of parchment paper. Transfer paper with dough to a baking sheet or large piece of cardboard; wrap (baking sheet and dough) with plastic wrap. Chill 8 hours. Cut chilled dough lengthwise into 4 (3-inch-wide) strips, and crosswise into 20 (½-inch-wide) strips, using a pastry wheel or knife, forming about 80 (3- x ½-inch) strips. Prick tops of strips with the tines of a fork, forming a decorative pattern. Place on lightly greased baking sheets. Omit whole pine nuts. Bake as directed. Makes about 6½ dozen.

Wine Pairings

■ Pesto Shortbread and Herbed-Feta Cheese Shortbread pair nicely with Riesling.
■ Blue Cheese-Walnut Shortbread sparkles with a full-bodied Merlot.
■ Jalapeño-Pecan Shortbread and Cajun-Benné Seed Shortbread partner well with a Sauvignon Blanc, one of the most versatile wines.

Shrimp: The Flavor of the South

From the Gulf Coast waters to the Atlantic Ocean, the South is blessed with delectable shrimp. If you live near the coast during harvest season, you can purchase shrimp fresh from the water. (The "fresh" shrimp we find in our grocery stores are flash-frozen on the boat to preserve freshness, then thawed.)

We selected three favorite recipes that showcase distinct regional styles: Fried Shrimp from Port St. Joe, Florida; Shrimp Creole, one of the grandes dames of New Orleans cooking; and Shrimp Burgers, a South Carolina twist on the crab cake (recipe on following page).

FRIED SHRIMP

chef recipe • family favorite
MAKES 6 SERVINGS
Prep: 30 min., Cook: 1 min. per batch

    2 pounds unpeeled, large fresh shrimp
    1 (12-ounce) package fish-fry mix
    1 tablespoon Greek seasoning
    Vegetable oil

PEEL shrimp, and devein, if desired, leaving shells on, if desired. Combine fish-fry mix and Greek seasoning. Dredge shrimp in mixture.
POUR oil to a depth of 1½ inches into a Dutch oven or large saucepan; heat to 360°. Fry shrimp, a few at a time, 1 minute; drain on paper towels, and serve immediately.

NOTE: For testing purposes only, we used Zatarain's Wonderful FISH-FRI and Cavender's Greek Seasoning.

CHARLENE MATRE
DOCKSIDE CAFE
PORT ST. JOE, FLORIDA

SHRIMP CREOLE

MAKES 6 TO 8 SERVINGS
Prep: 25 min., Cook: 35 min.

    2 pounds unpeeled, medium-size fresh shrimp
    2 cups chopped onion
    1 cup chopped green bell pepper
    1 cup chopped celery
    2 garlic cloves, minced
    ¼ cup vegetable oil
    1 (6-ounce) can tomato paste
    1½ cups low-sodium, fat-free chicken broth, divided
    1 (14.5-ounce) can diced tomatoes, undrained
    1 (8-ounce) can tomato sauce
    2 bay leaves
    1 teaspoon ground red pepper
    1 teaspoon Worcestershire sauce
    ½ teaspoon salt
    2 tablespoons all-purpose flour
    Hot cooked rice

PEEL shrimp, and devein, if desired; set shrimp aside.
SAUTÉ onion and next 3 ingredients in hot oil in a large skillet over medium-high heat 5 minutes or until tender. Add tomato paste, and cook, stirring constantly, 1 minute. Stir in 1 cup chicken broth and next 6 ingredients; bring to a boil. Reduce heat, and simmer, stirring occasionally, 20 minutes.
STIR together remaining ½ cup chicken broth and flour. Whisk into tomato mixture, and cook, stirring occasionally, 5 minutes.
ADD shrimp; cook 4 minutes or until shrimp turn pink. Remove and discard bay leaves; serve shrimp over rice.

WALKER OGLESBY
TAMPA, FLORIDA

Shrimp Burgers

chef recipe

MAKES 6 SERVINGS

Prep: 20 min., Chill: 2 hrs., Cook: 8 min.
per batch

Finely chopping the shrimp and chilling the patties for at least 2 hours will help them stay together while cooking.

- 1 pound unpeeled, medium-size fresh shrimp, cooked
- 3 tablespoons chopped celery
- 2 tablespoons chopped green onions
- 2 tablespoons chopped fresh parsley
- 1½ teaspoons grated lemon rind
- 1 cup cornbread crumbs or soft breadcrumbs
- 3 tablespoons mayonnaise
- 1 large egg, beaten
- ¼ teaspoon salt
- ⅛ teaspoon pepper
- ⅛ teaspoon hot sauce
- 2 tablespoons vegetable oil
- Hamburger buns
- Toppings: lettuce leaves, tomato slices, tartar sauce

PEEL shrimp, and devein, if desired; finely chop.
COMBINE shrimp and next 4 ingredients in a large bowl. Add cornbread crumbs and next 5 ingredients; stir mixture until well blended.
SHAPE mixture into 6 patties. Place patties on a wax paper-lined baking sheet; cover and chill at least 2 hours.
HEAT oil in a large nonstick skillet over medium-high heat. Cook shrimp patties 4 minutes on each side or until golden. Drain on paper towels. Serve on hamburger buns with desired toppings.

ROBERT STEHLING
HOMINY GRILL
CHARLESTON, SOUTH CAROLINA

Spring Garden Party

When spring blossoms appear, consider taking the party outside. Our menu is simple with straightforward recipes that don't require heavy-duty effort. Our delicate finger foods free you from the kitchen, allowing you plenty of time to catch up with friends. Whether you choose the lawn or patio, great fun is bound to fill the air.

Pesto Goat Cheese

MAKES ABOUT 3 CUPS

Prep: 25 min., Chill: 2 hrs.

Test Kitchens professional Rebecca Gordon shared this favorite spread.

- 2 (3-ounce) logs goat cheese, softened
- 1 (8-ounce) package cream cheese, softened
- 1 (7-ounce) jar basil pesto sauce, drained
- 1 tablespoon fresh lemon juice
- 1 tablespoon chopped fresh parsley
- 1 (¾-ounce) package fresh thyme sprigs
- Assorted crackers

STIR together first 5 ingredients until well blended. Remove ¼ cup mixture, and wrap in plastic wrap; chill. Press remaining cheese mixture into a 6-cup or 1.5-liter plastic wrap-lined bowl. Cover and chill 2 hours.
REMOVE plastic wrap from chilled ¼ cup cheese mixture. Shape heaping teaspoonfuls of cheese mixture into eggs. Cover and chill until ready to serve.
UNMOLD cheese mixture; remove plastic wrap, and place on a serving platter. Press a 2-inch indentation into center of cheese mold. Press thyme sprigs around top edge and sides of mold to resemble a nest. Arrange eggs in center of nest. Serve with crackers.

From-the-Heart Petits Fours

MAKES 28 PETITS FOURS

Prep: 1 hr., 30 min.; Cook: 10 min.; Chill: 1 hr.

Petits fours are simply bite-size frosted cakes. You'll find marzipan in the spice aisle of your supermarket. The glaze on these hearts works best when heated only once, so prepare all your cakes, and then glaze in one final step.

- 2 (10¾-ounce) frozen pound cakes, thawed and cut into 1-inch-thick slices
- ¾ cup seedless raspberry jam
- 1½ tablespoons water
- 4 ounces marzipan
- 7 cups sifted powdered sugar
- ⅔ cup water
- ¼ cup light corn syrup
- 1 drop red liquid food coloring

CUT 2 heart shapes from each cake slice, using a 1½-inch heart-shaped cookie cutter. Reserve excess cake for another use.
COOK jam and 1½ tablespoons water in a small saucepan over medium-low heat, stirring until smooth. Remove from heat, and let cool slightly. Place cake hearts on a wire rack in a wax paper-lined 15- x 10-inch jellyroll pan. Brush jam mixture evenly over tops and sides of cake hearts.
KNEAD marzipan gently; place between 2 sheets of plastic wrap, and roll to a ¹⁄₁₆-inch thickness. Remove plastic wrap, and cut out 28 hearts, using a 1½-inch heart-shaped cookie cutter. Place marzipan hearts over cake hearts. Cover and chill 1 hour.
COMBINE powdered sugar, ½ cup water, and corn syrup in a large saucepan; cook, stirring constantly, over low heat until mixture is translucent. Add remaining water as needed, 1 tablespoon at a time, until glazing consistency. Stir in red liquid food coloring until blended.
SPOON icing evenly over cake hearts, coating completely.

CUCUMBER-SALMON-WATERCRESS SANDWICHES

MAKES 12 SANDWICHES

Prep: 30 min., Chill: 2 hrs.

- ½ (8-ounce) package cream cheese, softened
- 3 tablespoons finely chopped cucumber
- 3 ounces cold smoked salmon, thinly sliced
- 1 teaspoon trimmed, minced watercress
- ½ teaspoon lemon juice
- ⅛ teaspoon ground red pepper
- 12 whole wheat bread slices
- 3 tablespoons butter or margarine, softened
- ½ cup trimmed, minced watercress

PROCESS cream cheese in a food processor until smooth, stopping to scrape down sides. Add finely chopped cucumber and next 4 ingredients; process until well blended.
CUT 2 rounds out of each bread slice using a 2-inch biscuit cutter. Spread cheese mixture evenly on 1 side of half of bread rounds. Top with remaining bread rounds. Carefully spread the cut outer edges of sandwiches with butter. Dip edges in ½ cup minced watercress, coating evenly. Cover and chill 2 hours.

HONEY ANGEL BISCUITS

MAKES 5 DOZEN

Prep: 30 min., Stand: 5 min., Bake: 10 min.

Honey Butter sweetens these tasty biscuits.

- 1 (¼-ounce) envelope active dry yeast
- 2 tablespoons warm water (100° to 110°)
- 5 cups all-purpose flour
- 1 tablespoon baking powder
- 1 teaspoon baking soda
- 1 teaspoon salt
- 1 cup shortening
- 2 cups buttermilk
- 3 tablespoons honey
- Honey Butter

COMBINE yeast and 2 tablespoons warm water in a 1-cup measuring cup; let stand 5 minutes.
COMBINE flour and next 3 ingredients in a large bowl; cut in shortening with a pastry blender or 2 forks until mixture is crumbly.
COMBINE yeast mixture, buttermilk, and honey; add to dry ingredients, stirring just until moistened.
TURN dough out onto a lightly floured surface, and knead 1 minute.
ROLL dough to a ½-inch thickness. Cut with a 2-inch round biscuit cutter, and place on ungreased baking sheets.
BAKE at 400° for 10 minutes or until golden. Serve with Honey Butter or chicken salad.

Honey Butter:

MAKES ⅔ CUP

Prep: 5 min.

- ½ cup butter or margarine, softened
- ¼ cup honey

STIR together butter and honey in a small bowl until blended.

The Secret to Gumbo

Two ingredients—flour and oil—make roux. The slow-cooked blend contributes a rich depth of flavor to Creole and Cajun cookery and is the heart of every real gumbo. Plan to spend from 30 to 40 minutes whisking the precious thickener depending on the size of your pot, the amount of oil, and the temperature. You can't rush that smoky, nutty flavor. If the heat is too high, the roux will burn, and then you'll have to start over.

Store roux in an airtight container in the refrigerator up to two weeks. Any time you want gumbo, you're ahead of the game. We've included a recipe for one of our favorites here.

ROUX

MAKES ABOUT 3½ CUPS

Cook: 30 min.

- 1½ cups vegetable oil
- 2 cups all-purpose flour

HEAT oil in a large cast-iron skillet over medium heat; gradually whisk in flour, and cook, whisking constantly, until flour is a dark mahogany color (about 30 minutes). Proceed with the gumbo recipe below, or cool roux completely, and store in an airtight container in the refrigerator up to 2 weeks.

SHRIMP-CRAB GUMBO

MAKES ABOUT 1¼ GALLONS

Prep: 35 min.; Cook: 3 hrs., 30 min.

- Roux (recipe above)
- 9 (14½-ounce) cans chicken broth
- 2½ cups chopped onions
- 1 cup chopped green onions
- ½ cup chopped celery
- 2 garlic cloves, chopped
- 1 (10-ounce) can diced tomatoes with green chiles
- 1 (8-ounce) can tomato sauce
- 1 (16-ounce) package frozen sliced okra (optional)
- 3 pounds unpeeled, medium-size fresh shrimp
- 1 (16-ounce) container lump crabmeat
- ½ cup chopped fresh parsley
- 1 tablespoon filé powder (optional)
- Hot cooked rice

STIR together first 8 ingredients and okra, if desired; bring to a boil. Reduce heat, and simmer, stirring occasionally, 3 hours.
PEEL shrimp, and devein, if desired. Add shrimp to broth mixture; cook, stirring often, 15 minutes or just until shrimp turn pink. Stir in crabmeat and parsley. Remove from heat; stir in filé powder, if desired. Serve over hot cooked rice.

Cornbread and Cast Iron

Some Southern foods just wouldn't be the same cooked in anything except cast iron. The recipe for roux on the previous page is one example, and cornbread is another. Cast iron's ability to distribute heat evenly, as well as to stand up to high temperatures, makes it an admirable addition to any kitchen.

After baking, immediately place the cornbread upside-down onto a plate. This allows the steam to escape, preventing the crust from getting soggy. You'll want the rest of the meal to be on the table when this happens—cornbread loses quality as it cools, and while still tasty an hour later, it never regains its fresh-from-the-oven flavor and texture.

If you prefer an even crispier version, try Hot-Water Cornbread. Pan-fried in small rounds, it has a dense crust with just a touch of tenderness inside. Naturally, there is no better cookware for frying it than a cast-iron skillet.

If you haven't baked cornbread in cast iron before, you should give it a try. For the best crust, heat the pan first, and add a small amount of bacon grease or oil. It's likely you'll never go back to a baking pan again.

SKILLET CORNBREAD

family favorite • fast fixin's

MAKES 6 SERVINGS
Prep: 15 min., Bake: 15 min.

This superb recipe, adapted from *Hoppin' John's Lowcountry Cooking* by John Martin Taylor (Houghton Mifflin, 2000), is one of our favorites. If you love to crumble cornbread into buttermilk and eat it with a spoon, this is a great recipe.

- **2 to 3 teaspoons bacon drippings**
- **2 cups buttermilk**
- **1 large egg**
- **1¾ cups white cornmeal**
- **1 teaspoon baking powder**
- **1 teaspoon baking soda**
- **1 teaspoon salt**

COAT bottom and sides of a 10-inch cast-iron skillet with bacon drippings; heat in a 450° oven.
WHISK together buttermilk and egg. Add cornmeal, stirring well. Whisk in baking powder, soda, and salt. Pour batter into hot skillet.
BAKE at 450° for 15 minutes or until cornbread is golden.

HOT-WATER CORNBREAD

family favorite • fast fixin's

MAKES 9 SERVINGS
Prep: 5 min., Cook: 6 min. per batch

This ranked as one of our Top 5 winners in the Family Favorites category in Our Top 25 Recipes in 25 Years. See the special section at the end of the book for more on this classic recipe.

- **2 cups white cornmeal**
- **¼ teaspoon baking powder**
- **1¼ teaspoons salt**
- **1 teaspoon sugar**
- **¼ cup half-and-half**
- **1 tablespoon vegetable oil**
- **1 to 2 cups boiling water**
- **Vegetable oil**
- **Softened butter**

COMBINE cornmeal, baking powder, salt, and sugar in a large bowl; stir in half-and-half and 1 tablespoon vegetable oil. Gradually add 1 to 2 cups boiling water to mixture, stirring until batter is the consistency of grits.
POUR vegetable oil to a depth of ½ inch into a large cast-iron skillet over medium-high heat.
DROP batter by ¼-cupfuls into hot oil; fry cornbread, in batches, 2 to 3 minutes on each side or until golden. Drain on paper towels. Serve with softened butter.

Ironclad Rules

■ To season new cast iron, scrub with steel wool soap pads; then wash with dish soap and hot water. Dry thoroughly. Spread a layer of vegetable shortening on the inside, including the underside of the lid. Bake at 250° for 15 minutes. Remove from oven, and wipe out shortening with a paper towel. Bake for 2 more hours. Remove from oven, and cool to room temperature. Repeat two or three times.
■ Once your cast iron is seasoned, never use soap to clean it—and never put it in a dishwasher.
■ Clean with a plastic scrubber or stiff brush under hot running water. Dry immediately, and rub with a thin coating of vegetable oil.
■ If your skillet loses its seasoning, you can repeat the seasoning procedure—or just fry something in it.
■ If you don't want to season new cookware, Lodge Manufacturing Company makes preseasoned cast iron that's ready to use.

Zesty Fish Po'boys, page 120

Sun-Dried Tomato Cheesecake, page 118

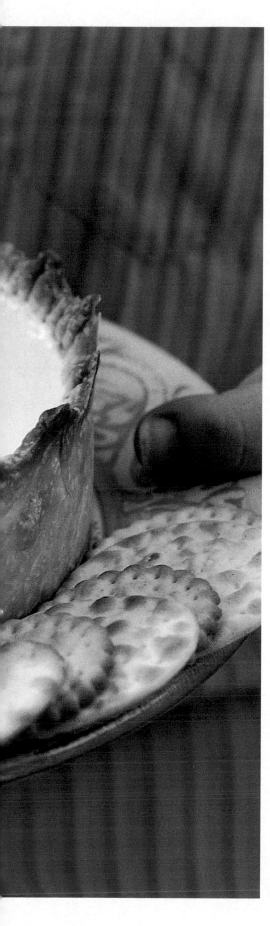

Classic Mint Julep,
page 129

Blueberry Bread Pudding, page 119

Orange Chiffon Cake With Orange
Icebox Pie Filling, page 105

Lime Icebox Pie Cake,
page 104

116

Gather Friends for Brunch

Choose a picturesque corner of your garden or deck to serve this elegant meal.

Special Occasion Brunch

Serves 10 to 12

Champagne Punch   Iced tea

Sun-Dried Tomato Cheesecake

Molasses-Coffee Glazed Ham or Turkey Breast

Lemon-Marinated Asparagus

Grand Oranges and Strawberries   Grits   Biscuits

Blueberry Bread Pudding

We all know there are many special occasions to celebrate in the spring—weddings, Mother's Day, and graduations, just to name a few. But why wait for a big event when a glorious morning is reason enough to throw a party? Forget fussing with a complicated menu—our six recipes showcase much of the season's plentiful produce, making them the perfect collection for a warm-weather brunch.

CHAMPAGNE PUNCH

fast fixin's

MAKES ABOUT 2 QUARTS

Prep: 10 min.

If you prefer a punch that's a little less on the sweet side, add additional sparkling water to taste.

- 1 (11.5-ounce) can frozen pineapple-orange juice concentrate, thawed and undiluted
- 1 (6-ounce) can frozen lemonade concentrate, thawed and undiluted
- 1 (12-ounce) can or 1½ cups ginger ale, chilled
- 1 (750-milliliter) bottle Champagne or sparkling white grape juice, chilled
- 2 cups bottled sparkling water, chilled

STIR together concentrates in punch bowl. Add remaining ingredients, stirring gently. Serve immediately.

LINDA DAVIDSON
MERIDIAN, MISSISSIPPI

SUN-DRIED TOMATO CHEESECAKE

make ahead

MAKES 20 TO 24 APPETIZER SERVINGS

Prep: 15 min., Freeze: 30 min., Bake: 47 min., Cool: 20 min., Chill: 8 hrs. *(pictured on page 114)*

- ½ cup minced dried tomatoes in oil
- 1 (15-ounce) package refrigerated piecrusts
- 2 (8-ounce) packages cream cheese, softened
- 3 large eggs
- 1 (5-ounce) package shredded Swiss cheese
- 3 green onions, chopped (about ¼ cup)
- ½ teaspoon salt
- ½ teaspoon black pepper
- ¼ teaspoon ground red pepper
- 1¾ cups sour cream
- Garnishes: edible pansies, marigolds, and nasturtiums, fresh chives, green onion stems, fresh mint leaves

DRAIN tomatoes well, pressing between paper towels. Set aside.

UNFOLD piecrusts; place 1 piecrust on a lightly floured surface, and brush with water. Top with remaining crust. Roll into 1 (12½-inch) circle. Press piecrust on bottom and up sides of a lightly greased 9-inch springform pan. Press out folds in piecrust on sides of pan; turn edge over ½ inch toward the inside, and gently press. Crimp with a fork, if desired. Freeze piecrust 30 minutes.

BAKE at 450° for 7 minutes. Remove piecrust from oven, and reduce oven temperature to 350°.

BEAT cream cheese at medium speed with an electric mixer 2 to 3 minutes or until light and fluffy. Add eggs, 1 at a time, beating well after each addition. Stir in tomatoes, Swiss cheese, and next 4 ingredients, mixing well. Pour into baked piecrust.

BAKE on lower rack at 350° for 35 to 40 minutes or until golden brown and set. Spread sour cream over top. Cool on a wire rack for 20 minutes; cover and chill 8 hours. Place cheesecake on serving plate; release and remove sides of pan. Garnish, if desired. Serve with crackers.

CARLIE STEIN
BIRMINGHAM, ALABAMA

Molasses-Coffee Glazed Ham

family favorite

MAKES 10 TO 12 SERVINGS

Prep: 20 min., Bake: 2 hrs., Stand: 30 min.

- **1 cup molasses**
- **1 (12-ounce) jar apricot jam**
- **2 tablespoons cider vinegar**
- **1 tablespoon Dijon mustard**
- **1 teaspoon salt**
- **1 teaspoon vanilla extract**
- **¾ cup brewed strong coffee**
- **1 (8- to 9-pound) bone-in, fully cooked smoked ham half**

STIR together first 7 ingredients until blended. Reserve 1 cup molasses-coffee sauce in a small bowl; set reserved sauce aside.

TRIM ham, and, if desired, score top of ham in a diamond pattern. Place ham in a lightly greased 13- x 9-inch pan. Pour remaining molasses-coffee sauce evenly over ham.

BAKE on lower rack at 350° for 2 hours or until a meat thermometer inserted in ham registers 140°, basting with sauce in pan every 15 minutes. Cover ham loosely with lightly greased aluminum foil the last 30 minutes to prevent excessive browning, if necessary.

REMOVE ham from baking pan; let stand at room temperature 30 minutes. Heat reserved molasses-coffee sauce, and serve with ham.

NOTE: For tips on choosing and storing a ham, as well as some great recipes that use leftover ham, see "Start With a Ham" on page 82.

MOLASSES-COFFEE GLAZED TURKEY BREAST: Substitute 1 (5- to 5½-pound) bone-in turkey breast with skin for ham. Place turkey in a lightly greased 11- x 7-inch pan. Proceed as directed, covering loosely with aluminum foil before baking. Bake at 350° for 1 hour; uncover and bake 1 to 1½ more hours or until a meat thermometer inserted in thickest portion registers 170°, basting with molasses-coffee sauce every 15 minutes. Serve with warm reserved molasses-coffee sauce. Makes 10 to 12 servings. Prep: 20 min.; Bake: 2 hrs., 30 min.; Cook: 5 min.

Lemon-Marinated Asparagus

make ahead

MAKES 10 TO 12 SERVINGS

Prep: 20 min., Chill: 10 hrs., Cook: 3 min.

We limited the marinating time to 2 hours because lemon juice tends to discolor and toughen asparagus.

- **½ cup fresh lemon juice**
- **3 tablespoons olive oil**
- **2 tablespoons sugar**
- **¼ teaspoon salt**
- **¼ teaspoon pepper**
- **1 garlic clove, minced**
- **1 (14-ounce) can artichoke heart quarters, drained**
- **1 (4-ounce) jar diced pimiento, drained**
- **2 pounds fresh asparagus**
- **Garnish: lemon rind strips**

WHISK together first 6 ingredients ingredients in a large bowl; add artichoke quarters and diced pimiento; gently toss. Cover and chill 8 hours or overnight.

SNAP off tough ends of asparagus; cook in boiling salted water to cover 3 minutes or until crisp-tender.

DRAIN asparagus, and plunge into ice water to stop cooking process; drain. Place cooked asparagus in a large zip-top freezer bag, and store overnight in refrigerator, if desired.

ADD asparagus to artichoke mixture, and gently toss. Cover and chill 2 hours. Garnish, if desired.

Grand Oranges and Strawberries

make ahead

MAKES 10 TO 12 SERVINGS

Prep: 30 min., Chill: 8 hrs.

- **½ cup orange marmalade**
- **1½ cups sparkling white grape juice, chilled**
- **¼ cup orange liqueur**
- **10 to 12 large navel oranges, peeled and sectioned**
- **2 cups sliced fresh strawberries**

MELT marmalade in a small saucepan over low heat, stirring constantly; remove pan from heat, and cool marmalade slightly.

STIR together marmalade, grape juice, and liqueur in a large serving dish or bowl until blended. Add orange sections; gently stir. Cover and chill 8 hours.

ADD strawberries to oranges in bowl, and gently stir. Serve with a slotted spoon.

NOTE: For testing purposes only, we used Grand Marnier for orange liqueur.

JULIA MITCHELL
BIRMINGHAM, ALABAMA

Blueberry Bread Pudding

make ahead

MAKES 10 TO 12 SERVINGS

Prep: 15 min, Chill: 8 hrs., Bake 1 hr., Stand: 5 min.

Make this easy, decadent recipe the day before, and chill; then bake and serve hot. *(pictured on page 115)*

- **1 (16-ounce) French bread loaf, cubed**
- **1 (8-ounce) package cream cheese, cut into pieces**
- **3 cups fresh blueberries, divided**
- **6 large eggs**
- **4 cups milk**
- **½ cup sugar**
- **¼ cup butter or margarine, melted**
- **¼ cup maple syrup**
- **1 (10-ounce) jar blueberry preserves**
- **Garnishes: fresh mint leaves, edible pansies**

ARRANGE half of bread cubes in a lightly greased 13- x 9-inch pan. Sprinkle evenly with cream cheese and 1 cup blueberries; top with remaining bread cubes.

WHISK together eggs, milk, sugar, butter, and maple syrup; pour over bread mixture, pressing bread cubes to absorb egg mixture. Cover and chill 8 hours.

BAKE, covered, at 350° for 30 minutes. Uncover and bake 30 more minutes or until lightly browned and set. Let stand 5 minutes before serving.

STIR together remaining 2 cups blueberries and blueberry preserves in a saucepan over low heat until warm. Serve blueberry mixture over bread pudding. Garnish, if desired.

Meal Starters From the Freezer

Shorten your dinner prep time with these great entrée and dessert recipes.

What's in your freezer that could be tonight's supper? I don't mean heat-and-eat TV dinners—I'm talking about jump-start frozen foods such as fish and chicken tenders. With recipes such as these, you can think of the freezer as your second pantry, stocked with quick supper ingredients for time-stretched nights.

FIESTA FRIED CHICKEN SALAD

family favorite • fast fixin's

MAKES 6 SERVINGS

Prep: 30 min.

For another night's supper, make chicken tenders as directed. Prepare fresh veggie dippers such as carrot and celery sticks and cauliflower. Serve the dressing as a dipping sauce for the vegetables and the chicken.

- 1 (2-pound) package frozen breaded chicken tenders
- 1 teaspoon garlic powder
- 1 teaspoon chili powder
- 1 teaspoon crushed oregano leaves
- ¼ teaspoon ground cumin
- 1 head iceberg lettuce, shredded
- ⅓ cup thinly sliced green onions
- 4 plum tomatoes, seeded and diced
- ½ (8-ounce) package shredded Mexican four-cheese blend
- 1 to 2 large avocados, sliced
- ⅓ cup chopped fresh cilantro
- 1 cup Ranch dressing
- ⅔ cup fire-roasted tomato salsa or taco sauce

COMBINE first 5 ingredients in a large zip-top plastic bag; seal and shake to coat. Bake seasoned chicken tenders according to package directions.
ARRANGE lettuce on 6 serving plates; sprinkle with green onions and next 4 ingredients. Combine Ranch dressing and salsa; drizzle over salad. Top with chicken, and serve immediately.

MARY LOU COOK
WELCHES, OREGON

ZESTY FISH PO'BOYS

family favorite • fast fixin's

MAKES 4 SERVINGS

Prep: 20 min. *(pictured on page 113)*

- 2 (11-ounce) packages frozen breaded fish fillets
- 2 (12-inch) French bread loaves
- 1 cup regular or light mayonnaise
- 3 tablespoons lemon juice
- 1 tablespoon Creole mustard
- 1 tablespoon sweet pickle relish
- 1 teaspoon chopped fresh or ½ teaspoon dried parsley
- ¼ teaspoon dried tarragon
- ½ teaspoon hot sauce
- 4 lettuce leaves

BAKE fish fillets according to package directions. Set aside, and keep warm.
CUT bread in half crosswise. Split each half lengthwise, and toast.
STIR together mayonnaise and next 6 ingredients. Spread mixture evenly over cut side of bread halves. Place lettuce and fish on bottom bread halves; top with remaining bread halves. Serve immediately.

NOTE: For testing purposes only, we used Gorton's Southern Fried Country Style Breaded Fish Fillets.

CHOCOLATE MINT SUNDAES

family favorite • fast fixin's

MAKES 4 SERVINGS

Prep: 5 min.

Keep ice cream and a bag of peppermint patties in the freezer to create this quick dessert.

- 12 (0.25-ounce) chocolate-covered peppermint patties
- 2 tablespoons milk
- Vanilla ice cream

PLACE peppermint patties and milk in a small microwave-safe glass bowl. Cover and microwave at HIGH 1 minute or until patties melt, stirring every 15 seconds. Serve over ice cream.

NOTE: For testing purposes only, we used York Peppermint Patties.

LIZ CHIZ
LOS ANGELES, CALIFORNIA

Give Your Freezer a Makeover

If your freezer doesn't have any built-in organizational features, create your own with these tips.

■ Take stock of what you have; then purchase inexpensive plastic storage containers to group like foods together. Label bins to make finding what you need even easier.
■ If there isn't a rack, add plastic-coated, free-standing wire shelves to increase the storage space.

Food and Family Ties

Family reunions are serious business in the South. These events are times for preserving ties and visiting with loved ones. They're also opportunities to enjoy our favorite foods. We selected these top-rated recipes for their great taste and make-ahead convenience. Of course, feel free to make the pork the day of, if time permits—few things rival the aroma of an outdoor barbecue.

Follow the golden rule of food safety when transporting the dishes to the event: Keep hot foods hot and cold foods cold. This will ensure everyone has a great time at your next family get-together.

SMOKED PORK

family favorite • make ahead

MAKES 8 TO 10 SERVINGS

Prep: 40 min.; Soak: 1 hr.; Cook: 7 hrs., 25 min.

Most barbecue sauces have either a ketchup or mustard base; this one has both.

Hickory wood chunks
2 cups prepared mustard
1½ cups ketchup
¾ cup cider vinegar
2 tablespoons sugar
2 tablespoons Worcestershire sauce
1 tablespoon hot sauce
2 tablespoons butter or margarine
1 (5- to 6-pound) Boston butt pork roast
5 garlic cloves, chopped
2 tablespoons salt
1 tablespoon pepper

SOAK wood in water 1 hour.
COOK mustard and next 6 ingredients in a large saucepan over low heat, stirring often, 20 minutes; remove from heat.
CUT several deep slits in roast using a paring knife. Stir together garlic, salt, and pepper; rub on all sides of roast.

PREPARE charcoal fire in smoker; let burn 15 to 20 minutes.
DRAIN wood; place on coals. Place water pan in smoker; add water to fill line.
PLACE pork roast in center of lower food rack. Pour 1 cup mustard mixture over roast.
COOK, covered with smoker lid, 6 to 7 hours or until a meat thermometer inserted into thickest portion registers 165°, adding additional wood and charcoal every hour as needed. Remove roast from smoker; cool slightly. Chop and serve with remaining mustard sauce.

JAY POOLE
GASTON, SOUTH CAROLINA

ORANGE-POPPY SEED SALAD

family favorite

MAKES 6 SERVINGS

Prep: 25 min., Bake: 25 min.

1 egg white
¼ cup sugar
1 cup sliced almonds
2 tablespoons butter or margarine
1 head Bibb lettuce, torn
1 head Green or Red Leaf lettuce, torn
1 (11-ounce) can mandarin oranges, drained
1 (16-ounce) package strawberries, thinly sliced
1 green onion, chopped
¾ cup olive oil
¼ cup red wine vinegar
1 teaspoon grated orange rind
1 tablespoon fresh orange juice
½ teaspoon poppy seeds
⅛ teaspoon salt
⅛ teaspoon pepper

BEAT egg white at high speed with an electric mixer until foamy. Add sugar, 1 tablespoon at a time, beating 2 to 4 minutes or until stiff peaks form and sugar dissolves. Fold in almonds.
MELT butter in a 9-inch square pan in a 325° oven. Add almonds to pan, and bake, stirring every 5 minutes, 20 to 25 minutes or until lightly browned and dry. Cool in pan on a wire rack.
TOSS together Bibb lettuce and next 4 ingredients in a large bowl.

WHISK together oil and next 6 ingredients; drizzle half over salad, tossing gently. Sprinkle with sugared almonds, and serve immediately with remaining dressing.

RITA MARSH
LOUISVILLE, KENTUCKY

WIXIE'S YEAST ROLLS

family favorite • make ahead

MAKES 2 DOZEN

Prep: 30 min., Stand: 12 min., Chill: 8 hrs., Rise: 1 hr., Bake: 15 min.

½ cup shortening
3½ to 4 cups all-purpose flour
1 (¼-ounce) envelope active dry yeast
⅓ cup sugar
1¼ teaspoons salt
1½ cups warm water (100° to 110°)
¼ cup butter or margarine, melted

CUT shortening into 3½ cups flour with a pastry blender or fork until crumbly.
COMBINE yeast and next 3 ingredients in a bowl; let stand 10 to 12 minutes or until bubbly. Gradually stir in flour mixture to make a soft dough, adding more flour if necessary. Cover and chill 8 hours.
TURN dough out onto a lightly floured surface, and knead until smooth and elastic (about 1 to 2 minutes). Shape dough into 1½-inch balls, and place in a lightly greased 13- x 9-inch pan.
COVER and let rise in a warm place (85°), free from drafts, 1 hour or until doubled in bulk.
BAKE at 450°for 15 minutes or until golden. Brush with melted butter.

RUTH RHYNE SMULL
ALEXANDRIA, VIRGINIA

Mangoes Sweet, Juicy, and Versatile

This tropical fruit is as close as your local market.

Mangoes were once considered as exotic as the countries where they grew. Their deep golden flesh reminded us of the sunny climates required to ripen them into juicy sweetness. They still bring to mind warm breezes, but mangoes have now become a staple in Southern supermarkets. Although their peak season runs from May to September, many times they can be found year-round in the produce section, along with jars of mango slices. Jarred slices can often be substituted, but don't be intimidated by fresh mangoes. We've included a tip box on how to cut them with ease.

A ripe mango should have a faintly sweet aroma and yellow skin blushed with red. To ripen, keep at room temperature, or store in a paper bag. (Don't refrigerate until they're fully ripe.) Enjoy their delectable flavor in these fantastic recipes.

Cutting a Mango

To slice, hold the fruit firmly with the narrow side up, and cut in half. Remove the large seed. Score a crisscross pattern in pulp of each half, cutting to, but not through, the skin. Release the cubes by folding the skin almost inside out.

MANGO CREAM PIE

family favorite • make ahead

MAKES 1 (9-INCH) PIE

Prep: 10 min., Bake: 7 min., Cook: 10 min., Chill: 8 hrs.

This terrific dessert is a cinch to prepare and sure to become a family favorite. Mango nectar can be found in the Mexican-food section of most grocery stores.

- ½ (15-ounce) package refrigerated piecrusts
- 2½ cups mango nectar
- 1 cup whipping cream
- 3 egg yolks
- ¾ cup sugar
- ⅓ cup cornstarch
- ⅛ teaspoon salt
- 2 tablespoons butter or margarine
- 1½ teaspoons vanilla extract
- Garnishes: whipped cream, fresh mango slices, fresh mint leaves

FIT piecrust into a 9-inch pieplate according to package directions; fold edges under, and crimp.

BAKE at 425° for 7 minutes or until lightly browned; cool.

COMBINE nectar and next 5 ingredients in a medium saucepan. Bring to a boil over medium heat, whisking constantly; boil, whisking constantly, 1 minute or until mixture thickens. Remove from heat.

STIR in butter and vanilla. Cover tightly with plastic wrap, and cool to room temperature. Spoon mixture into prepared piecrust; cover and chill 8 hours. Garnish, if desired.

MANGO SMOOTHIE

make ahead

MAKES 3 CUPS

Prep: 10 min., Chill: 2 hrs.

A large peeled, seeded, and chopped mango yields about 2 cups of fruit.

- 2 cups chopped mango (1 large)*
- ½ cup cold water
- 2 tablespoons lemon juice
- 1 (8-ounce) container vanilla yogurt
- ¼ cup sugar

PROCESS first 3 ingredients in a blender until smooth, stopping to scrape down sides. Add yogurt and sugar; process until smooth. Cover and chill 2 hours.

*Substitute 2 cups chopped refrigerated mango slices, drained, if desired.

GAIL HARRIS
MIAMI BEACH, FLORIDA

MANGO SALAD

make ahead

MAKES 6 SERVINGS

Prep: 30 min., Chill: 2 hrs.

- 3 cups chopped mango (about 2 medium)*
- 2 tomatoes, chopped
- ½ red onion, chopped
- 2 cucumbers, seeded and chopped
- 1½ cups fresh corn kernels (about 3 ears)
- ½ cup shredded fresh basil
- ½ cup olive oil
- ¼ cup rice vinegar
- 2 tablespoons sugar
- 3 tablespoons fresh lime juice
- 1 garlic clove, chopped
- ½ teaspoon salt
- ½ teaspoon pepper
- 1 bunch watercress, torn
- 1 head Bibb lettuce, torn

COMBINE first 13 ingredients in a large bowl; toss to coat. Cover and chill 2 hours. Serve over watercress and lettuce.

*Substitute 3 cups chopped refrigerated mango slices, drained, if desired.

MANGO-CHICKEN PITA SANDWICHES

fast fixin's

MAKES 8 SANDWICHES

Prep: 20 min.

    1 (10-ounce) package shredded
      angel hair cabbage slaw
    1 Granny Smith apple, diced
    ½ cup plain yogurt
    1 teaspoon grated lemon rind
    ½ teaspoon dry mustard
    4 pita bread rounds, halved
    4 grilled chicken breasts, cut into
      thin strips*
    1 cup warm Mango Chutney**

COMBINE first 5 ingredients. Layer pita halves evenly with chicken, Mango Chutney, and slaw mixture.

*Substitute 1 roasted chicken for grilled chicken breasts, if desired. Remove meat from bones, and chop.

**Substitute 1 cup commercial mango chutney for Mango Chutney, if desired.

THOMAS HAMMONS
JACKSON, MISSISSIPPI

MANGO CHUTNEY

make ahead

MAKES 2 CUPS

Prep: 30 min., Cook: 35 min.

    1½ cups orange juice
    1 cup golden raisins
    3 cups chopped mango (2 medium)*
    2 to 3 jalapeño peppers, seeded and
      chopped
    1 medium-size red onion, chopped
    2 tablespoons brown sugar
    2 to 3 tablespoons lime juice
    2 teaspoons ground coriander
    1 teaspoon ground cumin
    1 teaspoon ground ginger
    ¼ teaspoon ground cloves
    ¼ teaspoon ground nutmeg
    ⅛ teaspoon ground red pepper

COMBINE all ingredients in a medium saucepan.
COVER mixture, and bring to a boil over medium heat, stirring occasionally. Reduce

heat, and simmer, uncovered, 30 minutes or until mixture thickens, stirring occasionally; cool slightly. Serve immediately with Mango-Chicken Pita Sandwiches, or cover and chill up to 1 week.

*Substitute 3 cups chopped refrigerated mango slices, if desired.

AMY FITZGERALD
BIRMINGHAM, ALABAMA

Quick & Easy

Pasta Bowls

This is terrific food—quick homemade meals served in bowls. While the pasta cooks, get everything else ready. If you want to make it even faster next time, cook extra pasta, drain, and freeze it. After a dunk into hot water, it's ready.

RANCH HOUSE FETTUCCINE

MAKES 4 SERVINGS

Prep: 15 min., Cook: 25 min.

All you need to make this tasty dish a complete meal is a couple of crisp breadsticks.

    8 ounces fettuccine
    1 (16-ounce) package fresh broccoli
      florets
    1 medium-size red bell pepper, diced
    2 tablespoons olive oil
    1 garlic clove, minced
    ¾ cup cooked ham, cut into thin strips
    1 (6-ounce) package grilled chicken
      breast strips
    4 dried tomato halves in oil, drained
      and chopped
    2 teaspoons minced fresh rosemary
    1 (8-ounce) bottle Ranch-style
      dressing, divided
    ¼ cup freshly grated Parmesan cheese

PREPARE pasta according to package directions. Drain and keep warm.
SAUTÉ broccoli and bell pepper in hot oil in a large skillet over medium-high

heat 7 minutes or until crisp-tender; add garlic, and sauté 2 minutes.
STIR in ham, chicken, and tomatoes; sprinkle with rosemary. Cook, stirring occasionally, until thoroughly heated.
TOSS together warm pasta, broccoli mixture, and ½ cup Ranch dressing; add cheese, tossing well. Serve in bowls with remaining Ranch dressing.

HELEN CONWELL
FAIRHOPE, ALABAMA

SPAGHETTI CARBONARA

family favorite • fast fixin's

MAKES 6 SERVINGS

Prep: 10 min., Cook: 20 min.

Traditionally, the ingredients for this dish are simply stirred into hot pasta and served. In our Test Kitchens, we tossed the raw egg mixture with spaghetti and reheated it in a skillet to ensure safety.

    12 ounces spaghetti
    ½ pound bacon, cut into 1-inch
      pieces
    1 small onion, chopped
    1 garlic clove, minced
    1 cup half-and-half
    ½ cup milk
    ½ cup whipping cream
    1 large egg, lightly beaten
    ¼ teaspoon salt
    ¼ teaspoon pepper
    ½ cup grated Parmesan cheese
    2 tablespoons chopped parsley

PREPARE spaghetti according to package directions; drain and keep warm.
COOK bacon in a large skillet over high heat until crisp. Reduce heat to medium; add onion and garlic, and sauté 5 minutes.
STIR together half-and-half and next 5 ingredients; toss in spaghetti.
ADD spaghetti mixture and ¼ cup cheese to onion mixture in skillet. Cook over low heat, stirring occasionally, until thoroughly heated. Sprinkle with remaining ¼ cup Parmesan cheese and parsley. Serve in bowls.

RENEE TREMPE
WEST BLOOMFIELD, MICHIGAN

EASY TACO PASTA

family favorite • fast fixin's

MAKES 4 TO 6 SERVINGS

Prep: 5 min., Cook: 20 min.

Grill some Texas toast to serve alongside this hearty one-dish dinner that'll be ready in less than half an hour.

- 1 (16-ounce) package ground pork sausage
- 1 (15.5-ounce) can chili hot beans
- 1 (10-ounce) can diced tomatoes and green chiles, drained
- 1 (10-ounce) can enchilada sauce
- ½ (1.25-ounce) package taco seasoning
- 3 cups cooked pasta shells
- 1 cup (4 ounces) shredded colby cheese
- ½ cup (2 ounces) shredded sharp Cheddar cheese

COOK sausage in a large skillet, stirring until meat crumbles and is no longer pink; drain. Stir in chili beans and next 3 ingredients; cook 3 minutes.

ADD pasta to sausage mixture, and cook over medium heat 3 minutes. Stir in colby and Cheddar cheeses until melted and well blended. Serve in bowls.

NOTE: For testing purposes only, we used Bush's Best Chili Hot Beans.

STACEY BOOTH
HERMITAGE, TENNESSEE

Casual Menu From the Grill

Invite the neighbors over, and welcome the season at a laid-back gathering with great food.

Fuss-Free Dinner From the Grill

Serves 6

Citrus Party Olives

Rosemary Grilled Flank Steak
or Lamb Chops

Italian Eggplant Vinaigrette

Smoked Mozzarella Pasta Salad

Very Berry Sundaes

Entertaining is easy when you take it outside. If you need a stress-free evening with friends, here's a great menu. Let your budget help you choose between lamb chops (more expensive) or flank steak (a nice cut, but less costly per pound than the chops). The joy of this party is the make-ahead aspect—you can do everything except cook the meat beforehand. As you finish up, friends can join you to enjoy that fresh-from-the-grill aroma.

While the atmosphere is casual, the food is stellar. You'll love what the smoky flavor adds to the pasta salad and eggplant vinaigrette. Bring out your favorite beverages, and you're set. Refreshing berry sundaes offer a sweet, cool ending to the meal. So go ahead—invite your friends to supper from the grill.

CITRUS PARTY OLIVES

make ahead

MAKES 6 SERVINGS

Prep: 20 min., Chill: 8 hrs., Stand: 30 min.

Flecks of grated orange and lemon rind hint at the flavor of these marinated olives.

- 4 garlic cloves, chopped
- ½ cup olive oil
- 1 tablespoon grated orange rind
- 2 teaspoons grated lemon rind
- ⅓ cup fresh orange juice
- 3 tablespoons fresh lemon juice
- 1½ teaspoons chopped fresh rosemary
- 1 teaspoon coarse salt
- ½ teaspoon freshly ground pepper
- 4 (6-ounce) cans pitted ripe olives, drained
- Garnish: fresh rosemary sprigs

STIR together first 10 ingredients in a large bowl.

COVER and chill 8 hours. Let stand 30 minutes at room temperature before serving. Garnish, if desired. Serve with a slotted spoon.

DIANNE BUSH
HOPE HULL, ALABAMA

ROSEMARY GRILLED FLANK STEAK

MAKES 6 TO 8 SERVINGS

Prep: 20 min., Chill: 2 hrs., Grill: 20 min.

We found that this delicious grilled lamb chop recipe works equally well with flank steak.

- 1 cup red wine
- ½ cup olive oil
- ½ teaspoon Worcestershire sauce
- 2 tablespoons chopped fresh parsley
- 2 bay leaves
- 2 green onions, chopped
- 3 garlic cloves, minced
- 1 teaspoon dried oregano
- 1 teaspoon salt
- ½ teaspoon pepper
- 2 pounds flank steak
- Rosemary sprigs
- 2 tablespoons fresh lemon juice

COMBINE first 10 ingredients. Reserve ⅓ cup red wine mixture.

PLACE flank steak in a large shallow dish or a large zip-top plastic bag. Pour red wine mixture over steak. Cover or seal bag, and chill 2 to 4 hours, turning occasionally.

REMOVE flank steak from marinade, discarding marinade.

GRILL, covered with grill lid, over medium-high heat (350° to 400°) for 8 to 10 minutes on each side or to desired degree of doneness, brushing with reserved wine mixture using rosemary sprigs. Cut steak diagonally across the grain into thin strips. Squeeze juice over steak before serving.

ROSEMARY GRILLED LAMB CHOPS: Place 8 (1½-inch-thick) lamb chops (about 2 pounds) in a large zip-top plastic bag. Add red wine mixture, reserving ⅓ cup. Seal bag, and chill 2 hours, turning occasionally. Remove lamb chops from marinade, discarding marinade. Grill chops, covered with grill lid, over medium-high heat (350° to 400°) 8 to 10 minutes on each side or to desired degree of doneness, brushing with reserved wine mixture using rosemary sprigs. Squeeze juice over chops before serving.

GEORGIA THORSTENSON
HERNDON, VIRGINIA

ITALIAN EGGPLANT VINAIGRETTE

make ahead

MAKES 6 SERVINGS

Prep: 25 min., Stand: 1 hr., Grill: 19 min., Chill: 8 hrs.

- 2 large eggplants
- 2½ teaspoons salt, divided
- 2 small zucchini
- 2 yellow squash
- 4 tablespoons olive oil
- 4 garlic cloves, minced (about 2 tablespoons)
- ¼ cup chopped fresh basil
- ¼ cup chopped fresh mint
- 3 tablespoons balsamic vinegar
- Garnishes: halved grape tomatoes, fresh basil sprigs

CUT eggplants crosswise into ½-inch slices; sprinkle cut sides with 1½ teaspoons salt. Place slices in a single layer on paper towels; let stand 1 hour.

CUT zucchini and squash lengthwise into ⅛- to ¼-inch-thick slices; set aside.

PROCESS ½ teaspoon salt, 4 tablespoons olive oil, minced garlic, chopped basil, chopped mint, and balsamic vinegar in a food processor, stopping to scrape down sides.

RINSE eggplant slices with water, and pat dry. Brush slices with olive oil mixture; sprinkle with ¼ teaspoon salt.

ARRANGE eggplant in a single layer on a lightly greased grill.

GRILL eggplant slices, covered with grill lid, over medium-high heat (350° to 400°) 10 to 12 minutes or until lightly browned, turning and brushing with olive oil mixture. Remove from grill.

SPRINKLE zucchini and squash slices with remaining ¼ teaspoon salt, brush with olive oil mixture. Arrange slices in a single layer on a lightly greased grill.

GRILL zucchini and squash slices, covered with grill lid, over medium-high heat 5 minutes; turn and grill 2 more minutes.

ARRANGE grilled eggplant, zucchini, and squash in an even layer in a 13- x 9-inch baking dish. Pour remaining olive oil mixture over vegetables. Cover and chill 8 hours. Garnish, if desired.

GILDA LESTER
WILMINGTON, NORTH CAROLINA

Easy Tabletop Touches

We found the supplies for smart-looking table touches at a combination crafts-fabric store.

■ Give new life to napkins you already have. Thread beads and buttons onto embroidery floss, then sew onto one corner of each napkin. Accent pastel colors with bright, primary colors.

■ Answer guests' question of "Is the tea sweet or unsweet?" or "Does this have alcohol?" with beverage labels. Braid embroidery floss, and attach it to a paper label using stationery sealing wax pressed with a decorative stamp. Follow package directions for using wax. For a quick alternative, use decorative stickers. Label each beverage, including water, to follow through with the idea.

■ Help partygoers keep track of their wine glasses. To make your own wine glass charms, string one color button for each guest onto fine gauge wire along with beads. Tie onto the stemware with a ribbon.

■ Send friends home with a treat. Pick up scrapbook paper, small organza bags, ribbons, embroidery floss, and a hole puncher to make party favor bags. Fill each one with Jordan almonds.

SMOKED MOZZARELLA PASTA SALAD

make ahead • vegetarian

MAKES 6 SERVINGS

Prep: 20 min., Cook: 12 min., Chill: 1 hr.

- 1 (6-ounce) jar marinated artichoke hearts
- 1 (8-ounce) package rotini pasta, cooked
- 1 (7-ounce) jar roasted red bell peppers, drained and cut into strips
- ½ pound smoked mozzarella cheese, cut into ½-inch cubes*
- ½ (5-ounce) bag baby spinach leaves (about 1½ cups)
- ½ (4.5-ounce) can chopped green chiles, drained
- ½ cup mayonnaise
- ½ cup grated Parmesan cheese
- ¼ cup pine nuts, toasted
- 1 garlic clove, minced
- ½ teaspoon pepper
- Garnishes: tomato wedges, baby spinach leaves

DRAIN artichokes, reserving marinade. Cut artichokes into strips, and place in a large bowl. Add pasta and next 4 ingredients, and gently toss.

STIR together reserved artichoke marinade, mayonnaise, and next 4 ingredients until blended. Add to pasta mixture, stirring to combine. Cover and chill 1 hour. Garnish, if desired.

*Substitute ½ pound smoked Gouda or Cheddar cheese for smoked mozzarella, if desired.

ROBERTA FRANK
CASTROVILLE, CALIFORNIA

VERY BERRY SUNDAES

make ahead

MAKES 6 SERVINGS

Prep: 10 min., Chill: 2 hrs.

We used blueberries, blackberries, and raspberries for mixed fresh berries.

- 2¼ cups fresh strawberries, halved
- 2¼ cups mixed fresh berries
- 3 tablespoons sugar
- 2 tablespoons orange liqueur
- 2 teaspoons grated orange rind
- ½ teaspoon chopped mint
- 3 cups fruit sorbet
- Garnishes: orange zest, fresh mint sprigs

COMBINE first 6 ingredients, tossing lightly to combine. Cover and chill up to 2 hours.

SCOOP ½ cup sorbet into each of 6 serving dishes. Spoon two-thirds cup of berries over sorbet in each dish. Garnish, if desired. Serve immediately.

JOY MAURER
CLERMONT, GEORGIA

Coffee Cake Reinvented

Reader Jennifer Dale of Clarksville, Tennessee, asked us to transform her family's favorite dense, buttery sour cream breakfast treat into one loaded with flavor, not tons of fat and calories. We used fat-free sour cream and cream cheese to provide moisture and a creamy tang. Her original recipe called for three sticks of butter, but our version gets lots of buttery flavor with just half a stick. For fresh flavor and fragrance, we relied on a splash of orange juice. We hope you enjoy this wonderful lightened version as much as we did.

SOUR CREAM COFFEE CAKE

make ahead

MAKES 16 SERVINGS

Prep: 30 min.; Bake: 50 min.; Cool: 1 hr. 10 min.

- Vegetable cooking spray
- 1 cup coarsely chopped pecans, toasted
- 1 cup firmly packed light brown sugar
- 1 tablespoon ground cinnamon
- 3 cups all-purpose flour
- 1½ teaspoons baking soda
- 1½ teaspoons baking powder
- ¾ teaspoon salt
- ¼ cup butter, softened
- 1 (8-ounce) package fat-free cream cheese, softened
- 1½ cups granulated sugar
- 1 large egg
- ½ cup egg substitute
- 2 teaspoons vanilla extract
- 1 (16-ounce) container fat-free sour cream
- 1 cup powdered sugar
- 1 tablespoon orange juice

COAT a 12-cup nonstick Bundt pan with cooking spray.

COMBINE pecans, brown sugar, and cinnamon; set aside.

COMBINE flour, baking soda, baking powder, and salt.

BEAT butter, cream cheese, and sugar at medium speed with an electric mixer until creamy. Add egg, and beat until blended. Add egg substitute and vanilla, beating until blended. Add flour mixture to butter mixture alternately with sour cream, beginning and ending with flour mixture. Beat on high 1 minute.

POUR one-third of batter into prepared pan. Sprinkle batter with half of pecan mixture. Repeat layers twice, ending with batter.

BAKE at 350° for 50 minutes or until a wooden pick inserted in center comes out clean. Cool in pan on a wire rack 10 minutes. Run a knife around edges to loosen sides. Gently turn cake out onto wire rack. Cool 1 hour. Transfer to a serving plate.

WHISK together powdered sugar and orange juice. Drizzle over cake.

Calories 372 (23% from fat); Fat 9.5g (sat 2.8g, mono 1.1g, poly 0.4g); Protein 7.9g; Carb 64g; Fiber 1.3g; Chol 25mg; Iron 1.7mg; Sodium 429mg; Calc 102mg

World-Class Sides

Try some fun ingredients from the international aisle when your side dishes need a lift. These mouthwatering recipes combine familiar favorites such as pasta, peanuts, and zucchini with more global ingredients such as tomatillos, couscous, and orzo. If you've never cooked orzo (rice-shaped pasta) or couscous (tiny, granulated pasta), don't worry—it couldn't be easier. They both boil up just like regular pasta, only faster.

SOUTHWESTERN STUFFED ZUCCHINI

MAKES 6 SERVINGS

Prep: 30 min., Bake: 30 min.

Southwestern Stuffed Zucchini gets its flair from Mexican tomatillos.

- 6 medium zucchini or yellow squash
- ¾ teaspoon salt
- ¾ cup (3 ounces) shredded Monterey Jack cheese
- ½ cup chopped green onions
- 5 bacon slices, cooked and crumbled
- 3 small tomatillos, husked and chopped
- ½ teaspoon pepper
- ½ cup breadcrumbs
- 2 to 3 tablespoons butter or margarine, melted

CUT zucchini in half lengthwise, and remove seeds. Microwave in batches in an 11- x 7-inch glass dish at HIGH 5 to 7 minutes or until tender. Scoop out pulp, keeping shells intact; reserve pulp. Sprinkle shells with salt.

STIR together reserved pulp, cheese, and next 4 ingredients.

FILL shells with pulp mixture; place in a 13- x 9-inch baking dish. Sprinkle evenly with breadcrumbs; drizzle with butter.

BAKE at 375° for 30 minutes.

LILLIAN GOODSTEIN
GEORGETOWN, TEXAS

MEDITERRANEAN COUSCOUS SALAD

fast fixin's

MAKES 4 SERVINGS

Prep: 15 min., Cook: 2 min., Stand: 5 min.

- ¾ cup vegetable or chicken broth
- 1 cup uncooked couscous
- 2 tablespoons olive oil
- 1 (14-ounce) can quartered artichoke hearts, drained and coarsely chopped
- 1 (10-ounce) can diced tomatoes and green chiles, drained
- ½ cup crumbled feta cheese
- ¼ cup pine nuts, toasted
- ¼ cup pitted kalamata olives
- 2 green onions, chopped
- 1 garlic clove, minced
- 2 tablespoons chopped fresh basil
- 2 tablespoons chopped fresh mint
- 2 tablespoons chopped fresh parsley
- Romaine or baby spinach leaves (optional)

BRING broth to a boil in a saucepan; stir in couscous. Cover, return to a boil, and remove from heat. Let stand 5 minutes. Drizzle with olive oil, and fluff with a fork. Let cool.

COMBINE couscous, artichokes, and next 9 ingredients, tossing gently. Serve over lettuce or spinach, if desired.

CYNTHIA GRIPPAIDI
SPRING HILL, FLORIDA

LENTIL-AND-ORZO SALAD

fast fixin's • make ahead

MAKES 4 SERVINGS

Prep: 15 min., Chill: 2 hrs.

- ¼ cup vinaigrette dressing
- 2 tablespoons fresh lemon juice
- ½ teaspoon ground cumin
- ½ teaspoon salt
- ½ teaspoon ground black pepper
- ¼ teaspoon dried crushed red pepper
- 2 cups cooked lentils
- 1 cup cooked orzo
- ½ red bell pepper, diced
- ½ small red onion, diced
- 1½ tablespoons chopped fresh cilantro

WHISK together first 6 ingredients in a large bowl; add lentils and remaining ingredients, tossing gently to coat.
COVER and chill 2 hours.

DANIELLA DRAUGHOH
PLANTATION, FLORIDA

ASIAN PEANUT-AND-PASTA SALAD

MAKES 4 SERVINGS

Prep: 25 min., Cook: 10 min., Chill: 30 min.

- 1 (7-ounce) package spaghetti
- 1 cup roasted peanuts, coarsely chopped and divided
- 1 cup fresh orange juice
- 2 tablespoons rice wine vinegar
- 2 tablespoons teriyaki marinade and sauce
- 1 tablespoon sesame oil
- ½ teaspoon freshly grated orange rind
- ½ teaspoon garlic powder
- ½ teaspoon dried crushed red pepper
- 1 cup thinly sliced radishes
- 1 carrot, coarsely shredded
- 2 green onions, sliced
- 2 tablespoons chopped fresh cilantro
- 1 avocado, thinly sliced

COOK pasta according to package directions; drain and rinse with cold water; set aside.
PROCESS ½ cup peanuts, orange juice, and next 6 ingredients in a blender until smooth, stopping to scrape down sides.
COMBINE pasta, half of dressing, remaining ½ cup peanuts, radishes, and next 3 ingredients, gently tossing to coat. Cover and chill 30 minutes. Serve salad with remaining dressing and avocado slices.

NOTE: For testing purposes only, we used Kikkoman Teriyaki Marinade and Sauce.

ROXANNE CHAN
ALBANY, CALIFORNIA

Mexican for Supper

These zesty recipes, full of spicy, colorful ingredients, will have you saying *que rico* (yummy)!

Light Mexican Menu

Serves 6 to 8

Beefy Taco Salad or
Pork Tacos With Pineapple Salsa

Smashed Pinto Beans   Tex-Mex Rice With Corn

Light beer

BEEFY TACO SALAD

family favorite

MAKES 6 SERVINGS

Prep: 30 min., Cook: 16 min., Bake: 20 min. per batch, Cool: 5 min. per batch

Oven-safe bowls, cooking spray, and flour tortillas are all you need to create crispy, low-fat edible tortilla bowls.

- 1 pound extra lean ground beef
- Vegetable cooking spray
- 1 small onion, chopped
- 1 garlic clove, pressed
- 1 tablespoon fajita seasoning
- 1 (12-ounce) jar salsa verde, divided
- 6 (8-inch) flour tortillas
- Smashed Pinto Beans (recipe on facing page)*
- ½ head iceberg lettuce, shredded
- Chunky Avocado Sauce
- Garnish: chopped fresh tomatoes

BROWN beef in a nonstick skillet coated with cooking spray 7 minutes, stirring until beef crumbles and is no longer pink. Drain and pat dry with paper towels; set beef aside. Wipe skillet clean.

SAUTÉ onion in skillet coated with cooking spray 5 minutes. Add garlic, and sauté 1 minute. Return beef to skillet. Add fajita seasoning and ½ cup salsa verde. Cook over medium-high heat 3 minutes or until thoroughly heated and liquid is evaporated.

COAT both sides of 1 tortilla with cooking spray. Place tortilla inside a 7-inch oven-safe bowl. Place on a baking sheet. BAKE at 350° for 10 to 15 minutes or until golden. Remove tortilla from bowl; bake 5 more minutes. Remove from oven, and let cool 5 minutes. Repeat with remaining tortillas and cooking spray. (You can prepare 2 or 3 bowls at a time in your oven.)

SPREAD ¼ cup Smashed Pinto Beans on each tortilla shell. Sprinkle with lettuce and beef mixture. Top with Chunky Avocado Sauce. Serve with remaining salsa verde. Garnish, if desired.

*Substitute canned fat-free refried beans, if desired.

NOTE: Look for salsa verde, also called green salsa, in the Mexican food aisle of supermarkets.

Chunky Avocado Sauce:

MAKES 1½ CUPS

Prep: 10 min.

- 2 small avocados, chopped
- 2 large tomatoes, chopped
- ½ cup nonfat sour cream
- 2 tablespoons fresh lime juice
- 2 tablespoons nonfat buttermilk or fat-free milk
- 1 tablespoon chopped fresh cilantro
- ⅛ teaspoon salt

STIR together all ingredients.

Per salad: Calories 391 (34% from fat); Fat 15g (sat 3.6g, mono 2.5g, poly 0.6g); Protein 22g; Carb 45g; Fiber 8.6g; Chol 23mg; Iron 3.7mg; Sodium 993mg; Calc 135mg

PORK TACOS WITH PINEAPPLE SALSA

MAKES 8 SERVINGS

Prep: 30 min., Grill: 8 min., Stand: 10 min.

- 1 tablespoon curry powder
- ½ teaspoon garlic powder
- ¼ teaspoon salt
- ¼ teaspoon freshly ground pepper
- ⅛ teaspoon ground red pepper
- 6 (4-ounce) boneless pork loin chops, trimmed
- Vegetable cooking spray
- Pineapple Salsa
- 8 (8-inch) fat-free flour tortillas, warmed

COMBINE first 5 ingredients; sprinkle over pork chops. Coat pork evenly with cooking spray.

GRILL, covered with grill lid, over medium-high heat (350° to 400°) 3 to 4 minutes on each side or until done. Let stand 10 minutes. Coarsely chop pork.

SERVE with Pineapple Salsa and tortillas.

Pineapple Salsa:

MAKES 2 CUPS

Prep: 15 min.

- ¼ cup orange juice
- 2 tablespoons lemon juice
- 1 tablespoon honey
- ¼ teaspoon salt
- ¼ teaspoon ground pepper
- 2 cups chopped fresh pineapple
- 2 tablespoons chopped fresh cilantro
- ¼ small red onion, chopped

WHISK together first 5 ingredients. Stir in pineapple, cilantro, and onion.

Per taco: Calories 288 (18% from fat); Fat 6g (sat 2g, mono 2.5g, poly 0.5g); Protein 24g; Carb 34g; Fiber 4g; Chol 55mg; Iron 1.5mg; Sodium 417mg; Calc 25mg

SMASHED PINTO BEANS

MAKES 14 (¼-CUP) SERVINGS

Prep: 15 min., Cook: 20 min.

- 1 medium onion, chopped
- 1 teaspoon olive oil
- 2 garlic cloves, minced
- ½ cup tomato sauce
- 2 (15-ounce) cans pinto beans, rinsed and drained
- 1 cup beef broth
- 1 tablespoon hot sauce
- ¼ teaspoon salt
- ¼ teaspoon ground cumin
- ½ teaspoon pepper
- 1 to 2 tablespoons red wine vinegar

SAUTÉ chopped onion in hot olive oil in a Dutch oven over medium-high heat 5 minutes or until onion is tender. Add minced garlic, and sauté 1 minute. Stir in tomato sauce and remaining ingredients.
BRING to a boil; reduce heat, and simmer 8 minutes.
MASH bean mixture with a potato masher until thickened, leaving some beans whole.

Calories 47 (12% from fat); Fat 0.7g (sat 0.1g, mono 0.3g, poly 0.3g); Protein 2.9g; Carb 7.6g; Fiber 2.5g; Chol 0mg; Iron 0.6mg; Sodium 171mg; Calc 17mg

TEX-MEX RICE WITH CORN

MAKES 9 (½-CUP) SERVINGS

Prep: 15 min., Cook: 30 min., Stand: 10 min.

- 1 small onion, chopped (about ½ cup)
- ½ small green bell pepper, chopped
- 2 teaspoons olive oil
- 2 garlic cloves, minced
- 1 cup uncooked long-grain rice
- 1 cup chunky salsa
- 1 (14-ounce) can low-sodium, fat-free chicken broth
- 1 cup frozen whole kernel corn
- 1 teaspoon chicken bouillon granules
- ¼ teaspoon pepper

SAUTÉ onion and bell pepper in hot oil in a medium-size heavy saucepan over medium-high heat 5 minutes; add garlic, and sauté 1 minute. Add rice and salsa; sauté 2 to 3 minutes or until most of liquid is absorbed.
ADD broth and remaining ingredients. Cover, reduce heat, and simmer 15 to 20 minutes or until liquid is absorbed. Stir once to combine ingredients. Cover, remove from heat, and let stand 10 minutes.

Calories 135 (12% from fat); Fat 1.8g (sat 0.4g, mono 0.9g, poly 0.2g); Protein 3.6g; Carb 26g; Fiber 1.4g; Chol 1mg; Iron 1mg; Sodium 315mg; Calc 22mg

BEATRIZ SWIRSKY
SUNRISE, FLORIDA

Taste of the South

Mint Juleps

Kentucky Derby is celebrated the first Saturday in May with visitors from around the world gathering at the race track and all over Louisville. As "My Old Kentucky Home" plays before the race, julep cups are raised high. To Kentuckians, a mint julep is more than a drink; it's a cup of emotion, full of tradition.

The classic version is served in silver julep cups. These are filled to the rim with a refreshing concoction of the finest bourbon, simple syrup, fresh mint, and crushed ice. "Neophytes taking their first sips should know this is a bourbon cocktail that's very traditional, so it will be robust," says Chris Morris, master distiller in training for Brown-Forman Corporation.

This drink is best made individually "to taste" using only fresh ingredients. While Kentucky Colonel mint is commonly used, other varieties work too. The ingredients remain constant, but opinions are varied as to the proper way to make them. Many crush the mint and sugar together (referred to as muddling), while others insist that the mint should be smelled not tasted.

Chill cups before filling with crushed ice to prevent the ice from melting quickly. Julian P. Van Winkle, III, president of Old Rip Van Winkle Distillery in Frankfort, Kentucky, prefers his ice in small chunks.

Before tasting, insert a cocktail straw or coffee stirrer near the mint sprig. Inhale a deep breath, and slowly sip until someone says, "May I fix you another mint julep?"

CLASSIC MINT JULEP

fast fixin's

MAKES 1 (8-OUNCE) JULEP

Prep: 10 min.

Leftover simple syrup keeps in the refrigerator about one week and perfectly sweetens iced tea, in addition to these mighty juleps. *(pictured on page 115)*

- 3 fresh mint leaves
- 1 tablespoon Mint Simple Syrup
- Crushed ice
- 1½ to 2 tablespoons (1 ounce) bourbon
- 1 (4-inch) cocktail straw or coffee stirrer
- 1 fresh mint sprig
- Powdered sugar (optional)

PLACE mint leaves and Mint Simple Syrup in a chilled julep cup. Gently press leaves against cup with back of spoon to release flavors. Pack cup tightly with crushed ice; pour bourbon over ice. Insert straw, place mint sprig directly next to straw, and serve immediately. Sprinkle with powdered sugar, if desired.

Mint Simple Syrup:

MAKES 2 CUPS

Prep: 5 min., Cook: 10 min., Chill: 24 hrs.

- 1 cup sugar
- 1 cup water
- 10 to 12 fresh mint sprigs

BRING sugar and water to a boil in a medium saucepan. Boil, stirring often, 5 minutes or until sugar dissolves. Remove from heat; add mint, and let cool completely. Pour into a glass jar; cover and chill 24 hours. Remove and discard mint.

NOTE: For testing purposes only, we used Woodford Reserve Distiller's Select Bourbon.

Can-Do Grilled Chicken

These great recipes begin with canned drinks.

Chicken grilled over a can of cola or beer is tender and full of flavor. These recipes are adapted from Steven Raichlen's book *Beer-Can Chicken* (Workman Publishing Company, 2002).

BASIC BEER-CAN CHICKEN

MAKES 2 TO 4 SERVINGS

Prep: 10 min.; Grill: 1 hr., 15 min.; Stand: 5 min.

- **2 tablespoons All-Purpose Barbecue Rub, divided**
- **1 (3½- to 4-pound) whole chicken**
- **1 tablespoon vegetable oil**
- **1 (12-ounce) can beer**

SPRINKLE 1 teaspoon All-Purpose Barbecue Rub inside body cavity and ½ teaspoon inside neck cavity of chicken. Rub oil over skin. Sprinkle with 1 tablespoon All-Purpose Barbecue Rub, and rub over skin.

POUR out half of beer (about ¾ cup), and reserve for another use, leaving remaining beer in can. Make 2 additional holes in top of can. Spoon remaining 1½ teaspoons rub into beer can. Beer will start to foam.

PLACE chicken upright onto the beer can, fitting can into cavity. Pull legs forward to form a tripod, allowing chicken to stand upright.

PREPARE a fire by piling charcoal on one side of grill, leaving other side empty. (For gas grills, light only one side.) Place a drip pan on unlit side, and place food rack on grill. Place chicken upright over drip pan. Grill, covered with grill lid, 1 hour and 15 minutes or until golden and a meat thermometer inserted in thigh registers 180°.

REMOVE chicken from grill, and let stand 5 minutes; carefully remove can.

All-Purpose Barbecue Rub:

MAKES ABOUT 1 CUP

Prep: 5 min.

- **¼ cup coarse salt**
- **¼ cup firmly packed dark brown sugar**
- **¼ cup sweet paprika**
- **2 tablespoons pepper**

COMBINE all ingredients. Store mixture in an airtight jar, away from heat, up to 6 months.

COLA-CAN CHICKEN

family favorite

MAKES 2 TO 4 SERVINGS

Prep: 20 min.; Grill: 1 hr., 15 min.; Stand: 5 min.

- **2 tablespoons Barbecue Rub, divided**
- **1 (3½- to 4-pound) whole chicken**
- **3 tablespoons vegetable oil**
- **1 (12-ounce) can cola**
- **Cola Barbecue Sauce**

SPRINKLE 1 teaspoon Barbecue Rub inside body cavity and ½ teaspoon inside neck cavity of chicken.

RUB oil over skin. Sprinkle with 1 tablespoon Barbecue Rub, and rub over skin. Pour out half of cola (about ¾ cup), and reserve for Cola Barbecue Sauce, leaving remaining cola in can. Make 2 additional holes in top of can. Spoon remaining 1½ teaspoons rub into cola can. Cola will start to foam.

PLACE chicken upright onto the cola can, fitting can into cavity. Pull legs forward to form a tripod, allowing chicken to stand upright.

PREPARE a fire by piling charcoal on one side of grill, leaving other side empty. (For gas grills, light only one side.) Place a drip pan on unlit side, and place food rack on grill. Place chicken upright over drip pan. Grill, covered with grill lid, 1 hour and 15 minutes or until golden and a meat thermometer inserted in thigh registers 180°.

REMOVE chicken from grill, and let stand 5 minutes; carefully remove can. Serve with Cola Barbecue Sauce.

Barbecue Rub:

MAKES 3 TABLESPOONS

Prep: 5 min.

- **1 tablespoon mild chili powder**
- **2 teaspoons salt**
- **2 teaspoons light brown sugar**
- **1 teaspoon pepper**
- **1 teaspoon ground cumin**
- **½ teaspoon garlic powder**
- **¼ teaspoon ground red pepper**

COMBINE all ingredients.

Cola Barbecue Sauce:

MAKES ABOUT 1½ CUPS

Prep: 15 min., Cook: 8 min.

- **1 tablespoon butter**
- **½ small onion, minced**
- **1 tablespoon minced fresh ginger**
- **1 garlic clove, minced**
- **¾ cup reserved cola**
- **¾ cup ketchup**
- **½ teaspoon grated lemon rind**
- **2 tablespoons fresh lemon juice**
- **2 tablespoons Worcestershire sauce**
- **2 tablespoons steak sauce**
- **½ teaspoon liquid smoke**
- **½ teaspoon pepper**
- **Salt to taste**

MELT butter in a heavy saucepan over medium heat. Add onion, ginger, and garlic; sauté 3 minutes or until tender.

STIR in reserved cola; bring mixture to a boil. Stir in ketchup and remaining ingredients; bring to a boil. Reduce heat, and simmer 5 minutes.

NOTE: For testing purposes only, we used A1 Steak Sauce.

Stir-and-Drop Cookies

The kids are home from school, the cookie jar is empty, and you need to produce a sweet snack now. Fear not. These recipes offer speed and flavor from just a few ingredients. Simply put all the ingredients in a large bowl, stir well, and then drop onto baking sheets. The recipes are so easy, even the kids can do it—although they may need mom's or dad's muscle for stirring. Your family will call it fun, and you'll call it child's play.

CREAM CHEESE COOKIES

family favorite • fast fixin's

MAKES 4½ TO 5 DOZEN

Prep: 5 min., Bake: 15 min. per batch

Use the smallest holes of a grater to grate lemon rind; be careful not to get the bitter white flesh that's underneath the yellow skin.

- 1 cup butter, softened
- 1 (8-ounce) package cream cheese, softened
- 2 cups sugar
- 2 cups all-purpose flour
- 2 teaspoons grated lemon rind
- 1 teaspoon vanilla extract

STIR together butter and cream cheese in a large bowl until smooth; stir in sugar and remaining ingredients. Drop by teaspoonfuls onto ungreased baking sheets.
BAKE at 350° for 13 to 15 minutes or until light brown. Remove to wire racks to cool.

NOTE: For easier stirring, allow cream cheese to soften at room temperature for 30 minutes, or remove wrap and microwave at HIGH 15 to 20 seconds.

CREAM CHEESE-CHOCOLATE CHIP COOKIES: Omit lemon rind, and add 1 cup semisweet chocolate morsels. Bake as directed.

BARBARA SHERRER
BAY CITY, TEXAS

SOFT COCONUT MACAROONS

fast fixin's

MAKES 2½ TO 3 DOZEN

Prep: 10 min., Bake: 20 min. per batch

Clear vanilla extract keeps the macaroons pearly white, but regular vanilla works fine.

- 4 egg whites
- 2⅔ cups sweetened flaked coconut
- ⅔ cup sugar
- ¼ cup all-purpose flour
- ½ teaspoon clear vanilla extract
- ¼ teaspoon salt
- ¼ to ½ teaspoon almond extract

STIR together all ingredients in a large bowl, blending well. Drop dough by teaspoonfuls onto lightly greased baking sheets.
BAKE at 325° for 18 to 20 minutes. Remove to wire racks to cool.

PATRICIA A. ODAM
GREENVILLE, CALIFORNIA

QUICK PEANUT BUTTER COOKIES

family favorite • fast fixin's

MAKES 2½ TO 3 DOZEN

Prep: 10 min., Bake: 10 min. per batch, Cool: 2 min.

- 1½ cups powdered sugar
- 1 cup smooth peanut butter
- 1 large egg
- 1 teaspoon vanilla extract

STIR together all ingredients in a large bowl, blending well.
ROLL cookie dough into ¾-inch balls, and place on lightly greased or parchment paper-lined baking sheets. Lightly press cookies with a fork.
BAKE at 325° for 10 minutes. Let cool 2 minutes on baking sheets; remove to wire racks to cool completely.

LAURA MORRIS
BUNNELL, FLORIDA

CRISPY PRALINE COOKIES

family favorite • fast fixin's

MAKES ABOUT 2 DOZEN

Prep: 10 min., Bake: 15 min. per batch, Cool: 1 min.

Let the butter sit at room temperature for several hours, or soften it in the microwave at HIGH for 10 to 20 seconds (do not melt).

- 1 cup all-purpose flour
- 1 cup firmly packed dark brown sugar
- 1 large egg
- 1 cup chopped pecans
- ½ cup butter, softened
- 1 teaspoon vanilla extract

STIR together all ingredients in a large bowl, blending well. Drop cookie dough by tablespoonfuls onto ungreased baking sheets.
BAKE at 350° for 13 to 15 minutes. Cool on baking sheets 1 minute; remove cookies to wire racks to cool completely.

CRISPY PRALINE-CHOCOLATE CHIP COOKIES: Add 1 cup semisweet chocolate morsels. Bake as directed.

JULIA PENNINGTON
FORT WORTH, TEXAS

Cook's Notes

- Make cleanup quick by lining baking sheets with parchment paper. This versatile tool is perfectly sized for baking sheets, comes in rolls, and can be reused. If it's not available in a large supermarket in your area, ask the store manager to order it for you.
- If you don't have wire cooling racks, line your counter with a towel, and top it with wax paper. Allow cookies to cool there after removing from pan.

from our kitchen

Thank goodness we can find tortillas everywhere now. The Mexican flatbread has become a staple in most of our kitchens. Whether you like corn tortillas or soft flour ones, they can be heated in the oven or microwave, steamed, fried, or grilled.

- Use flour tortillas instead of noodles in lasagna.
- Turn tortillas into edible serving bowls. Press them into fluted pans, and bake. Pans are available by mail order through Chef's Catalog (1-800-338-3232). Or turn to "Living Light" on page 128 for instructions on making them using heat-proof bowls.
- Cut leftover tortillas into triangles, and deep-fry or bake for chips. For a tasty baked version, spray triangles with butter-flavored cooking spray. Combine ½ teaspoon dried basil, ½ teaspoon garlic powder, and ½ teaspoon ground cumin in a zip-top plastic bag. Add the tortilla pieces; shake to coat. Place chips on a baking sheet. Bake at 400° for 5 minutes or until crisp. Transfer to a wire rack to cool.
- Cut tortillas into thin strips; bake or fry for salad or soup toppings.
- Use them as sandwich wraps. We like the dried tomato and spinach flavors. Look for these with other fresh (not frozen) flour tortillas.

The Ripe Time for Avocados

More avocados are consumed in the month of May than any other time because of Cinco de Mayo. Whether you celebrate the holiday or not, now is a great time to add avocados to your menus. They're delicious sliced and served on top of grilled burgers or BLTs or tossed with salad greens and drizzled with balsamic vinegar. If you haven't had experience with this fruit, here's how to handle it.

- Cut it lengthwise around the seed. Twist the halves in opposite directions to separate. Slide a spoon under the seed to remove it. Slide a spoon between the skin and the fruit to scoop it away from the peel.
- Drizzle cut avocado pieces with lemon or lime juice to retard discoloration. Without the acid, the beautiful bright green color will turn a dark olive-drab.
- Ripe avocados have very dark green skins and feel soft to the touch. If you get some that aren't ready yet, place them in a paper bag with an apple for two to three days at room temperature.
- Store ripe avocados in the refrigerator up to three days. To store them in the freezer, mash and add 1 teaspoon lemon juice per avocado; seal in an airtight container.

The Ingredient List

A recipe isn't so easy if an ingredient is unfamiliar or isn't clear. Here's help interpreting some of our ingredient listings.

Frozen seasoning blend—a bag of mixed chopped onion, bell pepper, and celery located in the freezer among frozen vegetables. It's mainly available in the Southeast. You can substitute 1 chopped onion, 1 chopped bell pepper, and a chopped celery rib if you can't find the frozen blend.

All-purpose baking mix—products such as Bisquick or Pioneer baking mixes that have the leavening agents already included. They make fast work of pancakes, biscuits, shortcakes, etc.

Greek seasoning—a blend of dried oregano, garlic, mint, onion, salt, and parsley. Two brands offering this seasoning blend are McCormick and Cavender's.

Tips and Tidbits

- The next time you cook green beans, steam them. Besides being a fat-free method, steaming preserves their flavor and most of the nutrients. They'll also keep that beautiful green color. If you don't have a steamer basket, use your metal colander or strainer inside a large saucepan or Dutch oven with a tight-fitting lid. Fill the pot with about 1 inch of water, making sure the water does not touch the bottom of the basket or colander. Bring the water to a boil; then place the beans in the basket, and place it over the boiling water. Cover and steam 4 to 5 minutes or until they crunch the way you like them. Remove the basket with pot-holders as soon as the beans are done. Sprinkle with a little salt, drizzle with butter, and serve immediately. You could also cool them completely, seal in an airtight container, and refrigerate for tomorrow's salad plate.

Share the Flavors of Summer

It's easier than you think with these divine jams and jellies.

There's just something rewarding about making homemade spreads. But most of us don't want to sweat over the stove all day, no matter how much we like our friends. Fret not. We've chosen recipes that are made in small batches, and most can be ready in less than 40 minutes. These recipes are perfect for first-time "jammies" as well as seasoned preservers. The best part? Everyone will think you've been in the kitchen all day jarring these sweet jewels. *(pictured on pages 150-151)*

CARROT-ORANGE MARMALADE

MAKES 7 (½-PINT) JARS

Prep: 15 min., Cook: 25 min., Process: 10 min.

- 4 cups sugar
- 3 large oranges, thinly sliced
- 1 (10-ounce) bag matchstick carrots
- 2 teaspoons lemon rind (rind from 1 lemon)
- 2 tablespoons fresh lemon juice

BRING all ingredients to a full rolling boil over medium heat in a Dutch oven, stirring occasionally, until sugar is dissolved and syrup thickens. Reduce heat, and simmer, stirring occasionally, 15 to 20 minutes. Remove from heat; skim off any foam.

POUR hot marmalade immediately into hot, sterilized jars, filling to ¼ inch from top. Remove air bubbles; wipe jar rims. Cover at once with metal lids, and screw on bands.

PROCESS in boiling-water bath 10 minutes.

BARBARA ANDERSON
NORWELL, MASSACHUSETTS

PEACH-ROSEMARY JAM

MAKES 7 (½-PINT) JARS

Prep: 25 min., Cook: 10 min., Process: 10 min.

- 4 cups peeled and chopped fresh peaches or nectarines
- 1 teaspoon grated lime rind
- ¼ cup fresh lime juice
- 2 rosemary sprigs
- 1 (1¾-ounce) package powdered fruit pectin
- 5 cups sugar

BRING first 5 ingredients to a full rolling boil in a Dutch oven. Boil 1 minute, stirring constantly. Add sugar to peach mixture, and bring to a full rolling boil; boil 1 minute, stirring constantly. Remove from heat. Remove and discard rosemary sprigs; skim off any foam.

POUR hot mixture immediately into hot, sterilized jars, filling to ¼ inch from top. Remove air bubbles; wipe jar rims. Cover at once with metal lids, and screw on bands.

PROCESS in boiling-water bath 10 minutes.

RITA GIBBON
BIRMINGHAM, ALABAMA

STRAWBERRY-PORT JAM

MAKES 7 (½-PINT) JARS

Prep: 15 min., Cook: 10 min., Process: 10 min.

We first made this recipe with fresh strawberries, but they didn't hold their shape as well as frozen ones.

- 2 (10-ounce) packages frozen unsweetened strawberries, thawed
- 1½ cups ruby port
- 1 teaspoon grated lemon rind
- ½ teaspoon ground nutmeg
- 1 (1¾-ounce) package powdered fruit pectin
- 4 cups sugar

CHOP or crush thawed strawberries in a 4-cup measuring cup. Add water to strawberries to measure 2½ cups.

STIR together strawberry mixture, ruby port, grated lemon rind, and ground nutmeg in a large saucepan. Stir in fruit pectin.

BRING mixture to a full rolling boil, and boil, stirring constantly, 1 minute. Add sugar, stirring constantly, and bring to a full rolling boil. Boil 1 minute. Remove from heat, and skim off any foam.

POUR hot jam immediately into hot, sterilized jars, filling to ¼ inch from top. Remove air bubbles; wipe jar rims. Cover at once with metal lids, and screw on bands.

PROCESS in boiling-water bath 10 minutes.

NOTE: Ruby port is a deep red-colored sweet wine typically enjoyed as an after-dinner drink. It's usually sold in liquor stores because of a higher alcohol content than other wines.

LYNN YOUNG
KNOXVILLE, TENNESSEE

Canning Can-dos

■ For a kit that contains everything but the pot, Wal-Mart offers the Back to Basics Home Canning Kit for $12.86. It's only available on their Web site, **www.walmart.com**

■ For lots more on making canning easy and fun, read "From Our Kitchen" on page 148. Also visit **www.homecanning.com** for great canning tips.

SPICY BLUEBERRY-CITRUS MARMALADE

MAKES 5 (½-PINT) JARS

Prep: 15 min., Cook: 40 min., Process: 10 min.

- 1 orange
- 1 lemon
- 1 lime
- 2 cups water
- ½ teaspoon dried crushed red pepper
- 2 cups fresh blueberries*
- 2 cups sugar

CUT rinds from citrus fruit into thin strips. Set aside.

SQUEEZE juice and pulp from orange, lemon, and lime into a bowl. Set aside.

BRING rind strips, 2 cups water, and red pepper to a boil in a saucepan. Cover, reduce heat, and simmer 25 minutes or until rinds are very tender.

ADD blueberries, sugar, and citrus pulp and juice to saucepan. Bring to a full rolling boil; boil, uncovered and stirring often, 15 minutes or until a gel forms. Remove from heat; skim off any foam.

POUR hot mixture immediately into hot, sterilized jars, filling to ¼ inch from top. Remove air bubbles; wipe jar rims. Cover at once with metal lids, and screw on bands.

PROCESS in boiling-water bath 10 minutes.

*Substitute 2 cups frozen blueberries, thawed, if desired.

EASIEST PEPPER JELLY

MAKES 1 CUP

Prep: 5 min., Cook: 5 min., Chill: 8 hrs.

- ½ cup apple jelly
- ½ cup orange marmalade
- 1 teaspoon apple cider vinegar
- 1 tablespoon seeded and chopped jalapeño pepper
- 1 tablespoon chopped green onion

STIR together all ingredients in a large saucepan over low heat until jelly and marmalade are melted and mixture is blended. Cool. Cover and chill 8 hours.

NANCY SMITH
BLUE RIDGE, GEORGIA

TART BASIL JELLY

fast fixin's

MAKES 7 (½-PINT) JARS

Prep: 5 min., Cook: 10 min., Process: 5 min.

Serve this jelly or any of the other variations atop goat cheese or cream cheese with crispy crackers for a last-minute appetizer.

- 6¼ cups sugar
- 2 cups water
- 1 cup white vinegar
- 1 cup loosely packed fresh basil leaves
- 6 drops green liquid food coloring
- 2 (3-ounce) packages liquid fruit pectin

BRING first 5 ingredients to a boil in a large saucepan. Add pectin, and bring to a full rolling boil. Boil 1 minute. Remove from heat. Remove and discard basil leaves; skim off any foam.

POUR hot mixture immediately into hot, sterilized jars, filling to ¼ inch from top. Remove air bubbles; wipe jar rims. Cover at once with metal lids, and screw on bands.

PROCESS in boiling-water bath 5 minutes.

SOUTHWEST JELLY: Add 1 seeded and thinly sliced jalapeño pepper, and substitute 1 cup cilantro leaves for 1 cup basil leaves. Substitute 20 drops red liquid food coloring for 6 drops green food coloring.

MINT JELLY: Substitute 1 cup mint leaves for 1 cup basil leaves.

NOTE: Jellies usually require only 5 minutes of processing because of their higher acid content.

LYNN YOUNG
KNOXVILLE, TENNESSEE

Tasty Southern Sides

The next time you need something in a hurry, whether for a weeknight supper or weekend gathering, try these easy recipes. Two of the dishes get a jump start with convenience products: Italian Mashed Potatoes start with a frozen mashed potato base, and frozen cut okra can be substituted for fresh in Nutty Okra. The red potatoes used in Vegetable Potato Salad require only a short cooking time, and the basil and feta cheese provide a refreshing change of taste. All these recipes feature family-friendly flavors and are ready in about 30 minutes.

ITALIAN MASHED POTATOES

family favorite • fast fixin's

MAKES 4 SERVINGS

Prep: 20 min.

- 1 (22-ounce) package frozen mashed potatoes
- 2⅔ cups milk
- ¾ cup shredded Parmesan cheese, divided
- ¾ teaspoon salt
- ½ teaspoon pepper
- ½ cup refrigerated pesto

COMBINE mashed potatoes and milk in a large glass bowl.

MICROWAVE, uncovered, at HIGH for 12 minutes. Stir in ½ cup cheese, salt, and pepper.

SPREAD half of potato mixture in a lightly greased 8- x 8-inch dish. Spoon pesto over potato mixture. Top evenly with remaining potato mixture. Sprinkle with the remaining ¼ cup cheese; microwave at HIGH 2 minutes.

MARY MARGARET RUSSO
LAFAYETTE, LOUISIANA

NUTTY OKRA

MAKES 4 SERVINGS

Prep: 10 min., Fry: 4 min. per batch

Use a food processor to effortlessly chop the peanuts.

- **1 cup all-purpose baking mix**
- **½ cup finely chopped dry-roasted, salted peanuts**
- **1 teaspoon salt**
- **½ teaspoon pepper**
- **1 pound fresh okra, cut into ¼-inch pieces***
- **Peanut oil**

STIR together baking mix, chopped peanuts, salt, and pepper in a large bowl. Add okra, tossing to coat; gently press peanut mixture into okra.

POUR oil to a depth of 2 inches into a Dutch oven or cast-iron skillet; heat to 375°. Fry okra, in batches, 4 minutes or until golden; drain on paper towels.

*Substitute 1(16-ounce) package frozen cut okra, thawed, for fresh, if desired.

JINA BREAZEALE
GUYTON, GEORGIA

VEGETABLE POTATO SALAD

MAKES 6 SERVINGS

Prep: 20 min., Cook: 11 min.

We like our green beans crisp, but if you prefer more tender beans, lengthen the cook time.

- **1 pound fresh green beans, trimmed**
- **2 pounds small red potatoes, quartered**
- **1 pint cherry tomatoes, halved**
- **¼ cup crumbled feta cheese**
- **½ teaspoon salt**
- **¼ teaspoon pepper**
- **⅓ cup olive oil**
- **2 tablespoons balsamic vinegar**
- **1 garlic clove, minced**
- **1 tablespoon fresh chopped basil**

COOK green beans in boiling salted water to cover 3 minutes or until crisp-tender;

drain. Plunge into ice water to stop the cooking process; drain well, and set aside.
COOK quartered potatoes in boiling salted water to cover 8 minutes or until tender. Drain.
COMBINE beans and potatoes in a bowl. Add tomatoes and next 3 ingredients; gently toss.
WHISK together olive oil and remaining 3 ingredients. Drizzle half of dressing over bean mixture, and gently toss. Drizzle with remaining dressing just before serving.

MATT LANKES
AUSTIN, TEXAS

Spontaneous Party

The lazy days of summer speak to the soul, encouraging us to spend more time under a canary-colored sun, swapping stories with guests. It's the time of year when a brief chat with a neighbor turns into a full-fledged conversation and simply spotting a friend at the supermarket leaves you longing for time to catch up. Why not take advantage of the weather by extending your summer socializing with an easy, unplanned party?

Casual, outdoor gatherings help you slow down and reconnect. Fortunately, not every get-together mandates mailed invitations. A delightful summer gathering can be a simple endeavor, where everyday fare spruced up with one succulent standout, such as our Lamb Kabobs, can make a marvelous meal. Just marinate the meat, and don't worry about it until you're ready to grill.

As for accompaniments, rely on low-maintenance staples such as steamed rice and a side salad. Not only are these perfect companion dishes, but they'll keep you out of the kitchen and in the yard—conversing with neighbors and catching the sunset.

For this type of fun, no-frills party, even your dessert can be seasonal and simple. Instead of baking, line a platter with crisp watermelon wedges. This fruit will enhance the laid-back feel while giving guests a sweet yet healthy end. Or

another classic option is serving scoops of creamy vanilla ice cream.

To decorate for a spur-of-the-moment dinner, don't overwhelm yourself with extravagant centerpieces. A few strategically placed citronella candles (which light up the setting as they hold bugs at bay) can serve as attractive, practical, and decorative elements. A single vase filled with flowers gathered from your garden or purchased at the supermarket will spruce up your table just fine.

Remember, this get-together is about enjoying your friends and the always-inviting outdoors.

LAMB KABOBS

MAKES 8 SERVINGS

Prep: 20 min., Chill: 3 hrs., Grill: 20 min.

You often can find cubes of lamb in the supermarket, but if not, cut them from a leg rather than the more expensive chops.

- **2½ pounds lamb, cut into 1½-inch cubes**
- **¼ cup olive oil**
- **4 fresh rosemary sprigs**
- **8 (12-inch) wooden skewers**
- **2 red onions, quartered**
- **1 green bell pepper, cut into 1-inch pieces**
- **½ pound fresh mushrooms**
- **1 lemon, quartered and cut into 1-inch pieces**
- **1 cup drained pineapple chunks**
- **1 teaspoon salt**
- **Vegetable cooking spray**

COMBINE first 3 ingredients in a large shallow dish or freezer bag; cover or seal, and chill 3 hours. Soak wooden skewers in water during last 30 minutes of chilling lamb.
REMOVE lamb from dish, discarding marinade. Thread lamb cubes, onions, and next 4 ingredients alternately onto skewers. Sprinkle kabobs evenly with salt.
COAT grill rack with cooking spray; place on grill over medium-high heat (350° to 400°). Place lamb kabobs on rack, and grill, covered with grill lid, 5 minutes on each side or to desired degree of doneness.

Taste of the South

She-Crab Soup

This delectable recipe will have you clamoring for more.

A culinary icon of Charleston, South Carolina, she-crab soup was traditionally a rich combination of cream, crabmeat, roe (eggs), and a splash of sherry. The meat from a female crab is said to be sweeter, but it was the addition of her red-orange roe that created the dish's depth of flavor and beautiful pale color and resulted in the name "she-crab" soup.

These days, roe is not harvested in an ecological effort to preserve the supply of crabs. Is it still she-crab soup if there's no roe? Yes and no. The heart of the recipe remains the same. But when you can, try it made with roe, and savor every precious spoonful.

You'll find some variations, but purists know the basic recipe is the true Southern tradition. Fresh crabmeat is essential. For all of you lucky enough to catch your own crabs, you'll need about a dozen. If you remove the shell of the female crab and discover what looks like a mass of tiny red-orange beads inside, you've struck gold—or roe, that is. Remove it carefully; stir it into the soup with the crabmeat. (Note: Female crabs with roe on the outside must be returned to the water.)

Whether your crabmeat is from crabs you caught yourself or from the supermarket, enjoy a taste of the region with a bowl of this creamy soup.

Blue Crabs 101

Blue crabs are the star of this soup. If you're lucky enough to get the meat from fresh crabs, keep these tips in mind.

- Choose live crabs that are active and heavy for their size.
- For steamed crabs, combine ¼ cup plus 2 tablespoons coarse sea salt, ¼ cup plus 2 tablespoons Old Bay seasoning, 3 tablespoons pickling spice, 2 tablespoons celery seeds, and 1 tablespoon crushed red pepper flakes (optional). Bring 1 cup water and 1 cup white vinegar to a boil in a stockpot. Place a rack in stockpot. Add 1 dozen live crabs; sprinkle with seasoning mixture. Cover and cook for 20 to 25 minutes or until crabs turn bright red. Rinse with cold water; drain well.
- To get to the cooked meat, twist off crab legs and claws. Crack claws; remove meat with a small fork. Next, remove the apron, or tail flap, from the underside; discard. Insert thumb under shell by apron hinge; remove top shell. Pull away the gray gills; discard them along with internal organs. Break the body; remove meat from pockets. Pick through meat to remove all shell fragments.

SHE-CRAB SOUP

MAKES ABOUT 6 CUPS

Prep: 10 min.; Cook: 1 hr., 20 min.

The classic dish originally contained roe (crab eggs). These days, however, roe is not harvested in order to preserve the supply of crabs. While technically it's not she-crab soup without the roe, the heart of the recipe remains the same.

> 1 quart whipping cream
> ⅛ teaspoon salt
> ⅛ teaspoon pepper
> 2 fish bouillon cubes
> 2 cups boiling water
> ¼ cup unsalted butter
> ⅓ cup all-purpose flour
> 2 tablespoons lemon juice
> ¼ teaspoon ground nutmeg
> 1 pound fresh crabmeat, drained
> Garnish: chopped parsley
> ⅓ cup sherry (optional)

COMBINE first 3 ingredients in a heavy saucepan; bring to a boil over medium heat. Reduce heat, and simmer 1 hour. Set aside.

STIR together fish bouillon cubes and 2 cups boiling water until the bouillon dissolves.

MELT butter in a large, heavy saucepan over low heat; add flour, stirring until smooth. Cook 1 minute, stirring constantly. Gradually add hot fish broth; cook over medium heat until thickened. Stir in cream mixture, and cook until thoroughly heated. Add lemon juice, nutmeg, and crabmeat. Ladle into individual serving bowls. Garnish, if desired. Add a spoonful of sherry to each serving, if desired.

NOTE: For testing purposes only, we used Knorr Fish Bouillon. It's important to use good-quality sherry, not cooking sherry, for this soup.

Burgers in the Backyard

Put a new twist on an old-fashioned cookout.

PROCESS first 6 ingredients in a food processor until smooth, stopping to scrape down sides.

SPREAD bacon mixture into a 1-quart baking dish or a 9-inch pieplate.

BAKE at 350° for 20 minutes; sprinkle cheese evenly over top, and bake 5 more minutes. Serve immediately with chips.

ROBIN BASKETTE
LEXINGTON, KENTUCKY

An Easy Backyard Cookout

Serves 8 to 10

Barbecue Bean Dip and chips

Barbara's Big Juicy Burgers   flavored ketchups

Horseradish Spread   Pimiento Cheese

Marinated Green Tomatoes   Grilled Red Onions

Five-Bean Bake   Potato Cobb Salad

Over-the-Moon Banana Pudding

Homemade Orange Soda

BARBARA'S BIG JUICY BURGERS

family favorite

MAKES 10 SERVINGS

Prep: 20 min., Grill: 18 min.

Shape into 12 patties for smaller, quarter-pound burgers.

- 1 (11.5-ounce) can lightly tangy vegetable juice
- 3 white sandwich bread slices, torn into pieces
- 3 pounds ground chuck or ground round
- 1 large egg
- 1½ teaspoons salt
- 1 teaspoon pepper
- 10 hamburger buns
- Vegetable cooking spray

MICROWAVE vegetable juice in a glass bowl at HIGH 1 minute. Add bread pieces; let cool. Combine, using hands.

COMBINE vegetable juice mixture, ground chuck, and next 3 ingredients. Shape into 10 patties.

GRILL patties, covered with grill lid, over medium-high heat (350° to 400°) 6 to 8 minutes on each side or until beef is no longer pink.

SPRAY cut sides of buns with cooking spray; place buns, cut sides down, on grill rack; grill 2 minutes or until lightly browned. Serve hamburgers on buns.

NOTE: For testing purposes only, we used V-8 for vegetable juice.

BARBARA MANNING
BIRMINGHAM, ALABAMA

When's the last time you and your friends toppled over each other trying to win a sack race or dodge a ball? Too far back to remember? This summer, plan to do it again—invite them over for a cookout; then chill out, and have a ball in your backyard.

Play up the let's-have-a-ball theme on the tables by making beaded napkin rings and flower centerpieces that are reminiscent of beach balls. For long-lasting decorations, make one-panel, tie-on chair covers, or carve out enough time to build a whimsical picnic table. (For more detailed instructions, see Terrific Touches on page 140.)

On the menu, serve cookout favorites that feature unexpected tastes. Grill juicy burgers, and serve with toppings such as Marinated Green Tomatoes, Pimiento Cheese, and Sweet-Hot Ketchup. Prepare what you can the day before to keep party-day tasks to a minimum.

After the last scoop of Over-the-Moon Banana Pudding has been enjoyed, you'll hear, "Wow, I had a ball," as neighbors stroll home from a day of summer fun.

BARBECUE BEAN DIP

make ahead

MAKES 8 SERVINGS

Prep: 15 min., Cook: 25 min.

To make ahead, stir together bean mixture the day before; cover and chill. Let sit at room temperature 30 minutes before baking.

- 4 bacon slices, cooked and crumbled
- 1 small sweet onion, chopped
- 1 (14.5-ounce) can great Northern beans, rinsed and drained
- ¼ cup spicy barbecue sauce
- ¼ cup tomato sauce
- ¼ teaspoon garlic powder
- ½ cup (2 ounces) shredded Cheddar cheese
- Corn chip scoops

TOP-NOTCH TOPPINGS

Offer guests several of our flavored ketchups and simple spreads alongside classic burger condiments.

SPICY PEACH KETCHUP: Stir together 1 cup ketchup, ½ cup thick-and-spicy barbecue sauce, and ½ cup peach preserves until blended. Cover and chill 2 hours. (Makes 2 cups. Prep: 10 min., Chill: 2 hrs.)

SWEET-HOT KETCHUP: Stir together 1 cup ketchup, 2 tablespoons to ¼ cup honey, 1 tablespoon lime juice, and 1 teaspoon chipotle chile pepper seasoning until blended. Cover and chill 2 hours. (Makes 1⅓ cups. Prep: 10 min., Chill: 2 hrs.)

NOT-SO-SECRET SAUCE: Stir together 1 cup mayonnaise, ⅓ cup ketchup, and 3 tablespoons sweet pickle relish until blended. Cover and chill 2 hours. This is also good on fish sandwiches. (Makes 1½ cups. Prep: 10 min., Chill: 2 hrs.)

HORSERADISH SPREAD: Stir together 1 (8-ounce) package cream cheese, softened; 2 tablespoons Dijon mustard; and 2 tablespoons prepared horseradish until well blended. Cover and chill 1 hour. (Makes 1½ cups. Prep: 10 min., Chill: 1 hr.)

MARY PAPPAS
RICHMOND, VIRGINIA

PIMIENTO CHEESE: Stir together 1 (8-ounce) package sharp Cheddar cheese, shredded; 3 tablespoons mayonnaise; 2 sliced green onions; and 1 (2-ounce) jar diced pimiento, drained, until blended. Cover and chill 1 hour. (Makes 2 cups. Prep: 15 min., Chill: 1 hr.)

CYNTHIA GIVAN
FORT WORTH, TEXAS

MARINATED GREEN TOMATOES

MAKES 8 TO 10 SERVINGS

Prep: 15 min., Chill: 1 hr.

- 4 large green tomatoes (about 2 pounds)*
- 2 tablespoons sugar
- 1 teaspoon salt
- ⅛ teaspoon pepper
- ¼ cup tarragon vinegar

CUT tomatoes into ¼-inch-thick slices. Arrange half of slices in a large shallow serving dish; sprinkle with half each of sugar, salt, and pepper. Top with remaining tomato slices; sprinkle with remaining sugar, salt, and pepper. Drizzle vinegar evenly over tomatoes. Cover and chill 1 hour. Turn tomato slices, coating with vinegar mixture, before serving.

*Substitute red or yellow tomatoes for green ones, or use a mixture of all three varieties, if desired.

NORA HENSHAW
OKEMAH, OKLAHOMA

GRILLED RED ONIONS

MAKES 6 SERVINGS

Prep: 20 min., Chill: 8 hrs., Grill: 10 min.

If you've tried to grill onions only to have the rings separate and end up in the fire, then we have a solution. Insert a skewer through an onion slice to hold the rings together.

- 12 (8-inch) wooden skewers
- 3 medium-size red or sweet onions
- 1½ cups dry white wine
- 2 to 4 tablespoons butter or margarine
- 1 teaspoon chopped fresh thyme
- ⅛ teaspoon pepper

INSERT 4 wooden skewers (1 at a time) through each onion about ½ inch apart to create horizontal segments. Cut onions into slices between skewers. (Leave skewers in place to hold onion slices together during marinating and cooking.)

PLACE slices in a shallow container; add wine. Cover and chill 8 hours, turning occasionally. Drain.

MELT butter in a small saucepan; stir in thyme and pepper. Brush onion slices with butter mixture, reserving some for basting.

GRILL onions, covered with grill lid, over medium-high heat (350° to 400°) 6 to 10 minutes, turning and basting often with reserved butter mixture.

FIVE-BEAN BAKE

family favorite

MAKES 8 SERVINGS

Prep: 20 min.; Cook: 10 min.; Bake: 1 hr., 30 min.

- 8 bacon slices, chopped
- 1 large onion, diced
- 1 (28-ounce) can pork and beans
- 1 (19.75-ounce) can black beans, rinsed and drained
- 1 (16-ounce) can chickpeas, rinsed and drained
- 1 (15.5-ounce) can kidney beans, rinsed and drained
- 1 (15.25-ounce) can lima beans, rinsed and drained
- 1 cup ketchup
- ½ cup firmly packed brown sugar
- ½ cup water
- ¼ cup cider vinegar

COOK chopped bacon slices in a large skillet over medium-high heat until crisp; remove bacon, reserving 2 tablespoons drippings in skillet. Add diced onion, and sauté in hot drippings 5 minutes or until tender.

COMBINE bacon, onion, pork and beans, black beans, chickpeas, kidney beans, lima beans, ketchup, brown sugar, ½ cup water, and cider vinegar in a lightly greased 13- x 9-inch baking dish.

BAKE, covered, at 350° for 1 hour; uncover and bake 30 more minutes.

PAT SHOREY
ROSWELL, GEORGIA

Terrific Touches

Flower Power
Buy florist foam balls in varied sizes, and soak in water. Clip flower stems to within a few inches of blooms. (Mums, daisies, and carnations work well.) Press stems into florist foam until the entire ball is covered.

Havin' a Ball
For your table, decorate with wooden spheres in all shapes, sizes, and colors. Add florist foam balls adorned with flowers, and make simple beaded napkin rings.

Svelte Sacks
Potato sacks have never looked so good. Choose bright burlap and coordinating ribbon. Cut sack front and back (ours are 4 x 2 feet). Tip: When cutting burlap, use pinking sheers to prevent fraying.

Pin front and back together, right sides facing. With a sewing machine, stitch sides and bottom of sack together, leaving top open. Turn inside out. About 4 inches down from the top of the sack, use scissors to make small slits for ribbon, and thread ribbon.

Fabric Accents
Anytime you bring together food and family, there are bound to be thrills and spills. Deter stains by having your fabric laminated. We had some terrific fabric treated before crafting a runner and cushions. Check with your local fabric store.

To make a table runner, measure enough fabric to run length of table plus 2 feet for overhang (1 foot on each side). Fold runner ends toward underside to make a triangle, and hot glue edges together for a finished look. Sew beads at each pointed edge. Place laminated cushions on wooden benches.

Quick Covers
Use your leftover fabric from the potato sacks to create simple slipcovers for chairs. Cut a piece of burlap to cover back and seat of chair, allowing extra for overhang. Prevent edges from fraying by cutting them with pinking sheers or hemming them. Stitch two strips of burlap to each of the top corners, and wrap them around top of chair. Tie in knots.

Neat Napkins
To craft a set of napkin rings, purchase inexpensive wooden beads from a crafts store. Cover them with high-gloss spray paint in the color of your choice. Let dry, and use string or wire to thread beads. Alternate bead color for interest. Make sure beaded strand is long enough to fit around a rolled napkin. Cut wire, allowing room to secure at ends, and slip over a rolled napkin.

Burger Bar
Step right up to a build-your-best burger bar. A tiered shelf pulls double-duty—creating a focal point to draw folks to the table and serving as a clever buffet for burger fixings. If you don't have a shelf, or it's a windy day, try sturdy, short benches stacked on the table.

POTATO COBB SALAD

MAKES 8 TO 10 SERVINGS

Prep: 30 min., Cook: 30 min., Chill: 2 hrs.

- 3 pounds Yukon gold potatoes
- ¾ teaspoon salt
- 1 (16-ounce) bottle olive oil-and-vinegar dressing, divided
- 8 cups mixed salad greens
- 2 large avocados
- 1 tablespoon fresh lemon juice
- 3 large tomatoes, seeded and diced
- 12 small green onions, sliced
- 2 cups (8 ounces) shredded sharp Cheddar cheese
- 4 ounces crumbled blue cheese
- 6 to 8 bacon slices, cooked and crumbled
- Freshly ground pepper to taste

COOK potatoes in boiling salted water to cover 30 minutes or until tender. Drain and cool slightly. Peel and cut into cubes.
SPRINKLE potatoes evenly with ¾ teaspoon salt. Pour 1 cup dressing over potatoes; gently toss. Set aside remaining dressing. Cover potato mixture; chill at least 2 hours or overnight.
ARRANGE salad greens evenly on a large serving platter. Peel and chop avocados; toss with lemon juice.
ARRANGE potatoes, avocados, tomatoes, and next 4 ingredients in rows over salad greens. Sprinkle with pepper. Serve with remaining dressing.

OVER-THE-MOON BANANA PUDDING

family favorite

MAKES 12 TO 15 SERVINGS

Prep: 20 min., Cook: 10 min., Stand: 20 min., Chill: 2 hrs.

- 2 (4.6-ounce) packages cook-and-serve vanilla pudding mix
- 4 cups milk
- 1 (8-ounce) container sour cream
- 8 (2.75-ounce) chocolate-marshmallow sandwiches, cut into eighths
- 3 bananas, sliced
- 1 (8-ounce) container frozen whipped topping, thawed

COOK pudding mix and 4 cups milk in a saucepan according to package directions. Remove pan from heat; let stand 10 minutes. Whisk in sour cream; let stand until pudding thickens.

POUR half of pudding into a 2-quart dish. Layer about 40 chocolate-marshmallow sandwich wedges evenly over pudding. Top evenly with banana slices and remaining half of pudding. Top with whipped topping. Arrange remaining sandwich wedges around outer edge of dish. Cover and chill at least 2 hours or overnight.

NOTE: For testing purposes only, we used MoonPies for chocolate-marshmallow sandwiches.

HOMEMADE ORANGE SODA

family favorite • fast fixin's

MAKES ABOUT 4½ QUARTS

Prep: 5 min.

Stir this refreshing beverage occasionally to keep the ingredients thoroughly mixed. *(pictured on page 153)*

- 1 (12-ounce) can frozen, pulp-free orange juice concentrate, thawed and undiluted
- 2 (2-liter) bottles lemon-lime soft drink, chilled
- 1 to 2 oranges, thinly sliced

STIR together orange juice concentrate and lemon-lime soft drink when ready to serve. Serve over ice in individual glasses with an orange slice.

Clever Containers

Reader Janet Hayes of Macon, Georgia, sent us this idea for serving condiments at cookouts. Slice the tops off bell peppers, and rinse to remove seeds; reserve tops. Fill with mustard, mayonnaise, and ketchup; cover with reserved tops, and refrigerate until ready to serve.

Sparkling Summer Punch

Dress up this fruity beverage with an elegant, easy-to-make ice ring.

Across the South, punch is served for almost every occasion: church socials, ladies luncheons, and most certainly at weddings. Here, we offer a reader's punch recipe perfect for any celebration. Garnish with an exquisite ice ring made with assorted fruits, and adorn the bowl with a ring of fragrant flowers for a beautiful presentation.

CHAMPAGNE PUNCH

make ahead

MAKES 20 SERVINGS

Prep: 15 min., Chill: 8 hrs. *(pictured on page 149)*

- 2 cups cranberry juice cocktail
- 1 (12-ounce) can frozen orange juice concentrate, thawed
- 1 cup lemon juice
- 1 cup sugar
- 1 (375-milliliter) bottle Sauterne or dessert wine*
- 2 (750-milliliter) bottles Champagne, chilled
- Ice Ring

COMBINE first 4 ingredients, stirring well; chill at least 8 hours.

POUR juice mixture into a chilled punch bowl. Gently stir in Sauterne and Champagne just before serving. Float Ice Ring, fruit side up, in punch.

*Substitute either (375 ml) Bonny Doon, Vin de Glacière or (375 ml) Quady, Electra, if desired.

Ice Ring:

Prep: 10 min., Freeze: 10 hrs.

- 1½ to 2 cups orange juice
- ½ cup cranberry juice
- 6 to 8 seedless red grape clusters
- 10 to 12 orange slices, seeded
- 8 to 10 whole strawberries
- Fresh mint sprigs

COMBINE juices. Line bottom of a 6-cup ring mold with grape clusters and half of orange slices, using grapes to stand orange slices vertically. Pour a thin layer of juices into mold, and freeze until firm, about 2 hours.

ARRANGE remaining orange slices, strawberries, and mint sprigs around grapes. Pour remaining juices around fruit almost to top of mold. Freeze 8 hours.

UNMOLD by dipping bottom half of mold in several inches of warm water 5 to 10 seconds to loosen, repeating as necessary to release ring. (Do not immerse entire mold in water.) Invert ring onto plate.

EASY ICE RING: Combine juices. Fill a 6-cup ring mold with 2 cups crushed ice. Lay grape clusters over ice. Arrange orange slices, strawberries, and fresh mint sprigs around grapes. Pour juices around fruit almost to top of mold. Freeze 8 hours or until firm.
Prep: 10 min., Freeze: 8 hrs.

BOOTS ABERCROMBIE
HOOVER, ALABAMA

Italian Supper Tonight

Put tonight's meal in a bowl with these easy recipes.

Casual Weeknight Supper

Serves 8

Meatball Lasagna

Roasted Onion Salad

Parmesan Crisps

Ice cream

Show your flair for Italian fare with this hearty meal. The base of the lasagna is purchased pasta sauce and frozen meatballs. Blue cheese and caramelized onions combine in the Roasted Onion Salad, a great accompaniment for the lasagna. Top the salad with Parmesan Crisps—whole or crumbled—for a delightful crunch.

PARMESAN CRISPS

fast fixin's

MAKES 2 DOZEN

Prep: 20 min., Bake: 8 min.

> 1½ cups (6 ounces) finely shredded
>   Parmesan cheese
> Vegetable cooking spray

SPRINKLE about 1 tablespoon Parmesan cheese, forming a 2-inch round, on an aluminum-foil lined baking sheet coated with cooking spray. Repeat with remaining cheese, leaving 1 inch between rounds.

BAKE at 350° for 8 minutes or until lightly browned. Quickly remove cheese crisps from baking sheet with a spatula. Cool on a wire rack. Store in an airtight container.

ROASTED ONION SALAD

MAKES 8 SERVINGS

Prep: 15 min., Bake: 15 min., Cool: 5 min.

> 5 medium onions, peeled and cut into
>   ½-inch-thick slices
> ¼ cup olive oil
> 8 cups gourmet mixed salad greens
> ½ cup chopped walnuts, toasted
> 1 (4-ounce) package crumbled blue
>   cheese
> Garlic Vinaigrette

ARRANGE onion slices in a lightly greased roasting pan. Drizzle evenly with olive oil.

BAKE at 450° for 12 to 15 minutes or until onion slices are lightly charred. Cool 5 minutes.

COMBINE salad greens, walnuts, and blue cheese; toss gently. Top with onion slices; drizzle with Garlic Vinaigrette.

Garlic Vinaigrette:

MAKES 1 CUP

Prep: 10 min.

> 3 garlic cloves
> 2 shallots
> ¼ cup chopped fresh parsley
> 2 tablespoons white wine vinegar
> ½ teaspoon dried crushed red
>   pepper
> ½ teaspoon salt
> ½ teaspoon freshly ground black
>   pepper
> ⅔ cup olive oil

PULSE garlic and shallots in a food processor 3 or 4 times. Add parsley and next 4 ingredients; process 20 seconds, stopping once to scrape down sides. With processor running, gradually pour olive oil in a slow, steady stream through food chute until blended.

MEATBALL LASAGNA

family favorite

MAKES 8 SERVINGS

Prep: 15 min.; Bake: 1 hr., 10 min.; Stand: 15 min.

> 1 (15-ounce) container ricotta
>   cheese
> 1 (8-ounce) container soft onion-and-
>   chive cream cheese
> ¼ cup chopped fresh basil
> ½ teaspoon garlic salt
> ½ teaspoon seasoned pepper
> 1 large egg, lightly beaten
> 2 cups (8 ounces) shredded
>   mozzarella cheese, divided
> 1 (3-ounce) package shredded
>   Parmesan cheese, divided
> 2 (26-ounce) jars tomato-basil pasta
>   sauce, divided
> 1 (16-ounce) package egg roll
>   wrappers
> 60 to 64 frozen cooked Italian-style
>   meatballs

STIR together first 6 ingredients until blended. Stir in ½ cup mozzarella cheese and ½ cup Parmesan cheese; set aside.

SPREAD 1 cup pasta sauce in a lightly greased 13- x 9-inch baking dish. Cut egg roll wrappers in half; arrange 10 halves over pasta sauce. (Wrappers will overlap.) Top with meatballs. Spoon 3 cups pasta sauce over meatballs; sprinkle with ¾ cup mozzarella cheese. Arrange 10 wrappers evenly over mozzarella. Spread ricotta cheese mixture over wrappers; top with remaining wrappers and pasta sauce.

BAKE at 350° for 1 hour. Top with remaining ¾ cup mozzarella cheese and ½ cup Parmesan cheese. Bake 10 more minutes. Let stand 15 minutes before serving.

NOTE: For testing purposes, we used Rosina Italian Style Meatballs and Classico Tomato & Basil Pasta Sauce.

GROUND SIRLOIN LASAGNA: Substitute 2 pounds ground sirloin, cooked until no longer pink, drained, and seasoned with 1 teaspoon salt and 1 teaspoon Italian seasoning for frozen meatballs. Proceed as directed.

What's for Supper?

Satisfying Salads

No matter how you toss it, a simple salad becomes dinner in a bowl when you add a great source of protein such as chicken or pork. Take advantage of deli-roasted meats and canned products to make these salads all the more doable. With fabulous flavors, these recipes are super for hot weather suppers.

PORK-AND-RICE SALAD WITH SPICY TOMATO DRESSING

MAKES 8 SERVINGS

Prep: 25 min., Chill: 30 min.

  1½ pounds deli-roasted pork
    tenderloin, cut into strips*
  2 cups cooked white rice, chilled
  2 (15-ounce) cans black beans, rinsed
    and drained
  1 (15.25-ounce) can whole kernel corn,
    drained
  1½ cups (6 ounces) shredded colby-
    Jack cheese
  1 small red onion, chopped
  2 teaspoons sugar
  2 tablespoons fresh lime juice
  1 ripe avocado, chopped
  ½ cup chopped fresh cilantro,
    divided
  1 tablespoon Cajun seasoning
  Spicy Tomato Dressing
  8 romaine lettuce leaves

STIR together first 6 ingredients in a large bowl.
WHISK together sugar and lime juice; gently stir in avocado, ¼ cup cilantro, and Cajun seasoning. Add to pork mixture; stir in Spicy Tomato Dressing, and gently toss. Cover and chill 30 minutes.
SERVE salad on lettuce leaves, and sprinkle with remaining ¼ cup cilantro.

Spicy Tomato Dressing:

MAKES 2 CUPS

Prep: 5 min., Chill: 30 min.

  1 (10-ounce) can diced tomatoes and
    green chiles with lime and cilantro
  1 cup olive oil
  ½ cup minced celery
  ¼ cup red wine vinegar
  1 tablespoon Cajun seasoning

PROCESS all ingredients in a blender until smooth. Cover and chill 30 minutes.

*Substitute 1½ pounds pork tenderloin or boneless ½-inch-thick pork chops, cut into ½-inch strips and cooked in 2 tablespoons oil in a large skillet over medium-high heat for 7 minutes, if desired.

GLORIA BRADLEY
NAPERVILLE, ILLINOIS

NOODLE CHICKEN SALAD

MAKES 4 TO 6 SERVINGS

Prep: 20 min., Broil: 5 min., Cook: 8 min.

We received several clever versions of this Oriental chicken salad recipe. With so many good ideas, we couldn't settle on just one. So, we blended Cheryl Murphy's recipe with Mary Ellen Stokes's optional ingredients and lettuce base.

  2 (3-ounce) packages chicken-flavored
    ramen noodle soup mix
  1 (2- to 3-pound) roasted whole
    chicken
  2 tablespoons butter or margarine,
    divided
  ½ cup sliced almonds
  ¼ cup sesame seeds
  ⅓ cup vegetable oil
  2 tablespoons sesame oil
  ½ cup red wine vinegar
  ¼ cup sugar
  ¼ cup lite soy sauce
  ½ teaspoon pepper
  1 head romaine lettuce, torn
  5 green onions, sliced
  Optional ingredients: 1 (10-ounce) can
    mandarin oranges, drained; 1 cup
    sliced mushrooms; ½ cup sliced
    celery

REMOVE flavor packets from soup mixes, reserving 1 packet. Break noodles apart on a baking sheet. Broil 5½ inches from heat 4 to 5 minutes or until browned, stirring every minute.
PULL chicken from bones, and coarsely chop; set aside.
MELT 1 tablespoon butter in a large skillet over medium heat, and add almonds and sesame seeds; cook, stirring constantly, 3 minutes or until lightly browned. Remove from skillet, and set aside.
ADD remaining 1 tablespoon butter and chicken, and cook 4 to 5 minutes or until thoroughly heated.
WHISK together seasoning packet, oils, vinegar, and next 3 ingredients in a large bowl. Add lettuce, green onions, sesame seed mixture, chicken, and noodles, tossing to coat. Add optional ingredients, if desired. Serve immediately.

CHERYL MURPHY
HIGH POINT, NORTH CAROLINA

MARY ELLEN STOKES
ROANOKE, VIRGINIA

Real Men Cook

If you can't attend one of the events held around the U.S. this Father's Day, celebrate at home with these great-tasting recipes.

These recipes are favorites of dads who are celebrating their special day at a fun-filled food tasting hosted by the Atlanta Real Men Cook group. These men serve a huge feast honoring African American inner-city fathers and their contributions to the community. Started 14 years ago in a small Chicago neighborhood, Real Men Cook has become the largest national urban Father's Day celebration. Members include leading radio, TV, and sports celebrities in 11 cities who generate more than $700,000 for local charities. National sponsors—State Farm Insurance, Volvo, and Lawry's—help fund the annual events. Here's a sample of the feast.

JAMBALAYA

family favorite

MAKES 6 TO 8 SERVINGS
Prep: 15 min.; Cook: 40 min.

> 1 (16-ounce) package spicy hickory-smoked sausage, cut into ½-inch slices
> 1 large onion, chopped
> 1 small green bell pepper, chopped
> 3 garlic cloves, minced
> 2 cups uncooked rice
> 1 (32-ounce) container chicken broth
> 1 (14½-ounce) can stewed tomatoes, undrained and chopped
> 1 (8-ounce) can tomato sauce
> 2 teaspoons Cajun seasoning
> 1 teaspoon hot sauce
> 1 pound unpeeled, medium fresh shrimp
> 3 tablespoons chopped green onions

BROWN sausage in a large Dutch oven over medium-high heat. Drain, reserving 3 tablespoons drippings in pan. Add onion and bell pepper, and sauté 2 to 3 minutes or until tender. Add garlic, and sauté 1 more minute.
ADD rice and chicken broth. Bring to a boil; cover, reduce heat to low, and simmer 20 minutes. Stir in tomatoes and next 3 ingredients.
PEEL shrimp, and devein, if desired.
STIR in shrimp and green onions; cook 2 to 3 minutes or just until shrimp turn pink.

JOSEPH LARCHÉ
ATLANTA, GEORGIA

FIRECRACKER SHRIMP

fast fixin's

MAKES 2 TO 3 SERVINGS
Prep: 10 min., Cook: 7 min.

> 1 pound unpeeled, large shrimp
> ½ teaspoon Creole seasoning
> ¼ teaspoon salt
> ¼ teaspoon ground black pepper
> ⅛ teaspoon ground red pepper
> 1 tablespoon olive oil
> 2 garlic cloves, minced
> 2 tablespoons chopped green onions
> 1 cup whipping cream
> 2 tablespoons chopped fresh parsley
> 3 tablespoons lemon juice
> Hot cooked rice or pasta

PEEL shrimp, and devein, if desired.
COMBINE Creole seasoning and next 3 ingredients; sprinkle over shrimp.
SAUTÉ shrimp in hot oil in a large skillet 3 minutes. Add garlic and green onions; sauté 1 minute. Add cream, and cook 2 minutes, stirring often. Stir in parsley and lemon juice. Serve immediately over rice or pasta.

D.C. WILLIAMS
DALLAS, TEXAS

ISLAND BREEZE CHEESECAKE

MAKES 10 TO 12 SERVINGS

Prep: 25 min.; Bake: 1 hr., 10 min.; Chill: 8 hrs.

This is a dense New York-style cheesecake.

> 1 cup graham cracker crumbs
> 1 cup finely chopped almonds
> ¼ cup butter, melted
> 3 tablespoons sugar
> 4 (8-ounce) packages cream cheese, softened
> 1 cup sugar
> 3 tablespoons all-purpose flour
> 1 tablespoon vanilla extract
> 4 large eggs
> 1 cup sour cream
> Fruit Topping
> Garnish: toasted coconut

STIR together graham cracker crumbs, chopped almonds, melted butter, and sugar. Press crumb mixture into bottom and 1 inch up sides of a lightly greased 9-inch springform pan.

BAKE crust at 350° for 10 minutes. Cool on a wire rack.

BEAT softened cream cheese at medium speed with an electric mixer until smooth. Gradually add 1 cup sugar, flour, and vanilla.

ADD eggs, 1 at a time, beating until blended after each addition. Add sour cream, and beat just until blended. Pour mixture into prepared crust.

BAKE at 350° for 1 hour or until center is almost set. Remove cheesecake from oven; cool on wire rack. Cover and chill 8 hours. Gently run a knife around edge of cheesecake, and release sides of pan; spoon chilled Fruit Topping over top. Garnish, if desired.

Fruit Topping:

MAKES 3 CUPS

Prep: 20 min., Chill: 1 hr.

- 1 small papaya
- 1 mango
- 2 kiwifruit
- 1 (12-ounce) jar apricot preserves
- 1 tablespoon rum
- 1 cup pineapple tidbits

PEEL and cut papaya, mango, and kiwifruit into small chunks.

STIR together apricot preserves and rum in a large bowl; add papaya, mango, kiwifruit, and pineapple, tossing to coat. Cover and chill 1 hour. Drain before spooning on top of cheesecake.

KEVIN ASHFORD
ATLANTA, GEORGIA

Don't Wait for Delivery

Save time and money by making these fast, flavor-packed pizzas instead of ordering out.

In the time it takes to get a delivery chain on the phone, you can combine good-for-you ingredients to create a quick and satisfying homemade pizza the entire family will enjoy. Use these recipes as a guide to add your family's favorite toppings for a custom-made creation.

MEATY PIZZA PIE

family favorite • fast fixin's

MAKES 4 SERVINGS

Prep: 10 min., Bake: 30 min., Cool: 5 min.

Use your family's favorite leftover spaghetti meat sauce for this hearty weeknight meal. Serve with a green salad, if desired.

- 1 (15-ounce) package refrigerated piecrusts
- 2 cups spaghetti meat sauce
- 16 pepperoni slices
- 1 cup (4 ounces) shredded mozzarella cheese

UNFOLD piecrusts; stack piecrusts, and press together. Place piecrust on a parchment-lined baking sheet; spread spaghetti meat sauce evenly over crust, leaving a 1-inch border; top with pepperoni slices. Fold crust edges slightly over filling.

BAKE on lower rack at 425° for 15 minutes. Sprinkle with cheese, and bake 15 more minutes or until bubbly and golden.

COOL 5 minutes. Cut into wedges.

GREEK PIZZA

fast fixin's

MAKES 4 SERVINGS

Prep: 10 min., Bake: 15 min.

Buy pita bread fresh, or keep it in the freezer and microwave to thaw.

- 4 (8-inch) pita rounds
- 1 (8-ounce) container regular or garlic-flavored hummus
- 4 ounces sliced deli ham, cut into strips
- ¼ small red onion, sliced
- 4 pepperoncini peppers, sliced
- 1 cup grape tomatoes, halved
- 1 (2¼-ounce) can sliced ripe olives, drained
- 1 (4-ounce) package crumbled feta cheese

SPREAD 1 side of each pita round evenly with hummus; top evenly with deli ham and remaining ingredients.

BAKE at 400° for 10 to 15 minutes.

NOTE: For testing purposes only, we used Tribe of Two Sheiks Hummus with Roasted Garlic, which can be found in the deli department of large supermarkets.

SOUTHWESTERN PIZZA

fast fixin's

MAKES 4 SERVINGS

Prep: 10 min., Bake: 15 min.

For bold, smoky flavor, try this with two sliced, grilled chicken breasts.

8 (10-inch) flour tortillas*
1 (8-ounce) package shredded Mexican four-cheese blend
1 cup thick and chunky picante sauce
Black Bean Salsa
2 cups chopped cooked chicken
Garnishes: sour cream, chopped avocado

TOP 4 flour tortillas evenly with 1 cup cheese; top with remaining flour tortillas. Divide picante sauce, Black Bean Salsa, chicken, and remaining 1 cup cheese over flour tortillas. Bake at 400° for 15 minutes, or until cheese is bubbly. Garnish, if desired.

*Substitute 2 (11.5-ounce) cans refrigerated corn sticks for tortillas, if desired. Unroll and press perforations to seal into a lightly greased jellyroll pan to create a rectangular crust. Bake at 375° on lower oven rack 10 minutes. Add toppings, and bake 15 more minutes. Makes 8 pieces.

Black Bean Salsa:

MAKES 3 CUPS

Prep: 10 min.

1 (15-ounce) can black beans, rinsed and drained
½ cup frozen corn, thawed
2 plum tomatoes, seeded and chopped
1 green onion, chopped
2 tablespoons fresh lime juice
1 tablespoon chopped fresh cilantro
1 garlic clove, pressed
½ teaspoon Creole seasoning

STIR together all ingredients. Cover and chill until ready to serve.

Living Light

Trim and Terrific Recipes

Busy mom and cookbook author Holly Clegg shows how weeknight meals can be both tasty and healthy.

If you're juggling a job, family, and activities, these recipes are for you. This selection from *The Holly Clegg Trim & Terrific Cookbook* (Running Press, 2002) will convince you that good flavor and good for you can go hand-in-hand.

We sampled several recipes from the book including Grilled Flank Steak and yummy German Chocolate Sheet Cake topped with creamy frosting. When you're cutting back on fat and calories, it's not always easy to prepare recipes your family raves about, but Holly has managed to do so quite nicely.

GRILLED FLANK STEAK

chef recipe

MAKES 6 SERVINGS

Prep: 10 min., Chill: 8 hrs., Grill: 14 min., Stand: 5 min.

2 tablespoons dry red wine
1 tablespoon red wine vinegar
1 tablespoon prepared horseradish
1 tablespoon ketchup
1 teaspoon dried thyme
1 teaspoon minced garlic
½ teaspoon pepper
2 pounds flank steak

COMBINE first 7 ingredients in a shallow dish or freezer bag; add steak. Cover or seal, and chill 8 hours, turning occasionally.

REMOVE steak from marinade, discarding marinade.

GRILL, covered with grill lid, over high heat (400° to 500°) about 7 minutes on each side or to desired degree of doneness. Let stand 5 minutes. Cut diagonally across the grain into thin slices.

Calories 231 (43% from fat); Fat 11g (sat 4.7g, mono 4.4g, poly 0.4g); Protein 29g; Carb 1g; Fiber 0.2g; Chol 72mg; Iron 3mg; Sodium 118mg; Calc 13mg

SHRIMP RÉMOULADE

chef recipe • fast fixin's

MAKES 8 (¼-CUP) SERVINGS

Prep: 15 min.

¼ cup light mayonnaise
1 bunch green onions, sliced
⅓ cup chopped fresh parsley
2 tablespoons prepared horseradish
2 tablespoons Creole mustard
2 tablespoons Dijon mustard
1 tablespoon lemon juice
2 pounds peeled cooked shrimp

STIR together first 7 ingredients; add shrimp, tossing to coat. Cover and chill until ready to serve.

Calories 143 (25% from fat); Fat 4g (sat 0.4g, mono 0g, poly 0g); Protein 25g; Carb 2g; Fiber 0.5g; Chol 225mg; Iron 4mg; Sodium 421mg; Calc 41mg

Dirty Rice

chef recipe • family favorite

MAKES 6 SERVINGS

Prep: 25 min., Cook: 40 min.

- 1 pound lean ground beef
- 2 garlic cloves, minced
- 2 celery ribs, chopped (about ½ cup)
- 1 medium onion, chopped
- 1 tablespoon chopped fresh parsley
- 1 green bell pepper, chopped
- 1 teaspoon salt
- ¼ teaspoon ground red pepper
- ¼ teaspoon ground black pepper
- 1 tablespoon Worcestershire sauce
- 1 cup uncooked rice
- 1 (14.5-ounce) can beef broth
- ¾ cup water

COOK first 6 ingredients in a large skillet over medium-high heat, stirring until beef crumbles and is no longer pink.
ADD salt and next 3 ingredients, stirring well. Add rice, broth, and ¾ cup water, stirring well. Bring to a boil; cover, reduce heat, and simmer 25 to 30 minutes or until rice is tender.

Calories 267 (24% from fat); Fat 7g (sat 2.8g, mono 3g, poly 0.4g); Protein 20g; Carb 30g; Fiber 1.6g; Chol 28mg; Iron 3.4mg; Sodium 775mg; Calc 36mg

Barbecued Pork Roast

chef recipe • family favorite

MAKES 8 SERVINGS

Prep: 25 min.; Bake: 1 hr., 20 min.; Stand: 15 min.

- 1 (3-pound) boneless, rolled pork loin roast
- 3 large garlic cloves, thinly sliced
- 1 teaspoon pepper
- 1 teaspoon dried thyme
- 1 onion, sliced
- Vegetable cooking spray
- ½ cup fat-free chicken broth
- ½ cup cider vinegar
- 1 (6-ounce) can tomato paste
- ¼ cup lemon juice
- 2 tablespoons light brown sugar
- 2 tablespoons Worcestershire sauce
- 1 tablespoon Dijon mustard
- ½ teaspoon paprika
- Garnishes: lemon wedges, Italian parsley

TRIM any excess fat from roast. Cut deep slits in roast, using a paring knife; insert garlic slices. Stir together pepper and thyme; rub over all sides of roast, and set aside.
SAUTÉ onion in a nonstick skillet coated with cooking spray over medium heat until tender. Stir in chicken broth and next 7 ingredients; bring to a boil, stirring constantly. Remove from heat.
PLACE roast in a lightly greased large Dutch oven; pour sauce over roast.
BAKE, covered, at 350° for 1 hour and 20 minutes or until a meat thermometer registers 170°. Let stand 15 minutes. Slice and serve with sauce; garnish, if desired.

Calories 364 (47% from fat); Fat 19g (sat 6.9g, mono 8.4g, poly 1.7g); Protein 36g; Carb 11g; Fiber 1.5g; Chol 105mg; Iron 2.4mg; Sodium 363mg; Calc 53mg

Honey-Pecan Chicken

chef recipe • family favorite

MAKES 6 SERVINGS

Prep: 20 min., Bake: 20 min.

- 2 tablespoons lite soy sauce
- 2 tablespoons honey
- 2 cups wheat cereal squares, crushed
- ⅓ cup finely chopped pecans
- 1 teaspoon salt
- 1 teaspoon pepper
- 6 skinned and boned chicken breast halves
- Vegetable cooking spray

STIR together soy sauce and honey; set mixture aside.
COMBINE cereal crumbs and pecans.
SPRINKLE salt and pepper evenly over chicken. Dip both sides of chicken breast in soy sauce mixture; dredge in crumb mixture to coat.
ARRANGE chicken breasts on an aluminum-foil lined baking sheet coated with cooking spray.
BAKE at 425° for 15 to 20 minutes.

Calories 235 (25% from fat); Fat 7g (sat 0.8g, mono 3.1g, poly 1.9g); Protein 29g; Carb 16g; Fiber 2g; Chol 68mg; Iron 4.3mg; Sodium 732mg; Calc 41mg

German Chocolate Sheet Cake

chef recipe • family favorite

MAKES 48 SERVINGS

Prep: 25 min., Bake: 17 min.

- 1 (18.25-ounce) package German chocolate cake mix
- 1 large egg
- 2 egg whites
- 1¾ cups water
- Vegetable cooking spray
- 1 (14-ounce) can fat-free sweetened condensed milk
- ⅓ cup sweetened flaked coconut
- ⅓ cup chopped pecans
- ¼ cup margarine, softened
- 1 (16-ounce) package powdered sugar
- ⅓ cup unsweetened cocoa
- 1 teaspoon vanilla extract
- 3 to 4 tablespoons fat-free milk

BEAT first 4 ingredients at medium speed with an electric mixer 3 to 4 minutes or until creamy. Pour batter into a 15- x 10-inch jellyroll pan coated with cooking spray.
BAKE at 350° for 15 minutes.
COMBINE condensed milk, coconut, and pecans; spread over warm cake.
BROIL, on lowest rack in oven, about 2 minutes or until golden. Remove from oven, and cool.
BEAT margarine and next 3 ingredients at medium speed with an electric mixer until blended; gradually add fat-free milk, beating mixture until smooth. Spread over cake.

NOTE: For testing purposes only, we used Duncan Hines Moist Deluxe German Chocolate Cake Mix.

Calories 128 (23% from fat); Fat 3.3g (sat 1g, mono 1.3g, poly 0.6g); Protein 2g; Carb 23g; Fiber 0.4g; Chol 12mg; Iron 0.5mg; Sodium 103mg; Calc 36mg

from our kitchen

Beautiful jars of all shapes and sizes are available for home canning. Our instructions refer to jars with flat metal lids and screw bands. If you want to use the clamp-lid type, be sure to follow the manufacturer's directions. Some of these may be better for use as food storage containers.

Now you're ready to can—but what type of spread are you filling those jars with? Jelly is made from fruit juice and is translucent. Jam is usually softer than jelly and is made with crushed or finely chopped fruit. Jams and preserves are similar except that preserves contain larger pieces of fruit. Preserves are sometimes made from whole fruits. A conserve is a mixture of fruits, nuts, and sugar cooked together until thick.

Canning Tips

There's something comforting about preserving foods. If you've never done home canning, see "Share the Flavors of Summer" on page 134 for some great recipes. Don't be intimidated—just follow these easy steps.

■ Wash jars, lids, and bands in hot soapy water; rinse well before use.

■ Place lids in a small saucepan of simmering water until ready to use. Remove lids one at a time as needed.

■ When a recipe calls for sterilized jars, it simply means the jars should be submerged in a large pot of water and boiled for 10 minutes. Remove jars one at a time as needed. (Sterilizing jars is necessary if they are used for foods that are processed for less than 10 minutes. If the recipe is processed for 10 minutes or longer, the jars only need to be heated in a large saucepan of simmering water until ready to use, removing one at a time as needed.)

■ Hot food should be put in hot jars.

■ When filling jars, leave a 1-inch headspace (the airspace between the food and the inside of the lid) for low-acid foods, vegetables, and meats; $\frac{1}{2}$-inch for high-acid foods and fruits, and $\frac{1}{4}$-inch for juices, jams, jellies, pickles, and relishes. Overfilled jars will cause liquid to boil out during processing, while too much air may prevent a proper vacuum seal.

■ It's okay to reuse jars, but always use new lids.

■ Process filled jars in a boiling-water bath—this can be done in any Dutch oven or stockpot deep enough to hold a rack to set the jars on and allow enough water to cover them by 1 to 2 inches.

■ Remove jars from boiling-water bath to a towel to cool. Don't retighten bands or check for seal while jars are hot. (You may hear the lids pop as the vacuum seal forms while cooling.)

■ After 24 hours, check lids for proper seal (sealed lids curve downward). Reprocess any unsealed jars. Label and store jars of food in a cool, dry, dark place. Use within one year.

■ Altitude will affect processing times when using the boiling-water method, so be sure to find out what adjustments need to be made if altitude is a factor for you.

Tips and Tidbits

■ Get all the fresh blueberries you can while they're at their prime. Store them covered in the refrigerator, and wash just before using. To freeze, use berries that are unwashed and dry; seal in airtight containers. Rinse frozen berries, pat dry, and stir into batter just before cooking to retard color streaks. Toss berries in a little flour before adding them to batter to keep them from sinking to the bottom.

■ Flowers Bakeries, maker of Nature's Own bread, has introduced Reduced Carbohydrate Premium Wheat bread and Calcium Plus Ultra Wheat bread. The Thomasville, Georgia, company created these great-tasting options to fit consumers' individual dietary needs.

■ Gerry and Bill Alexander of Columbus, Indiana, visited Sally Lunn's in Bath, England. This restaurant claims to be the home of the Sally Lunn bread that we featured in "Taste of the South: A Sweet Little Bread" on page 27. Visit **www.sallylunns.co.uk** to learn more. If you're not into history, skip the reading, and just bake Sally Lunn bread for a sweet treat.

Champagne Punch, page 141

149

Peach-Rosemary Jam, Tart Basil Jelly,
Strawberry-Port Jam, and Carrot-Orange
Marmalade, pages 134-135

Spicy Blueberry-Citrus Marmalade,
page 135

Easiest Pepper Jelly,
page 135

clockwise from top: Shrimp Rolls, page 162; Marinated Green Beans With Tomatoes, Olives, and Feta; and Potato Salad, page 163

152

Mediterranean Wrap, page 168

Homemade Orange Soda,
page 141

Smoky Barbecue Brisket, page 160

Beef-and-Lime Rice Salad, page 172

Fried Green Tomatoes,
page 173

Raspberry, Cantaloupe, and Pineapple
Sorbets, page 171

July

Fresh From the Farmers Market

Summer produce makes suppertime special and shopping a bushel of fun.

On the edge of downtown, the Dallas Farmers Market is a vision of produce that excites the senses. Peruse the stalls of family farmers, and taste the fruits of their labor. Baskets of tomatoes, peppers, squash, peaches, plums, and melons compete for your attention. J. T. and Carolyn Lemley have 25 years experience growing tomatoes, peaches, green beans, and squash, while Pat Sherlock offers a variety of shelled peas and beans at Pat's Pea Patch. These recipes are from our friends at the market and our readers. Let them help you enjoy the bounty of fresh goodies this season.

FRIED EGGPLANT

MAKES 6 TO 8 SERVINGS

Prep: 15 min., Stand: 30 min., Soak: 30 min., Cook: 3 min. per batch

  2 eggplants, peeled and cut into
     ¼-inch-thick slices
  1 teaspoon salt
  1 cup buttermilk
  ¾ cup self-rising flour
  ½ cup self-rising cornmeal
  ½ teaspoon pepper
  ½ teaspoon salt
  Vegetable oil

SPRINKLE both sides of eggplant slices evenly with salt; place on layers of paper towels, and let stand 30 minutes. Rinse and pat dry.
SOAK eggplant slices in buttermilk about 30 minutes.

COMBINE flour and next 3 ingredients. Drain eggplant slices, and dredge in flour mixture.
POUR oil to a depth of 1½ inches into a large cast-iron skillet, heat to 375°. Fry eggplant slices 3 minutes or until golden.

CURTIS AIKEN
NOVATO, CALIFORNIA

GREEN BEANS AND RED POTATOES

family favorite

MAKES 8 SERVINGS

Prep: 20 min., Cook: 1 hr.

  ½ pound smoked ham hocks
  3 quarts chicken broth
  2½ pounds fresh whole green beans,
     trimmed
  1 large onion, sliced
  1½ pounds small red potatoes, halved
  1 to 1½ teaspoons salt
  ½ bay leaf
  Freshly ground pepper (optional)
  Salt to taste

BRING ham hocks and chicken broth to a boil in a large Dutch oven; reduce heat to low, and simmer about 20 minutes.
ADD green beans and next 4 ingredients; bring to a boil. Reduce heat, and simmer about 30 minutes or until beans and potatoes are tender. Sprinkle with freshly ground pepper, if desired. Add salt to taste. Discard bay leaf.

BARBARA J. SCHOTT
CASTROVILLE, TEXAS

TOMATO-AND-OKRA BAKE

family favorite

MAKES 6 SERVINGS

Prep: 25 min., Cook: 10 min., Bake: 25 min.

Six ounces of any pasta can be used. Cooking the pasta first makes prep a breeze for this vegetable rendition of mac-and-cheese.

  ⅓ cup butter or margarine
  1 small onion, chopped
  1 small green bell pepper, chopped
  1 tablespoon all-purpose flour
  1 teaspoon salt
  ½ teaspoon pepper
  2 cups diced fresh tomatoes
  8 ounces pasteurized prepared cheese
     product, cubed and divided
  1 teaspoon chopped fresh basil
  1½ cups sliced fresh okra
  6 ounces cooked tiny penne pasta
  ¼ cup fine, dry breadcrumbs

MELT butter in a large skillet over medium-high heat. Add onion and green pepper; sauté until tender. Stir in flour, salt, and pepper.
ADD tomatoes, half of cheese, and basil. Cook 3 to 4 minutes or until thickened. Stir in okra and pasta. Pour mixture into a 1-quart casserole dish. Top evenly with breadcrumbs.
BAKE at 350° for 20 minutes. Top with remaining cheese, and bake 5 more minutes or until cheese melts.

CAROLYN LEMLEY
CANTON, TEXAS

TOMATO TART

MAKES 4 TO 6 SERVINGS

Prep: 45 min.; Stand: 10 min.; Bake: 1 hr., 24 min.

  ½ (15-ounce) package refrigerated
     piecrusts
  1 garlic bulb
  ½ teaspoon olive oil
  1½ cups shredded fontina cheese,
     divided
  4 large tomatoes
  ½ teaspoon salt
  ¼ teaspoon pepper

PRESS refrigerated piecrust on bottom and up sides of a 9-inch square tart pan. Bake at 450° for 9 minutes or until piecrust is lightly browned; set aside.
CUT off pointed end of garlic bulb; place garlic on a piece of aluminum foil, and drizzle with olive oil. Fold foil to seal.
BAKE garlic at 425° for 30 minutes; cool. Squeeze pulp from garlic cloves into bottom of baked piecrust.
SPRINKLE ½ cup fontina cheese over the garlic.
SLICE tomatoes, and sprinkle evenly with salt and pepper. Place on folded paper towels, and let stand 10 minutes. Arrange tomato slices over shredded cheese. Sprinkle tomato slices with remaining 1 cup cheese.
BAKE at 350° for 45 minutes or until tart is lightly browned.

CAROLYN LEMLEY
CANTON, TEXAS

AFTERBURNERS

MAKES 6 APPETIZER SERVINGS

Prep: 20 min., Broil: 14 min.

Afterburners are fiery appetizers of bacon-wrapped jalapeño peppers stuffed with shrimp. Serve with a spicy queso dip.

- 12 unpeeled, medium-size fresh shrimp
- 12 jalapeño peppers
- 6 bacon slices, halved lengthwise

PEEL shrimp, and devein, if desired.
CUT a slit in each jalapeño pepper; remove seeds and membranes. Carefully place 1 shrimp in cavity of each jalapeño pepper.
WRAP each pepper with 1 bacon piece, and secure with a wooden pick. Place in a 15-x 10-inch jellyroll pan.
BROIL 5½ inches from heat 6 to 7 minutes on each side or until bacon is cooked. Serve warm.

GEORGE E. HOLY
MONTGOMERY, ALABAMA

BEST PINTO BEANS

MAKES 8 SERVINGS

Prep: 15 min.; Cook: 1 hr., 25 min.

- 1 pound fresh pinto beans, sorted and rinsed*
- 1 smoked ham hock
- 1 (10-ounce) can diced tomatoes and green chiles
- 1 (32-ounce) container chicken broth
- 1 green bell pepper, chopped
- 1 celery rib, chopped
- ½ onion, chopped
- Dash of red hot sauce
- 1 teaspoon salt
- 1 teaspoon garlic powder
- 1 teaspoon oregano
- ½ teaspoon thyme
- ½ teaspoon black pepper
- 1 teaspoon Worcestershire sauce
- Hot cooked rice

PLACE beans in a large Dutch oven, and add water to cover. Bring to a boil, and cook, uncovered, 30 minutes. Drain.
ADD ham hock, tomatoes, broth, and next 10 ingredients to Dutch oven with beans; cook 55 minutes or until beans are tender. Serve over rice.

*Substitute dried pinto beans for fresh, if desired.

LARRY D. HEDGE
FORT WORTH, TEXAS

SUMMER VEGETABLE GRATIN

family favorite

MAKES 6 SERVINGS

Prep: 30 min., Bake: 55 min., Stand: 10 min

- 2 garlic cloves, finely chopped
- 4 to 5 plum tomatoes, cut into ¼-inch slices
- 3 to 4 small red potatoes, cut into ⅛-inch slices (about ½ pound)
- 1 small red onion, thinly sliced
- 1 (7-ounce) jar roasted red bell peppers, drained and chopped
- 2 medium zucchini, thinly sliced
- 1 cup sliced fresh mushrooms
- ¾ teaspoon salt
- ¾ teaspoon pepper
- 3 tablespoons olive oil, divided
- ½ cup finely crumbled cornbread
- 1 tablespoon Dijon mustard
- ¼ cup grated Parmesan cheese
- 2 tablespoons Italian seasoning

SPRINKLE bottom of a lightly greased 11- x 7-inch baking dish evenly with garlic. Layer with tomatoes and next 5 ingredients, sprinkling with ⅛ teaspoon each of salt and pepper between layers. Drizzle with 2 tablespoons oil.
BAKE at 350° for 45 minutes. Combine cornbread, next 3 ingredients, and remaining 1 tablespoon olive oil. Sprinkle over vegetable mixture; bake 10 more minutes or until top is golden. Let stand 10 minutes before serving.

KATHAN DEARMAN
NEW ORLEANS, LOUISIANA

Barbecue Made Easy

From brisket in the oven to slow-cooker ribs, these make-ahead favorites offer ease and flavor.

Homemade weeknight barbecue is doable. No need for a fire or coals—just use your oven or slow cooker. Pop the barbecue in the refrigerator, and reheat in a day or two. Complete your meal with deli sides, corn on the cob, and sweet tea to satisfy your 'cue craving.

SLOW-COOKER BARBECUE RIBS

family favorite • make ahead

MAKES 6 TO 8 SERVINGS

Prep: 15 min., Cook: 6 to 7 hrs.

Put these on before you leave for work, or cook them overnight and refrigerate until dinnertime. If you reheat in the microwave, use 50% power.

- 4 pounds bone-in country-style pork ribs
- 2 teaspoons salt, divided
- 1 medium onion, chopped
- 1 cup firmly packed light brown sugar
- 1 cup apple butter
- 1 cup ketchup
- ½ cup lemon juice
- ½ cup orange juice
- 1 tablespoon steak sauce
- 1 teaspoon coarse ground pepper
- 1 teaspoon minced garlic
- ½ teaspoon Worcestershire sauce

CUT ribs apart, if necessary, and trim; sprinkle 1 teaspoon salt evenly over ribs, and set aside.
STIR together remaining 1 teaspoon salt, chopped onion, and next 9 ingredients until blended. Pour half of mixture into a 5-quart slow cooker. Place ribs in slow cooker, and pour remaining mixture over ribs.
COVER and cook on HIGH 6 to 7 hours.

NOTE: For testing purposes only, we used A.1. Steak Sauce.

ALLISON SINCLAIR
WESTFIELD, NORTH CAROLINA

SMOKY BARBECUE BRISKET

family favorite • make ahead

MAKES 8 SERVINGS

Prep: 10 min., Chill: 8 hrs., Bake: 6 hrs.

This is even better if it stays in your refrigerator a day after cooking to absorb the flavors. Slice and reheat in the oven or microwave. *(pictured on page 154)*

- 1 (4- to 6-pound) beef brisket, trimmed
- 1 (5-ounce) bottle liquid smoke
- 1 onion, chopped
- 2 teaspoons garlic salt
- 1 to 2 teaspoons salt
- ⅓ cup Worcestershire sauce
- 1 (12- to 18-ounce) bottle barbecue sauce

PLACE brisket in a large shallow dish or extra-large, zip-top freezer bag; pour liquid smoke over brisket. Sprinkle evenly with chopped onion, garlic salt, and salt. Cover or seal, and chill 8 hours, turning occasionally.
REMOVE brisket, and place on a large piece of heavy-duty aluminum foil, discarding liquid smoke mixture. Pour Worcestershire sauce evenly over brisket, and fold foil to seal; place wrapped brisket in a roasting pan.
BAKE at 275° for 5 hours. Unfold foil; pour barbecue sauce evenly over brisket. Bake 1 more hour, uncovered.

LINDA PUGLIANO
FORT WORTH, TEXAS

OVEN-BAKED BARBECUE CHICKEN

family favorite • make ahead

MAKES 8 TO 10 SERVINGS

Prep: 10 min., Cook: 15 min., Bake: 2 hrs.

Make this up to two days ahead, and reheat in the oven or microwave. Use the leftovers in tacos or wraps with Cheddar cheese and bacon.

- 3 cups spicy tomato juice
- ½ cup cider vinegar
- 3 tablespoons vegetable oil
- 2 to 3 garlic cloves, minced
- 1 bay leaf
- 2 teaspoons salt
- 1 teaspoon sugar
- ½ teaspoon pepper
- ¼ teaspoon ground red pepper (optional)
- 4½ teaspoons Worcestershire sauce
- 2 cups all-purpose flour
- 10 chicken thighs, skin removed
- 10 chicken legs, skin removed

STIR together first 10 ingredients in a saucepan over medium-high heat; bring to a boil. Reduce heat, and simmer 10 minutes.
PLACE flour in a shallow dish; dredge chicken pieces on both sides. Arrange thighs, bone-side up, and legs in a roasting pan. Pour tomato juice mixture evenly over chicken.
BAKE at 350° for 1½ to 2 hours, basting occasionally. Discard bay leaf.

DONNA RICHARDSON
JAMESTOWN, NORTH CAROLINA

Plum Delicious

Take a bite of summer.

A good plum seems magical. The contrast between its tart skin and sweet flesh can turn an everyday dish into something extraordinary. These recipes make the most of one of Assistant Foods Editor Kate Nicholson's favorite fruit selections. As summer's rich bounty urges you to buy, don't overlook the glorious plum.

PLUM PRESERVES

make ahead

MAKES 2 (1-QUART) JARS

Prep: 15 min.; Cook: 1 hr., 40 min.; Process: 20 min.

- 4 pounds plums
- 4 cups sugar
- 2 tablespoons grated orange rind
- ¾ cup fresh orange juice
- ⅓ cup fresh lemon juice
- 1 (15-ounce) package raisins

CUT plums in half. Remove and discard plum pits.

BRING 2 cups sugar, orange rind, and juices to a full rolling boil in a Dutch oven, stirring constantly, 4 to 5 minutes or until sugar dissolves. Reduce heat, and add remaining 2 cups sugar, plum halves, and raisins; simmer, stirring occasionally, 1 hour and 15 minutes to 1 hour and 30 minutes or until thickened, skimming off any foam.

POUR hot mixture immediately into hot, sterilized jars, filling to ¼ inch from top. Remove air bubbles; wipe jar rims. Cover at once with metal lids, and screw on bands.

PROCESS in a boiling-water bath 20 minutes.

NOTE: Store unopened preserves in a cool, dry place up to one year.

SUZAN L. WIENER
SPRING HILL, FLORIDA

PLUM COBBLER

MAKES 6 SERVINGS

Prep: 25 min., Bake: 35 min.

- 1 cup orange juice
- ½ cup sugar
- 1 tablespoon cornstarch
- ½ teaspoon ground cinnamon
- 4 cups sliced plums (about 12 medium)
- 1½ cups all-purpose baking mix
- 2 tablespoons sugar
- ½ cup milk
- 2 tablespoons butter or margarine, melted

BRING first 4 ingredients to a boil in a saucepan. Remove from heat; stir in plums. Pour into an 8-inch square baking dish.

COMBINE baking mix and 2 tablespoons sugar; stir in milk and butter. Spoon over plum mixture.

BAKE at 400° for 30 to 35 minutes or until golden.

BRENDA RUSSELL
SIGNAL MOUNTAIN, TENNESSEE

CHILLED PLUM SOUP

MAKES ABOUT 6½ CUPS

Prep: 15 min., Cook: 5 min., Chill: 8 hrs.

Garnish this soup with fresh mint leaves for a beautiful presentation.

- 2½ pounds plums, coarsely chopped
- 3 cups whipping cream, divided
- 2 tablespoons raspberry vinegar
- ⅓ cup honey

PROCESS half of plums in a blender or food processor until smooth, stopping to scrape down sides; spoon into a large saucepan. Process remaining plums, 1 cup whipping cream, and vinegar until smooth, stopping to scrape down sides.

ADD plum mixture, remaining 2 cups whipping cream, and honey to plum puree in saucepan; simmer, stirring often, over medium heat 5 minutes or until blended. Cover and chill, stirring occasionally, 8 hours.

NOTE: For a sweeter tasting soup, add 1 to 2 more tablespoons of honey.

CRISP PLUM SALAD

MAKES 4 SERVINGS

Prep: 25 min., Chill: 2 hrs.

The sweet, nutty taste of raw jícama adds flavor and crunch to this salad.

- 1 teaspoon grated lime rind
- 6 tablespoons fresh lime juice
- 2 tablespoons olive oil
- 1 teaspoon salt
- 1 teaspoon sugar
- ¼ teaspoon ground red pepper
- 1 pound jícama, peeled and chopped
- 4 green onions, chopped
- 2 tablespoons chopped fresh cilantro
- 6 plums, chopped
- Garnishes: plum slices, fresh cilantro leaves

WHISK together first 6 ingredients in a large bowl; add jícama, green onions, and cilantro; toss. Add plums, tossing gently to coat. Cover and chill 2 hours. Garnish, if desired.

Summer Suppers.

Simple, refreshing menus for supper and beyond are in store for you this season. Whether you're feeding a crowd for breakfast, planning an outdoor lunch, or taking a walk on the international side for dinner, these recipes will become favorites. And don't miss our decorative beverage-cooler project—it'll help you chill out when the Southern summer heats up.

Home for the Fourth

Feast for the Fireworks

Serves 8

Shrimp Rolls

Sweet-and-Savory Burgers

Potato Salad

Fresh sliced tomatoes

Marinated Green Beans With Tomatoes, Olives, and Feta

Chewy Red, White, and Blue Cookies

Fresh Blackberry Pie   Berry Blue Fizz

The Fourth of July is a peak summer experience. It's a chance to savor a day of vacation pleasures—sleeping late, cooking out, and spending time with your family. We celebrate this day of our country's founding (and our independence from work and school) with fireworks and lots of fun.

This menu will complement your holiday activities with the season's favorite foods—burgers, shrimp, fresh tomatoes, green beans, and blackberries. Most of the recipes can be made the day before. However, the pie should be assembled and served on the same day for best results. You can prepare the hamburger patties ahead also, but cook them at mealtime for burgers that are deliciously hot and juicy.

SHRIMP ROLLS
---
family favorite • make ahead

MAKES 6 TO 8 SERVINGS

Prep: 35 min., Cook: 5 min., Chill: 2 hrs., Bake: 10 min.

These are a delicious Southern twist on New England's lobster rolls. *(pictured on page 152)*

- 3 quarts water
- 1 (3-ounce) package crab and shrimp boil seasoning
- 2 pounds unpeeled, large fresh shrimp
- 1/3 cup light mayonnaise
- 1 small onion, finely chopped
- 2 celery ribs, finely chopped
- 2 tablespoons lemon juice
- 1/2 teaspoon salt
- 1/4 teaspoon seasoned pepper
- 3 tablespoons butter, softened
- 1 garlic clove, minced
- 8 French rolls, split
- 8 Green Leaf lettuce leaves (optional)
- 3 avocados, cubed (optional)

BRING 3 quarts water and crab seasoning to a boil in a Dutch oven; add shrimp, and cook, stirring occasionally, 3 to 5 minutes or just until shrimp turn pink. Drain and cool.

PEEL cooked shrimp, and devein, if desired; coarsely chop shrimp.

STIR together mayonnaise and next 5 ingredients in a large bowl; stir in shrimp. Chill 2 hours.

STIR together butter and garlic, and spread evenly on cut side of bread halves. Bake at 375° for 10 minutes or until toasted.

LINE each roll with a lettuce leaf, if desired. Spoon shrimp mixture evenly on each roll. Top with avocado, if desired.

CARRIE MCCORMICK
DURHAM, NORTH CAROLINA

CHEWY RED, WHITE, AND BLUE COOKIES

family favorite • make ahead

MAKES 5 DOZEN

Prep: 35 min., Bake: 15 min. per batch

You can find red, white, and blue candies at supermarkets and discount stores before the Fourth of July.

    1 cup firmly packed light brown sugar
    1 cup sugar
    ½ cup butter or margarine, softened
    3 large eggs
    1½ cups smooth peanut butter
    1 teaspoon vanilla extract
    1 teaspoon light corn syrup
    4½ cups uncooked regular oats
    1 cup semisweet chocolate morsels
    1 cup (6 ounces) red, white, and blue
       candy-coated chocolate pieces
    2 teaspoons baking soda

BEAT sugars and butter at low speed with an electric mixer until creamy. Add eggs and next 3 ingredients, beating until combined. Stir in oats and remaining ingredients.

DROP by tablespoonfuls onto ungreased baking sheets.

BAKE, in batches, at 350° for 15 minutes. Remove to wire racks to cool.

NOTE: For testing purposes only, we used red, white, and blue M&Ms.

NANCY WILEY
JEFFERSON CITY, MISSOURI

POTATO SALAD

family favorite • make ahead

MAKES 8 TO 10 SERVINGS

Prep: 25 min., Cook: 20 min. *(pictured on page 152)*

    3 pounds red potatoes
    ⅓ cup olive oil
    2 tablespoons fresh lemon juice
    2 tablespoons mayonnaise
    1 teaspoon dried oregano
    1 teaspoon dry mustard
    1 teaspoon salt
    3 green onions, chopped
    ½ red or green bell pepper, finely
       chopped
    2 tablespoons chopped parsley
    ½ teaspoon black pepper
    Salt to taste

COMBINE potatoes and water to cover in a Dutch oven; bring to a boil, and cook 20 minutes or until tender. Drain and cool. Cut potatoes into 1-inch cubes.

STIR together olive oil and next 5 ingredients in a large bowl, blending well. Add potatoes, green onions, and remaining ingredients, gently tossing to coat. Serve at room temperature or chilled.

GLENN ULRICH
CHARLESTON, SOUTH CAROLINA

SWEET-AND-SAVORY BURGERS

family favorite • make ahead

MAKES 8 SERVINGS

Prep: 15 min., Chill: 4 hrs., Grill: 10 min. *(pictured on page 152)*

    ¼ cup soy sauce
    2 tablespoons corn syrup
    1 tablespoon lemon juice
    ½ teaspoon ground ginger
    ¼ teaspoon garlic powder
    2 green onions, thinly sliced
    2 pounds ground beef
    ¼ cup chili sauce
    ¼ cup jalapeño jelly
    8 hamburger buns
    Toppings: grilled sweet onions, grilled
       pineapple slices

STIR together first 6 ingredients; pour into a shallow pan or baking dish.

SHAPE beef into 8 patties; place in a single layer in marinade, turning to coat both sides. Cover and chill 4 hours. Drain, reserving marinade.

GRILL patties over medium-high heat (350° to 400°) 5 minutes on each side or until beef is no longer pink, brushing several times with reserved marinade. Stir together chili sauce and jelly. Serve patties on buns with chili sauce mixture and toppings.

HAZEL J. KING
NACOGDOCHES, TEXAS

MARINATED GREEN BEANS WITH TOMATOES, OLIVES, AND FETA

make ahead

MAKES 8 TO 10 SERVINGS

Prep: 30 min., Cook: 9 min., Chill: 3 hrs. *(pictured on page 152)*

    2 pounds fresh green beans,
       trimmed
    1½ teaspoons salt, divided
    2 garlic cloves, minced
    ¼ cup olive oil
    1 cup kalamata olives, sliced
    2 tomatoes, seeded and chopped
    2 tablespoons red wine vinegar
    1 tablespoon fresh oregano, finely
       chopped
    ¼ teaspoon pepper
    2 (4-ounce) packages crumbled feta
       cheese
    Garnish: fresh oregano sprigs

PLACE beans in boiling water seasoned with 1 teaspoon salt; cook 6 to 8 minutes or until crisp-tender. Drain. Plunge beans into ice water to stop the cooking process. Place in a shallow serving dish.

COOK garlic in hot oil in a skillet over medium heat 30 seconds or just until fragrant; remove from heat. Stir in olives, next 4 ingredients, and remaining ½ teaspoon salt. Pour mixture over beans, tossing to coat. Chill at least 3 hours or overnight. Sprinkle with feta cheese. Garnish, if desired.

BERRY BLUE FIZZ

fast fixin's

MAKES 8 SERVINGS

Prep: 10 min.

Kids will love this thick, brightly colored drink created by young Zack Levine.

- 3 cups water
- 4 (3-ounce) packages blueberry gelatin
- 5 (12-ounce) cans lemon-lime soft drink
- 6 cups pineapple sherbet

MICROWAVE 3 cups water in a large microwave-safe bowl at HIGH 5 minutes or until it boils. Stir in blueberry gelatin until dissolved. Cool slightly, and stir in lemon-lime soft drink.

SCOOP ¾ cup sherbet into each of 8 (16-ounce) glasses. Pour gelatin mixture over sherbet. Serve immediately.

ZACK LEVINE
HENDERSONVILLE, NORTH CAROLINA

FRESH BLACKBERRY PIE

family favorite

MAKES 8 SERVINGS

Prep: 30 min.; Bake: 9 min.; Cook: 8 min.; Chill: 10 hrs., 30 min.

Though this pie should be assembled and served the same day, you can get a head start by combining the berries and sugar and chilling them the night before.

- 1½ cups fresh blackberries
- 1¼ cups sugar, divided
- ½ (15-ounce) package refrigerated piecrusts
- 3 tablespoons cornstarch
- 1¼ cups water
- ½ teaspoon vanilla extract
- 1 (3-ounce) package raspberry gelatin
- 4 drops blue liquid food coloring
- Sweetened whipped cream (optional)

GENTLY toss berries and ¼ cup sugar in a large bowl; cover and chill 8 hours. Drain.
FIT piecrust into a 9-inch pieplate according to package directions; fold edges under, and crimp. Prick bottom and sides of piecrust with a fork. Bake at 450° for 7 to 9 minutes or until lightly browned.
STIR together cornstarch and remaining 1 cup sugar in a small saucepan; slowly whisk in 1¼ cups water and vanilla. Cook over medium heat, whisking constantly, 7 to 8 minutes or until mixture thickens.
STIR together raspberry gelatin and blue liquid food coloring in a small bowl; whisk into the warm cornstarch mixture.
SPOON blackberries into piecrust. Pour glaze evenly over berries, pressing down gently with a spoon to be sure all berries are coated. Chill 2½ hours. Serve with whipped cream, if desired.

KARYN M. DARDAR
MONTEGUT, LOUISIANA

Ice It Down

Keeping beverages cold at a gathering can be a challenge, especially if you're short on refrigerator space. For canned drinks, fill items you have around the yard, such as buckets, terra-cotta pots, or a wheelbarrow, with ice and use as coolers. (Be sure to clean thoroughly first.) To chill bottles, make individual decorative coolers following these instructions.

Items to Freeze

Consider using materials that will fit between the plastic container and empty wine bottle:

- fresh flowers
- small seashells
- sliced citrus fruit
- summer berries
- fresh herbs

NICELY ICED

Supplies:
An empty 3-liter clear plastic soft drink bottle or other large, wide plastic container
An empty 750-milliliter wine bottle, air dried
Plastic wrap
Heavy-duty tape
Items to Freeze (See shaded box.)
Wooden skewers
Funnel
Distilled water (to prevent cloudiness)
Scissors

CUT the plastic container 2 inches above the desired height of the finished cooler.
WRAP the empty wine bottle in the plastic wrap.
PLACE wrapped bottle in center of the plastic container.
SECURE heavy-duty tape to 1 side of plastic container. Continue up 1 side and over the top of the wine bottle, securing tape on opposite side of plastic container. Repeat procedure, forming an X across top of bottle. (This holds wine bottle in place when water is poured into plastic container.)
FILL the space between plastic container and wine bottle tightly, in a decorative fashion, with selected objects. Use wooden skewers to push items snugly in the bottom curves of the plastic container and to readjust once water is added, if necessary.
USING the funnel, pour the distilled water 2 inches from the top of the plastic container.
FREEZE at least 24 hours.
REMOVE from freezer, and let stand at room temperature 20 minutes. Remove heavy-duty tape, and hold bottle under cool running water to loosen plastic container. If you have trouble removing the plastic, cut the plastic bottle, beginning at the top edge, and continue cutting down side to remove.
FILL wine bottle with hot water, and let stand for 10 minutes, twisting bottle to dislodge. Discard wine bottle and plastic wrap. Place chilled bottle in cooler to serve. Frozen coolers will last 2 to 3 hours.

A Blending of Flavors

Familiar ingredients and Indian recipes create a vibrant fusion of tastes and culture.

Sejal Patel, of Roswell, Georgia, was thrilled to share her family's traditional recipes with *Southern Living*. She quickly added that if we wanted the really good stuff, we'd better talk to her mom, Ranjan Patel. Once we received Ranjan's mouthwatering recipes, we substituted more widely available ingredients for some of the less common ones she uses.

COOL CUCUMBER SALAD

MAKES 3½ CUPS

Prep: 10 min., Chill: 2 hrs.

Known as raita (RI-tah), this refreshing saucy dish balances spicy meats.

- 2 cups plain yogurt
- 1 large cucumber, peeled, seeded, and diced
- 1 medium-size sweet onion, chopped
- ½ to 1 small jalapeño pepper, seeded and minced
- ¼ cup chopped fresh cilantro
- 1 teaspoon cumin seeds*
- 1 teaspoon lemon pepper
- ½ teaspoon salt
- Garnishes: fresh cilantro sprigs, cucumber slices

STIR together first 8 ingredients in a bowl. Cover and chill at least 2 hours. Garnish, if desired.

*Substitute ½ teaspoon ground cumin, if desired.

SPICY SKILLET FISH

MAKES 6 SERVINGS

Prep: 10 min., Chill: 30 min., Cook: 10 min. per batch

For a different variation, prepare this recipe as directed, and make fish soft tacos with warmed flour or corn tortillas. Drizzle with fresh lime juice, and serve with your favorite rice.

- 2 garlic cloves
- 1 (2-inch) piece fresh ginger, peeled and chopped (about 2 tablespoons chopped)
- ½ cup chopped fresh cilantro
- 1 small jalapeño pepper, seeded
- 1 teaspoon salt
- ½ teaspoon ground paprika
- ½ teaspoon ground turmeric
- ½ teaspoon ground coriander
- 2 teaspoons vegetable oil
- 2 pounds catfish, grouper, or flounder fillets (about 6 fillets)
- 2 tablespoons vegetable oil
- Fresh lemon or lime wedges (optional)

PROCESS first 9 ingredients in a food processor until finely chopped.
SPREAD 2 teaspoons spice mixture evenly over both sides of each fillet. Cover and chill 30 minutes.
COOK fish, in batches, in 2 tablespoons hot vegetable oil in a large nonstick skillet over medium-high heat 5 minutes on each side or until fish flakes with a fork. Serve with fresh lemon or lime wedges, if desired.

TANDOORI CHICKEN

MAKES 8 SERVINGS

Prep: 20 min., Chill: 8 hrs., Bake: 35 min.

This spicy chicken dish calls for quite a few ingredients, but it's well worth it. High-heat roasting makes for a short cooking time.

- 6 tablespoons fresh lime juice (about 3 limes)
- 3 tablespoons plain yogurt
- 1 to 2 small jalapeño or serrano chile peppers, seeded and minced
- 1½ teaspoons salt
- 1 teaspoon ground turmeric
- 1 teaspoon ground coriander
- 1 teaspoon ground cumin
- ½ teaspoon ground ginger
- ½ teaspoon garlic powder
- ½ teaspoon ground red pepper
- ¼ teaspoon ground cinnamon
- ¼ teaspoon ground cloves
- 2 tablespoons vegetable oil, divided
- 3 pounds chicken pieces
- Garnishes: lime wedges, jalapeño or serrano chile peppers

STIR together first 12 ingredients and 1 tablespoon vegetable oil in a large bowl until blended.
SKIN chicken breasts. Remove breast bones by inserting a sharp knife tip between bone and meat, cutting gently to remove as much meat as possible. Cut breast halves into thirds. Cut deep slits, 1-inch apart, into remaining chicken pieces. (Do not skin pieces.) Place chicken in a large bowl with spice mixture. Thoroughly rub spice mixture into slits. Cover and chill 8 hours.
DRIZZLE remaining 1 tablespoon oil in a large aluminum foil-lined roasting pan. Arrange chicken in a single layer in pan. Bake chicken at 450° for 35 minutes or until done.
ARRANGE chicken on a serving platter. Garnish, if desired.

NOTE: For testing purposes only, we used Butterball Best of the Fryer, a cut-up mix of chicken breasts, thighs, legs, and wings.

Simple Stir-Fried Okra

fast fixin's

MAKES 4 TO 6 SERVINGS

Prep: 10 min., Cook: 20 min.

We prepared this recipe with frozen whole okra. The results were consistently tender, fragrant, and fresh-tasting.

1 medium-size sweet onion, chopped
1 teaspoon mustard seeds*
½ teaspoon ground cumin
¼ teaspoon dried crushed red pepper
2 tablespoons vegetable oil
1 (16-ounce) package frozen okra, thawed, or 1 pound fresh okra
¾ teaspoon salt

SAUTÉ first 4 ingredients in hot oil in a large skillet over medium-high heat 5 minutes or until onion is tender.
ADD okra; sauté 15 minutes or until okra is lightly browned. Stir in salt.

*Substitute ½ teaspoon dry mustard for 1 teaspoon mustard seeds, if desired.

Morning at the Lake

Before a day of fun on the water, Rosalie Nicholson fuels her hungry crew with this terrific menu.

Sunday Brunch

Serves 8 to 10

Bacon-and-Egg Casserole   Pigs in a Blanket
Quick Double-Cheese Grits   Sliced fresh tomatoes
Fresh Fruit Salad With Orange-Ginger Syrup
Peach Streusel Muffins
Coffee   Orange juice

Peach Yogurt Refresher

fast fixin's

MAKES 5 CUPS

Prep: 5 min.

Known in India as lassi (lah-see), this shakelike beverage is usually prepared with mango. It's a healthy way to start your day.

3 cups plain yogurt
1 cup sliced fresh peaches*
½ cup water
6 tablespoons sugar

PROCESS all ingredients in a blender until smooth, stopping to scrape down sides. Serve over ice.

*Substitute 1 cup fresh mango slices, if desired.

Bacon-and-Egg Casserole

family favorite • make ahead

MAKES 8 TO 10 SERVINGS

Prep: 25 min., Chill: 8 hrs., Stand: 30 min., Bake: 35 min.

Assemble this hearty dish the night before, and bake the next morning.

1 (16-ounce) Hawaiian bread loaf, cut into ¾-inch cubes
2 cups (8 ounces) finely shredded Mexican four-cheese blend
½ pound bacon, cooked and crumbled (8 slices)
8 large eggs
2½ cups milk
½ teaspoon salt
½ teaspoon pepper
1 teaspoon dry mustard
½ teaspoon Worcestershire sauce
Salsa or sliced fresh tomatoes

ARRANGE bread cubes in a lightly greased 13- x 9-inch baking dish. Sprinkle with shredded cheese and crumbled bacon.
WHISK together eggs, milk, salt, pepper, mustard, and Worcestershire sauce. Pour over prepared dish; press down bread cubes with a spoon to allow bread to soak up liquid. Cover and chill 8 hours. Let stand 30 minutes before baking.
BAKE at 350° for 35 minutes or until set and golden. Serve with salsa or sliced fresh tomatoes.

NOTE: Hawaiian bread can be found in the deli section of the supermarket. Substitute 10 to 12 white bread slices, cubed, for Hawaiian bread, if desired.

PIGS IN A BLANKET

family favorite

MAKES 8 TO 10 SERVINGS

Prep: 30 min., Cook: 10 min., Bake: 15 min.

- 1 pound uncooked small link breakfast sausage
- 2 (8-ounce) cans refrigerated crescent rolls
- ½ cup coarse-ground mustard
- ¼ cup light mayonnaise
- 2 tablespoons honey

COOK sausage in a large skillet over medium-high heat 10 minutes or until browned and thoroughly cooked. Drain on paper towels.

DIVIDE crescent rolls into individual triangles. Place 1 cooked sausage link in center of each dough triangle. Roll up, starting at wide end. Arrange on an ungreased baking sheet.

BAKE at 350° for 10 to 15 minutes or until golden brown.

STIR together mustard, mayonnaise, and honey in a bowl. Serve with sausage rolls.

QUICK DOUBLE-CHEESE GRITS

family favorite • fast fixin's

MAKES 8 SERVINGS

Prep: 15 min., Cook: 5 min.

- 6 cups water
- ½ teaspoon salt
- 1½ cups quick-cooking grits
- 1 cup (4 ounces) shredded extra-sharp Cheddar cheese
- 1 cup (4 ounces) shredded Monterey Jack cheese
- 2 tablespoons butter or margarine
- ½ teaspoon pepper

BRING 6 cups water and salt to a boil in a large saucepan. Gradually stir in grits. Cook 4 to 5 minutes, stirring often, until thickened. Remove from heat. Add shredded cheeses, butter, and pepper, stirring until blended. Serve cheese grits immediately.

NOTE: Grits may be chilled and reheated. Whisk ¼ cup warm water into grits over medium-heat, adding more water as necessary.

FRESH FRUIT SALAD WITH ORANGE-GINGER SYRUP

fast fixin's

MAKES 8 TO 10 SERVINGS

Prep: 25 min.

- 1 large cantaloupe, cut into 2-inch cubes
- 2 pints fresh strawberries, halved
- 1 pint fresh blueberries
- 1 pineapple, peeled, cored, and cut into 2-inch cubes
- Orange-Ginger Syrup

COMBINE cantaloupe, strawberries, blueberries, and pineapple in a large bowl. Serve with chilled Orange-Ginger Syrup.

Orange-Ginger Syrup:

MAKES ¾ CUP

Prep: 10 min., Cook: 5 min., Stand: 15 min., Chill: 1 hr.

Make this citrusy-sweet syrup up to three days ahead. It's also tasty in unsweetened iced tea.

- 1 cup sugar
- ½ cup water
- 2 tablespoons chopped fresh ginger
- 2 teaspoons orange rind
- ¼ teaspoon lemon juice

COOK all ingredients in a small saucepan over low heat until sugar dissolves. Bring to a boil; reduce heat, and simmer 1 minute.

REMOVE from heat; let stand 15 minutes. Remove and discard ginger and orange rind. Cool syrup; chill 1 hour or up to 3 days.

NOTE: Remove rind from an orange using a vegetable peeler or paring knife. Avoid the white, bitter pith as much as possible.

PEACH STREUSEL MUFFINS

family favorite

MAKES 1 DOZEN

Prep: 20 min., Bake: 20 min.

If you're using frozen peach slices, thaw them; then drain any liquid before chopping.

- ¼ cup butter or margarine, softened
- ⅓ cup sugar
- 1 large egg
- 2⅓ cups all-purpose flour
- 1 tablespoon baking powder
- ½ teaspoon salt
- ¾ cup milk
- 1 teaspoon vanilla extract
- 1½ cups chopped fresh or frozen peeled peaches
- ¼ cup sugar
- 3 tablespoons all-purpose flour
- ¼ teaspoon ground cinnamon
- 2½ tablespoons chilled butter or margarine

BEAT ¼ cup butter at medium speed with an electric mixer until creamy; gradually add ⅓ cup sugar, beating until light and fluffy. Add egg, beating mixture until blended.

COMBINE 2⅓ cups flour, baking powder, and salt. Add flour mixture to butter mixture alternately with milk, stirring well after each addition. Stir in vanilla, and fold in chopped peaches.

SPOON muffin batter into a greased or paper-lined muffin pan, filling two-thirds full.

COMBINE ¼ cup sugar, 3 tablespoons flour, and cinnamon; cut in 2½ tablespoons butter with a pastry blender or fork until mixture resembles crumbs. Sprinkle evenly over muffin batter.

BAKE at 375° for 20 minutes or until golden. Remove from pan, and cool on wire racks.

Good Food Is a Breeze

Lee Guinn and his wife, Jane, of Corpus Christi, Texas, enjoy spending the day with dear friends and family aboard their sailboat stocked with tasty food from their cafe and juice bar, Somethin' Healthy. Dickinson Merkle, Jr., manager of the eatery and friend of the Guins, bought these recipes along on this summer cruise.

Wrappin' Picnic

Serves 3

Garden Wrap, Turkey Wrap, or Mediterranean Wrap

Chilled Watermelon Soup

Sticky Fingers

Apple Lemonade   Cayenne Lemonade

GARDEN WRAP

chef recipe • fast fixin's

MAKES 1 SERVING

Prep: 15 min.

- 2 to 3 tablespoons hummus
- 1 (9-inch) whole wheat-and-honey wrap
- ¼ cup shredded carrot
- ⅓ cup shredded Monterey Jack cheese
- ¼ cup shredded red cabbage
- ¼ cucumber, peeled and chopped
- 2 tablespoons chopped red bell pepper
- 1 tablespoon lemon juice
- ¼ teaspoon salt
- ¼ teaspoon pepper

SPREAD hummus over 1 side of wrap. **STIR** together carrot and next 7 ingredients. Sprinkle over hummus. Roll up tightly. Cut diagonally in half.

NOTE: Hummus can be found in the refrigerated deli section of the supermarket, near the gourmet cheeses. We used pre-shredded carrots found in (10-ounce) packages in the produce section of the supermarket.

TURKEY WRAP

chef recipe • fast fixin's

MAKES 1 SERVING

Prep: 10 min.

- 2 tablespoons ⅓-less-fat cream cheese
- 1 (9-inch) spinach or tomato-basil wrap
- 1 tablespoon Dijon mustard
- 5 smoked turkey breast slices (about 5 ounces)
- 4 tomato slices
- 1 cup chopped fresh baby spinach
- ⅓ cup shredded Monterey Jack cheese
- 1 to 2 tablespoons chopped fresh basil

SPREAD cream cheese over half of 1 side of wrap. Spread mustard over cream cheese and remaining half of wrap. Top with turkey and remaining ingredients. Roll up tightly. Cut diagonally in half.

MEDITERRANEAN WRAP

chef recipe • fast fixin's

MAKES 1 SERVING

Prep: 15 min. *(pictured on page 153)*

- 1 tablespoon ⅓-less-fat cream cheese
- 1 (9-inch) spinach or tomato-basil wrap
- ¾ cup chopped fresh baby spinach
- ½ small avocado, sliced
- ⅓ cup crumbled feta cheese
- ¼ cup chopped tomato
- 2 tablespoons sliced black olives
- 1 to 1½ tablespoons chopped fresh basil
- 1 tablespoon wine vinaigrette

SPREAD cream cheese over 1 side of wrap. Top with chopped spinach and remaining ingredients. Roll up wrap tightly. Cut diagonally in half.

NOTE: For testing purposes only, we used Brianna's Blush Wine Vinaigrette.

CHILLED WATERMELON SOUP

chef recipe

MAKES 4 CUPS

Prep: 30 min., Chill: 1 hr.

We added fresh lime juice for tang and honey for extra sweetness. If your watermelon is sweet, omit the honey. For a pretty presentation, garnish the soup with watermelon balls and fresh mint sprigs.

- 4 cups seeded watermelon cubes
- ⅓ cup apple juice
- 2 tablespoons fresh lime juice
- 1 teaspoon chopped fresh mint
- ¼ to ½ teaspoon ground ginger
- 1 tablespoon honey (optional)
- ⅓ cup plain nonfat yogurt

PROCESS first 5 ingredients and honey, if desired, in a blender or food processor until smooth, stopping to scrape down sides. Cover and chill 1 hour. Serve in individual bowls with a dollop of yogurt.

STICKY FINGERS

chef recipe • fast fixin's

MAKES 3 SERVINGS

Prep: 10 min.

For nonSticky Fingers, top with another slice of banana bread, and cut into three sandwiches.

- 1 tablespoon peanut butter
- 3 (½-inch-thick) slices banana bread
- ½ large banana, sliced
- 3 tablespoons toasted sweetened coconut
- 1 tablespoon honey
- Garnish: fresh fruit

SPREAD peanut butter evenly over banana bread; top with banana and coconut. Drizzle with honey. Serve at room temperature, or heat in microwave at HIGH 10 seconds, and serve warm. Garnish, if desired.

NOTE: For testing purposes only, we used Pepperidge Farm Banana Swirl Bread for banana bread.

APPLE LEMONADE

chef recipe • fast fixin's

MAKES 4½ CUPS

Prep: 10 min.

At their cafe and juice bar, the Guinn's use fresh apples for this recipe, but we used bottled juice.

- 1 quart apple juice, chilled
- ½ cup fresh lemon juice (about 3 lemons)
- Mint sprigs (optional)
- Lemon slices (optional)

COMBINE fruit juices. Serve over ice with mint sprigs and lemon slices, if desired.

CAYENNE LEMONADE

chef recipe • fast fixin's

MAKES 6 CUPS

Prep: 5 min.

Pepper in lemonade? Surprisingly, yes. The zing actually heightens the sweetness and fresh lemon flavor.

- 1 cup fresh lemon juice (4 to 6 lemons)
- 1 cup pure maple syrup
- 4 cups water
- ⅛ to ¼ teaspoon ground red pepper

STIR together ingredients. Serve over ice.

Afternoon Picnic

STRAWBERRY-LEMONADE SLUSH

family favorite

MAKES ABOUT 2 QUARTS

Prep: 20 min., Stand: 30 min.

- 2 (16-ounce) containers fresh strawberries, sliced
- 1½ cups sugar
- 2 cups water
- 1½ cups fresh lemon juice (6 to 9 medium lemons)
- 4 cups ice cubes

STIR together sliced strawberries and sugar; let stand 30 minutes.
PROCESS half of strawberry mixture, 1 cup water, ¾ cup lemon juice, and 2 cups ice in a blender until smooth. Repeat procedure with remaining ingredients. Serve immediately.

OPEN-FACED COLESLAW REUBENS

fast fixin's

MAKES 8 SERVINGS

Prep: 25 min., Bake: 6 min.

Buy an unsliced loaf of rye bread in the deli section of your grocery store or bakery, and cut thick slices with a serrated or bread knife.

- ¾ cup mayonnaise, divided
- 8 green onions, sliced
- 2 tablespoons white vinegar
- ½ teaspoon salt
- ½ teaspoon pepper
- 1 (10-ounce) package finely shredded cabbage
- ¼ cup Dijon mustard
- 8 (1-inch-thick) rye bread slices, lightly toasted
- 16 (¾-ounce) Swiss cheese slices
- 16 ounces thinly sliced corned beef

STIR together ½ cup mayonnaise and next 4 ingredients in a large bowl; stir in shredded cabbage, and set aside, or chill until ready to serve.
STIR together mustard and remaining ¼ cup mayonnaise. Spread evenly on 1 side of each bread slice. Layer evenly with 1 cheese slice and corned beef; top with remaining cheese slices. Place on a baking sheet.
BAKE at 450° for 5 to 6 minutes or until cheese is melted. Spoon coleslaw mixture evenly over cheese, and serve immediately.

MILDRED BICKLEY
BRISTOL, VIRGINIA

CHOCOLATE-CREAM CHEESE CUPCAKES

family favorite

MAKES 2½ DOZEN

Prep: 30 min., Bake: 25 min.

Dollop cupcakes with whipped topping, and add your favorite sprinkles.

- 1 (18.25-ounce) package Swiss chocolate cake mix
- 1 (8-ounce) package cream cheese, softened
- ⅓ cup sugar
- 1 large egg
- 1 cup semisweet chocolate morsels

PREPARE cake mix according to package directions. Spoon batter into paper-lined muffin pans, filling two-thirds full.
BEAT cream cheese and sugar at medium speed with an electric mixer until fluffy. Add egg, beating well; stir in chocolate morsels. Spoon 1 heaping teaspoon cream cheese mixture into center of batter.
BAKE at 350° for 25 minutes. Remove from pans, and cool on wire racks. Store in refrigerator.

NOTE: For testing, we used Duncan Hines Swiss Chocolate Cake Mix.

Pair Veggies With Pasta

Savor these snappy suppers any night of the week.

As the weather gets warmer, schedules get busier. We've combined pasta with this season's fresh vegetables to help you put a satisfying supper on the table in 45 minutes or less. These dishes are perfect for fast-fix entrées. While the pasta cooks, just heat a loaf of crusty garlic bread and make an easy salad to complete your meal.

LINGUINE WITH SAUSAGE AND PEPPERS

family favorite

MAKES 6 SERVINGS

Prep: 25 min., Cook: 20 min.

Jan Kimbell uses extra virgin olive oil to pack this dish with even more flavor.

- 1 pint grape or cherry tomatoes, halved
- ¾ teaspoon coarse-grained sea salt or kosher salt
- 1 (12-ounce) package linguine
- 1 (16-ounce) package mild Italian turkey sausage links
- 1 red bell pepper, seeded and diced
- 1 green bell pepper, seeded and diced
- 1 medium-size sweet onion, diced
- 1 (8-ounce) package sliced fresh mushrooms
- 3 garlic cloves, minced
- ¼ teaspoon dried crushed red pepper
- 1 tablespoon olive oil
- 1½ cups shredded Parmesan cheese

STIR together tomatoes and salt; set aside, stirring occasionally.
COOK linguine in a Dutch oven, according to package directions. Drain and return to Dutch oven; keep warm.

REMOVE and discard casings from sausage. Brown sausage, bell peppers, onion, and mushrooms in a large skillet over medium-high heat, stirring until sausage crumbles and is no longer pink. Add garlic; cook 2 minutes. Drain.
TOSS together linguine, sausage mixture, tomatoes, crushed red pepper, olive oil, and ½ cup Parmesan cheese. Serve immediately with remaining Parmesan cheese.

JAN KIMBELL
VESTAVIA HILLS, ALABAMA

SPAGHETTINI WITH GREEN BEANS AND WALNUT BROWN BUTTER

family favorite

MAKES 4 SERVINGS

Prep: 15 min., Cook: 20 min.

- 1 (8-ounce) package spaghettini
- ½ pound small fresh green beans, trimmed*
- 5 tablespoons butter, cut into pieces
- ⅔ cup chopped walnuts
- ½ teaspoon salt
- 2 garlic cloves, minced
- ¼ teaspoon pepper
- 2 lemons, halved
- 2 green onions, chopped (optional)
- ½ cup freshly grated Parmesan cheese

COOK spaghettini in a large Dutch oven, according to package directions, adding green beans the last 4 minutes; drain. Keep warm.
MELT butter in a small skillet over medium-high heat. Add walnuts and salt; cook, stirring occasionally, 2 minutes, until butter is golden brown. Stir in garlic and pepper. Pour over spaghettini mixture, tossing well. Squeeze juice of 2 lemons evenly over top of spaghettini mixture; discard lemons. Top with green onions, if desired. Serve with cheese.

*Substitute asparagus for green beans, if desired.

MARY PAPPAS
RICHMOND, VIRGINIA

PENNE WITH SPINACH AND FETA

fast fixin's

MAKES 4 SERVINGS

Prep: 15 min., Cook: 15 min.

- 1 (8-ounce) package penne pasta
- 5 large plum tomatoes, seeded and chopped
- 2 cups fresh spinach
- 4 green onions, chopped
- 2 tablespoons olive oil
- 2 teaspoons dried or 1 tablespoon chopped fresh oregano
- 2 teaspoons dried or 1 tablespoon chopped fresh basil
- ½ teaspoon salt
- ¼ teaspoon pepper
- 1 (6-ounce) package basil-and-tomato crumbled feta cheese

PREPARE pasta in a large Dutch oven, according to package directions; drain. Return to Dutch oven.
STIR in tomatoes and next 7 ingredients; cook 2 minutes over medium heat or until thoroughly heated. Top with cheese. Serve immediately.

NOTE: For testing purposes only, we used Athenos Basil & Tomato crumbled feta cheese.

SHARON GEANULEAS
ROUND ROCK, TEXAS

Lip-Smackin' Sorbets

These icy concoctions burst with the flavors of your favorite citrus fruits, melons, and berries. Unlike its cousins ice cream and sherbet, sorbet is made without cream or eggs, so it's the perfect pick-me-up for the dog days of summer.

Sugar is the key to a good sorbet—too little and the crystals will be too big, too much and the sorbet will be slushy. Make sure you select the ripest, most fragrant fruits to add even more punch. Cover leftover sorbet with plastic wrap (directly on the surface), and store in a plastic container in the freezer up to two weeks.

WATERMELON SORBET

family favorite • make ahead

MAKES ABOUT ½ GALLON

Prep: 15 min., Cook: 5 min., Chill: 2 hrs., Freeze: about 1 hr. *(pictured on page 156)*

- **3 cups water**
- **1 cup sugar**
- **4 cups seeded, chopped watermelon**
- **¼ cup lime juice**

BRING 3 cups water and sugar just to a boil in a medium saucepan over high heat, stirring until sugar dissolves. Remove from heat. Cool.

PROCESS sugar syrup and watermelon, in batches, in a blender until smooth. Stir in lime juice. Cover and chill 2 hours.

POUR mixture into the freezer container of a 1-gallon ice-cream maker, and freeze according to manufacturer's instructions.

GRAPEFRUIT SORBET: Substitute 3 cups fresh grapefruit juice and 1 teaspoon chopped fresh mint for watermelon and lime juice. Proceed as directed.

PINEAPPLE SORBET: Substitute 2 cups chopped pineapple for watermelon and lime juice. Strain and discard pulp after processing mixture in blender, if desired. Proceed as directed.

LEMON SORBET: Substitute ½ cup of fresh lemon juice and 2 teaspoons grated lemon rind for watermelon and lime juice. Proceed as directed.

ORANGE SORBET: Substitute 3 cups fresh orange juice and 2 teaspoons grated orange rind for watermelon and lime juice. Proceed as directed.

STRAWBERRY SORBET: Substitute 5 cups fresh or frozen strawberries and 2 tablespoons lemon juice for watermelon and lime juice. Proceed as directed.

CANTALOUPE SORBET: Substitute 4 cups chopped cantaloupe for watermelon and lime juice. Proceed as directed.

CHERRY SORBET: Substitute 1 (6-ounce) can frozen lemonade concentrate, prepared, and 1 (16-ounce) jar maraschino cherries, drained, for watermelon and lime juice. Strain and discard pulp, if desired. Proceed as directed.

RASPBERRY SORBET: Substitute 5 cups fresh or frozen raspberries for watermelon and lime juice. Proceed as directed.

A Ritzy Mojito

When it comes to drinks, Southerners enjoy just about anything, so long as it sits on cubes of ice. Iced tea reigns as the table wine of our region, but we also like Coca-Cola, lemonade, coffee, punch, orange juice, and all manner of other drinks on the rocks.

Our fondness for ice may, at least somewhat, explain our preferences in imbibing. While the rest of the country drinks room-temperature wine and hot toddies, the South swoons over drinks famed not so much for their potency as for their cooling effects. The latest iced spirit embraced by Southerners is Cuba's mojito. The mojito (pronounced "moe-HEE-toe") was a favorite drink of Ernest Hemingway. It's something of a cross between a mint julep and a limeade, excepting all that rum, of course. Light, cool, and refreshing, the mojito is the perfect summer drink. Nearly every swank hotel and restaurant in Florida touts a mojito on their list of specialty cocktails. Ordering one elsewhere in the South may be dicey, but then, such is the penalty of being hip to new fads. Better still, impress your friends by making your own at home. Good luck out there.

A RITZY MOJITO

chef recipe • fast fixin's

MAKES 1 SERVING

Prep: 5 min.

After sampling almost every mojito in South Florida, Travel Editor Morgan Murphy found his favorite at The Ritz-Carlton Key Biscayne, near Miami. The hotel has kindly shared its one-serving recipe with us. The hotel also serves their now-famous mojito martini—essentially the same drink but with vodka instead of rum. Watch out!

- **10 mint leaves**
- **2 tablespoons sugar**
- **Juice from ½ lime**
- **1½ ounces rum**
- **Ice**
- **Splash of club soda**
- **Garnish: fresh mint sprig**

MIX mint leaves, sugar, and lime juice in a small mortar bowl; crush mint.
ADD rum, and stir.
POUR into a glass with ice.
ADD a splash of club soda, and garnish, if desired.

Quick & Easy

Fresh Takes on Supper

Pick up some ground beef for fast, delicious meals.

This column is designed to simplify meal planning and preparation for our busy lives. Most recipes included each month are ready to serve in about 45 minutes. When they take longer, we offer make-ahead, timesaving tips.

Here we focus on an old standard—ground beef—but there's certainly nothing old or standard about these dishes. Recipes from our readers offer quick, updated versions of a main dish salad, meat loaf, and soft tacos for your family's meals.

BEEF-AND-LIME RICE SALAD

make ahead

MAKES 4 SERVINGS

Prep: 15 min., Cook: 35 min.

This salad can be served right away or chilled and served cold. *(pictured on page 155)*

- 1 pound lean ground beef
- 3 cups water
- ½ teaspoon salt
- ½ teaspoon ground cumin
- 1½ cups long-grain rice
- 1 teaspoon grated lime rind
- 1 tablespoon fresh lime juice
- Toppings: salsa, shredded Cheddar cheese, tortilla chips, sour cream, chopped tomatoes, chopped green onions, avocado slices

COOK beef in a 3-quart saucepan over medium-high heat, stirring until it crumbles and is no longer pink. Drain and pat dry with paper towels. Wipe pan clean.

ADD 3 cups water, salt, and cumin to saucepan. Bring to a boil, and add rice; cover, reduce heat, and cook 20 to 25 minutes or until water is absorbed and rice is tender. Stir in beef, lime rind, and lime juice. Serve salad with desired toppings.

TAMY WHITE
HARTWELL, GEORGIA

TACOS WRAPIDOS

family favorite

MAKES 4 SERVINGS

Prep: 20 min., Cook: 20 min.

- 1 (4.3-ounce) package quick-cooking Spanish rice
- 1 pound lean ground beef
- 1 teaspoon fajita seasoning
- 4 (10-inch) flour tortillas
- 1 avocado, cut into 8 slices
- 1 cup (4 ounces) shredded Cheddar cheese
- 1 cup shredded lettuce
- ½ cup diced tomatoes

PREPARE rice according to package directions.
TOSS ground beef with fajita seasoning. Cook in a large nonstick skillet over medium-high heat, stirring until beef crumbles and is no longer pink; drain. Stir in cooked rice.
SPREAD beef mixture evenly over 1 side of each tortilla. Top with avocado slices, cheese, lettuce, and tomatoes. Roll up.

MARLA CLARK
MORIARTY, NEW MEXICO

TERIYAKI MEAT LOAF

family favorite • make ahead

MAKES 4 SERVINGS

Prep: 15 min., Bake: 40 min.

To prepare ahead, combine the ingredients, and shape into a loaf the night before or in the morning. Remove from the refrigerator to stand while you heat the oven.

- ⅔ cup orange marmalade
- 3 tablespoons teriyaki sauce, divided
- 2 tablespoons seasoned rice wine vinegar
- ¼ teaspoon dried crushed red pepper
- 1 pound ground beef
- 1 cup soft breadcrumbs
- ½ cup finely chopped roasted peanuts
- 1 tablespoon fresh lime juice
- ½ teaspoon ground ginger
- ½ teaspoon minced garlic
- 1 large egg
- Hot cooked rice or mashed potatoes

STIR together marmalade, 2 tablespoons teriyaki sauce, vinegar, and red pepper. Set aside.
COMBINE ground beef, next 6 ingredients, and remaining 1 tablespoon teriyaki sauce. Shape into a 7- x 4-inch loaf, and place in a 9-inch square pan or baking dish.
BAKE at 350° for 30 minutes. Remove from oven, and pour reserved marmalade mixture over meat; bake 8 to 10 more minutes or until done. Serve with hot cooked rice or mashed potatoes, and drizzle with pan juices, if desired.

ROXANNE CHAN
ALBANY, CALIFORNIA

Taste of the South

Fried Green Tomatoes

Senior Writer Donna Florio is embarrassed to admit this, but before she came to work at *Southern Living* seven years ago, she had never tasted a fried green tomato. Call her deprived, but for some reason she had never found the gumption to sample this traditional Southern favorite. To her way of thinking, tomatoes ought to be red and fresh, not green and fried.

That all changed one day at taste testing. Test Kitchens' professional Vanessa McNeil was frying a mess of tomatoes, pulling them out of the skillet in batches just as the Foods staff arrived to sample the day's recipes. "Y'all please eat these right away," she said. "I want you to taste them while they're still hot." They were golden and crisp, with a pleasingly rugged exterior. Some of the staff started munching on the inviting medaillons before they made it to the table. The combination of fried cornmeal and flour encasing hot, tart, juicy tomato was exquisite.

Donna was hooked. She vowed to learn what it takes to make a great fried green tomato. So she obtained the fine recipe you see here, then asked Vanessa for some pointers. It seems she has frying down to an art. "I use a cast-iron skillet at home, but have found that any good, heavy skillet works fine," she says. "Actually, an electric skillet is great—it keeps an even heat, so the tomatoes all cook nicely."

Vanessa also recommends using firm tomatoes and frying them in fairly shallow oil, about ¼- to ½-inch deep. "You don't want to cover the tomatoes with grease," she says. "And keep the temperature at 360° to 375°. If you like, you can add about three tablespoons bacon grease for more flavor." Salt the fried tomatoes as they drain, and serve them hot. "They retain their heat for a while, so let them cool just a little before you eat them," Vanessa adds. "After that, all you need is a fork."

FRIED GREEN TOMATOES

MAKES 4 TO 6 SERVINGS

Prep: 20 min., Cook: 4 min. per batch

If your family has a large appetite, you may want to double this recipe. *(pictured on page 155)*

> 1 large egg, lightly beaten
> ½ cup buttermilk
> ½ cup all-purpose flour, divided
> ½ cup cornmeal
> 1 teaspoon salt
> ½ teaspoon pepper
> 3 medium-size green tomatoes, cut into ⅓-inch slices
> Vegetable oil
> Salt to taste

COMBINE egg and buttermilk; set aside.
COMBINE ¼ cup flour, cornmeal, 1 teaspoon salt, and pepper in a shallow bowl or pan.
DREDGE tomato slices in remaining ¼ cup flour; dip in egg mixture, and dredge in cornmeal mixture.
POUR oil to a depth of ¼ to ½ inch in a large cast-iron skillet; heat to 375°. Drop tomatoes, in batches, into hot oil, and cook 2 minutes on each side or until golden. Drain on paper towels or a rack. Sprinkle hot tomatoes with salt.

Served Hot

Novelist Fannie Flagg modeled her book *Fried Green Tomatoes at the Whistle Stop Cafe*, Random House 1987, after Birmingham's Irondale Cafe, which her great-aunt operated for nearly 40 years. Owner Jim Dolan says his crew cooks about 135 pounds of fried green tomatoes a day. The book and movie helped the dish's popularity—visitors come from all over the country to sample this Southern specialty.

Shortcut Casseroles

Assistant Foods Editor Cynthia Ann Briscoe still cooks the comfort foods from her childhood, but today she uses shortcuts whenever possible to lessen preparation time while still maintaining the same great tastes. Using items such as deli-roasted chicken, prepared salsa, and packaged shredded cheese means these dishes can be assembled in 25 minutes or less.

SOUTHWESTERN CHICKEN LASAGNA

family favorite

MAKES 6 TO 8 SERVINGS

Prep: 15 min., Stand: 15 min., Cook: 8 min., Bake: 30 min.

> 2 cups shredded deli-roasted chicken
> 1 tablespoon lime juice
> 1½ teaspoons chili powder
> 1 teaspoon salt
> ½ teaspoon pepper
> 1 small onion, chopped
> 2 garlic cloves, chopped
> 1 tablespoon vegetable oil
> 1 (16-ounce) jar salsa
> 1 (15-ounce) can chili with beans
> 1 (4.5-ounce) can chopped green chiles
> 9 (6-inch) flour tortillas
> 1 (8-ounce) package shredded Mexican four-cheese blend

COMBINE first 5 ingredients; let stand 5 minutes. Set aside.
SAUTÉ onion and garlic in hot oil in a large skillet over medium-high heat 3 to 4 minutes or until tender. Add salsa, chili, and green chiles; reduce heat, and simmer 3 to 4 minutes.
LINE bottom of an 11- x 7-inch baking dish with 3 tortillas; layer with one-half chili mixture, one-half chicken mixture, and one-third cheese. Repeat layers; top with remaining tortillas. Sprinkle remaining cheese on top.
BAKE at 350° for 25 to 30 minutes; let stand 5 to 10 minutes before serving.

HAM TETRAZZINI

family favorite

MAKES 6 TO 8 SERVINGS

Prep: 25 min., Cook: 10 min., Bake 25 min.

Prepare an extra casserole to freeze for later.

- 2 (7-ounce) packages thin spaghetti, uncooked*
- ¼ cup butter or margarine
- 1 (8-ounce) package sliced fresh mushrooms
- 6 green onions, chopped
- 3 garlic cloves, minced
- ½ teaspoon salt
- ½ teaspoon pepper
- 3 tablespoons all-purpose flour
- 2 cups half-and-half or whipping cream
- 2 cups (8 ounces) shredded Cheddar cheese
- ½ cup shredded Parmesan cheese
- 2 cups chopped cooked ham

COOK pasta according to package directions. Drain and set aside.

MELT butter in a large skillet over medium-high heat; add sliced mushrooms, chopped green onions, and minced garlic; sauté 3 to 4 minutes or until tender. Add salt and pepper.

WHISK in flour gradually until blended. Gradually whisk in half-and-half until smooth. Stir in Cheddar cheese and ¼ cup Parmesan cheese until melted; stir in ham and pasta. Pour mixture into a lightly greased 13- x 9-inch baking dish. Sprinkle with remaining ¼ cup Parmesan cheese.

BAKE at 350° for 20 to 25 minutes.

*Substitute 1 (12-ounce) package thin egg noodles for spaghetti, if desired. Cook according to package directions.

JANICE HODGES
SCOTTSBORO, ALABAMA

Living Light

Hearty, Healthy Entrées

These satisfying recipes are sure to please even the hungriest folks at your table.

If you're trying to eat more vegetables but have a tough time coming up with substantial meat-free dishes, here's a terrific selection of recipes. All are prepared with ingredients such as beans, mushrooms, and eggplant that are so satisfying, you'll never miss the meat. Beans help lower your LDL (bad) cholesterol. Eggplant and portobello mushrooms offer a smoky flavor and meaty texture, making them good meat alternatives.

EGGPLANT PARMESAN WITH FETA

vegetarian

MAKES 6 SERVINGS

Prep: 35 min., Cook: 15 min., Bake: 56 min.

- ½ small eggplant
- ¾ teaspoon salt, divided
- 1 teaspoon pepper, divided
- 1 cup Italian-seasoned breadcrumbs
- ½ cup grated Parmesan cheese, divided
- ½ cup egg substitute
- Vegetable cooking spray
- 1 medium onion, chopped
- 2 garlic cloves, minced
- 1 (28-ounce) can crushed tomatoes
- 1 teaspoon sugar
- 1 teaspoon dried basil
- ½ teaspoon dried oregano
- 1 (16-ounce) container 1% low-fat cottage cheese*
- ½ cup crumbled feta cheese

CUT eggplant crosswise into ⅛-inch-thick slices. Sprinkle evenly with ½ teaspoon salt and ½ teaspoon pepper.

COMBINE breadcrumbs and 3 tablespoons Parmesan cheese. Dip eggplant into egg substitute. Dredge in breadcrumb mixture. Coat eggplant evenly on both sides with cooking spray. Arrange slices on a rack coated with cooking spray; place rack inside a roasting pan.

BAKE at 375° for 16 minutes, turning after 8 minutes.

SAUTÉ onion and garlic in a large saucepan coated with cooking spray over medium-high heat 5 minutes or until onion is tender. Add tomatoes, remaining ¼ teaspoon salt, remaining ½ teaspoon pepper, sugar, basil, and oregano; bring to a boil. Reduce heat, and simmer, stirring often, 10 minutes or until thickened.

SPOON 1 cup tomato mixture into an 8-inch square baking dish coated with cooking spray; arrange one-third of eggplant slices in a single layer over tomato mixture.

STIR together cottage cheese and feta cheese; spoon ⅓ cup cheese mixture over eggplant. Spoon 1 cup tomato mixture over cheese mixture. Repeat layers twice, ending with tomato mixture. Sprinkle with remaining Parmesan cheese.

BAKE at 350° for 35 to 40 minutes or until bubbly and golden brown.

*Substitute part-skim ricotta cheese for cottage cheese, if desired.

Calories 279 (25% from fat); Fat 7.6g (sat 3.8g, mono 1.6g, poly 0.7g); Protein 22.2g; Carb 32g; Fiber 5g; Chol 20mg; Iron 3.7mg; Sodium 1,215mg; Calc 299mg

CRUSTLESS VEGGIE SAUSAGE QUICHE

vegetarian

MAKES 8 SERVINGS

Prep: 20 min., Cook: 5 min., Bake: 35 min., Cool: 10 min.

Look for vegetable sausage patties next to other meatless products in the frozen-food section of your supermarket.

> 1 (8-ounce) package vegetable breakfast patties*
> 1 tablespoon light butter or margarine
> ½ pound sliced fresh mushrooms
> ½ large sweet onion, chopped
> 1 cup egg substitute
> 1 (8-ounce) container light sour cream
> 1 cup 1% low-fat cottage cheese
> 3 tablespoons all-purpose flour
> 3 tablespoons grated Parmesan cheese
> 1 teaspoon hot sauce
> 1½ cups (6 ounces) reduced-fat Cheddar cheese
> Vegetable cooking spray

PREPARE patties according to package directions; crumble and set aside.

MELT butter in a large skillet over medium-high heat; add mushrooms and onion, and sauté 5 minutes or until tender.

PROCESS egg substitute, sour cream, and next 4 ingredients in a food processor until smooth, stopping to scrape down sides.

STIR together crumbled breakfast patties, mushroom mixture, egg substitute mixture, and Cheddar cheese. Spoon into a 10-inch quiche pan coated with cooking spray.

BAKE at 350° for 35 minutes or until golden. Cool 10 minutes. Cut quiche into 8 wedges.

*If you'd rather have the meat, substitute 1 cup lean chopped cooked ham for vegetable breakfast patties.

NOTE: Individual wedges may be reheated in the microwave at MEDIUM (50% power) 1 minute or until thoroughly heated.

Calories 244 (44% from fat); Fat 12g (sat 6g, mono 1.7g, poly 1.8g); Protein 23g; Carb 11g; Fiber 2g; Chol 31mg; Iron 2.3mg; Sodium 585mg; Calc 261mg

PORTOBELLO PIZZA

vegetarian

MAKES 6 SERVINGS

Prep: 15 min., Cook: 7 min., Bake: 23 min.

Baking the crust on the bottom rack will keep it from becoming soggy.

> 2 large portobello mushroom caps, sliced*
> ½ large onion, sliced
> ½ teaspoon salt
> ½ teaspoon pepper
> Vegetable cooking spray
> 1 tablespoon balsamic vinegar
> 2 tablespoons yellow cornmeal
> 1 (10-ounce) can refrigerated pizza crust dough
> 2 tablespoons basil pesto
> 2 tablespoons plain nonfat yogurt
> ¼ cup chopped fresh basil
> 6 fresh mozzarella cheese slices (6 ounces)**
> 5 plum tomatoes, chopped
> 2 tablespoons shredded Parmesan cheese

SAUTÉ first 4 ingredients in a large skillet coated with cooking spray over medium-high heat 5 minutes or until onion is tender. Add balsamic vinegar; cook 2 minutes or until liquid is evaporated. Set aside.

SPRINKLE cornmeal in a 15- x 10-inch jellyroll pan; spread out pizza dough almost to the edges. Bake on bottom oven rack at 425° for 5 minutes.

STIR together pesto and yogurt. Spread over pizza crust, leaving a 1-inch border. Sprinkle with mushroom mixture and fresh basil. Top with mozzarella cheese and tomatoes. Sprinkle with Parmesan cheese.

BAKE at 425° on bottom oven rack for 18 minutes or until edges are golden brown and cheese is melted.

*Substitute 1 (8-ounce) package sliced button mushrooms for portobello mushroom caps, if desired.

**Substitute 1½ cups (6 ounces) shredded part-skim mozzarella cheese for fresh mozzarella, if desired.

Calories 292 (35% from fat); Fat 11.3g (sat 5.3g, mono 0.2g, poly 0.1g); Protein 12.3g; Carb 35g; Fiber 2.4g; Chol 24mg; Iron 2.4mg; Sodium 667mg; Calc 210 mg

SPICY BEANS WITH COCONUT MILK

vegetarian

MAKES 6 SERVINGS

Prep: 20 min., Cook: 37 min.

Reader Judy Johnson enjoys this dish spicy and tangy, but feel free to adjust the curry paste and lime juice to your liking. This recipe is an excellent source of fiber—you need at least 25 grams per day.

> 1 sweet onion, chopped
> Vegetable cooking spray
> 2 garlic cloves, minced
> 1 to 2 tablespoons red curry paste
> 2 (15-ounce) cans kidney beans, rinsed and drained
> 1 (14.5-ounce) can diced tomatoes, undrained
> 1 (13.5-ounce) can lite coconut milk
> 1 teaspoon grated lime rind
> 2 to 3 tablespoons fresh lime juice
> 2 tablespoons sugar
> 1 to 1½ teaspoons salt
> 4 cups hot cooked basmati or long-grain rice
> Toppings: 2 green onions, chopped; 2 tablespoons chopped fresh cilantro (optional)

SAUTÉ chopped onion in a Dutch oven coated with cooking spray over medium-high heat 5 minutes; add garlic, and sauté 1 minute. Add red curry paste; sauté 1 minute. Stir in kidney beans, diced tomatoes, coconut milk, and next 4 ingredients. Bring to a boil; reduce heat, and simmer 30 minutes. Serve over basmati rice, and sprinkle with toppings, if desired.

NOTE: Red curry paste can be found in the Asian section of large supermarkets or in Asian markets.

JUDY JOHNSON
BIRMINGHAM, ALABAMA

Calories 335 (11% from fat); Fat 4.2g (sat 2.2g, mono 0.2g, poly 0.1g); Protein 11g; Carb 64g; Fiber 11g; Chol 0mg; Iron 2.3mg; Sodium 495mg; Calc 40mg

from our kitchen

Get out of the house this weekend, and make supper a picnic. No need for special equipment—you can create a great picnic basket from items you may already have. Try these tips for an easy outdoor meal.
- Recycle a gift basket or one from the farmers market.
- Jars with tight-fitting lids make great containers for potato, pasta, and chicken salads.
- If you don't have reusable ice packs, freeze bottles of water to keep foods cold. Later, the refreshing drinking water will be a bonus.
- Carry a large, colorful disposable cloth for the table or a spot under a tree. For speedy cleanup, put all trash on the cloth, and tie up the ends.

Portobello Mushrooms

The flavor of portobellos—large crimini (brown) mushrooms—lives up to their size. If you buy them wrapped in plastic, remove them and immediately refrigerate in a paper bag. (Plastic holds too much moisture and speeds deterioration.) Rinse or wipe off portobellos with a damp paper towel. Their stems can be sliced lengthwise and cooked the same as the caps.

To roast: Brush caps and stems with oil or your favorite sauce, such as Italian salad dressing or teriyaki sauce. Place gill-side down on a baking sheet. Roast at 425° for 15 to 20 minutes.

To grill or broil: Brush with oil, and season with salt and pepper or your favorite sauce. Grill or broil 4 to 6 inches from heat for 4 to 6 minutes on each side, brushing once or twice.

To sauté: Cook sliced, chopped, or whole in a skillet with a little oil or butter over medium-high heat about 5 to 6 minutes.

Storing Fresh Produce

A trip to the farmers market is good for heart and soul (see page 158). All that fresh produce inspires us to experiment with new recipes and cook for pure pleasure.

To keep your purchases in prime condition for as long as possible, it's important to know how to store them properly. Learn what to keep at room temperature, what to refrigerate or freeze immediately, and whether to wash items before storage.
- Berries should be refrigerated *unwashed* until ready to eat.
- Store tomatoes at room temperature for best flavor. (A bowl of the plump, red beauties makes a wonderful centerpiece.)
- Remove corn from the cob as soon as possible to preserve its tender sweetness.
- Refrigerate okra, peas, and beans *unwashed* until ready to cook.
- Peaches, plums, and nectarines can be washed, dried, and stored in the refrigerator.
- Fresh basil should be stored at room temperature, not in the refrigerator (it will turn black). Place stems in a glass with a little water to keep fresh.
- All other fresh herbs can be stored in the refrigerator up to five days. Wash, shake off excess water, wrap in a damp paper towel, and place in an airtight container or zip-top plastic bag.

Ice Cream

Thank goodness July is National Ice Cream Month—it gives us a terrific reason to indulge our cravings. Make your own ice cream and sorbet with a countertop machine.

Foods Editor Scott Jones prefers the Donvier Ice Cream Maker. It produces a quart of ice cream, frozen yogurt, or sorbet in just 20 minutes. His 3-year-old daughter, Tallulah, loves it because she can turn the crank. Simply freeze the canister, and you're set. All it requires is a few turns of the crank every few minutes, and the result is perfectly smooth, delicious frozen dessert.

Foods Editor Andria Scott Hurst really likes the electric Cuisinart model. There's no cranking required—just plug it in to enjoy ice cream in about 20 minutes. The average price is about $50 for whichever brand you select. You'll find both of these at department stores, kitchen shops, and discount stores. For terrific sorbet recipes, see page 171.

Hot-and-Spicy Hints

- The makers of McCormick seasonings suggest that spices in the red pepper family, such as paprika and chili powder, be stored in the refrigerator. The cold helps retain the color and guard against infestation of spice bugs. This is especially important during summer months and in hot climates.
- Measure seasonings into a bowl; then add them to the pot. Don't sprinkle spices and herbs directly from the bottles over a steaming pot. Steam gets into the bottle and speeds the loss of flavor and aroma of the spices. Steam also causes spices to cake.

Fried Chicken and Fixin's

Enjoy some of the best flavors of the South in this menu.

Southern Supper

Serves 4

Our Best Southern Fried Chicken

Tee's Corn Pudding   Baby Blue Salad

Key Lime Pie

OUR BEST SOUTHERN FRIED CHICKEN

MAKES 4 SERVINGS

Prep: 25 min., Chill: 8 hrs., Fry: about 30 min.
(pictured on page 189)

This is one of our Top 5 winners in the Ultimate Southern Recipes category in our Top 25 Recipes in 25 Years. See the special section at the end of the book.

- 3 quarts water
- 1 tablespoon salt
- 1 (2½ to 3-pound) broiler-fryer, cut up
- 1 teaspoon salt
- 1 teaspoon pepper
- 1 cup all-purpose flour
- 2 cups vegetable oil
- ¼ cup bacon drippings

COMBINE water and 1 tablespoon salt; add chicken. Cover and chill 8 hours. Drain chicken; rinse with cold water, and pat dry.
COMBINE 1 teaspoon salt and pepper; sprinkle half of pepper mixture over chicken. Combine remaining pepper mixture and flour in a large freezer bag. Place 2 pieces of chicken in bag; seal. Shake to evenly coat. Remove chicken, and repeat procedure with remaining chicken, 2 pieces at a time.
COMBINE oil and bacon drippings in a 12-inch cast-iron skillet or chicken fryer; heat to 360°. Add chicken, a few pieces at a time, skin side down. Cover and cook 6 minutes; uncover and cook 9 minutes. Turn chicken pieces; cover and cook 6 minutes. Uncover and cook 5 to 9 minutes, turning pieces during the last 3 minutes for even browning, if necessary. Drain on paper towels.

JOHN EGERTON
SOUTHERN FOOD
UNIVERSITY OF NORTH CAROLINA PRESS, 1987
NASHVILLE, TENNESSEE

TEE'S CORN PUDDING

MAKES 8 SERVINGS

Prep: 15 min., Bake: 45 min., Stand: 5 min.
(pictured on page 189)

- ¼ cup sugar
- 3 tablespoons all-purpose flour
- 2 teaspoons baking powder
- 1½ teaspoons salt
- 6 large eggs
- 2 cups whipping cream
- ½ cup butter or margarine, melted
- 6 cups fresh corn kernels (about 12 ears)

COMBINE first 4 ingredients.
WHISK together eggs, cream, and butter. Gradually add sugar mixture, whisking until smooth; stir in corn. Pour into a lightly greased 13- x 9-inch baking dish.
BAKE at 350° for 40 to 45 minutes or until golden and set. Let stand 5 minutes.

BABY BLUE SALAD

chef recipe

MAKES 6 SERVINGS

Prep: 10 min. *(pictured on page 189)*

This ranked as one of our Top 5 winners in the Family Favorite category in Our Top 25 Recipes in 25 Years. See the special section at the end of the book.

- ¾ pound gourmet mixed salad greens
- 1 (4-ounce) package crumbled blue cheese
- 2 oranges, peeled and cut into slices
- 1 pint fresh strawberries, quartered
- Sweet-and-Spicy Pecans
- Balsamic Vinaigrette

TOSS together first 5 ingredients in a large bowl. Drizzle with desired amount of Balsamic Vinaigrette, gently tossing to coat. Serve with remaining Balsamic Vinaigrette.

Sweet-and-Spicy Pecans:

MAKES 1 CUP

Prep: 5 min., Soak: 10 min., Bake: 10 min.

- ¼ cup sugar
- 1 cup warm water
- 1 cup pecan halves
- 2 tablespoons sugar
- 1 tablespoon chili powder
- ⅛ teaspoon ground red pepper

STIR together ¼ cup sugar and 1 cup warm water until sugar dissolves. Add pecans, and soak 10 minutes. Drain, discarding syrup.
COMBINE 2 tablespoons sugar, chili powder, and red pepper. Add pecans, tossing to coat. Place pecans on a lightly greased baking sheet.
BAKE at 350° for 10 minutes or until golden brown, stirring once.

Balsamic Vinaigrette:

MAKES 2 CUPS

Prep: 5 min.

- ½ cup balsamic vinegar
- 3 tablespoons Dijon mustard
- 3 tablespoons honey
- 2 large garlic cloves, minced
- 2 small shallots, minced
- ¼ teaspoon salt
- ¼ teaspoon pepper
- 1 cup olive oil

WHISK together first 7 ingredients until blended. Gradually whisk in olive oil, blending well.

FRANKLIN BIGGS
HOMEWOOD GOURMET
HOMEWOOD, ALABAMA

KEY LIME PIE

MAKES 1 (9-INCH) PIE

Prep: 20 min., Bake: 38 min., Chill: 8 hrs.

- 1¼ cups graham cracker crumbs
- ¼ cup firmly packed light brown sugar
- ⅓ cup butter or margarine, melted
- 2 (14-ounce) cans sweetened condensed milk
- 1 cup fresh Key lime juice
- 2 egg whites
- ¼ teaspoon cream of tartar
- 2 tablespoons granulated sugar

COMBINE first 3 ingredients. Press into a 9-inch pieplate. Bake piecrust at 350° for 10 minutes or until lightly browned; cool.
STIR together sweetened condensed milk and lime juice until blended. Pour into prepared crust. Set aside.
BEAT egg whites and cream of tartar at high speed with an electric mixer just until foamy. Add granulated sugar gradually, 1 tablespoon at a time, beating until soft peaks form and sugar dissolves (2 to 4 minutes). Spread meringue over filling. Bake at 325° for 25 to 28 minutes. Chill 8 hours.

Summertime Snacks

CHESAPEAKE BAY PARTY NUTS

MAKES 2 CUPS

Prep: 15 min., Bake: 30 min.

- 2 tablespoons butter, melted
- 2 teaspoons Old Bay seasoning
- 2 tablespoons Worcestershire sauce
- ½ teaspoon garlic powder
- ¼ to ½ teaspoon hot sauce
- 2 cups pecan halves or whole almonds

STIR together melted butter, Old Bay seasoning, Worcestershire sauce, garlic powder, and hot sauce; add pecans, tossing to coat. Place nuts in an aluminum foil-lined 15- x 10-inch jellyroll pan.
BAKE nuts at 300° for 30 minutes, stirring twice. Cool. Store in an airtight container.

ROBIN RICH-COATES
MACHIPONGO, VIRGINIA

EGG SALAD SANDWICHES

MAKES ABOUT 44 FINGER SANDWICHES

Prep: 20 min., Chill: 3 hrs.

- 5 large hard-cooked eggs, grated
- 2 tablespoons finely chopped celery
- 2 tablespoons sweet pickle relish
- 2 tablespoons mayonnaise
- 1 tablespoon sour cream
- 1 tablespoon grated onion
- ¾ teaspoon dried salad seasoning
- ½ teaspoon Dijon mustard
- ¼ teaspoon salt
- ¼ teaspoon sugar
- ⅛ teaspoon ground black pepper
- 22 thin white sandwich bread slices

COMBINE first 11 ingredients in a bowl until blended. Cover and chill 3 hours.
SPREAD 2 tablespoons egg mixture evenly on 1 side of 11 bread slices. Top with remaining 11 bread slices. Cut each sandwich into 4 finger sandwiches.

NOTE: For testing, we used McCormick Salad Supreme Seasoning and Pepperidge Farm Very Thin Sliced White Bread.

SALLY HOWARD
VIRGINIA BEACH, VIRGINIA

STRAWBERRY-ORANGE POPS

freezeable

MAKES 12 POPS

Prep: 10 min., Freeze: 8 hrs.

- 2 cups orange juice
- ½ cup low-fat vanilla yogurt
- 1 cup frozen whole strawberries, thawed

STIR together orange juice and yogurt.
PROCESS berries in a blender or food processor until smooth, stopping to scrape down sides. Stir into juice mixture. Spoon mixture evenly into 12 (3-ounce) plastic pop molds; insert plastic pop sticks, and freeze 8 hours.

NOTE If desired, place 12 (3-ounce) paper cups in a muffin pan. Spoon mixture into cups; freeze 30 minutes. Insert a stick into center of each. Freeze 8 hours. Peel off cups.

LOOKS-LIKE WATERMELON: Hollow out lime halves, leaving rinds intact. Spoon pop mixture into rinds. Sprinkle with semisweet chocolate mini-morsels and freeze 8 hours. Cut frozen halves in half with a bread knife.

CRISPY CHEESE BITES

MAKES 5 DOZEN

Prep: 25 min., Bake: 20 min.

- 1 cup butter, softened
- 1 cup (4 ounces) shredded sharp Cheddar cheese
- 1 cup (4 ounces) shredded Monterey Jack cheese
- 2 cups all-purpose flour
- 2 cups crisp rice cereal
- ½ teaspoon salt
- ¼ teaspoon ground red pepper

STIR together butter and cheeses until blended. Stir in flour and remaining ingredients. (Dough will be stiff.)
SHAPE dough into ¾-inch balls, and place on an ungreased baking sheet.
BAKE at 325° for 20 minutes. Cool on wire racks. Store in an airtight container.

CHRISTINE MCDONALD
VICTORIA, TEXAS

Easy Freezer Meals

Sharon Gray, of Mount Juliet, Tennessee, created her own method of "investment cooking." She shops for grocery meat specials, cooks in large quantities, and freezes food in various stages.

Make It Work for You

Here are some of Sharon's specific investment cooking tips and recipes as well as instructions for using a rub and marinade. For information on safe freezing times, see "From Our Kitchen" on page 186.

Baked, grilled, or stir-fried chicken: Buy boneless, skinless breasts. Make several different recipes of marinades and rubs. Prick chicken several times with a fork to allow flavors to penetrate the meat. Combine marinade and breast halves in labeled zip-top freezer bags. Seal bags, and knead the meat to circulate the marinade. Lay bags flat with meat side by side in a flat pan with sides. Marinate for desired time in refrigerator. Place pan in freezer; freeze bags flat. Remove frozen bags from pan, and stack in freezer. For kabobs or stir-fry, cut breast halves into cubes or strips, and follow the same instructions.

Cooked chicken for casseroles, etc.: Bring 2 whole chickens and water to cover to a boil in a large stockpot. Add 2 celery ribs, 2 carrots, 1 onion, and 4 garlic cloves. Reduce heat; cover and simmer 40 minutes. Remove chicken; discard vegetables, reserving broth. Remove chicken from bones, and shred. Place 2 cups shredded chicken in labeled quart-size zip-top freezer bags. Seal and freeze. Strain broth, cool, and refrigerate. Freeze broth in zip-top freezer bags for use in other recipes.

ZESTY CHICKEN MARINADE

fast fixin's • make ahead

MAKES ABOUT ½ CUP

Prep: 10 min.

- 4 garlic cloves, minced
- 1 small onion, finely chopped
- ⅓ cup chopped fresh cilantro
- ¼ cup olive oil
- 1½ teaspoons paprika
- 1 teaspoon ground cumin
- 1 teaspoon dried parsley
- ½ teaspoon salt
- ½ teaspoon ground red pepper

COMBINE all ingredients.

CHICKEN KABOBS: Cut 2 pounds skinned and boned chicken breast halves into 1-inch cubes. Place chicken pieces and Zesty Chicken Marinade in a large zip-top freezer bag. Seal; chill 8 hours. (For investment cooking, freeze; thaw before grilling.) Soak 8 (8-inch) wooden skewers in water 30 minutes. Remove chicken from marinade, discarding marinade. Thread chicken onto skewers, leaving ¼-inch space between pieces. Grill, covered with grill lid, over medium-high heat (350° to 400°) 6 to 8 minutes on each side or until done. Serve on pita bread with lettuce and tomatoes. Prep: 20 min., Chill: 8 hrs., Soak: 30 min., Grill: 16 min.

ITALIAN MARINADE

fast fixin's • make ahead

MAKES 1¼ CUPS

Prep: 10 min.

- 1 cup olive oil
- ¼ cup red wine vinegar
- 3 shallots, peeled and chopped
- 6 garlic cloves, chopped
- 1 tablespoon chopped fresh rosemary
- 1 tablespoon soy sauce
- 2 teaspoons pepper

COMBINE all ingredients. Use to marinate poultry, beef, or lamb.

ITALIAN STEAK: Place 1 (2-pound) flank steak and Italian Marinade in a large zip-top freezer bag. Seal; chill 2 hours. (For investment cooking, freeze up to 6 months; thaw before grilling.) Grill, covered with grill lid, over medium-high heat (350° to 400°) 8 minutes on each side or to desired doneness. Cut into thin slices, and serve immediately. Prep: 5 min., Chill: 2 hrs., Grill: 16 min.

MEDITERRANEAN RUB

fast fixin's • make ahead

MAKES ¼ CUP

Prep: 5 min.

- 2 teaspoons ground sage
- 2 teaspoons dried thyme
- 2 teaspoons pepper
- 1 teaspoon salt
- 1 teaspoon garlic powder
- 1 teaspoon dried rosemary, crushed

COMBINE all ingredients. Store in airtight container. Use for lamb, chicken, or beef.

MEDITERRANEAN STEAK: Stir together Mediterranean Rub and 1 tablespoon olive oil; rub over 1 (2-pound) flank or sirloin steak. (For investment cooking, freeze up to 6 months. Thaw before grilling.) Grill, covered with lid, over medium-high heat (350° to 400°) 8 minutes on each side or to desired doneness. Prep: 10 min., Grill: 16 min.

SOUTHWESTERN SPICE BLEND

fast fixin's • make ahead

MAKES ¼ CUP

Prep: 5 min.

- 1 tablespoon salt
- 2 teaspoons garlic powder
- 2 teaspoons chili powder
- 2 teaspoons ground cumin
- 2 teaspoons pepper
- ½ teaspoon unsweetened cocoa

COMBINE all ingredients. Store in an airtight container. Use as a meat or poultry rub or to flavor chili and soups.

SOUTHWESTERN CHICKEN: Rub Southwestern Spice Blend over 6 skinned and boned chicken breast halves. (For investment cooking, freeze in a zip-top freezer bag up to 6 months. Thaw before grilling.) Grill, covered with grill lid, over medium-high heat (350° to 400°) 6 to 7 minutes on each side or until done. Prep: 10 min., Grill: 14 min.

Taste of the South

Frogmore Stew

When Frogmore Stew was first cooked in the 1960s, Frogmore was a hamlet on St. Helena Island, near Beaufort, South Carolina. Richard Gay, whose family owns Gay Fish Company on St. Helena, created the dish. "I was on weekend duty in the National Guard," he says, "and I'd sometimes get a lot of shrimp, put it in a pot with sausage and corn, and boil it. Within an hour, we'd have a complete meal for 100 people. The boys joked that since I was from Frogmore, we'd name it Frogmore Stew.

The dish at its most basic contains shrimp, seafood seasoning, smoked sausage, corn on the cob, and potatoes. But onions, crab, and butter are other additions. We used a loose, finely ground seasoning blend in our stew and the results were delicious.

Richard is justifiably proud of his creation and its popularity. Ten years ago, he petitioned the South Carolina senate to have Frogmore Stew named the state seafood dish. "There was a state dog, flag, and flower," he says, "but no seafood dish." He let the matter drop when he moved to Tulsa, but he still dreams of the day when his boil will be the state's official seafood dish, proudly bearing the name Frogmore Stew.

FROGMORE STEW

MAKES 12 SERVINGS

Prep: 10 min., Cook: 30 min.

We found that the sausage adds plenty of richness to this dish, so we omitted the butter.

5 quarts water
¼ cup Old Bay seasoning
4 pounds small red potatoes
2 pounds kielbasa or hot smoked link sausage, cut into 1½-inch pieces
6 ears fresh corn, halved
4 pounds unpeeled, large fresh shrimp
Old Bay seasoning
Cocktail sauce

BRING 5 quarts water and ¼ cup Old Bay seasoning to a rolling boil in a large covered stockpot. Add potatoes; return to a boil, and cook, uncovered, for 10 minutes.
ADD sausage and corn, and return to a boil. Cook 10 minutes or until potatoes are tender. Add shrimp to stockpot; cook 3 to 4 minutes or until shrimp turn pink. Drain. Serve with Old Bay seasoning and cocktail sauce.

Lighter Side of the Season

These top-notch *Southern Living* recipes underwent a nutrition makeover without compromising taste. We reduced the amount of oil and butter, and chose low-fat dairy products.

GRILLED PORK TENDERLOIN WITH ORANGE MARMALADE

MAKES 6 SERVINGS

Prep: 20 min., Chill: 1 hr., Cook: 10 min., Grill: 25 min.

1 cup pineapple juice
¼ cup apple cider vinegar
¼ cup lite soy sauce
1 (1½-pound) package pork tenderloins
3 bell peppers (1 each of red, green, and yellow), cut into strips
½ red onion, thinly sliced
Vegetable cooking spray
1 (12-ounce) jar orange marmalade*

COMBINE first 3 ingredients in a shallow dish or large zip-top freezer bag; add pork tenderloins. Cover or seal, and chill 1 hour.
SAUTÉ peppers and onion in a nonstick skillet coated with cooking spray over medium-high heat, 5 minutes or until tender. Stir in marmalade; bring to a boil and cook until melted. Reserve ¼ cup mixture for basting. Remove pork from marinade; discard marinade.
GRILL pork, covered with grill lid, over medium-high heat (350° to 400°) 25 minutes or until a meat thermometer inserted into thickest portion registers 160°, basting with reserved marmalade mixture the last 5 minutes. Serve with remaining marmalade mixture.

*Substitute 1 (10.5-ounce) jar red pepper jelly or 1 (10.5-ounce) jar jalapeño jelly for orange marmalade, if desired.

Calories 317 (14% from fat); Fat 5.1g (sat 1.8g, mono 2g, poly 0.5g); Protein 25g; Carb 43g; Fiber 1.2g; Chol 75.2mg; Iron 1.4 mg; Sodium 141mg; Calc 18mg

CHICKPEA-CHIPOTLE TOSTADAS

MAKES 12 SERVINGS

Prep: 35 min., Cook: 14 min., Bake: 20 min.

12 corn tortillas
Vegetable cooking spray
1 medium onion, chopped
½ red bell pepper, chopped
2 teaspoons olive oil
2 garlic cloves, chopped
1½ (16-ounce) cans chickpeas, rinsed and drained
1 cup fat-free reduced-sodium chicken broth
2 tablespoons chopped fresh cilantro
2 chipotle peppers in adobo sauce, minced
½ teaspoon salt
2 tablespoons lime juice
1 (8-ounce) container light sour cream
½ cup salsa verde
½ head iceberg lettuce, shredded
6 plum tomatoes, chopped
½ (8-ounce) package feta cheese, crumbled

COAT tortillas evenly on both sides with cooking spray. Arrange on baking sheets in a single layer.
BAKE at 375° for 20 minutes or until crisp and golden. Remove from oven; set aside.
SAUTÉ onion and bell pepper in hot oil in a large skillet over medium-high heat 5 minutes or until tender. Add garlic; sauté 1 minute. Add chickpeas and next 4 ingredients; bring to a boil. Reduce heat, and simmer 5 minutes.
PROCESS chickpea mixture in a food processor or with a hand blender until smooth. Return mixture to skillet. Simmer, stirring occasionally until thickened. Stir in lime juice, and cook 2 to 3 minutes. Stir together sour cream and ½ cup salsa verde.
SPREAD chickpea mixture evenly over tortillas. Top with lettuce and tomatoes. Drizzle with sour cream mixture, and sprinkle with cheese. Serve immediately.

NOTE: Find chipotle peppers in adobo sauce and salsa verde (green salsa) in the Mexican section of the supermarket.

Calories 189 (31% from fat); Fat 6.5g (sat 3.2g, mono 1.3g, poly 0.7g); Protein 6.6g; Carb 27.4g; Fiber 4.2g; Chol 18.2mg; Iron 1.3 mg; Sodium 438mg; Calc 155mg

SAVORY SUMMER PIE

MAKES 8 SERVINGS

Prep: 20 min., Cook: 6 min., Bake: 52 min.,
Stand: 5 min.

 4 phyllo pastry sheets, thawed
 Vegetable cooking spray
 1 small red bell pepper, chopped
 ½ small sweet onion, chopped
 2 garlic cloves, minced
 3 tablespoons chopped fresh basil
 1 cup egg substitute
 1 cup whole milk
 ½ teaspoon salt
 ½ teaspoon pepper
 1½ cups (6 ounces) shredded part-
   skim mozzarella cheese
 ¼ cup shredded Parmesan cheese
 2 large plum tomatoes, cut into
   ¼-inch-thick slices

PLACE 1 phyllo sheet in a 9-inch tart
pan, gently pressing on bottom and up
sides of pan. (Phyllo will hang over edge
of pan.) Lightly coat with cooking spray.
Repeat with 3 more sheets of phyllo,
coating with cooking spray between layers. Trim phyllo dough 3 to 4 inches over
edge of pan. Quickly fold edges under.
(Phyllo dries out quickly.)
BAKE at 425° for 6 to 7 minutes.
Remove from oven; set aside.
SAUTÉ bell pepper and onion in a large
skillet coated with cooking spray over
medium-high heat 4 to 5 minutes. Add
garlic; sauté 1 minute. Stir in basil.
WHISK together egg substitute and next
3 ingredients in a large bowl; stir in
sautéed vegetables, mozzarella cheese,
and Parmesan cheese. Pour into prepared tart shell; top with tomato slices.
BAKE at 375° for 45 minutes or until set.
Let stand 5 minutes before serving.

Calories 155 (41% from fat); Fat 7g (sat 3.7g, mono 2.2g, poly
0.8g); Protein 13g; Carb 10g; Fiber 0.8g; Chol 18mg; Iron 1.2mg;
Sodium 418mg; Calc 248mg

BLUEBERRY CHEESECAKE

MAKES 12 SERVINGS

Prep: 20 min.; Bake: 1 hr., 15 min.; Stand: 30 min.,
Cool: 30 min.; Chill: 8 hrs. *(pictured on page 192)*

Though not really low-fat, this dessert has less than
half the calories and one-third the fat of the original.

 1 cup graham cracker crumbs
 3 tablespoons butter, melted
 1 tablespoon sugar
 Vegetable cooking spray
 2 (8-ounce) packages ⅓-less-fat
   cream cheese
 1 (8-ounce) package fat-free cream
   cheese
 1 cup sugar
 3 tablespoons all-purpose flour
 ½ teaspoon salt
 2 large eggs
 2 egg whites
 1 (8-ounce) container light sour cream
 1 teaspoon vanilla extract
 1 tablespoon grated lemon rind
 1½ cups fresh or frozen blueberries
 1 cup fat-free frozen whipped topping,
   thawed
 ¼ cup light sour cream

COMBINE graham cracker crumbs, butter,
and 1 tablespoon sugar. Press on bottom and
1½ inches up sides of a 9-inch springform
pan coated with cooking spray. Bake at 350°
for 5 minutes. Remove from oven; set aside.
BEAT cream cheeses at medium speed
with an electric mixer until smooth.
COMBINE 1 cup sugar, flour, and salt.
Add to cream cheese, beating until
blended. Add eggs, 1 at a time, beating
well after each addition. Add egg whites,
beating until blended.
ADD 8-ounce container sour cream,
vanilla, and lemon rind, beating just
until blended. Gently stir in blueberries.
Pour mixture into prepared pan.
BAKE at 300° for 1 hour and 10 minutes
or until center of cheesecake is firm. Turn
off oven; let cheesecake stand in oven,
with door partially open, 30 minutes.
REMOVE cheesecake from oven; cool in pan
on a wire rack 30 minutes. Cover cheesecake; chill 8 hours. Release sides of pan.
STIR together whipped topping and
¼ cup sour cream. Spread over cheesecake.

Calories 315 (45% from fat); Fat 15.6g (sat 9.5g, mono 1.5g, poly
0.5g); Protein 10.2g; Carb 33.4g; Fiber 0.8g; Chol 83mg; Iron
0.6mg; Sodium 469mg; Calc 110mg

ICE CREAM-TOFFEE DESSERT

make ahead

MAKES 8 SERVINGS

Prep: 15 min., Freeze: 8 hrs.

 2 (3-ounce) packages ladyfingers
 2 tablespoons instant coffee
   granules
 ¼ cup hot water
 3 (1.4-ounce) toffee candy bars,
   divided
 ½ gallon sugar-free low-fat vanilla
   ice cream, softened
 2 tablespoons coffee liqueur
   (optional)
 1 (8-ounce) container fat-free frozen
   whipped topping, thawed

STAND ladyfingers around edge of a 9-
inch springform pan; line bottom of pan
with remaining ladyfingers.
COMBINE coffee granules and ¼ cup hot
water in a small bowl, stirring until dissolved; cool completely.
CHOP 2 candy bars into small pieces.
Stir chopped candy and coffee into ice
cream. Spoon into pan. Cover with plastic wrap, and freeze 8 hours.
STIR liqueur into whipped topping, if
desired. Dollop around edge of dessert.
FINELY chop remaining candy bar. Sprinkle evenly over top of ice-cream mixture.

Calories 418 (33% from fat); Fat 15.2g (sat 8.3g, mono 4.2g, poly
0.8g); Protein 8.7g; Carb 58.2g; Fiber 0.4g; Chol 108mg; Iron
0.8mg; Sodium 210mg; Calc 285mg

Living Light

Updated Burger Menu

Sometimes you just want a big, juicy
burger piled high with your favorite
toppings. When nothing else will do, try
our bold gyro recipe. Served with creamy
potato salad and sweet-and-sour tomatoes,
you simply can't go wrong. So satisfy
your craving with this fantastic variation,
and round out the meal with two deliciously cool sides.

LAYERED POTATO SALAD

family favorite • make ahead

MAKES 12 SERVINGS

Prep: 15 min., Cook: 30 min., Chill: 1 hr.

- 4 pounds red potatoes, unpeeled
- 1 (8-ounce) container fat-free sour cream
- ¾ cup light mayonnaise
- 2 tablespoons Creole mustard
- ¼ teaspoon salt
- ½ teaspoon pepper
- 1 bunch green onions, chopped
- ¾ cup chopped Italian parsley
- 3 reduced-fat, reduced-sodium bacon slices, cooked and crumbled

BRING potatoes and water to cover to a boil in a large Dutch oven over medium-high heat. Boil 25 minutes or until tender. Drain and let cool.

STIR together sour cream and next 4 ingredients. Layer one-third each of potatoes, sour cream mixture, green onions, and parsley in a large glass bowl. Repeat layers twice, ending with parsley. Cover and chill 1 hour. Sprinkle with bacon just before serving.

PARKER STORY
HOOVER, ALABAMA

Calories 192 (27% from fat); Fat 5.8g (sat 1g, mono 0g, poly .01g); Protein 4.8g; Carb 30g; Fiber 3.4g; Chol 8mg; Iron 1.5mg; Sodium 270mg; Calc 51mg

FIRE-AND-ICE TOMATOES

MAKES 6 SERVINGS

Prep: 20 min., Cook: 3 min., Chill: 1 hr.

If you're serving a bunch, this dish can easily be doubled.

- 4 large tomatoes, quartered
- 1 large sweet onion, thinly sliced
- ¾ cup white vinegar
- ¼ cup cold water
- 4½ teaspoons sugar
- 1½ teaspoons mustard seeds
- 1½ teaspoons celery seeds
- ½ teaspoon salt
- ⅛ teaspoon dried crushed red pepper
- ⅛ teaspoon black pepper

PLACE tomato and onion in a serving dish. Set aside.

BRING vinegar and next 7 ingredients to a boil in a saucepan over medium-high heat. Boil 1 minute.

POUR vinegar mixture over tomato mixture. Cover and chill at least 1 hour.

JUDY CARTER
WINCHESTER, TENNESSEE

Calories 53 (7% from fat); Fat 0.1g (sat 0g, mono 0.2g, poly 0.2g); Protein 1.7g; Carb 12g; Fiber 2.2g; Chol 0mg; Iron 0.9mg; Sodium 207mg; Calc 25mg

GYRO BURGERS WITH TAHINI SAUCE

MAKES 4 SERVINGS

Prep: 20 min., Grill: 12 min.

- 1 pound extra-lean ground beef
- 1 teaspoon Greek seasoning
- 4 (6-inch) pita rounds
- 4 lettuce leaves
- 8 large tomato slices
- 4 thin red onion slices
- Tahini Sauce
- ¼ cup crumbled feta cheese

COMBINE beef and seasoning. Shape into 4 patties. Grill, covered with grill lid, over medium-high heat (350° to 400°) 5 to 6 minutes on each side or until beef is no longer pink.

CUT off 2 inches of bread from 1 side of each pita round, forming a pocket. Line each with 1 lettuce leaf, 2 tomato slices, and 1 red onion slice. Add burger. Drizzle each with 2 tablespoons Tahini Sauce; sprinkle with 1 tablespoon cheese.

Tahini Sauce:

MAKES ½ CUP

Prep: 10 min.

- ¼ cup tahini paste
- ¼ cup water
- 2 tablespoons fresh lemon juice
- ⅛ teaspoon garlic powder
- ¼ teaspoon salt

WHISK together all ingredients.

MARLA CLARK
MORIARTY, NEW MEXICO

Calories 377 (31% from fat); Fat 13g (sat 2.8g, mono 4.7g, poly 4.3g); Protein 26.4g; Carb 41g; Fiber 3g; Chol 48mg; Iron 4mg; Sodium 551mg; Calc 81mg

Cool, Creamy Chocolate

We loved this pudding so much that we came up with two more scrumptious versions by making a couple of substitutions.

CHOCOLATE COOKIE PUDDING

MAKES 6 TO 8 SERVINGS

Prep: 15 min., Chill: 5 min.

- 1 (5.9-ounce) package chocolate instant pudding mix
- 2 cups milk
- 1 (3-ounce) package cream cheese, softened
- 1 (8-ounce) container frozen whipped topping, thawed
- 16 double-stuffed cream-filled chocolate sandwich cookies, crushed
- ¾ cup chopped pecans, toasted

WHISK together pudding mix and milk for 2 minutes. Cover and chill 5 minutes. Stir together cream cheese and whipped topping.

PLACE 1 cup crushed cookies on bottom of an 8-cup bowl. Spread half of cream cheese mixture on top; sprinkle with half of pecans. Spread all of pudding over top; spread remaining cream cheese mixture over pudding. Sprinkle with remaining cookies and pecans. Chill. (For testing, we used Oreo Double Stuff for sandwich cookies.)

MARGIE CRISP
RINGGOLD, GEORGIA

MOCHA-CHOCOLATE COOKIE PUDDING: Crush 16 coffee-flavored cream-filled chocolate sandwich cookies. Stir 2 tablespoons strong coffee into cream cheese mixture. Omit pecans. Proceed as directed. (For testing, we used Double Delight Oreo Coffee 'n Creme for sandwich cookies.)

CHOCOLATE-PEANUT BUTTER COOKIE PUDDING: Crush 16 peanut butter cream-filled chocolate sandwich cookies. Substitute ¼ cup peanut butter for cream cheese and 1 cup chopped dry roasted peanuts for pecans. Proceed as directed. (For testing, we used Double Delight Oreo Peanut Butter & Chocolate for sandwich cookies.)

What's for Supper?

Homemade Fast Food

BUFFALO HOT WINGS

MAKES 4 TO 6 SERVINGS

Prep: 35 min., Bake: 55 min.

- **3 pounds chicken wings**
- **2 (0.7-ounce) envelopes Italian dressing mix, divided**
- **½ cup butter, melted**
- **½ to ¾ cup hot sauce**
- **2 tablespoons lemon juice**
- **½ teaspoon dried basil**
- **Ranch dressing**

CUT off wingtips, and discard; cut wings in half at joint, if desired. Place 1 package dressing mix in a large zip-top plastic bag; add wings, and shake to coat. Place wings in a single layer in a lightly greased aluminum foil-lined 15- x 10-inch jellyroll pan.

BAKE at 425° for 25 minutes or until browned. Remove pan from oven, and reduce heat to 350°.

STIR together remaining package of dressing mix, butter, and next 3 ingredients. Pour over wings; bake at 350° for 30 more minutes. Serve with Ranch dressing.

AMY STRAUTMAN
TUCSON, ARIZONA

BUFFALO TENDERS: Substitute 1 (28-ounce) package crispy chicken strips for wings. Place tenders on a lightly greased rack in a broiler pan. Bake at 400° for 15 minutes or until browned. Pour sauce over tenders, and bake at 400° for 5 more minutes. Makes 4 to 6 servings. Prep: 20 min., Bake: 20 min.

BUFFALO TENDERS SALAD: Toss together romaine and iceberg lettuces, tomato wedges, sliced cucumber, and chopped onion. Top with Buffalo Tenders and croutons, and drizzle with Ranch or blue cheese dressing.

LEMON CHICKEN TENDERS

family favorite

MAKES 4 SERVINGS

Prep: 30 min., Bake: 20 min., Cook: 5 min.

- **½ teaspoon paprika**
- **½ teaspoon salt**
- **¼ teaspoon pepper**
- **3 large skinned and boned chicken breast halves, cut into 2-inch strips**
- **2 large eggs, lightly beaten**
- **1 cup Italian-seasoned breadcrumbs**
- **½ cup sugar**
- **½ cup lemon juice**
- **1¼ to 1½ teaspoons curry powder**

COMBINE first 3 ingredients; sprinkle on chicken strips.

DIP chicken pieces in egg, and dredge in breadcrumbs. Arrange chicken in a single layer in an aluminum foil-lined 15- x 10-inch jellyroll pan.

BAKE at 400° for 15 minutes, turning chicken once.

COOK sugar, lemon juice, and curry powder in a small saucepan 5 minutes over medium-low heat, stirring until sugar dissolves. Drizzle over chicken; bake 5 more minutes.

RHONA BRIVIK
SARASOTA, FLORIDA

NUTTY STUFFED CELERY

fast fixin's

MAKES 4 SERVINGS

Prep: 15 min.

- **3 ounces ⅓-less-fat cream cheese, softened**
- **1 tablespoon half-and-half**
- **½ teaspoon onion powder**
- **½ teaspoon seasoned salt**
- **¼ teaspoon curry powder**
- **4 celery stalks, cut into 4-inch pieces**
- **¼ cup coarsely chopped honey-roasted peanuts**

STIR together first 5 ingredients. Cover and chill until ready to serve.

SPREAD mixture on celery pieces, and sprinkle with peanuts.

LAURA MORRIS
BUNNELL, FLORIDA

Quick & Easy

Versatile Veggie Plate

BAKED MACARONI AND CHEESE

family favorite • make ahead

MAKES 4 TO 6 SERVINGS

Prep: 15 min., Bake: 45 min.

- **2 teaspoons butter or margarine**
- **¼ cup chopped onion**
- **1 (10¾-ounce) can condensed Cheddar cheese soup**
- **¼ cup milk**
- **¼ teaspoon hot sauce**
- **2 cups shredded mild Cheddar cheese**
- **3 cups cooked elbow macaroni**

MELT butter over medium heat in a 3-quart saucepan. Add onion; cook, stirring often, 2 minutes or until tender. Whisk in soup, milk, hot sauce, and half of cheese, stirring just until cheese melts. Stir in macaroni; pour into a lightly greased 9-inch square baking dish. Top with remaining cheese.

BAKE at 375° for 30 to 45 minutes or until golden and bubbly.

ANGELLA KNOLL
PENSACOLA, FLORIDA

SQUASH SALAD

fast fixin's

MAKES 6 SERVINGS

Prep: 10 min.

- **2 small yellow squash, thinly sliced**
- **2 small zucchini, thinly sliced**
- **1 red bell pepper, sliced into rings**
- **1 small sweet onion, thinly sliced**
- **¼ cup water**
- **1 cup Italian salad dressing**

PLACE first 5 ingredients in a 1-quart glass bowl. Cover with heavy-duty plastic wrap; fold back a small edge to let steam escape. Microwave at HIGH 2 minutes. Drain. Pour salad dressing over vegetables; toss to coat. Cover and chill.

Pesto Green Beans

fast fixin's

MAKES 8 SERVINGS

Prep: 20 min., Cook: 10 min.

Purchase trimmed fresh beans to save time.

- 2 pounds fresh green beans, trimmed
- ¼ cup butter or margarine
- 2 garlic cloves, pressed
- 1 teaspoon dried pesto seasoning
- ½ teaspoon salt

ARRANGE green beans in a steamer basket over boiling water. Cover and steam 6 minutes or until crisp-tender.
MELT butter in a large skillet over medium-low heat. Stir in garlic, pesto seasoning, and salt; sauté about 1 minute. Add green beans, and sauté 2 minutes or until thoroughly heated. Serve immediately.

NOTE: For testing purposes only, we used McCormick Gourmet Collection Pesto Seasoning.

SHEILA SUDERS
WILLIAMSBURG, VIRGINIA

Chili Corn on the Cob

fast fixin's

MAKES 4 SERVINGS

Prep: 15 min., Stand: 2 min.

- ¼ cup butter or margarine, softened
- 1 tablespoon chopped fresh chives
- 1 teaspoon chili powder
- 4 ears fresh corn, husks removed
- ¼ teaspoon salt
- ¼ teaspoon pepper

STIR together butter, chives, and chili powder; set aside.
WRAP each ear of corn in plastic wrap; arrange, spoke fashion, on a glass plate.
MICROWAVE at HIGH 7 minutes, turning after 3½ minutes. Let stand 2 minutes. Remove plastic wrap; brush with butter mixture. Sprinkle with salt and pepper.

CHARLOTTE BRYANT
GREENSBURG, KENTUCKY

Cheese Garlic Biscuits

family favorite • fast fixin's

MAKES 10 TO 12 BISCUITS

Prep: 10 min., Bake: 10 min.

- 2 cups all-purpose baking mix
- ⅔ cup milk
- ½ cup (2 ounces) shredded Cheddar cheese
- ¼ cup butter, melted
- ¼ teaspoon garlic powder

STIR together first 3 ingredients until soft dough forms. Stir vigorously 30 seconds. Drop by tablespoonfuls onto an ungreased baking sheet.
BAKE at 450° for 8 to 10 minutes.
STIR together butter and garlic powder; brush over warm biscuits.

M.E. O'NEILL
ABERDEEN, MARYLAND

Hooked on Catfish

Layered Catfish Dip

fast fixin's

MAKES 12 APPETIZER SERVINGS

Prep: 15 min., Cook: 5 min.

- 3 cups water
- 2 (8-ounce) catfish fillets
- 1 (8-ounce) package cream cheese, softened
- 1 (3-ounce) package cream cheese, softened
- 2 tablespoons Worcestershire sauce
- 2 tablespoons mayonnaise
- 1 tablespoon lemon juice
- ⅛ teaspoon garlic salt
- ⅓ cup chopped onion
- 1 cup chili sauce
- Garnish: fresh lemon slice

BRING 3 cups water to a boil in a large skillet; add fillets, and return to a boil. Cover, reduce heat, and simmer 5 minutes or until fish flakes with a fork.

Remove fish from skillet; drain well, and cool. Flake with a fork; set aside.
STIR together cream cheeses and next 4 ingredients until blended. Stir in onion. Spread cream cheese mixture in a shallow dish. Add chili sauce, and top with pieces of fish. Garnish, if desired.

THE CATFISH INSTITUTE
INDIANOLA, MISSISSIPPI

Pecan Catfish With Lemon Sauce

MAKES 4 SERVINGS

Prep: 20 min., Chill: 8 hrs., Cook: 16 min.

- 3 cups milk
- ⅛ teaspoon hot sauce
- 4 (6-ounce) catfish fillets
- 1 large egg, lightly beaten
- ¾ cup all-purpose flour
- 2 teaspoons salt
- 1 teaspoon ground red pepper
- 1 teaspoon ground black pepper
- 1 cup pecans, finely chopped
- Vegetable oil
- ½ cup dry white wine or chicken broth
- ½ cup whipping cream
- ¼ cup lemon juice
- 1 tablespoon all-purpose flour
- ¼ teaspoon garlic powder
- 2 tablespoons butter, cut into pieces

COMBINE milk and hot sauce in a shallow dish; add catfish. Cover and chill 8 hours, turning occasionally.
REMOVE catfish from milk mixture. Whisk egg into milk mixture.
COMBINE ¾ cup flour and next 3 ingredients; dredge catfish in flour mixture, shaking off excess. Dip in egg mixture; coat with pecans.
POUR oil to a depth of 2 inches into a Dutch oven; heat to 360°. Fry 3 minutes on each side or until fish flakes with a fork. Drain on paper towels.
BRING wine, whipping cream, and lemon juice to a boil, stirring constantly. Whisk in 1 tablespoon flour and garlic powder, and simmer, stirring often, 8 to 10 minutes or until thickened. Remove from heat; whisk in butter. Serve over fish.

MARY PAPPAS
RICHMOND, VIRGINIA

from our kitchen

As you can see from "Easy Freezer Meals" on page 179, homemade supper items waiting in your freezer can make life easier. You can adapt many kinds of recipes—from casseroles that use cooked, shredded chicken to meatloaf that just needs to be thawed and baked—to the investment cooking method. Be sure to wrap your food in freezer-safe packages, label them with the date, and keep them only for the appropriate amount of time. This chart will help you know how long an item can stay in your freezer.

FREEZER STORAGE TIMES

- Combination dishes (such as rice and spaghetti dishes, lasagna, stuffed peppers, meat pies, casseroles): 4 to 6 months
- Ground beef, cooked and uncooked: 2 to 3 months
- Chicken (whole, breasts, pieces), uncooked: 6 months
- Meatloaf, baked or unbaked: 3 to 4 months
- Smoked sausage: 1 to 2 months (Note: Freezing sausage may alter flavor.)
- Beef steaks: 6 to 12 months
- Pork chops: 3 to 6 months
- Ham and other cured meats: Not recommended for freezing; may lose color when frozen and become rancid more quickly than other meats

Sources: Clemson University and University of Missouri-Columbia Cooperative Extension Service

Hot Jalapeño Jelly

One of the great advantages of working in the *Southern Living* Test Kitchens is having the opportunity to try new food products. High on our list of favorites is hot jalapeño jelly, a feisty first cousin of the milder red and green pepper jellies often paired with cream cheese as an appetizer. Hot jalapeño jelly combines the heat of jalapeño peppers with the sassy boldness of a sweet-and-sour sauce and can transform everyday ingredients into company fare in a matter of minutes. It's naturally fat free and terrific tossed with hot grilled vegetables or steamed green beans. It packs a concentrated punch, so start with a small amount and adjust according to taste.

The next time you're preparing stir-fry, add a few tablespoons of the jelly to the skillet after browning the meat. It can also add a kick to caramelized onions or a pot of baked beans. Whisk a little into your favorite dressing for marinated vegetables, or use it to glaze carrots—the possibilities are almost endless. Here are three of our most popular recipes using this delicious product.

SPICY SUMMER SALSA: Whisk together ⅓ cup hot jalapeño jelly, 3 tablespoons fresh lime juice, ½ cup diced red onion, and ¼ cup chopped fresh cilantro. Stir in 2 cups coarsely chopped mango, 1 cup fresh sliced strawberries, and 1 large avocado, chopped. Serve over a platter of hot grilled chicken cutlets for a quick and colorful entrée. Fresh nectarines make a great substitution for mango. Makes 4 cups.

JALAPEÑO-GLAZED PORK TENDER-LOIN: Sprinkle 2 (12-ounce) pork tenderloins with salt and pepper, and brown in 2 tablespoons hot oil in a large skillet over medium-high heat. Transfer to a lightly greased 13- x 9-inch baking pan. Whisk together 1 (10.5-ounce) jar hot jalapeño jelly and 2 tablespoons Dijon mustard, and pour over the pork tenderloins. Bake at 350° for 20 to 25 minutes or until a meat thermometer inserted into thickest portion registers 160°, basting occasionally. Let stand 10 minutes; slice and serve with sauce from pan. Makes 6 servings. (If you're a fan of Buffalo Chicken, you'll love this glaze as a dip for fried chicken strips. To serve warm, just pop in the microwave for a few seconds on HIGH.)

SPICY SWEET-AND-SOUR MEATBALLS: Whisk together 1 (10.5-ounce) jar hot jalapeño jelly and 1 (12-ounce) jar cocktail sauce in a Dutch oven. Stir in ½ (3-pound) package frozen cooked meatballs, and simmer over low heat, stirring occasionally, 25 to 30 minutes, or until thoroughly heated. Makes 8 to 10 appetizer servings.

Braswell's, a Georgia-based company, makes a terrific hot jalapeño jelly. You can find it in the jelly section of your local supermarket or order it directly from the Web site at **www.braswells.com**

Tips and Tidbits

- Make quick work of buttering corn on the cob for a crowd by melting the butter in a 13- x 9-inch baking dish. Stir in your favorite seasonings; then add hot corn, and roll.
- Save the wide rubber bands that come on fresh vegetables for other uses. Snap one or two around the lid of a hard-to-open jar to get a better grip. Rebecca Kracke Gordon of our Test Kitchens uses them to separate bundles of uncooked spaghetti and fettuccine inside her pasta jar.

September

Texas-Style Brisket

You'll get fabulous flavor with this slow-smoked cut of beef.

Ask a Texan about barbecue, and it's beef brisket, not pork, that's on the tip of his or her tongue. If you're not from those parts, you're missing out on some good eating. All it takes is one bite, and you'll be hooked.

Our Assistant Garden Design Editor, Troy Black, isn't from Texas, but you wouldn't know it by his brisket. Troy's Traditional Brisket recipe contains all the prerequisites of a true Texas brisket—a great rub, a juicy mop, and a long, slow smoking time. He's got the technique down to a science, too.

TRADITIONAL BRISKET

family favorite

MAKES 8 SERVINGS
Prep: 40 min., Chill: 8 hrs., Soak: 8 hrs.,
Smoke: 6½ hrs., Stand: 1½ hrs.

Smoke brisket 1 hour and 15 minutes per pound at 225° to 250° until the internal temperature reaches 190°. *(pictured on page 190)*

- 1 (5¾-pound) trimmed beef brisket flat
- Brisket Rub
- Hickory smoking chips
- Brisket Mopping Sauce
- Mop
- Brisket Red Sauce (optional)

SPRINKLE each side of beef with ¼ cup Brisket Rub; rub thoroughly into meat. Wrap brisket in plastic wrap, and chill 8 hours.

SOAK hickory chips in water for 8 hours. Drain.

PREPARE smoker according to manufacturer's directions, regulating temperature with a thermometer to 225°; allow it to maintain that temperature for 1 hour before adding beef.

REMOVE beef from refrigerator, and let stand 30 minutes.

PLACE brisket on smoker rack, fat side up. Insert thermometer horizontally into thickest portion of beef brisket. Maintain smoker temperature between 225° and 250°.

ADD a handful (about ¼ cup) of hickory chips about every hour.

BRUSH beef liberally with Brisket Mopping Sauce when beef starts to look dry (internal temperature will be about 156°). Mop top of brisket every hour. When internal temperature reaches 170°, place brisket on a sheet of heavy-duty aluminum foil; mop liberally with Brisket Mopping Sauce. Wrap tightly, and return to smoker.

REMOVE brisket from smoker when internal temperature reaches 190° with an instant-read thermometer. Let stand 1 hour. Cut into very thin (⅛- to ¼-inch-thick) slices. Serve with Brisket Red Sauce, if desired.

NOTE: Mops can be found in the grilling supply section of supermarkets, in restaurant-supply stores, and in the grilling accessory section of sporting goods stores. For testing purposes only, we used the Weber Smokey Mountain Cooker Smoker.

Brisket Rub:

MAKES 2 CUPS
Prep: 5 min.

This makes enough for about three briskets.

- ¼ cup kosher salt
- ¼ cup sugar
- ¼ cup black pepper
- ¾ cup paprika
- 2 tablespoons garlic powder
- 2 tablespoons garlic salt
- 2 tablespoons onion powder
- 2 tablespoons chili powder
- 2 teaspoons ground red pepper

COMBINE all ingredients. Store in an airtight container.

Brisket Mopping Sauce:

MAKES 4 CUPS
Prep: 10 min.

This is enough sauce for about two briskets, so make half the recipe if you're preparing just one.

- 1 (12-ounce) bottle beer
- 1 cup apple cider vinegar
- 1 onion, minced
- 4 garlic cloves, minced
- ½ cup water
- ½ cup Worcestershire sauce
- ¼ cup vegetable oil
- 2 tablespoons Brisket Rub

STIR together all ingredients until blended.

Brisket Red Sauce:

MAKES 3½ CUPS
Prep: 10 min.

- 1½ cups apple cider vinegar
- 1 cup ketchup
- ½ teaspoon ground red pepper
- ¼ cup Worcestershire sauce
- 1 teaspoon salt
- ½ teaspoon black pepper
- ½ teaspoon onion powder
- ½ tablespoon garlic powder
- ½ tablespoon ground cumin
- 2 tablespoons unsalted butter, melted
- ½ cup firmly packed brown sugar

STIR together all ingredients until blended. Serve sauce heated or at room temperature.

Our Best Southern Fried Chicken, Tee's Corn Pudding,
Baby Blue Salad, page 178

Southwestern Brunch
Casserole, page 197

190

Marinated vegetables,
grilled alongside Chicken
Kabobs, page 180

Zesty Santa Fe Salsa, page 198

191

Blueberry Cheesecake, page 182

Start With Convenience Veggies

Have you noticed the enormous variety of vegetables in your supermarket's freezer section? Going with frozen produce shortens prep times and allows you to try new vegetables, even when they're out of season.

We used a variety of frozen veggies to create dishes your whole family will love. So enjoy your recommended five servings of vegetables and fruits per day.

CORN-AND-POBLANO CHOWDER

MAKES 4 (1-CUP) SERVINGS

Prep: 20 min., Broil: 6 min., Stand: 10 min., Cook: 20 min.

Frozen creamed corn and fat-free cream cheese are the base for this spicy-sweet, creamy chowder. Have a cupful for a light lunch, or serve it alongside a sandwich for a more substantial supper.

- 1 large poblano pepper, cut in half lengthwise
- 1 (20-ounce) tube frozen creamed corn, thawed
- 1½ cups 1% low-fat or fat-free milk
- ¼ teaspoon salt
- ⅛ to ¼ teaspoon ground red pepper
- ¼ teaspoon ground cumin
- 1½ to 2 cups reduced-sodium, fat-free chicken broth
- ½ (8-ounce) package fat-free cream cheese, softened
- Garnishes: thinly sliced jalapeño pepper strips, ground black pepper

BROIL poblano pepper halves, skin side up, on an aluminum foil-lined baking sheet 6 inches from heat 5 to 6 minutes or until pepper looks blistered. Fold aluminum foil over pepper to seal, and let stand 10 minutes. Peel pepper; remove and discard seeds. Coarsely chop pepper; set aside.

BRING creamed corn and next 4 ingredients to a boil in a 3-quart saucepan over medium-high heat, stirring constantly. Reduce heat to low, and simmer, stirring often, 10 minutes.

STIR 1½ cups chicken broth into mixture. Whisk in softened cream cheese and chopped poblano pepper; cook, whisking often, 5 minutes or until cream cheese melts and mixture is thoroughly heated. Whisk in additional chicken broth, if necessary, to reach desired consistency; garnish, if desired. Serve chowder immediately.

Calories 222 (37% from fat); Fat 9.2g (sat 0.9g, mono 0.1g, poly 0.2g); Protein 12.5g; Carb 37.5g; Fiber 4.3g; Chol 8mg; Iron 1.2mg; Sodium 803mg; Calc 244mg

CREAMY HASH BROWN CASSEROLE

family favorite

MAKES 6 SERVINGS

Prep: 10 min., Bake: 1 hr., Stand: 10 min.

- 1 (32-ounce) package frozen hash brown potatoes
- 1 (10¾-ounce) can fat-free cream of chicken soup
- 1 (8-ounce) container light sour cream
- 1 small onion, chopped
- 1 (5-ounce) can low-fat evaporated milk
- ¼ cup light butter or margarine, melted
- ½ teaspoon salt
- ¼ teaspoon pepper
- 1 teaspoon dried rosemary (optional)
- Vegetable cooking spray
- 1 cup (4 ounces) shredded reduced-fat Cheddar cheese

STIR together first 8 ingredients, and rosemary, if desired, in a large bowl.

SPOON mixture into an 11- x 7-inch baking dish coated with cooking spray. Sprinkle cheese evenly over top.

BAKE at 350° for 1 hour or until bubbly and golden. Remove from oven, and let stand 10 minutes.

SHARON JONES
HOMEWOOD, ALABAMA

Calories 308 (37% from fat); Fat 13g (sat 7.4g, mono 0.4g, poly 0.5g); Protein 13g; Carb 37g; Fiber 2.6g; Chol 44mg; Iron 1.7mg; Sodium 811mg; Calc 230mg

LETTUCE-WRAPPED PICADILLO

MAKES 6 SERVINGS

Prep: 10 min., Cook: 30 min.

Pronounced *pee-cah-DEE-yo*, this warm and zesty ground beef mixture is very tasty rolled in crisp iceberg lettuce leaves. Also try it in whole wheat tortillas layered with fat-free refried beans, fat-free sour cream, and your favorite salsa.

- 1 pound extra-lean ground beef*
- 2 garlic cloves, minced
- Vegetable cooking spray
- ½ (10-ounce) package frozen onion-and-pepper medley, thawed
- ½ cup golden raisins
- ½ cup tomato sauce
- 2 to 3 teaspoons hot sauce
- ½ teaspoon ground cumin
- ½ teaspoon salt
- ¼ teaspoon pepper
- Iceberg lettuce leaves
- Lime wedges (optional)

COOK ground beef and minced garlic in a large nonstick skillet coated with cooking spray over medium-high heat 10 minutes or until beef crumbles and is no longer pink. Drain, remove from skillet, and pat with paper towels.

ADD onion-and-pepper medley to skillet; cook over medium-high heat, stirring often, 10 minutes or until onions are tender.

STIR in beef mixture, raisins, and next 5 ingredients. Bring mixture to a boil. Reduce heat, and simmer 10 minutes or until most of liquid evaporates. Serve beef mixture in the lettuce leaves. Serve with lime wedges, if desired.

*Substitute lean ground pork for extra-lean ground beef. Use trimmed boneless pork loin chops; cut into chunks, and process in food processor until ground. Cook according to recipe.

NOTE: For testing purposes only, we used McKenzie's Seasoning Blend. If you can't find it in your market, substitute 1 onion, chopped; 1 green bell pepper, chopped; and 1 celery rib, chopped.

KENT BRENNER
BIRMINGHAM, ALABAMA

Calories 175 (29% from fat); Fat 5.6g (sat 2.2g, mono 2.4g, poly 0.3g); Protein 14.5g; Carb 17g; Fiber 2.2g; Chol 22mg; Iron 2.7mg; Sodium 351mg; Calc 39mg

Shortcakes for Fall

Stack the flavors of the season
in these fruit-filled favorites.

Cooler temperatures remind us that fall, along with its delicious harvest, is on its way. These shortcakes incorporate an array of the season's fruit—apples, cranberries, and pears—complemented by the rich flavors of cinnamon and cloves.

Flaky sweetened biscuits sandwich these wonderful fruit fillings. Assemble while the biscuits are still warm, and savor the contrast of tender, flaky shortcakes and fragrant fruit combinations. Enjoy them year-round by substituting other fruits, but do try these recipes this fall. Then cherish the essence of the season.

CINNAMON-CRUNCH SHORTCAKES

family favorite

MAKES 12 SERVINGS

Prep: 20 min., Bake: 15 min.

- 2½ cups all-purpose baking mix
- 3 tablespoons granulated sugar
- ½ cup milk
- 4 tablespoons butter, melted and divided
- ¼ cup chopped pecans
- 2 tablespoons brown sugar
- ¼ teaspoon ground cinnamon

STIR together baking mix, granulated sugar, milk, and 3 tablespoons butter until a soft dough forms. Turn out onto a lightly floured surface; knead 3 or 4 times.
PAT dough to a ¼-inch thickness; cut with a 2¾-inch round biscuit cutter. Place on lightly greased baking sheets.
COMBINE pecans, brown sugar, cinnamon, and remaining tablespoon butter; pat onto biscuit tops.

BAKE at 375° for 12 to 15 minutes or until lightly browned.

CINNAMON-CRUNCH SHORTCAKES WITH FRUIT COMPOTE: Prepare 1 recipe Cinnamon-Crunch Shortcakes. Melt 1 tablespoon butter in a large nonstick skillet over medium-high heat. Stir in ½ cup apple juice; ¼ cup firmly packed brown sugar; 2 ripe Bosc pears, peeled and sliced; 2 Rome apples, peeled and sliced; ¼ cup dried cranberries; and ¼ teaspoon ground cinnamon. Bring to a boil; reduce heat to low, and simmer, stirring occasionally, 10 to 15 minutes or until fruit is tender. Split each baked shortcake in half. Layer half of biscuit halves with fruit compote and whipped cream; top with remaining biscuit halves.

HELEN WOLT
COLORADO SPRINGS, COLORADO

CARAMEL-APPLE SHORTCAKES

family favorite

MAKES 12 SERVINGS

Prep: 15 min., Cook: 18 min.

If you're short on time, use purchased caramel sauce for ease.

- 1 tablespoon butter
- 5 Gala apples, peeled and sliced
- ½ cup apple juice
- 3 tablespoons brown sugar
- ¼ teaspoon ground cinnamon
- Caramel Sauce
- 1 recipe Cinnamon-Crunch Shortcakes
- Whipped cream

MELT butter in a large skillet over medium-high heat; add apples, tossing to coat. Stir in apple juice, brown sugar, and cinnamon. Bring to a boil; reduce heat to low, and simmer 10 to 15 minutes or until apples are tender.
POUR ½ cup Caramel Sauce over apples, tossing to coat. Split Cinnamon-Crunch Shortcakes in half. Layer half of biscuit halves with apple mixture and whipped cream. Top with remaining biscuit halves. Drizzle with the remaining Caramel Sauce.

Caramel Sauce:

MAKES 4 CUPS

Prep: 5 min., Cook: 20 min.

- 3 cups sugar
- 1 cup water
- 2 cups whipping cream

POUR sugar into a heavy 3.5-quart saucepan. Stir in 1 cup water. Bring mixture to a boil, and cook, without stirring, 15 to 20 minutes or until mixture turns a caramel color. Swirl mixture around pan until it turns golden amber in color. Remove from heat, and slowly add cream, stirring constantly with a long wooden spoon. (If caramel begins to clump and harden, return to low heat, and stir until smooth.)

GINGER-PEAR SHORTCAKES

family favorite

MAKES 12 SERVINGS

Prep: 20 min., Bake: 12 min.

Dust the knife with sugar before chopping the ginger to keep it from sticking.

- 2½ cups all-purpose baking mix
- 1 tablespoon sugar
- ½ cup plus 2 tablespoons milk
- 2 tablespoons molasses
- ¼ cup chopped walnuts
- 3 tablespoons chopped crystallized ginger
- 1 tablespoon butter, melted
- ¼ teaspoon ground cinnamon
- ¼ teaspoon ground cloves
- Sautéed Pears
- Whipped cream

STIR together baking mix, sugar, milk, and molasses until a soft dough forms; turn out onto a lightly floured surface, and knead 3 or 4 times.

PAT dough to a ¼-inch thickness, and cut with a 2¾-inch round biscuit cutter. Place on a lightly greased baking sheet.

COMBINE walnuts and next 4 ingredients; pat onto biscuit tops.

BAKE at 375° for 12 minutes or until lightly browned. Cool.

SPLIT shortcakes in half. Layer half of biscuit halves with Sautéed Pears and whipped cream; top with remaining biscuit halves.

Sautéed Pears:

MAKES ABOUT 2½ CUPS

Prep: 20 min., Cook: 10 min.

 6 Bosc pears, peeled and sliced
 2 tablespoons lemon juice
 3 tablespoons butter
 3 tablespoons brown sugar
 1 tablespoon vanilla extract
 ⅛ teaspoon salt

TOSS together pears and lemon juice.

MELT butter in a large skillet over medium-high heat. Add pear mixture, tossing to coat, and cook about 2 minutes; add brown sugar. Bring to a boil; reduce heat to low, and simmer 5 minutes or until pears are soft and sauce thickens slightly. Stir in vanilla and salt.

Grown-up Peanut Butter

While some might consider peanut butter just a children's snack or lunchbox staple, it can also add wonderful flavor to a variety of grown-up dishes. The evidence is in these recipes. Nutty-spicy Peanut Butter Salad Dressing perks up ordinary greens. A fiber-rich Peanut Butter-Banana Muffin doubles as breakfast on the run and dessert, and the Chocolate-Peanut Bars melt in your mouth.

PEANUT BUTTER-BANANA MUFFINS

family favorite • freezeable

MAKES ABOUT 1½ DOZEN

Prep: 20 min., Stand: 5 min., Bake: 30 min.

These muffins are a hit as a snack or a light dessert. Freeze them up to one month; thaw in the refrigerator overnight, or defrost in the microwave.

 2 cups shreds of wheat bran cereal
 1¾ cups milk
 1½ cups all-purpose flour
 ¾ cup sugar
 1 tablespoon baking powder
 ¼ teaspoon salt
 1 medium-size ripe banana, mashed
 ½ cup crunchy peanut butter
 ¼ cup vegetable oil
 1 large egg
 Streusel Topping

STIR together cereal and milk; let stand 5 minutes.

COMBINE flour and next 3 ingredients in a large bowl; make a well in center of mixture.

STIR banana and next 3 ingredients into cereal mixture; add to dry ingredients, stirring just until moistened. Spoon into greased muffin pans, filling two-thirds full. Sprinkle Streusel Topping evenly over batter.

BAKE at 350° for 25 to 30 minutes. Remove from pans immediately, and cool on wire racks.

Streusel Topping:

MAKES 1¼ CUPS

Prep: 5 min.

 ½ cup all-purpose flour
 ½ cup firmly packed light brown sugar
 ¼ cup butter or margarine
 2 tablespoons peanut butter

COMBINE flour and brown sugar. Cut butter and peanut butter into flour mixture with a pastry blender or fork until mixture resembles small peas.

NOTE: For testing purposes only, we used Kellogg's All-Bran cereal for shreds of wheat bran cereal.

MARY CHAMBLISS
HOUSTON, TEXAS

CHOCOLATE-PEANUT BARS

family favorite • make ahead

MAKES ABOUT 4 DOZEN

Prep: 10 min., Cook: 3 min., Chill: 1 hr., Stand: 10 min.

 1 cup butter or margarine, softened
 1 cup crunchy peanut butter
 1 (16-ounce) package powdered sugar
 1½ cups vanilla wafers, crushed (about 45 cookies)
 1 (12-ounce) package semisweet chocolate morsels
 ½ cup whipping cream

BEAT butter and peanut butter at medium speed with an electric mixer until blended. Add powdered sugar and vanilla wafer crumbs; beat until blended. Press mixture evenly into a lightly greased 13- x 9-inch pan lined with wax paper.

STIR together chocolate morsels and whipping cream in a medium saucepan over low heat until melted and smooth. Spread evenly on top of peanut butter mixture. Chill 1 hour or until firm.

REMOVE from refrigerator, and let stand at room temperature 10 minutes or until slightly softened. Cut into 48 bars.

SHERRI MITCHELL
HOOVER, ALABAMA

PEANUT BUTTER SALAD DRESSING

fast fixin's • make ahead

MAKES 1⅓ CUPS

Prep: 10 min.

 ⅔ cup vegetable oil
 ⅓ cup fresh orange juice
 2 tablespoons honey
 2 tablespoons creamy peanut butter
 1 teaspoon dried crushed red pepper
 ½ teaspoon minced fresh ginger
 ¼ teaspoon salt
 Mixed salad greens

WHISK together first 7 ingredients in a bowl until blended and smooth. Serve over mixed salad greens.

ASHLEY TURKHEIMER
NEW ORLEANS, LOUISIANA

The *Southern Living* Cooking School invites you to gather family and friends and enjoy doable recipes for easy weeknights and gracious parties too. Let's eat!

Supper's Ready

Southern Living has put together a variety of recipes to fit your needs. Also included are seven unique menus designed to spark creativity in your kitchen.

SAVORY TOMATO-BACON BISCUIT BITES

fast fixin's

MAKES 32 APPETIZER SERVINGS

Prep: 20 min., Bake: 10 min.

2 cups BISQUICK Original All-Purpose Baking Mix
⅓ cup grated Parmesan cheese
1 tablespoon sugar
1 teaspoon Italian seasoning
¼ teaspoon ground red pepper
⅔ cup mayonnaise, divided
¼ cup milk
4 large plum tomatoes, each cut into 8 slices
10 bacon slices, cooked and crumbled
Thinly sliced green onions (optional)

COMBINE first 5 ingredients in a medium bowl; stir in ⅓ cup mayonnaise and milk with a fork until moistened. Turn dough out onto a lightly floured surface, and knead 5 or 6 times.

PAT or roll dough to a ¼-inch thickness; cut with a 1¾-inch round cutter, and place on a lightly greased baking sheet. **BAKE** at 425° for 8 to 10 minutes or until golden brown. Cool slightly. **SPREAD** each biscuit evenly with half of remaining ⅓ cup mayonnaise; top with a tomato slice. Spread tomato slices with remaining mayonnaise; sprinkle with bacon and, if desired, sliced green onions.

SHRIMP-AND-ARTICHOKE QUICHE

MAKES 6 TO 8 SERVINGS

Prep: 15 min., Bake: 35 min., Stand: 10 min.

¾ pound frozen cooked shrimp, thawed and coarsely chopped (1½ cups)
3 small green onions, sliced
1 (4-ounce) package shredded Swiss cheese
1 (4-ounce) package shredded Parmesan cheese
1 cup BISQUICK Original All-Purpose Baking Mix
2 large eggs
1 cup milk
1½ teaspoons Cajun seasoning
1 (14-ounce) can small artichoke hearts, drained and cut in half lengthwise

SPRINKLE shrimp and green onions in a lightly greased 9-inch pieplate. **COMBINE** Swiss and Parmesan cheeses; sprinkle half of cheese mixture evenly over shrimp mixture. **WHISK** together baking mix and next 3 ingredients until blended. Pour evenly over cheeses in pieplate; top with artichoke heart halves, cut sides down, and remaining cheese mixture. **BAKE** at 400° for 30 to 35 minutes or until a knife inserted in center comes out clean. Let stand 10 minutes before serving.

PINEAPPLE-TURKEY MELTS

MAKES 6 SANDWICHES

Prep: 20 min., Cook: 15 min.

1 (20-ounce) can DOLE Pineapple Slices
2 tablespoons butter or margarine
½ teaspoon salt
½ teaspoon pepper
1 (8-ounce) container soft chive-and-onion cream cheese
2 (8-ounce) French bread loaves, split
1 pound sliced deli turkey or chicken
1 (8-ounce) package Swiss cheese slices

DRAIN pineapple slices, and cut each slice in half.
MELT butter in a skillet over medium heat; add pineapple, and sauté 2 to 3 minutes. Sprinkle pineapple evenly with salt and pepper.

SPREAD cream cheese on each French bread half. Layer bottom bread halves with pineapple, turkey, and Swiss cheese slices; top with French bread halves.
COOK sandwiches on a lightly greased griddle over medium heat 5 minutes on each side or until bread is toasted and cheese melts. Cut sandwiches into thirds.

NOTE: For testing purposes only, we used 1 (16-ounce) package Pepperidge Farm Hot 'n' Crusty Twin French Bread.

SOUTHWESTERN BRUNCH CASSEROLE

family favorite

MAKES 8 TO 10 SERVINGS
Prep: 30 min., Cook: 10 min., Bake: 55 min., Cool: 25 min. *(pictured on page 190)*

1⅔ cups water
1 cup milk
2 tablespoons butter or margarine
1 teaspoon salt
¼ teaspoon pepper
⅔ cup uncooked quick-cooking grits
2 cups (8 ounces) shredded Mexican
    cheese blend, divided*
2 garlic cloves, pressed
¼ teaspoon dried oregano
8 large eggs
1½ cups chopped cooked ham
1 (4.5-ounce) can chopped green chiles
1½ cups milk, divided
3 cups BISQUICK Original All-Purpose
    Baking Mix
1 (8-ounce) container sour cream
1 teaspoon hot sauce
Salsa (optional)

BRING first 5 ingredients to a boil in a medium saucepan; gradually stir in grits. Cover, reduce heat, and simmer, stirring occasionally, 5 to 7 minutes. Add ½ cup cheese, garlic, and oregano, stirring until the cheese melts; let cool 10 to 15 minutes. Stir in 2 eggs, and pour into a lightly greased 13- x 9-inch baking dish.
BAKE at 350° for 20 minutes; remove baking dish from oven. Increase oven temperature to 400°.

A Week of Menu Suggestions

Game-Day Menu
Serves 6

Sweet 'n' Savory Snack Mix

Zesty Santa Fe Salsa with
red and blue tortilla chips

Pineapple-Turkey Melts

Double-Chip Oatmeal Cookies

South-of-the-Border Brunch
Serves 6 to 8

Southwestern Brunch Casserole

Tomato Grits   Mixed fruit salad

Pineapple-Coconut Coffee Cake

Wedding Brunch
Serves 6 to 8

Curried Pineapple

Shrimp-and-Artichoke Quiche

Vinaigrette over gourmet mixed greens

Croissants

Orange juice, sparkling wine

Weeknight Meatless Menu
Serves 6

Blue cheese dressing over gourmet
mixed greens

Spanish-Style Lentils and Rice

Breadsticks   Choco Cupcakes

Casual Supper Club
Serves 6 to 8

Savory Tomato-Bacon
Biscuit Bites

Chicken-and-Sausage Jambalaya,
Light Italian Casserole, or
Chicken-and-Pepper Pasta

Tossed salad

French bread

Peanut Butter-Brownie Trifle

Elegant Supper Club
Serves 8

Savory Tomato-Bacon
Biscuit Bites

2 (4- to 5-pound)
whole deli-roasted chickens

Pear-and-Cranberry Wild Rice
Salad (double recipe)

Dinner rolls

Store-bought cheesecake
and fresh strawberries

Southwestern Dinner
Serves 6

Zesty Santa Fe Salsa with
red and blue tortilla chips

Grilled steaks   Tomato Grits

Tex-Mex Layered Salad

Lime sherbet

SPRINKLE remaining 1½ cups cheese, ham, and chiles evenly over grits crust. Whisk together remaining 6 eggs and ½ cup milk; pour into baking dish.
STIR together remaining 1 cup milk and the next 3 ingredients; spoon the milk mixture evenly over egg mixture, slightly spreading with back of a spoon.

(The baking mix mixture will be very thick.)
BAKE at 400° for 35 minutes. Cool 10 minutes; cut into squares. Serve with salsa, if desired.

*Substitute 2 cups (8 ounces) shredded Cheddar cheese, if desired.

PINEAPPLE-COCONUT COFFEE CAKE

freezeable

MAKES 2 (8-INCH) CAKES (ABOUT 8 SERVINGS PER CAKE)

Prep: 15 min., Bake: 40 min., Cool: 10 min., Broil: 5 min.

Because this recipe makes two coffee cakes, you could freeze one to use later. They also make great gifts.

- 2 (20-ounce) cans DOLE Crushed Pineapple, divided
- ½ cup butter or margarine, softened
- 1 cup granulated sugar
- 1 cup firmly packed brown sugar
- 2 large eggs
- 2½ cups all-purpose flour
- 1 teaspoon baking powder
- 1 teaspoon baking soda
- ¼ teaspoon salt
- 1 (3½-ounce) can sweetened flaked coconut
- 1¼ cups chopped pecans, toasted and divided
- 1 teaspoon vanilla extract
- 2 cups powdered sugar
- ¼ cup sweetened flaked coconut

DRAIN pineapple, reserving 2 tablespoons juice; set pineapple and reserved juice aside.

BEAT butter at medium speed with an electric mixer until creamy; gradually add granulated sugar and brown sugar, beating well. Add eggs, 1 at a time, beating after each addition.

COMBINE flour and next 3 ingredients; gradually add to butter mixture, beating well. Stir in 1½ cups drained pineapple, 3½-ounce can coconut, 1 cup pecans, and vanilla.

SPOON batter into 2 greased and floured 8-inch round cakepans.

BAKE at 350° for 35 to 40 minutes or until a wooden pick inserted in center comes out clean. Cool in pans on wire racks 10 minutes.

STIR together powdered sugar, remaining pineapple, reserved juice, remaining chopped pecans, and ¼ cup coconut. Spread evenly over cakes.

BROIL 5½ inches from heat 3 to 5 minutes or until lightly browned and bubbly. Cool completely in pans on wire racks.

ZESTY SANTA FE SALSA

MAKES 4½ CUPS

Prep: 15 min., Cook: 20 min.

Top an ordinary baked potato with this salsa, sour cream, and shredded cheese for a super Tex-Mex meal. *(pictured on page 191)*

- 1 large onion, thinly sliced
- 4 garlic cloves, minced
- 2 tablespoons vegetable oil
- 1 (14.5-ounce) can HUNT'S Petite Diced Tomatoes with Mild Green Chilies
- ½ jalapeño pepper, seeded and minced
- 1 teaspoon chopped canned chipotle peppers in adobo sauce
- 2 teaspoons adobo sauce (from canned chipotle peppers)
- 1 (15-ounce) can black beans, rinsed and drained
- ½ cup frozen whole kernel corn
- ¼ teaspoon salt
- ¼ cup chopped fresh cilantro
- 2 tablespoons lime juice
- Garnish: jalapeño pepper, seeded and sliced lengthwise, forming a fan
- Tortilla or corn chips

SAUTÉ onion and garlic in hot oil in a large saucepan over medium-high heat 5 minutes or until tender. Add tomatoes and next 3 ingredients; bring to a boil. Reduce heat to medium low, and cook, covered, 10 minutes, stirring occasionally.

PROCESS 1 cup tomato mixture in a blender until smooth, stopping to scrape down sides; return to saucepan.

STIR in black beans, corn, and salt; cook 3 minutes or until thoroughly heated. Stir in cilantro and lime juice. Garnish salsa, if desired. Serve with chips.

LIGHT ITALIAN CASSEROLE

family favorite

MAKES 6 TO 8 SERVINGS

Prep: 20 min., Cook: 20 min., Bake: 30 min.

We lightened this casserole by using lean ground beef, light pasteurized prepared cheese product, light sour cream, and light cream cheese.

- 6 ounces wide egg noodles
- 6 green onions, chopped
- 2 pounds lean ground beef or ground round
- 2 cups pasta sauce
- 1 (14.5-ounce) can HUNT'S Diced Tomatoes with Green Pepper, Celery & Onions
- ½ teaspoon Italian seasoning
- 1 (16-ounce) loaf light pasteurized prepared cheese product
- 1 (8-ounce) container light sour cream
- 1 (8-ounce) package light cream cheese, softened

COOK egg noodles according to package directions; drain. Stir together egg noodles and chopped green onions; set aside.

COOK ground beef in a large skillet over medium heat, stirring until it crumbles and is no longer pink; drain and return to skillet. Stir in pasta sauce, diced tomatoes, and Italian seasoning.

CUT cheese loaf into ½-inch cubes; reserve and set aside 1 cup. Stir together remaining cheese cubes, sour cream, and cream cheese.

SPOON one-third of beef mixture into a 13- x 9-inch baking dish; top with half of noodle mixture and half of sour cream mixture. Repeat layers.

SPOON remaining one-third of ground beef mixture over sour cream mixture, and sprinkle evenly with reserved 1 cup of cheese cubes.

BAKE at 350° for 30 minutes or until cheese is melted and bubbly.

Tomato Grits

make ahead

MAKES: 6 SERVINGS

Prep: 5 min., Cook: 30 min, Stand: 5 min.

To make ahead, prepare the recipe in its entirety, and cool. Cover grits, and refrigerate. To reheat, microwave until thoroughly heated.

- 2 bacon slices, chopped
- 2 (14½-ounce) cans chicken broth
- ½ teaspoon salt
- 1 cup quick-cooking grits
- 1 (14.5-ounce) can HUNT'S Petite Diced Tomatoes
- ¼ (16-ounce) loaf pasteurized prepared cheese product with jalapeño peppers, cubed

COOK bacon in a heavy saucepan until crisp, reserving drippings in pan. Gradually add broth and salt, and bring to a boil.
STIR in grits and diced tomatoes; return to a boil, stirring often. Reduce heat; simmer, stirring often, 15 to 20 minutes.
STIR in cheese; cover and let stand 5 minutes or until cheese melts. Stir mixture until blended.

Pear-and-Cranberry Wild Rice Salad

make ahead

MAKES 6 SERVINGS

Prep: 10 min., Cook 25 min., Chill: 1 hr.

Bosc pears have a slender neck, wide base, and reddish-yellow skin.

- 1 (6-ounce) package long-grain and wild rice mix
- ½ cup sweetened dried cranberries
- PAM Original No-Stick Cooking Spray
- ½ cup sliced almonds
- ½ small red onion, chopped
- 1 shallot, chopped
- 1 tablespoon dried parsley flakes
- ½ teaspoon salt
- ¼ teaspoon pepper
- 1 Bosc pear, chopped

COOK rice with dried cranberries according to package directions, omitting the seasoning packet and butter. Reserve the seasoning packet for another use.
SPRAY a small skillet with cooking spray; heat over medium-high heat. Add almonds, and sauté 3 to 5 minutes or until toasted. Remove from pan, and set aside. Wipe skillet clean with a paper towel.
SPRAY skillet with cooking spray, and heat over medium-high heat. Add onion and shallot, and sauté 6 minutes or until tender.
STIR together rice mixture, onion, shallot, and next 3 ingredients in a large bowl, and stir well. Cover mixture, and chill 1 hour.
STIR in sliced almonds and pear just before serving.

Sweet 'n' Savory Snack Mix

fast fixin's

MAKES 8 CUPS

Prep: 5 min., Bake 12 min.

- 3 cups crispy corn or rice cereal squares
- 1 cup small pretzels
- 1 (6-ounce) can roasted almonds
- 1 (8-ounce) jar salted peanuts
- ⅓ cup firmly packed light brown sugar
- 1½ tablespoons Worcestershire sauce
- PAM Butter Flavor No-Stick Cooking Spray
- 1 cup bear-shaped graham crackers
- ½ cup raisins

COMBINE first 4 ingredients in a large bowl. Stir together brown sugar and Worcestershire sauce until blended; pour over cereal mixture. Spray a 15- x 10-inch jellyroll pan with cooking spray; spread cereal mixture in a single layer in pan, stirring to coat.
BAKE at 325° for 12 minutes, stirring every 5 minutes. Stir in graham crackers and raisins. Store snack mix in an airtight container.

Chicken-and-Pepper Pasta

family favorite

MAKES 6 SERVINGS

Prep: 15 min., Cook: 30 min.

Spray the water with cooking spray before adding and cooking the pasta to keep the noodles from sticking together.

- 8 ounces uncooked linguine
- 4 skinned and boned chicken breast halves, cut into 1-inch pieces
- 1½ teaspoons pesto seasoning
- PAM Original No-Stick Cooking Spray
- 1 small green bell pepper, cut into strips
- 1 small red bell pepper, cut into strips
- 1 small yellow bell pepper, cut into strips
- ½ sweet onion, chopped
- 1 (14½-ounce) can chicken broth
- ¾ cup white wine
- ¾ cup (3 ounces) shredded Parmesan cheese

COOK linguine according to package directions; drain and set pasta aside.
TOSS together chicken pieces and pesto seasoning.
SPRAY a large skillet with cooking spray, and heat over medium-high heat. Cook chicken, stirring often, 10 minutes or until done. Remove chicken from skillet, and keep warm.
SPRAY skillet with cooking spray, and heat over medium-high heat. Add bell peppers and onion, and sauté 6 minutes or until tender.
STIR in broth and wine, and simmer, stirring occasionally, 10 to 15 minutes or until liquid is slightly reduced. Add chicken and pasta, and toss. Sprinkle with cheese, and toss. Serve pasta immediately.

SOUTHERN LIVING COOKING SCHOOL

PEANUT BUTTER-BROWNIE TRIFLE

family favorite

MAKES 6 TO 8 SERVINGS

Prep: 30 min., Bake: 30 min., Chill: 30 min.

- 1 (19-ounce) package fudge brownie mix*
- 2 cups whipping cream, divided
- 1⅔ cups (11-ounce package) NESTLÉ TOLL HOUSE Peanut Butter & Milk Chocolate Morsels
- 2 teaspoons vanilla extract
- 1½ cups Peanut Butter NESTLÉ TREASURES, chopped
- 1 (8-ounce) container frozen whipped topping, thawed
- 1⅔ cups (11-ounce package) NESTLÉ TOLL HOUSE Peanut Butter & Milk Chocolate Morsels (optional)

PREPARE and bake brownie mix according to package directions; cool. Cut into 2-inch squares.

COOK ⅔ cup whipping cream and 1⅔ cups morsels in a small saucepan over low heat, stirring constantly, until blended; remove from heat, and stir in vanilla. Chill 30 minutes.

BEAT remaining 1⅓ cups whipping cream at high speed with an electric mixer until soft peaks form. Stir one-third of whipped cream into chocolate mixture. Fold in remaining whipped cream.

LAYER half of brownies in a 3½-quart trifle dish or bowl; top with half of chocolate mixture, half of chopped peanut butter treasures, and half of whipped topping. Repeat procedure with remaining brownies, chocolate mixture, chopped peanut butter treasures, and whipped topping.

SPRINKLE 1⅔ cups morsels in an even layer on a parchment- or wax paper-lined baking pan. Bake at 200° for 2 minutes or until morsels are evenly melted; chill 1 hour or until firm. Break into large pieces. Garnish trifle with peanut butter-chocolate pieces, if desired.

*Substitute 2 (18-ounce) packages NESTLÉ TOLL HOUSE Refrigerated Brownie Bar Dough for brownie mix. Prepare and bake according to package directions.

CHOCO CUPCAKES

MAKES ABOUT 1½ DOZEN

Prep: 15 min., Bake: 15 min.

- 1 (18.25-ounce) package chocolate cake mix
- 3 large eggs
- 1¼ cups water
- ½ cup vegetable oil
- 1 cup (6 ounces) NESTLÉ TOLL HOUSE Semi-Sweet Chocolate Morsels
- Chocolate Filling
- Buttercream Frosting

BEAT first 4 ingredients at low speed with an electric mixer 2 minutes; then beat at medium speed 3 minutes or until blended. Stir in chocolate morsels. Spoon batter evenly into 16 to 18 paper-lined muffin pans.

BAKE at 350° for 15 minutes.

REMOVE from oven. Make a small indentation in center of each hot cupcake. Spoon 2 teaspoons Chocolate Filling into each center. Remove from pans, and let cool completely on a wire rack.

SPREAD cupcakes with Buttercream Frosting.

Chocolate Filling:

MAKES ABOUT 1 CUP

Prep: 5 min., Cook: 5 min., Cool: 20 min.

- 1 cup (6 ounces) NESTLÉ TOLL HOUSE Semi-Sweet Chocolate Morsels
- ¼ cup whipping cream
- 2 tablespoons butter or margarine

COMBINE all ingredients in a small saucepan. Cook over low heat, stirring constantly, until blended. Cool filling 20 minutes.

Buttercream Frosting:

MAKES 3 CUPS

Prep: 10 min.

- ½ cup butter or margarine, softened
- 1 (16-ounce) package powdered sugar
- ¼ cup whipping cream
- ¼ teaspoon salt
- 1 teaspoon coconut extract

BEAT butter at medium speed with an electric mixer; gradually add powdered sugar, beating until blended. Stir in whipping cream, salt, and coconut extract.

DOUBLE-CHIP OATMEAL COOKIES

family favorite

MAKES 1½ DOZEN

Prep: 15 min., Bake: 16 min. per batch

Lots of chocolate and peanut butter chips in these cookies will guarantee that this is your most requested recipe.

- ¾ cup butter or margarine, softened
- ¼ cup shortening
- ¾ cup granulated sugar
- ¾ cup firmly packed light brown sugar
- 2 large eggs
- 1 teaspoon vanilla extract
- 2¼ cups all-purpose flour
- 1 teaspoon baking soda
- ¼ teaspoon salt
- 1⅔ cups (11-ounce package) NESTLÉ TOLL HOUSE Peanut Butter & Milk Chocolate Morsels
- 2 cups (12-ounce package) NESTLÉ TOLL HOUSE Semi-Sweet Chocolate Morsels
- ½ cup uncooked regular oats
- ½ cup chopped pecans, toasted

BEAT butter and shortening at medium speed with an electric mixer until creamy; gradually add sugars, beating until blended. Add eggs and vanilla, beating until blended.

COMBINE flour, baking soda, and salt; gradually add to butter mixture, beating well. Stir in morsels, oats, and pecans.

STOP

DROP dough by ¼ cupfuls onto lightly greased baking sheets. Bake at 350° for 15 to 16 minutes or until golden around edges. Remove cookies to wire racks to cool completely.

CURRIED PINEAPPLE

fast fixin's

MAKES 4 CUPS

Prep: 5 min., Cook: 20 min.

- 2 (20-ounce) cans DOLE Pineapple Chunks
- 1 cup firmly packed light brown sugar
- 2 tablespoons butter or margarine
- 1 teaspoon curry powder
- 1 cup chopped pecans, toasted

DRAIN pineapple, reserving juice. Place pineapple in a large serving bowl, and set aside.
BRING 1 cup reserved juice, brown sugar, butter, and curry powder to a boil in a saucepan; reduce heat, and simmer, uncovered, 20 minutes. Pour mixture over pineapple, tossing to coat. Sprinkle with chopped pecans. Serve warm or at room temperature.

CHICKEN-AND-SAUSAGE JAMBALAYA

family favorite

MAKES 6 SERVINGS

Prep: 15 min., Cook: 40 min.

- 1 deli-roasted whole chicken
- 1 pound smoked sausage, cut into ¼-inch-thick slices
- 1 medium-size green bell pepper, chopped
- 1 small onion, chopped
- 2 (10-ounce) cans ROTEL Milder Diced Tomatoes & Green Chilies
- 1 (14½-ounce) can chicken broth
- 1 cup water
- 1 teaspoon garlic powder
- 1 teaspoon Cajun seasoning
- 2 cups uncooked long-grain rice

REMOVE chicken from bones; cut chicken into bite-size pieces, and set aside.
COOK sausage in a Dutch oven over medium heat, stirring occasionally, 5 minutes. Add bell pepper and onion; cook, stirring occasionally, 3 minutes or until vegetables are tender.
STIR in tomatoes and green chilies, broth, 1 cup water, garlic powder, and Cajun seasoning; bring to a boil, stirring occasionally. Stir in chicken and rice. Cover, reduce heat, and simmer 30 minutes or until rice is tender.

TEX-MEX LAYERED SALAD

family favorite

MAKES 8 SERVINGS

Prep: 25 min., Chill: 1 hr.

This is a great dish to take to your next potluck supper.

- 1 (10-ounce) can ROTEL Mexican Festival Diced Tomatoes, drained
- 1 (8-ounce) container sour cream
- 1 (3-ounce) package cream cheese, softened
- 1 teaspoon ground cumin
- 1 garlic clove, pressed
- 4 cups shredded romaine lettuce
- 1 (15-ounce) can black beans, rinsed and drained
- 1 (15-ounce) can whole kernel corn, drained
- 1 avocado, peeled and chopped
- 1 (4-ounce) jar diced pimiento, drained
- 1 cup (4 ounces) shredded sharp Cheddar cheese
- 2 (4-ounce) cans sliced ripe olives, drained
- Chopped green onions (optional)

PROCESS first 5 ingredients in a blender or food processor until smooth, stopping to scrape down sides; chill.
LAYER lettuce and next 6 ingredients in a 3-quart bowl; spoon tomato mixture evenly over top. Sprinkle with green onions, if desired. Cover and chill 1 hour.

SPANISH-STYLE LENTILS AND RICE

vegetarian

MAKES 6 SERVINGS

Prep: 20 min., Cook: 30 min., Bake: 20 min.

Lentils, in combination with rice, make this a protein-complete dish.

- 3½ cups water
- 1 cup uncooked long-grain white rice
- 1 cup dried lentils
- 1 teaspoon salt
- 1 medium onion, diced
- 1 green bell pepper, diced
- ½ teaspoon ground cumin
- ½ teaspoon chili powder
- ¼ teaspoon garlic powder
- 1 (10-ounce) can ROTEL Mexican Festival Diced Tomatoes
- 1 cup (4 ounces) shredded sharp Cheddar cheese

BRING first 4 ingredients to a boil in a medium saucepan; reduce heat, cover, and simmer 20 to 25 minutes or until lentils are tender.
SAUTÉ onion and bell pepper in a large lightly greased nonstick skillet over medium-high heat until tender. Add cumin, chili powder, and garlic powder; cook, stirring constantly, 2 minutes.
STIR onion mixture and tomatoes into rice mixture, and spoon into a lightly greased 13- x 9-inch baking dish.
BAKE at 350° for 15 minutes; top evenly with Cheddar cheese, and bake 5 more minutes.

Supper Swap

Cook only one night a week. We'll show you how.

You want to prepare exciting, nutritious meals throughout the week, but busy schedules often mean the same ho-hum recipes. Wouldn't it be nice to have a fresh, home-cooked supper delivered a few nights a week? A cooking co-op could be the answer, and it's easier to set up than you might think.

"The idea is pretty simple," says nine-year co-op veteran Leigh Fran Jones of Indian Springs, Alabama. "You cook a big meal once a week to share with your co-op and, depending on the number of people in your group, you get two or three in return. That means you save trips to the grocery store and really mess up the kitchen only once," she says with a big smile. For the rest of the week, Leigh Fran and fellow co-op member Ruthann Betz-Essinger take advantage of leftovers or prepare simpler meals.

"The co-op meals usually consist of a main dish, vegetable, and starch. Sometimes we include dessert," explains Susan Franco of Atlanta, who, along with a couple of friends, formed the Supper Sisters two years ago. In addition to saving money, Susan believes the co-op has allowed her family to consistently eat a wider variety of foods.

"Learning to cook for 10 to 15 people took some getting used to," Susan remembers. "However, I picked recipes I could handle and that easily doubled (such as the ones featured here). In no time at all, my confidence grew, and my time spent in the kitchen dropped dramatically."

All of these recipes are from readers, many of whom use them in their own co-ops. We've also included handy tips on starting a co-op, as well as reheating instructions and serving suggestions.

CALZONES WITH ITALIAN TOMATO SAUCE

family favorite • freezeable

MAKES 6 SERVINGS

Prep: 30 min., Cook: 10 min., Bake: 30 min.

Deliver with potato chips and fresh fruit.

- 1 pound lean ground beef
- 3½ cups (14 ounces) shredded mozzarella cheese, divided
- 1 (6-ounce) can low-sodium tomato paste
- ½ cup frozen chopped spinach, thawed and drained
- 2 teaspoons Italian seasoning
- 2 (10-ounce) cans refrigerated pizza crust
- Olive oil
- Italian Tomato Sauce

COOK ground beef in a large skillet over medium-high heat, stirring until it crumbles and is no longer pink. Drain.
COMBINE beef, 2½ cups cheese, and next 3 ingredients.
UNROLL each pizza crust, and cut each crust into thirds. Roll each portion into a 5-inch circle. Spread ¾ cup of meat mixture evenly over half of each circle. Moisten edges with water; fold dough over, pressing or crimping edges to seal. Place on a lightly greased baking sheet, and cut slits in tops to allow steam to escape. Brush with olive oil.
BAKE at 375° for 25 to 30 minutes or until golden. Top with Italian Tomato Sauce; sprinkle with remaining cheese. Melt cheese under broiler, if desired.

Italian Tomato Sauce:

Prep: 5 min., Cook: 5 min.

- 1¼ cups tomato sauce
- ¼ cup tomato paste
- 1 garlic clove, minced
- 1 teaspoon Italian seasoning

COOK all ingredients in a small saucepan over medium heat 5 minutes or until thoroughly heated.

NOTE: Freeze baked calzones up to 1 month, if desired. Thaw in refrigerator overnight. Wrap calzones in aluminum foil, and bake at 300° for 1 hour or until thoroughly heated.

BEEF-AND-PEPPERONI CALZONES: Substitute 1 (3.5-ounce) package pepperoni slices for spinach.

RUTHANN BETZ-ESSINGER
BIRMINGHAM, ALABAMA

SALISBURY STEAK WITH MUSHROOM GRAVY

family favorite • make ahead

MAKES 6 SERVINGS

Prep: 20 min., Cook: 20 min., Bake: 25 min.

Deliver with mashed potatoes (for convenience, we prefer frozen) and a vegetable.

- 1 large onion, chopped and divided (about 2 cups)
- 3 tablespoons vegetable oil, divided
- 1 garlic clove, minced
- 2 pounds ground beef
- 2 large eggs, lightly beaten
- ¼ cup fine, dry breadcrumbs
- 2 teaspoons prepared mustard
- 2 teaspoons Worcestershire sauce
- 1 teaspoon salt, divided
- 1 teaspoon pepper, divided
- 1 (8-ounce) package sliced fresh mushrooms
- 3 tablespoons all-purpose flour
- ½ cup dry red wine
- 1½ cups low-sodium beef broth

SAUTÉ half of chopped onion in 1 tablespoon hot oil in a medium skillet over medium-high heat until tender. Add garlic, and sauté 30 seconds. Remove from heat, and let cool.
COMBINE onion mixture, beef, next 4 ingredients, ¼ teaspoon salt, and ½ teaspoon pepper. Shape into 6 patties.
COOK patties in remaining 2 tablespoons hot oil over medium-high heat 3 minutes on each side or until browned. (Do not cook until done.) Remove patties, and set aside.

ADD remaining half of chopped onion to drippings in skillet, and sauté over medium heat until tender; add mushrooms, and sauté 3 minutes. Whisk in flour, and cook, stirring constantly, 1 minute; whisk in wine, broth, and remaining ¾ teaspoon salt and ½ teaspoon pepper. Bring to a boil; reduce heat to low, and simmer, stirring occasionally, 5 minutes.

PLACE patties in a lightly greased baking dish; top evenly with gravy.

BAKE, covered, at 350° for 25 minutes or until done.

NOTE: To reheat, bake, covered, at 350° for 45 minutes or until bubbly.

VIVIAN WATERS
THOMASVILLE, GEORGIA

CRISPY CHICKEN-AND-RICE CASSEROLE

family favorite • freezeable

MAKES 8 TO 10 SERVINGS

Prep: 30 min., Bake: 30 min.

Deliver with a tossed green salad and French bread.

> 1 cup uncooked long-grain rice
> 2 cups chopped cooked chicken
> 2 (10¾-ounce) cans cream of mushroom soup
> 1 (8-ounce) can sliced water chestnuts, drained
> 1 (3½-ounce) can sliced mushrooms, drained
> 1 cup chopped celery
> ¾ cup mayonnaise
> 1 small onion, chopped
> ½ cup sliced almonds
> 1 tablespoon lemon juice
> 1 teaspoon salt
> 1 cup crushed cornflakes cereal
> Garnish: chopped fresh parsley

COOK rice according to package directions. Stir together cooked rice and next 10 ingredients in a bowl. Spoon into a lightly greased 13- x 9-inch baking dish. Sprinkle evenly with cereal.

BAKE at 350° for 30 minutes or until golden and bubbly. Garnish, if desired.

NOTE: Freeze casserole up to 1 month, if desired. Thaw casserole in refrigerator overnight. Bake, covered with aluminum foil, at 350° for 45 minutes. Remove foil, and bake 15 more minutes or until thoroughly heated.

RUTHANN BETZ-ESSINGER
BIRMINGHAM, ALABAMA

Tips for Co-Op Success

Getting Started:

■ Keep the group small (a co-op of three or four families of similar size is ideal).
■ Meet to plan at least one month of menus, and establish planning calendars to maintain a variety.
■ Create your own general guidelines (such as vegetarian, nothing too spicy, or no fish).
■ Make the group aware of allergies and nutritional needs.
■ Set up delivery times that are convenient for everyone, such as when picking up kids from school.
■ Be honest. If your family doesn't like something, tell the group so no one wastes time and effort.

Food Preparation:

■ Try to include at least one vegetable and one starch (other than bread) with every meal.
■ Deliver a meal that's ready to go except for reheating or that requires only minimal work to finish.
■ Package food in containers that are both freezeable and reheatable.
■ Most recipes yield 6 to 8 servings, so you may need to double or make recipes twice to serve everyone in the co-op.

For more information check out **www.co-opcooking.com.** The Web site is produced by Dee Sarton Bower and Mary Eileen Wells, co-authors of *Homemade To Go: The Complete Guide to Co-op Cooking* (Purrfect Publishing, 1997).

What's for Supper?

Mighty Good Meat Loaf

When the craving for meat loaf hits, you've just gotta make it. The beauty of this satisfying dish is that once you spend 15 minutes or so to prepare it, you're free for about an hour while it bakes.

SWEET KETCHUP-AND-BACON-TOPPED MEAT LOAF

family favorite

MAKES 6 TO 8 SERVINGS

Prep: 15 min.; Bake: 1 hr., 10 min.; Stand: 10 min.

We adapted this recipe from one called Mizner Meatloaf in *Savor the Moment* by The Junior League of Boca Raton, Florida. For special occasions, make it with 1 pound each ground beef and ground veal and 2 tablespoons chopped fresh basil, chives, or parsley substituted for dried Italian seasoning.

> 2 pounds lean ground beef
> ½ cup soft breadcrumbs
> ½ medium onion, finely chopped
> 2 large eggs, lightly beaten
> 2 teaspoons salt
> 1 teaspoon pepper
> 1 teaspoon dried Italian seasoning
> 4 bacon slices
> ⅓ cup firmly packed brown sugar
> ½ cup ketchup
> ½ cup molasses

STIR together first 7 ingredients in a large bowl. Shape mixture into a 10- x 4-inch loaf; place in a lightly greased aluminum foil-lined 15- x 10-inch jelly-roll pan.

BAKE at 375° for 20 minutes. Arrange bacon slices over top of loaf. Stir together brown sugar, ketchup, and molasses; spread mixture evenly over meat loaf.

BAKE at 375° for 50 minutes or until meat is no longer pink in center. Let stand 10 minutes before serving.

CHEESEBURGER MEAT LOAF

family favorite

MAKES 4 SERVINGS

Prep: 15 min., Bake: 1 hr., 10 min., Stand: 10 min.

- 1 pound lean ground beef
- ¾ cup uncooked regular oats
- ½ cup milk
- 2 tablespoons minced onion
- 1 large egg
- 1 teaspoon Worcestershire sauce
- ½ teaspoon salt
- ¼ teaspoon dry mustard
- ¼ teaspoon garlic salt
- ¼ teaspoon pepper
- 1 (12-ounce) bottle chili sauce
- 3 packaged Cheddar cheese slices, cut into 1-inch strips

STIR together first 10 ingredients in a large bowl just until combined. Place in a 9- x 5-inch loafpan.

BAKE at 350° for 40 to 45 minutes. Pour chili sauce over meat loaf, and bake 20 to 25 more minutes or until meat is no longer pink in center.

ARRANGE cheese slices in a crisscross pattern on top of meat loaf. Let stand 10 minutes before slicing.

NOTE: For testing purposes only, we used Heinz Chili Sauce.

CYNTHIA GIVAN
FORT WORTH, TEXAS

MEAT LOAVES WITH SPAGHETTI SAUCE

family favorite

MAKES 6 TO 8 SERVINGS

Prep: 20 min., Bake: 50 min., Stand 10 min.

- 1½ cups spaghetti sauce, divided
- 1½ pounds lean ground beef
- ½ cup Italian-seasoned breadcrumbs
- 1 small onion, minced
- 1 large egg
- 1½ teaspoons salt
- ¼ teaspoon pepper
- 1 tablespoon brown sugar
- 1½ tablespoons white vinegar
- 1 tablespoon prepared mustard
- 2 teaspoons Worcestershire sauce

STIR together ½ cup spaghetti sauce, ground beef, breadcrumbs, and next 4 ingredients just until combined. Shape mixture into 2 (8-inch) loaves, and place in a lightly greased 13- x 9-inch baking dish.
BAKE at 350° for 25 minutes.
STIR together remaining 1 cup spaghetti sauce, brown sugar, and next 3 ingredients. Pour sauce evenly over meat loaves, and bake 25 more minutes or until beef is no longer pink in center. Let stand 10 minutes before serving.

MARGARET MCNEIL
MEMPHIS, TENNESSEE

Top-Rated Menu

Harvest Breakfast

Fall Brunch

Serves 6 to 8

Balsamic Pork Chops With Apples

Farmer's Oven-Baked Omelet

Cornbread Waffles

Jalapeño-Pecan-Mustard Butter

BALSAMIC PORK CHOPS WITH APPLES

MAKES 6 TO 8 SERVINGS

Prep: 20 min., Cook: 20 min.

- 8 (½-inch-thick) boneless pork loin chops
- 1 teaspoon salt
- 1 teaspoon seasoned pepper
- ½ cup all-purpose flour
- 3 tablespoons vegetable oil
- 4 large Granny Smith apples, peeled and diced
- ⅔ cup balsamic vinegar
- ½ cup chicken broth

SPRINKLE pork chops evenly with salt and seasoned pepper; dredge in flour.
COOK pork in hot oil in a large skillet over medium-high heat 3 to 4 minutes on each side or until lightly browned. Remove from skillet; keep warm.
ADD apples to skillet, and sauté for 5 minutes; add vinegar and broth, and cook, stirring often, 5 to 7 minutes, or until slightly thickened. Spoon over pork, and serve.

FARMER'S OVEN-BAKED OMELET

MAKES 10 TO 12 SERVINGS

Prep: 20 min., Bake: 35 min.

- 12 large eggs
- ½ cup sour cream
- 2 tablespoons chopped fresh thyme
- 1 teaspoon salt
- ¾ teaspoon freshly ground pepper
- ¼ teaspoon baking powder
- 2 tablespoons butter or margarine
- 6 small plum tomatoes, seeded and chopped
- 8 ounces farmer's cheese, shredded
- ½ cup chopped fresh basil
- Garnish: fresh basil leaves

BEAT first 6 ingredients at medium speed with an electric mixer 2 to 3 minutes or until well blended.
MELT butter in a 12-inch ovenproof skillet; add egg mixture.
BAKE at 350° for 15 minutes. Remove from oven; sprinkle with tomatoes, cheese, and chopped basil. Return to oven, and bake 15 to 20 more minutes or until set. Garnish, if desired; serve immediately.

NOTE: Farmer's cheese is a mild, part-skim, semisoft cheese available in 8-ounce rounds. Substitute Havarti or Monterey Jack cheese, if desired.

SPINACH, CHEDDAR, AND BACON OMELET: Substitute 1 (10-ounce) package frozen, thawed, and well-drained chopped spinach for thyme. Omit farmer's cheese and fresh basil. Top with 8 ounces shredded Cheddar cheese and ½ cup cooked, crumbled bacon.

CORNBREAD WAFFLES

fast fixin's

MAKES 12 (4-INCH) WAFFLES

Prep: 10 min., Cook: 20 min.

- 1½ cups plain white cornmeal
- ½ cup all-purpose flour
- 2 tablespoons sugar
- 2½ teaspoons baking powder
- ¾ teaspoon salt
- 1 large egg
- 1½ cups milk

STIR together first 5 ingredients in a large bowl. Stir together egg and milk; add to cornmeal mixture, stirring just until dry ingredients are moistened.
COOK in a preheated, oiled waffle iron just until crisp.

JALAPEÑO-PECAN-MUSTARD BUTTER

fast fixin's

MAKES 2½ CUPS

Prep: 10 min., Bake: 5 min.

- ½ cup chopped pecans
- 2 cups butter or margarine, softened
- ⅓ cup Creole mustard
- ¼ cup minced red onion
- 2 garlic cloves
- 2 jalapeño peppers, seeded and minced
- Garnish: fresh thyme sprigs

BAKE pecans in a shallow pan at 350°, stirring occasionally, 5 minutes or until toasted; cool.
STIR together pecans, butter, and next 4 ingredients in a large bowl until well blended. Garnish, if desired.

Quick & Easy

Skillet Pork Chops

The skillet-cooked pork chop is your friend when trying to get supper on the table in a hurry. The chops in these recipes require just a few minutes of cook time. Avoid overcooking the pork—thicker chops require perhaps an extra minute, while thinner ones cook super-fast. Although more expensive, thick chops tend to be much juicier. Aim to have some pink color in the meat when you're done.

LEMONY PAN-FRIED PORK CHOPS

family favorite • fast fixin's

MAKES 6 TO 8 SERVINGS

Prep: 10 min., Cook: 7 min.

- ½ cup all-purpose flour
- 1 teaspoon seasoned salt
- 1 teaspoon seasoned pepper
- 1½ pounds wafer-thin boneless pork chops (about 12)
- ¼ cup vegetable oil
- ¾ cup chicken broth
- ¼ cup fresh lemon juice

COMBINE first 3 ingredients in a shallow dish; dredge pork chops in flour mixture.
FRY pork chops, in 3 batches, in hot oil in a large skillet over medium-high heat 1 minute on each side or until browned. Drain on paper towels.
ADD broth and lemon juice to skillet. Bring to a boil, and stir to loosen particles from bottom of skillet. Serve sauce over pork chops.

TUSCAN PORK CHOPS

family favorite • fast fixin's

MAKES 4 SERVINGS

Prep: 10 min., Cook: 10 min.

- ¼ cup all-purpose flour
- 1 teaspoon salt
- ¾ teaspoon seasoned pepper
- 4 (1-inch-thick) boneless pork chops
- 1 tablespoon olive oil
- 3 to 4 garlic cloves, minced*
- ⅓ cup balsamic vinegar
- ⅓ cup chicken broth
- 3 plum tomatoes, seeded and diced
- 2 tablespoons capers
- Garnish: fresh parsley sprigs

COMBINE first 3 ingredients in a shallow dish; dredge pork chops in the flour mixture.
COOK pork chops in hot oil in a large nonstick skillet over medium-high heat 1 to 2 minutes on each side or until golden brown. Remove chops from skillet.
ADD garlic to skillet, and sauté 1 minute. Add vinegar and broth, stirring to loosen particles from bottom of skillet; stir in tomatoes and capers.
RETURN pork chops to skillet; bring sauce to a boil. Cover, reduce heat, and simmer 4 to 5 minutes or until pork is done. Serve pork chops with tomato mixture. Garnish, if desired.

*Substitute 1 tablespoon bottled minced garlic, if desired.

CONNIE VICKERS
DALLAS, TEXAS

SPICY BROWN MUSTARD PORK CHOPS

family favorite • fast fixin's

MAKES 6 SERVINGS

Prep: 10 min., Cook: about 6 min.

This recipe will serve three hearty eaters. Dijon mustard or coarse-grained mustard may be substituted to vary the flavor.

- ½ teaspoon salt
- ½ teaspoon garlic powder
- ¼ teaspoon pepper
- ½ cup spicy brown mustard
- 6 (½-inch-thick) boneless pork chops
- 1 cup all-purpose flour
- ¼ cup vegetable or canola oil

COMBINE first 3 ingredients. Spread mustard evenly on both sides of pork chops, and sprinkle with salt mixture.
PLACE flour in a shallow dish; dredge chops in flour.
COOK pork chops in hot oil in a large skillet over medium-high heat 2 to 3 minutes on each side or until golden brown. Drain on paper towels, and serve immediately.

NANCY MULLINS
PLANO, TEXAS

Gather at the Beach

Labor Day weekend is the perfect time to relax with friends and no-fuss food.

Spend some time with the Campbell, Conroy, Elliott, Fitz, Sears, and Sions families on the Outer Banks of North Carolina, and you'll laugh until your cheeks hurt. It started 21 years ago, when a few college friends enjoyed a beach weekend. It has turned into a yearly reunion for them.

When everyone gets together, video cameras roll, and snapshots are taken. Trish Conroy sums up the experience best: "This group has become so congenial that on one trip, three people shared the same book using three different bookmarks. That's magic, isn't it?"

How do that many people get along in one rented beach house? "The key is organization, patience, and a desire for a relaxing vacation," says Trish. "Great food keeps everyone in good spirits," she adds. We've shared some of their favorite recipes, including Trish's Beach Barbecue and Kathy Sears's Chocolate 'Eclair Cake.

STEAMED SHRIMP

fast fixin's

MAKES 8 SERVINGS

Prep: 15 min., Cook: 15 min., Stand: 2 min.

We used 16- to 20-count shrimp per pound when testing this recipe.

- 6 cups water
- 1 (12-ounce) bottle beer
- 1 large onion, quartered
- 4 to 6 tablespoons Old Bay seasoning
- 6 pounds unpeeled, jumbo fresh shrimp
- Cocktail sauce (optional)
- Lemon wedges (optional)

BRING first 4 ingredients to a boil in a large Dutch oven. Add shrimp, and cook, covered, 10 minutes or just until shrimp turn pink, stirring often. Turn off heat, and let stand 2 minutes; drain. Serve shrimp with cocktail sauce and lemon wedges, if desired.

CARMEN CAMPBELL
PORTSMOUTH, VIRGINIA

TRISH'S BEACH BARBECUE

freezeable • make ahead

MAKES 10 SERVINGS

Prep: 20 min., Cook: 2 hrs., Stand: 10 min.

Trish prepares and freezes both the meat and sauce. To reheat, place in a 13- x 9-inch baking dish. Cover and bake at 350° for 30 minutes or until bubbly.

- 1 (4-pound) eye of round roast
- 1 teaspoon salt
- 3 (8-ounce) cans tomato sauce
- 1 (12-ounce) bottle chili sauce
- 1 medium onion, chopped
- ½ cup white vinegar
- ¼ cup firmly packed brown sugar
- ¼ cup butter or margarine
- ¼ cup lemon juice
- 2 tablespoons Worcestershire sauce
- ½ teaspoon dry mustard
- ½ teaspoon chili powder
- ½ teaspoon paprika
- Hamburger buns

PLACE roast in large Dutch oven, and sprinkle with salt; add water to cover, and bring to a boil. Cover, reduce heat to medium, and cook 2 hours or until tender, adding more water as needed after 1 hour.

STIR together tomato sauce and next 10 ingredients in a large saucepan; bring to a boil. Reduce heat to low, and simmer 1 hour, stirring occasionally.

REMOVE roast from Dutch oven, and let stand 10 minutes before serving. Shred or slice meat, and serve on hamburger buns with sauce.

NOTE: For testing purposes only, we used Heinz Chili Sauce.

TRISH CONROY
LYNCHBURG, VIRGINIA

CHOCOLATE ÉCLAIR CAKE

family favorite • make ahead

MAKES 12 SERVINGS

Prep: 15 min., Chill: 8 hrs.

One box of graham crackers contains three individually wrapped packages of crackers; use one package for each layer of this indulgent dessert.

- 1 (14.4-ounce) box honey graham crackers
- 2 (3.4-ounce) packages French vanilla instant pudding mix
- 3 cups milk
- 1 (12-ounce) container frozen whipped topping, thawed
- 1 (16-ounce) container ready-to-spread chocolate frosting

LINE bottom of an ungreased 13- x 9-inch baking dish with one-third of honey graham crackers.

WHISK together pudding mix and milk; add whipped topping, stirring until mixture thickens. Spread half of pudding mixture over graham crackers. Repeat layers with one-third of graham crackers and remaining pudding mixture. Top with remaining graham crackers. Spread with chocolate frosting. Cover and chill 8 hours.

NOTE: To lighten, use reduced-fat graham crackers, sugar-free pudding mix, fat-free milk, and fat-free frozen whipped topping.

KATHY SEARS
RICHMOND, VIRGINIA

LAYERED NACHO DIP

fast fixin's

MAKES 8 CUPS

Prep: 15 min.

This classic 1981 *Southern Living* recipe has stood the test of time with the group.

> 1 (16-ounce) can refried beans
> 2 teaspoons taco seasoning mix
> 1 (6-ounce) container avocado dip
> 1 (8-ounce) container sour cream
> 1 (4.5-ounce) can chopped ripe olives, drained
> 2 large tomatoes, diced
> 1 small onion, diced
> 1 (4-ounce) can chopped green chiles
> 1½ cups (6 ounces) shredded Monterey Jack cheese
> Corn or tortilla chips

STIR together beans and seasoning mix; spread mixture in an 11- x 7-inch dish. Spread avocado dip and sour cream evenly over bean mixture. Sprinkle with olives and next 4 ingredients. Serve with chips.

FRESH HERB-RUBBED SALMON FILLETS

MAKES 4 SERVINGS

Prep: 15 min., Chill: 1 hr., Grill: 10 min.

This fish cooks up in minutes and requires few additional ingredients.

> ¼ cup tightly packed fresh parsley leaves
> ¼ cup tightly packed fresh cilantro leaves
> ¼ cup chopped onion
> 2 garlic cloves, pressed
> 3 tablespoons olive oil
> 1½ teaspoons chili powder
> 1 teaspoon dried oregano
> ½ teaspoon salt
> 6 (6-ounce) salmon fillets

PROCESS first 8 ingredients in a food processor until smooth.
PLACE salmon fillets, skin side down, in a 13- x 9-inch dish. Spread herb mixture over fillets; cover and chill 1 hour.

GRILL, skin side down, covered with grill lid, over high heat (400° to 500°) 6 to 10 minutes or until fish flakes with a fork.

TRISH CONROY
LYNCHBURG, VIRGINIA

Hot Bread in a Hurry

These big-flavored breads are just right for fall, and each takes 15 minutes or less to prepare for baking.

PIZZA SCONES

family favorite

MAKES 12 SCONES

Prep: 15 min., Bake: 20 min.

> 2 cups all-purpose baking mix
> ¾ cup (3 ounces) shredded sharp Cheddar cheese
> ¼ cup dried tomatoes, thinly sliced
> ¼ cup sliced black olives
> ¼ cup chopped salami
> 2 tablespoons cornmeal
> ½ teaspoon onion powder
> ½ teaspoon Italian seasoning
> 3 tablespoons shredded Parmesan cheese, divided
> ¾ cup buttermilk
> 1½ teaspoons olive oil
> ¼ teaspoon black pepper
> 1 cup pizza sauce (optional)

COMBINE first 8 ingredients and 2 tablespoons Parmesan cheese; add buttermilk. Stir until a soft dough forms.
TURN dough out onto a lightly floured surface. Pat into an 8-inch circle; place on a lightly greased baking sheet. Brush with oil; sprinkle evenly with pepper and remaining 1 tablespoon Parmesan cheese. Cut into 12 even wedges. (Do not separate wedges.)
BAKE at 400° for 15 to 20 minutes or until golden brown. Separate wedges, and serve with pizza sauce, if desired.

SHERLYNE HUTCHINSON
CORNELIUS, OREGON

SPICY KICKIN' BISCUITS

fast fixin's

MAKES 18 BISCUITS

Prep: 10 min., Bake: 15 min.

> 3½ cups all-purpose baking mix
> 1 to 2 tablespoons taco seasoning mix
> 1 (10-ounce) can diced tomatoes and green chiles, drained
> 1 cup (4 ounces) shredded Monterey Jack cheese with peppers
> 1 cup milk
> Butter (optional)

COMBINE baking mix and taco seasoning mix in large bowl; add tomatoes, cheese, and milk, stirring until a soft dough forms. Drop dough by 2 tablespoonfuls onto ungreased baking sheets 2 to 3 inches apart.
BAKE at 425° for 12 to 15 minutes or until biscuits begin to brown. Serve warm with butter, if desired.

PAMELA HINKLE
ATLANTA, GEORGIA

SWEET BEER BREAD

MAKES 1 LOAF

Prep: 5 min., Bake: 55 min.

To make a Sweet Beer Bread gift kit, place dry ingredients in a zip-top bag, then tie the bag and recipe to a bottle of beer.

> 3 cups self-rising flour
> ½ cup sugar
> 1 (12-ounce) bottle beer*
> ¼ cup butter or margarine, melted

STIR together first 3 ingredients; pour into a lightly greased 9- x 5-inch loafpan.
BAKE at 350° for 45 minutes. Pour melted butter over top. Bake 10 more minutes.

*Substitute nonalcoholic or light beer, if desired.

CHEDDAR-CHIVE BEER BREAD: Add ¾ cup shredded sharp Cheddar cheese and 2 tablespoons chopped fresh chives to dry ingredients. Proceed as directed.

MARISA STONE
JACKSON, MISSISSIPPI

from our kitchen

A Space of One's Own

If you long for the sleek surface of a professional kitchen, take a close look at the Chef Station: a 20- x 22-inch stainless steel work area that fits most kitchen countertops. It's a favorite with Foods Editor Scott Jones and his wife, Deanna, who enjoy having a space for making breads and pasta. The Chef Station retails for $69.95 and comes with a dishwasher-safe nonskid mat, flexible cutting board, hardwood rolling pin, and dough scraper. For more information, call toll free 1-866-448-8324, or visit the web site at **www.chefstation.com**

BASIL PUREE: Process 4 cups loosely packed basil leaves and 1 cup olive oil or 1 (8-ounce) can tomato sauce in a food processor until basil is finely chopped. Spoon mixture into ice-cube trays, and freeze. Store frozen cubes in freezer bags up to 6 months. Makes about 1 cup or 8 (2-tablespoon) cubes.

Use anywhere you need a burst of fresh basil flavor: in soups, sauces, or salad dressings. Thaw and add to marinades, or drizzle over grilled meats and vegetables.

BASIL PESTO: Process 4 cups loosely packed basil leaves, 6 garlic cloves, ¼ teaspoon salt, and 1 cup each of shredded Parmesan cheese, toasted pine nuts, and olive oil in a food processor until smooth, stopping to scrape down sides. Spoon mixture into ice-cube trays, and freeze. Store cubes in freezer bags up to 6 months. Makes 2 cups or 16 (2-tablespoon) cubes.

Pesto is great to have on hand for last-minute hors d'oeuvres. It can stand alone as a dip and also works as a spread for pizzas and sandwiches.

BASIL-GARLIC BUTTER: Process 1 cup softened butter and 2 garlic cloves in a food processor until smooth. Add ½ cup firmly packed basil leaves, and pulse 3 or 4 times or until basil is finely chopped. Store in the refrigerator up to 1 week, or freeze in airtight containers up to 4 months. Makes 1 cup. If desired, shape butter into a log; wrap in wax paper, and chill. When firm, slice into smaller rounds, and freeze.

Serve with hot crusty French bread or baked potatoes. Toss with hot, cooked pasta and Parmesan cheese or steamed vegetables. Try it on a grilled cheese, with mozzarella, sliced tomatoes, and crumbled bacon.

PESTO-GOAT CHEESE SPREAD: Process 1 (11-ounce) log goat cheese, 1 (8-ounce) package softened cream cheese, 2 cups loosely packed basil leaves, ½ cup toasted pine nuts, 3 garlic cloves, and 2 tablespoons balsamic vinegar in a food processor until smooth. Chill 2 hours before serving. Makes 3 cups. Store in refrigerator up to 1 week, or freeze in airtight containers up to 4 months. Serve with toasted pita chips or sliced baguettes.

Shape cheese mixture into logs, and wrap in wax paper; slice chilled logs into ½-inch rounds. Dip cheese rounds in lightly beaten egg, and dredge in Italian breadcrumbs. Pan-fry over medium-high heat in a little butter 1 minute on each side or until golden, and serve warm over a crisp, green salad.

LEMON-BASIL MAYONNAISE: Process 2 cups mayonnaise and 1 garlic clove in a food processor until smooth. Add ½ cup firmly packed basil leaves and 1 tablespoon grated lemon rind; pulse 3 or 4 times or until basil is finely chopped. Store in refrigerator up to 1 week. Makes 2 cups.

Even though this won't freeze, it's unbelievably delicious with a bowl of grape tomatoes or on a turkey sandwich. Use it in place of plain mayonnaise in deviled eggs or main dish salads; it's also great with chicken, shrimp, or tuna. Try this flavorful mayonnaise instead of tartar sauce the next time you serve your favorite fish.

October

Celebrate Fall

Maximize the fun and minimize the effort with our friendly menu and easy decorating ideas.

The Season's Best Menu

Serves 6

Hot Spiced Wine

Trick or Treat Popcorn

Assorted Cheddar cheeses and crackers

Flank Steak With Tomato-Olive Relish

Garlic Grits

Mixed green salad with
Creamy Garlic Salad Dressing

Roasted Pumpkin Seeds

Crispy Sticks

Pumpkin Cake With Little Ghosts

On a chilly October afternoon, before the little goblins come knocking for treats, summon friends to your neck of the woods for a little merriment. Take a wonderfully warm beverage and a tasty, crunchy snack along on a hayride, and bask in the brilliant beauty of fall. Afterward, serve a scrumptious meal that features simple, flavorful flank steak over grits, and end with a cake that's simply "spook-tacular." Costume the setting with jack-o'-lantern luminarias, and offer a grab bag of disguises for guests. With our great recipes and party ideas, the only thing frightening will be the ghost stories told around the flickering flames of a campfire.

HOT SPICED WINE

fast fixin's

MAKES 9 CUPS

Prep: 5 min., Cook: 20 min.

> 2 (750-milliliter) bottles red wine
> 2 cups apple juice
> 1 cup sugar
> 6 tablespoons mulling spice

BRING all ingredients to a boil in a Dutch oven; reduce heat, and simmer 15 minutes. Pour mixture through a wire-mesh strainer into a pitcher, discarding mulling spices. Serve wine hot.

NOTE: For best results, use a fruity red wine, such as Beaujolais or Pinot Noir.

TRICK OR TREAT POPCORN

fast fixin's

MAKES 19 CUPS

Prep: 10 min., Bake: 15 min.

To serve this snack in style, roll squares of brown craft paper into cones, staple, and tie with raffia. *(pictured on page 227)*

> 3 cups pecan halves
> 2 tablespoons butter or margarine, melted
> 2 tablespoons Worcestershire sauce
> 2 teaspoons garlic powder
> 1 teaspoon ground cumin
> ½ teaspoon ground red pepper
> 1 (6-ounce) package sweetened dried cranberries
> 3 (4-ounce) packages caramel corn

COMBINE first 6 ingredients in a large bowl, tossing to coat. Spread mixture in a 15- x 10-inch jellyroll pan.
BAKE at 375° for 8 to 10 minutes, stirring once. Stir in cranberries, and bake 5 more minutes. Spread on paper towels to cool.
TOSS pecan mixture with caramel corn. Store in airtight containers.

NOTE: For testing purposes only, we used Crunch 'n Munch Buttery Toffee Popcorn with Peanuts for caramel corn.

NORMA PARTRIDGE
SHAWNEE, OKLAHOMA

FLANK STEAK WITH TOMATO-OLIVE RELISH

MAKES 6 SERVINGS

Prep: 10 min., Cook: 27 min. *(pictured on page 226)*

> 1½ pounds flank steak
> ¾ teaspoon salt
> ¾ teaspoon coarsely ground pepper
> 3 tablespoons olive oil
> 2 garlic cloves, thinly sliced
> ½ cup red wine or chicken broth
> 1 (14½-ounce) can Italian-style diced tomatoes
> ½ cup pitted oil-cured black olives, sliced
> 1 tablespoon balsamic vinegar
> 3 tablespoons minced fresh parsley

SPRINKLE flank steak evenly with salt and pepper.

COOK steak in hot oil in a large skillet over medium-high heat 6 to 8 minutes on each side or to desired degree of doneness.

DRAIN, reserving 1 tablespoon drippings in skillet; add garlic, and sauté 1 minute. Add wine, tomatoes, olives, and vinegar; cook 10 minutes or until reduced by half. Stir in parsley.

CUT steak diagonally across grain into thin slices, and serve with tomato mixture.

DOLORES VACCARO
PUEBLO, COLORADO

GARLIC GRITS

fast fixin's

MAKES 6 (1-CUP) SERVINGS

Prep: 10 min., Cook: 15 min. *(pictured on page 226)*

- 6 cups half-and-half
- 1 teaspoon salt
- ½ teaspoon garlic powder
- ½ teaspoon pepper
- 1½ cups uncooked quick-cooking grits
- 2 (3-ounce) packages cream cheese, cubed
- ½ teaspoon hot sauce

BRING first 4 ingredients to a boil in a Dutch oven; gradually stir in grits. Return to a boil; cover, reduce heat, and simmer, stirring occasionally, 5 to 7 minutes or until thickened.

ADD cream cheese and hot sauce, stirring until cream cheese melts. Serve immediately.

CREAMY GARLIC SALAD DRESSING

MAKES ABOUT 1 CUP

Prep: 5 min., Chill: 1 hr. *(pictured on page 226)*

- 1 teaspoon salt
- 3 garlic cloves, minced
- ½ cup mayonnaise
- 3 tablespoons white vinegar
- 3 tablespoons oil

COMBINE salt and garlic in a small bowl, pressing with the back of a spoon to form a paste. Whisk in remaining ingredients. Cover and chill 1 hour.

IRENE BAUGH
NORMAN, OKLAHOMA

Little Ghost Templates *(recipe on following page)*

enlarge 200%

ROASTED PUMPKIN SEEDS

fast fixin's

MAKES 2 CUPS

Prep: 20 min., Bake: 12 min.

- 2 cups fresh pumpkin seeds
- 2 tablespoons dried rosemary
- 2 tablespoons olive oil
- 2 tablespoons coarse-grain sea salt

RINSE pumpkin seeds in water, and drain on paper towels to dry. Toss with remaining ingredients, and spread on a baking sheet.

BAKE at 350° for 10 to 12 minutes or until crisp. Cool. Store in an airtight container.

CRISPY STICKS

family favorite • fast fixin's

MAKES 24 BREADSTICKS

Prep: 10 min., Bake: 10 min. *(pictured on page 226)*

- ½ cup olive oil
- 2 garlic cloves, minced
- 1 tablespoon chopped fresh Italian parsley
- 1 tablespoon chopped fresh rosemary
- ¼ teaspoon coarsely ground pepper
- ¼ teaspoon salt
- 2 (6-ounce) French bread loaves, halved lengthwise
- ¼ cup shredded Parmesan cheese

COMBINE first 6 ingredients.

CUT bread halves into ½-inch slices. Place on baking sheets. Brush with oil mixture, and sprinkle with cheese.

BAKE at 425° for 7 to 10 minutes or until cheese melts.

PUMPKIN CAKE WITH LITTLE GHOSTS

MAKES 8 TO 10 SERVINGS

Prep: 20 min., Bake: 1 hr., Cool: 15 min.

Cutting the vanilla coating with a knife (using the templates on page 211) is the easiest way to create the Little Ghosts. *(pictured on page 227)*

2 cups sugar
2 cups all-purpose flour
2 teaspoons baking powder
1 teaspoon baking soda
½ teaspoon salt
½ teaspoon ground cinnamon
½ teaspoon ground cloves
¼ teaspoon ground allspice
¼ teaspoon ground ginger
4 large eggs
1 (15-ounce) can pumpkin
1 cup vegetable oil
1 cup wheat bran cereal
1 cup semisweet chocolate morsels
1 cup coarsely chopped pecans
Simple Chocolate Ganache
Little Ghosts

COMBINE first 9 ingredients.
BEAT eggs at medium speed with an electric mixer until foamy. Add pumpkin, oil, and cereal, beating until combined. Add dry ingredients, beating just until moistened. Stir in morsels and pecans. Pour into a greased and floured 10-inch Bundt pan.
BAKE at 350° for 1 hour or until a wooden pick inserted in the center comes out clean. Cool in pan 15 minutes before removing. Drizzle Simple Chocolate Ganache over top of cake, allowing it to run down sides. Arrange Little Ghosts around center of cake.

Simple Chocolate Ganache:

MAKES 1 CUP

Prep: 5 min., Stand: 10 min.

½ cup whipping cream
1 cup semisweet chocolate morsels

MICROWAVE cream in a 2-cup glass measuring cup at HIGH 1 minute.
ADD chocolate morsels, stirring until melted. Let stand 10 minutes before drizzling over cake.

Little Ghosts:

MAKES 6 (3½-INCH GHOSTS)

Prep: 20 min.; Stand: 1 hr., 30 min.

1 (24-ounce) package vanilla bark coating
Semisweet chocolate mini-morsels
6 (10-inch) wooden skewers

MICROWAVE vanilla coating in a glass bowl at HIGH 1½ minutes or until melted, stirring twice. Pour onto wax paper, spreading into a 16- x 8-inch rectangle. Let stand 15 minutes or until firm to the touch. Cut 6 ghost shapes, using a lightly greased paring knife (see templates on previous page). Gently press mini-morsels into ghosts for eyes and mouths. Let stand 15 minutes or until completely hardened.
REMOVE trimmings around ghosts, starting at outside edge. Carefully lift each ghost, gently removing from rectangle. Reserve trimmings.
MELT reserved trimmings; spread a small amount on back of each ghost. Attach wooden skewers. Let stand 1 hour.

VITA LEFLER
OXFORD, MISSISSIPPI

Living Light

Oven-Fried Goodness

COCONUT-PECAN SHRIMP WITH ORANGE DIPPING SAUCE

MAKES 6 SERVINGS

Prep: 25 min., Bake: 15 min.

1½ pounds unpeeled, large fresh shrimp
1 teaspoon seasoned salt
3 egg whites
1½ cups sweetened flaked coconut
⅔ cup ground pecans
2 tablespoons all-purpose flour
Vegetable cooking spray
Orange Dipping Sauce

PEEL shrimp, leaving tails on, and devein, if desired.
SPRINKLE shrimp evenly with seasoned salt.
WHISK egg whites in a small bowl until frothy.
COMBINE coconut, pecans, and flour in a shallow bowl.
PLACE a wire rack coated with cooking spray in an aluminum foil-lined 15- x 10-inch jellyroll pan.
DIP shrimp, 1 at a time, in egg whites, and dredge in coconut mixture. Arrange shrimp on rack. Coat shrimp evenly with cooking spray.
BAKE at 425° for 10 to 15 minutes or just until shrimp turn pink, turning after 5 to 7 minutes. Serve with Orange Dipping Sauce.

Orange Dipping Sauce:

MAKES ABOUT 1 CUP

Prep: 5 min.

¾ cup orange marmalade
¼ cup orange juice
2 tablespoons lemon juice
1 teaspoon stone-ground mustard
½ teaspoon dried crushed red pepper

MICROWAVE marmalade in a small glass bowl at HIGH 20 seconds or until melted.
STIR in orange juice, lemon juice, mustard, and red pepper. Serve immediately.

(Per serving of shrimp with sauce) Calories 415 (38% from fat); Fat 18g (sat 8g, mono 4.9g, poly 3g); Protein 23g; Carb 44g; Fiber 2.4g; Chol 144mg; Iron 3.3 mg; Sodium 357mg; Calc 81mg

SPICY "FRIED" CATFISH WITH LEMON CREAM

MAKES 6 SERVINGS

Prep: 25 min., Bake: 30 min.

6 (6-ounce) catfish fillets
½ teaspoon salt, divided
¼ teaspoon black pepper
1½ cups panko breadcrumbs*
¼ teaspoon garlic powder
¼ teaspoon ground red pepper
4 egg whites
Vegetable cooking spray
Lemon Cream
Garnishes: lemon slices, fresh parsley sprigs

SPRINKLE catfish evenly with ¼ teaspoon salt and ¼ teaspoon black pepper.
COMBINE breadcrumbs, remaining ¼ teaspoon salt, ¼ teaspoon garlic powder, and ¼ teaspoon ground red pepper in a shallow bowl.
WHISK egg whites in a shallow bowl until frothy. Dip fillets in egg whites, and dredge in breadcrumb mixture.
ARRANGE fillets on a wire rack coated with cooking spray in an aluminum foil-lined 15- x 10-inch jellyroll pan. (Do not overlap fillets.) Lightly coat fillets evenly on both sides with cooking spray.
BAKE at 375° for 25 to 30 minutes or until fish is golden brown and flakes with a fork. Serve with Lemon Cream. Garnish, if desired.

*Substitute 1 cup plain dry breadcrumbs for panko, Japanese-style breadcrumbs.

Lemon Cream:
MAKES ABOUT 1 CUP
Prep: 10 min.

- 1 (8-ounce) container light sour cream
- 1 tablespoon chopped fresh parsley
- ½ teaspoon grated lemon rind
- 2 tablespoons fresh lemon juice
- ¼ teaspoon salt

STIR together ingredients until blended. Cover; chill until ready to serve.

(Per serving of fish with Lemon Cream) Calories 337 (28% from fat); Fat 10.1g (sat 4.1g, mono 1.4g, poly 1.5g); Protein 35g; Carb 24.6g; Fiber 1g; Chol 118mg; Iron 0.6mg; Sodium 480mg; Calc 93mg

SALTY ROSEMARY FRIES

family favorite

MAKES 4 SERVINGS

Prep: 10 min., Bake: 40 min.

- 2 large baking potatoes
- 2 tablespoons olive oil
- 1 large garlic clove, minced
- 2 teaspoons dried rosemary
- 1½ teaspoons kosher salt*
- ¾ teaspoon freshly ground pepper
- Vegetable cooking spray

CUT each potato lengthwise into 10 to 12 wedges. Drizzle with oil, and sprinkle with next 4 ingredients; toss to coat.

ARRANGE potato wedges, skin side down, in a single layer on a baking sheet coated with cooking spray.
BAKE at 450° for 35 to 40 minutes or until golden brown.

*Substitute ¾ teaspoon iodized salt for 1½ teaspoons kosher salt.

Calories 230 (28% from fat); Fat 7.3g (sat 1.1g, mono 5.4g, poly 0.7g); Protein 3.6g; Carb 39g; Fiber 4g; Chol 0mg; Iron 2.3mg; Sodium 718mg; Calc 25mg

BUTTERMILK OVEN-FRIED CHICKEN

family favorite

MAKES 8 SERVINGS

Prep: 25 min., Chill: 8 hrs., Bake: 45 min.

- 3 skinned and boned chicken breast halves (about 1⅓ pounds)
- 5 skinned and boned chicken thighs (about 1¼ pounds)
- 2 cups fat-free buttermilk
- 1 cup all-purpose flour
- 1 tablespoon poultry seasoning
- 1 teaspoon lemon pepper
- 4 egg whites
- 6 cups cornflakes cereal, coarsely crushed
- Vegetable cooking spray

PLACE chicken and buttermilk in a large bowl or zip-top plastic bag, turning chicken to coat all sides. Cover or seal, and chill 8 hours. Drain chicken, discarding buttermilk.
COMBINE flour, poultry seasoning, and lemon pepper in a bowl. Set aside.
WHISK egg whites in a medium bowl until frothy.
DREDGE chicken in flour mixture, dip in egg whites; gently press chicken in crushed cereal.
ARRANGE chicken on a wire rack coated with cooking spray in an aluminum foil-lined 15- x 10-inch jellyroll pan. (Do not overlap chicken.) Lightly coat chicken evenly on both sides with cooking spray.
BAKE at 375° for 45 minutes or until chicken is done.

Calories 431 (13% from fat); Fat 5.7g (sat 1.5g, mono 1.5g, poly 1.3g); Protein 66g; Carb 24g; Fiber 0.7g; Chol 180mg; Iron 3.3mg; Sodium 426mg; Calc 53mg

EGGPLANT PARMESAN SANDWICHES

MAKES 6 SERVINGS

Prep: 30 min., Bake: 25 min., Broil: 2 min.

Panko (Japanese-style breadcrumbs) create a light, crisp coating.

- 1 medium eggplant, cut into ⅛-inch-thick slices
- ¼ teaspoon salt
- ½ teaspoon pepper, divided
- 2 large egg whites
- 1 cup panko breadcrumbs*
- ½ cup freshly grated Parmesan cheese
- 1 teaspoon Italian seasoning
- Vegetable cooking spray
- 1 (14-ounce) French bread loaf, halved horizontally
- 2 cups pasta sauce
- 1 cup (4 ounces) shredded part-skim mozzarella cheese
- Pasta sauce (optional)

SPRINKLE eggplant evenly on both sides with salt and ¼ teaspoon pepper.
WHISK egg whites in a shallow bowl until frothy. Set aside.
COMBINE breadcrumbs, Parmesan cheese, Italian seasoning, and remaining ¼ teaspoon pepper in a bowl.
DIP eggplant slices in egg whites; dredge in breadcrumb mixture. Arrange on a wire rack coated with cooking spray in an aluminum foil-lined 15- x 10-inch jellyroll pan. Lightly coat eggplant slices on both sides with cooking spray.
BAKE at 375° for 20 to 25 minutes or until golden brown and eggplant is tender, adding split bread halves to oven during the last 5 minutes.
SPREAD 2 cups pasta sauce on cut sides of bread. Arrange eggplant on bottom half of bread; sprinkle with mozzarella cheese.
BROIL 6 inches from heat 2 minutes or until cheese melts. Cover with top half of bread. Cut into 6 sandwiches, and serve with pasta sauce, if desired.

*Substitute 1 cup Italian breadcrumbs for panko breadcrumbs.

Calories 337 (15% from fat); Fat 5.5g (sat 2.5g, mono 1.5g, poly 0.4g); Protein 15g; Carb 56g; Fiber 3.2g; Chol 11mg; Iron 2.3mg; Sodium 822mg; Calc 187mg

One-Dish Wonders

This busy mom shares her favorite recipes for family-friendly weeknight meals that are great for company, too.

Charlotte Skelton has a lot in common with many *Southern Living* readers. This on-the-go mother of three (including two teens) from Cleveland, Mississippi, juggles the responsibilities of an active family with a successful career. She also faces the universal challenge of serving her family a variety of great-tasting meals throughout the week. Charlotte's solution: stocking her freezer with one-dish meals. In fact, she's built a career around it.

"In 1992, I started making casseroles and gift baskets out of my house. Business took off pretty quickly, so I found a building downtown," remembers Charlotte. Today, A la Carte Alley is home to one of the Delta's most popular restaurants, along with a gift shop stocked with Southern necessities for the kitchen and table. Though her business has grown, the one thing that hasn't changed is Charlotte's love of recipes she can make ahead, freeze, and reheat. "They're convenient for weeknight meals—even for my finicky teens—and they make great gifts," she says.

Charlotte's recipes were a big hit with our Foods staff, and we think they'll be a home run with your friends and family too. Her passion for Southwest flavors explodes in Chicken Enchiladas. "This is one of my favorites, especially when company's coming," she explains. She also enjoys Italian-inspired Beef Lombardi for a hearty weeknight meal. All of the recipes freeze well and can be easily lightened.

CHICKEN ENCHILADAS

family favorite • make ahead

MAKES 4 TO 6 SERVINGS

Prep: 30 min., Cook: 30 min., Bake: 25 min.

- 2 tablespoons butter
- 2 large onions, thinly sliced
- 2 cups chopped cooked chicken
- ½ cup diced roasted red bell pepper
- 2 (3-ounce) packages cream cheese, cubed
- ¼ teaspoon salt
- ¼ teaspoon pepper
- 4 (4.5-ounce) cans diced green chiles
- 1 small onion, chopped
- 2 garlic cloves, minced
- 2 teaspoons dried oregano
- 1 teaspoon ground cumin
- ½ teaspoon sugar
- 1 (14½-ounce) can chicken broth
- ½ cup salsa
- 10 (7-inch) flour tortillas
- 2 cups (8 ounces) shredded Cheddar cheese

MELT butter in a large skillet over medium-high heat, stirring often; add sliced onions, and cook 20 minutes or until caramelized. Reduce heat to low; add chopped chicken and next 4 ingredients, stirring until combined. Set aside.

PULSE chiles and next 5 ingredients in a blender or food processor several times until combined.

BRING chile mixture and chicken broth to a boil in a saucepan over high heat; cook 5 minutes or until slightly thickened. (Mixture should be the consistency of a thin gravy.) Remove from heat, and stir in salsa.

SPREAD one-third chile mixture evenly in a lightly greased 13- x 9-inch baking dish.

SPOON chicken mixture evenly down center of each tortilla; roll up, and place seam side down in prepared baking dish. Top with remaining chile mixture; sprinkle with cheese.

BAKE at 375° for 20 to 25 minutes or until bubbly.

NOTE: Freeze chile mixture and filled tortillas separately up to 1 month, if desired. Thaw in refrigerator overnight. Prepare and bake as directed.

TO LIGHTEN: Substitute ⅓-less-fat cream cheese, 2% reduced-fat Cheddar cheese, and fat-free tortillas.

BEEF LOMBARDI

freezeable • make ahead

MAKES 6 SERVINGS

Prep: 10 min., Cook: 41 min., Bake: 40 min.

- 1 pound lean ground beef
- 1 (14½-ounce) can chopped tomatoes
- 1 (10-ounce) can diced tomatoes and green chiles
- 2 teaspoons sugar
- 2 teaspoons salt
- ¼ teaspoon pepper
- 1 (6-ounce) can tomato paste
- 1 bay leaf
- ½ (12-ounce) package medium egg noodles
- 6 green onions, chopped (about ½ cup)
- 1 cup sour cream
- 1 cup (4 ounces) shredded sharp Cheddar cheese
- 1 cup shredded Parmesan cheese
- 1 cup (4 ounces) shredded mozzarella cheese
- Garnish: fresh parsley sprigs

COOK beef in a large skillet over medium heat 5 to 6 minutes, stirring until it crumbles and is no longer pink. Drain.

STIR in chopped tomatoes and next 4 ingredients; cook 5 minutes. Add tomato paste and bay leaf, and simmer 30 minutes. Discard bay leaf.

COOK egg noodles according to package directions; drain.

STIR together cooked egg noodles, chopped green onions, and sour cream until blended.

PLACE noodle mixture in bottom of a lightly greased 13- x 9-inch baking dish. Top with beef mixture; sprinkle evenly with cheeses.

BAKE, covered with aluminum foil, at 350° for 35 minutes. Uncover casserole, and bake 5 more minutes. Garnish, if desired.

NOTE: Freeze casserole up to 1 month, if desired. Thaw in refrigerator overnight. Bake as directed.

TO LIGHTEN: Substitute low-fat or fat-free sour cream and 2% reduced-fat Cheddar cheese. Reduce amount of cheeses on top to ½ cup each.

Charlotte's Kitchen and Entertaining Tips

■ Double the recipe when preparing items such as chili, gumbo, and spaghetti sauce. It doesn't really take much time, and you can easily freeze the extra batch for heat-and-eat weeknight meals.

■ For easy uniform slices, freeze boneless, skinless chicken breasts, pork tenderloin, or steak for 10 minutes. Then slice for a stir-fry or quick sauté.

■ Refrigerate brown sugar (with a half slice of bread in the bag) to keep it from clumping and getting hard.

■ Save time and eliminate clutter while cooking by cleaning as you go.

■ Simple garnishes such as fresh chopped herbs, nuts, or slices of fruit are easy ways to dress up weeknight recipes for company. Decorative serving dishes also provide a pop of color and visual interest.

■ Set aside space in your refrigerator for make-ahead dishes before you prepare the recipe.

■ If you plan to freeze a casserole, line the baking dish with aluminum foil. This makes removing and freezing the casserole easier and cuts down on cleanup.

To purchase a copy of Charlotte's cookbook, *Absolutely a la Carte* (Wimmer, 1999), call (662) 843-6510, or visit **www.gritlit.com.**

ONE-DISH BLACK-EYED PEA CORNBREAD

freezeable • make ahead

MAKES 12 APPETIZER OR 6 MAIN-DISH SERVINGS

Prep: 20 min., Cook: 5 min., Bake: 1 hr.

This uniquely Southern recipe works as a tasty appetizer when cut into small squares or as a main dish when paired with a tossed green salad.

- 1 pound spicy ground pork sausage
- 1 medium onion, diced
- 1 cup white cornmeal
- ½ cup all-purpose flour
- 1 teaspoon salt
- ½ teaspoon baking soda
- 2 large eggs, lightly beaten
- 1 cup buttermilk
- ½ cup vegetable oil
- 1 (15-ounce) can black-eyed peas, drained
- 2 cups (8 ounces) shredded Cheddar cheese
- ¾ cup cream-style corn
- ¼ cup chopped pickled jalapeño peppers
- 1 (4.5-ounce) can chopped green chiles

COOK sausage and onion in a large skillet over medium-high heat 5 minutes, stirring until sausage crumbles and is no longer pink. Drain.

COMBINE cornmeal, flour, salt, and baking soda.

STIR together eggs, buttermilk, and oil until combined. Add to dry ingredients, stirring just until moistened. (Batter will not be smooth.) Add sausage mixture, peas, and remaining ingredients to batter, stirring well.

POUR into a greased 13- x 9-inch baking dish.

BAKE at 350° for 1 hour or until golden and set.

NOTE: Freeze baked cornbread up to 1 month, if desired. Thaw in refrigerator overnight. Bake, covered, at 350° for 30 minutes. Uncover and bake 10 more minutes or until thoroughly heated. To reheat directly from the freezer, bake, covered, at 350° for 1 hour. Uncover and bake 10 more minutes or until thoroughly heated.

TO LIGHTEN: Substitute 1 (12-ounce) package reduced-fat sausage, fat-free buttermilk, ½ cup egg substitute, and 2% reduced-fat Cheddar cheese. Reduce oil to 2 tablespoons. Prepare and bake as directed.

Cook's Corner

Don't let the busy holiday entertaining season sneak up on you—make a quick phone call, send an envelope, or visit the Web sites featured here, and these timely, helpful brochures will soon be yours.

You Can Make Ordinary Meals Extraordinary

Pepperidge Farm has compiled a sumptuous collection of 10 sweet and savory recipes using puff pastry.

This handy booklet will give you a head start on planning family meals and entertaining menus. Savory recipes include Parmesan Cheese Twists, Brie en Croûte, and Spinach-Cheese Swirls as perfect appetizer selections. The sweet assortment includes Chocolate Bundles and Chocolate Mini-Puffs. This essential brochure is available by calling 1-800-762-8301 or visiting **www.puffpastry.com.**

Cheese Pairing Guide

The Southeast Dairy Association is offering a savvy guide to help pair cheeses with wines. It's a cool slide-rule-style gadget that has cheese and wine pairings on one side and cheese descriptions on the other. Also included are suggestions for serving different types of fruit, breads, and nuts to complement both your cheese and wine selections. Whether you are hosting a wine-and-cheese party or simply looking for the right cheese to go with the right wine for a hostess gift basket, this will meet your needs. To order, call 1-800-651-6455, or visit **www.ilovecheese.com** and request the cheese pairing guide. You may also send a self-addressed, stamped, business-size envelope to Cheese Pairing Guide Offer, c/o Southeast Dairy Association, 5340 West Fayetteville Road, Atlanta, GA 30349.

The Pork Kitchen Companion: An Essential Guide to Cooking Pork

The National Pork Board is offering a guide to shopping for and preparing pork. This booklet contains valuable resource information that covers the storage and freezing of pork, a cooking chart for a variety of cuts, and definitions of cooking methods. The recipes from six nationally known chefs, along with basic recipes from the National Pork Board, will be staples in your meal planning. To receive the free booklet, go to the National Pork Board Web site, **www.otherwhitemeat.com,** and click on "brochure offers." You also can send a self-addressed, stamped, business-size envelope to the National Pork Board, P.O. Box 9114, Des Moines, IA 50306.

Tricks to Great Treats

Test Kitchens professional James Leo Schend has Penny P. Patrick's Praline Parlor to thank for his love of caramel apples. While working at this shop within Six Flags Great America amusement park, he made over 50,000 of them. That job taught him a few tricks of the trade.

CARAMEL APPLES

make ahead

MAKES 6 APPLES

Prep: 20 min., Cool: 5 min., Chill: 30 min.

- 6 large Granny Smith apples
- 6 wooden craft sticks
- 1 (14-ounce) package caramels, unwrapped
- 1 tablespoon vanilla extract
- 1 tablespoon water
- 2 cups chopped pecans, toasted
- 1 (12-ounce) package semisweet chocolate morsels
- Pecan halves (optional)

WASH and dry apples; remove stems. Insert a craft stick into stem end of each apple; set aside.

COMBINE caramels, vanilla, and 1 tablespoon water in a microwave-safe glass bowl. Microwave at HIGH 90 seconds or until melted, stirring twice.

DIP each apple into the caramel mixture quickly, allowing excess caramel to drip off. Roll in chopped pecans; place on lightly greased wax paper. Chill at least 15 minutes.

MICROWAVE chocolate morsels at HIGH 90 seconds or until melted, stirring twice; cool 5 minutes. Pour chocolate where craft stick and apple meet, allowing chocolate to drip down sides of apples. Press pecan halves onto chocolate, if desired. Chill 15 minutes or until set.

NOTE: For testing purposes only, we used Kraft Caramels.

BLACK-AND-WHITE CARAMEL APPLES: Microwave 6 ounces white chocolate morsels at HIGH 60 seconds or until melted, stirring once; drizzle evenly over semisweet chocolate.

CALYPSO CARAMEL APPLES: Substitute 1 cup chopped toasted macadamia nuts and 1 cup toasted coconut for pecans.

THE BEST EVER CARAMEL SAUCE

fast fixin's

MAKES 1¼ CUPS

Prep: 10 min., Cook: 10 min.

Toss apple slices in pineapple juice before serving to prevent browning. This recipe is adapted from *Discover Dinnertime: Your Guide to Building Family Time Around the Table* (Wimmer, 1998).

- ½ cup butter or margarine
- 1 cup firmly packed light brown sugar
- ½ cup whipping cream
- 1 tablespoon vanilla extract
- Apple slices

COOK butter and brown sugar in a heavy saucepan over medium heat, stirring occasionally, until sugar melts.

ADD whipping cream, stirring occasionally. Bring to a boil, and stir mixture occasionally. Remove from heat. Stir in vanilla. Serve with apple slices.

Cook's Notes

- Lightly scrub apples with mild soap and a soft scrub brush to remove waxy coating.
- Hot caramel won't stick to a wet apple, so make sure apples are dry.
- Don't get the caramel too hot, or you'll end up with a thin layer on your apple and the rest sliding off.
- Scrape excess caramel off the sides of your apple before rolling in nuts. Don't forget to scrape the bottom of the apple too.

Entertain With Ease

Autumn Menu

Serves 4

Glazed Roasted Chicken

Sweet Onion Risotto   Snow peas

Lemon Chess Pie

Before the rush of the holidays, get together with friends, and enjoy our jazzed up chicken and rice menu. Hearty Sweet Onion Risotto is a creamy complement to Glazed Roasted Chicken. Add a vegetable of your choice and end the meal with Lemon Chess Pie.

GLAZED ROASTED CHICKEN

MAKES 4 SERVINGS

Prep: 20 min., Chill: 8 hrs., Bake: 45 min. *(pictured on page 225)*

- ½ cup lite teriyaki sauce
- ¼ cup frozen orange juice concentrate, thawed and undiluted
- 3 tablespoons dark sesame oil
- 4 garlic cloves, minced
- 1 (4-pound) whole chicken
- 1 teaspoon salt
- ½ teaspoon freshly ground pepper

STIR together first 4 ingredients; reserve half of mixture.
CUT chicken in half, and sprinkle evenly with salt and pepper. Place chicken in a large freezer bag, and pour half of teriyaki mixture over chicken; seal bag, and chill 8 hours, turning chicken, if desired.

REMOVE chicken from marinade, discarding marinade. Place chicken, skin side up, on an aluminum foil-lined 15- x 10-inch jellyroll pan.
BAKE at 450° for 45 minutes or until a meat thermometer inserted in chicken thigh registers 180°. Brush with reserved teriyaki mixture.

SWEET ONION RISOTTO

MAKES 6 SERVINGS

Prep: 10 min.; Cook: 1 hr., 10 min.

Arborio rice is located with other rice products in the grocery store. Its short, smooth grain and high starch content give risotto a creamy texture. *(pictured on page 225)*

- 3 large sweet onions, chopped
- 3 tablespoons olive oil, divided
- 2 garlic cloves, pressed
- 1 (16-ounce) package Arborio rice
- 8 cups warm chicken broth
- 1 cup dry white wine
- ½ cup shredded Parmesan cheese
- 2 tablespoons butter or margarine
- 1 teaspoon salt

COOK onions in 2 tablespoons hot oil in a Dutch oven over medium heat, stirring occasionally, 30 to 35 minutes or until caramelized. Remove from pan, and set aside.
HEAT remaining 1 tablespoon oil in Dutch oven; add garlic, and sauté 2 minutes. Add rice; cook, stirring constantly, 2 minutes.
REDUCE heat to medium; add 1 cup chicken broth. Cook, stirring often, until liquid is absorbed. Repeat procedure with remaining chicken broth, 1 cup at a time. (This takes about 30 minutes.) Stir in onions.
ADD wine; cook, stirring gently, until liquid is absorbed. Stir in cheese, butter, and salt. Serve immediately.

LEMON CHESS PIE

MAKES 8 TO 10 SERVINGS

Prep: 25 min.; Bake: 1 hr., 2 min.

A blend of butter, sugar, and eggs makes this an all-time favorite. *(pictured on page 225)*

- ½ (15-ounce) package refrigerated piecrusts
- 2 cups sugar
- ½ cup butter or margarine, melted
- ¼ cup milk
- ⅓ cup lemon juice
- 2 teaspoons grated lemon rind
- 2 tablespoons cornmeal
- 1 tablespoon all-purpose flour
- 1 tablespoon white vinegar
- ½ teaspoon vanilla extract
- ¼ teaspoon salt
- 4 large eggs, lightly beaten

FIT piecrust into a 9-inch pieplate according to package directions; fold edges under, and crimp.
LINE pastry with aluminum foil, and fill with pie weights or dried beans.
BAKE at 425° for 4 to 5 minutes. Remove weights and foil. Bake 2 more minutes or until golden. Cool crust completely.
STIR together sugar and next 9 ingredients until blended. Add eggs, stirring well. Pour filling into piecrust.
BAKE at 350° for 50 to 55 minutes, shielding edges with foil after 10 minutes to prevent excessive browning. Cool completely on a wire rack.

Pick a Potato Casserole

Your family will love these delicious dishes made from convenience products.

Speed meal preparation by starting in the frozen food section of your local grocery store. We've used frozen hash browns and mashed potatoes to streamline this collection of recipes. Try one or all of these great dishes. They include a breakfast or brunch casserole, two versions of a side dish, and a kid-friendly one-dish meal. We think these versatile casseroles will become permanent additions to your recipe files.

SAUSAGE-HASH BROWN BREAKFAST CASSEROLE

family favorite

MAKES 10 SERVINGS

Prep: 30 min., Bake: 40 min.

- 1 pound mild ground pork sausage
- 1 pound hot ground pork sausage
- 1 (30-ounce) package frozen hash browns
- 1½ teaspoons salt, divided
- ½ teaspoon pepper
- 1 cup (4 ounces) shredded Cheddar cheese
- 6 large eggs
- 2 cups milk

COOK sausages in a large skillet over medium-high heat, stirring until sausage crumbles and is no longer pink. Drain sausage well.
PREPARE hash browns according to package directions, using ½ teaspoon salt and pepper.
STIR together hash browns, sausage, and cheese. Pour into a lightly greased 13- x 9-inch baking dish.

WHISK together eggs, milk, and remaining 1 teaspoon salt. Pour evenly over potato mixture.
BAKE at 350° for 35 to 40 minutes.

BRENDA AUSTIN MASON
AUSTIN, TEXAS

BEEFY POTATO CASSEROLE

family favorite

MAKES 5 SERVINGS

Prep: 15 min., Cook: 10 min., Bake: 30 min.

Teresa's potato tots casserole recipe inspired this version, which is like a shepherd's pie.

- 1 (22-ounce) package frozen mashed potatoes
- 2 tablespoons butter
- 1 teaspoon salt, divided
- 1 pound lean ground beef
- 1 small onion, chopped
- ½ teaspoon seasoned pepper
- 2 cups (8 ounces) shredded Cheddar cheese, divided
- 1 (11-ounce) can whole kernel corn, drained
- 1 (10¾-ounce) can cream of mushroom soup, undiluted
- ½ cup milk

PREPARE mashed potatoes according to package directions. Stir in butter and ½ teaspoon salt; set aside.
COOK ground beef, onion, and pepper in a large skillet over medium-high heat, stirring until beef crumbles and is no longer pink; drain and return to skillet. Add 1 cup cheese, corn, soup, milk, and remaining ½ teaspoon salt, stirring well.

POUR beef mixture into a lightly greased 13- x 9-inch baking dish. Spread mashed potatoes evenly over beef mixture.
BAKE at 350° for 20 minutes. Sprinkle with remaining 1 cup cheese, and bake 10 more minutes.

TERESA HUBBARD
RUSSELLVILLE, ALABAMA

CHEESY HASH BROWN CASSEROLE

family favorite

MAKES 4 TO 6 SERVINGS

Prep: 10 min., Bake: 55 min.

- 1 (30-ounce) package frozen shredded hash browns
- 1 cup (4 ounces) shredded colby-Jack cheese
- 1 (5-ounce) package shredded Swiss cheese
- 1 large onion, minced
- 1 teaspoon minced garlic
- 1½ cups milk
- 1 (10¾-ounce) can cream of chicken soup, undiluted
- ½ cup beef broth
- 2 tablespoons butter, melted
- 1½ teaspoons salt
- ½ teaspoon pepper

COMBINE first 5 ingredients in a large bowl.
STIR together milk and next 5 ingredients; pour over hash brown mixture. Pour into a lightly greased 13- x 9-inch baking dish.
BAKE at 350° for 45 to 55 minutes or until golden.

PEPPER JACK-POTATO CASSEROLE: Omit colby-Jack and Swiss cheeses, onion, and beef broth. Substitute 1 (8-ounce) package Monterey Jack cheese with peppers, shredded. Proceed as directed. Bake at 350° for 45 to 50 minutes or until bubbly.

TERRI MATHEWS
LEEDS, ALABAMA

Five Fast Dinners Begin With One Vegetable Mix

Connie Sorie Dana of Tyler, Texas, developed a dish that she hoped would encourage her husband, Tom, to eat eggplant, a vegetable she likes but he doesn't. What she ended up with was a base for a week of meals. "I just came up with a batch of something that's like ratatouille," she says, "and I realized it would be good over shrimp. Then I stirred some beans and chili powder into it to make soup or added ground beef and Italian seasonings for spaghetti sauce."

Connie enjoys making food that she describes as simple "but not boring." She says, "When I made a recipe that we could eat for a week and not get tired of it, I knew I had a winner."

DAY-BY-DAY VEGETABLE MEDLEY

fast fixin's

MAKES ABOUT 12 CUPS

Prep: 10 min., Cook: 20 min.

Use this dish as a base for the recipes that follow. It makes enough to use in four recipes.

- 3 medium onions, chopped (about 4½ cups)
- 2 red bell peppers, chopped (about 3 cups)
- 2 green bell peppers, chopped (about 3 cups)
- 5 tablespoons olive oil, divided
- 1 large eggplant, unpeeled and chopped (about 8 cups)
- 1 pound fresh mushrooms, sliced (about 6 cups)
- 4 (10-ounce) cans mild diced tomatoes and green chiles
- ¼ cup Greek seasoning

SAUTÉ onions and bell peppers in 1 tablespoon hot olive oil in a Dutch oven over medium-high heat 5 minutes. Place onion mixture in a large bowl, and set aside.

SAUTÉ eggplant in 2 tablespoons hot olive oil in Dutch oven over medium heat 5 minutes. Add eggplant to onion mixture in bowl.

SAUTÉ mushrooms in remaining 2 tablespoons hot oil in Dutch oven over medium heat 5 minutes.

ADD tomatoes and green chiles, Greek seasoning, and vegetable mixture to Dutch oven, and cook 5 minutes or until thoroughly heated.

SPOON 3 cups mixture into each of 4 freezer bags; seal and freeze up to 1 month.

NOTE: For testing purposes only, we used Cavender's All Purpose Greek Seasoning.

INDIVIDUAL PIZZAS: Place 6 (5-ounce) Italian bread shells on a baking sheet. Brush each with 1 teaspoon olive oil. Spread ½ cup Day-by-Day Vegetable Medley, thawed, over each crust. Sprinkle each with ¼ cup shredded mozzarella cheese and your favorite toppings. Bake at 450° for 15 to 20 minutes or until cheese is melted.

GREEK-STYLE CHICKEN STEW: Bring 4 cups chopped cooked chicken; 3 cups Day-by-Day Vegetable Medley, thawed; and 1 (14½-ounce) can chicken broth to a boil in a large saucepan. Stir in 1 cup cooked diced potatoes and 1 cup whipping cream. Reduce heat, and simmer 20 minutes or until thoroughly heated. Salt to taste.

SHRIMP WITH RICE: Heat 3 cups Day-by-Day Vegetable Medley, thawed, and 1 cup vegetable broth in a large saucepan; add 1 (16-ounce) package peeled frozen shrimp, thawed, and cook until thoroughly heated. Spoon mixture over hot cooked rice. Serve immediately.

BEEF-AND-VEGETABLE SUPPER: Cook 1 pound lean ground beef in a large skillet, stirring until it crumbles and is no longer pink; drain. Stir in 3 cups Day-by-Day Vegetable Medley, thawed; 1 cup chicken broth; and 1 (8-ounce) can tomato paste. Reduce heat; cover and simmer 30 minutes. Serve over your favorite cooked pasta or noodles. Salt to taste.

BLACK BEAN SOUP: Bring 2 (15-ounce) cans black beans, drained; 3 cups Day-by-Day Vegetable Medley, thawed; and 2 cups chicken broth to a boil. Stir in ¼ cup lime juice, 1 tablespoon chopped fresh cilantro, 1 teaspoon ground cumin, and ½ teaspoon chili powder. Reduce heat; cover and simmer 45 minutes. Serve with chopped fresh cilantro and chopped onion. Salt to taste.

Veggie Shopping

- When selecting fresh produce, look for bright color and crisp appearance.

- Smaller vegetables tend to be sweeter and more tender than larger ones in the same family.

- Generally speaking, buy firm vegetables rather than soft.

- Avoid vegetables that are bruised. If vegetables are limp when you buy them, chances are they won't improve when you get them home.

Favorite Turnip Greens

These luscious greens have all the makings of a simple Southern dish—four ingredients and a lot of love.

As the daughter of an Air Force pilot, Shannon Sliter Satterwhite was fortunate to live in various regions of the country. She spent much time in the South where her dad was stationed most often. She grew up enjoying down-home Southern food as her family moved from state to state, but it wasn't until she met her Georgia-native husband, Scott, that she truly experienced her first bowl of turnip greens.

One day, Scott took her to a local meat-and-three where turnip greens were the specialty. When their order arrived, she marveled at how excitedly he doused his treasured greens with pepper sauce and hastily crumbled cornbread into his bowl as if it were his last meal. Intrigued by his frenzy, she curiously followed suit and quickly found herself emotionally involved with every bite.

Since then, she's learned the fundamentals of preparing her own pot of greens. Most agree that turnip greens are best during the peak season, typically October through February.

The first step is washing them—a time-consuming task, but it's well worth the trouble. To ease the removal of dirt and grit from the leaves, Test Kitchens professional Angela Sellers recommends chopping the greens first, then soaking them. It's best to soak and rinse the leaves four or five times. The result is perfectly clean greens.

Choosing the proper seasoning, however, can be a touchy subject in the South. Some argue that it's better to add salt pork to the pot, while others insist on ham hocks. Some cooks opt to embellish their greens with other ingredients, such as chicken broth, bacon, garlic, onions, and even wine, though purists prefer to keep it simple.

We tried several variations, and after much debate at the taste-testing table, we unanimously gave the nod to Southern Turnip Greens and Ham Hocks. Thanks to her husband, Shannon will forever enjoy this quintessential Southern dish.

Turnip Greens 101

▪ Choose crisp greens with even color. Avoid those that are wilted, yellowing, or have dark green, slimy patches.

▪ Store fresh greens in a tightly sealed, large plastic bag in the refrigerator up to 3 days.

▪ As with any leafy green vegetable, turnip greens are an excellent source of vitamins A and C, important antioxidants known to help prevent heart disease and certain types of cancer. Greens also contain significant amounts of fiber, calcium, and folic acid.

SOUTHERN TURNIP GREENS AND HAM HOCKS

MAKES 8 TO 10 SERVINGS

Prep: 30 min., Cook: 3 hrs.

We simmered the ham hocks for about 2 hours until the meat easily pulled away from the bones. If you want to save time, just simmer 30 to 45 minutes to release the flavor. *(pictured on page 228)*

- 1¾ pounds ham hocks, rinsed
- 2 quarts water
- 2 bunches fresh turnip greens with roots (about 10 pounds)
- 1 tablespoon sugar

BRING ham hocks and 2 quarts water to a boil in an 8-quart Dutch oven. Reduce heat, and simmer 1½ to 2 hours or until meat is tender.

REMOVE and discard stems and discolored spots from greens. Chop greens, and wash thoroughly; drain. Peel turnip roots, and cut in half.

ADD greens, roots, and sugar to Dutch oven; bring to a boil. Reduce heat; cover and simmer 45 to 60 minutes or until greens and roots are tender.

Creamy Fall Soups

Soups offer soul-satisfying contentment. In fact, they should share top billing with the usual choices of best-loved comfort foods. These soup recipes use a variety of fall and winter produce, such as squash, apples, and pumpkin, to create rich flavors that are perfect for the season. What's more, the soups can be frozen and then easily thawed and warmed for chilly days.

CURRIED ACORN SQUASH-AND-APPLE SOUP

freezeable • make ahead

MAKES 3 QUARTS

Prep: 40 min., Bake: 45 min., Cook: 50 min., Cool: 10 min.

Our Test Kitchens honored this rich and creamy soup with their highest rating.

- 2 medium acorn squash (about 3 pounds), halved
- ¼ cup butter or margarine
- 4¾ cups chicken broth, divided
- 4 Granny Smith apples, peeled and coarsely chopped
- 2 baking potatoes, peeled and coarsely chopped
- 1½ tablespoons curry powder
- ¾ teaspoon ground red pepper
- ½ teaspoon ground cinnamon
- 1 teaspoon salt
- 2 cups whipping cream
- 2 tablespoons honey

PLACE squash halves, cut side down, on an aluminum foil-lined baking sheet.
BAKE at 350° for 45 minutes or until tender. Scoop out pulp, discarding shells; set pulp aside.
MELT butter in a Dutch oven over medium heat; add 4 cups chicken broth, apples, and next 5 ingredients. Cook, stirring often, 25 to 30 minutes or until apples and potatoes are tender. Remove from heat, and let cool slightly (about 5 to 10 minutes).

PROCESS squash pulp, apple mixture, and remaining ¾ cup chicken broth, in batches, in a food processor or blender until smooth, stopping to scrape down sides.
RETURN puree to Dutch oven. Stir in whipping cream and honey, and simmer, stirring occasionally, 15 to 20 minutes or until thoroughly heated.

KELLY K. BROWN
DENVER, COLORADO

CREAMY SOUTHWESTERN PUMPKIN SOUP

freezeable • make ahead

MAKES 10 CUPS

Prep: 15 min., Cook: 55 min., Cool: 10 min.

- 2 tablespoons butter or margarine
- 1 large onion, chopped (about 2 cups)
- 1 jalapeño pepper, seeded and chopped
- 2 garlic cloves, minced
- 5 cups chicken broth
- 1 large baking potato, peeled and chopped (about 2 cups)
- 1¼ teaspoons salt
- ½ teaspoon chili powder
- ½ teaspoon ground cumin
- 1 (15-ounce) can pumpkin
- ¼ cup chopped fresh cilantro
- 2 cups milk
- 3 tablespoons fresh lime juice
- Garnishes: sour cream, fresh cilantro sprig

MELT butter in a Dutch oven over medium heat. Add onion, jalapeño pepper, and garlic; sauté 15 minutes. Add chicken broth and next 4 ingredients; cook, stirring often, 30 minutes or until potato is tender. Remove from heat, and let cool slightly (about 5 to 10 minutes).
PROCESS potato mixture, pumpkin, and cilantro, in batches, in a food processor or blender until smooth, stopping to scrape down sides.
RETURN to Dutch oven; stir in milk, and simmer 10 minutes or until thoroughly heated. Stir in lime juice; garnish, if desired.

GINGERED CARROT-AND-PARSNIP SOUP

freezeable • make ahead

MAKES 4 QUARTS

Prep: 15 min.; Cook: 1 hr., 15 min.; Cool: 10 min.

This recipe is adapted from *Revenge of the Barbeque Queens* (St. Martin's Press, 1997) by Lou Jane Temple.

- 2 celery ribs, chopped
- 1 medium onion, chopped
- 1 tablespoon olive oil
- 1 (2-inch) piece fresh ginger, peeled and sliced
- 1½ pounds carrots, cut into 1-inch pieces
- 1 pound parsnips, cut into 1-inch pieces
- 10 cups chicken broth
- 1 cup half-and-half
- ¾ teaspoon kosher salt or ½ teaspoon salt
- ¼ teaspoon ground white pepper
- Pinch of ground allspice (optional)
- Pinch of ground nutmeg (optional)

SAUTÉ celery and onion in hot oil in a large Dutch oven over medium-high heat 10 to 15 minutes or until tender. Add ginger, and cook 5 minutes.
ADD carrots, parsnips, and chicken broth to Dutch oven; bring to a boil. Reduce heat, and simmer, stirring occasionally, 45 minutes or until carrots and parsnips are tender. Remove from heat; let cool slightly (about 5 to 10 minutes).
PROCESS mixture, in batches, in a food processor or blender until smooth, stopping to scrape down sides.
RETURN puree to Dutch oven. Stir in half-and-half, salt, pepper, and, if desired, allspice and nutmeg; simmer, stirring occasionally, over low heat 10 minutes or until thoroughly heated.

LOU JANE TEMPLE
KANSAS CITY, MISSOURI

Quick & Easy

Dressed-Up Chicken

Make a tried-and-true classic extra-special when you shape biscuits into simple bowls.

Casual creamed chicken—or chicken à la king, as it's sometimes called—will wow guests and family alike when you serve it in our biscuit bowls. This dinner will only look like you worked hard. It might even inspire you to get out the china, stemmed glassware, and real napkins. Add a parsley garnish, toss a salad, and a special yet simple supper is on the table.

Biscuit Bowls
fast fixin's
MAKES 8 SERVINGS

Prep: 5 min., Bake: 14 min.

1 (16.3-ounce) can refrigerated
    jumbo flaky biscuits
Vegetable cooking spray

ROLL each biscuit into a 5-inch circle (photo 1).
INVERT 8 (6-ounce) custard cups or ramekins, several inches apart, on a lightly greased baking sheet.
Coat outside of cups with cooking spray (photo 2).
MOLD flattened biscuits around outside of custard cups (photo 3), and bake at 350° for 14 minutes.
COOL slightly, and remove biscuit bowls from cups.

NOTE: Frozen biscuits may be substituted. Let thaw at room temperature for 30 minutes or overnight in the refrigerator. Biscuits may be slightly sticky; lightly flour before rolling out. Bake at 350° for 16 to 18 minutes.

CREAMED CHICKEN IN BISCUIT BOWLS

family favorite • fast fixin's
MAKES 8 SERVINGS

Prep: 10 min., Cook: 20 min.

You can also serve Creamed Chicken over toast points, split biscuits, cornbread, waffles, or puff pastry shells.

2 tablespoons butter or margarine
½ cup finely chopped onion
    (about 1 small onion)
½ cup finely chopped celery
½ cup sliced fresh mushrooms
1 (10¾-ounce) can cream of chicken
    soup
½ cup milk
¼ teaspoon dried tarragon
1 cup (4 ounces) shredded sharp
    Cheddar cheese
2½ cups chopped cooked chicken
½ (16-ounce) package frozen peas
    and carrots, thawed
1 (2-ounce) jar diced pimiento,
    drained
¼ teaspoon salt
½ teaspoon pepper
Biscuit Bowls (see box)

MELT butter in a large skillet over medium-high heat; add onion, celery, and mushrooms, and sauté 2 to 3 minutes or until tender.
WHISK in soup, milk, and tarragon; cook over medium-low heat 3 to 4 minutes, stirring occasionally. Add Cheddar cheese, stirring constantly, until cheese melts. Stir in chicken, peas and carrots, pimiento, salt, and pepper. Cook over low heat, stirring often, 10 minutes or until thoroughly heated.
SPOON warm chicken mixture evenly into Biscuit Bowls.

CHICKEN POT PIE IN BISCUIT BOWLS: Substitute 1 (10-ounce) thawed package frozen mixed vegetables for peas and carrots. Add ½ teaspoon dried thyme and ½ teaspoon poultry seasoning. Omit tarragon, sliced mushrooms, and pimiento. Proceed with recipe as directed.

ANN MCFARLAND
SPRING, TEXAS

Home-Style Brownies

Need a quick treat? Let brownies come to the rescue. Using a cake mix in one recipe and self-rising flour in the other jump-starts these easy desserts. Choose Cream Cheese Brownie Sundaes topped with ice cream and chocolate sauce or Fudge Cake Brownies dusted with powdered sugar.

Bars such as these Fudge Cake Brownies are great in care packages because they don't crumble easily. Place in a plastic bag when cool, and hand deliver to friends; or package carefully and mail.

CREAM CHEESE BROWNIE SUNDAES

family favorite

MAKES 12 SERVINGS

Prep: 15 min., Bake: 40 min.

> 1 (18.25-ounce) package chocolate
>   cake mix
> 3 large eggs, divided
> ½ cup butter or margarine, melted
> 1 (8-ounce) package cream cheese,
>   softened
> 1 (16-ounce) package powdered sugar
> ⅓ cup unsweetened cocoa
> Mint chocolate-chip ice cream
> Chocolate sauce

BEAT cake mix, 1 egg, and melted butter with an electric mixer at medium speed until combined. Press mixture into the bottom of a lightly greased 13- x 9-inch baking dish.
BEAT cream cheese and sugar at medium speed until smooth. Add remaining 2 eggs, 1 at a time, beating well after each addition. Gradually add cocoa, beating until blended. Pour mixture evenly over chocolate layer.
BAKE at 350° for 35 to 40 minutes or until a wooden pick inserted in center comes out clean. Cool. Cut into squares. Serve with mint chocolate-chip ice cream and chocolate sauce.

BRENDA J. BICKING
COATESVILLE, PENNSYLVANIA

FUDGE CAKE BROWNIES

family favorite

MAKES 16 SQUARES

Prep: 10 min., Bake: 30 min.

Place brownies in the freezer for 45 minutes or until firm for cleaner slices.

> 6 tablespoons unsweetened cocoa
> 1 cup sugar
> ½ cup butter or margarine, melted
> 2 large eggs, lightly beaten
> ½ cup self-rising flour
> 1 tablespoon vanilla extract
> ½ cup chopped pecans, toasted
> Powdered sugar

COMBINE cocoa and sugar. Add melted butter and next 4 ingredients, stirring just until combined. Pour mixture into a lightly greased 8-inch square pan.
BAKE at 350° for 25 to 30 minutes. Cool. Cut into 2-inch squares, and dust with powdered sugar before serving.

SHARON SCOGGINS
ANNISTON, ALABAMA

Cheesy Bites

If you have a passion for anything with cheese, then you've just turned to the right page.

CHEESY CROSTINI

fast fixin's

MAKES 40 APPETIZER SERVINGS

Prep: 15 min., Bake: 12 min.

> 1 cup (4 ounces) shredded Swiss
>   cheese
> ½ cup mayonnaise
> ½ cup sour cream
> 1 (0.7-ounce) envelope Italian dressing
>   mix
> 1 (16-ounce) French bread loaf, cut
>   into 40 slices
> 1 small green bell pepper, diced
> 1 small red bell pepper, diced
> Ripe olive slices (optional)

STIR together first 4 ingredients. Spread 1 side of each bread slice evenly with cheese mixture; sprinkle with diced bell peppers. Place bread slices on a baking sheet.
BAKE at 350° for 10 to 12 minutes. Top with olive slices, if desired. Serve crostini immediately.

JENNY MAGUIRE
POQUOSON, VIRGINIA

BEER-AND-CHEDDAR FONDUE

fast fixin's

MAKES ABOUT 6 CUPS

Prep: 10 min., Cook: 10 min.

Stir occasionally when serving to keep blended.

> ½ pound ground pork sausage
> 6 tablespoons butter
> 1 onion, chopped
> 1 garlic clove, chopped
> 6 tablespoons all-purpose flour
> 2 cups milk
> 2 (8-ounce) blocks Cheddar cheese,
>   shredded
> 1 cup beer*
> 1 (4-ounce) can chopped green chiles
> ½ teaspoon salt
> ¼ teaspoon ground red pepper
> Cubed French bread or sliced pears

COOK sausage in a large saucepan over medium heat, stirring until it crumbles and is no longer pink. Drain and remove sausage from pan.
MELT butter in saucepan over medium heat; add onion and garlic, and sauté until tender.
ADD flour, stirring until smooth. Cook, stirring constantly, 1 minute. Gradually add milk, stirring until thickened. Add cheese, stirring until melted. Remove from heat; stir in sausage, beer, and next 3 ingredients. Transfer to a fondue pot or slow cooker; keep warm on LOW. Serve with cubed French bread or sliced pears.

*Substitute nonalcoholic beer for regular beer, if desired.

SUSAN HEIN
KENOSHA, WISCONSIN

from our kitchen

Fresh boiled shrimp are quick and easy hors d'oeuvres, but they need to be kept cold. When entertaining a crowd, this can be a problem. We found an attractive solution—the Puget Sound Seafood Server ($69.95), a three-piece set of stackable stoneware bowls designed with a drainage hole in the serving section that allows the water from melting ice to collect in a bowl below. The Seafood Server also can be used as an ovenproof baking dish. For more information, visit **www.pugetsoundseafoodserver.com** or call toll free 1-877-251-1508.

Serve boiled shrimp with an assortment of homemade dipping sauces. Look for some of our favorite recipes at **southernliving.com/features.** If you're short on time, you can usually have your grocer season and steam the shrimp for you, or you can pick up a bag of frozen cooked shrimp.

Simple Pleasures

Not far from where we work is Gilchrist, a tiny landmark cafe with a six-stool soda fountain. For more than 75 years they have served white bread sandwiches and tomato aspic salad plates. Their specialty, though, is fresh limeade that's incredibly delicious and unlike any other in town. The secret might be in the sugar syrup they use, or the tap water, or the fact that each one is made to order with a handheld citrus press.

When we discovered these colorful juicers in the Williams-Sonoma catalog, we couldn't resist buying one to make our own limeades. Of course, they aren't *exactly* the same, but close enough to set you dreaming about life's simple pleasures. You may want to adjust the proportions to suit your personal taste, but start with the juice from half a lime. Stir in ¼ cup of sugar syrup and a generous splash or two of tap water. Then add a big handful of crushed ice, and enjoy.

To make 3 cups of sugar syrup, stir together 2 cups of water and 2 cups of sugar in a saucepan. Bring to a boil over medium heat, continuing to stir until sugar dissolves. Boil 1 minute; remove from heat, and cool. Sugar syrup can be stored in the refrigerator for several weeks. Used with abandon, it will make a shockingly sweet glass of iced tea as well.

Citrus presses for lemons and oranges also are available. One squeeze and the juices are extracted, turning the rind inside out and leaving the seeds behind. In less time than it takes to order a latte, you can treat yourself to a glass of fresh orange juice every morning. Citrus presses sell for around $15 and can be found in many specialty stores or ordered from **www.williams-sonoma.com.**

Frozen Roll Dough

The package of Rich's Homestyle Roll Dough provides instructions for shaping all sorts of clever rolls, from cloverleaf to Parker House, but what they don't tell you is that their dough also makes terrific little sandwich buns. Instead of buying expensive cocktail buns at local bakeries, you can make them yourself for a fraction of the cost. Divide the frozen balls of dough from 1 (25-ounce) package between 2 greased baking sheets, leaving ample space for rising between each roll. Follow the package directions for thawing and baking, and you'll end up with two dozen beautiful little buns.

In the Test Kitchens, we all have our favorite ways of serving them, whether we're splurging for a formal affair with beef tenderloin and horseradish sauce or grilling baby hamburgers for a backyard full of wild and crazy kids. For a taste of New Orleans, Laura Martin makes miniature po'boys and tucks them alongside bowls of steaming hot gumbo. Vanessa McNeil stuffs them with Texas barbecue. Filled with deli meats and cheeses or homemade chicken salad, they're the perfect size for boxed lunches.

Tips and Tidbits

■ The promise of first frost gets us thinking about fresh turnip and collard greens (see "Taste of the South" about turnip greens on page 220). A less familiar seasonal offering that's available in the produce market this fall is arugula. Popular in Italian cuisine, the deep green leaves are rich in vitamins A and C. Arugula has an assertive peppery flavor similar to that of watercress, and it's usually sold in small bunches. Add it to salads or sandwiches—it's especially good with the sweetness of roasted peppers and goat cheese.

■ Slow cookers are a great way to keep foods moist and hot. On sleepy Saturday mornings when you're having weekend guests or serving breakfast in shifts, crank up that slow cooker, and fill it with hot cooked oatmeal or grits. Set out some toppings, such as fresh or dried fruit and yogurt for oatmeal, or shredded cheese, crumbled bacon, and diced tomatoes for grits. Then let people serve themselves.

Glazed Roasted Chicken, Sweet Onion Risotto, snowpeas, page 217

Crispy Sticks, page 211; Garlic Grits, page 211; Flank Steak With Tomato-Olive Relish, page 210; mixed green salad with Creamy Garlic Salad Dressing, page 211

Pumpkin Cake With Little Ghosts, page 212

Trick or Treat Popcorn, page 210

227

Southern Turnip Greens and
Ham Hocks, page 220

228

November

Our Ultimate Thanksgiving Feast

Thanksgiving Menu

Serves 8

Roasted Butternut Squash Bisque With Marmalade Cream

Apple Brandy Turkey   Cornbread Dressing

Double Cranberry-Apple Sauce

Green Beans With Grape Tomatoes

Potato Casserole With Caramelized Onions

Buttery Herb-Cheese Muffins

Ginger-Pear Cobbler

ROASTED BUTTERNUT SQUASH BISQUE

freezeable • make ahead

MAKES 8 SERVINGS

Prep: 30 min., Bake: 45 min., Cook: 30 min., Chill: 8 hrs. *(pictured on page 267)*

1 large butternut squash
2 Granny Smith apples, peeled and cut into 8 wedges
2 large onions, peeled and cut into 1-inch pieces
2 to 2½ cups chicken broth
1 cup fresh orange juice
2 teaspoons grated orange rind
2 teaspoons curry powder
1 teaspoon salt
½ teaspoon freshly ground black pepper
1 cup whipping cream
½ cup milk
Marmalade Cream

CUT squash in half; remove seeds. Place squash, cut side down, apples, and onions on a lightly greased foil-lined baking sheet.
BAKE at 400° for 45 minutes or until squash is tender. Remove from oven; cool. Scoop out squash pulp, discarding shells.

COMBINE pulp, roasted apples, onions, broth, and next 5 ingredients in a Dutch oven. Bring to a boil; reduce heat to medium-low, and simmer, stirring often, 5 minutes. Remove mixture from heat; cool.
PROCESS squash mixture, 1 cup at a time, in a food processor until smooth. Return puree to Dutch oven, and chill 8 hours, if desired. (Or freeze up to 1 month, if desired. Thaw overnight in refrigerator.)
HEAT soup in Dutch oven over low heat. Slowly add cream and milk, stirring constantly until thoroughly heated and smooth. Remove from heat, and top with Marmalade Cream. Serve immediately.

Marmalade Cream:

MAKES 1 CUP
Prep: 10 min.

1 cup sour cream
½ teaspoon curry powder
¼ teaspoon ground nutmeg
2 tablespoons orange marmalade

COMBINE all ingredients, blending well. Cover and chill 8 hours, if desired.

SHERI L. CASTLE
RALEIGH, NORTH CAROLINA

APPLE BRANDY TURKEY

MAKES 10 TO 12 SERVINGS

Prep: 40 min.; Cook: 20 min.; Chill: 8 hrs.; Bake: 3 hrs., 15 min.; Stand: 15 min. *(pictured on page 266)*

1 (12-pound) whole turkey
5 cups apple juice
½ cup firmly packed light brown sugar
¼ cup cider vinegar
Cheesecloth
½ cup chicken broth
¼ cup apple brandy
3 tablespoons honey
¼ cup all-purpose flour
Salt and pepper to taste

DISCARD giblets and neck from turkey. Rinse turkey with cold water; pat dry.
STIR together ½ cup apple juice and brown sugar in a large saucepan over low heat until sugar dissolves. Remove from heat, and add cider vinegar and remaining 4½ cups apple juice.
PLACE turkey in a large roasting pan; cover with cheesecloth. Pour juice mixture over cheesecloth, coating completely. Cover and chill at least 8 hours, spooning marinade over turkey occasionally.
REMOVE turkey from pan, discarding cheesecloth and reserving 3¼ cups marinade. Place turkey on a rack in a large roasting pan. Pour 2½ cups reserved apple cider marinade over turkey.
BAKE at 325° for 3 hours and 15 minutes or until a meat thermometer inserted into thigh registers 172°, basting every 30 minutes with pan juices. Shield with aluminum foil to prevent excessive browning, if necessary. Let stand 15 minutes or until meat thermometer registers 180°.
REMOVE turkey to a serving platter, reserving 2 cups pan drippings. Pour reserved drippings through a wire-mesh strainer into a saucepan, discarding solids. Add ¼ cup reserved marinade, chicken broth, brandy, and honey to saucepan, whisking until smooth.
STIR together flour and remaining ½ cup reserved marinade; stir into broth mixture. Bring to a boil, stirring constantly. Reduce heat to low; cook, stirring often, 15 minutes or until thickened. Add salt and pepper to taste. Serve with turkey.

LISA MARIE STROUP
MARIETTA, GEORGIA

CORNBREAD DRESSING

freezeable • make ahead

MAKES 16 TO 18 SERVINGS

Prep: 45 min.; Cook: 7 min.; Bake: 1 hr., 15 min.

This classic recipe was featured in our "Taste of the South" column last year. It makes one large and one small pan of dressing, so freeze one pan for another meal. *(pictured on page 266)*

    1 cup butter or margarine, divided
    3 cups self-rising white cornmeal mix
    1 cup all-purpose flour
    7 large eggs
    3 cups buttermilk
    3 cups soft, white breadcrumbs
    2 large sweet onions, diced
    4 celery ribs, diced
    ¼ cup finely chopped fresh sage
    ¼ cup finely chopped fresh parsley
    1 tablespoon seasoned pepper
    7 cups chicken broth

PLACE ½ cup butter in a 13- x 9-inch pan; heat in oven at 425° for 4 minutes.
STIR together cornmeal and flour; whisk in 3 eggs and buttermilk.
POUR hot butter into batter, and stir until blended. Pour batter into pan.
BAKE at 425° for 30 minutes or until golden brown. Cool. Crumble cornbread into a large bowl; stir in breadcrumbs, and set aside.
MELT remaining ½ cup butter in a skillet over medium heat; add onions and celery, and sauté 5 minutes. Stir in sage, parsley, and seasoned pepper; sauté 1 minute. Remove from heat, and stir into cornbread mixture.
WHISK together broth and remaining 4 eggs; stir into cornbread mixture. Pour evenly into 1 lightly greased 13- x 9-inch pan and 1 lightly greased 8-inch square pan.
BAKE at 400° for 35 to 40 minutes or until golden brown.

NOTE: For testing purposes only, we used White Lily Self-Rising Buttermilk Cornmeal Mix.

DOUBLE CRANBERRY-APPLE SAUCE

make ahead

MAKES ABOUT 5 CUPS

Prep: 20 min., Cook: 20 min.
(pictured on page 266)

    6 large Granny Smith apples, peeled
        and diced
    1 (12-ounce) package fresh
        cranberries
    1 small lemon, sliced and seeded
    1 cup sugar
    ½ cup water
    ¾ cup sweetened dried cranberries

STIR together first 5 ingredients in a large saucepan; bring to a boil over medium-high heat, stirring often.
REDUCE heat; simmer, stirring often, 15 minutes or until cranberries pop and mixture starts to thicken. Remove from heat, and stir in dried cranberries. Cool. Cover and chill until ready to serve.

NOTE: Mixture can be stored in the refrigerator up to 2 weeks.

BETSY SHROAT
UNION, KENTUCKY

GREEN BEANS WITH GRAPE TOMATOES

make ahead

MAKES 8 SERVINGS

Prep: 15 min., Cook: 18 min.

Grape tomatoes are small and have a sweet flavor like summer tomatoes. Look for them at your local supermarket. *(pictured on page 266)*

    2 pounds fresh green beans, trimmed
    6 tablespoons butter or margarine
    1 pint grape tomatoes, halved
    1 tablespoon chopped fresh thyme
    2 teaspoons sugar
    1 teaspoon salt
    ½ teaspoon pepper

COOK beans in boiling salted water 8 minutes or until crisp-tender; drain. Plunge into ice water to stop the cooking process; drain and set aside.
MELT butter in a large skillet over medium heat 6 to 7 minutes or until butter begins to brown. Add green beans, and sauté until tender. Stir in grape tomatoes and remaining ingredients. Serve immediately.

JANE MENENDEZ
BIRMINGHAM, ALABAMA

POTATO CASSEROLE WITH CARAMELIZED ONIONS

make ahead

MAKES 10 TO 12 SERVINGS

Prep: 45 min., Cook: 55 min., Bake: 35 min.

    ¾ cup butter, divided
    ¼ cup olive oil
    6 large sweet onions, diced
    1 tablespoon sugar
    4 pounds baking potatoes, peeled and
        cubed
    4 cups chicken broth
    1 cup whipping cream
    1 cup sour cream
    4 large eggs, lightly beaten
    ½ teaspoon salt

MELT ¼ cup butter in a large skillet over medium heat. Add olive oil, onions, and sugar. Cook, stirring often, 25 to 30 minutes or until onions are deep golden brown. Remove from heat, and set aside.
BRING potatoes and chicken broth to a boil in a Dutch oven; cook 20 minutes or until tender. Drain. Reserve broth for another use, if desired.
ADD remaining ½ cup butter to potatoes; mash with a potato masher until smooth. Whisk together whipping cream and next 3 ingredients; add to potato mixture, stirring until blended.
SPOON half of potato mixture into a lightly greased 13- x 9-inch baking dish. Spoon caramelized onions evenly over potatoes. Spoon remaining potatoes evenly over onions.
BAKE at 350° for 30 to 35 minutes or until golden.

NOTE: Casserole can be prepared up to 2 days ahead and refrigerated. Remove from refrigerator 30 minutes before baking. Bake at 350° for 40 to 45 minutes or until golden brown.

MICHELL VALENTINE
LITTLE ROCK, ARKANSAS

Cook's Timeline

Prepare a few things each day so making your Thanksgiving feast won't seem so overwhelming.

5 days ahead:
- Plan decorative accents and centerpiece.
- Select serving pieces, table linens, and napkins.

4 days ahead:
- Shop for grocery staples. Purchase produce and fresh herbs.
- Thaw turkey in the refrigerator.
- Prepare Double Cranberry-Apple Sauce, and chill.
- Prepare Cornbread Dressing (do not bake), and freeze.

3 days ahead:
- Bake Buttery Herb-Cheese Muffins, wrap in foil, and freeze.
- Prepare Roasted Butternut Squash Bisque up to puree stage (do not add whipping cream, milk, or Marmalade Cream). Freeze.

2 days ahead:
- Cook green beans until crisp-tender. Place damp paper towels over beans. Cover tightly, and chill.
- Prepare potato casserole (do not bake). Cover and chill.

1 day ahead:
- Cover turkey with cheesecloth; soak with brandy-juice mixture. Chill.
- Prepare Ginger-Pear Cobbler filling, and chill.
- Prepare Marmalade Cream; chill.
- Remove Cornbread Dressing and Roasted Butternut Squash Bisque puree from the freezer. Place in the refrigerator to thaw.
- Set table.
- Pick up flowers, if necessary, and keep in a cool place.

The day of the dinner:
- Roast turkey according to recipe. Keep warm until ready to serve.
- Remove muffins from freezer; thaw at room temperature.
- Remove pear filling from refrigerator. Roll piecrusts according to directions; bake cobbler. Let stand at room temperature until serving.

1½ hours before serving:
- Remove potato casserole and dressing from refrigerator. Let stand at room temperature 30 minutes before baking. Remove from oven; keep warm until serving.

1 hour before serving:
- Heat soup on low. Slowly add whipping cream and milk, stirring constantly until heated.

35 minutes before serving:
- Sauté cooked green beans, then add remaining ingredients.
- Heat muffins until warm.
- Prepare gravy, and slice turkey.

BUTTERY HERB-CHEESE MUFFINS

family favorite

MAKES 2½ DOZEN

Prep: 10 min., Bake: 25 min.

The secret to delectable Buttery Herb-Cheese Muffins is a garlic-and-herb cheese spread from the grocery store. *(pictured on page 266)*

- **2 cups self-rising flour**
- **1 cup butter, melted**
- **1 (6.5-ounce) package garlic-and-herb spreadable cheese, softened**
- **½ cup sour cream**

STIR together all ingredients just until blended.

SPOON muffin batter into lightly greased miniature muffin pans, filling to the top.

BAKE at 350° for 25 minutes or until lightly browned.

NOTE: For testing purposes only, we used Alouette Garlic et Herbes Gourmet Spreadable Cheese.

GINGER-PEAR COBBLER

make ahead

MAKES 10 SERVINGS

Prep: 45 min., Cook: 10 min., Bake: 25 min.

This recipe was inspired by a pie from Caroline Kennedy of Newborn, Georgia. We tweaked it in our Test Kitchens to create a cobbler.

- **12 large firm Bosc pears, peeled and sliced**
- **1 cup firmly packed light brown sugar**
- **¼ cup all-purpose flour**
- **¼ cup butter or margarine**
- **½ cup chopped pecans, toasted**
- **1 tablespoon grated fresh ginger**
- **1 teaspoon grated lemon rind**
- **1 (15-ounce) package refrigerated piecrusts**
- **1 large egg**
- **1 tablespoon water**

TOSS sliced pears with brown sugar and flour.

MELT butter in a large skillet over medium-high heat; add pear mixture, and cook, stirring often, 10 minutes or until tender. Remove from heat, and stir in pecans, ginger, and lemon rind.

SPOON mixture into a lightly greased 2-quart baking dish.

ROLL piecrusts to press out fold lines; cut into ½-inch strips. Arrange strips in a lattice design over filling. Reroll remaining strips and scraps. Cut leaf shapes from piecrust using a small 1-inch leaf-shaped cookie cutter. Use a paring knife to gently score designs in leaves, if desired. Arrange leaves around inner edge of baking dish, forming a decorative border over ends of lattice.

WHISK together egg and 1 tablespoon water; brush over piecrust.

BAKE at 425° for 20 to 25 minutes or until golden brown.

Chill-Chasing Beverages

The season's festivities and cold weather go hand in hand, making this the perfect time of year to enjoy warm drinks. We've chosen this delicious selection with holiday flavors in mind.

HOLIDAY CRANBERRY TEA

fast fixin's

MAKES 8 TO 10 SERVINGS

Prep: 5 min., Cook: 10 min.

- 1 (48-ounce) bottle cranberry juice cocktail
- 1 cup firmly packed brown sugar
- 1 cup orange juice
- 1 cup lemonade
- 1 cup pineapple juice
- 3 to 4 (3-inch) cinnamon sticks

COMBINE all ingredients in a Dutch oven over low heat. Cook, stirring occasionally, 10 minutes or until sugar dissolves. Remove cinnamon sticks before serving. Serve warm.

LISA RUST
LUMBERTON, NORTH CAROLINA

HOT CIDER PUNCH

MAKES 8 SERVINGS

Prep: 5 min., Cook: 1 hr.

- 1 (64-ounce) bottle apple cider
- 2 cups orange juice
- ¾ cup fresh lemon juice
- ¼ cup honey
- 10 whole allspice
- 5 whole cloves
- 1 (2½-inch) cinnamon stick
- 1 lemon, sliced

BRING first 7 ingredients to a boil in a Dutch oven; reduce heat, and simmer 1 hour. Pour mixture through a wire-mesh strainer into a container; discard spices. Add lemon slices to punch just before serving. Serve warm.

MULLED WINE

fast fixin's

MAKES 10 SERVINGS

Prep: 5 min., Cook: 15 min.

Four women on Hilton Head Island formed Yuletide Publishing to raise money for health and human services agencies on the island. We adapted this fabulous recipe from their book, *Yuletide on Hilton Head* (Yuletide Publishing Committee, Inc., 1999). Order it from your local bookseller or from **www.coastaldiscovery.org.**

- 2 cups water
- 2 cups sugar
- 1 orange, sliced
- 1 lemon, sliced
- 2 (2½-inch) cinnamon sticks
- 12 whole cloves
- 12 allspice berries
- 2 (750-milliliter) bottles or 1 (1.5-liter) bottle dry red wine
- Garnish: cinnamon sticks

COMBINE first 7 ingredients in a Dutch oven over medium heat; bring to a boil, reduce heat, and simmer 5 minutes. Add wine; simmer 10 minutes. Pour mixture through a wire-mesh strainer into a container; discard solids. Garnish, if desired.

NOTE: For testing purposes only, we used Gallo Hearty Burgundy wine.

BOURBON-BARREL COFFEE

fast fixin's

MAKES 4 SERVINGS

Prep: 10 min.

This recipe is inspired by a coffee drink served by The Oakroom restaurant at The Seelbach Hilton Hotel in Louisville. For a gentler brew, omit the ¾ cup bourbon.

- ¾ cup bourbon
- Bourbon Syrup
- 3 cups hot brewed coffee
- Whipped cream

PLACE 3 tablespoons bourbon and 2 tablespoons Bourbon Syrup in each of 4 coffee cups. Stir ¾ cup hot brewed coffee into each mug. Top with whipped cream.

Bourbon Syrup:

MAKES 2 CUPS

Prep: 5 min., Cook: 10 min.

Use leftover syrup on waffles, pancakes, roasted bananas, or ice cream. Or add to iced tea along with fresh mint for a refreshing tea julep. You can purchase superfine sugar at the supermarket, or make your own by processing granulated sugar in a food processor until powdery.

- 1 cup superfine sugar
- 1 cup firmly packed light brown sugar
- 1 cup water
- 1 cup bourbon

BRING superfine sugar, brown sugar, and 1 cup water to a boil in a small saucepan over medium-high heat; cook 10 minutes until reduced by half. Remove from heat, and stir in bourbon.

NOTE: For testing purposes only, we used Maker's Mark Bourbon.

Breadmaking Made Simple

Here's how to surprise your guests
(and yourself) with a homemade loaf of bread
or a plate of pleasing sweet rolls.

Assistant Foods Editor Joy Zacharia suggested writing a from-scratch bread story because she thinks she's challenged in the bread-baking department. Fortunately, Rebecca Gordon, one of our Test Kitchens professionals, took the mystery out of baking bread by documenting every step in understandable language. Try and savor these fantastic recipes. You'll definitely want to bake the heavenly sweet roll variations. They start with frozen bread dough, so they're super-easy to make, and the taste is nothing less than awesome.

BRAIDED EGG BREAD

MAKES 2 LOAVES

Prep: 25 min., Stand: 5 min., Rise: 1 hr.,
Bake: 25 min.

This slightly sweet bread is also known as challah (pronounced KHAH-lah). It's delicious for French toast. (pictured on pages 262–263)

- 1½ cups fat-free milk
- 2 (¼-ounce) envelopes active dry yeast
- 5½ cups all-purpose flour
- 1 teaspoon salt
- ¼ cup shortening
- ½ cup egg substitute
- 1 egg yolk
- ½ cup honey
- All-purpose flour
- 1 egg, lightly beaten
- 1 teaspoon sesame seeds (optional)

PREHEAT oven to 200°.

MICROWAVE 1½ cups milk at HIGH in a microwave-safe glass bowl 2 to 3 minutes or until heated. Stir in yeast; let stand 5 minutes.

COMBINE 5½ cups flour and salt in a large bowl; stir in yeast mixture. Add shortening and next 3 ingredients. Beat at low speed with an electric mixer 1 to 2 minutes. Beat at medium speed 5 more minutes.

SPRINKLE dough with additional flour, and remove from bowl. (Dough will be very sticky.) Place dough in a lightly greased bowl, turning to grease top. Turn off oven. Cover bowl with plastic wrap, and let rise in oven 30 minutes or until doubled in bulk. Remove from oven. Remove and discard plastic wrap.

PUNCH dough down, and divide in half. Divide each half into 3 equal portions. Roll each portion into a 14-inch-long rope; pinch 3 ropes together at 1 end to seal, and braid. Repeat with remaining dough portions. Place braids on a parchment paper-lined baking sheet.

COVER braids with plastic wrap, and let rise in a warm place, free from drafts, 25 to 30 minutes or until doubled in bulk. Brush evenly with beaten egg, and sprinkle with sesame seeds, if desired.

BAKE at 350° for 25 minutes or until golden. (A wooden pick should come out clean.)

PENNY ABRAMS
SARASOTA, FLORIDA

POTATO-CARAMELIZED ONION BUNS

MAKES ABOUT 2 DOZEN

Prep: 35 min., Stand: 5 min., Rise: 50 min.,
Bake: 18 min.

We added caramelized onions to reader Virginia Ann Towne's wonderful Potato Bread recipe. Serve meaty cheeseburgers or grilled fish inside these delicious buns. (pictured on pages 262–263)

- 2 cups warm water (100° to 110°)
- 3 (¼-ounce) envelopes active dry yeast
- 1 cup refrigerated or frozen mashed potatoes, thawed and warmed
- 2 tablespoons sugar
- 2 tablespoons butter, melted
- 7 cups plus 1 tablespoon all-purpose flour
- 1 tablespoon salt
- Caramelized Onions
- 1 egg, lightly beaten
- 1½ teaspoons poppy seeds (optional)

PREHEAT oven to 200°.

STIR together 2 cups warm water and yeast in a large mixing bowl of a heavy-duty electric stand mixer until dissolved. Let stand 5 minutes.

ADD potatoes, sugar, and butter to yeast mixture; beat at medium speed, using dough hook attachment, until blended. Add 7 cups flour and salt; beat at low speed 2 minutes. Add Caramelized Onions, and beat at medium speed 5 minutes. (Dough will be very sticky.) Sprinkle dough with remaining 1 tablespoon flour, and remove from bowl.

SHAPE into a ball, and place in a lightly greased bowl, turning to grease top. Turn off oven. Cover bowl with plastic wrap, and let rise in oven 30 minutes or until doubled in bulk.

REMOVE from oven. Remove and discard plastic wrap. Punch dough down, and turn out onto a lightly floured surface. Divide into 21 portions.

SHAPE each portion into a ball with floured hands. Place no more than 8 balls on each parchment paper-lined baking sheet. Cover with plastic wrap; let rise again in a warm place, free from drafts, for 15 to 20 minutes or until doubled in bulk. Brush with egg, and sprinkle with poppy seeds, if desired.

BAKE buns at 350° for 15 to 18 minutes or until golden brown. Remove from pans, and cool on wire racks.

Caramelized Onions:

MAKES 2 CUPS

Prep: 10 min., Cook: 20 min.

¼ cup butter
2 large sweet onions, chopped
½ teaspoon salt

MELT butter in a large skillet over medium heat; add onions and salt, and sauté 20 minutes or until caramel-colored. Cool.

VIRGINIA ANN TOWNE
LANSING, MICHIGAN

DRIED CHERRY-WALNUT SWEET ROLLS

MAKES ABOUT 2 DOZEN

Prep: 10 min., Rise: 30 min., Bake: 15 min.
(pictured on pages 262–263)

1 (25-ounce) package frozen roll dough, thawed according to package instructions
½ cup chopped walnuts
¼ cup butter, melted
1 (3-ounce) package dried cherries, chopped
3 tablespoons granulated sugar
¾ teaspoon pumpkin pie spice
2 cups powdered sugar
3 tablespoons hot water

PREHEAT oven to 200°.
PLACE dough balls in 2 greased 9-inch round cakepans. Turn off oven. Cover dough balls with plastic wrap; let rise in oven 25 to 30 minutes or until doubled in bulk. Remove from oven. Remove and discard plastic wrap.
STIR together walnuts and next 4 ingredients. Sprinkle over dough in pans.
BAKE at 350° for 12 to 15 minutes or until golden brown. Cool.
STIR together powdered sugar and 3 tablespoons hot water. Drizzle evenly over rolls.

PECAN-GOLDEN RAISIN SWEET ROLLS: Omit walnuts, cherries, sugar, and pumpkin pie spice. Replace with 1½ cups chopped pecans, ½ cup golden raisins, ½ cup firmly packed dark brown sugar, and ¾ teaspoon apple pie spice, stirring together with melted butter. Proceed as directed.

APRICOT-ORANGE SWEET ROLLS: Omit walnuts, cherries, 1 tablespoon granulated sugar, and pumpkin pie spice. Replace with 1 (6-ounce) package dried apricots, chopped, and 1 tablespoon grated orange rind, stirring together with melted butter. Proceed as directed. Omit hot water, and replace with 3 tablespoons fresh orange juice, stirring together with powdered sugar. Proceed as directed.

NOTE: For testing purposes only, we used Rich's Enriched Homestyle Roll Dough.

Quick & Easy

Pizza at Home

CHICKEN FAJITA PIZZA

family favorite

MAKES 4 TO 6 SERVINGS

Prep: 15 min., Cook: 10 min., Bake: 12 min.

½ (24-ounce) package refrigerated pizza crusts
2 skinned and boned chicken breast halves, cut into strips
1 tablespoon vegetable oil
2 teaspoons chili powder
1 teaspoon salt
½ teaspoon garlic powder
1 small onion, sliced
1 small green bell pepper, chopped
1 cup salsa
1 (8-ounce) package shredded Monterey Jack cheese
Toppings: diced tomatoes, shredded lettuce, sour cream

PLACE crust on a lightly greased baking sheet.

SAUTÉ chicken in hot oil in a skillet over medium-high heat 5 minutes or until tender. Stir in chili powder, salt, and garlic powder. Remove from skillet; set aside.
ADD onion and bell pepper to skillet; sauté 5 minutes or until tender.
SPREAD crust with salsa; top with chicken, onion mixture, and cheese.
BAKE at 425° for 10 to 12 minutes or until cheese melts. Serve with desired toppings.

NOTE: For testing purposes only, we used Mama Mary's Gourmet Pizza Crusts.

TAMORA CORNWALL
CHARLOTTE, NORTH CAROLINA

PEPPERS-AND-CHEESE PIZZA

family favorite

MAKES 4 TO 6 SERVINGS

Prep: 15 min., Cook: 5 min., Bake: 18 min.

1 medium onion, diced
1 medium-size green bell pepper, diced
1 large banana pepper, diced
3 garlic cloves, minced
¼ cup olive oil, divided
4 ounces cream cheese, softened
2 ounces feta cheese, crumbled
1 tablespoon dried basil
1 tablespoon dried oregano
1 tablespoon dried sage
¼ teaspoon salt
½ (24-ounce) package refrigerated pizza crusts
½ cup shredded Parmesan cheese

SAUTÉ first 4 ingredients in 2 tablespoons olive oil in a large skillet over medium-high heat 5 minutes or until tender. Remove from heat, and set aside.
STIR together remaining 2 tablespoons olive oil, cream cheese, feta cheese, and next 4 ingredients until blended.
PLACE crust on a lightly greased baking sheet. Spread with cream cheese mixture; sprinkle with onion mixture and Parmesan cheese.
BAKE at 400° for 15 to 18 minutes or until cheese is melted.

NOTE: For testing purposes only, we used Mama Mary's Gourmet Pizza Crusts.

MARIAN LOVENE GRIFFEY
GAINESVILLE, FLORIDA

SEAFOOD ALFREDO PIZZA

family favorite

MAKES 4 TO 6 SERVINGS

Prep: 20 min., Cook: 12 min., Bake: 12 min., Stand: 5 min.

- 1 (16-ounce) package dry Alfredo sauce mix
- 1 pound unpeeled, medium-size fresh shrimp
- 3 bacon slices
- 1 medium onion, thinly sliced
- 2 garlic cloves, minced
- 2 ounces bay scallops
- 1 teaspoon dried oregano
- ¼ teaspoon pepper
- 1 (16-ounce) package prebaked Italian pizza crust
- ⅓ cup shredded Parmesan cheese
- 1 teaspoon dried parsley
- 2 plum tomatoes, chopped
- 1 (8-ounce) package shredded mozzarella cheese

PREPARE Alfredo sauce according to package directions.

PEEL shrimp, and devein, if desired.

COOK bacon in a nonstick skillet until crisp; remove bacon, reserving drippings in skillet. Drain bacon on paper towels; crumble.

ADD onion and garlic to skillet, and sauté over medium-high heat until tender. Add scallops and shrimp, and sauté 2 minutes. Stir in oregano and pepper. Remove from heat.

PLACE crust on a baking sheet; spread with Alfredo sauce. Sprinkle evenly with seafood mixture, bacon, Parmesan cheese, and remaining ingredients.

BAKE at 400° for 12 minutes or until cheese is melted. Let stand 5 minutes.

NOTE: For testing purposes only, we used Boboli for prebaked pizza crust.

JOHN KENNEY
MARCO ISLAND, FLORIDA

Living Light

Supper With All the Trimmings

Nowadays it's not unusual to have a family member or friend who doesn't eat meat. Here, Crescent Dragonwagon of Arkansas shares a few of the more than 1,000 recipes from her cookbook, *Passionate Vegetarian* (Workman Publishing Company, Inc., 2002). This menu is so good, you'll gladly serve it to meat lovers too. It's perfect with Thanksgiving dinner or anytime you want to impress.

BUTTERNUT SQUASH-LIME SOUP

vegetarian

MAKES 6 SERVINGS

Prep: 20 min., Cook: 35 min., Bake: 5 min.

Make peeling butternut squash easy by cutting off ends, then standing squash on wide end and cutting off peel from top to bottom using a sharp knife. Once peeled, cut horizontally in half, remove seeds, and cut into pieces. This recipe is adapted from Crescent's Lime Soup Yucatán.

- 8 cups vegetable broth
- 1 butternut squash, peeled and cut into ¾-inch pieces
- ½ cup fresh lime juice
- 1 teaspoon dried sage leaves
- 3 to 6 whole cloves
- 1 garlic bulb, chopped and divided
- 1 large onion, chopped
- Vegetable cooking spray
- 1 to 2 serrano or jalapeño peppers, seeded and minced
- ½ cup canned diced tomatoes
- 4 (6-inch) corn tortillas, cut into ½-inch strips
- ½ cup fresh cilantro leaves
- ½ teaspoon pepper
- ¼ teaspoon salt
- 1 teaspoon Dragon Salt
- 1 lime, thinly sliced (optional)

BRING first 5 ingredients and half of garlic to a boil in a Dutch oven; reduce heat, and simmer 20 minutes. Remove and discard cloves.

SAUTÉ onion in a large skillet coated with cooking spray over medium-high heat 5 minutes or until tender. Add peppers and remaining garlic; sauté 1 to 2 minutes. Add ½ cup broth mixture, stirring to loosen particles from bottom of skillet. Stir onion mixture and diced tomatoes into soup.

PLACE tortilla strips on a baking sheet. Bake at 350° for 5 minutes or until crisp.

ADD cilantro, pepper, salt, and 1 teaspoon Dragon Salt to soup. Ladle into bowls; top with toasted tortilla strips and, if desired, lime slices.

Dragon Salt:

MAKES ABOUT 1½ CUPS

Prep: 5 min.

This mixture is terrific as a dry rub for steaks, chicken, and pork chops, and even sprinkled on hot popcorn.

- ⅓ cup coarse-grain sea salt
- ⅓ cup coarsely ground black pepper
- ¼ cup ground red pepper
- ¼ cup dried dillweed
- 2 tablespoons paprika
- 1 tablespoon dried basil
- 1 tablespoon celery seeds

COMBINE all ingredients. Store in an airtight container.

Calories (per 2-cup serving of soup) 116 (9% from fat); Fat 1.3g (sat 0g, mono 0g, poly 0.2g); Protein 3.6g; Carb 25g; Fiber 4.2g; Chol 0mg; Iron 1.8mg; Sodium 862mg; Calc 109mg

---

Vegetarian Dinner

Serves 6

Butternut Squash-Lime Soup

Polenta Lasagna With Cream Sauce

Salad With Dijon Vinaigrette

POLENTA LASAGNA WITH CREAM SAUCE

vegetarian

MAKES 6 SERVINGS

Prep: 20 min., Cook: 10 min., Bake: 40 min., Broil: 5 min., Stand: 15 min.

This recipe is adapted from Crescent's Polenta Lasagna With Sauce Soubise.

- ½ pound fresh shiitake mushrooms
- ½ large onion, sliced
- Vegetable cooking spray
- ½ (8-ounce) container fresh button mushrooms, sliced
- ¾ cup 1% low-fat milk
- 2 tablespoons cornstarch
- 2 tablespoons 1% low-fat milk
- ¼ cup ⅓-less-fat cream cheese, softened
- ¼ cup dry white wine
- ¾ teaspoon salt
- ¼ teaspoon freshly ground pepper
- ¼ teaspoon ground nutmeg
- Cream Sauce
- 2 (17-ounce) tubes plain or pesto-flavored polenta, cut into ½-inch slices
- ½ cup grated Parmesan cheese, divided

REMOVE stems from shiitake mushrooms, and thinly slice.

SAUTÉ onion in a large nonstick skillet coated with cooking spray over high heat 3 minutes. Add shiitake and button mushrooms, and sauté 3 to 4 minutes or until onion is tender. Add ¾ cup milk, and bring to a simmer.

WHISK together cornstarch and 2 tablespoons milk; stir into mushroom mixture. Add cream cheese and wine, stirring until blended. Remove from heat. Stir in salt, pepper, and nutmeg.

SPREAD 3 tablespoons Cream Sauce in a 13- x 9-inch baking dish coated with cooking spray. Layer one-third of polenta slices over sauce. Sprinkle ¼ cup Parmesan cheese over polenta. Top with mushroom mixture. Top with one-third of polenta slices and remaining Cream Sauce; top sauce with remaining polenta slices.

BAKE at 375° for 35 to 40 minutes or until bubbly. Sprinkle with remaining ¼ cup Parmesan. Broil at high 3 to 5 minutes or until cheese is lightly browned. Remove from heat. Cover loosely with aluminum foil, and let stand 15 minutes before serving.

NOTE: For testing purposes only, we used Marjon Original Polenta found in the produce section of the supermarket.

Cream Sauce:

MAKES 5 CUPS

Prep: 20 min.; Cook: 1 hr., 15 min.

- 3 large onions, diced
- 2 teaspoons water
- ¼ teaspoon soy sauce
- Vegetable cooking spray
- 3¾ cups unflavored soymilk, divided
- ¾ medium onion, unpeeled
- 1 celery rib, cut into 3-inch pieces
- 6 whole cloves
- 3 bay leaves
- ¼ teaspoon ground nutmeg
- 2 tablespoons butter or margarine
- 2 tablespoons all-purpose flour
- 4½ teaspoons cornstarch
- 1 teaspoon salt
- ¾ teaspoon pepper

COOK first 3 ingredients in a large non-stick skillet coated with cooking spray, covered, over low heat 45 minutes or until onions are very tender, stirring occasionally. Remove from heat.

RESERVE 2 tablespoons soymilk, and set aside. Bring remaining soymilk, unpeeled onion, and next 4 ingredients to a gentle boil in a medium saucepan; reduce heat, and simmer 15 minutes.

MELT butter in a nonstick skillet over medium heat. Stir in flour, and cook, stirring constantly, 2 to 3 minutes or until flour is lightly browned.

POUR soymilk mixture through a wire-mesh strainer into a bowl, discarding solids. Whisk soymilk mixture into butter mixture; bring to a boil. Reduce heat, and simmer 6 minutes or until thickened.

STIR together cornstarch and reserved 2 tablespoons soymilk until smooth. Whisk cornstarch mixture into soymilk mixture, whisking until thickened. Remove from heat. Stir in diced onion mixture, salt, and pepper.

Calories 374 (25% from fat); Fat 11g (sat 5.3g, mono 2.8g, poly 2g); Protein 17g; Carb 51g; Fiber 5.3g; Chol 23mg; Iron 3.2mg; Sodium 1,255mg; Calc 219mg. Reduce sodium by omitting salt when preparing this recipe. Packaged polenta contains salt.

SALAD WITH DIJON VINAIGRETTE

fast fixin's • vegetarian

MAKES 6 SERVINGS

Prep: 15 min.

This recipe is adapted from Crescent's Salad of Local Greens With Sharp Classic Vinaigrette With a Bite.

- 6 to 8 cups mixed salad greens
- 1 cup very thinly sliced red or green cabbage
- Dijon Vinaigrette
- 1 lemon, halved (optional)
- Freshly ground black pepper to taste
- ¼ cup freshly grated Parmesan cheese

PLACE salad greens and cabbage in a large bowl. Drizzle 2 to 3 tablespoons Dijon Vinaigrette over greens, and squeeze lemon over salad, if desired. Sprinkle with pepper and cheese. Serve immediately.

Dijon Vinaigrette:

MAKES ABOUT 1¾ CUPS

Prep: 5 min.

- ½ cup cider vinegar
- ¼ cup coarse-grained Dijon mustard
- 4 to 6 garlic cloves
- ½ teaspoon salt
- ¼ to ½ teaspoon pepper
- 1 cup extra-virgin olive oil

PROCESS first 5 ingredients in a blender or food processor until smooth. With blender or processor running, add oil in a slow, steady stream; process until smooth.

NOTE: Store remaining dressing in refrigerator up to 1 week.

Calories (including 1 tablespoon dressing) 108 (78% from fat); Fat 9.4g (sat 1.8g, mono 6.5g, poly 0.8g); Protein 2.9g; Carb 4.1g; Fiber 2.1g; Chol 2.6mg; Iron 1.2mg; Sodium 171mg; Calc 96mg

Make a Party Around These Appetizers

If you're planning a party, you can't go wrong with these make-ahead appetizers. Two of our favorites are Baby Hot Browns and hearty pork tenderloin with a zesty mustard sauce served with Quick Whipping Cream Biscuits. The Cranberry-Cheese Box is a breeze to prepare, but creating the look of a package will take extra time. If you're in a hurry, just roll it into a ball or log, then serve with crackers. Accompany with Pinot Noir or Viognier wine.

CRANBERRY-CHEESE BOX

make ahead

MAKES 12 TO 16 APPETIZER SERVINGS

Prep: 20 min., Chill: 8 hrs. *(pictured on page 264)*

- 1 (16-ounce) block sharp Cheddar cheese, shredded
- 1 cup mayonnaise
- ½ cup chopped onion
- ¼ teaspoon salt
- ¼ teaspoon black pepper
- ¼ to ½ teaspoon ground red pepper
- 1 cup chopped pecans, toasted
- 1 (8-ounce) can whole-berry cranberry sauce
- Garnishes: green onion strips, fresh cranberries, orange curls
- Crackers or bread rounds

BEAT first 6 ingredients at medium speed with an electric mixer until blended; stir in pecans. Shape mixture into a 5- x 2-inch box, or spoon into a 5-cup mold. Cover and chill 8 hours or up to 2 days.

SPOON cranberry sauce over cheese mixture; garnish, if desired. Serve with crackers or bread rounds.

NOTE: To decorate the box, cut white part from 4 green onions. Blanch green onion tops in boiling water 1 minute or until tender, saving white part for other uses. Drain. Press 1 green onion strip into base of center of 1 side of box, pressing up sides until it meets center of top of box. Remove and discard excess green onion. Repeat with remaining green onion strips. Top center with fresh cranberries, orange curls, and additional strips of green onion, if desired.

BABY HOT BROWNS

make ahead

MAKES 2 DOZEN

Prep: 30 min., Broil: 4 min., Cook: 10 min., Bake: 2 min.

This warm sandwich combines turkey, a rich cheese sauce, bacon, and tomatoes. *(pictured on page 264)*

- 24 pumpernickel party rye bread slices
- 3 tablespoons butter or margarine
- 3 tablespoons all-purpose flour
- 1 cup milk
- 1½ cups (6 ounces) shredded sharp Cheddar cheese
- 1½ cups diced cooked turkey
- ¼ teaspoon salt
- ¼ teaspoon ground red pepper
- ½ cup freshly grated Parmesan cheese
- 6 bacon slices, cooked, crumbled, and divided
- 5 plum tomatoes, thinly sliced

ARRANGE bread slices on a lightly greased baking sheet. Broil 6 inches from heat for 3 to 4 minutes.

MELT butter in a saucepan over low heat; add flour, and cook, whisking constantly, until smooth. Gradually whisk in milk; cook over medium heat, whisking constantly, until mixture is thickened and bubbly. Add Cheddar cheese, whisking until cheese melts. Stir in diced turkey, salt, and ground red pepper.

TOP bread evenly with warm cheese-turkey mixture. Sprinkle evenly with Parmesan cheese and half of bacon.

BAKE at 500° for 2 minutes or until Parmesan is melted. Top with tomato slices, and sprinkle evenly with remaining bacon.

TO MAKE AHEAD: Prepare the cheese-turkey mixture, cook the bacon, and grate the Parmesan the day before. To reheat cheese mixture, place pan over low heat, stirring constantly, until smooth and warm. Assemble and proceed as directed.

PORK TENDERLOIN WITH MUSTARD SAUCE

MAKES 12 APPETIZER SERVINGS

Prep: 10 min., Stand: 40 min., Grill: 24 min.

- 1½ pounds pork tenderloins
- ¼ cup soy sauce
- ¼ cup bourbon or apple juice
- 2 tablespoons brown sugar
- ⅓ cup sour cream
- ⅓ cup mayonnaise
- 1 tablespoon dry mustard
- 1 tablespoon minced onion
- 1½ teaspoons white vinegar

PRICK pork tenderloins several times with a fork. Combine soy sauce, bourbon, and sugar in a shallow dish or zip-top freezer bag; add tenderloins. Cover or seal; let stand 30 minutes at room temperature, or, if desired, chill 8 hours.

REMOVE pork from marinade, discarding marinade.

GRILL, covered with grill lid, over medium-high heat (350° to 400°) 12 minutes on each side or until a meat thermometer inserted into thickest portion registers 155°. Let stand 10 minutes before slicing.

STIR together sour cream and next 4 ingredients; serve with pork.

NOTE: Pork tenderloins can be baked at 500° for 20 to 25 minutes instead of grilled.

QUICK WHIPPING CREAM BISCUITS

fast fixin's • make ahead

MAKES 2 DOZEN

Prep: 10 min., Bake: 15 min.

- 1 cup butter or margarine
- 4 cups self-rising flour
- 1¾ to 2 cups whipping cream
- ½ cup butter or margarine, melted

CUT 1 cup butter into flour with a pastry blender or fork until crumbly. Add whipping cream, stirring just until dry ingredients are moistened.

TURN dough out onto a lightly floured surface, and knead lightly 3 or 4 times. Roll or pat dough to ¾-inch thickness. Cut with a 2-inch round cutter, and place biscuits on a lightly greased baking sheet.

BAKE at 400° for 13 to 15 minutes. Brush warm biscuits with melted butter.

Tricks With Turkey

Every holiday season leaves us with the question: What to do with all the leftovers? The turkey, in particular, seems to remain in abundance, even after feeding family, friends, and neighbors. Here are some recipes to help with the answer. Refreshing salad, cornbread dumpling soup, and a simple casserole will help you enjoy your leftovers in a whole new way. For another great turkey recipe, see "What's for Supper?" on page 257.

TURKEY SOUP WITH CORNBREAD DRESSING DUMPLINGS

family favorite

MAKES ABOUT 4 QUARTS

Prep: 20 min., Cook: 45 min.

See "From Our Kitchen" on page 274 for tips on adding fresh flavor to canned chicken broth.

> 1 tablespoon butter or margarine
> 1 large sweet onion, diced (about 1½ cups)
> 1 garlic clove, minced
> 1 celery rib, diced
> 2½ quarts chicken broth
> 3 cups chopped cooked turkey
> 1 cup frozen green peas
> 3 carrots, sliced
> 2 medium potatoes, peeled and diced
> 1 teaspoon pepper
> Cornbread Dressing Dumpling Dough

MELT butter in a large 8-quart stockpot. Add onion, garlic, and celery; sauté over medium-high heat 3 minutes. Add chicken broth and next 5 ingredients. Bring to a boil; reduce heat, and simmer 20 minutes, stirring occasionally.

DROP Cornbread Dressing Dumpling Dough by tablespoonfuls into simmering soup. Cook 5 minutes. Cover and cook 15 more minutes or until dumplings are done.

Cornbread Dressing Dumpling Dough:

MAKES ABOUT 1½ CUPS DOUGH

Prep: 10 min., Cook: 3 min.

> 2 tablespoons butter or margarine
> 1 celery rib, diced
> ½ small sweet onion, diced (about ¼ cup)
> ½ teaspoon rubbed sage
> ¾ cup cornmeal
> ½ cup all-purpose flour
> 1 teaspoon baking powder
> 1 teaspoon seasoned pepper
> ½ teaspoon salt
> 1 large egg, lightly beaten
> ⅓ cup milk

MELT butter in a small skillet. Add celery, onion, and sage; sauté over medium-high heat 3 minutes.

COMBINE cornmeal and next 4 ingredients in a medium bowl; add egg, milk, and celery mixture, stirring until dry ingredients are moistened.

CHARLES STENSRUD
SLIDELL, LOUISIANA

TURKEY-WALNUT SALAD

MAKES 10 SERVINGS

Prep: 15 min., Chill: 30 min. *(pictured on page 265)*

> 2 cups chopped cooked turkey
> ½ cup dried cranberries
> ½ cup light mayonnaise
> ¼ cup chopped walnuts, toasted
> 3 tablespoons chopped fresh parsley
> 2 tablespoons Dijon mustard
> 2 celery ribs, sliced
> 1 small red onion, chopped (about ½ cup)
> ¼ teaspoon salt
> ¼ teaspoon freshly ground pepper
> Mixed salad greens

STIR together first 10 ingredients in a large bowl.

COVER and chill at least 30 minutes. Serve over salad greens.

NORIE BERNDT
PEARLAND, TEXAS

TURKEY-AND-SAUSAGE WILD RICE CASSEROLE

family favorite

MAKES 6 SERVINGS

Prep: 40 min., Cook: 30 min., Bake: 30 min.

> 1 (6-ounce) package long-grain and wild rice mix
> 1 pound hot or mild ground pork sausage
> 1 medium onion, chopped
> ⅓ cup red bell pepper, diced
> 1 cup sliced fresh mushrooms
> 1 (8-ounce) can sliced water chestnuts, drained
> ¼ cup all-purpose flour
> ¼ teaspoon pepper
> 1½ cups chicken broth
> ¾ cup milk
> 2 cups chopped cooked turkey
> Fresh chopped parsley (optional)

COOK rice according to package directions. Set aside.

BROWN sausage in a large skillet over medium heat about 10 minutes, stirring until sausage crumbles and is no longer pink. Add onion and bell pepper to sausage mixture, and sauté 3 minutes or until vegetables are tender. Drain. Return sausage mixture to skillet over medium-high heat, and add mushrooms and water chestnuts. Sauté 3 minutes or until mushrooms are tender.

WHISK in flour and pepper; cook, s constantly, 1 minute. Whisk in chicken broth and milk; cook 7 to 8 minutes or until thickened and bubbly. Remove from heat. Stir together rice, sausage mixture, and turkey. Transfer to a lightly greased 13- x 9-inch baking dish. Bake at 350° for 25 to 30 minutes or until thoroughly heated. Top with parsley, if desired.

LINDA MORTEN
KATY, TEXAS

HOLIDAY DINNERS®

Celebrate Southern food and style with these fantastic recipes and great tips. Whether you need easy appetizers for an open house, an impressive dessert for a potluck, or an entire menu for a special dinner, this is your guide to the most delicious time of the year.

Food, Fun, and Tradition

Festive Feast

Serves 6 to 8

Extra-Creamy Dried Beef Dip

Marinated Beef Tenderloin

Sugar-and-Spice Acorn Squash

Italian Green Beans With Onion and Basil

Spinach-and-Strawberry Salad With Tart Poppy Seed Dressing

For almost 30 years, a group of 16 friends from Midwest City, Oklahoma, has met once a month to share a meal and a good time. The tradition began with a birthday party. "We found out that we all got along, so one thing led to another, and we started having dinner together every month," says Bette Leone. "Along the way, we've lent each other a helping hand and offered advice on raising kids—now it's the grandchildren."

"We definitely have similar tastes in food and cooking," says Pat Padgham. "Plus, we're all pretty good in the kitchen,

so that makes it fun," she adds with a big smile. The group finds there's no better time to celebrate their special kinship than during the Christmas season. According to Pat, some of their favorite holiday recipes over the years have been Marinated Beef Tenderloin, Spinach-and-Strawberry Salad With Tart Poppy Seed Dressing, and Italian Green Beans With Onion and Basil, all of which we're happy to share with you. Through these wonderful recipes, you and your family can enjoy a little bit of Oklahoma-style charm and hospitality.

EXTRA-CREAMY DRIED BEEF DIP

MAKES 8 TO 10 SERVINGS
Prep: 15 min., Bake: 20 min.

This updated version of a classic dip uses bell pepper, garlic powder, and pecans for a flavor boost.

- 2 (8-ounce) packages cream cheese, softened
- 1 (8-ounce) container sour cream
- ¼ cup milk
- ¼ teaspoon garlic powder
- ¼ teaspoon pepper
- 2 (2-ounce) jars dried beef, chopped
- 1 green or red bell pepper, chopped (about ½ cup)
- ¼ cup finely chopped onion
- ½ cup chopped pecans
- Assorted crackers or bagel chips

BEAT first 5 ingredients at medium speed with an electric mixer until blended; stir in beef, bell pepper, and onion. Spoon into a 2½-quart baking dish; sprinkle with pecans.

BAKE at 350° for 20 minutes. Serve immediately with crackers or bagel chips.

EXTRA-CREAMY SMOKED SALMON DIP: Substitute 4 ounces smoked salmon for dried beef, dried chives for finely chopped onion, and add ¼ teaspoon salt to mixture. Omit chopped pecans.

PAT PADGHAM
MIDWEST CITY, OKLAHOMA

MARINATED BEEF TENDERLOIN

family favorite • make ahead

MAKES 8 SERVINGS

Prep: 15 min., Chill: 8 hrs., Bake: 50 min.,
Stand: 10 min.

Determine doneness with an instant-read meat
thermometer. Our tenderloin registered about 135°
after 40 minutes. Let it stand until the temperature
reaches 145° (medium rare). *(pictured on page 1)*

- 1 cup port wine
- 1 cup soy sauce
- ½ cup olive oil
- 1 teaspoon pepper
- 1 teaspoon dried thyme
- ½ teaspoon hot sauce
- 4 garlic cloves, minced
- 1 bay leaf
- 1 (5-pound) trimmed beef tenderloin

COMBINE first 8 ingredients in a large
shallow dish or zip-top freezer bag; add
beef. Cover or seal, and chill 8 hours,
turning occasionally.
REMOVE beef from marinade, discarding marinade. Place on a rack in a roasting pan.
BAKE at 425° for 40 to 50 minutes or to
desired degree of doneness. Cover
loosely with foil, and let tenderloin stand
10 minutes before slicing.

JEAN ISON
MIDWEST CITY, OKLAHOMA

SUGAR-AND-SPICE ACORN SQUASH

MAKES 8 SERVINGS

Prep: 10 min., Bake: 47 min.

This simple recipe works well with a spicy entrée
or other more intensely flavored sides.

- 2 large acorn squash (about 2 pounds each)
- ¼ teaspoon salt
- ¼ teaspoon pepper
- ¼ cup butter or margarine, melted
- ¼ cup firmly packed brown sugar
- ¼ to ½ teaspoon ground nutmeg

CUT each squash into fourths lengthwise; remove and discard seeds and
membranes. Sprinkle evenly with salt
and pepper. Place, cut side down, on an
aluminum foil-lined baking sheet.
BAKE at 400° for 40 minutes or until
squash is tender.
COMBINE butter, brown sugar, and nutmeg. Turn squash, cut side up, on baking sheet; sprinkle evenly with butter
mixture. Bake 5 to 7 more minutes or
until browned.

GWEN PIERSALL
STILLWATER, OKLAHOMA

ITALIAN GREEN BEANS WITH ONION AND BASIL

family favorite

MAKES 6 TO 8 SERVINGS

Prep: 5 min., Cook: 30 min.

Basil and onion add a nice flavor to these beans
that are sautéed in butter and olive oil.

- 1 tablespoon butter
- 1 tablespoon olive oil
- 1 small white onion, chopped
- 3 (10-ounce) packages frozen Italian-style green beans, thawed
- 1 cup vegetable stock
- 1 tablespoon chopped fresh or 2 teaspoons dried basil
- 1 teaspoon salt
- ½ teaspoon pepper

MELT butter with oil in a large skillet
over medium heat; add onion, and sauté
5 minutes or until tender. Add green
beans and remaining ingredients to skillet; cook 20 to 25 minutes or until beans
are tender.

JEAN ISON
MIDWEST CITY, OKLAHOMA

SPINACH-AND-STRAWBERRY SALAD WITH TART POPPY SEED DRESSING

family favorite • fast fixin's

MAKES 8 SERVINGS

Prep: 15 min.

We love this perennial favorite in our Test
Kitchens.

- 2 (10-ounce) packages fresh spinach
- 1 quart fresh strawberries, cut in half
- ⅓ cup sliced almonds, toasted
- Tart Poppy Seed Dressing

PLACE spinach, strawberries, and
toasted almonds in a large bowl, and
toss. Drizzle with Tart Poppy Seed
Dressing just before serving.

Tart Poppy Seed Dressing:

MAKES 1 CUP

Prep: 5 min.

- ⅓ cup sugar
- ¼ cup white vinegar
- 1½ teaspoons chopped onion
- ¼ teaspoon paprika
- ¼ teaspoon Worcestershire sauce
- ½ cup vegetable oil
- 1 tablespoon poppy seeds

PROCESS first 5 ingredients in a blender
for 30 seconds. With blender running,
pour oil through food chute in a slow,
steady stream, and process until smooth.
Stir in poppy seeds.

PAT PADGHAM
MIDWEST CITY, OKLAHOMA

Southwestern Holiday Gathering

Great food brings these families together as business associates and as friends.

The Christmas season in Austin is the time for a special get-together at the home of Ron and Peggy Weiss. The couple and their children share a holiday meal with their friends and business associates David and Jennifer Garrido and their children. David is executive chef for Ron and Peggy's renowned restaurant, Jeffrey's.

"It's one of the few times during the year when we take the time to be together and appreciate each other's company," Ron says. "We get to do the same things with our families that we do for our customers every night."

Holiday Fiesta

Serves 8

Asparagus-and-Mushroom Tostadas With Goat Cheese

Pistachio-Crusted Lamb Rack With Cranberry-Black Bean Relish

Ancho Mashers

Roasted Root Vegetables

Hazelnut-Chocolate Truffles

Fig-Walnut Pudding With Rum Sauce

ASPARAGUS-AND-MUSHROOM TOSTADAS WITH GOAT CHEESE

chef recipe

MAKES 8 SERVINGS

Prep: 25 min., Cook: 8 min., Bake: 5 min.

David uses Texas goat Gouda cheese, but he says goat cheese or Monterey Jack also works.

- **4 fresh asparagus spears**
- **2 tablespoons chopped onion**
- **2 tablespoons olive oil**
- **1 garlic clove, finely chopped**
- **2 cups sliced shiitake or crimini mushrooms**
- **2 tablespoons white wine**
- **1 teaspoon chopped fresh basil**
- **1 teaspoon chopped fresh marjoram**
- **1 teaspoon chopped fresh thyme**
- **16 round tortilla chips**
- **4 ounces goat cheese, crumbled***

SNAP off tough ends of asparagus spears. Cook asparagus in boiling water 3 minutes or until crisp-tender. Plunge into ice water to stop the cooking process; drain and cut into ½-inch pieces.
SAUTÉ onion in hot oil over medium heat in a large skillet 30 seconds or until tender. Add garlic and mushrooms, and sauté for 1 to 2 minutes or until mushrooms are tender. Add wine, and cook 2 minutes, stirring to loosen particles from bottom of skillet. Stir in basil, marjoram, thyme, and asparagus.
PLACE tortilla chips in a single layer on a baking sheet. Spoon 1 teaspoon mushroom mixture onto each chip; top with cheese.
BAKE at 375° for 5 minutes or until cheese melts.

*Substitute Monterey Jack cheese, cut into 16 pieces.

CHEF DAVID GARRIDO
JEFFREY'S
AUSTIN, TEXAS

PISTACHIO-CRUSTED LAMB RACK

chef recipe

MAKES 8 SERVINGS

Prep: 10 min., Chill: 2 hrs., Cook: 2 min. per batch, Bake: 30 min., Stand: 5 min.

- **¾ cup fine, dry breadcrumbs**
- **½ cup pistachios**
- **2 tablespoons chopped fresh marjoram**
- **4 (4-rib) lamb rib roasts (12 to 16 ounces each), trimmed**
- **¼ cup Dijon mustard**
- **Salt and pepper to taste**
- **¼ cup olive oil**
- **Cranberry-Black Bean Relish**

PROCESS first 3 ingredients in a food processor 30 seconds or until finely ground. Transfer to a shallow dish or pan.
BRUSH lamb with Dijon mustard, and sprinkle with salt and pepper. Roll in crumb mixture, coating well. Chill 2 hours.
COOK lamb, in batches, in hot oil in a large skillet over medium-high heat 1 minute on each side or until light brown. Transfer to 2 (13- x 9-inch) lightly greased baking dishes.
BAKE lamb at 350° for 24 minutes or until a meat thermometer inserted into thickest portion registers 135°, or bake 30 to 35 minutes or until a meat thermometer inserted into thickest portion registers 145° (medium rare).
REMOVE from oven; cover loosely with aluminum foil, and let stand 5 minutes or until thermometer registers 145° (medium rare) or 160° (medium). Cut into chops, and serve with Cranberry-Black Bean Relish.

Cranberry-Black Bean Relish:

MAKES 1½ CUPS

Prep: 5 min., Chill: 2 hrs.

1 cup canned black beans, rinsed and
    drained
½ cup dried cranberries, chopped
2 tablespoons chopped fresh cilantro
2 tablespoons olive oil
1 tablespoon lime juice
1 tablespoon honey
Salt to taste

STIR together all ingredients in a bowl;
chill at least 2 hours.

CHEF DAVID GARRIDO
JEFFREY'S
AUSTIN, TEXAS

ANCHO MASHERS

chef recipe

MAKES 8 SERVINGS

Prep: 25 min., Cook: 36 min.

8 medium Yukon gold potatoes
    (about 4 pounds)
½ onion, chopped
2 garlic cloves, chopped
2 tablespoons olive oil
1 ancho chile, seeded
1 chipotle chile in adobo sauce,
    stemmed and seeded
½ tomato, quartered
1 teaspoon sugar
Salt to taste
¾ cup whipping cream
¼ cup half-and-half
½ cup butter
Pepper to taste

PEEL and quarter potatoes. Bring potatoes and salted water to cover to a boil in
a Dutch oven; cook 20 to 30 minutes
over medium heat or until tender. Drain.
SAUTÉ onion and garlic in hot oil in a
large skillet over medium-high heat 2
minutes or until tender. Add chiles,
tomato, and sugar; cook 2 to 4 minutes
or until chiles begin to soften.
TRANSFER mixture to a blender, and
process until smooth, stopping to scrape

down sides. Pour mixture through a wire
mesh strainer into a bowl. Salt to taste.
BEAT potatoes, whipping cream, half-
and-half, and butter at medium speed
with an electric mixer just until smooth.
Spoon chile puree over mashed potatoes,
and gently swirl with a knife for a mar-
bled effect. Add pepper to taste.

CHEF DAVID GARRIDO
JEFFREY'S
AUSTIN, TEXAS

ROASTED ROOT VEGETABLES

chef recipe

MAKES 8 SERVINGS

Prep: 20 min., Bake: 45 min.

1 large celery root, peeled and cut into
    1-inch cubes
4 parsnips, peeled and cut into 1-inch
    cubes
8 shallots, peeled and quartered
3 tablespoons olive oil, divided
2 beets, peeled and cut into 1-inch cubes
2 tablespoons chopped fresh parsley
1 tablespoon chopped fresh basil
2 tablespoons shredded Parmesan
    cheese

TOSS first 3 ingredients with 2 tablespoons olive oil; place in a single layer
in a 15- x 10-inch jellyroll pan, leaving
space at 1 end of pan for beets.
TOSS beets with remaining 1 tablespoon
olive oil; arrange beets at empty end of
jellyroll pan, apart from other vegetables.
BAKE at 375° for 45 minutes or until
vegetables are tender.
TRANSFER vegetables to a large serving
dish; toss with herbs and Parmesan
cheese.

CHEF DAVID GARRIDO
JEFFREY'S
AUSTIN, TEXAS

HAZELNUT-CHOCOLATE TRUFFLES

chef recipe

MAKES 20 TRUFFLES

Prep: 20 min., Chill: 2 hrs., Bake: 10 min.

Test Kitchens professional Angela Sellers wears
plastic gloves so she can roll each truffle in
melted chocolate in her palm.

¾ cup whipping cream
1 cup finely chopped bittersweet
    chocolate
1 tablespoon unsalted butter
2 tablespoons hazelnut liqueur
¾ cup hazelnuts
1 (3-ounce) dark chocolate bar,
    chopped*

BRING cream to a boil in a medium
saucepan over medium-high heat; whisk
in bittersweet chocolate, butter, and
hazelnut liqueur until well combined.
Chill at least 2 hours.
PLACE hazelnuts on a baking sheet.
Bake at 350° for 10 minutes or until
hazelnuts are toasted. Place warm hazelnuts in a dish towel, and rub vigorously
to remove skins.
PROCESS toasted hazelnuts in a food
processor until ground. Place in a shallow dish.
SHAPE chocolate mixture into 1-inch
balls. Melt chopped dark chocolate bar
in a small saucepan over low heat. Roll
each ball in 1 teaspoon of melted dark
chocolate, and immediately roll in
toasted, ground hazelnuts.
COVER and chill truffles until ready to
serve.

NOTE: For testing purposes only, we
used Ghirardelli Dark Chocolate for
dark chocolate bar.

*Substitute ½ cup semisweet morsels
for dark chocolate bar, if desired.

CHEF DAVID GARRIDO
JEFFREY'S
AUSTIN, TEXAS

FIG-WALNUT PUDDING

chef recipe

MAKES 8 SERVINGS

Prep: 20 min.; Stand: 20 min.; Cook: 5 min.;
Bake: 1 hr., 4 min.

Challah is a braided Jewish egg bread. You can substitute any braided loaf or soft French bread.

- 12 to 14 dried figs
- 8 to 10 (½-inch) challah bread slices
- 1 cup walnuts
- 2 cups milk
- 1 cup whipping cream
- 1 cup sugar, divided
- 6 large eggs
- ½ cup honey
- 2 tablespoons vanilla extract
- ½ teaspoon ground nutmeg
- Pinch of ground cloves
- Rum Sauce (optional)

PLACE figs in a heat-proof bowl with boiling water to cover; let stand 20 minutes or until plump. Drain figs, and slice.

PLACE bread and walnuts in a 15- x 10-inch jellyroll pan; bake at 500° for 3 to 4 minutes or until toasted. Remove from oven, and set aside. Reduce heat to 350°.

HEAT milk, cream, and ¾ cup sugar in a medium saucepan over medium heat. (Do not boil.)

WHISK together eggs and next 4 ingredients in a large bowl; slowly whisk in milk mixture.

LAYER half of bread and half of walnuts evenly in a lightly greased 11- x 7-inch baking dish or 10-inch pieplate, slightly overlapping slices; layer half of figs evenly over bread. Pour half of milk mixture evenly over figs. Repeat procedure with remaining bread, figs, and milk mixture. Press lightly with a spatula. Sprinkle remaining half of walnuts and remaining ¼ cup sugar evenly over top.

COVER loosely with foil, leaving corners uncovered to brown edges (if using a pieplate, loosely cover with foil, allowing edges to brown).

BAKE at 350° for 45 minutes or until set. Remove foil, and bake 15 more minutes. Serve pudding warm with Rum Sauce, if desired.

Rum Sauce:

MAKES 1¼ CUPS

Prep: 15 min., Cook: 10 min.

- ½ cup butter
- ⅓ cup firmly packed brown sugar
- ½ cup whipping cream
- 2 tablespoons rum
- ¼ teaspoon orange rind
- Pinch of ground cloves

MELT butter and sugar in a heavy saucepan over low heat, stirring until smooth. Stir in remaining ingredients. Cook, stirring constantly, 10 minutes or until thickened.

DAVID GARRIDO
JEFFREY'S
AUSTIN, TEXAS

Showstopping Desserts

Here we offer a variety of recipes to help you present a sweet creation.

CHOCOLATE BREAD PUDDING WITH CUSTARD SAUCE

chef recipe

MAKES 6 SERVINGS

Prep: 30 min., Cook: 5 min., Cool: 15 min., Bake: 45 min.

Vagn Nielsen, executive chef of Proof of the Pudding in Atlanta, shares this recipe. Pulse bread slices in a food processor to make fresh breadcrumbs.

- 1 cup whipping cream
- 1 (8-ounce) package semisweet chocolate, coarsely chopped
- ⅔ cup sugar, divided
- ½ cup unsalted butter, cut into pieces
- 5 large eggs, separated
- 1 tablespoon vanilla extract
- 2 cups soft white breadcrumbs (5 bread slices)
- Custard Sauce

BRING whipping cream to a simmer in a medium saucepan. Remove from heat; cool 5 minutes.

PROCESS chocolate in a food processor 15 to 20 seconds or until finely chopped. With processor running, slowly add cream; process until smooth. Add ⅓ cup sugar and butter. Add egg yolks, 1 at a time; process until smooth. Add vanilla, and process until blended.

COMBINE breadcrumbs and chocolate mixture, stirring until blended.

BEAT egg whites at medium speed with an electric mixer until soft peaks form. Gradually add remaining ⅓ cup sugar, and beat until mixture is glossy and stiff peaks form.

FOLD one-third of egg white mixture into chocolate mixture. Fold in remaining egg white mixture until blended. Spoon into a greased 8-inch square pan. Place pan in a broiler pan; add enough water to broiler pan to reach halfway up sides of square pan.

BAKE, on center oven rack, at 325° for 45 minutes or until a knife inserted in center comes out clean. Cool on a wire rack 10 minutes. Carefully invert onto a serving platter. Serve with Custard Sauce.

NOTE: For testing purposes only, we used Ghirardelli Semi-Sweet Chocolate.

Custard Sauce:

fast fixin's • make ahead

MAKES 2 CUPS

Prep: 10 min., Cook: 10 min.

This can be prepared a day ahead and chilled.

- 6 egg yolks
- ⅔ cup sugar, divided
- 2 cups milk
- 1 tablespoon brandy
- 1 teaspoon vanilla extract

WHISK together egg yolks and ⅓ cup sugar in a large bowl 3 minutes or until blended.

BRING milk and remaining ⅓ cup sugar to a boil in a medium saucepan, whisking constantly.

STIR about one-fourth of hot milk mixture gradually into yolks; add to remaining hot mixture, stirring constantly. Cook over medium-low heat, stirring constantly, 10 minutes or until custard is thick enough to coat back of a wooden spoon. Remove from heat. Pour through a fine wire-mesh strainer into a bowl. Stir in brandy and vanilla.

CHEF VAGN NIELSEN
PROOF OF THE PUDDING
ATLANTA, GEORGIA

APRICOT-CREAM CHEESE PASTRIES

MAKES ABOUT 4 DOZEN

Prep: 30 min., Chill: 1 hr., Bake: 25 min., Cool: 15 min.

Known as rugalach (pronounced RUGH-uh-luhkh), this treat turns anyone into a baker. If you don't have a food processor, cut cream cheese and butter into flour and granulated sugar using a pastry blender until crumbly. Form into a dough, and proceed with recipe as directed.

- 2½ cups all-purpose flour
- 1 (8-ounce) package cream cheese, cut into 1-inch cubes
- 1 cup butter or margarine, cut into 1-inch cubes
- 2 tablespoons granulated sugar
- 1 cup pecans, finely chopped and toasted
- 1 cup golden raisins
- 1 cup granulated sugar
- 2 tablespoons ground cinnamon
- 1 (12-ounce) jar apricot jam
- ⅓ cup butter or margarine, melted
- Powdered sugar

PULSE first 4 ingredients in a food processor until crumbly. Combine mixture by hand, forming a dough.
DIVIDE dough into 4 equal portions. Shape each portion into a ball; cover and chill 1 hour.
PLACE 1 portion between 2 sheets of lightly floured wax paper; roll into a 15- x 10-inch rectangle. Repeat with remaining portions.

COMBINE pecans and next 3 ingredients. Spread each rectangle evenly with jam, leaving a 1-inch border; sprinkle evenly with pecan mixture.
ROLL UP, jellyroll fashion, and place seam side down on a lightly greased baking sheet, tucking ends under to keep jam from seeping out. Brush with melted butter.
BAKE at 375° for 20 to 25 minutes or until golden. Remove to a wire rack, and cool 15 minutes.
CUT each roll into 1-inch slices using a serrated knife; sprinkle with powdered sugar.

SHERRON GOLDSTEIN
BIRMINGHAM, ALABAMA

BLACKBERRY-RASPBERRY TRUFFLE CAKE

MAKES 12 TO 15 SERVINGS

Prep: 1 hr.; Bake: 40 min.; Cool: 15 min.; Cook: 15 min.; Chill: 1 hr., 30 min.

- 2 (18.25-ounce) packages devil's food cake mix
- 6 large eggs
- 1 cup vegetable oil
- 1⅓ cups water
- 1¼ cups light sour cream
- 1 (12-ounce) package semisweet chocolate morsels
- 1½ cups whipping cream
- ½ cup seedless blackberry jam
- ½ cup seedless raspberry jam
- ¼ cup water
- 1 (8-ounce) package cream cheese, softened
- ⅓ cup powdered sugar
- 1 (16-ounce) container frozen whipped topping, thawed
- 1 teaspoon vanilla extract
- 3 to 3½ cups chopped pecans, toasted
- Garnish: ¼ cup blackberry and raspberry candies

BEAT first 5 ingredients at medium speed with an electric mixer 2 minutes or until blended.

GREASE 3 (9-inch) parchment or wax paper-lined round cakepans. Pour batter into cakepans.
BAKE at 350° for 35 to 40 minutes or until a wooden pick inserted in center comes out clean. Cool cake layers in pans on wire racks 15 minutes. Remove from pans, and remove paper. Cool completely on wire racks.
COMBINE chocolate morsels and whipping cream in a medium saucepan over medium heat, whisking constantly, 10 minutes or until mixture is smooth. Pour into a mixing bowl; cover and chill 1½ hours or until mixture begins to thicken.
COOK jams and ¼ cup water in a small saucepan over medium heat, stirring constantly, 5 minutes or until jam melts. Brush tops of cake layers with warm jam mixture.
BEAT chocolate mixture at medium speed with an electric mixer about 20 seconds or until stiff peaks form. (Do not overbeat.)
PLACE 1 layer, glazed side up, on a cake platter. Spread with half of chocolate mixture. Top with another cake layer, glazed side down; spread with remaining chocolate mixture. Top with the remaining cake layer, glazed side down.
BEAT cream cheese and powdered sugar at medium speed with an electric mixer until smooth. Add whipped topping and vanilla, beating until smooth. Working quickly, frost top and sides of cake with cream cheese mixture. Press pecans around sides of cake. Garnish, if desired.

NOTE: For testing purposes only, we used Betty Crocker SuperMoist Devil's Food Cake Mix and Jelly Belly Confections Blackberries and Raspberries for candy. Candies can be found at Cracker Barrel, in the bulk candy aisle of supermarkets, or in specialty stores.

CONNIE COBERN
HENDERSONVILLE, TENNESSEE

Casual Breakfast Buffet

Irene Smith of Covington, Georgia, is passionate about entertaining. She and her husband, Billy, also have a commitment to helping others. Here's a sampling of the brunch Irene donates when charities host fund-raisers with silent auctions.

Pecan-Raisin Mini-Tarts

family favorite

MAKES 45 TARTS

Prep: 10 min., Bake: 25 min. *(pictured on page 267)*

- 1 cup sugar
- ¼ cup butter or margarine, melted
- 2 large eggs, lightly beaten
- 1 tablespoon white vinegar
- ½ teaspoon ground cinnamon
- ½ teaspoon ground nutmeg
- 1 cup golden raisins
- 1 cup chopped pecans, toasted
- 3 (2.1-ounce) packages frozen mini phyllo tart shells
- Garnishes: whipped cream, ground nutmeg

STIR together first 6 ingredients in a large bowl. Stir in raisins and pecans.
SPOON filling evenly into frozen tart shells. Place on a large baking sheet.
BAKE tarts at 325° for 20 to 25 minutes or until golden. Cool. Garnish, if desired.

NOTE: For testing purposes only, we used Athens Foods Mini Fillo Dough Shells.

PECAN-RAISIN TARTS: Substitute 3 (10-ounce) packages tart shells. Bake at 325° for 35 to 40 minutes or until golden. Makes 10 servings.

NOTE: For testing purposes only, we used Dutch Ann frozen tart shells.

Brunch Egg Nests

family favorite

MAKES 6 SERVINGS

Prep: 30 min., Cook: 10 min.

- ½ tablespoon butter
- ½ cup sliced mushrooms
- ½ cup chopped cooked ham
- 1 (10-ounce) container refrigerated Alfredo sauce
- ¼ cup sour cream
- ¼ cup milk
- 1 (10-ounce) package frozen puff pastry shells, baked
- 4 hard-cooked eggs, coarsely chopped
- Pepper, paprika, and parsley (optional)

MELT butter in a medium saucepan over medium-high heat; add mushrooms and ham, and sauté 7 minutes or until tender. Reduce heat to low; whisk in Alfredo sauce, sour cream, and milk, stirring until thoroughly heated. (Do not boil.)
FILL each pastry shell with ⅓ cup mixture. Sprinkle evenly with chopped egg. If desired, sprinkle with pepper, paprika, and parsley.

Garlic Shrimp and Grits

fast fixin's

MAKES 10 TO 12 SERVINGS

Prep: 10 min., Cook: 15 min.

- 1 pound unpeeled, medium-size fresh shrimp, cooked
- 3 cups water
- 1 cup whipping cream
- ¼ cup butter or margarine
- 1 teaspoon salt
- 1 cup quick-cooking grits, uncooked
- 1 cup (4 ounces) extra-sharp shredded Cheddar cheese
- 2 garlic cloves, minced
- Garnishes: fresh chives, peeled and cooked shrimp

PEEL shrimp, and devein, if desired.
BRING 3 cups water, whipping cream, butter, and salt to a boil in a large saucepan over medium-high heat. Reduce heat to medium, and whisk in grits. Cook, whisking constantly, 7 to 8 minutes or until mixture is smooth. Stir in shrimp, cheese, and garlic, and cook 1 to 2 minutes or until thoroughly heated. Garnish, if desired.

Cooking for a Crowd

Donna Daniel Teague of Oviedo, Florida, has loved cooking for crowds since she was in high school. The "crowd" Donna is cooking for refers to a group of 100 here, but these recipes can easily be divided for smaller groups. For instructions on how to prepare these recipes to serve eight, visit Donna's Web site at www.sweetsandsavories.com.

Spinach Salad

family favorite

MAKES 100 SERVINGS

Prep: 1 hr., Cook: 15 min.
(pictured on page 261)

- 6 (15-ounce) jars spinach salad dressing
- 16 (10-ounce) bags fresh baby spinach
- 3 dozen hard-cooked eggs, chopped
- 5 pounds bacon, cooked and crumbled
- 4 large red onions, sliced (optional)

HEAT salad dressing on low heat until warm. Arrange spinach leaves on plates. Serve with chopped eggs, crumbled bacon, and, if desired, onions. Drizzle with warm dressing.

NOTE: For testing purposes only, we used Marzetti's Original Spinach Salad Dressing.

CINNAMON ROLLS

family favorite

MAKES 96 ROLLS

Prep: 30 min., Rise: 20 min., Bake: 25 min.

- 2 recipes Cinnamon Roll Dough,
      prepared 1 at a time
- 2 recipes Cinnamon Roll Filling
- ¼ cup butter, melted
- 2 recipes Cinnamon Roll Icing

DIVIDE Cinnamon Roll Dough into 6 equal portions. Roll each portion into a 13- x 9-inch rectangle on a lightly floured surface. Spread each rectangle with ⅔ cup Cinnamon Roll Filling, using back of a spoon. Roll up, jellyroll fashion. Cut each roll into 16 slices. (An electric knife works best.) Place rolls, cut sides up, in 2 buttered 15- x 10-inch jellyroll pans. Cover and let rise in a warm place (85°), free from drafts, 15 to 20 minutes.
BAKE rolls at 350° for 20 to 25 minutes. Remove from oven, brush with butter, and drizzle with Cinnamon Roll Icing.

Cinnamon Roll Dough:

MAKES 48 ROLLS

Prep: 20 min., Rise: 1 hr.

- 1 (¼-ounce) package rapid-rise yeast
- ⅓ cup sugar
- ½ teaspoon salt
- 3½ cups bread flour, divided
- ¼ cup shortening
- ¼ cup butter
- 1 cup boiling water
- 1 large egg, lightly beaten

COMBINE yeast, sugar, salt, and 2 cups flour in a large mixing bowl.
STIR together shortening, butter, and 1 cup boiling water until melted. Cool to 120° to 130°.
ADD butter mixture and egg to flour mixture, and beat at medium speed with a heavy-duty mixer 1 minute. Remove beater, and replace with dough hook attachment. Add remaining 1½ cups flour, beating 3 to 5 minutes. Cover and let rise in a warm place (85°), free from drafts, 1 hour or until dough is doubled in bulk.
PUNCH down dough.

Cinnamon Roll Filling:

MAKES ABOUT 2 CUPS

Prep: 10 min.

- ½ cup butter, softened
- ½ cup granulated sugar
- ½ cup firmly packed brown sugar
- 6 tablespoons all-purpose flour
- 1½ tablespoons ground cinnamon

COMBINE all ingredients, stirring until blended.

Cinnamon Roll Icing:

MAKES ABOUT 1½ CUPS

Prep: 10 min.

- 3 cups powdered sugar
- 3 tablespoons milk

STIR together sugar and milk until smooth. Spoon icing into a zip-top freezer bag. Snip 1 corner of bag, and drizzle icing over warm rolls.

BAKED CURRIED FRUIT

family favorite

MAKES 100 SERVINGS

Prep: 40 min., Bake: 1 hr.
(pictured on page 261)

- 10 (20-ounce) cans pineapple chunks
- 8 (29-ounce) cans sliced peaches
- 4 (29-ounce) cans sliced pears
- 4 (16-ounce) jars maraschino cherries, drained
- 5 cups firmly packed brown sugar
- 1¼ cups cornstarch
- 3 tablespoons curry powder
- 2 tablespoons ground cinnamon
- 2½ cups butter or margarine, melted

DRAIN pineapple, peaches, and pears, reserving 10 cups juice mixture.
ARRANGE pineapple, peaches, and pears evenly in 2 (15- x 12-inch) roasting pans. Top with cherries.
WHISK together reserved 10 cups juice, brown sugar, and remaining ingredients. Pour evenly over each pan of fruit mixture.
BAKE at 350° for 1 hour.

CHICKEN POT PIE

family favorite

MAKES 100 (⅔-CUP) SERVINGS

Prep: 10 min., Bake: 40 min., Stand: 15 min.
(pictured on page 261)

- 2 recipes Pot Pie Filling, prepared
      1 at a time
- 4 (15-ounce) packages refrigerated
      piecrusts

DIVIDE filling evenly among 4 (15- x 12-inch) disposable aluminum roasting pans. Top each pan with 2 round piecrusts. Cut slits in piecrusts.
BAKE at 400° for 30 to 40 minutes or until golden. Let stand 15 minutes before serving.

Pot Pie Filling:

MAKES 32 CUPS

Prep: 1 hr., Cook: 15 min.

- 3 cups butter or margarine
- 2 large onions, chopped
- 6 celery ribs, chopped
- 3 cups all-purpose flour
- 2 (49-ounce) cans chicken broth
- 5 cups milk
- 16 cups chopped cooked chicken
      (about 8 roasted whole chickens)
- 3½ cups sliced carrots, cooked (about
      1 pound)
- 3½ cups frozen green peas,
      thawed
- 1 to 2 tablespoons salt
- 1 tablespoon pepper
- 1½ teaspoons poultry seasoning
- 2 teaspoons hot sauce

MELT butter in a 4- to 6-gallon stockpot over medium heat; add onions and celery, and sauté until tender.
ADD flour, stirring until blended; cook, stirring constantly, 2 minutes. Stir in broth and milk, stirring constantly. Bring to a boil, stirring constantly, and cook 2 minutes. Stir in chicken, sliced carrots, and remaining ingredients.

Friends Toast the Season

Turn your next gathering into an event featuring food and wine pairings. It's sure to be a success if you take your cue from the African American Wine Tasting Society (AAWTS), organized by Reneé Rowe of Powder Springs, Georgia. "I was so excited after attending Anita LaRaia's Wine School," explains Reneé. "I wanted to share the fun of learning about wine."

The Atlanta group explores 6 to 12 wines during monthly meetings at area restaurants. When they share recipes, as they did here, the tasting becomes a party.

CAMEMBERT CREMES

MAKES 32 (1-INCH) BALLS

Prep: 45 min., Chill: 1 hr.

Serve with Rancho Zabaco Sauvignon Blanc, a crisp white wine.

- 2 (3-ounce) packages cream cheese, softened
- ⅓ cup minced red onion
- ⅓ cup finely chopped fresh parsley
- ½ teaspoon salt
- ½ teaspoon pepper
- 2 (8-ounce) rounds Camembert or Brie cheese, divided
- 1½ cups finely crushed Italian-seasoned croutons
- Chopped fresh parsley

STIR together first 5 ingredients in a small bowl. Set cream cheese mixture aside.

TRIM rind from cheese rounds. Cut each round into 16 wedges.

PLACE cheese wedges on wax paper, and flatten and shape wedges into 3-inch circles. Place 1 teaspoon cream cheese mixture in center of each circle. Gently wrap cheese sides around filling, and roll into balls. Roll in crushed croutons and parsley. Chill 1 hour.

JUMBO SHRIMP ROLLS WITH SWEET SOY SAUCE

family favorite

MAKES 28 APPETIZERS

Prep: 45 min., Fry: 3 min. per batch

Rancho Zabaco Sauvignon Blanc was served with this appetizer, too.

- 28 unpeeled, jumbo fresh shrimp
- ¼ cup minced fresh cilantro
- 2 garlic cloves, minced
- 2 teaspoons red curry paste
- 28 won ton wrappers
- 1 egg white, lightly beaten
- Vegetable oil
- Sweet Soy Sauce

PEEL shrimp, leaving tails on; devein, if desired, and set aside.

COMBINE cilantro, garlic, and curry paste.

BRUSH 1 side of each won ton wrapper with egg white. Spoon ¼ teaspoon cilantro mixture in center of each wrapper. Top with 1 shrimp. Fold wrapper around shrimp; leave tail exposed, and press wrapper to seal.

POUR oil to a depth of 3 inches in a Dutch oven; heat to 350°. Fry won tons, in small batches, 2 to 3 minutes or until golden, turning once. Drain on wire racks over paper towels. Serve with Sweet Soy Sauce.

Sweet Soy Sauce:

MAKES ½ CUP

Prep: 5 min.

- ½ cup soy sauce
- ⅛ to ¼ teaspoon dried red pepper flakes
- 2 teaspoons honey

COMBINE soy sauce, red pepper flakes, and honey, stirring well.

WHITE FRUITCAKE

make ahead • freezeable

MAKES 10 SERVINGS (2 LOAVES)

Prep: 25 min., Stand: 30 min., Bake: 1 hr., Cool: 10 min.

Rich, blossom-scented Domaine de Coyeaux Muscat complements this fruited, pound-cakelike dessert.

- 1 cup dark raisins
- 1 cup golden raisins
- 1 cup canned pineapple tidbits, drained
- ½ cup currants
- ¼ cup orange juice
- 1 cup butter, softened
- 1 cup sugar
- 5 large eggs
- 2½ cups all-purpose flour
- 1 teaspoon baking powder
- ½ teaspoon salt
- 2 teaspoons grated lemon rind
- 2 teaspoons grated orange rind
- ½ cup candied green cherries, quartered
- ¼ cup candied red cherries, quartered
- Orange-Bourbon Glaze

STIR together first 5 ingredients; cover and let stand 30 minutes.

BEAT butter at medium speed with an electric mixer 2 minutes or until creamy. Gradually add sugar, beating 5 to 7 minutes or until blended. Add eggs, 1 at a time, beating just until yellow disappears.

STIR together flour, baking powder, and salt; remove ½ cup flour mixture. Gradually add remaining flour mixture to butter mixture, beating at low speed just until blended after each addition. Stir in lemon and orange rind.

DRAIN raisin mixture, and stir in cherries. Toss raisin mixture with reserved ½ cup flour mixture, and fold into batter. Spoon batter into 2 lightly greased 8- x 4-inch loafpans.

BAKE at 325° for 45 minutes to 1 hour or until a wooden pick inserted in center comes out clean. Brush hot cakes evenly with Orange-Bourbon Glaze until absorbed. Cool in pans 10 minutes;

invert cakes onto a wire rack, and cool completely. (Wrap and freeze up to 1 month, if desired.)

Orange-Bourbon Glaze:

MAKES ¼ CUP

Prep: 2 min., Cook: 2 min.

¼ cup orange juice
2 tablespoons sugar
2 tablespoons bourbon

COOK orange juice and sugar in a small saucepan over medium heat 2 minutes or until sugar is dissolved. Remove orange juice mixture from heat, and stir in bourbon.

Learn More About It

For AAWTS information, call Reneé Rowe at (770) 943-3649, or visit **www.aawts.org.** Anita L. LaRaia's book is *Wine FAQs: Real Questions, Real Answers* (1st Books Library, 2001).

Holiday Wine Guide

Folks enjoy wine year-round, but during the holidays, things get particularly festive. Though the market is loaded with wines to fit any budget, there's an impressive selection of quality wines that costs less than $12 a bottle. Look for reliable producers such as Columbia Crest, Woodbridge by Robert Mondavi, Beringer Founders' Estate, Wolf Blass, Lindeman's, and Rosemount Estate. For a Southern twist, try regional favorites such as Château Élan, Biltmore

Estate, Linden, Valhalla, Westbend, Becker Vineyards, and Llano Estacado.

For more suggestions on wine, check out the Food & Wine Resource Guide Web site at **southernliving.com/features.** For a copy of *Southern Living® Wine Guide & Journal,* contact a *Southern Living At HOME* consultant near you, or visit the Web site, **southernlivingathome.com.**

Saving Leftover Wine
The key to preserving an opened bottle of wine is to limit its exposure to air. You can recork the wine, but the seal is not very tight. The wine will not last more than a day or two. The most economical way to preserve an opened bottle is to use a hand-pump vacuum sealer to remove excess air from the bottle. The pump is available in most kitchenware sections of department and grocery stores (for about $12) and allows you to enjoy the wine for an extra two or three days.

What's the Right Glass?
A basic white wine glass has a tulip shape, while a glass for red wine has a larger balloon shape. However, for most wine drinkers, one thin, clear, all-purpose glass of either shape with a capacity of about 10 to 12 ounces will do. The one exception is the Champagne flute. Its narrow shape concentrates the wine's bubbles and bouquet and helps maintain its chill. When serving wine, don't fill glasses more than halfway. The remaining space allows for swirling and the development of the wine's bouquet.

Sparkle With the Season
All Champagne is sparkling wine, but not all sparkling wine is Champagne. In order for a sparkling wine to be called Champagne, it must be made with specific grapes from the Champagne region of northeast France. As a general rule, *méthode champenoise* is the phrase you're looking for on a label of sparkling wine (the term basically means the wine is made in the style of Champagne). The most notable Italian sparklers are Prosecco (pro-SECK-oh) and spumante (the Italian word for bubbly wine). Spain's easy-drinking Cava (KAH-vuh) may be

one of the best values around—it can often be found for less than $10.

Wine After Dinner
Bottom line: Feel free to serve whatever wine you or your guests prefer. However, there are traditional after-dinner wines such as port from Portugal and sherry from Spain. Both wines are fortified, which means they've had alcohol added to stop fermentation, leaving behind residual sugar and sweetness. If you're looking for a gift-giving idea (or just wanting to splurge), try the 1998 Quinta do Vesuvio vintage port or Graham's Tawny Port Centennial box set, which includes a bottle each of 10-year, 20-year, 30-year, and 40-year port.

Serving Temperature: What's Best?

Proper temperature is a big deal when it comes to serving wine. Most reds are best served between 62° to 65°, so don't be afraid to stick a bottle in the refrigerator for 10 or 15 minutes before popping the cork. However, avoid chilling reds for more than 15 minutes. A cold bottle of red wine is downright unpleasant, playing up the wine's natural astringent quality (called tannins). On the other hand, Beaujolais, a smooth, fruity holiday favorite from France, is one of the few exceptions to the rule—it's actually made to be served slightly chilled (around 58°).

White wines should be served between 58° to 62°. There's a tendency to drink or serve ice-cold white wine, but it's best to avoid this mistake. Whites that are too cold will taste flat and lifeless. Champagne and sparkling wines are the exception; they're best served well chilled at around 45°.

Family Christmas in New Orleans

Creole Christmas Dinner

Serves 8

Spicy-Sweet Smoked Turkey Breast

Cranberry Jezebel Sauce

Shrimp-and-Ham Stuffed Mirlitons

Louise's Cornbread Dressing

After-the-Dance Pralines

Joan and Maurice Hartson III always host a magnificent celebration on Christmas Day at their historic home on Prytania Street in New Orleans. Surrounded by their daughters, sons-in-law, and 14 grandchildren, they fill the hours with family traditions and delicious food.

For example, Maurice's family started a tradition of hanging the Christmas tree from the ceiling. "When I was a young boy, my mother asked me where we should put the Christmas tree that year. I responded, sort of kidding, that we should hang it from the ceiling," Maurice recalls.

The day starts with a flurry of pajama-clad kids and adults opening presents. With 24 folks involved, the scene can be chaotic. The group nibbles on brunch items well into the afternoon. Then everyone retires for a short rest. Late in the afternoon, the family gathers for a large feast. True to their South Louisiana heritage, they always enjoy stuffed mirlitons, cornbread dressing with andouille sausage, and a twist on smoked turkey and Jezebel sauce. Pralines round out the menu. As the day comes to an end, the entire Hartson clan gives thanks for their abundant blessings.

SPICY-SWEET SMOKED TURKEY BREAST

family favorite

MAKES 16 SERVINGS

Prep: 10 min., Soak: 1 hr., Smoke: 6 hrs., Stand: 10 min.

> **Hickory wood chunks**
> **2 tablespoons coarsely ground pepper**
> **2 (6-pound) bone-in turkey breasts***
> **2 (5-ounce) bottles sweet pepper sauce**

SOAK wood chunks in water 1 hour. Prepare charcoal fire in smoker; let burn 20 to 25 minutes.

RUB pepper evenly over turkey breasts. Pour sauce evenly over breasts.

DRAIN wood chunks, and place on coals. Place water pan in smoker; add water to depth of fill line. Place turkey breasts, side by side, on upper food grate; cover with smoker lid.

SMOKE 5 to 6 hours or until a meat thermometer inserted in thickest portion registers 170°, adding additional water to depth of fill line, if necessary. Remove from smoker; let stand 10 minutes before slicing.

*Substitute 2 (6-pound) fully cooked or fully cooked smoked bone-in turkey breasts, if desired. Proceed as directed, reducing smoking time to 1 hour or until thoroughly heated.

NOTE: For testing purposes only, we used Pickapeppa Sauce.

JOAN HARTSON
NEW ORLEANS, LOUISIANA

CRANBERRY JEZEBEL SAUCE

fast fixin's

MAKES ABOUT 3 CUPS

Prep: 5 min., Cook: 15 min.

This fabulous sauce to serve over smoked turkey doubles as an appetizer when poured over cream cheese and served with assorted crackers. *(pictured on page 1)*

> **1 cup water**
> **½ cup granulated sugar**
> **½ cup firmly packed light brown sugar**
> **1 (12-ounce) bag fresh or frozen cranberries**
> **½ cup pineapple preserves**
> **3 tablespoons prepared horseradish**
> **1 tablespoon Dijon mustard**

BRING first 3 ingredients to a boil, stirring often, in a saucepan over medium-high heat; add cranberries.

RETURN to a boil. Reduce heat, and simmer, stirring often, 10 minutes or until cranberry skins begin to pop and mixture begins to thicken. Remove from heat.

STIR in preserves, horseradish, and mustard; remove pan from heat, and let sauce cool. Cover and chill until ready to serve.

NOTE: Sauce can be stored in an airtight container in the refrigerator up to 2 weeks.

JOAN HARTSON
NEW ORLEANS, LOUISIANA

SHRIMP-AND-HAM STUFFED MIRLITONS

MAKES 8 SERVINGS

Prep: 40 min., Cook: 45 min., Bake: 20 min.

This was adapted from *The Plantation Cookbook* by the Junior League of New Orleans.

- 4 large mirlitons
- 1 pound unpeeled, medium-size fresh shrimp
- ⅓ cup minced onion
- ¼ cup chopped fresh parsley
- 4 green onions, chopped
- 3 garlic cloves, minced
- 2 tablespoons bacon drippings
- 8 ounces cooked ham, coarsely chopped
- 1¼ cups soft breadcrumbs, divided
- 1 tablespoon Creole seasoning
- 1 large egg, lightly beaten
- 2 tablespoons butter, melted

BRING mirlitons and water to cover to a boil in a Dutch oven; boil 25 to 30 minutes or until tender.

PEEL shrimp, and devein, if desired. Set shrimp aside.

DRAIN and cool mirlitons. Cut in half lengthwise; remove seeds, and discard. Scoop out pulp, leaving ½-inch-thick shells; chop pulp.

SAUTÉ onion and next 3 ingredients in hot bacon drippings 3 minutes. Add shrimp and ham; cook, stirring constantly, 3 to 5 minutes or until shrimp turn pink. Stir in mirliton pulp, ¾ cup breadcrumbs, and Creole seasoning; cook, stirring occasionally, 5 minutes. Let cool slightly; stir in egg. Stuff mirliton mixture evenly into mirliton shells.

STIR together remaining ½ cup breadcrumbs and butter. Sprinkle evenly over stuffed mirlitons. Place in a lightly greased 13- x 9-inch baking dish.

BAKE at 375° for 15 to 20 minutes or until lightly browned.

NOTE: Unbaked mirliton mixture may be spooned into a lightly greased 11- x 7-inch baking dish (discard mirliton shells), and then baked as directed.

LOUISE'S CORNBREAD DRESSING

family favorite • make ahead

MAKES 16 SERVINGS

Prep: 45 min., Cook: 20 min., Bake: 1 hr.

- 1 cup butter or margarine, divided
- 4 cups white cornmeal
- 2 tablespoons sugar
- 4 large eggs
- 3 cups buttermilk
- 1 (12-ounce) package andouille sausage, chopped
- 8 green onions, thinly sliced
- 3 large celery ribs, diced
- 1 large sweet onion, diced
- 1 medium-size green bell pepper, diced
- 1 (8-ounce) package fresh mushrooms, diced
- 1 cup dry sherry (optional)
- 2 cups chopped pecans, toasted
- ¼ cup chopped fresh parsley
- 2 tablespoons Creole seasoning
- 2 (14-ounce) cans low-sodium chicken broth

PLACE ½ cup butter in a 13- x 9-inch pan; heat in oven at 425° for 4 minutes.

COMBINE white cornmeal and sugar in a large bowl; whisk in 2 eggs and buttermilk. Pour hot butter into batter, stirring until blended. Pour batter into pan.

BAKE at 425° for 30 minutes or until golden brown. Cool and crumble into a large bowl.

SAUTÉ chopped andouille sausage in a large skillet over medium-high heat 3 to 4 minutes or until lightly browned.

ADD sliced green onions, diced celery, diced onion, and diced green bell pepper to skillet; sauté 5 minutes or until vegetables are tender. Spoon sausage mixture into bowl with cornbread mixture.

MELT remaining ½ cup butter in skillet; add diced mushrooms, and sauté 5 minutes. If desired, reduce sauté time to 3 minutes, and add 1 cup dry sherry to skillet. Cook, stirring often, until liquid is reduced by half.

ADD mushroom mixture, chopped pecans, chopped parsley, and Creole seasoning to cornbread mixture in bowl.

WHISK together remaining 2 eggs and chicken broth; add to cornbread mixture, and stir gently until moistened. Spoon into 1 lightly greased 13- x 9-inch baking dish and 1 lightly greased 8-inch square baking dish.

BAKE, uncovered, at 350° for 30 minutes or until golden brown.

TO MAKE AHEAD: Chill prepared, unbaked dressing in the refrigerator overnight. Let dressing stand until room temperature, then bake as directed.

NOTE: For testing purposes only, we used White Lily Buttermilk Cornmeal Mix and Tony's Creole Seasoning.

JOAN HARTSON
NEW ORLEANS, LOUISIANA

AFTER-THE-DANCE PRALINES

MAKES 20 PRALINES

Prep: 10 min., Stand: 8 hrs.

This beloved Louisiana confection got its name from the tradition of young women in New Orleans making them before going to a ball and then enjoying them with friends (and beaux) at their homes afterward.

- 1 cup firmly packed light brown sugar
- 1 egg white, beaten
- 1½ cups chopped pecans, lightly toasted

PREHEAT oven to 400°.

STIR together brown sugar and beaten egg white, and fold in chopped pecans.

DROP by heaping tablespoonfuls onto a heavy-duty aluminum foil-lined baking sheet.

TURN off oven; place baking sheet in oven, and let pralines stand 8 hours in oven.

JOAN HARTSON
NEW ORLEANS, LOUISIANA

Caring for Community

This small town knows the meaning of sharing.

Residents of tiny Latta, South Carolina, head for the local community center each year on the Friday before Christmas. Everyone is welcome to free meals throughout the day, all paid for, prepared, and served by a group of their neighbors.

Henry Brunson and 49 other men have been carrying on the tradition for about 30 years. "We view it as our gift back to the community," Henry says. He is so devoted to the gathering that he grows, harvests, washes, and helps cook the seven pickup truck loads of collards it takes to feed the entire town. The group's members simply call themselves "the sponsors," each contributing $125 and innumerable hours.

John Kirby explains that Allan Brigman, then-mayor of Latta, and Chester Taylor started cooking barbecue to share with shut-ins. Claude Graham adds, "We began cooking for the shut-ins and invited our friends in to eat the leftovers. Over the years, it turned into thousands of friends!"

The group prepares the food in a cook house equipped with burners that can accommodate huge kettles and stockpots as well as several large smokers.

Rescue squad members and other volunteers deliver 450 take-out meals to the aged and the ailing. "Most of the people are bedridden and can't get out," says a member of the Floydale Rescue Squad. Melinda Roberts says, "I've been coming since I was in the sixth grade, and now my own son is in third grade. It's a tradition." Claude Graham couldn't agree more. His face wears a satisfied smile when he says, "Our community has really enjoyed this thing." Here are a few of their recipes so that you can enjoy a taste of the event.

COUNTRY-STYLE COLLARDS

MAKES 8 TO 10 SERVINGS
Prep: 45 min.; Cook: 1 hr., 10 min.

Henry Brunson's original recipe started with a pickup truck load of collards, but we whittled it down to a family-size proportion.

- 2 large bunches fresh collard greens (about 5 pounds each)
- ½ pound fatback, sliced
- ½ pound hog jowl
- 1 tablespoon vegetable oil
- 4 cups water
- 2 tablespoons sugar
- 2 teaspoons salt
- ½ teaspoon pepper

REMOVE and discard stems and discolored spots from greens. Wash greens thoroughly; drain and cut into ½-inch strips. Set aside.

COOK fatback and hog jowl in hot oil in a 6-quart Dutch oven over medium heat, stirring often, 8 to 10 minutes or until fatback is crisp. Remove fatback and jowl, and set aside. Drain, reserving ¼ cup drippings.

BRING 4 cups water, next 3 ingredients, and ¼ cup reserved drippings to a boil in Dutch oven over medium-high heat. Add one-third of greens, stirring often, 2 to 3 minutes or until wilted. Repeat procedure twice with remaining greens. Reduce heat to low; cover and cook, stirring occasionally, 45 minutes or until collards are tender. Add additional sugar and salt to taste, if desired.

KEITH ALLEN AND HENRY BRUNSON
LATTA, SOUTH CAROLINA

COLESLAW

MAKES 10 TO 12 SERVINGS
Prep: 20 min.

The cooks at Latta Middle/High School are known for this tasty slaw.

- 1 cup mayonnaise
- 2½ tablespoons sugar
- 3 tablespoons sweet pickle cubes
- 1 (3-pound) cabbage, finely chopped

STIR together first 3 ingredients.
ADD cabbage; toss well to coat. Cover and chill until ready to serve.

NOTE: For testing purposes only, we used Miracle Whip Salad Dressing for mayonnaise.

PORK BACKBONE AND RICE

MAKES 6 TO 8 SERVINGS
Prep: 5 min., Cook: 2 hrs.

This richly flavored dish is similar to chicken bog, a regional favorite.

- 2 pounds pork backbones
- 1 pound boneless pork loin, cut into 1½-inch cubes
- 6 cups water
- 1½ teaspoons salt
- 1 teaspoon pepper
- 2 cups uncooked rice

BRING first 5 ingredients to a boil in a Dutch oven over medium-high heat. Cover, reduce heat to low, and simmer, stirring occasionally, 1½ hours or until meat is tender.
STIR in rice; cover and cook over low heat 20 to 25 minutes or until rice is done. (Do not stir.) Fluff rice with a fork, and serve.

NOTE: Pork backbones are also sold as "country-style ribs."

VIC BETHEA III
LATTA, SOUTH CAROLINA

Southern Cooks Share Their Secrets

Because the holidays are a busy time for many, we've asked our editors and faithful readers, chefs and home cooks alike, to share their tips for making the holiday season enjoyable.

The Home Cook
Several weeks in advance, Marie Davis of Charlotte prepares two grocery lists—one of nonperishable items to purchase ahead of time and another of perishables to buy just a few days before the holiday.

Marie also spends some time shopping for unique things to include in personalized gift baskets. "Gift baskets are inexpensive, thoughtful, and full of fresh ingredients."

Her favorite baskets to assemble are a bread lover's basket (bread, starter, jams, flavored butters) and a spaghetti dinner basket (dried pasta, homemade sauce, a large wedge of Parmesan, and a cheese grater). For teachers' gifts, Marie suggests giving gift baskets of homemade apple jelly. The possibilities are endless—just tailor the gifts to the recipient's taste.

For tree-decorating parties, Marie makes easy homemade soups such as oyster stew or hearty winter vegetable soup, fresh bread, and fruit salad. Marie also likes to make iced coffee in advance, freeze it, and then serve coffee slushes to drop-in guests. "Serve with some cheese mousse, crackers, dips, and baked Brie all set in front of the fire," she suggests.

The Caterer
Kelven Book, a high-profile caterer in Washington, D.C., offers a myriad of creative and practical ideas for successful entertaining.

He suggests buying or making holiday decorations in neutral, festive tones such as silver, white, and gold. These colors can be reused for special occasions such as graduations, weddings, showers, and anniversaries.

"Lighting," Kelven states, "is probably the most important aspect of decorating. If you're on a budget, put out a few decorations, dim your lights, and place candles of all sizes around the house. It's festive, cozy, elegant, and romantic all at once."

He also recommends setting up a cookie-decorating table for kids and adults. Be sure to have small boxes with tissue paper available for guests to take home their cookie favors.

The Chef
Chef Adolfo Garcia of RioMar restaurant in New Orleans always carefully plans his menu before starting home entertaining. "If I really want brussels sprouts, let's say, I'll start from there. Then I think about what would go well . . . pork, duck, goose, maybe. And then I think about the cooking method.

"If I'm going to pan roast the sprouts on the cooktop, I look for a dish that will be baked in the oven: goose, perhaps, slow-cooked with apples and hard cider. To round out the menu, I try to come up with something cold that can be made one or two days ahead of time. Then I make a sweet potato casserole the day before, and I've got a whole meal."

Adolfo's most important advice, though, is take time to relax. We often get so overwhelmed that we forget what this time of year is really all about. So, whether hosting an intimate dinner, a kids' party, or a fabulous extravaganza, remember the holidays are a time to treasure family and friends.

Personalized Confetti

Use these playful trimmings with all kinds of seasonal projects.

Use family pictures to enhance your party or celebration with Confoti confetti. It's versatile and fun to use. Visit online at **www.confoti.com,** load in your digital photos, and in a short time, you'll receive customized cheer with about 3,200 pieces in each bag. This fun accent features your friends' and families' faces from the digital photos. A bag using up to 10 of your photos costs $16.95 and will cover an 8-foot round table for a quick, festive feel. These packages also make unique favors and hostess gifts. Join the confetti excitement, and make each celebration a one-of-a-kind party.

Great Tips from Our Editors

- Roast turkey breast side down for extremely tender white meat.
- Keep carcasses of roasted turkeys and chickens to make rich, flavorful stocks. Freeze some of the stock in ice cube trays for easy use in sauces and soups.
- Foods Editor Scott Jones loves his Staub teapot (for warming and pouring sauces) and Silpat® nonstick, reusable baking mats.

Creative Ways With Grits

Most folks would agree that hot cooked grits rank high among adored Southern sides. The addition of cheese and eggs over the years has made them a must at brunch. These recipes, however, pair this old favorite with unique ingredients to create delightfully different memories. So have fun serving this down-home side in new and clever ways.

CHEESE GRITS WITH CHICKEN SAUSAGE AND SHIITAKE MUSHROOMS

MAKES 6 SERVINGS

Prep: 15 min., Cook: 25 min., Bake: 50 min.

This tasty recipe is really a basic cheese grits casserole transformed by the addition of unexpected ingredients.

- 9 ounces fully cooked smoked chicken sausage with apples and Chardonnay
- 6 ounces shiitake mushrooms
- ½ cup butter or margarine, divided
- 3 cups water
- ¾ cup uncooked quick-cooking grits
- 1 (8-ounce) loaf pasteurized prepared cheese product, cubed
- 2 large eggs, lightly beaten
- ½ teaspoon dried rosemary
- ¼ teaspoon seasoned salt
- Sliced ripe olives (optional)

CUT sausage into ½-inch-thick slices; cut slices into quarters. Cut stems from mushrooms and, if desired, reserve for another use; cut mushroom caps into slices.

MELT 1 tablespoon butter in a nonstick skillet over medium-high heat; add sausage, and sauté 7 minutes or until lightly browned. Remove sausage from skillet. Add mushroom caps to skillet, and sauté 5 minutes or until tender.

BRING 3 cups water to a boil in a Dutch oven. Gradually stir in grits; return to a boil. Reduce heat, and simmer, stirring occasionally, 5 minutes or until thickened. Add remaining 7 tablespoons butter and cheese; cook, stirring often, 5 minutes or until melted and blended. Remove from heat; stir in eggs, rosemary, and seasoned salt until blended. Stir in sausage and mushrooms; pour mixture into a lightly greased 11- x 7-inch baking dish.

BAKE at 350° for 45 to 50 minutes or just until set. Sprinkle top with olives, if desired.

NOTE: For testing purposes only, we used Gerhard's Smoked Chicken Sausage with Apples & Chardonnay.

MARY CLARKE
NASHVILLE, TENNESSEE

SHRIMP 'N' GRITS TARTS

MAKES 36 TARTS

Prep: 30 min., Cook: 25 min., Bake: 35 min.

- 3½ cups chicken broth, divided
- 1 cup milk
- ¼ cup butter or margarine, divided
- ½ teaspoon white pepper
- 1 cup uncooked coarse-ground or regular grits
- ⅔ cup shredded Parmesan cheese
- ⅔ cup diced smoked ham
- 3 tablespoons all-purpose flour
- 3 tablespoons chopped fresh parsley
- ¾ teaspoon white wine Worcestershire sauce
- 36 medium-size peeled and cooked shrimp
- Garnish: chopped parsley

BRING 2 cups chicken broth, milk, 2 tablespoons butter, and white pepper to a boil in a large saucepan over medium-high heat. Gradually whisk in grits; return to a boil. Reduce heat, and simmer, stirring occasionally, 5 to 10 minutes or until thickened. Add Parmesan cheese, and whisk until melted and blended.

SPOON 1 rounded tablespoonful of grits-and-cheese mixture into each lightly greased cup of 3 (12-cup) miniature muffin pans.

BAKE at 350° for 20 to 25 minutes or until lightly browned. Make an indentation in centers of warm grits tarts, using the back of a spoon. Let cool completely in pans. Remove tarts from muffin pans, and place tarts on a 15- x 10-inch jelly-roll pan.

MELT remaining 2 tablespoons butter in a medium saucepan over medium-high heat; add ham, and sauté 1 to 2 minutes. Sprinkle 3 tablespoons flour evenly over ham, and cook, stirring often, 1 to 2 minutes or until lightly brown. Gradually add remaining 1½ cups chicken broth, stirring until smooth.

REDUCE heat, and cook, stirring often, 5 to 10 minutes or until thickened. Stir in 3 tablespoons chopped parsley and white wine Worcestershire sauce, and spoon evenly into tarts. Top each with 1 shrimp.

BAKE at 350° for 5 to 10 minutes or just until warm. Garnish, if desired.

NOTE: For testing purposes only, we used Cumberland Gap Diced Ham.

MARY GREENE
COLUMBIA, SOUTH CAROLINA

These Ladies Do Lunch

Jenny Joseph's poem "Warning" sets the tone for the Red Hat Society, a national organization of fun-loving women who are over the age of 50. The poem begins, "When I am an old woman I shall wear purple/With a red hat which doesn't go and doesn't suit me." Helen Naismith and Dorothy Lee started their chapter of the Red Hat Society in Hiawassee, Georgia.

"The only requirements," says Helen, "are to wear a red hat, a purple dress, and a big smile to enjoy food and fellowship.

We have a great time, and the food is always delicious."

The ladies' luncheon was held at Arkaquah Valley Inn, near Blairsville, Georgia. The inn's owner, Nancie Concato, provided the recipes for the succulent stuffed pork tenderloin as well as two delicious sides.

To locate a chapter in your area, you can visit the group's Web site at **www.redhatsociety.com.**

Sugar Snap Peas With Bell Peppers

fast fixin's

MAKES 6 SERVINGS

Prep: 10 min., Cook: 10 min. *(pictured on page 1)*

- ½ cup water
- 1 large red bell pepper, cut into thin strips
- 1 pound fresh sugar snap peas
- 1 garlic clove, minced
- 2 tablespoons butter
- 2 tablespoons fresh lemon juice
- ½ teaspoon salt

BRING ½ cup water to a boil in a large skillet. Add red bell pepper strips, sugar snap peas, and minced garlic to skillet. Cook, covered, over medium heat 5 to 7 minutes until crisp-tender. Toss with butter, lemon juice, and salt.

Russian Potatoes

make ahead

MAKES 6 SERVINGS

Prep: 30 min., Bake: 30 min.

- 2 (22-ounce) packages frozen mashed potatoes
- 1½ teaspoons salt
- 4 tablespoons butter
- 3 large garlic cloves, minced
- 2 cups sour cream
- 3 tablespoons butter, cut into pieces
- 2 cups (8 ounces) shredded sharp Cheddar cheese (optional)

COOK potatoes according to package directions, omitting salt. Stir in 1½ teaspoons salt.

MELT 4 tablespoons butter in a small skillet over high heat; add garlic, and sauté 2 minutes. Stir garlic and sour cream into mashed potatoes.

TRANSFER potato mixture to a lightly greased 13- x 9-inch baking dish. Dot with 3 tablespoons butter. (Cool completely, cover, and refrigerate up to 24 hours, if desired.)

BAKE at 350° for 25 minutes. Top evenly with cheese, if desired, and bake 5 more minutes or until cheese is melted.

Festive Pork Loin Roast

MAKES 12 TO 14 SERVINGS

Prep: 45 min., Bake: 1 hr., Stand: 15 min.

- 2 (4-pound) center cut boneless pork loins
- 1 teaspoon salt
- 1 teaspoon pepper
- Sausage Stuffing
- 3 white bread slices
- 1 cup chopped pecans
- 3 tablespoons bourbon
- 1 cup chicken broth
- Juice of 1 lemon
- Mushroom Sauce
- Garnishes: decoratively cut orange, fresh cranberries, fresh kale

CUT pork loins in half lengthwise; sprinkle pork with salt and pepper.

SPOON 2 cups Sausage Stuffing evenly on each bottom half. Place each top half over stuffing, and tie firmly with kitchen string.

PULSE together bread, pecans, and bourbon in a food processor 6 times or until crumbly. Spread half of bread mixture evenly over top of each roast. Place roasts on a rack in a roasting pan. Pour chicken broth and lemon juice into bottom of pan.

BAKE, covered with aluminum foil, at 425° for 30 minutes. Remove foil, and bake 30 more minutes or until a meat thermometer registers 160°. Remove

roasts, reserving pan drippings. Let roasts stand 15 minutes before slicing. Serve with Mushroom Sauce. Garnish, if desired.

Sausage Stuffing:

MAKES 4 CUPS

Prep: 10 min., Cook: 15 min.

- 7 white bread slices
- 1 pound ground pork sausage
- 1 large onion, finely chopped
- 3 celery ribs with leaves, finely chopped
- 1 cup chicken broth
- 1 tart apple, diced
- 1 teaspoon poultry seasoning

REMOVE crusts from bread slices. Cut bread into cubes.

COOK sausage in a large skillet, stirring until it crumbles and is no longer pink. Add onion and celery, and cook until tender. Remove from heat; stir in bread, broth, apple, and seasoning.

Mushroom Sauce:

MAKES 3 CUPS

Prep: 10 min., Cook: 20 min.

- ½ cup butter
- 1½ (8-ounce) packages sliced fresh mushrooms (3¾ cups)
- 1 large onion, finely chopped
- 1 bunch green onions, chopped
- ½ cup chopped fresh parsley
- 2 large garlic cloves, finely chopped
- ½ teaspoon salt
- 1½ cups white wine
- ½ cup reserved pan drippings or chicken broth

MELT butter in a large skillet over medium heat; add mushrooms and next 4 ingredients, and sauté 6 to 7 minutes or until tender. Stir in salt, wine, and pan drippings; cook 10 minutes.

Pass the Rolls

Mattie H. Scott, who according to her daughter, Foods Editor Andria Scott Hurst, makes some of the best bread in the world, shared her roll recipes with us.

EASY YEAST ROLLS

family favorite

MAKES 3 DOZEN

Prep: 40 min., Stand: 5 min., Rise: 2 hrs., Bake: 18 min.

> 2 (¼-ounce) envelopes active dry yeast
> ½ cup warm milk (100° to 110°)
> 1 cup milk
> ½ cup sugar
> ½ cup shortening, melted
> 2 large eggs, beaten
> 1 teaspoon salt
> 5½ cups all-purpose flour
> ½ cup butter, melted and divided

COMBINE yeast and ½ cup warm milk in a 2-cup liquid measuring cup; let stand 5 minutes.

COMBINE yeast mixture, 1 cup milk, sugar, and next 3 ingredients in a large bowl. Gradually add 1 cup flour, stirring until smooth. Gradually stir in enough remaining flour to make a soft dough. Place in a well-greased bowl, turning to grease top of dough.

COVER and let rise in a warm place (85°), free from drafts, 1 hour or until doubled in bulk.

TURN dough out onto a floured surface; knead 5 or 6 times. Divide dough in half. Roll each dough portion on a lightly floured surface to ¼-inch thickness. Cut with a 2-inch round cutter. Brush rounds evenly with ¼ cup melted butter, and fold in half. Place rolls in 3 lightly greased 9-inch round cakepans.

COVER and let rise in a warm place, free from drafts, 1 hour or until doubled in size.

BAKE at 375° for 15 to 18 minutes or until golden. Brush with remaining ¼ cup melted butter.

CITRUS-PECAN ROLLS

family favorite

MAKES ABOUT 5 DOZEN

Prep: 1 hr., Rise: 2 hrs., Bake: 18 min.

> 2 cups granulated sugar
> ½ cup grated orange rind
> ¼ cup grated lime rind
> 1 recipe Easy Yeast Rolls dough
> ½ cup butter, melted
> 1½ cups finely chopped pecans, toasted
> 2½ cups powdered sugar
> 2 tablespoons grated orange rind
> ¼ cup fresh orange juice
> 2 tablespoons lime juice

COMBINE 2 cups granulated sugar, ½ cup grated orange rind, and ¼ cup grated lime rind, and set aside.

PREPARE 1 recipe Easy Yeast Rolls dough, letting it rise once for 1 hour. Turn dough out onto a lightly floured surface; knead 5 or 6 times. Divide dough in half. Roll each dough portion on a lightly floured surface into an 18- x 24-inch rectangle.

BRUSH dough rectangles with ¼ cup melted butter each. Spread half of granulated sugar mixture evenly over 1 dough rectangle; sprinkle with half of pecans. Cut dough rectangle in half crosswise, forming 2 (18- x 12-inch) rectangles; roll up, jellyroll fashion, starting at long edges. Repeat procedure with second dough rectangle.

CUT each dough log into 16 (1¼-inch-thick) slices. Place slices in lightly greased 8-inch round cakepans (12 rolls per cakepan).

LET rise, uncovered, in a warm place 1 hour or until doubled in size.

BAKE at 375° for 15 to 18 minutes or until rolls are lightly browned. Cool slightly in pans.

STIR together powdered sugar and remaining ingredients until blended. Drizzle powdered sugar mixture evenly over warm rolls, and serve immediately.

Perfect Giblet Gravy

GIBLET GRAVY

MAKES 4 CUPS

Prep: 10 min.; Cook: 1 hr., 5 min.

We used egg yolks and flour as thickeners in this luscious recipe.

> Giblets and neck from 1 turkey
> 4 cups water
> ½ cup butter or margarine
> 1 small onion, chopped
> 1 celery rib, chopped
> 1 carrot, chopped
> ¼ cup all-purpose flour
> 2 egg yolks
> ½ cup half-and-half
> ½ teaspoon salt
> ½ teaspoon pepper
> ½ teaspoon poultry seasoning
> Garnish: fresh parsley sprig

BRING giblets, neck, and 4 cups water to a boil in a medium saucepan over medium heat. Cover, reduce heat, and simmer 45 minutes or until tender. Drain, reserving broth. Chop giblets and neck meat, and set aside.

MELT butter in a large skillet over medium heat; add chopped vegetables, and sauté 5 minutes. Add flour, stirring until smooth. Add reserved broth; cook, stirring constantly, 10 minutes or until thickened. Reduce heat to low. Remove vegetables using a handheld, wire-mesh strainer, and discard, leaving gravy in skillet.

WHISK together egg yolks and half-and-half. Gradually stir about one-fourth of hot gravy into yolk mixture; add to remaining hot gravy. Add giblets and neck meat; cook, stirring constantly, 4 to 5 minutes or until a thermometer registers 160°. Stir in salt, pepper, and seasoning. Serve immediately. Garnish, if desired.

Make-Ahead Pasta Casseroles

Create heat-and-eat suppers your family will love.

Casseroles are invaluable during the holidays because of their make-ahead ease, and these mouthwatering dishes deliver just that. All of the recipes can be made the night before, if desired. Allow the casseroles to stand at room temperature for 30 minutes before baking. Or you can follow our easy freezing instructions for advance preparation up to a month.

If you enjoy the traditional flavors of lasagna, be sure to try Cheesy Sausage-and-Tomato Manicotti. Laura Martin of our Test Kitchens discovered an easy way to fill the manicotti shells. Simply slice each noodle lengthwise, fill, and fold the noodle back together. Then place the cut side down in the casserole dish. Stuffing pasta shells has never been easier.

CHEESY SAUSAGE-AND-TOMATO MANICOTTI

freezeable • make ahead

MAKES 6 SERVINGS

Prep: 25 min., Cook: 9 min., Bake: 20 min., Stand: 10 min.

- **1 (8-ounce) package uncooked manicotti noodles**
- **1 (15-ounce) can tomato sauce**
- **1 (10-ounce) can diced tomatoes and green chiles with garlic, oregano, and basil**
- **1 pound Italian sausage**
- **1 (8-ounce) package cream cheese**
- **1 cup ricotta cheese**
- **4 cups (16 ounces) shredded mozzarella cheese, divided**
- **½ cup chopped fresh parsley (optional)**

COOK pasta according to package directions; rinse with cold water. Drain.
PROCESS tomato sauce and diced tomatoes in a blender 20 seconds or until smooth. Set aside.
REMOVE casings from sausage, and discard. Cook sausage in a large skillet over medium-high heat, stirring until meat crumbles and is no longer pink. Stir in cream cheese, ricotta cheese, and 2 cups mozzarella cheese. Spoon into manicotti shells; arrange stuffed shells in a lightly greased 13- x 9-inch baking dish.
POUR tomato mixture over shells; sprinkle with remaining 2 cups mozzarella cheese.
BAKE at 350° for 20 minutes or until cheese is melted and bubbly. Let casserole stand 10 minutes before serving. Sprinkle with chopped fresh parsley, if desired.

NOTE: Casserole can be assembled and frozen up to 1 month. Thaw in the refrigerator overnight; bake, covered, at 350° for 30 minutes. Uncover and bake 15 more minutes or until cheese is melted and bubbly. If you prefer a smaller casserole, use 2 (11- x 7-inch) baking dishes. Proceed as directed.

GROUND BEEF-AND-TOMATO MANICOTTI: Substitute 1 pound lean ground beef for sausage. Stir in ½ teaspoon dried Italian seasoning, 1 teaspoon salt, 1 teaspoon pepper, and 1 teaspoon fennel seed. Proceed as directed.

CHRISTINA VALENTA
FRIENDSWOOD, TEXAS

TURKEY TETRAZZINI

freezeable • make ahead

MAKES 8 SERVINGS

Prep: 20 min., Bake: 45 min., Stand: 10 min.

- **1 (10¾-ounce) can cream of mushroom soup**
- **⅔ cup milk**
- **1 (16-ounce) jar Alfredo sauce**
- **3½ cups chopped cooked turkey, chicken, or ham**
- **12 ounces thin spaghetti, cooked**
- **1 (10-ounce) package frozen petite peas, thawed**
- **1 (8-ounce) package sliced fresh mushrooms**
- **1½ cups shredded baby Swiss cheese**
- **1 cup shredded Parmesan cheese, divided**
- **½ cup crushed garlic-and-onion seasoned croutons**
- **¼ teaspoon paprika**

WHISK together soup and milk in a large bowl; whisk in Alfredo sauce. Stir in chopped turkey, next 4 ingredients, and ½ cup Parmesan cheese. Pour mixture into a lightly greased 15- x 10-inch baking dish.
STIR together remaining Parmesan cheese, crushed croutons, and paprika; sprinkle evenly over casserole.
BAKE, covered, at 375° for 30 minutes. Uncover and bake 15 more minutes or until golden brown and bubbly. Let stand 10 minutes before serving.

NOTE: Casserole can be assembled and frozen up to 1 month. Thaw in the refrigerator overnight; bake, covered, at 350° for 40 minutes. Uncover and bake 15 more minutes or until cheese is melted and bubbly. If you prefer a smaller casserole, use 2 (11- x 7-inch) baking dishes. Proceed as directed.

ELIZABETH KENNARD
NORTH BARRINGTON, ILLINOIS

No-Fuss Supper Club

Celebration Supper

Serves 6

Whiskey Sours

Potato-and-Blue Cheese Pastries

Skillet Filets Mignon

Buttery Broccoli Medley

Beer-Parmesan Rolls

Lemon Chess Pie

Supper clubs are a fabulous way to get together with friends on a regular basis and experiment with new recipes. In many groups, the guests simply show up with a bottle of wine or fresh flowers and enjoy the evening. If you're the hostess, however, you've probably been cleaning and cooking all day.

Start a laid-back, budget-friendly monthly gathering that's fun for all members (including the host). You create a menu and prepare the main dish as well as a fitting beverage. Then ask for volunteers or assign a dish for each guest to bring. You may even want to provide recipes, especially for the less-seasoned cooks. It's also not a bad idea to call your guests on party day to ensure they're coming with dish in tow. What's left? Set the table, dish out the goodies, and dig in.

WHISKEY SOURS

fast fixin's • make ahead

MAKES ABOUT 12½ CUPS

Prep: 5 min.

- **1 (6-ounce) can frozen orange juice concentrate, thawed**
- **1 (6-ounce) can frozen limeade concentrate, thawed**
- **1 (6-ounce) can frozen lemonade concentrate, thawed**
- **4⅓ cups water**
- **2 cups bourbon**
- **1 (33.8-ounce) bottle club soda, chilled**
- **Ice cubes**
- **Garnishes: orange, lime, lemon slices**

STIR together concentrates, 4⅓ cups water, and bourbon. Stir in club soda just before serving. Serve over ice, and garnish, if desired.

SLUSHY WHISKEY SOURS: Stir together first 5 ingredients. Pour into a large zip-top freezer bag; seal. Freeze 2 hours. Spoon into a pitcher. Stir in club soda, and serve immediately.

AGNES L. STONE
OCALA, FLORIDA

POTATO-AND-BLUE CHEESE PASTRIES

make ahead

MAKES 22 SERVINGS

Prep: 25 min., Cook: 12 min., Bake: 30 min.

- **1 (22-ounce) package frozen mashed potatoes**
- **5 ounces crumbled blue cheese**
- **¼ cup butter or margarine, softened**
- **½ teaspoon salt**
- **½ teaspoon freshly ground pepper**
- **1 small onion, chopped**
- **1 tablespoon vegetable oil**
- **2 garlic cloves, minced**
- **1 (17¼-ounce) package frozen puff pastry sheets, thawed**

PREPARE mashed potatoes according to package directions. Stir in blue cheese and next 3 ingredients.

SAUTÉ onion in hot oil in a small nonstick skillet over medium-high heat 10 minutes or until tender. Add minced garlic, and sauté 2 minutes; stir into potato mixture.

UNFOLD 1 pastry sheet on a lightly floured surface; roll into an 11- x 11-inch square.

SPREAD half of potato mixture evenly over pastry sheet, leaving a 1-inch border. Roll up, jellyroll fashion, forming a log. Repeat procedure with remaining pastry sheet and potato mixture.

CUT each log into 11 (1-inch-thick) slices with a serrated knife; place slices on a lightly greased aluminum foil-lined baking sheet.

BAKE at 400° for 30 minutes or until golden brown. Serve warm.

SKILLET FILETS MIGNON

MAKES 6 SERVINGS

Prep: 15 min., Cook: 20 min.

- **6 (6-ounce) beef tenderloin filets**
- **1 teaspoon salt**
- **1 teaspoon freshly ground pepper**
- **¼ cup butter or margarine, divided**
- **1 tablespoon olive oil**
- **1 (8-ounce) package fresh mushrooms, thinly sliced**
- **½ cup dry sherry***
- **½ cup whipping cream**
- **Garnish: fresh flat-leaf parsley sprigs**

SPRINKLE beef evenly with salt and freshly ground pepper.

MELT 2 tablespoons butter with oil in a large skillet over medium-high heat; add steaks, and cook 8 minutes. Turn and cook 5 more minutes or to desired degree of doneness. Remove steaks from skillet, reserving drippings in pan. Keep steaks warm.

MELT remaining 2 tablespoons butter in skillet over medium-high heat; add mushrooms, and sauté 3 to 4 minutes. Remove mushrooms from skillet.

ADD sherry and cream to skillet; cook, stirring constantly, over high heat 1 to 2 minutes or until thickened. Stir in mushrooms. Serve mixture over beef; garnish, if desired.

*Substitute ¼ cup beef broth.

MARY PAPPAS
RICHMOND, VIRGINIA

Supper Club Plan

Host:
- Have serving platters, baskets, and utensils ready for guests' dishes.
- Whiskey Sours: Prepare mixture ahead, adding club soda just before serving.
- Skillet Filets Mignons: Cook immediately before serving.

Guests:
- Potato-and-Blue Cheese Pastries: Have guest prepare ahead; bake according to recipe 30 minutes before dinner.
- Buttery Broccoli Medley: Have guest prepare ahead, but do not sprinkle with green onions; bake 20 minutes to reheat, and sprinkle with green onions before serving.
- Beer-Parmesan Rolls: Have guest prepare ahead. Reheat, as directed, just before serving.
- Lemon Chess Pie: Have guest bake ahead; serve at room temperature.

BUTTERY BROCCOLI MEDLEY

make ahead

MAKES 6 TO 8 SERVINGS

Prep: 30 min., Cook: 15 min.

- 1 pound fresh broccoli
- 1 head fresh cauliflower, broken into florets
- ⅓ cup butter or margarine
- 1 red bell pepper, chopped
- 2 garlic cloves, minced
- 2 tablespoons Dijon mustard
- ¼ to ½ teaspoon salt
- ½ teaspoon freshly ground pepper
- 3 green onions, chopped

CUT broccoli into florets, reserving stems for another use.

ARRANGE cauliflower and broccoli in a steamer basket over boiling water. Cover and steam 10 minutes or until crisp-tender.

MELT butter in a Dutch oven over medium-high heat; add bell pepper and garlic, and sauté 3 to 5 minutes or until tender. Stir in broccoli, cauliflower, mustard, salt, and pepper; sprinkle with onions.

NOTE: To make ahead, spoon broccoli mixture into a greased 11- x 7-inch baking dish (do not sprinkle with onions); cover and chill. Bake, covered, at 350° for 20 minutes or until heated. Sprinkle with onions before serving.

ALICE B. FLINT
PLEASANT VALLEY, NEW YORK

BEER-PARMESAN ROLLS

make ahead

MAKES 20 ROLLS

Prep: 20 min., Bake: 25 min.

- 3 cups biscuit mix
- 3 tablespoons sugar
- ⅓ cup (1½ ounces) shredded Parmesan cheese
- 1 cup beer
- 3 tablespoons butter or margarine, melted
- ½ teaspoon dried Italian seasoning
- 2 tablespoons butter or margarine (optional)

STIR together first 6 ingredients until moistened. Drop dough by ¼-cupfuls onto lightly greased baking sheets.

BAKE at 425° for 25 minutes or until golden. Brush rolls with 2 tablespoons melted butter, if desired.

NOTE: Rolls can be stored overnight in an airtight container. To reheat, brush rolls with butter and bake at 425° for 4 to 5 minutes.

LEMON CHESS PIE

make ahead

MAKES 8 SERVINGS

Prep: 20 min., Bake: 57 min.

- 1 unbaked 9-inch deep-dish frozen pastry shell
- ¼ cup butter or margarine, softened
- 1½ cups sugar
- 4 large eggs
- 1 tablespoon grated lemon rind
- ¼ cup fresh lemon juice
- 1 tablespoon cornmeal
- Garnishes: lemon slice and zest

BAKE pastry shell at 425° for 7 minutes or until light golden brown. Reduce oven temperature to 350°.

BEAT butter and sugar at medium speed with an electric mixer until creamy; add eggs and next 3 ingredients, beating just until blended. Pour mixture into pastry shell; place on a baking sheet.

BAKE at 350° for 45 to 50 minutes or until pie is firm, shielding edges with aluminum foil to prevent excessive browning, if necessary. Cool completely on a wire rack. Garnish, if desired.

MANOLA WHEELER
BIRMINGHAM, ALABAMA

Creative Classic Sides

Try these dishes with slow-cooked roast pork or fried chicken, or serve them with the traditional turkey or ham. We know you'll enjoy them as much as we did.

HOLIDAY SPINACH WITH RED PEPPER RIBBONS

MAKES 4 SERVINGS

Prep: 15 min., Bake: 30 min., Stand: 10 min., Cook: 10 min.

Drizzle this dish with a good quality extra-virgin olive oil just before serving.

- 2 red bell peppers
- 3 teaspoons minced garlic
- 1 tablespoon olive oil
- 3 (6-ounce) packages fresh baby spinach
- 1 teaspoon salt
- ½ teaspoon pepper
- ¼ cup pine nuts, toasted
- 2 teaspoons balsamic vinegar (optional)

BAKE peppers on a lightly greased aluminum foil-lined baking sheet at 400° for 30 minutes or until peppers look blistered.

PLACE peppers in a zip-top plastic bag, and seal. Let stand 10 minutes to loosen skins. Peel peppers; remove and discard seeds. Cut peppers into thin slices. Set aside.

SAUTÉ garlic in hot olive oil in a large skillet over medium heat 2 minutes. Add spinach, 1 bag at a time, and sauté just until spinach begins to wilt. Add salt and pepper. Cover and reduce heat to medium low. Cook 2 to 3 more minutes or until spinach is completely wilted.

DRAIN spinach and return to skillet. Stir in sliced roasted peppers, pine nuts, and, if desired, vinegar. Cook over medium heat 5 minutes or until thoroughly heated, gently tossing to coat.

KITCHEN EXPRESS: Substitute 1 (7-ounce) jar roasted red bell peppers, drained and sliced, for 2 red bell peppers. Omit baking procedure, and proceed as directed.

LUCINDA LUCAS
CHARLOTTE, NORTH CAROLINA

FALL VEGETABLES

MAKES 6 SERVINGS

Prep: 20 min., Bake: 30 min. *(pictured on page 1)*

- 6 red potatoes, cut into quarters
- 2 large sweet potatoes, peeled and cubed
- 2 cups fresh brussels sprouts, cut in half
- 1 cup baby carrots
- 1 cup pearl onions
- 2 tablespoons olive oil
- ½ teaspoon salt
- ¼ teaspoon pepper
- ¼ teaspoon dried crushed rosemary

COMBINE all ingredients in a large bowl, and gently toss. Spread into an aluminum foil-lined jellyroll pan.

BAKE at 425° for 30 minutes or until potatoes are tender.

PRALINE SWEET POTATOES AND APPLES

MAKES 4 SERVINGS

Prep: 10 min., Cook: 25 min.

Two to three large sweet potatoes should equal two pounds.

- ¼ cup butter
- 2 pounds sweet potatoes, peeled and cut into ¼-inch-thick slices
- 2 apples, peeled and cut into ¼-inch-thick slices
- ¼ cup granulated sugar
- ¼ cup firmly packed brown sugar
- ¼ cup pecans, chopped
- ¼ teaspoon ground cinnamon
- ⅛ teaspoon salt
- 2 tablespoons water

MELT butter in a large skillet over medium heat. Add sweet potatoes; cover and cook over medium heat 5 minutes or until golden. Turn potato slices over. Reduce heat; cover and cook 5 more minutes.

REMOVE potatoes from skillet. Add apples; cook 5 minutes on each side or until tender and golden.

RETURN potatoes to skillet. Add sugars, pecans, cinnamon, and salt, tossing to coat. Add 2 tablespoons water, stirring to loosen browned particles. Cook 5 minutes or until potatoes and apples are glazed and tender.

CHEF SHARON WORSTER
THE WOODLANDS, TEXAS

ROOT VEGETABLE MEDLEY

MAKES 4 TO 6 SERVINGS

Prep: 10 min., Bake: 1 hr.

This recipe takes advantage of root vegetables, which are at their peak in fall and winter.

- 3 medium leeks
- 1 fennel bulb
- 3 large carrots, peeled and cut into ½-inch pieces (about 2 cups)
- 2 large parsnips or turnips, peeled and diced (about 2 cups)
- 10 large garlic cloves
- 3 tablespoons olive oil
- 2 fresh thyme or rosemary sprigs
- 2 large beets, peeled and cut into quarters
- 2 teaspoons salt
- ½ teaspoon freshly ground pepper

REMOVE bulbs from leeks, reserving green parts for another use. Cut bulbs into 1½-inch pieces.

REMOVE and discard fennel fronds and outside layer of fennel bulb. Cut fennel into slices.

TOSS together sliced leek bulbs, fennel, carrots, and next 4 ingredients. Place in a 13- x 9-inch roasting pan. Add beets; sprinkle vegetables with salt and pepper.

BAKE at 400° for 1 hour or until vegetables are tender, stirring twice.

RICHARD TURKHEIMER
NEW ORLEANS, LOUISIANA

Chicken Pot Pie, Spinach Salad, and
Baked Curried Fruit, pages 246–247

Braided Egg Bread, Dried Cherry-Walnut Sweet Rolls, Apricot-Orange Sweet Rolls, and Potato-Caramelized Onion Buns, pages 234–235

Dried Cherry-Walnut Sweet Rolls, page 235

Potato-Caramelized Onion Buns, page 234

Cranberry-Cheese Box, page 238

Baby Hot Browns, page 238

Turkey-Walnut Salad, page 239

Apple Brandy Turkey, Double Cranberry-Apple Sauce, Buttery Herb-Cheese Muffins, Green Beans With Grape Tomatoes, and Cornbread Dressing, pages 230–232

Pecan-Raisin Mini-Tarts, page 246

Roasted Butternut Squash Bisque, page 230

Turtle Cake, page 287

Celebrate the Season With Pecans

If you think pie is the only use for pecans, then we have some mouthwatering news for you. These golden-brown gems add wonderful crunch to many other desserts as well.

The baked apple recipe gives details on toasting pecans, which deepens their natural buttery sweetness. To fend off spoilage, refrigerate shelled pecans (toasted or untoasted) in an airtight container up to three months, or freeze up to six months.

PECAN PRALINE CHEESECAKE

make ahead

MAKES 12 SERVINGS

Prep: 30 min.; Bake: 1 hr., 10 min.; Stand: 30 min.; Cool: 30 min.; Chill: 8 hrs *(pictured on page 1)*

- 1½ cups crushed gingersnaps (about 24 cookies)
- ½ cup butter or margarine, melted and divided
- 5 (8-ounce) packages cream cheese, softened
- 1 cup granulated sugar
- 6 tablespoons all-purpose flour, divided
- 4 large eggs
- 1 teaspoon vanilla extract
- ¼ teaspoon salt
- ¼ cup firmly packed light brown sugar
- ½ cup chopped pecans, toasted

STIR together gingersnaps and ¼ cup melted butter; press mixture into bottom of a 9-inch springform pan.

BEAT cream cheese, granulated sugar, and 2 tablespoons flour at medium speed with an electric mixer 2 minutes. Add eggs, vanilla, and salt; beat 3 minutes. Pour batter into prepared crust. Set aside.

STIR together brown sugar, pecans, remaining ¼ cup flour, and remaining ¼ cup melted butter until crumbly. Sprinkle around edge of cream cheese mixture.

BAKE at 300° for 1 hour and 10 minutes or until center is firm. Turn off oven. Leave cheesecake in oven 30 minutes. Remove cheesecake from oven; cool in pan on a wire rack 30 minutes. Cover and chill 8 hours.

ELLEN J. LEE
CONCORD, GEORGIA

PECAN-AND-DRIED FRUIT BAKED APPLES

MAKES 6 SERVINGS

Prep: 35 min.; Bake: 1 hr., 35 min.; Cook: 10 min.

- ¼ cup chopped pecans
- 6 large Gala or Rome apples, cored
- 1 tablespoon lemon juice
- 2 tablespoons butter, softened and divided
- ½ cup raisins
- ¼ cup dried cranberries
- ¼ cup firmly packed brown sugar
- ½ teaspoon ground cinnamon
- ¼ teaspoon ground nutmeg
- ½ cup apple cider
- ¼ teaspoon vanilla extract
- 2 tablespoons rum (optional)
- Garnishes: whipped cream, toasted pecans

PLACE pecans on a baking sheet, and bake at 350° for 12 to 15 minutes or until golden brown, stirring once. Set pecans aside.

MAKE 4 evenly spaced vertical cuts through each apple, stopping halfway from bottom. Brush insides of apples with lemon juice. Place apples in a 9-inch pieplate.

COMBINE 1 tablespoon butter, raisins, and next 4 ingredients. Stuff mixture evenly into apples, pressing into center of each apple. Top evenly with remaining 1 tablespoon butter. Pour cider, vanilla, and, if desired, rum around apples in pieplate.

BAKE at 350° for 1 hour and 20 minutes, basting twice every 30 minutes or until apples are tender. Transfer apples to a serving dish, reserving juices, and keep apples warm.

POUR juices through a wire-mesh strainer into a small saucepan. Bring to a boil; reduce heat, and simmer over medium heat 8 to 10 minutes or until mixture is thickened and is syrup consistency. Drizzle over warm apples; garnish, if desired. Serve immediately.

CLAIRE MORRIS
ATLANTA, GEORGIA

Cheese Appetizers

When it comes to appetizers, nothing satisfies like cheese. Choices such as Cheddar and Parmesan offer loads of mellow flavor.

CHEESE PUFFS

family favorite

MAKES 2 DOZEN

Prep: 15 min., Cook: 5 min., Bake: 12 min.

- 1 (16-ounce) loaf French bread
- ½ cup butter or margarine
- 1 cup (4 ounces) shredded sharp Cheddar cheese
- 1 (3-ounce) package cream cheese
- 2 egg whites

TRIM crust from bread; discard. Cut bread into 2-inch cubes, and place in a large bowl.

MELT butter and cheeses in a saucepan over low heat; stir occasionally.

BEAT egg whites at high speed with an electric mixer until stiff peaks form; fold one-fourth whites into cheese mixture. Fold into remaining whites. Pour over bread cubes, tossing to coat. Place bread cubes in a single layer on an ungreased baking sheet.

BAKE at 400° for 12 minutes or until golden.

CLARISSA MCCONNELL
ORLANDO, FLORIDA

QUICK ARTICHOKE DIP

make ahead

MAKES 2 CUPS

Prep: 5 min., Chill: 1 hr.

½ cup reduced-fat mayonnaise
½ cup reduced-fat sour cream
1 (0.6-ounce) envelope Italian dressing
    mix
1 (16-ounce) can quartered artichoke
    hearts, drained
¼ cup shredded Parmesan cheese

PROCESS first 3 ingredients in a food processor until blended, stopping to scrape down sides. Add artichokes and cheese, pulsing 5 to 7 times or just until artichokes are coarsely chopped.
SPOON mixture into a serving bowl; cover and chill 1 hour.

JOSIE FLYNN
VIENNA, VIRGINIA

Cook's Pound Cake Notes

■ If you've never used a heavy-duty stand mixer, such as those made by KitchenAid, here's a tip: Decrease the mixing time. This type of mixer will cream butter in 1 minute at medium speed; other stand mixers may take as long as 7 minutes at high speed (you'll have to stop and scrape the sides, lengthening the time spent). Less-expensive hand mixers (we used a 125-watt one) take 2 to 3 minutes at medium speed. Some of our readers like a hand mixer because you can scoot it around the bowl and have more control.
■ Mixers come in all price ranges. A KitchenAid heavy-duty stand mixer is the most powerful and has many built-in, trademark features. The most popular model ranges from $199 to $250. Less powerful stand and hand mixers cover the middle of the spectrum, beginning at $25 to $40 and going upward.
■ A lower wattage, less expensive mixer will usually need a little more time to achieve the desired results. As long as you understand the difference, you're guaranteed excellent results, regardless of your mixer's price.

Mixing Up a Perfect Pound Cake

Perhaps one of the mixer's most important jobs in the Southern kitchen is making a pound cake. So with holiday baking in full swing, we put one of our favorite recipes, Million Dollar Pound Cake, to the test, using a hand mixer, a mid-range stand mixer, and a heavy-duty stand mixer. We got excellent results in all three cakes. The trick is knowing how long to beat the cake batter and what visual cues to look for in the batter. Our recipe takes you through the entire process, step-by-step.

MILLION DOLLAR POUND CAKE

family favorite

MAKES 10 TO 12 SERVINGS

Prep: depends on your mixer;
Bake: 1 hr., 40 min.; Cool: 15 min.

For the best results, preheat your oven to 300° before you begin. We also soften butter at room temperature for 30 minutes.

1 pound butter, softened
3 cups sugar
6 large eggs
4 cups all-purpose flour
¾ cup milk
1 teaspoon almond extract
1 teaspoon vanilla extract

BEAT butter at medium speed with an electric mixer until creamy. (The butter will become a lighter yellow color; this is an important step, as the job of the mixer is to incorporate air into the butter so the cake will rise. It will take 1 to 7 minutes, depending on the power of your mixer.) Gradually add sugar, beating at medium speed until light and fluffy. (Again, the times will vary, and butter will turn a fluffy white.) Add eggs, 1 at a time, beating just until yellow yolk disappears.

ADD flour to butter mixture alternately with milk, beginning and ending with flour. Beat batter at low speed just until blended after each addition. (The batter should be smooth and bits of flour should be well incorporated; to rid batter of lumps, stir gently with a rubber spatula.) Stir in almond and vanilla extracts.
POUR into a greased and floured 10-inch tube pan. (Use vegetable shortening to grease the pan, getting every nook and cranny covered. Sprinkle a light coating of flour over the greased surface.)
BAKE at 300° for 1 hour and 40 minutes or until a long wooden pick inserted in center of cake comes out clean. Cool in pan on a wire rack 10 to 15 minutes. Remove from pan, and cool completely on a wire rack.

NOTE: For testing purposes only, we used White Lily All-Purpose Flour.

Pork Chops Tonight

The next time you want to prepare pork chops, forget about frying. Cooking, grilling, and baking on the cooktop will all give great results. And no matter how you decide to prepare them, feel free to use either bone-in or boneless chops that are as thick or as thin as you like. Both kinds are versatile and very flavorful. You probably have the ingredients for these recipes on hand, so give a familiar cut of meat a tasty new attitude.

CIDER PORK CHOPS

family favorite

MAKES 4 SERVINGS

Prep: 15 min., Cook: 5 min., Bake: 1 hr.

If you choose a thinner, less expensive chop, decrease the cooking time. Begin to check for doneness after 30 minutes.

- ½ cup all-purpose flour
- 1 teaspoon salt
- ¼ teaspoon pepper
- 4 (1-inch-thick) bone-in pork chops
- 3 tablespoons butter or margarine, divided
- 4 Granny Smith apples, thinly sliced
- 1 cup raisins (optional)
- 1 cup firmly packed dark brown sugar
- 1 cup apple cider

COMBINE flour, 1 teaspoon salt, and ¼ teaspoon pepper in a zip-top freezer bag; add pork chops. Seal and shake to coat. Remove chops.
MELT 2 tablespoons butter in a large skillet; add chops, and cook 5 minutes on each side or until browned.
GREASE a 13- x 9-inch baking dish with remaining 1 tablespoon butter. Place apple slices in bottom of dish; top with raisins, if desired, and sprinkle with brown sugar. Arrange chops over brown sugar, and drizzle with apple cider.
BAKE at 350° for 1 hour or until pork chops are done.

GRILLED ASIAN PORK CHOPS

family favorite

MAKES 6 SERVINGS

Prep: 10 min., Chill: 4 hrs., Grill: 8 min.

Boneless chops also work well in this recipe. If you splurge on thicker chops, you'll need to cook them a bit longer.

- 6 tablespoons soy sauce
- 6 garlic cloves, minced
- 1 teaspoon pepper
- 2 teaspoons toasted sesame oil
- 2 teaspoons fresh lime juice
- 6 (¼- to ½-inch-thick) bone-in pork chops

COMBINE first 5 ingredients in a large shallow dish or zip-top freezer bag; add pork chops. Cover or seal, and chill 4 hours.
REMOVE chops from marinade, discarding marinade.
GRILL chops, covered with grill lid, over medium-high heat (350° to 400°) 4 minutes on each side or until an instant-read thermometer inserted into thickest portion of meat registers 160°.

JUDY LEE
AUSTIN, TEXAS

ITALIAN PORK CHOPS

family favorite

MAKES 4 SERVINGS

Prep: 10 min., Cook: 40 min.

- 4 (6-ounce) center-cut pork chops
- 1 tablespoon vegetable oil
- 1 (15-ounce) can tomato sauce
- ½ cup water
- 1 small onion, sliced
- 1 teaspoon Italian seasoning
- ½ teaspoon salt
- ½ teaspoon pepper
- 1 (8-ounce) package sliced fresh mushrooms
- 1 green bell pepper, sliced

BROWN chops in hot oil in a large skillet over medium-high heat. Drain and remove chops from skillet.
ADD tomato sauce, ½ cup water, and next 6 ingredients to skillet, stirring to combine. Return pork chops to skillet. Bring to a boil; cover, reduce heat, and simmer 30 minutes or until pork chops are tender.

NANCY RUSSELL
MORO, ARKANSAS

Have Snacks, Will Travel

"Are we there yet?" How often have you heard that road-trip query? Probably more times than you care to count. Holidays often mean travel, and dealing with car crankiness can be a daunting task for even the most patient among us.

To please the kids and grown-ups alike, take along these nonmessy homemade treats. They're just right for folks en route.

CRISPY PEANUT BUTTER-CHOCOLATE TREATS

family favorite • fast fixin's

MAKES 16 SQUARES

Prep: 15 min., Cook: 5 min.

This recipe got our Test Kitchens' highest rating.

- 1½ cups sugar
- 1½ cups light corn syrup
- 1½ cups chunky peanut butter
- 6 cups crisp rice cereal
- 1 (12-ounce) package semisweet chocolate morsels

COOK first 3 ingredients in a large saucepan over medium-low heat, stirring constantly, until blended and mixture begins to bubble. Remove pan from heat.
COMBINE 6 cups cereal and chocolate morsels in a large bowl. Stir in hot peanut butter mixture until combined. Spread mixture into a plastic wrap-lined 13- x 9-inch pan. Cool completely; cut into squares.

SPICY NUT POPCORN

fast fixin's

MAKES 8 SERVINGS

Prep: 10 min., Cook: 5 min.

- 3 tablespoons butter or margarine
- 1 cup pine nuts or pecans
- ¾ cup slivered almonds
- 1 teaspoon chili powder
- ½ teaspoon salt
- ½ teaspoon grated lime rind
- 1 tablespoon fresh lime juice
- ¼ teaspoon ground cloves
- ¼ teaspoon pepper
- 1 (3-ounce) bag low-fat popcorn, popped

MELT butter in a large skillet over medium heat; add pine nuts and next 7 ingredients, and sauté 3 to 4 minutes. Pour warm mixture over popcorn, tossing to coat.

NOTE: For testing purposes only, we used Orville Redenbacher's Smart Pop Gourmet Popping Corn.

SPRING DE LEON
LISLE, ILLINOIS

WALNUT-DATE BARS

freezeable • make ahead

MAKES 16 SQUARES

Prep: 20 min., Bake: 35 min., Stand: 30 min.

Wrap these chewy treats in plastic wrap, and place them in a zip-top freezer bag; freeze up to three months, if desired.

- 1 (18.25-ounce) package yellow cake mix
- ⅔ cup firmly packed brown sugar
- 2 large eggs
- ¾ cup butter or margarine, melted
- 2 cups chopped dates, divided
- 2 cups chopped walnuts or pecans, divided

COMBINE cake mix and sugar in a mixing bowl. Add eggs and melted butter, beating at medium speed with an electric mixer until blended (batter will be stiff). Spoon half of batter into a lightly greased 13- x 9-inch pan; sprinkle with 1 cup each of dates and walnuts.
STIR remaining 1 cup each of dates and walnuts into remaining batter; spread over mixture in pan.
BAKE at 350° for 30 to 35 minutes or until golden. Run a knife around edge of pan to loosen sides. Let stand 30 minutes before cutting. Cut into squares, and store bars in an airtight container.

PAT ASAY
PHOENIX, ARIZONA

Taste of the South

Oysters Rockefeller

There is much ado over the original recipe for Oysters Rockefeller. We do know that it was invented by Jules Alciatore, the second-generation proprietor of Antoine's restaurant in New Orleans. We don't know, however, what exactly went into the original dish—just that there was a wealth of bright green herbs and it was rich, like John D. Rockefeller himself.

In restaurants today, we find a host of impostors, such as oysters masked in Parmesan cheese, parading around with pale artichoke hearts, or cavorting with anchovy paste.

These variations, although often delicious, are not the true taste of Oysters Rockefeller. A true Rockefeller is bold and strong with freshly blended ingredients including parsley, celery leaf, and fennel bulb. The addition of anise-flavored liqueur such as Pernod only enhances the green herbaceous flavor.

Over the years, there has been the spinach vs. watercress debate for this dish. Assistant Foods Editor Kim Sunée prefers, when in season, the edgy bite of crisp watercress. But if you favor spinach and no celery leaves or tarragon and no chervil, use what you like. When making these baked bivalves, it's important to choose the freshest oysters and herbs available.

Our version of Oysters Rockefeller, adapted from a wealth of provocative recipes, rated very highly in our Test Kitchens. It seems that this classic Southern taste, which has incited such debate, must be worth trying at least once.

OYSTERS ROCKEFELLER

MAKES 4 TO 6 SERVINGS

Prep: 45 min., Cook: 8 min., Bake: 15 min.

- 1 cup unsalted butter, divided
- ½ cup chopped flat-leaf parsley
- ¼ cup chopped green onions
- ¼ cup fennel bulb, chopped
- 1 teaspoon chopped fresh chervil or tarragon
- 2 to 3 chopped celery leaves
- 2 cups watercress or baby spinach leaves
- ⅓ cup fine, dry breadcrumbs
- 2 tablespoons anise-flavored liqueur
- ¼ teaspoon salt
- ¼ teaspoon pepper
- ⅛ to ¼ teaspoon hot sauce
- ½ (4-pound) box rock salt
- 2 dozen fresh oysters on the half shell
- Rock salt
- Garnish: lemon wedges

MELT 3 tablespoons butter in a skillet over medium-high heat; add parsley and next 4 ingredients. Sauté 2 to 3 minutes. Add watercress to skillet, and cook 2 to 3 minutes or until wilted. Cool.
PULSE parsley mixture in a food processor with the remaining 13 tablespoons butter, breadcrumbs, and liqueur until smooth, stopping to scrape down sides.
ADD salt, pepper, and hot sauce.
FILL pie pans or a large baking sheet with 2 pounds rock salt. Dampen salt slightly, and arrange oysters on the beds of salt.
TOP each oyster with a spoonful of parsley mixture.
BAKE at 450° about 12 to 15 minutes or until lightly browned and bubbly. Serve on a bed of rock salt, and garnish, if desired.

NOTE: For testing purposes, we used Pernod for anise-flavored liqueur.

Kid-Friendly Cookies

You'll cook up happy holiday memories with any of these recipes.

When Assistant Foods Editor Shannon Sliter Satterwhite was a kid, she couldn't wait for the holidays. It was always fun for her sister, Leslie, and her to help their mom make festive treats. Her nephew, Hunter, and his cousin, Rachel, experienced the same thrill preparing these cookie recipes. Your young chefs also will enjoy the fun of breaking Toffee Cookie Bites and powdering Peppermint Crescents. (Just leave the oven duty to the grown-ups.) Who knows? You might inspire the next Julia Child or Emeril Lagasse.

TOFFEE COOKIE BITES

family favorite • make ahead

MAKES ABOUT 4½ DOZEN

Prep: 10 min., Bake: 15 min., Chill: 2 hrs.

- 24 saltine crackers
- 1 cup butter
- 1 cup firmly packed light brown sugar
- 1 (12-ounce) package milk chocolate morsels
- ½ cup chopped pecans or walnuts, toasted

COVER bottom of a 13- x 9-inch aluminum foil-lined pan with crackers.

MICROWAVE butter and brown sugar in a microwave-safe glass bowl at HIGH for 3 to 4 minutes or until sugar dissolves, stirring occasionally. Pour butter mixture over crackers.

BAKE at 325° for 15 minutes or until bubbly. Remove from oven, and sprinkle with chocolate morsels, spreading as they melt. Sprinkle with pecans.

COVER and chill at least 2 hours. Cut toffee into 1-inch squares or break into pieces, and store in an airtight container in refrigerator.

PAM LUTGEN
LARGO, FLORIDA

PEPPERMINT CRESCENTS

family favorite • make ahead

MAKES 3 DOZEN

Prep: 30 min., Bake: 18 min. per batch, Cool: 5 min.

- 1 cup butter, softened
- 1⅔ cups powdered sugar, divided
- 1¼ teaspoons peppermint extract, divided
- ⅛ teaspoon salt
- 2 cups all-purpose flour
- Sifted powdered sugar
- 2 tablespoons milk
- Hard peppermint candies, crushed

BEAT butter at medium speed with an electric mixer until creamy. Gradually add ⅔ cup powdered sugar, 1 teaspoon peppermint extract, and salt, beating well. Gradually add flour, beating until blended.

DIVIDE dough into 3 portions; divide each portion into 12 pieces. Roll each piece into a 2-inch log, curving ends to form a crescent. Place crescents 2 inches apart on lightly greased baking sheets.

BAKE at 325° for 15 to 18 minutes or until lightly browned. Cool 5 minutes.

Carefully roll warm cookies in sifted powdered sugar. Cool completely on wire racks.

STIR together milk, remaining 1 cup powdered sugar, and remaining ¼ teaspoon extract until smooth. Drizzle cookies with icing, and sprinkle with crushed candies, gently pressing. Store in airtight containers.

SANDY RUSSELL
ORANGE PARK, FLORIDA

CHOCOLATE SNOWBALLS

family favorite • make ahead

MAKES ABOUT 7 DOZEN

Prep: 25 min., Bake: 10 min. per batch

- 1¼ cups butter, softened
- ⅔ cup granulated sugar
- 2 teaspoons vanilla extract
- 2 cups all-purpose flour
- ½ cup unsweetened cocoa
- ¼ teaspoon salt
- ½ cup finely chopped unsalted peanuts
- Sifted powdered sugar

BEAT butter at medium speed with an electric mixer until creamy; gradually add granulated sugar and vanilla, beating well.

COMBINE flour, cocoa, salt, and nuts; gradually add to butter mixture, beating until blended.

PORTION dough by teaspoonfuls, and roll into balls; place on ungreased baking sheets.

BAKE at 350° for 8 to 10 minutes. Roll warm cookies in sifted powdered sugar.

PENNY JUAREZ
COLORADO SPRINGS, COLORADO

from our kitchen

Creating Keepsake Cookbooks

We all have our favorite cookbooks, but dearest to the heart are those unpublished collections of familiar recipes that remind us of home. If you're in search of a special gift this holiday season, consider a hand-made cookbook. It's easier than ever to design your own. All you need to get started are a few clever ideas and some inexpensive supplies from an art-supply or crafts store.

■ Use a color copier to reproduce old black-and-white photographs and handwritten recipes. You'll be amazed at how closely they resemble the originals, and lucky relatives will be delighted to have duplicates of those treasures.

■ Group different types of recipes together for gift giving. You might want to create a small book filled with favorite cookie recipes or pasta casseroles. Assemble a collection of luncheon menus from members of your church circle, or celebrate the culinary skills of your supper club with a stylish volume of gourmet appetizers and entrées.

■ If you don't have family recipes to share, personalize a published cookbook with a colorful index of your favorite recipes attached inside the cover.

■ Scrapbooks, journals, and photo albums with acid-free paper and page protectors come in a wide variety of sizes and styles. Just arrange your recipes and photographs on decorative paper or vellum, and then add festive designs with self-adhesive borders and illustrations.

Note: For our albums, we used materials designed by artist Susan Branch (**www.susanbranch.com**). For a list of retail outlets in your area visit **www.colorbok.com**.

Tips and Tidbits

■ If you're doubling a recipe and discover your largest mixing bowl is too small for the task at hand, try using a roasting pan or a stockpot as a substitute. Disposable roasting pans are often on sale during the holidays.

■ When preparing a casserole for the freezer, line the baking dish with heavy-duty aluminum foil, leaving several inches of overhang around the sides. Freeze until firm; then remove the foil-lined frozen casserole from the baking dish, and store in a zip-top freezer bag. When ready to serve, remove the foil, and place the frozen casserole back into the original baking dish. Thaw in the refrigerator, and bake as directed.

■ For information on all things turkey, you can call the 24-hour Butterball Turkey Talk-Line at 1-800-BUTTERBALL (1-800-288-8372), or visit **www.butterball.com.** For concerns about food safety issues, call the USDA Meat and Poultry Hotline at 1-800-535-4555.

■ Take a break from the flurry of holiday preparations, and invite several close friends over for a simple supper of homemade soup and sandwiches. For easy-to-make recipes visit **southernliving.com/features.**

Blessings of Peace and Plenty

In the spirit of holiday and yuletide tradition, the Lindsay Olive Company offers a unique 20-inch wreath woven from fresh green olive branches. All profits from the sale of these wreaths will be donated to America's Second Harvest, the nation's largest domestic hunger-relief program. These are available exclusively through the Web site **www.lindsayolives.com** for $50 plus shipping.

Stocking Up on Flavor

A rich, full-bodied broth can add tremendous flavor to an otherwise ordinary recipe. If you don't have time to linger around the stove all day, start with 2 quarts of canned chicken broth. Add 1 cup each of coarsely chopped celery, carrots, and onion; $\frac{1}{2}$ cup chopped fresh parsley; 2 large garlic cloves, pressed; and the leftover bones and scraps from a roasted turkey or chicken. Bring the ingredients to a boil; reduce heat, and simmer broth 45 minutes, skimming the surface to remove excess fat and foam. Strain and chill up to two days or freeze up to one month.

Sentimental Favorites

For many of us, the holidays wouldn't be the same without these recipes. We thought we'd pass them along to you.

Home for the Holidays

Serves 6 to 8

Butternut Squash Soup

Creamy Crawfish Pasta

Garlic-Orange Roast Pork

Suppertime Pancakes   Nana's Collard Greens

Cranberry Conserve

Coconut Cake   Mama's Fudge

Stylish Holiday Blooms

Small arrangements lend themselves to a variety of flowers that are a bit different from standard holiday fare. When choosing blooms for a dinner table, remember to forego fragrance. Here are a few options.

- anemone
- green button chrysanthemums
- Ranunculus
- spray roses
- dendrobium orchids
- calla lilies

Whether you're just establishing your holiday traditions or simply looking to add an extra-special touch of seasonal spirit to a time-honored heritage, we'd like to share some of our own sentimental favorites. This mouthwatering collection of holiday dishes is sure to add sparkle to your table, as they do to ours.

The *Southern Living* family drew from the warm, childhood memories of Christmas past in putting together this menu for you. Quite simply, for our staff, the holidays wouldn't be the same without these recipes. Several of the classics received an update, while others were streamlined for your convenience. There's something for everyone regardless of your time, budget, or confidence in the kitchen.

Your only requirement is to round out the occasion with warmth and hospitality.

BUTTERNUT SQUASH SOUP

family favorite

MAKES 8 SERVINGS

Prep: 25 min., Cook: 50 min.

This rich, creamy soup is Greg Cosby's idea of comfort food. The Photo Services staffer says, "My mom, Priscilla, always roasted her squash, but I've managed to make my mom's recipe easier by using frozen butternut squash. It's very simple for the novice cook."

- 6 bacon slices
- 1 large onion, chopped
- 2 carrots, chopped
- 2 celery ribs, chopped
- 1 Granny Smith apple, peeled and finely chopped
- 2 garlic cloves, chopped
- 4 (12-ounce) packages frozen butternut squash, thawed*
- 1 (32-ounce) container low-sodium, fat-free chicken broth
- 2 to 3 tablespoons fresh lime juice
- 1½ tablespoons honey
- 2 teaspoons salt
- 1 teaspoon ground black pepper
- ⅛ teaspoon ground allspice
- ⅛ teaspoon ground nutmeg
- ⅛ teaspoon ground red pepper
- ¼ cup whipping cream
- Garnishes: sour cream, ground red pepper

COOK bacon slices in a Dutch oven until crisp; remove bacon, and drain on paper towels, reserving 2 tablespoons drippings in pan. Crumble bacon, and set aside.

SAUTÉ chopped onion and carrots in hot bacon drippings in Dutch oven over medium-high heat 5 minutes or until onion is tender.

ADD celery and apple to onion mixture, and sauté 5 minutes. Add garlic, and sauté 30 seconds.

ADD butternut squash and chicken broth. Bring mixture to a boil; reduce heat, and simmer 20 minutes or until carrots are tender.

PROCESS mixture, in batches, in a blender or food processor until smooth.

RETURN mixture to Dutch oven. Stir in lime juice and next 7 ingredients. Simmer 10 to 15 minutes or until thickened.

Top soup with crumbled bacon. Garnish, if desired.

*Substitute 3 pounds butternut squash, peeled, seeded, and chopped for frozen, if desired.

NOTE: For testing purposes only, we used McKenzie's Southland Frozen Butternut Squash.

PRISCILLA COSBY
ROGERSVILLE, ALABAMA

CREAMY CRAWFISH PASTA

MAKES 6 TO 8 SERVINGS
Prep: 20 min., Cook: 20 min.

Copy Chief Dawn Cannon credits her Aunt Vivian Barilleaux for this rich pasta dish. "I streamlined her recipe a bit and reduced the amount of butter to ½ cup. However, I did keep the whipping cream," Dawn says with a smile. To speed up prep time, she does all the chopping in a food processor.

    1 (8-ounce) package uncooked
        linguine
    ½ cup butter
    ⅓ cup all-purpose flour
    1 bunch green onions, finely
        chopped
    1 small onion, minced
    4 garlic cloves, minced
    ½ green bell pepper, minced
    2 celery ribs, minced
    1 chicken bouillon cube
    1 pint whipping cream
    1 (2-pound) package frozen
        crawfish tails, thawed*
    1 (10-ounce) can diced tomatoes
        and green chiles, drained
    1 tablespoon Creole seasoning
    1 tablespoon chopped fresh
        parsley
    ¼ teaspoon pepper
    ⅛ teaspoon salt
    Hot sauce (optional)
    Shredded Parmesan cheese
    Garnish: chopped fresh parsley

COOK linguine according to package directions; drain. Keep warm.
MELT butter in a Dutch oven over medium heat. Add flour, and cook, stirring constantly, 2 minutes or until blended.
ADD green onions and next 4 ingredients; sauté 5 minutes or until tender. Add bouillon cube and next 7 ingredients; cook 10 minutes or until thickened. Stir in hot sauce, if desired.
SERVE over linguine noodles; sprinkle with shredded Parmesan cheese. Garnish, if desired.

*Substitute 2 pounds peeled, medium-size fresh or frozen shrimp for crawfish tails, if desired.

VIVIAN BARILLEAUX
HARAHAN, LOUISIANA

GARLIC-ORANGE ROAST PORK

MAKES 8 TO 10 SERVINGS
Prep: 30 min.; Bake: 3 hrs., 55 min.;
Stand: 20 min.; Cook: 1 min.

This festive recipe from Assistant Foods Editor Kim Sunée combines the vibrant flavors of her childhood growing up in New Orleans. In fact, Kim's so fond of the recipe, she submitted it in last year's *Southern Living* Cook-Off (prior to joining our staff).

    2 cups chopped fresh parsley
    ¼ cup herbes de Provence
    2 tablespoons grated lemon rind
    ¼ cup fresh lemon juice
    1 (5- to 6-pound) Boston butt pork
        roast
    1 tablespoon salt, divided
    1 tablespoon pepper, divided
    10 garlic cloves, divided
    2 large oranges, sliced
    2 tablespoons olive oil
    2¼ cups orange juice, divided
    4 pints cherry tomatoes
    1 tablespoon cornstarch
    Garnishes: cilantro sprigs, fresh
        orange slices

COMBINE first 4 ingredients. Set aside.
BUTTERFLY roast by making a lengthwise cut down center of 1 flat side, cutting to within 1 inch of bottom. Open roast; sprinkle evenly with 1 teaspoon each of salt and pepper. Chop 2 garlic cloves, and sprinkle evenly over pork. Rub half of parsley mixture evenly over pork; fold pork over to close; tie pork at 1-inch intervals with string. Sprinkle evenly with remaining 2 teaspoons each of salt and pepper on outside of pork.
PLACE orange slices in bottom of a roasting pan with remaining 8 garlic cloves; drizzle with oil. Place pork on top of orange slices; pour 2 cups orange juice over pork.
BAKE at 450° for 15 minutes; reduce heat to 325°, and bake, basting every 20 minutes, for 1 hour and 30 minutes. Add tomatoes to pan, and bake 2 more hours or until a meat thermometer inserted into thickest portion registers 150°, basting occasionally with pan drippings. Remove pork from oven, and coat evenly with remaining parsley mixture.
BAKE 10 more minutes or until a meat thermometer registers 155°. Remove pork, orange slices, and tomatoes from pan; cover with aluminum foil, and let stand 20 minutes for temperature to rise to 160° and juices to settle. Reserve drippings in pan.
COMBINE cornstarch and remaining ¼ cup orange juice; stir into drippings. Bring mixture to a boil, and cook, stirring constantly, 1 minute or until thickened. Pour sauce through a wire-mesh strainer, if desired. Serve pork with tomatoes, orange slices, and sauce. Garnish, if desired.

SUPPERTIME PANCAKES

MAKES 14 PANCAKES

Prep: 20 min., Cook: 4 min. per batch

"My mom, Libby, always serves these during the holidays. She usually places two pancakes under slices of pork roast, fried pork chops, or boneless fried chicken breasts, and always smothered in gravy. I also like to serve them for breakfast, topped with over-easy eggs and salsa." Scott Jones, Foods Editor

- 1 tablespoon butter
- ½ medium onion, chopped
- 1 garlic clove, chopped
- ½ cup milk
- 1 tablespoon Dijon mustard
- 4 bacon slices, cooked and crumbled
- 4 large eggs*
- ⅛ teaspoon salt
- 1 teaspoon Creole or fajita seasoning
- ¼ teaspoon pepper
- 1 (10-ounce) package frozen chopped spinach, thawed and drained
- 1 cup fine, dry Italian-seasoned breadcrumbs
- ¼ cup shredded Parmesan cheese

MELT butter in a skillet over medium-high heat; add onion, and sauté until tender. Add garlic, and sauté 30 seconds. Remove skillet from heat; let cool.
STIR together milk and next 6 ingredients in a large bowl. Stir in cooled onion mixture, spinach, breadcrumbs, and Parmesan cheese.
POUR about ¼ cup batter into a hot, nonstick skillet over medium heat. (Batter will spread to about a 4-inch circle.) Cook pancakes 2 minutes on each side or until done. Serve immediately, or keep warm in oven.

*Substitute 1 cup egg substitute for eggs, if desired.

LIBBY TROMBLEY
APOPKA, FLORIDA

NANA'S COLLARD GREENS

MAKES 6 TO 8 SERVINGS

Prep: 20 min.; Cook: 1 hr., 15 min.

"My late grandmother, Cora Meadows, always used carrots to sweeten her greens," says Designer/Illustrator Christopher Davis, who updated the recipe by using fat-free chicken broth and a touch of balsamic vinegar. We think these greens would be great over grits too.

- 4 bacon slices
- 1 large carrot, chopped
- 1 large onion, chopped
- 2 garlic cloves, minced
- 2 to 3 tablespoons balsamic vinegar
- 4 (1-pound) packages fresh collard greens, washed, trimmed, and chopped
- 1½ cups low-sodium, fat-free chicken broth
- ½ teaspoon dried red pepper flakes
- ½ teaspoon salt
- ¼ teaspoon pepper

COOK bacon in a Dutch oven until crisp; remove bacon, and drain on paper towels, reserving 2 tablespoons drippings. Crumble bacon.
COOK carrot in hot bacon drippings in Dutch oven over medium-high heat, stirring occasionally, 5 minutes.
ADD onion, and cook, stirring occasionally, 5 minutes or until carrot and onion begin to caramelize.
ADD garlic, and cook, stirring constantly, 30 seconds. Add balsamic vinegar, and cook 30 seconds. Add collards, reserved bacon, broth, and remaining ingredients.
BRING to a boil; cover, reduce heat, and simmer 1 hour or until collards are tender.

CRANBERRY CONSERVE

MAKES 8 TO 10 SERVINGS

Prep: 10 min., Cook: 30 min., Chill: 3 hrs.

Senior Copy Editor Susan Roberts picked up this tangy-sweet spread from her grandmother, Georgia Roberts. "Sometimes I add a touch of apple juice or cider to punch up the flavor," she says. The conserve is also perfect with leftover turkey sandwiches.

- 4 cups fresh cranberries
- 1 cup water
- 1 orange
- 1 cup raisins
- 2½ cups sugar
- ½ cup finely chopped pecans

COMBINE cranberries and 1 cup water in a large saucepan; bring to a boil. Cover, reduce heat, and simmer 6 to 8 minutes or until cranberry skins pop.
GRATE rind of orange; peel, seed, and dice orange. Stir together cranberries, orange, grated rind, raisins, sugar, and pecans.
COOK over low heat, stirring often, 20 minutes or until mixture thickens. Remove from heat; cool. Cover and chill at least 3 hours.

GEORGIA ROBERTS
MONTICELLO, KENTUCKY

COCONUT CAKE

make ahead

MAKES 1 (4-LAYER) CAKE, 8 TO 10 SERVINGS

Prep: 20 min., Bake: 30 min., Chill: 3 days

"I never remember a Christmas without my mother's coconut cake," says Creative Development Director Valerie Fraser, who thinks this one is so easy because it starts with a mix. The frozen flaked coconut provides the cake's moist texture.

- 1 (18.25-ounce) package butter cake mix
- ½ teaspoon almond extract
- 3 (6-ounce) packages frozen flaked coconut, thawed
- 2 cups sugar
- 1 (8-ounce) container sour cream
- 1 (8-ounce) container frozen whipped topping, thawed
- Flaked coconut
- Garnish: halved kumquats

PREPARE cake mix batter according to package directions, adding almond extract to cake batter.

POUR batter into 2 greased and floured (8-inch) round cakepans.

BAKE at 375° for 28 to 30 minutes or until a wooden pick inserted in center comes out clean. (Do not overbake.) Cool in pans 10 minutes. Remove from pans, and cool completely on wire racks. Slice each cake layer in half horizontally. Set aside.

COMBINE 3 packages coconut, sugar, and sour cream, reserving 1 cup mixture.

SPREAD remaining mixture evenly between 3 cake layers. Fold whipped topping into reserved 1 cup mixture, and spread on top and sides of cake. Sprinkle top and sides of cake evenly with flaked coconut. Cover and chill 1 to 3 days before serving. Garnish, if desired.

NOTE: For testing purposes only, we used Duncan Hines Moist Deluxe Butter Recipe Golden.

NANNETTE FRASER
HARPERSVILLE, ALABAMA

MAMA'S FUDGE

MAKES ABOUT 20 (1-INCH) PIECES

Prep: 10 min., Cook: 20 min., Cool: 30 min.

"My grandmother, Ruth Pilgrim, taught my mother, Anne Kracke, how to make this fudge, and my mother, in turn, taught me," says Rebecca Kracke Gordon of the Test Kitchens. She adds that this decadent goodie is a staple gift during the holidays for teachers, neighbors, and friends.

2 cups sugar
⅔ cup milk
¼ cup unsweetened cocoa
1 tablespoon corn syrup
¼ teaspoon salt
3 tablespoons butter
1 teaspoon vanilla extract

STIR together first 5 ingredients in a 2-quart saucepan. Bring mixture to a boil over medium-high heat, and cook until a candy thermometer registers 240° (soft ball stage). Remove from heat; add butter, and let melt. (Do not

stir.) Let cool 10 to 15 minutes or until pan is cool to the touch. Stir in vanilla.

BEAT mixture with an electric mixer at medium-low speed 2 to 3 minutes or until mixture begins to lose its gloss. Working quickly, pour fudge onto a buttered 11- x 7-inch platter. Let cool 15 minutes. Cut into 1-inch pieces.

ANNE KRACKE
BIRMINGHAM, ALABAMA

What's for Supper?

'Twas the Night Before

A Simple Pasta Supper

Serves 6

Pasta With Sausage and Kale

Holiday Citrus and Greens

Toasted Pizza Crust Wedges

The stores have finally closed, and friends and family have settled in from out of town. Perhaps a lazy after-dinner drive to enjoy holiday lights or a church celebration is on the evening agenda. We put together a menu for you—a main dish, salad, and bread—that's simple to do yet special enough to win praise. Tie up this menu package by serving any one of the sweet treats you'll find in this issue.

PASTA WITH SAUSAGE AND KALE

MAKES 6 SERVINGS

Prep: 15 min., Cook: 25 min.

Kale is most often seen as a garnish. It has a mild cabbagelike flavor that's nice with sausage. To save a few minutes on cook time, use spinach, which doesn't require steaming. Cook pasta, chop onion, and toast pine nuts the day before. Rinse pasta with cold water to wash away starches that cause sticking and refrigerate in a zip-top freezer bag.

4 large kale leaves*
1 (12-ounce) package bow tie pasta
¾ pound hot Italian sausage
1 medium onion, chopped
4 garlic cloves, minced
¼ cup balsamic vinegar
1 (14½-ounce) can chicken broth
4 fresh basil leaves, thinly sliced
1 tablespoon chopped fresh or
   1 teaspoon dried oregano
⅛ teaspoon salt
¼ teaspoon pepper
3 tablespoons pine nuts, toasted
6 ounces crumbled feta cheese

ARRANGE kale in a steamer basket over boiling water; cover and steam 2 minutes. Drain. Remove heavy stems, and cut leaves into thin strips.

COOK pasta according to package directions; drain and set aside.

REMOVE and discard casings from sausage. Cook sausage in a Dutch oven over medium heat, stirring until it crumbles and is no longer pink; drain.

ADD onion to sausage in Dutch oven, and sauté 5 minutes. Add garlic, and sauté 1 minute. Add vinegar, and cook 3 minutes. Add chicken broth and kale; cook 5 minutes. Stir in basil and next 3 ingredients; cook 1 minute. Stir in pine nuts, pasta, and feta cheese; cook until thoroughly heated. Serve immediately.

*Substitute 1 (6-ounce) package fresh baby spinach for kale, if desired. Omit steaming procedure.

CAROLE JONES
SURF CITY, NORTH CAROLINA

HOLIDAY CITRUS AND GREENS

fast fixin's • make ahead

MAKES 6 TO 8 SERVINGS

Prep: 15 min.

- ¾ cup olive oil
- ¼ cup white wine vinegar
- 2 garlic cloves, minced
- 1 tablespoon sugar
- 3 tablespoons fresh orange juice
- 1 tablespoon fresh lemon juice
- ¼ teaspoon dried basil
- 1 teaspoon salt
- ¼ teaspoon freshly ground pepper
- 1 (10-ounce) package romaine lettuce
- 1 (5-ounce) package fresh baby spinach
- 1 cucumber, sliced
- 1 red bell pepper, sliced
- 3 navel oranges, peeled and sectioned
- 1 cup walnut halves, toasted

WHISK together first 9 ingredients. Layer lettuce and next 4 ingredients over dressing. (Cover and chill up to 12 hours, if desired.) Add walnuts, and toss before serving.

ALEXIS IWANISZIW
PHILADELPHIA, PENNSYLVANIA

TOASTED PIZZA CRUST WEDGES

fast fixin's

MAKES 6 TO 8 SERVINGS

Prep: 10 min., Cook: 7 min., Bake: 10 min.

- ⅓ cup butter
- 2 garlic cloves, minced
- ½ to 1 teaspoon dried Italian seasoning or rosemary
- 2 (14-ounce) Italian bread shells*
- ½ cup shredded Parmesan cheese

MELT butter in a small saucepan over medium heat; add garlic and Italian seasoning. Reduce heat, and simmer 5 minutes. Remove from heat.
BRUSH each bread shell with half of butter mixture; sprinkle with ¼ cup cheese. Cut each bread shell into 12 wedges. Place on a lightly greased baking sheet.
BAKE at 450° for 8 to 10 minutes or until crisp.

*Substitute 1 (16-ounce) French bread loaf, sliced, if desired.

Celebrate the Season

The *Southern Living® Cooking School* helps you welcome family and friends into your home with these easy recipes perfect for memorable holiday gatherings or casual weeknights.

Southern Living Cooking School has put together a wide variety of recipes sure to make party menu or supper decisions easy. You'll find choices for Italian, Southwestern, Asian, or down-home style dishes. We've even included recipes perfect for gift giving.

SOUTHWEST SALAD

make ahead

MAKES 6 SERVINGS

Prep: 20 min., Chill: 8 hrs.

This salad can be made and chilled a day in advance. In fact, a longer chilling time enhances the wonderful flavors.

- 1 (15-ounce) can black beans, rinsed and drained
- 1½ cups frozen whole kernel corn, thawed*
- 1½ cups chopped, seeded plum tomatoes
- ¾ cup thinly sliced green onions
- ⅓ cup minced fresh cilantro
- ½ cup CRISCO Oil
- ½ cup fresh lemon juice (1 to 2 lemons)
- 2 teaspoons salt

TOSS together first 5 ingredients in a medium bowl.
WHISK together oil, lemon juice, and salt; pour over black bean mixture, stirring gently to coat. Cover and chill at least 8 hours. Serve at room temperature or chilled.

*Substitute 1½ cups fresh corn kernels, cooked, if desired.

ASIAN GRILLED STEAKS WITH SPICY HERB SAUCE

MAKES 6 SERVINGS

Prep: 20 min., Chill: 1 hr., Grill: 10 min.

- ⅔ cup CRISCO Oil
- 3 garlic cloves, minced
- 3 tablespoons sugar
- 3 tablespoons cooking sherry
- 1 tablespoon sesame oil
- 1 teaspoon dried crushed red pepper
- ½ teaspoon salt, divided
- 6 (1-inch-thick) beef strip steaks
- ½ teaspoon ground black pepper
- Spicy Herb Sauce

WHISK together first 6 ingredients and ¼ teaspoon salt in a large shallow dish; add steaks, turning to coat. Cover and chill 1 hour, turning once.
REMOVE steaks from marinade, discarding marinade. Sprinkle evenly with remaining ¼ teaspoon salt and pepper.
GRILL steaks, covered with grill lid, over medium-high heat (350° to 400°) 4 to 5 minutes on each side or to desired degree of doneness. Serve with Spicy Herb Sauce.

Spicy Herb Sauce:

MAKES ABOUT 1 CUP

Prep: 5 min.

- ⅔ cup loosely packed fresh cilantro
- 3 garlic cloves, minced
- 1 small jalapeño pepper, seeded and coarsely chopped
- ⅓ cup CRISCO Oil
- 3 tablespoons soy sauce
- 1½ tablespoons fresh lime juice
- ¼ teaspoon sesame oil

PROCESS all ingredients in a blender or food processor 20 seconds or until smooth, stopping to scrape down sides.

ALMOND BRITTLE

MAKES ABOUT 1 POUND

Prep: 5 min., Cook: 15 min., Stand: 30 min.

Start with a heavy nonaluminum saucepan to encourage even cooking and to prevent the mixture from overbrowning.

- Butter
- 3 tablespoons butter or margarine
- 1¼ cups whole almonds
- 1 cup DOMINO Granulated Sugar
- ¼ cup water
- ½ teaspoon baking soda

LINE a baking sheet or 15- x 10-inch jellyroll pan with foil; grease foil with butter. Set aside.

MELT 3 tablespoons butter in a small skillet over medium heat. Add almonds, and cook, stirring constantly, 2 minutes. Remove from heat.

COOK sugar and ¼ cup water in a small heavy saucepan over medium-high heat, stirring constantly, until mixture starts to boil. (Use a small brush dipped in cold water to brush down sugar crystals that cling to sides of pan.) Boil without stirring about 10 minutes or until a candy thermometer registers 310° (hard-crack stage). (Mixture should be golden.) Remove from heat, and stir in almond mixture and baking soda.

POUR mixture immediately onto prepared baking sheet, spreading mixture quickly into an even layer with a metal spatula. Allow to stand 30 minutes or until hardened. Break into pieces.

HOLIDAY PUMPKIN BREAD

MAKES 2 LOAVES

Prep: 15 min., Bake: 55 min.

- 1 (15-ounce) can unsweetened pumpkin
- 1 cup CRISCO Oil
- 3 cups sugar
- 3 large eggs
- 3½ cups all-purpose flour
- 2 teaspoons baking soda
- 1 teaspoon baking powder
- 1 teaspoon ground cinnamon
- 1 teaspoon ground nutmeg
- ½ teaspoon salt
- ½ teaspoon ground cloves
- 1 cup chopped walnuts
- 1 cup raisins
- CRISCO No-Stick Cooking Spray
- Orange Glaze (optional)

BEAT first 11 ingredients at low speed with an electric mixer 1 to 2 minutes or until blended. Stir in walnuts and raisins. Pour batter into 2 (9- x 5-inch) dark, nonstick loafpans coated with cooking spray.

BAKE at 350° for 55 minutes or until a wooden pick inserted in center comes out clean. Cool in pans on wire racks 15 minutes; remove from pans, and cool. Drizzle with Orange Glaze, if desired.

Orange Glaze:

MAKES ABOUT 1 CUP

Prep: 5 min.

- 1½ cups powdered sugar
- 1 teaspoon grated orange rind
- 3 tablespoons fresh orange juice
- 2 tablespoons chopped walnuts

STIR together first 3 ingredients until blended; stir in walnuts.

NOTE: For light, shiny loafpans, bake 1 hour and 5 minutes or until a wooden pick inserted in center comes out clean.

HOLIDAY PUMPKIN MUFFINS: Spoon batter (about ¼ cup each) into lightly greased muffin pans. Bake at 350° for 20 to 25 minutes. Remove immediately, and cool on wire racks. Makes 3 dozen.

BROWN SUGAR POUND CAKE WITH CREAMY HOLIDAY GLAZE

MAKES 10 TO 12 SERVINGS

Prep: 20 min.; Bake: 1 hr., 30 min.; Cool: 10 min.

- 1 cup butter, softened
- 1 cup firmly packed DOMINO Dark Brown Sugar
- 1 cup DOMINO Granulated Sugar
- 5 large eggs
- 3 cups all-purpose flour
- ½ teaspoon baking powder
- ½ teaspoon baking soda
- ½ teaspoon salt
- 1 cup milk
- 2 teaspoons vanilla extract
- Creamy Holiday Glaze

BEAT butter at medium speed with an electric mixer until creamy; gradually add dark brown and granulated sugars, beating well. Add eggs, 1 at a time, beating until blended after each addition.

COMBINE flour and next 3 ingredients; add to butter mixture alternately with milk, beginning and ending with flour mixture. Beat at low speed until blended after each addition. Stir in vanilla. Pour batter into a greased and floured 10-inch tube pan.

BAKE at 325° for 1 hour and 30 minutes or until a wooden pick inserted in center comes out clean. Cool in pan on a wire rack 10 minutes. Remove from pan; cool completely on a wire rack. Serve with warm Creamy Holiday Glaze.

Creamy Holiday Glaze:

MAKES ABOUT 1½ CUPS

Prep: 5 min., Cook: 10 min.

- ½ cup DOMINO Granulated Sugar
- ½ cup firmly packed DOMINO Dark Brown Sugar
- ½ cup whipping cream
- ½ cup butter
- 1 to 2 tablespoons dark rum or
- ¼ teaspoon rum extract

COOK first 4 ingredients in a heavy saucepan over medium heat, stirring constantly, until butter melts and sugars dissolve. Increase heat, and bring to a boil; cook, stirring constantly, about 3 minutes or until slightly thickened. Stir in rum. Cool slightly.

Brie With Brown Sugar and Nuts

MAKES 8 APPETIZER SERVINGS

Prep: 10 min., Bake: 25 min., Cool: 10 min.

For a decorative top, cut shapes from remaining puff pastry sheet with a 2-inch star-shaped cutter. Arrange stars on top of pastry before baking.

- ¼ cup firmly packed DOMINO Light Brown Sugar
- ¼ cup chopped pecans
- 1 tablespoon bourbon
- ½ (17.3-ounce) package frozen puff pastry sheets, thawed
- 1 (13.2-ounce) round Brie
- French baguette slices, assorted crackers, apple and pear slices

STIR together first 3 ingredients.

PLACE puff pastry sheet on a lightly floured surface; roll out fold lines. Spread brown sugar-and-pecan mixture in a 5-inch circle in center of puff pastry sheet. Place Brie round on top of pecan mixture.

WRAP puff pastry around Brie round, pinching to seal tightly, and place on an aluminum foil-lined baking sheet, folded side down.

BAKE at 400° for 25 minutes or until pastry is lightly brown. Cool 10 minutes on baking sheet. Serve warm with French baguette slices, crackers, and apple and pear slices.

Coffee-Rubbed Strip Steaks

MAKES 4 SERVINGS

Prep: 10 min., Stand: 11 min., Cook: 15 min., Bake: 5 min.

- 2 (1-pound) beef strip steaks, trimmed and halved
- 2 teaspoons salt
- 1 tablespoon ground MILLSTONE Kona Blend Coffee
- 1 tablespoon cracked pepper
- 1 tablespoon vegetable oil
- ¼ cup minced onion
- ¼ cup bourbon
- 1 cup brewed MILLSTONE Kona Blend Coffee
- 2 tablespoons butter or margarine
- Chopped fresh parsley (optional)

SPRINKLE both sides of steaks evenly with salt, and let stand 10 minutes.

COMBINE ground coffee and cracked pepper; rub both sides of steaks with coffee mixture.

COOK steaks in hot oil in a large non-stick ovenproof skillet over high heat 2 minutes or until well browned. Remove skillet from heat, and turn steaks.

BAKE steaks in skillet, browned sides up, at 350° for 5 minutes or to desired degree of doneness. Remove steaks from skillet, and keep warm.

SAUTÉ onion in skillet 2 minutes or until tender. Remove skillet from heat; stir in bourbon, and let stand 30 seconds. Return skillet to heat, and cook, stirring often, until liquid almost evaporates. Add brewed coffee, and cook, stirring often, over medium heat, 5 minutes or until liquid is reduced by half. Remove skillet from heat, and stir in butter until melted. Pour sauce over steaks; sprinkle with parsley, if desired, and serve immediately.

French Vanilla Latte Pudding

fast fixin's

MAKES 6 SERVINGS

Prep: 20 min., Stand: 10 min.

- 3½ cups milk
- ½ cup ground MILLSTONE French Vanilla Coffee
- 1 (8-ounce) container sour cream
- 1 (5.1-ounce) package vanilla instant pudding mix
- 1 (8-ounce) container frozen whipped topping, thawed
- Chocolate-hazelnut cream-filled entertaining cookies (optional)

MICROWAVE milk at HIGH 3 minutes. Stir in ground coffee, and let stand 10 minutes.

POUR coffee mixture through a fine wire-mesh strainer into a bowl, discarding coffee grounds; cool completely.

WHISK together coffee mixture, sour cream, and pudding until thickened. Spoon into serving bowls; top with whipped topping, and, if desired, serve with cookies.

NOTE: For testing, we used Pepperidge Farm Chocolate-Hazelnut Cream-Filled Pirouettes for the cookies.

Vanilla-Nut Coffee Punch

MAKES ABOUT 15 CUPS

Prep: 15 min., Chill: 45 min.

- ¼ cup sugar
- 6 cups hot brewed MILLSTONE Vanilla Nut Cream Coffee
- ½ gallon vanilla ice cream
- ½ to ¾ cup coffee liqueur
- Toppings: whipped cream, chocolate syrup

STIR together sugar and hot coffee in a bowl until sugar dissolves. Cover and chill 30 to 45 minutes.

SPOON ice cream into a large punch bowl. Pour coffee mixture over ice cream; stir in coffee liqueur. Serve with desired toppings.

Macaroon Cookies

MAKES 4 DOZEN

Prep: 20 min., Chill: 1 hr., Bake: 13 min. per batch

Baking for 11 minutes will make soft, chewy cookies, while baking for 13 minutes will make crisper cookies.

- ⅓ cup butter or margarine, softened
- 1 (3-ounce) package cream cheese, softened
- ¾ cup sugar
- 1 egg yolk
- 2 teaspoons orange juice
- 1 to 2 teaspoons almond extract
- 1¼ cups all-purpose flour
- 2 teaspoons baking powder
- ¼ teaspoon salt
- 5 cups sweetened flaked coconut, divided
- 1 (10-ounce) package HERSHEY'S KISSES Chocolates, unwrapped

BEAT first 3 ingredients at medium speed with an electric mixer until blended. Add egg yolk, orange juice, and almond extract, beating until mixture is blended.

COMBINE flour, baking powder, and salt; gradually add to butter mixture, beating until blended. Stir in 3 cups coconut. Cover and chill 1 hour.

SHAPE dough into 1-inch balls; roll balls in remaining 2 cups coconut, and place on ungreased baking sheets.
BAKE at 350° for 11 to 13 minutes or until lightly browned. Remove from oven, and press 1 chocolate into center of each warm cookie. Cool on baking sheets 1 minute. Remove to wire racks to cool completely.

MINT CHOCOLATE MOUSSE TARTS

MAKES 6 SERVINGS

Prep: 30 min., Cook: 14 min., Stand: 1 hr., Chill: 4 hrs.

- 1½ cups miniature marshmallows*
- ⅓ cup milk
- 6 to 8 drops red liquid food coloring (optional)
- 36 HERSHEY'S KISSES Mint Chocolates, unwrapped
- 1 cup whipping cream
- 1 (4-ounce) package ready-made mini graham cracker crusts
- Garnish: fresh mint sprigs

COOK marshmallows and milk in a heavy saucepan over low heat, stirring constantly, 6 to 8 minutes or until marshmallows melt and mixture is smooth. Pour ⅓ cup mixture into a bowl, and, if desired, stir in food coloring; set aside.
STIR mint chocolates into remaining marshmallow mixture in saucepan, and cook, stirring constantly, over low heat 4 to 6 minutes or until chocolate melts. Remove pan from heat, and let stand 1 hour or until cool.
BEAT whipping cream at medium speed with an electric mixer until stiff peaks form. Fold 1 cup whipped cream into chocolate mixture in pan, and spoon evenly into ready-made mini graham cracker crusts.
FOLD remaining whipped cream into reserved ⅓ cup marshmallow mixture. Dollop marshmallow mixture evenly on top of chocolate mixture. Chill 3 to 4 hours or until set. Garnish, if desired.

*Substitute 15 large marshmallows, if desired.

NOTE: Substitute HERSHEY'S KISSES Chocolates for HERSHEY'S KISSES

Mint Chocolates for a variation, and add ¼ teaspoon almond extract or 2 teaspoons kirsch or other cherry liqueur to ⅓ cup marshmallow mixture. Prepare as directed, omitting the mini graham cracker crusts, and spoon evenly into 4 parfait glasses. Chill as directed.

CHOCOLATE CRESCENTS

family favorite • fast fixin's

MAKES 8 SERVINGS

Prep: 15 min., Bake: 10 min.

A three-ingredient treat—life is good!

- 1 (8-ounce) package refrigerated crescent dinner rolls
- 24 HERSHEY'S KISSES or HUGS Chocolates, unwrapped
- Powdered sugar

UNROLL refrigerated crescent dinner rolls, and separate each dough portion along center and diagonal perforations, forming 8 triangles.
PLACE 2 chocolates, points up, on wide end of each triangle; place a third chocolate between the 2 chocolates, point down. Starting at wide end of triangle, roll dough over chocolates, pinching edges to seal. Place rolls, sealed sides down, on an ungreased baking sheet. Shape into crescents.
BAKE at 375° for 10 minutes or until lightly browned. Cool crescents slightly, and sprinkle with powdered sugar. Serve warm.

CHEDDAR-POTATO SOUP

family favorite

MAKES ABOUT 3¾ CUPS

Prep: 20 min., Stand: 10 min., Cook: 10 min.

- 1 (11½-ounce) package STOUFFER'S Potatoes au Gratin
- 1 (10-ounce) package STOUFFER'S Welsh Rarebit
- 1 cup milk
- 1 tablespoon chopped green onions
- ⅛ teaspoon pepper
- ⅓ cup shredded Cheddar cheese

COOK potatoes in microwave at HIGH 4 minutes; stir and cook in microwave 2 to 4 more minutes or until potatoes are tender. Let stand in microwave 10 minutes. Set potatoes aside.
THAW Welsh rarebit in microwave at MEDIUM (50% power) 5 to 6 minutes. Stir together potatoes, Welsh rarebit, milk, green onions, and pepper in a medium saucepan over medium heat, and cook, stirring constantly, 10 minutes or until soup begins to simmer. Remove from heat; add cheese, and stir until cheese melts. Serve immediately.

BAKED APPLE FRENCH TOAST

family favorite

MAKES 6 SERVINGS

Prep: 15 min., Stand: 2 min., Bake 40 min.

This breakfast dish also makes a fabulous dessert.

- 2 (12-ounce) packages STOUFFER'S Harvest Apples
- ½ (16-ounce) package Italian bread loaf
- ⅓ cup firmly packed brown sugar
- 4 large eggs
- 1⅓ cups milk
- 1 teaspoon vanilla extract
- Garnishes: whipped cream, ground cinnamon, cinnamon sticks

THAW apples in microwave at MEDIUM (50% power) 6 to 7 minutes.
CUT Italian bread loaf, diagonally, into 6 equal slices; set aside.
STIR together apples and brown sugar. Spoon into a lightly greased 13- x 9-inch baking dish.
WHISK together eggs, milk, and vanilla in a shallow dish until blended. Place bread slices in egg mixture, and let stand 1 minute. Turn bread slices over, and let stand 1 more minute. Place bread slices in an even layer on top of apple mixture.
BAKE at 350° for 35 to 40 minutes or until bread centers are firm. Invert each serving, placing bread slices, bottom sides down, on individual plates. Garnish, if desired.

SENSATIONAL BEEF PIE

fast fixin's

MAKES 4 SERVINGS

Prep: 10 min., Bake: 20 min.

1 (25-ounce) package STOUFFER'S
    Skillet Sensations Homestyle
    Beef*
¼ cup water
¼ teaspoon pepper
½ (15-ounce) package refrigerated
    piecrusts

PLACE beef in a 9-inch microwave-safe pieplate; add ¼ cup water. Cover with plastic wrap, and microwave at HIGH 6 minutes, stirring after 3 minutes. Sprinkle beef evenly with ¼ teaspoon pepper. **UNFOLD** piecrust, and place on top of beef mixture; fold edges under, and crimp. Cut 4 slits in center of crust. **BAKE** at 425° for 18 to 20 minutes or until golden brown.

*Substitute STOUFFER'S Skillet Sensations Homestyle Chicken or STOUFFER'S Skillet Sensations Lean Cuisine Roasted Turkey, if desired.

FIESTA DIP

fast fixin's

MAKES 4 SERVINGS

Prep: 15 min.

For a clever presentation, serve in decorative margarita glasses. Coat the glass rims in fresh lime juice, and dip in margarita salt or fajita seasoning.

1 (10-ounce) can ROTEL Original
    Diced Tomatoes & Green Chilies,
    drained
1 (16-ounce) can refried beans
2 (8-ounce) containers guacamole
1 cup (4 ounces) shredded Cheddar
    cheese
2 green onions, sliced
¼ cup sour cream
1 (2¼-ounce) can sliced ripe olives,
    drained
Tortilla chips

RESERVE ¼ cup diced tomatoes and green chilies.

STIR together refried beans and remaining tomatoes and green chilies. Spoon refried bean mixture evenly into 4 (8- to 9-ounce) margarita glasses or small bowls; press mixture on bottom and up sides of glasses, if desired. Layer each glass with guacamole, cheese, reserved ¼ cup tomatoes and green chilies, green onions, sour cream, and olives. Serve with tortilla chips.

UPSIDE-DOWN PIZZA CASSEROLE

family favorite

MAKES 8 SERVINGS

Prep: 20 min., Cook: 12 min., Bake: 20 min.

2 (16-ounce) packages JIMMY DEAN
    Pork Sausage
2 medium onions, chopped
½ cup chopped green bell pepper
    (optional)
2 teaspoons dried basil (optional)
1 teaspoon fennel seeds (optional)
¼ cup all-purpose flour
1 (26-ounce) jar tomato-and-basil sauce
2 cups (8 ounces) shredded
    mozzarella cheese, divided
1 (10-ounce) can refrigerated pizza crust
1 tablespoon olive oil
2 tablespoons grated Parmesan
    cheese
1 teaspoon dried basil

COOK sausage, onions, and, if desired, bell pepper, 2 teaspoons basil, and fennel seeds in a large skillet over medium-high heat about 10 minutes, stirring until sausage crumbles and is no longer pink and onions are tender. Drain.
ADD flour, stirring until blended. Stir in tomato-and-basil sauce. Bring to a boil over medium-high heat, stirring constantly. Spoon mixture into a lightly greased 13- x 9-inch baking dish. Sprinkle mixture with 1½ cups mozzarella cheese.
UNROLL pizza crust, and place on top of sausage mixture. (Tuck edges into baking dish, if necessary.) Brush with olive oil, and sprinkle with remaining ½ cup mozzarella cheese, Parmesan cheese, and 1 teaspoon basil.
BAKE at 425° for 20 minutes or until golden brown.

GOLDEN SAUSAGE EGG ROLLS

MAKES 24 EGG ROLLS

Prep: 45 min., Cook: 10 min., Cool: 15 min., Fry: 32 min.

1 (16-ounce) package JIMMY DEAN
    Extra Mild Pork Sausage
2 (16-ounce) packages shredded
    coleslaw mix
3 tablespoons minced fresh ginger
3 tablespoons minced garlic
1 tablespoon pepper
1 teaspoon salt
24 egg roll wrappers
Vegetable oil
Condiments: sweet-and-sour sauce,
    spicy mustard, soy sauce

COOK sausage in a large skillet over medium-high heat about 10 minutes, stirring until sausage crumbles and is no longer pink. Spoon sausage into a colander, and let drain. Cool sausage 15 minutes.
STIR together sausage, coleslaw mix, and next 4 ingredients.
BRUSH water around outer edge of each egg roll wrapper. Spoon ⅓ cup sausage mixture in center of each egg roll wrapper. Fold bottom corner over filling, tucking tip of corner under filling; fold left and right corners over filling. Tightly roll filled end toward remaining corner; gently press to seal.
POUR oil to a depth of 3 inches in a Dutch oven; heat to 375°. Fry egg rolls, in 8 batches, 3 to 4 minutes or until golden brown; drain on paper towels. Serve immediately with desired condiments.

SPICY SHRIMP-AND-PINEAPPLE FRIED RICE

fast fixin's

MAKES 4 SERVINGS

Prep: 10 min., Cook: 20 min.

- 1 cup uncooked MAHATMA Jasmine Rice
- 1 (20-ounce) can pineapple tidbits, undrained
- 3 green onions, chopped
- 1 tablespoon chopped fresh cilantro
- 1 teaspoon dried crushed red pepper
- 2 cups unpeeled, medium-size fresh shrimp
- 3 tablespoons vegetable oil, divided
- 2 garlic cloves, minced
- 1 to 2 tablespoons fish sauce
- 2 tablespoons soy sauce
- 1 teaspoon sugar
- Garnish: green onion stem curls

PREPARE rice according to package directions; set aside.
COMBINE pineapple and next 3 ingredients in a bowl, and set aside.
PEEL shrimp, and devein, if desired. Sauté shrimp in 1 tablespoon hot oil in a large skillet 3 minutes. Remove shrimp from skillet, and set aside.
HEAT remaining 2 tablespoons oil in skillet over medium heat; add garlic, and sauté 2 minutes or until golden brown. Stir in rice, fish sauce, soy sauce, and sugar. Cook, stirring constantly, until thoroughly heated.

FOLD in pineapple mixture and shrimp, and cook until thoroughly heated. Garnish, if desired.

CREAMY RISOTTO

MAKES 6 SERVINGS

Prep: 10 min., Cook: 50 min.

Serve this delicious, creamy side dish with any beef, chicken, pork, or fish entrée.

- 1 (14½-ounce) can chicken broth
- 3 cups water
- ¼ cup butter or margarine, divided
- ½ cup chopped onion
- 1 cup uncooked MAHATMA White Rice
- ⅓ cup dry white wine (at room temperature)
- ½ cup whipping cream
- ¼ cup freshly grated Parmesan cheese
- ½ teaspoon pepper
- ¼ teaspoon salt

BRING chicken broth and 3 cups water to a boil in a saucepan. Reduce heat to low, and simmer.
MELT 2 tablespoons butter in a large saucepan over medium heat; add onion, and sauté until tender. Add rice, and sauté 2 to 3 minutes.
ADD wine, and cook, stirring constantly, until liquid is absorbed. Increase heat to medium-high. Add 1 cup hot broth mixture, and cook, stirring often, until liquid is absorbed. Repeat procedure, adding remaining broth mixture 1 cup at a time. (Cooking time is about 25 to 30 minutes.)
ADD remaining 2 tablespoons butter, whipping cream, and next 3 ingredients. Cook, stirring constantly, 2 minutes. Serve immediately.

OLD-FASHIONED RICE PUDDING

MAKES 6 SERVINGS

Prep: 20 min., Cook: 25 min., Stand: 15 min., Chill: 2 hrs.

This pudding is delicious served warm or cold.

- 1 (3.5-ounce) bag SUCCESS White or Brown Rice
- 3 tablespoons butter or margarine
- 1 (14½-ounce) can evaporated low-fat 2% milk, divided
- ⅓ cup sugar
- ¼ teaspoon salt
- ½ cup dried cherries*
- Boiling water
- 1 large egg
- 1½ teaspoons vanilla extract
- 1½ teaspoons ground cinnamon

PREPARE rice according to package directions.
STIR together rice, butter, 1 cup evaporated milk, sugar, and salt in a medium saucepan, and cook, stirring often, over medium heat 20 minutes or until thick and creamy.
PLACE cherries in a small bowl; add boiling water to cover, and let stand 15 minutes. Drain.
STIR together egg and remaining evaporated milk until blended; gradually pour into hot rice mixture in pan, stirring constantly. Cook, stirring often, 5 minutes. Remove from heat; stir in vanilla and cherries. Sprinkle evenly with cinnamon. Serve warm, or cover and chill at least 2 hours.

*Substitute ½ cup raisins, if desired.

Twelve Cakes for Christmas

We came up with one easy-to-make cake batter that bakes to become an incredibly delicious velvety-rich chocolate cake. Then we paired it with a dozen of our favorite frostings and toppings—one for each of the 12 days of Christmas. These cakes are doable for anyone—novice or pro.

CHOCOLATE VELVET CAKE BATTER

fast fixin's

MAKES ABOUT 8½ CUPS

Prep: 15 min.

The addition of hot water at the end of this recipe makes for an exceptionally moist cake.

- 1½ cups semisweet chocolate morsels
- ½ cup butter, softened
- 1 (16-ounce) package light brown sugar
- 3 large eggs
- 2 cups all-purpose flour
- 1 teaspoon baking soda
- ½ teaspoon salt
- 1 (8-ounce) container sour cream
- 1 cup hot water
- 2 teaspoons vanilla extract

MELT chocolate morsels in a microwave-safe bowl at HIGH for 30-second intervals until melted (about 1½ minutes total time). Stir until smooth.
BEAT butter and sugar at medium speed with an electric mixer, beating about 5 minutes or until well blended. Add eggs, 1 at a time, beating just until blended after each addition. Add melted chocolate, beating just until blended.
SIFT together flour, baking soda, and salt. Gradually add to chocolate mixture alternately with sour cream, beginning and ending with flour mixture. Beat at low speed just until blended after each addition. Gradually add 1 cup hot water in a slow steady stream, beating at low speed just until blended. Stir in vanilla. Use immediately, following directions for desired cake.

CHOCOLATE-MINT CAKE

MAKES 16 SERVINGS

Prep: 30 min., Bake: 30 min.

Don't be tempted to substitute peppermint extract for the peppermint oil used in this recipe. Peppermint oil, available from cake-supply stores, has an intense, highly concentrated flavor like that found in chocolate-covered peppermint patties.

- Chocolate Velvet Cake Batter
- ½ recipe Vanilla Buttercream Frosting
- ¼ teaspoon peppermint oil
- Chocolate Ganache

SPOON batter evenly into 2 greased and floured 10-inch round cakepans. Bake at 350° for 30 minutes or until a wooden pick inserted in center of cake comes out clean. Cool in pans on a wire rack 10 minutes; remove from pans, and let cool completely on wire rack.
STIR together Vanilla Buttercream Frosting and peppermint oil until well blended. Spread frosting mixture evenly between cake layers. Spread Chocolate Ganache evenly over top and sides of cake.

VANILLA BUTTERCREAM FROSTING

fast fixin's

MAKES ABOUT 6 CUPS

Prep: 10 min.

- 1 cup butter, softened
- 2 (16-ounce) packages powdered sugar
- ⅔ cup milk
- 1 tablespoon vanilla extract

BEAT butter at medium speed with an electric mixer until creamy; gradually add powdered sugar alternately with milk, beating at low speed until blended after each addition. Stir in vanilla.

BOURBON BUTTERCREAM FROSTING: Substitute ⅓ cup bourbon and ⅓ cup milk for ⅔ cup milk.

Melting Morsels

- Do not stir the morsels until finished microwaving.
- Melted morsels should retain a glossy sheen and some of their original shape. As you stir the morsels, they will continue to melt, becoming blended and smooth.

CHOCOLATE GANACHE

MAKES ABOUT 2 CUPS

Prep: 10 min., Stand: 20 min.

Ganache is a rich chocolate icing made by melting semisweet chocolate with whipping cream. *(pictured on page 4)*

- 1 (12-ounce) package semisweet chocolate morsels
- ½ cup whipping cream
- 3 tablespoons butter

MICROWAVE chocolate and whipping cream in a 2-quart microwave-safe bowl at MEDIUM (50% power) 2½ to 3 minutes or until chocolate begins to melt.
WHISK until chocolate melts and mixture is smooth. Whisk in butter; let stand 20 minutes. Beat at medium speed with an electric mixer 3 to 4 minutes or until mixture forms soft peaks.

CHOCOLATE VELVET "POUND" CAKE

freezeable

MAKES 12 TO 16 SERVINGS

Prep: 5 min.; Bake: 1 hr., 5 min.

Ice cream and warm Chocolate Ganache go perfectly with this cake. *(pictured on page 4)*

- Chocolate Velvet Cake Batter
- ¼ cup powdered sugar

SPOON batter evenly into a greased and floured 10-inch tube pan. Bake at 350° for 55 to 65 minutes or until a wooden pick inserted in center comes out clean. Cool in pan on a wire rack 10 minutes.

Remove from pan, and let cool completely on wire rack.

SIFT powdered sugar over top of cake.

CHOCOLATE VELVET CAKE WITH VANILLA BUTTERCREAM FROSTING

MAKES 12 SERVINGS

Prep: 20 min., Bake: 45 min.

You'll need 2 (9-inch) round cakepans that are at least 2 inches deep for this cake. If your pans are only 1½ inches deep, use 3 pans, and reduce baking time to 25 to 30 minutes.

> **Chocolate Velvet Cake Batter**
> **Vanilla Buttercream Frosting**

SPOON batter evenly into 2 greased and floured 9-inch round cakepans (pans must be 2 inches deep).

BAKE at 350° for 40 to 45 minutes or until a wooden pick inserted in center comes out clean. Cool in pans on a wire rack 10 minutes. Remove from pans, and let cool completely on wire rack. Spread Vanilla Buttercream Frosting between layers and on top and sides of cake.

CHOCOLATE-BOURBON-PECAN CAKE

MAKES 12 SERVINGS

Prep: 30 min., Bake: 30 min.

> **Chocolate Velvet Cake Batter**
> **Bourbon Buttercream Frosting**
> **2¾ cups chopped pecans, toasted**
> **1 (4-ounce) semisweet chocolate bar, chopped**

SPOON batter evenly into 3 greased and floured 9-inch square pans. Bake at 350° for 25 to 30 minutes or until a wooden pick inserted in center comes out clean. Cool in pans on a wire rack 10 minutes. Remove from pans, and let cool completely on wire rack.

SPREAD Bourbon Buttercream Frosting between layers and on top and sides of cake, sprinkling ¼ cup pecans on top of frosting for each of the layers. Press remaining pecans onto sides of cake. Sprinkle chopped chocolate over top of the cake.

WHITE CHOCOLATE-ALMOND CAKE

MAKES 12 SERVINGS

Prep: 30 min., Bake: 30 min., Chill: 30 min.

> **Chocolate Velvet Cake Batter**
> **1 (12-ounce) package white chocolate morsels**
> **1 cup coarsely chopped slivered almonds, toasted**
> **Vanilla Buttercream Frosting**

SPOON batter evenly into 3 greased and floured 8-inch square pans. Bake at 350° for 25 to 30 minutes or until a wooden pick inserted in center comes out clean. Cool in pans on a wire rack 10 minutes. Remove from pans, and let cool completely on wire rack.

MELT chocolate morsels in a microwave-safe bowl at HIGH for 30-second intervals until melted (about 1½ minutes total). Stir until smooth, and spread in a ¼-inch-thick layer on a foil-lined baking sheet. Sprinkle evenly with almonds. Chill 30 minutes or until firm. Remove from baking sheet, and chop.

SPREAD Vanilla Buttercream Frosting between layers and on top and sides of cake. Press chopped chocolate mixture onto top and sides of cake. If desired, tie a decorative ribbon around sides of cake.

CHOCOLATE-PEPPERMINT CANDY CUPCAKES

MAKES 36 CUPCAKES

Prep: 30 min., Bake: 18 min., Chill: 30 min.

> **Chocolate Velvet Cake Batter**
> **1 (12-ounce) package white chocolate morsels**
> **½ cup crushed peppermint candy canes**
> **Vanilla Buttercream Frosting**

PLACE 36 paper baking cups in muffin pans; spoon batter evenly into paper cups, filling two-thirds full. Bake at 350° for 18 minutes or until a wooden pick inserted in center of cupcake comes out clean. Remove cupcakes from pan, and let cool completely on wire racks.

MELT chocolate morsels in a microwave-safe bowl at HIGH for 30-second intervals until melted (about 1½ minutes total). Stir until smooth, and spread in a ¼-inch-thick layer on an aluminum foil-lined baking sheet. Sprinkle evenly with peppermint candy. Chill 30 minutes or until firm. Remove from baking sheet, and chop.

SPREAD cupcakes evenly with Vanilla Buttercream Frosting; sprinkle evenly with chopped candy mixture.

TURTLE CAKE

MAKES 12 SERVINGS

Prep: 30 min., Bake: 30 min.

> **Chocolate Velvet Cake Batter**
> **Caramel Filling**
> **1 cup chopped pecans, toasted**
> **Chocolate Ganache**

SPOON batter evenly into 3 greased and floured 9-inch round cakepans. Bake at 350° for 25 to 30 minutes or until a wooden pick inserted in center comes out clean. Cool in pans on a wire rack 10 minutes. Remove from pans, and let cool completely on wire rack.

PLACE 1 cake layer on a serving platter; spread top with 1 cup Caramel Filling, and sprinkle with ⅓ cup chopped pecans. Repeat procedure with remaining cake layers. Spread Chocolate Ganache evenly around sides of cake.

Caramel Filling:

MAKES ABOUT 3 CUPS

Prep: 5 min., Cook: 15 min., Chill: 2 hrs.

> **1 cup butter**
> **2 cups sugar**
> **2 tablespoons corn syrup**
> **1 cup whipping cream**

MELT butter in a heavy 3-quart saucepan over medium heat. Add sugar and corn syrup, and cook, stirring constantly, 6 to 8 minutes or until mixture turns a deep caramel color. Gradually add cream, and cook, stirring constantly, 1 to 2 minutes or until smooth. Remove from heat, and let cool. Chill 2 hours or until thickened and spreading consistency.

NOTE: Caramel Filling may be made up to three days ahead and refrigerated. Let stand at room temperature 1 hour or until spreading consistency.

CHOCOLATE VELVET CAKE WITH CREAM CHEESE-BUTTER PECAN FROSTING

MAKES 12 SERVINGS

Prep: 30 min., Bake: 30 min. *(pictured on cover)*

Chocolate Velvet Cake Batter (page 286)
Cream Cheese-Butter Pecan Frosting
Garnishes: sugared silk ivy leaves,
raspberry candies, toffee peanut
candies, cracked partially shelled
pecans

SPOON cake batter evenly into 3 greased and floured 8-inch round cakepans. Bake at 350° for 25 to 30 minutes or until a wooden pick inserted in center comes out clean.
COOL in pans on a wire rack 10 minutes; remove from pans, and let cool completely on wire rack.
SPREAD Cream Cheese-Butter Pecan Frosting between layers and on top and sides of cake. Garnish, if desired.

Cream Cheese-Butter Pecan Frosting:

MAKES ABOUT 7 CUPS

Prep: 15 min., Bake: 15 min.

2 cups chopped pecans
¼ cup butter, melted
2 (8-ounce) packages cream cheese,
softened
½ cup butter, softened
2 (16-ounce) packages powdered
sugar
2 teaspoons vanilla extract

STIR together chopped pecans and ¼ cup melted butter. Spread pecans in an even layer in a 13- x 9-inch pan. Bake at 350° for 15 minutes or until pecans are toasted. Remove pecans from oven, and let cool.
BEAT cream cheese and ½ cup butter at medium speed with an electric mixer until creamy. Gradually add powdered sugar, beating until light and fluffy. Stir in toasted pecans and vanilla.

NOTE: To sugar silk ivy leaves, brush leaves lightly with corn syrup, and sprinkle with granulated sugar. For how-to tips on garnish and instructions for baking and decorating our gift box cake, see "From Our Kitchen" on page 308.

CHOCOLATE-PRALINE PECAN CAKE

freezeable

MAKES 2 (9-INCH) CAKES
(ABOUT 9 SERVINGS EACH)

Prep: 30 min., Bake: 40 min., Cook: 10 min.

This must be baked in two 9-inch square pans that are at least 2 inches deep.

Chocolate Velvet Cake Batter (page 286)
2 cups firmly packed brown sugar
⅔ cup whipping cream
½ cup butter
2 cups powdered sugar, sifted
2 teaspoons vanilla extract
2 cups chopped pecans, toasted

SPOON batter evenly into 2 greased and floured aluminum foil-lined 9- x 9- x 2-inch square pans. Bake at 350° for 40 minutes or until a wooden pick inserted in center comes out clean. Cool in pans on a wire rack.
BRING brown sugar, whipping cream, and butter to a boil in a 3-quart saucepan over medium heat, stirring often; boil 1 minute. Remove from heat; whisk in powdered sugar and vanilla. Add pecans, stirring gently, 3 to 5 minutes or until mixture begins to cool and slightly thicken. Pour immediately over cakes in pans. Cool completely. Cut into squares.

MISSISSIPPI MUD CAKE

freezeable

MAKES 2 (9-INCH) CAKES
(ABOUT 9 SERVINGS EACH)

Prep: 30 min., Bake: 45 min., Cook: 5 min.

This must be baked in two 9-inch square pans that are at least 2 inches deep.

Chocolate Velvet Cake Batter (page 286)
4 cups miniature marshmallows
2 cups chopped pecans, toasted
½ cup butter or margarine
⅓ cup milk
3 tablespoons cocoa
1 (16-ounce) package powdered sugar,
sifted
1 teaspoon vanilla extract

SPOON batter into 2 greased and floured aluminum foil-lined 9- x 9- x 2-inch square pans. Bake at 350° for 40 minutes or until a wooden pick inserted in center comes out clean. Remove from oven; sprinkle each cake evenly with 2 cups marshmallows and 1 cup pecans. Return to oven, and bake 5 more minutes or just until marshmallows begin to melt. Remove from oven, and let cool on a wire rack.
BRING butter, milk, and cocoa to a boil in a large saucepan over medium heat, stirring until butter melts. Remove from heat; whisk in powdered sugar and vanilla. Drizzle evenly over cakes in pans. Let cool completely. Cut cakes into squares.

CHOCOLATE-CREAM CHEESE COFFEE CAKE

freezeable

MAKES 2 (9-INCH) CAKES (ABOUT 24 SERVINGS)

Prep: 30 min., Bake: 45 min.

1⅓ cups all-purpose flour
½ cup firmly packed brown sugar
½ cup cold butter, cut up
1 cup chopped pecans
1 (8-ounce) package cream cheese,
softened
¼ cup granulated sugar
1 tablespoon all-purpose flour
1 large egg
1 teaspoon vanilla extract, divided
Chocolate Velvet Cake Batter (page 286)
1 cup powdered sugar
2 tablespoons milk

STIR together 1⅓ cups flour and brown sugar in a small bowl. Cut butter into flour mixture with a pastry blender or fork until crumbly; stir in pecans. Set aside.
BEAT cream cheese at medium speed with an electric mixer until smooth; add granulated sugar and 1 tablespoon flour, beating until blended. Add egg and ½ teaspoon vanilla, beating until blended.
SPOON Chocolate Velvet Cake Batter evenly into 2 greased and floured 9-inch springform pans. Dollop cream cheese mixture evenly over cake batter; gently swirl through cake batter with a knife. Sprinkle pecan mixture evenly over batter.
BAKE at 350° for 45 minutes or until set. Cool on a wire rack.
WHISK together powdered sugar, milk, and remaining ½ teaspoon vanilla extract. Drizzle evenly over tops of coffee cakes.

CHOCOLATE VELVET CAKE WITH COCONUT-PECAN FROSTING

MAKES 12 SERVINGS

Prep: 20 min., Bake: 30 min.

**Chocolate Velvet Cake Batter (page 286)
Coconut-Pecan Frosting**

SPOON batter evenly into 3 greased and floured 9-inch round cakepans. Bake at 350° for 25 to 30 minutes or until a wooden pick inserted in center comes out clean. Cool in pans on a wire rack 10 minutes. Remove from pans, and let cool completely on wire rack.
SPREAD Coconut-Pecan Frosting between layers and on top and sides of cake.

Coconut-Pecan Frosting:

MAKES ABOUT 5 CUPS

Prep: 15 min., Cook: 17 min.

**1 (12-ounce) can evaporated milk
1½ cups sugar
¾ cup butter or margarine
6 egg yolks
1½ teaspoons vanilla extract
2 cups chopped pecans, toasted
1½ cups sweetened flaked coconut**

STIR together first 4 ingredients in a heavy 3-quart saucepan over medium heat; bring to a boil, and cook, stirring constantly, 12 minutes. Remove from heat; add remaining ingredients, and stir until frosting is cool and spreading consistency.

Cake Freezing Tips

■ Place baked, completely cooled, unfrosted round and square cake layers in large zip-top freezer bags or airtight containers, and freeze up to one month. (We recommend frosting cake layers while they're still partially frozen.)
■ Three of the cakes—Chocolate-Praline Pecan Cake, Mississippi Mud Cake, and Chocolate-Cream Cheese Coffee Cake (all on facing page)—can be baked, frozen, and frosted in pans.

Teachers' Gifts

Our eight-ingredient-or-less recipes are terrific treats to share with favorite teachers. From peanuts to red hot candies, these simple ingredients spell fun for a family project. With minimal cooking involved, all ages can lend a hand.

These recipes are quick to prepare, and it's tempting to sneak a bite of White Chocolate Party Mix or a spoonful of Peanut Butter Sauce while you're making them. Go ahead, it's part of the fun of creating homemade gifts. Most people give bought remembrances, but these goodies will be just as appreciated—and may have your children's teachers asking for the recipe.

SPICED CIDER MIX

fast fixin's

MAKES 3 CUPS

Prep: 10 min.

Tie a bag of cinnamon candies with a pretty ribbon and include it along with the mix and a gift card.

**1 cup orange breakfast drink mix
1 cup sugar
½ cup instant tea
1 (4-ounce) package sweetened
lemonade drink mix
½ teaspoon ground cinnamon
¼ teaspoon ground cloves
¼ teaspoon ground allspice
Red cinnamon candies**

COMBINE first 7 ingredients together in a large bowl, stirring well. Store in an airtight container. Mix can be frozen up to 1 month.

DIRECTIONS TO INCLUDE ON GIFT CARD:
Combine 3 tablespoons Spiced Cider Mix, 1 teaspoon red cinnamon candies and 1 cup boiling water. Stir well.

LOUISE MAYER
RICHMOND, VIRGINIA

PEANUT BUTTER SAUCE

fast fixin's

MAKES 2½ CUPS

Prep: 5 min., Cook: 10 min.

Serve warm over ice cream.

**1⅓ cups miniature marshmallows
1 (14-ounce) can sweetened
condensed milk
1 cup chunky peanut butter
⅓ cup light corn syrup**

MELT marshmallows and sweetened condensed milk in a small saucepan over medium heat, stirring constantly. Add peanut butter and corn syrup, stirring until blended. Store in the refrigerator up to 1 month, and reheat before serving.

WHITE CHOCOLATE PARTY MIX

MAKES 3 POUNDS

Prep: 15 min., Cool: 30 min.

We couldn't keep our hands off this crunchy sweet-and-salty snack.

**1 (14-ounce) package candy-coated
chocolate-covered peanuts
1 (9-ounce) package butter-flavored
pretzels
5 cups toasted oat O-shaped cereal
5 cups crispy corn cereal snack mix
1 (24-ounce) package almond bark
coating**

COMBINE first 4 ingredients in a large container; set aside.
MICROWAVE almond bark in a microwave-safe dish at HIGH 1 minute, stirring once. Microwave at HIGH for 1 more minute; stir until smooth. Pour over cereal mixture, stirring to combine. Spread onto wax paper, and let cool 30 minutes.
BREAK apart, and store in an airtight container.

NOTE: For testing purposes only, we used Snyder's of Hanover Butter Snaps Pretzels, Cheerios, and Corn Chex snack mix.

KARLENE BROWN
AUGUSTA, WISCONSIN

Lunch for a Bunch

Fixing a deliciously light meal for a crowd has never been so easy!

When you're feeding a crowd, it can be a real challenge to serve something that you know everyone will enjoy. We selected several delicious dishes that can be doubled or tripled, depending on the size of your guest list, and all of them can be made a day ahead. Best of all, these recipes also call for easy-to-find, low-fat ingredients such as lean ground beef and pork loin.

SMOKY KIDNEY BEANS AND RICE

MAKES 8 (1-CUP) SERVINGS

Prep: 30 min.; Cook: 1 hr., 45 min.; Stand: 1 hr.

Smoked ham replaces traditional high-fat sausage in this hearty one-dish meal. Double the recipe, if desired.

- 1 (16-ounce) package dried kidney beans
- ½ pound smoked ham, chopped
- 1 teaspoon olive oil
- 1 large onion, chopped
- 3 garlic cloves, minced
- 4 cups low-sodium chicken broth
- 2 bay leaves
- ½ teaspoon freshly ground pepper
- 4 cups hot cooked rice

BRING beans and water to cover to a boil in a Dutch oven; boil 2 minutes. Remove from heat; cover and let stand 1 hour. Drain beans; rinse well, and drain. Set aside.

BROWN ham in Dutch oven over medium heat. Add oil and onion, and sauté over medium-high heat 5 minutes or until onion is tender. Add garlic; sauté 1 minute. Stir in beans, broth, bay leaves, and pepper.

BRING to a boil; cover, reduce heat, and simmer 1 hour and 30 minutes or until beans are tender and mixture thickens. Remove and discard bay leaves. Serve over rice.

RENA P. MARSHALL
REX, GEORGIA

Calories per 1-cup beans and ½ cup rice 332 (7% from fat); Fat 2.7g (sat 0.8g, mono 0.5g, poly 0.4g); Protein 22g; Carb 55g; Fiber 15g; Chol 10mg; Iron 5.3mg; Sodium 435mg; Calc 104mg

GREEK SALAD

fast fixin's

MAKES 6 SERVINGS

Prep: 20 min.

Recipe can easily be doubled or tripled. Enjoy it alongside a soup or sandwich, or stuff into a pita half and drizzle with dressing.

- 1 large head romaine lettuce, torn
- ½ cup chopped fresh parsley
- 3 green onions, chopped
- 2 tomatoes, cubed
- 1 cucumber, sliced
- 1 tablespoon chopped fresh or 1 teaspoon dried mint leaves
- ½ cup crumbled reduced-fat feta cheese
- ¼ cup kalamata olives, pitted and chopped
- Greek Salad Dressing
- 3 (6-inch) pita rounds, halved and warmed (optional)

COMBINE first 6 ingredients in a large bowl or on a large platter. Top with cheese and olives. Serve with Greek Salad Dressing and, if desired, pita halves.

Calories including 2 tablespoons dressing 224 (56% from fat); Fat 14g (sat 2.5g, mono 8.8g, poly 1.4g); Protein 6.6g; Carb 21.1g; Fiber 3.7g; Chol 3.3mg; Iron 2.2mg; Sodium 506mg; Calc 105mg

Greek Salad Dressing:

MAKES 16 (2-TABLESPOON) SERVINGS

Prep: 10 min.

- 3 garlic cloves
- 1 teaspoon salt
- 1 teaspoon pepper
- 1¼ cups fresh lemon juice
- ¾ cup olive oil

PULSE first 3 ingredients in a blender or food processor until chopped. Add lemon juice, and pulse 3 times. With food processor running, pour oil through food chute in a slow, steady stream; process until smooth.

DOE'S PITA
CHARLESTON, SOUTH CAROLINA

STRAWBERRY-PRETZEL SALAD

MAKES 12 SERVINGS

Prep: 20 min., Bake: 15 min., Chill: 9 hrs.

- 1 cup crushed mini pretzels
- ¾ cup sugar, divided
- ¼ cup butter or margarine, melted
- Vegetable cooking spray
- 1 (8-ounce) package ⅓-less-fat cream cheese, softened
- 1 teaspoon vanilla extract
- 1 (8-ounce) container fat-free frozen whipped topping, thawed
- 1 (6-ounce) package strawberry-flavored gelatin
- 2 cups boiling water
- 2 (10-ounce) packages frozen strawberries in light syrup, thawed
- 1 (16-ounce) container fat-free sour cream
- ¼ cup chopped pecans, toasted

COMBINE crushed pretzels, 3 table-spoons sugar, and melted butter. Press mixture on bottom of a 13- x 9-inch pan coated with cooking spray. (Mixture will be crumbly.) Bake at 350° for 15 minutes; cool completely.

BEAT cream cheese, 5 tablespoons sugar, and vanilla at low speed with a mixer until sugar dissolves. Fold in whipped topping; spread over pretzel layer.

STIR together gelatin and 2 cups boiling water until dissolved; add strawberries. Chill 1 hour or until partially set. Spread gelatin mixture over cream cheese layer; cover and chill 8 hours or until set.

STIR together sour cream and remaining ¼ cup sugar; spread over top of strawberry layer; sprinkle with pecans.

*Reduce sodium by substituting low-sodium pretzels for regular.

Calories 329 (26% from fat); Fat 9.5g (sat 5g, mono 2.3g, poly 0.8g); Protein 6.4g; Carb 54g; Fiber 0.6g; Chol 22.5mg; Iron 0.9 mg; Sodium 401mg*; Calc 90mg

FRESH CITRUS SALSA

fast fixin's

MAKES 8 (¾-CUP) SERVINGS
Prep: 30 min.

Tempt the gang's appetite with this sweet and tangy salsa and baked tortilla chips for dipping.

- 2 red grapefruit, peeled, sectioned, and chopped
- 2 large navel oranges, peeled, sectioned, and chopped
- 3 plum tomatoes, chopped
- ½ each of a green, yellow, and red bell pepper, seeded and chopped
- 1 to 2 jalapeño peppers, seeded and minced
- ¼ medium-size red onion, chopped (about ⅓ cup)
- 2 to 3 tablespoons chopped fresh cilantro
- 2 teaspoons sugar
- ¼ teaspoon salt
- Baked tortilla chips (optional)

COMBINE first 9 ingredients in a large bowl. Serve with chips, if desired.

RECIPE COURTESY OF TEXASWEET CITRUS
MARKETING, INC.
MISSION, TEXAS

Calories per ¾-cup 58 (3% from fat); Fat 0.2g (sat 0g, mono 0g, poly 0.1g); Protein 1.2g; Carb 14.4g; Fiber 2.4g; Chol 0mg; Iron 0.3mg; Sodium 77mg; Calc 26mg

SPICY 3-BEAN CHILI

MAKES 16 (1-CUP) SERVINGS
Prep: 25 min., Cook: 1 hr.

Brenda Johnson enjoys this satisfying stew with warm flour tortillas and colorful toppings for lunch or supper. Keep on hand cans of beans, crushed tomatoes, chicken broth, and diced green chiles for quick one-dish suppers.

- 1 pound extra-lean ground beef
- 1 pound boneless pork loin chops, cut into bite-size pieces
- ½ teaspoon pepper
- ¼ teaspoon salt
- Vegetable cooking spray
- 2 onions, chopped
- 4 garlic cloves, minced
- 1 (15-ounce) can black beans, rinsed and drained
- 1 (15-ounce) can pinto beans, rinsed and drained
- 1 (15-ounce) can kidney beans, rinsed and drained
- 2 (4-ounce) cans diced green chiles
- 1 (28-ounce) can crushed tomatoes
- 1 (1.12-ounce) envelope fajita seasoning
- 1 (14.5-ounce) can fat-free reduced-sodium chicken broth
- 2 tablespoons fresh lime juice
- 2 teaspoons hot sauce
- Toppings: chopped fresh cilantro, chopped tomatoes, reduced-fat shredded Mexican 4-cheese blend

COOK first 4 ingredients in a Dutch oven coated with cooking spray until beef crumbles and is no longer pink. Drain. Return beef and pork to Dutch oven.

ADD onions and garlic to Dutch oven, and cook 5 to 7 minutes or until onions are tender.

STIR in black beans and next 8 ingredients. Bring to a boil; reduce heat, and simmer 30 to 40 minutes or until pork is tender. Serve with desired toppings.

NOTE: For testing purposes only, we used McCormick Fajita Seasoning Mix.

BRENDA JOHNSON
BIRMINGHAM, ALABAMA

Calories 169 (20% from fat); Fat 3.8g (sat 1.4g, mono 1.6g, poly 0.2g); Protein 17g; Carb 16.3g; Fiber 5g; Chol 31.3mg; Iron 1.5mg; Sodium 581mg; Calc 38.4mg

CHICKEN AND ROASTED RED PEPPER SALAD

make ahead

MAKES 10 (1-CUP) SERVINGS
Prep: 15 min., Chill: 1 hr.

We loved this salad alongside whole wheat melba rounds, tangy grapes, and crisp apple slices.

- 6 cups chopped cooked chicken (about 5 skinned and boned chicken breast halves)
- 1 bunch green onions, chopped (about ¾ cup)
- ⅔ cup light mayonnaise
- ½ cup diced jarred roasted red bell pepper
- ¼ cup chopped macadamia nuts, toasted
- 3 tablespoons Dijon mustard
- 3 tablespoons honey
- 2 teaspoons Worcestershire sauce
- 1 teaspoon hot sauce
- ½ teaspoon pepper
- ¼ teaspoon salt

STIR together all ingredients in a large bowl. Cover and chill at least 1 hour.

*Reduce fat by omitting nuts and using fat-free mayonnaise.

Calories 231(40% from fat); Fat 10.3g* (sat 1.9g, mono 2.7g, poly 0.7g); Protein 25g; Carb 8.8g; Fiber 0.8g; Chol 70.3mg; Iron 1mg; Sodium 387mg; Calc 22.2mg

Easy Appetizers

Serving appetizers that everyone will rave about is great, but what if you're time challenged? These tasty nibbles are easy to prepare and call for short prep times. You might as well make copies of these distinctly delicious recipes; your friends will be asking for them.

CITRUSY PECANS

fast fixin's

MAKES 2 CUPS

Prep: 15 min., Bake: 25 min.

These sweet, crunchy nuts are great by the handful, or you can also chop them and add to chicken or tuna salads. The sweet pecans can become a bit sticky if not stored in a sealed container or zip-top freezer bag.

- 1 egg white
- 2 cups pecan halves
- ½ cup firmly packed light brown sugar
- 2 teaspoons grated orange rind
- 2 tablespoons fresh orange juice
- ½ teaspoon salt
- ¼ teaspoon ground cinnamon

WHISK egg white in a medium bowl until frothy; toss with pecans.
STIR together brown sugar and next 4 ingredients in a large bowl. Add pecans, and toss. Drain well. Place pecans in a single layer on an aluminum foil-lined baking sheet coated with cooking spray.
BAKE at 325°, stirring occasionally, 20 to 25 minutes.

ANTIPASTO SQUARES

MAKES 8 SERVINGS

Prep: 15 min., Bake: 47 min.

Prep time is only 15 minutes because you start with refrigerated crescent rolls, meats from the deli, and vegetables in jars. We used reduced-fat versions of crescent rolls, deli meats, and Swiss cheese for a lighter, equally delicious pick-up appetizer.

- 2 (8-ounce) cans reduced-fat crescent rolls, divided
- ¼ pound sliced reduced-fat salami
- 1 (3-ounce) package reduced-fat pepperoni
- ¼ pound thinly sliced deli ham
- 1 (6.67-ounce) package reduced-fat Swiss cheese slices
- 1 (6-ounce) package Provolone cheese slices
- 2 large eggs
- 1 large egg, separated
- 1 (12-ounce) jar mild banana pepper rings, drained
- 1 (12-ounce) jar roasted red peppers, drained and cut into thin strips
- 1 (2¼-ounce) can sliced ripe olives, drained
- 1 teaspoon Italian seasoning
- ½ teaspoon garlic powder
- ¼ teaspoon ground red pepper
- ¼ teaspoon ground black pepper
- 2 teaspoons sesame seeds

UNROLL 1 can crescent rolls, and press into bottom of a lightly greased 13- x 9-inch pan.
BAKE at 350° for 12 minutes or until lightly browned. Cool slightly, and layer with sliced meats and cheeses.
WHISK together 2 eggs and 1 egg white. Pour over meat and cheeses. Stir together banana pepper rings and next 6 ingredients. Sprinkle over meat and cheese mixture.
UNROLL remaining can crescent rolls, and place over mixture in pan. Brush dough with lightly beaten egg yolk, and sprinkle with sesame seeds.
BAKE at 350° for 25 minutes; cover and bake 10 more minutes. Cool completely, and cut into 2-inch squares.

PHYLLIS MAGILL
MONROEVILLE, ALABAMA

QUICK PARTY SALSA

fast fixin's

MAKES 4 CUPS

Prep: 10 min.

Canned tomatoes shorten chopping time and allow you to enjoy the great flavors when juicy, fresh tomatoes aren't in season.

- 1 (28-ounce) can diced tomatoes with roasted garlic
- 1 small red onion, chopped
- 1 large jalapeño pepper, seeded and chopped
- 1 cup chopped fresh cilantro
- 2 tablespoons lemon juice
- 2 tablespoons lime juice
- 1 teaspoon ground cumin
- 1 teaspoon chili powder
- ¼ teaspoon salt
- 2 teaspoons sugar (optional)
- Tortilla chips

COMBINE first 9 ingredients and, if desired, sugar in a large bowl. Cover and chill until ready to serve. Serve with tortilla chips.

CHICKEN-BACON NUGGETS

family favorite

MAKES 6 SERVINGS

Prep: 15 min., Chill: 2 hrs., Bake: 20 min.

If you're trying to cut back on sodium, use reduced-sodium bacon and lite soy sauce.

- 2 large skinned and boned chicken breast halves
- 8 bacon slices, cut into thirds
- ½ cup orange marmalade
- ¼ cup soy sauce
- 2 tablespoons sesame oil
- 1 teaspoon ground ginger
- 1 garlic clove, minced
- Vegetable cooking spray

CUT chicken breasts into 24 (1-inch) cubes. Wrap each chicken cube with bacon, and secure with a wooden pick.
STIR together marmalade and next 4 ingredients in a shallow dish or large zip-top freezer bag; add chicken nuggets.

Cover or seal, and chill 2 hours, turning occasionally.
COAT a rack and broiler pan with cooking spray. Place chicken nuggets on rack in broiler pan.
BAKE at 450° for 10 minutes; turn, and bake 10 more minutes.

DENISE GIEGER
WOODSTOCK, GEORGIA

CREAMY CHICKPEA SPREAD

fast fixin's

MAKES 1¼ CUPS

Prep: 15 min.

This Middle Eastern dip, also known as hummus, contains tahini, a paste made of ground toasted sesame seeds. Look for it on the condiment aisle or in the ethnic food section of most supermarkets.

> 1 (16-ounce) can garbanzo beans, rinsed and drained
> 2 tablespoons lemon juice
> 1 large garlic clove, minced
> 1 tablespoon olive oil
> 1 tablespoon plain yogurt
> 1 to 2 tablespoons water
> 1 teaspoon tahini
> ½ teaspoon cumin seeds, toasted and ground*
> ½ teaspoon ground black pepper
> ⅛ teaspoon ground red pepper
> ¼ teaspoon salt
> Extra-virgin olive oil (optional)
> Pita bread triangles, pita chips, or assorted fresh vegetables

PROCESS first 11 ingredients in a food processor until smooth, stopping to scrape down sides. Drizzle with olive oil, if desired. Serve with pita bread, pita chips, or vegetables.

*Substitute ¼ teaspoon ground cumin, if desired.

Pass the Mashed Potatoes

We've eaten mashed potatoes all our lives, and we usually want them the way Mama made 'em. But if you're ready for something a little different, try these. Though they may not be quite the same as your mother's, they got top ratings in our Test Kitchens.

LEEK MASHED POTATOES

family favorite

MAKES 6 SERVINGS

Prep: 20 min., Cook: 25 min.

> 2 medium leeks
> ¼ cup dry sherry or chicken broth
> 1 tablespoon butter or margarine
> 4 large baking potatoes, peeled and cubed
> 4 cups water
> 1 tablespoon chicken bouillon granules
> 4 garlic cloves, chopped
> ¼ cup butter or margarine, softened
> 3 tablespoons half-and-half
> ¼ teaspoon seasoned salt

REMOVE root, tough outer leaves, and green tops from leeks. Cut leeks in half lengthwise; rinse and drain. Chop leeks.
COOK sherry and 1 tablespoon butter in a large saucepan over medium-high heat until butter melts; add leeks, and sauté 5 minutes. Add potatoes, 4 cups water, bouillon granules, and garlic. Bring to a boil; reduce heat, and cook 15 to 20 minutes or until potatoes are tender. Drain.
COMBINE potato mixture, ¼ cup butter, half-and-half, and salt in a large bowl; mash with a potato masher until smooth.

ALEXIS M. EIDSON
SAN ANTONIO, TEXAS

SWIRLED MASHED-POTATO BAKE

family favorite

MAKES 8 TO 10 SERVINGS

Prep: 20 min., Cook: 40 min., Bake: 30 min.

> 2½ pounds Yukon gold potatoes, peeled and cubed
> 2½ pounds sweet potatoes, peeled and cubed
> 1½ cups milk, divided
> 1 (8-ounce) package light cream cheese, divided
> 2 tablespoons butter or margarine, divided
> 2 green onions, finely chopped
> 1½ teaspoons salt, divided
> ¼ teaspoon pepper
> ½ teaspoon dried thyme
> Garnish: chopped green onions

BRING Yukon gold potatoes and water to cover to a boil in a large Dutch oven. Reduce heat, and cook 20 minutes or until tender; drain. Repeat procedure with sweet potatoes.
BEAT Yukon gold potatoes at medium speed with an electric mixer until mashed. Add ¾ cup milk, half of cheese, and 1 tablespoon butter, beating until smooth. Stir in chopped onions, 1 teaspoon salt, and pepper. Spoon into a lightly greased 3-quart oval baking dish.
BEAT sweet potatoes until mashed; add remaining ¾ cup milk, remaining cheese, and remaining 1 tablespoon butter, beating until smooth. Stir in remaining ½ teaspoon salt and thyme. Spread over Yukon gold potato mixture, and swirl gently with a knife. Cover and chill up to 8 hours, if desired.
BAKE at 350° for 25 to 30 minutes or until thoroughly heated. Garnish, if desired.

MARCIA LOOMIS
ST. LOUIS, MISSOURI

Christmas All Through the House

Within these pages, we share easy-going recipes and simple decorations.

An Easy Holiday Feast

Holiday Dinner

Serves 8

Baked Artichoke Dip (double recipe)

Rosemary Rib Roast

Creamy Lemon-Poppy Seed Mashed Potatoes

Asparagus Amandine   Bourbon Carrots

Lime-and-Macadamia Nut Tart   Winter Wassail

BAKED ARTICHOKE DIP

MAKES 4 TO 6 SERVINGS

Prep: 20 min., Bake: 30 min.

> 2 (14-ounce) cans artichoke hearts,
>   drained and chopped
> 2 garlic cloves, minced
> 2 tablespoons lemon juice
> ¾ cup mayonnaise
> ½ cup fine, dry breadcrumbs
> 1 cup freshly shredded Parmesan cheese
> ¼ cup freshly grated Parmesan cheese
> Crackers

COMBINE first 6 ingredients, stirring well. Spoon into a lightly greased 1-quart baking dish; sprinkle with grated Parmesan cheese. Bake at 350° for 30 minutes or until done. Serve with crackers.

PEGGY MORGAN
BIRMINGHAM, ALABAMA

ROSEMARY RIB ROAST

MAKES 8 SERVINGS

Prep: 10 min.; Bake: 1 hr., 35 min.;
Stand: 50 min.

Have the butcher remove the bone, and then tie it back on—this will give you the flavor from the bone, but allow you to easily remove it for carving.

> 6 garlic cloves, pressed
> 2 teaspoons salt
> 2 teaspoons pepper
> 1 teaspoon crushed rosemary
> 2 tablespoons olive oil
> 1 (7-pound) 4-rib prime rib roast, chine
>   bone removed
> 1 cup sour cream
> 2 tablespoons lemon juice
> 2 tablespoons prepared horseradish

COMBINE first 5 ingredients in a small bowl; rub over roast. Let roast stand at room temperature 30 minutes.

BAKE at 450° for 45 minutes on lower rack of oven. Reduce temperature to 350°, and bake 45 to 50 minutes or until meat thermometer inserted into roast registers 145° (medium rare), or 160° (medium). Let stand 20 minutes.

COMBINE sour cream, lemon juice, and horseradish; serve with roast.

CREAMY LEMON-POPPY SEED MASHED POTATOES

MAKES 8 SERVINGS

Prep: 15 min., Cook: 20 min..

You may substitute plain nonfat yogurt and extra lemon rind for the lemon yogurt used in this recipe

> 3 pounds Yukon gold potatoes, peeled
>   and cubed
> 1½ teaspoons salt
> ¼ cup low-fat milk
> 6 garlic cloves, peeled
> 1 bay leaf
> 1 (6-ounce) container lemon yogurt
> ½ cup milk
> ¼ cup chive-and-onion cream cheese
> 3 tablespoons butter or margarine
> 1 to 2 teaspoons poppy seeds
> 2 teaspoons grated lemon rind
> 1 teaspoon salt
> Garnishes: chopped fresh chives,
>   parsley sprigs, lemon rind strips

BRING first 5 ingredients and water to cover to a boil in a large saucepan; cook 15 to 20 minutes or until tender.

DRAIN, discarding bay leaf, and return potatoes and garlic to saucepan.

ADD yogurt and next 3 ingredients; beat at medium speed with an electric mixer until smooth.

STIR in poppy seeds, lemon rind, and salt. Garnish, if desired.

RICHARD J. BOULANGER
WILLISTON, VERMONT

ASPARAGUS AMANDINE

fast fixin's

MAKES 8 SERVINGS

Prep: 5 min., Cook: 15 min.

- 2 pounds fresh asparagus
- 2 tablespoons butter
- ¼ cup sliced almonds
- 2 tablespoons diced red bell pepper
- 1 tablespoon fresh lemon juice
- ½ teaspoon salt
- ½ teaspoon pepper

SNAP off tough ends of asparagus. Cook asparagus in boiling salted water to cover in a large skillet 3 minutes or until crisp-tender; drain.

PLUNGE asparagus into ice water to stop the cooking process; drain.

MELT butter in a large skillet over medium heat; add almonds, and sauté 2 to 3 minutes or until golden brown. Add asparagus and red bell pepper; cook 3 to 5 minutes. Toss with lemon juice, salt, and pepper, and serve immediately.

MILDRED SHERRER
BAY CITY, TEXAS

BOURBON CARROTS

fast fixin's

MAKES 8 SERVINGS

Prep: 5 min., Cook: 15 min.

- 3 cups water
- 1½ pounds baby carrots
- 1 tablespoon granulated sugar
- ½ teaspoon salt
- 2 tablespoons butter
- 3 tablespoons brown sugar
- 2 tablespoons bourbon
- Garnish: chopped fresh parsley

BRING 3 cups water to a boil in a 3-quart saucepan; add carrots, granulated sugar, and salt. Return to a boil, and cook 5 minutes, or until tender.

MELT butter and brown sugar in a large skillet over medium-high heat. Stir in carrots, and cook, stirring occasionally, 2 to 3 minutes or until well coated. Add bourbon, and cook, stirring occasionally, 3 more minutes. Garnish, if desired.

DEMETRA ECONOMOS ANAD
POTOMAC, MARYLAND

LIME-AND-MACADAMIA NUT TART

MAKES 8 SERVINGS

Prep: 25 min., Bake: 9 min., Cook: 8 min.,
Cool: 20 min., Chill: 4 hrs

- 1 (5⅓-ounce) package graham crackers, crushed (about 1½ cups)
- ½ cup macadamia nuts, finely chopped
- ¼ cup sugar
- 6 tablespoons butter, melted
- 6 large eggs
- 1½ tablespoons grated lime rind
- ½ cup fresh lime juice (about 6 large limes)
- 1 cup sugar
- 6 tablespoons butter or margarine
- 1 drop green liquid food coloring (optional)
- 1 drop yellow liquid food coloring (optional)
- Garnishes: whipped cream, toasted macadamia nuts

STIR together first 4 ingredients. Firmly press crumb mixture evenly on bottom and up sides of a 10-inch tart pan.

BAKE crust at 350° for 7 to 9 minutes. Cool on a wire rack.

WHISK together eggs, lime rind, and lime juice in a nonaluminum saucepan over low heat. Add 1 cup sugar, 6 tablespoons butter, and if desired, food coloring; cook, whisking constantly, 8 minutes or until lime mixture is thickened and bubbly. Let cool 15 to 20 minutes. Pour filling into prepared crust; cover and chill 4 hours or until set. Garnish, if desired.

J. MICHAEL MCLAUGHLIN
JOHN'S ISLAND, SOUTH CAROLINA

WINTER WASSAIL

fast fixin's • make ahead

MAKES 13 CUPS

Prep: 5 min., Cook: 20 min.

This will warm up a chilly morning and fill the house with spicy holiday aromas. Whole allspice and cloves are in the supermarket next to their ground counterparts.

- 2 teaspoons whole allspice
- 2 teaspoons whole cloves
- 6 cinnamon sticks
- 2 quarts apple cider
- 2 cups sugar
- 2 cups orange juice
- 1½ cups lemon juice
- 1 cup water

TIE first 3 ingredients together in a piece of cheesecloth or coffee filter.

BRING cider and sugar to a boil in a large saucepan. Add spice bag; reduce heat, and simmer, covered, 10 minutes. Remove spice bag; discard.

STIR in orange juice and remaining ingredients; simmer 5 minutes or until heated. Serve hot.

NOTE: Winter Wassail can be chilled 8 hours; reheat to serve.

FRANCES LEANNA PAFFORD
GAFFNEY, SOUTH CAROLINA

Light Up the Night

Whether it's twinkling icicles raining from tree branches or candles shimmering in window boxes, outdoor lights produce incomparable magic and mystique. The options are mind-boggling, but the bottom line is this: Holiday illuminations, in every shape and form, are just plain fun. Use them to showcase your architecture, personality, and sense of style.

Turn an afternoon working on your outdoor decor into a winter picnic. Enlist your spouse or a friend to help—they'll bring merriment and make the completed task doubly satisfying. Reward yourselves with soothing soup and a hearty sandwich, ending with spicy-sweet gingerbread to add the best flavors of the season.

The Secrets of Candlelight

Candles exude gracious hospitality and generate a warm welcome when used outdoors. Here are a few ideas to incorporate them into your decorations, as well as a few safety tips.

■ Always place candles in windproof containers.
■ Place inexpensive hurricane globes in large clay pots filled with sand. Chunky candles inside the globes and clipped greenery around the outer edges complete the arrangement. Line a walkway or stagger the containers on entry stairs for quick, easy illumination.
■ Dress up a winter window box with votives. Wrap wire around the glass container and attach it to a bamboo or wire plant stake.
■ Keep candles a safe distance from shrubs, dry leaves, and other holiday decorations.

YUKON GOLD-CHEESE CHOWDER

MAKES 6 CUPS

Prep: 15 min., Cook: 35 min.

- 1 cup diced carrots
- ½ cup chopped green onions
- ½ cup diced fennel
- 2 tablespoons olive oil
- 2 medium Yukon gold potatoes, peeled and diced (about 2 cups)
- 3 (14.5-ounce) cans chicken broth
- 1 cup milk
- 2 tablespoons all-purpose flour
- ½ teaspoon salt
- ¼ teaspoon ground white pepper
- ⅛ teaspoon ground nutmeg
- ⅛ teaspoon ground red pepper
- 1 cup (4 ounces) shredded Cheddar cheese
- ½ cup (2 ounces) shredded Swiss cheese
- Garnish: chopped green onions

SAUTÉ carrots, green onions, and fennel in hot oil in a large Dutch oven over medium heat 5 minutes or until tender. Add potatoes and broth, and bring to a boil. Reduce heat, and simmer 15 minutes, uncovered, or until potatoes are tender.

STIR together milk and next 5 ingredients in a small bowl; gradually stir into chowder, and cook, stirring constantly, 5 minutes.

STIR in cheeses until melted. Garnish, if desired.

ALFRED LESTER
WILMINGTON, NORTH CAROLINA

GRILLED ROAST BEEF-AND-BRIE SANDWICHES

MAKES 6 SERVINGS

Prep: 15 min., Cook: 25 min.

Though eye-of-round roast gives this sandwich great flavor and texture, deli roast beef can be substituted. Keep these sandwiches warm by wrapping them in foil and placing them in a slow cooker.

- 1 large red onion, sliced
- 1 teaspoon sugar
- ½ teaspoon salt
- 6 hoagie rolls, split
- 3 tablespoons butter, melted
- 1 (8-ounce) round Brie, cut into 6 slices
- 1 pound Classic Roast Beef, thinly sliced
- 1 cup Dijon Horseradish Sauce

SAUTÉ first 3 ingredients in a medium nonstick skillet over medium-high heat 8 minutes or until onion is tender.

BRUSH cut sides of rolls evenly with melted butter, and cook, buttered sides down, in a skillet or on a griddle over medium heat, 5 minutes or until lightly browned. Turn roll halves over in skillet; layer cut sides of bottom halves evenly with Brie slices, onion mixture, and roast beef. Remove rolls from skillet.

SPREAD 1 tablespoon Dijon Horseradish Sauce on cut side of each top half, and place sauce side down on top of roast beef. Serve with remaining sauce.

Classic Roast Beef:

MAKES 6 TO 8 SERVINGS

Prep: 5 min., Bake: 1 hr., Stand: 1 hr.

- 1 (3½ -pound) eye-of-round roast
- 1½ tablespoons salt
- 2 teaspoons pepper

LET roast stand at room temperature 45 minutes.

PREHEAT oven to 450°.

PLACE roast, fat side up, on a rack in a roasting pan. Sprinkle with salt and pepper. Add ¼ inch water to pan.

REDUCE oven temperature to 350°, and bake on middle oven rack 1 hour or until a meat thermometer inserted into roast registers 145° (medium rare), or to desired degree of doneness. Remove from oven, and let stand loosely covered with foil 10 to 15 minutes. Slice thinly for sandwiches.

Dijon Horseradish Sauce:

MAKES 1 CUP

Prep: 5 min.

- **1 cup sour cream**
- **1 teaspoon prepared horseradish**
- **1 tablespoon Dijon mustard**
- **¼ teaspoon salt**
- **¼ teaspoon black pepper**

STIR together all ingredients in a small bowl; cover and chill until ready to serve.

APPLE-GINGERBREAD SQUARES

MAKES 12 SERVINGS

Prep: 15 min., Bake: 45 min.

- **½ cup butter or margarine, softened**
- **¾ cup granulated sugar**
- **⅓ cup firmly packed dark brown sugar**
- **1 large egg**
- **2 cups all-purpose flour**
- **2 tablespoons crystallized ginger, minced**
- **2 teaspoons ground ginger**
- **1½ teaspoons baking soda**
- **1 teaspoon ground cinnamon**
- **1 teaspoon ground cloves**
- **½ teaspoon salt**
- **1 cup molasses**
- **1 cup boiling apple cider**
- **Ginger-Molasses Whipped Cream**

BEAT butter at medium speed with an electric mixer until creamy; gradually add sugars, beating well. Add egg, beating until blended.
ADD flour and next 8 ingredients; beat at medium speed until smooth. Pour into a greased and floured 13- x 9-inch pan.
BAKE at 325° for 35 to 45 minutes or until a wooden pick inserted in center comes out clean. Cool on a wire rack. Cut into 3-inch squares. Serve with Ginger-Molasses Whipped Cream.

Ginger-Molasses Whipped Cream:

MAKES 1½ CUPS

Prep: 5 min.

- **1 cup whipping cream**
- **1 tablespoon powdered sugar**
- **1 tablespoon molasses**
- **¼ teaspoon ground ginger**

BEAT all ingredients at high speed with an electric mixer until soft peaks form.

Merry and Bright

There has never been a more diverse array of outdoor lights, and the decorating options are endless. Get started with these ideas.

- Hang icicle lights from tree limbs where they have room to dangle between branches.
- Wrap a tomato cage in rope lights, spiraling them from bottom to top. Use small 3-foot cages in decorative pots at an entrance. Choose larger ones to place among shrubs or along the driveway.
- Turn off standard lights, and dangle star and snowflake lights from the ceiling of a covered entryway for celestial sparkle.
- Double strands of icicle lights, and hang them from a fence.
- Wind cluster lights into a garland before draping it around the front door.

A Stolen Moment

You've shopped till you dropped, finished baking, and wrapped every gift. Now you can cuddle up on the sofa with your honey, share a soothing hot toddy, and munch a cookie—just the two of you. What better time to catch up on the day's events and anticipate the fun yet to come? After all, it's Christmas.

SOFT-AND-CHEWY CARAMELS

MAKES 64 PIECES

Prep: 5 min., Cook: 20 min., Stand: 3 hrs.

These rich candies are more tender than their store-bought cousins.

- **Vegetable cooking spray**
- **1 cup butter**
- **1 (16-ounce) package light brown sugar**
- **1 (14-ounce) can sweetened condensed milk**
- **1 cup light corn syrup**

LINE an 8-inch square pan with aluminum foil, extending foil over edges of pan. Generously coat foil with cooking spray; set aside.
MELT 1 cup butter in a 3-quart saucepan over low heat. Stir in sugar, condensed milk, and corn syrup until smooth. Bring to a boil. Cook over medium heat, stirring often, until a candy thermometer registers 235° (soft ball stage).
REMOVE mixture from heat; stir by hand 1 minute or until mixture is smooth and no longer bubbling. Quickly pour mixture into prepared pan; let stand 3 hours or until completely cool.
LIFT foil and caramel out of pan. Cut caramels into 1-inch pieces with a buttered knife. Wrap each piece with plastic wrap.

MARCIA WHITNEY
HOUSTON, TEXAS

SUGAR COOKIES

family favorite

MAKES ABOUT 7 DOZEN
Prep: 30 min., Bake: 11 min. per batch

These sugar cookies are so good that we offer some fun variations.

- 1 cup butter, softened
- 1 cup powdered sugar
- 1 cup granulated sugar
- 2 large eggs
- 1 cup vegetable oil
- 2 teaspoons vanilla extract
- 1 tablespoon fresh lemon juice
- 5¼ cups all-purpose flour
- 1 teaspoon cream of tartar
- 1 teaspoon baking soda
- ¼ teaspoon salt
- Colored sugar

BEAT butter at medium speed with an electric mixer until fluffy; add sugars, beating well. Add eggs, oil, vanilla, and lemon juice, beating until blended.
COMBINE flour and next 3 ingredients; gradually add to sugar mixture, beating until blended.
SHAPE dough into 1-inch balls; roll in colored sugar, and place about 2 inches apart on lightly greased baking sheets.
BAKE in batches at 350° for 9 to 11 minutes or until set. (Do not brown.) Remove to wire racks to cool.

CHOCOLATE KISS COOKIES: Omit colored sugar. After baking, immediately place an unwrapped milk chocolate kiss in center of each cookie, and cool.

PEANUT BUTTER CUP COOKIES: Omit colored sugar. After baking, immediately place 1 unwrapped miniature peanut butter cup in the center of each cookie, and cool.

LEMON COOKIES: Omit vanilla and colored sugar. Increase lemon juice to ¼ cup, and add 1 teaspoon grated lemon rind to dough. Proceed as directed.

LEMON THUMBPRINT COOKIES: Prepare Lemon Cookies; press thumb in center of each cookie to make an indentation.

Bake and cool as directed. Spoon ½ teaspoon raspberry jam into each indentation.

JANET TELLEEN
RUSSELL, IOWA

FIRESIDE COFFEE

fast fixin's

MAKES 4 (6-OUNCE) SERVINGS
Prep: 5 min., Cook: 2 min., Stand: 1 min.

This creamy concoction is inspired by Ruth Traweek's Brandy Coffee from 1997's *Southern Living® Annual Recipes.*

- 1 cup half-and-half
- 1 (1-ounce) unsweetened chocolate baking square, chopped
- 1 cup hot brewed coffee
- 6 tablespoons bourbon
- ¼ to ½ cup sugar
- ⅓ cup whipping cream
- ½ teaspoon vanilla extract
- Whipped cream (optional)

MICROWAVE half-and-half in a 2-cup glass measuring cup on HIGH 1 to 2 minutes or until steamy. Pour over chocolate; let stand 1 minute, and whisk until smooth. Stir in coffee and next 4 ingredients; top with whipped cream, if desired. Serve immediately.

A Festive Tree Trimming

When the tree comes indoors, Christmas kicks into high gear. Trimming sweetly scented boughs mingles memories, laughter, and timeless fun. Lights twist, twinkle, and set the atmosphere aglow like no other aspect of holiday decorating. Prepare a few simple appetizers to share with loved ones.

CANDY CANE-CHEESE LOGS

MAKES 12 TO 16 APPETIZER SERVINGS
Prep: 20 min., Chill: 2 hrs.

These colorful logs were inspired by reader Clairiece Humphrey's recipe for bite-size cheese balls.

- 1 pound sharp Cheddar cheese, grated
- 1 (8-ounce) package cream cheese, softened
- 4 ounces Roquefort cheese
- 2 tablespoons diced onion
- 1 tablespoon Worcestershire sauce
- ¼ to ½ teaspoon ground red pepper
- ¼ teaspoon salt
- ¼ teaspoon pepper
- 1 cup finely chopped dried cranberries
- 1 cup sesame seeds, toasted
- Assorted crackers

PROCESS first 8 ingredients in a blender or food processor until smooth, stopping to scrape down sides. Cover and chill 1 hour.
SHAPE cheese mixture into 3 (10-inch) logs. Press opposite sides of each log in chopped cranberries; press remaining sides in sesame seeds. Gently twist log to form spiral stripes.
CURVE 1 end to form a cane. Place on a wax paper-lined baking sheet. Cover and chill 1 hour. Serve with assorted crackers.

CLAIRIECE GILBERT HUMPHREY
CHARLOTTESVILLE, VIRGINIA

SOUTHWESTERN PULL-APART RING

MAKES 12 TO 16 APPETIZER SERVINGS

Prep: 15 min., Cook: 10 min., Bake: 15 min., Stand: 10 min.

- 1 (12-ounce) package ground hot or mild pork sausage
- 1 red bell pepper, diced
- 1 green bell pepper, diced
- 1 (1-ounce) package fajita seasoning mix
- 2 (12-ounce) cans refrigerated biscuits
- 1½ cups (6 ounces) shredded Mexican four-cheese blend

SOUTHWESTERN PULL-APART RING

MAKES 12 TO 16 APPETIZER SERVINGS

Prep: 15 min., Cook: 10 min., Bake: 15 min., Stand: 10 min.

- 1 (12-ounce) package ground hot or mild pork sausage
- 1 red bell pepper, diced
- 1 green bell pepper, diced
- 1 (1-ounce) package fajita seasoning mix
- 2 (12-ounce) cans refrigerated biscuits
- 1½ cups (6 ounces) shredded Mexican four-cheese blend

COOK sausage in a skillet over medium heat, stirring until it crumbles and is no longer pink. Stir in peppers, and cook 3 to 5 minutes or until tender. Sprinkle with seasoning mix, and cook 1 to 2 more minutes; drain well, pressing with paper towels.
SEPARATE biscuits; and cut into quarters; place in a large mixing bowl. Fold in sausage mixture, tossing to coat.
LAYER biscuit mixture and cheese in a lightly greased 10-inch tube pan.
BAKE at 400° for 15 minutes or until golden brown. Let stand for 5 to 10 minutes. Turn mold onto a serving plate, and serve immediately.

Great-Looking Tree Ideas

Here are a few tips to fill out your tree branches.

- Tuck magnolia leaves in branches for classy textural contrast. For extra pizzazz, lightly spray-paint the leaves gold.
- Angel hair and spray-on snow turns a not-so-perfect tree into shimmering gossamer.
- Wrap small boxes in shiny paper, and tuck them deep into the tree for a bit of dazzle.
- Check flea markets and antiques stores for vintage ornaments.

Illuminating Tips

Birmingham expert Ray Jordan of Christmas and Company shares his personal tips for lighting a Christmas tree.

- Begin lights at the bottom of the tree and work up to the top.
- Use only 300 lights per extension cord—this is the maximum number that string sets are designed to handle. When possible, use 50-light strands; they don't tangle as easily and burn out less frequently.
- Tuck white lights close to the trunk—they highlight the tree's depth. Add colored and specialty lights on the outer branches, wrapping lights around tips.
- For more great tips, visit Christmas and Company's Web site at **www.christmasandco.com**.

PESTO-GARBANZO DIP

MAKES 3 CUPS

Prep: 10 min.; Chill: 30 min.

- 1 (7-ounce) container pesto sauce
- 1 (15.5-ounce) can garbanzo beans, rinsed and drained
- 2 garlic cloves
- ¼ cup olive oil
- 3 tablespoons lemon juice
- 2 tablespoons finely chopped fresh cilantro
- Salt and pepper to taste
- Pita chips, assorted vegetables

REMOVE and discard top layer of oil from prepared pesto sauce.
PROCESS beans and garlic in a blender or food processor until smooth, stopping to scrape down sides. With processor running, pour oil, pesto sauce, and lemon juice through food chute, blending well. Transfer to a serving bowl; stir in cilantro and salt and pepper to taste.
COVER and chill 30 minutes, if desired.
SERVE with pita chips and assorted vegetables.

NOTE: For testing purposes only, we used DiGiorno Basil Pesto Sauce.

JAYSHREE SETH
WOODBURY, MINNESOTA

HAM BALLS

MAKES ABOUT 50 APPETIZERS

Prep: 40 min.; Chill: 1 hr.; Cook: 30 min.; Bake: 50 min.

- 1 pound diced ham
- 1 pound ground pork
- 2 cups fine, dry breadcrumbs
- 1 cup milk
- 2 large eggs, beaten
- ¾ teaspoon salt
- ¼ teaspoon ground red pepper
- 6 tablespoons vegetable oil, divided
- ½ cup firmly packed brown sugar
- ½ cup water
- ½ cup white vinegar
- 1 teaspoon dry mustard

PROCESS ham in a food processor until coarsely ground; add pork and next 5 ingredients, and pulse to combine. Chill 1 hour. Shape into 1-inch balls. Cook, in batches, in 2 tablespoons hot oil in a large skillet over medium heat 3 minutes on each side, adding oil as needed. Place in a lightly greased 13- x 9-inch baking dish.
COMBINE brown sugar and next 3 ingredients in a large saucepan over medium heat; cook about 5 minutes or until thoroughly heated. Pour sauce over balls.
BAKE, covered, at 350° for 20 minutes. Uncover and bake 30 more minutes.

JUDIE COVINGTON
MCCALL CREEK, MISSISSIPPI

Guests Are Coming

BUTTER MINTS

freezeable • make ahead

MAKES 20 DOZEN

Prep: 20 min., Cook: 5 min., Stand: 4 hrs.

Freeze extra mints in a zip-top freezer bag for up to three months.

- ½ (8-ounce) package cream cheese
- 2 tablespoons butter
- 1 (16-ounce) package powdered sugar
- ¼ teaspoon peppermint extract
- ⅛ teaspoon vanilla extract

MELT cream cheese and butter in a large saucepan over low heat, stirring constantly until smooth. Gradually stir in powdered sugar; add peppermint and vanilla extracts, stirring until well blended.

DIVIDE cream cheese mixture into 10 (¼-cup) portions; roll into a 12-inch rope. Cut into ½-inch pieces. Let stand, uncovered, 4 hours or until firm.

SUSAN THOMS
SPARTANBURG, SOUTH CAROLINA

CHRISTMAS PECANS

fast fixin's

MAKES 2 CUPS
Prep: 5 min., Bake: 20 min.

Double this recipe so there will be plenty to snack on.

- 5 tablespoons sugar, divided
- ¼ cup butter or margarine, melted
- 1 tablespoon pumpkin pie spice
- 1 tablespoon grated orange rind
- 2 cups pecan halves

STIR together 4 tablespoons granulated sugar, butter, spice, and orange rind. Add pecan halves; toss to coat.

PLACE on a lightly greased aluminum foil-lined baking sheet. Sprinkle evenly with remaining 1 tablespoon sugar.
BAKE at 350° for 20 minutes, stirring pecans once.

TOASTED PECANS: Toss 3 cups pecan halves with 1½ tablespoons melted butter. Place in an aluminum foil-lined jelly-roll pan. Bake at 325° for 10 minutes. Sprinkle 1 tablespoon coarse salt evenly over pecans, and bake 10 more minutes, stirring once.

CHRISTINE PATTERSON
ASHLAND, ALABAMA

Easy Dried Flower Wreath

Holiday decorations can be easily overlooked in a guest room. Instead of worrying about fresh flowers, place an everlasting wreath in the window—it looks good throughout the season.

Materials:

Florist wire
2 paperwhite bulbs
12-inch grapevine wreath
Dried roses
Glue gun
Spanish moss
Ribbon or raffia
1 clear or white pushpin

- Push a piece of florist wire through each paperwhite bulb, and attach it to the wreath base.
- Place the wreath flat on a table. Remove stems from the dried roses, and cluster the buds on each side of the bulbs, attaching them with the glue gun.
- Tuck Spanish moss around the bulbs and flowers, tacking it in place with the glue gun.
- Suspend the decoration from ribbon or raffia, attaching it to the window frame with a pushpin.

The Extra Touches

Be sure your guest room is well-stocked. Spend a quiet hour relaxing there yourself to discover which additional amenities you want to add. Here are a few suggestions.

- CD player/FM radio—relaxing music and station guide
- Scented candle, matches, and snuffer
- Current magazines
- Quick-read books (*The Little Prince, A Child's Christmas in Wales*)
- Spa-style shampoo and soap
- Extra pillows
- Slippers
- Postcards and stamps
- Assorted tea bags
- A thermos or teapot of hot water
- Snacks for between meals or before bedtime

It's the little things that make guests feel welcome. Set up their room as a private retreat where a quiet cup of tea and quick catnap are pure pleasure.

Providing for guests' minute-to-minute needs with beverages, snacks, toiletries, extra pillows, and blankets will ensure their comfort and give you some quiet time as well. In fact, while you're playing concierge, tuck one of these tasty treats into your room to enjoy at the end of a busy day. Such special touches will assure you and your visitors of sweet dreams.

Southern-Fried Stuffed Chicken With Roasted Red
Pepper-and-Vidalia Onion Gravy, page 322

301

Spicy Tex-Mex Chicken Cobbler, page 324

302

Tex-Mex Egg Rolls
With Creamy Cilantro
Dipping Sauce,
page 327

Melt-in-Your-Mouth Braised and Barbecued Chicken, page 326

Cream Cheese Flan, page 328

Pancakes With Dad

Saturdays and holidays are great times to stay home with the children, especially during the Christmas break. Plan a special morning when everyone relaxes around the table rather than rushes out the door. Give Dad a chance to shine in the kitchen, leaving Mom free to sleep in.

Our easy pancake breakfast includes yummy bacon with a sweet apple butter topping. Cooking the bacon in the oven leaves hands free to make the hotcakes. The Orange Jubilee takes only a few minutes to whip into a sweet, foamy favorite.

After breakfast, retrieve the day's treat hidden inside the Advent calendar, then count the days left until Christmas. By now, the children will be counting the minutes until playtime, and Dad will be ready to put up his feet.

Easy Advent Calendar

Kids love surprises, and an Advent calendar promises a daily treat. Make this child's version with baby socks hanging from a laundry line in only a few hours—then string it in front of a flat surface like a window.

Materials:

12 pairs 100% cotton white infant socks
Red dye
Stick-on numerals (1-24)
Decorative buttons, pom-poms, rickrack
Glue gun or needle and thread
Heavy string or laundry line
2 tacks or 2 suction cups with hooks
Miniature clothespins
24 small treats (candy, trinkets, or toys)

■ Tint socks following instructions on dye package. Once dry, gently stretch each one to loosen the fibers.
■ Number each sock 1 through 24.
■ Attach buttons, pom-poms, and rickrack using a glue gun or needle and thread.
■ Fasten string or laundry line with tacks or with suction cups stuck on glass or another smooth material. In a narrow area string two lines—one below the other—to accommodate all the socks.
■ Fasten each sock to the line with a clothespin, and drop a treat in each one.

CHRISTMAS TREE HOTCAKES

fast fixin's

MAKES 12 HOTCAKES

Prep: 5 min., Cook: 18 min.

To make these pancakes without cookie cutters, pour batter by ¼ cupfuls onto a hot griddle.

 1 cup all-purpose flour
 1 tablespoon baking powder
 2 teaspoons sugar
 1 teaspoon salt
 1⅛ cups milk (more for thinner batter)
 1 large egg, lightly beaten
 2 to 4 (4½- to 5-inch) metal cookie cutters

COMBINE first 4 ingredients in a bowl; whisk in 1⅛ cups milk and egg, whisking until blended.
LIGHTLY grease heavy metal cookie cutters, and place on a hot (375°), lightly greased griddle. Pour approximately 2 tabelsppons batter into each cutter. Using tongs, remove cutters after 1 minute (cutters will be hot); cook pancakes 2 more minutes. Turn and cook 2 to 3 minutes or until done.

PECAN PANCAKES: Stir ½ cup chopped toasted pecans into batter. Proceed as directed.

BANANA PANCAKES: Stir 1 cup chopped banana (2 bananas) into batter. Proceed as directed.

SHIRLEY PERKINS
MIDLAND, TEXAS

SWEET APPLE BACON

family favorite

MAKES 16 SLICES

Prep: 5 min., Bake: 50 min.

 1 pound thick-cut bacon
 ¼ cup apple butter
 2 tablespoons dark brown sugar

PLACE bacon slices in a single layer on rack in a broiler pan.

BAKE at 350° for 30 minutes. Turn slices; brush with apple butter, and sprinkle with brown sugar. Bake 15 to 20 more minutes or until lightly browned.

CANDACE SCHLOSSER
BIRMINGHAM, ALABAMA

ORANGE JUBILEE

fast fixin's

MAKES 4½ CUPS

Prep: 5 min.

 1 (6-ounce) can frozen orange juice concentrate, thawed and undiluted
 2¼ cups milk
 ½ teaspoon vanilla extract
 ¼ cup powdered sugar
 1 cup ice cubes

PROCESS all ingredients in a blender until smooth, stopping to scrape down sides. Serve immediately.

JOHNSIE FORD
ROCKINGHAM, NORTH CAROLINA

Make-Ahead Holiday Breakfast

Enjoy a relaxing Christmas morning with these delicious recipes. We've even included a few ideas for a great-looking table.

On Christmas morning, mayhem reigns. The children are in noisy high gear after weeks of anticipation, neighbors are likely to drop by for a cup of coffee, and family members are visiting from out of town. The living room is awash in scattered toys, reams of discarded wrapping paper, and ribbon.

We've assembled a collection of recipes that can be mostly made ahead, then either baked or reheated just before serving—they're perfect for large or small gatherings. Mix and match them to suit your family's tastes, or offer the entire spread of holiday bounty. Then sit back, enjoy the compliments, and bask in the pleasures of this most special time with those you love.

HASH BROWN BREAKFAST CASSEROLE

make ahead

MAKES 8 SERVINGS

Prep: 15 min., Cook: 12 min., Chill: 8 hrs., Bake: 1 hr., Stand: 5 min.

If you need to keep this casserole warm until the excitement dies down, you can cover it with foil, and put the cassrole in a 200° oven while the presents are being opened.

- 1 pound ground hot pork sausage
- ¼ cup chopped onion
- 2½ cups frozen cubed hash browns
- 5 large eggs, lightly beaten
- 2 cups (8 ounces) shredded sharp Cheddar cheese
- 1¾ cups milk
- 1 cup all-purpose baking mix
- ¼ teaspoon salt
- ¼ teaspoon pepper
- Toppings: picante sauce or green hot sauce, sour cream
- Garnish: fresh parsley sprigs

COOK sausage and onion in a large skillet over medium-high heat 5 minutes or until meat crumbles. Stir in hash browns, and cook 5 to 7 minutes or until sausage is no longer pink and potatoes are lightly browned. Drain mixture well on paper towels; spoon into a greased 13- x 9-inch baking dish.

STIR together eggs and next 5 ingredients; pour evenly over sausage mixture, stirring well. Cover and chill 8 hours.

BAKE, covered with nonstick foil, at 350° for 45 minutes. Uncover and bake 10 to 15 more minutes, or until a wooden pick inserted in the center comes out clean. Remove from oven, and let stand 5 minutes. Serve casserole with desired toppings. Garnish, if desired.

MICHELE MCCLAIN
FLOWER MOUND, TEXAS

LEMON-RASPBERRY MUFFINS

make ahead

MAKES 1 DOZEN

Prep: 20 min., Bake: 25 min.

You can mix up the dry ingredients and the streusel topping for these delicious muffins up to two days before you bake them, and store in zip-top freezer bags.

- 2¼ cups all-purpose flour, divided
- ½ cup sugar
- 2½ teaspoons baking powder
- ½ teaspoon salt
- 1 (8-ounce) container lemon yogurt
- ½ cup vegetable oil
- 2 large eggs
- 1 teaspoon grated lemon rind
- 1 (6-ounce) package fresh raspberries (about 1¼ cups), or 1 (6-ounce) package frozen raspberries, unthawed*
- 3 tablespoons sugar
- 1 tablespoon cold butter or margarine

COMBINE 2 cups flour, ½ cup sugar, baking powder, and salt in a large bowl; make a well in center of mixture.

STIR together yogurt and next 3 ingredients; add to dry ingredients, stirring just until moistened.

TOSS together 2 tablespoons flour and raspberries; fold into batter. Spoon into lightly greased muffin pans, filling two-thirds full.

COMBINE remaining 2 tablespoons flour and 3 tablespoons sugar; cut butter into mixture with a pastry blender or fork until crumbly, and spoon evenly over batter in muffin pans.

BAKE at 375° for 20 to 25 minutes or until golden. Remove muffins from pans immediately, and cool on wire racks.

*Substitute blueberries for raspberries, if desired.

JUDY BOYD MILLS
LONGWOOD, FLORIDA

HOT FRUIT COMPOTE

make ahead

MAKES 12 SERVINGS

Prep: 20 min., Bake 45 min.

To make preparation easy, crush the gingersnaps and toast the almonds the night before. We purchased fresh pineapple chunks from the supermarket produce department.

- 2 tablespoons butter, softened
- 2 to 2½ cups small crunchy gingersnap cookies (about 48 cookies)
- 1 (15.25-ounce) can peeled apricots, drained
- 1 fresh pineapple, cored and cut into small chunks
- 2 pears, peeled and cut into small chunks
- 1 (15-ounce) can sweet dark cherries, drained and halved
- ¼ cup firmly packed light brown sugar
- ½ cup amaretto liqueur
- ¼ cup butter, melted
- ½ cup slivered almonds, toasted
- Garnish: fresh mint sprig

GREASE a 3-quart baking dish with 2 tablespoons softened butter.

PROCESS gingersnaps in a food processor until crushed.

REMOVE pits and stems from apricots, and coarsely chop. Combine apricots, and next 3 ingredients in a large bowl. Spread one-third of gingersnap crumbs in prepared baking dish. Layer with half of fruit mixture and one-third of gingersnap crumbs. Top with remaining fruit mixture, and sprinkle evenly with remaining gingersnap crumbs. Sprinkle evenly with brown sugar, and drizzle with liqueur.

BAKE at 350° for 35 minutes. Drizzle with ¼ cup melted butter, and bake 10 more minutes. Sprinkle with toasted almonds, and garnish, if desired. Serve warm.

JULIE Y. BENSON
LOUISVILLE, KENTUCKY

CARAMEL-SOAKED FRENCH TOAST

make ahead

MAKES 10 SERVINGS

Prep: 20 min., Cook: 5 min., Chill: 8 hrs., Bake: 50 min., Stand: 10 min.

This luscious breakfast treat is a staff favorite from *Southern Living Our Best Five-Star Recipes*. Serve it with bacon or sausage to complement the sweet flavor and custardlike texture.

- 1½ cups firmly packed brown sugar
- ¾ cup butter or margarine
- ¼ cup plus 2 tablespoons light corn syrup
- 10 (1½-inch-thick) French bread slices, or 1 (10-ounce) loaf French bread, cut into 1½-inch-thick slices
- 4 large eggs
- 2½ cups milk
- 1 tablespoon vanilla extract
- ¼ teaspoon salt
- 3 tablespoons granulated sugar
- 1½ teaspoons ground cinnamon
- ¼ cup butter or margarine, melted
- Garnish: fresh raspberries

STIR together first 3 ingredients in a medium saucepan over medium heat, and cook, stirring constantly, 5 minutes or until mixture is bubbly. Pour mixture evenly into a lightly greased 13- x 9-inch baking dish. Arrange bread slices over syrup.

WHISK together eggs, milk, vanilla, and salt; gradually pour over bread slices. Cover and chill at least 8 hours.

STIR together granulated sugar and cinnamon; sprinkle evenly over bread. Drizzle evenly with ¼ cup melted butter.

BAKE at 350° for 45 to 50 minutes or until golden and bubbly. Let stand 10 minutes before serving. Garnish, if desired.

SPICE COOKIES

freezeable • make ahead

MAKES ABOUT 4 DOZEN

Prep: 30 min., Chill: 2 hrs., Bake: 10 min. per batch

We added a sweet orange glaze to Jeanne Wood's original recipe. Make and freeze these up to 6 weeks ahead.

- 1¾ cups sugar, divided
- 1 cup butter or margarine, softened
- 2 large eggs
- 1 tablespoon milk
- 4 cups all-purpose flour
- 1½ teaspoons baking soda
- 1½ teaspoons ground cinnamon
- ½ teaspoon ground nutmeg
- ¼ teaspoon ground cloves
- 1 cup dried currants or raisins
- Orange Glaze

BEAT 1½ cups sugar and butter at medium speed with an electric mixer until smooth. Add eggs, beating until blended. Add milk; beat at low speed until blended.

COMBINE flour and next 4 ingredients; gradually add to butter mixture, beating until blended. Stir in currants. Shape dough into a ball; wrap in plastic wrap, and chill 2 hours.

TURN dough out onto a lightly floured surface, and roll to ⅛-inch thickness; sprinkle top with remaining ¼ cup sugar. Cut dough with a 2½-inch round or other desired shape cutter. Place 2 inches apart on baking sheets.

BAKE at 350° for 8 to 10 minutes or until lightly browned. Cool on baking sheets 3 to 4 minutes. Remove to wire racks, and let cool completely. Drizzle Orange Glaze evenly over cookies.

Orange Glaze:

MAKES ¾ CUP

Prep: 5 min.

- 1½ cups powdered sugar
- 1 tablespoon orange juice
- ¼ teaspoon vanilla extract

STIR together all ingredients until smooth.

JEANNE WOOD
NEW ORLEANS, LOUISIANA

from our kitchen

Holiday Gift Box Cake

To create our festive Holiday Gift Box Cake, pictured on the cover and at right, we used a ruler to make a set of cardboard templates and then cut decorative strips from 1 (15-ounce) package of refrigerated piecrusts. Three (9-inch) square layers of Chocolate Velvet Cake With Cream Cheese-Butter Pecan Frosting (page 288) form the base of the box. After frosting the cake, follow these easy steps, and you'll end up with one delicious centerpiece for your holiday table.

Cut 1 (12- x 1-inch) strip and 1 (12- x ½-inch) strip from a piece of cardboard or poster board.

Step 1: Unfold 1 piecrust on a lightly floured surface; gently roll to press out fold lines. Cut piecrust in half; reserve and set aside one half. Using the 12- x ½-inch cardboard template as a guide, begin at the straight edge of 1 piecrust half, and cut 8 (½-inch-wide) strips. Cut each of the 8 strips into as many 3-inch-long pieces as possible. You will need a total of 20 (3- x ½-inch) pieces. Gather together any remaining scraps, and set aside.

Step 2: Arrange cut pieces on a baking sheet. Bake at 425° for 4 minutes or until golden. Cool 10 minutes on a wire rack. Dip the top side of each warm pastry piece in powdered sugar. Let cool completely on a wire rack.

Step 3: Unfold the second piecrust on a lightly floured surface; gently roll to press out fold lines. Whisk together 1 large egg and 2 tablespoons water. Brush egg mixture lightly over piecrust. Sprinkle piecrust evenly with ½ cup finely chopped pecans and 2 tablespoons white sparkling sugar. Using the 12- x 1-inch cardboard template, cut the piecrust into 1-inch-wide strips. Repeat the procedure with the reserved piecrust half, sprinkling with ¼ cup nuts and 1 tablespoon sparkling sugar. Cut 4 of the strips into 9½ x 1-inch pieces. Cut the remaining strips into as many 3-inch-long pieces as possible. You will need a total of 20 (3- x 1-inch) pieces.

Step 4: Arrange the cut pieces on a lightly greased baking sheet. Bake at 425° for 5 minutes or until golden. Cool on a wire rack.

To make gift tags, roll the reserved scraps of piecrust to ⅛-inch thickness on a lightly floured surface. Using a 2½- to 3-inch cookie cutter, cut decorative shapes from the piecrust. Place on a lightly greased baking sheet. Press the end of a plastic drinking straw into each tag, creating a round opening. Brush lightly with the egg mixture, and sprinkle with white sparkling sugar. Bake at 425° for 5 minutes or until golden. Cool on a wire rack.

Step 5: Prepare a half recipe of Vanilla Buttercream Frosting (page 286). Carefully spread a small amount of frosting on the back of each pastry piece. Gently press 1 9½-inch-long pastry piece horizontally on each side of the cake to form the rim of the box's lid. Gently press 3-inch pastry pieces, alternating pecan and powdered sugar pieces, on each side of the cake in a vertical pattern. Sprinkle the top of the cake with ½ cup finely chopped, toasted pecans and 2 tablespoons white sparkling sugar. If desired, use remaining frosting to add a decorative design to the gift tag or to pipe a narrow border around the bottom of the cake. Garnish the top with gold and silver wire-edged ribbon, fresh mint, and red candy-coated chocolate pieces.

Top 25 Recipes *in 25 Years*

Top 25 Recipes in 25 Years

Just imagine being on the taste panel to narrow down the heavy-hitting recipe nominations for the all-time favorites in the history of this book series! Now you can enjoy the winners in your own home.

Challenged with how to celebrate 25 years of publishing *Southern Living Annual Recipes,* we naturally thought about more taste-testing. But in the history of this book series, we've run over 25,000 recipes. Where to start?

With the polished palates of our veteran staff, of course. Eight former or present employees (profiles on facing page) worked on the magazine Foods staff for 12 or more of the past 25 years. We asked them to nominate their five favorite recipes in each of our five categories.

We narrowed down the recipes that garnered two or more independent nominations and put them to the test . . . again . . . in our kitchens. The aromas wafting down the hallway directed the staff selected as judges exactly where to go, but once at the tasting table, decisions were much more difficult to make. But, somehow, they managed.

It's nice to be reminded of old favorite recipes and even better to be reminded of a few forgotten favorites. We hope you enjoy them as much as we did.

Top 5 Ultimate Southern Recipes

DOUBLE CRUST PEACH COBBLER

MAKES 8 SERVINGS

Prep: 12 min., Cook: 12 min., Bake: 30 min.

Double Crust Peach Cobbler debuted in our June 1977 issue, before this book series started. It made such an impression on our staff in 1990 that we shared it in that December issue as an All-Time Best Desserts marking the 25th anniversary of *Southern Living.* Its double crust and perfectly sweetened and spiced peach filling made it a winner in this race, too.

- **8 cups sliced fresh peaches (about 5 pounds peaches)**
- **2 cups sugar**
- **3 tablespoons all-purpose flour**
- **½ teaspoon ground nutmeg**
- **1 teaspoon almond or vanilla extract**
- **⅓ cup butter or margarine**
- **Pastry for double-crust 9-inch pie**

STIR together first 4 ingredients in a Dutch oven; set aside until syrup forms. Bring peach mixture to a boil; reduce heat to low, and cook 10 minutes or until tender. Remove from heat; add almond extract and butter, stirring until butter melts.

ROLL half of pastry to ⅛-inch thickness on a lightly floured surface; cut into a 9-inch square. Spoon half of peaches into a lightly buttered 9-inch square pan; top with pastry square. Bake at 475° for 12 minutes or until lightly browned. Spoon remaining peaches over baked pastry square.

ROLL remaining pastry to ⅛-inch thickness, and cut into 1-inch strips; arrange in lattice design over peaches. Bake 15 to 18 more minutes or until browned.

OUR BEST SOUTHERN FRIED CHICKEN

Recipe with a menu on page 178

Our Best Southern Fried Chicken lives up to its name. It was the brainchild of Nashville author and food historian John Egerton, who fried it up in our Test Kitchens for the September 1995 issue. He combined techniques from several respected sources to create this one. Don't skip the overnight soak in salty water because that's the secret to making the chicken extra tender and juicy. Buy a chicken that hasn't been injected with a salty solution or your chicken may be too salty. Our homemade brine is more effective and easy to do. Just refrigerate the chicken overnight in a large pitcher; then drain and pat it dry before breading.

CHICKEN FRIED STEAK

recipe with menu on page 72

Chicken-Fried Steak might just be the national entrée of Texas, so we challenged Lone Star State native Vanessa McNeil from our Test Kitchens to develop the definitive version for our February 2001 issue. That she did, and our discriminating taste panel for these Top 25 Recipes tipped their hats to her recipe again. Vanessa recommends using an electric skillet to keep the frying temperature even, and she says the breading works well with chicken, too. Leftovers make great sandwiches; her dad piles chopped jalapeños on his.

FRIED OKRA

fast fixin's

MAKES 4 SERVINGS

Prep: 11 min., Cook: 3 min. per batch

We'd almost forgotten about this Fried Okra recipe submitted by Shirley Ryer of Canton, Texas, in our May 1987 issue, but Diane and Patty still make it for their families and refreshed our memories. The sliced okra is dipped in beaten egg whites and breaded with homemade soft breadcrumbs before being fried into the crispiest morsels you'll ever taste. Add a light sprinkling of salt, and your family will devour these golden nuggets.

1 pound fresh okra
3 tablespoons all-purpose flour
2 egg whites
1½ cups soft breadcrumbs (homemade)
Vegetable oil
Salt

WASH okra, and drain well. Remove tips and stem ends; cut okra into ½-inch slices. Place okra and flour in a zip-top plastic bag. Seal bag, and shake until okra is coated.
BEAT egg whites at high speed with an electric mixer until stiff peaks form; fold in okra. Stir in breadcrumbs, coating well.
POUR oil to a depth of 2 inches into a large skillet or Dutch oven; heat to 375°. Fry okra, in batches, 3 minutes or until golden brown, stirring as little as necessary for even browning. Drain on paper towels. Sprinkle with salt.

Recipe Nominators

Our Southern Living *experts, who have been on staff for at least half of the 25 years of the book's production, spent hours pouring over recipes to come up with a list of nominations for the best of the best. Below are the current or former staff who nominated favorites.*

Kaye Mabry Adams: After her 8-year tenure as *Southern Living* Test Kitchens Director, Kaye joined the editorial side as Executive Editor before recently taking early retirement.

Susan Dosier: Susan joined *Southern Living* in 1986. She left as Foods Editor in 1995, when her children were young, and returned as Executive Editor a couple of years ago.

Judy Feagin: In 1996, Judy became Assistant Test Kitchens Director after 10 years testing recipes. Readers may be familiar with Judy's hospitable voice and recipe recommendations, as she handled countless reader inquiries before retiring early.

Diane Hogan: A 20-year veteran of the *Southern Living* Test Kitchens, Diane retired as Assistant Foods Editor in 1999. Readers who admired our beautiful frosted cake swirls over the years likely have Diane to thank because she was our resident cake decorator extraordinaire.

Jean Wickstrom Liles: *Southern Living* Senior Foods Editor for 20 years, Jean worked on the original plan for beginning this book series. She retired early from the company but still peruses every word of *Southern Living® Annual Recipes* on a freelance basis.

Susan Carlisle Payne: Susan began testing recipes in the Test Kitchens a year before the *Annual Recipes* series started and prior to becoming Foods Editor at *Southern Living*. Currently Executive Editor at Oxmoor House, Susan has been involved with the book for the entire 25 years.

Peggy Smith: Our original *Southern Living* recipe tester, Peggy has the longest tenure and spent her early years testing recipes in between administrative duties. After years in the Test Kitchens, which fortunately grew in staff over time, Peggy retired as Assistant Foods Editor.

Patty M. Vann: Before we had electronic methods for tracking our favorite recipes, Patty was marking all of our very favorites in her *Southern Living® Annual Recipes* book each year. Patty spent many years in the Test Kitchens before taking early retirement as Assistant Foods Editor.

CREAM CHEESE POUND CAKE

MAKES 1 (10-INCH) CAKE

Prep: 15 min.; Bake 1 hr., 45 min.

Postman Eddy McGee of Elkin, North Carolina, bakes Cream Cheese Pound Cake every Christmas for the lucky folks on his route and shared it in our November 1995 issue. We gave it our highest rating then in a tube pan, and again in November 2001 when submitted by Yolanda Powers of Decatur, Alabama, in a shapely Bundt pan and with a brazen double the amount of vanilla extract. The baking time is the same in either pan, so you can take your pick.

    1½ cups butter, softened
    1 (8-ounce) package cream cheese,
        softened
    3 cups sugar
    6 large eggs
    3 cups all-purpose flour
    ⅛ teaspoon salt
    1 tablespoon vanilla extract

BEAT butter and cream cheese at medium speed with an electric mixer until creamy. Gradually add sugar, beating well. Add eggs, 1 at a time, beating just until yellow disappears.
COMBINE flour and salt; gradually add to butter mixture, beating at low speed just until blended. Stir in vanilla. Spoon batter into a greased and floured 10-inch Bundt or tube pan.
BAKE at 300° for 1 hour and 45 minutes or until a long wooden pick inserted in center comes out clean. Cool in pan on a wire rack 15 minutes; remove from pan, and let cool completely on wire rack.

Top 5 Family Favorites

ADAMS' RIBS

make ahead

MAKES 8 TO 10 SERVINGS

Prep: 30 min.; Grill: 2 hrs., 30 min.

Anne-Marie Adams and her now late husband, Oscar, shared Adams' Ribs with us in September 1995, Anne-Marie perfecting the sauce with her Cajun background and Oscar strategizing the grilling technique. The grilling takes time, but the distinctive spice rub and two sauces are quick to stir together so the recipe's definitely worth the time investment. Leftover sauce will keep in the refrigerator up to a week and is great on chicken and beef. Be sure to keep the portion you baste the raw meat with separate to make sure the leftover portion is free of meat juices.

    Hickory wood chunks
    5 pounds spareribs
    1 tablespoon garlic powder
    1 tablespoon Creole seasoning
    2 tablespoons ground black pepper
    1 tablespoon Worcestershire sauce
    Grill Basting Sauce
    The Sauce

SOAK wood chunks in water to cover 30 minutes. Drain.
PREPARE a hot fire by piling charcoal on 1 side of grill, leaving other side empty. Place wood chunks on charcoal. Place food rack on grill.
REMOVE thin membrane from back of ribs by slicing into it with a knife and then pulling.
COMBINE garlic powder and next 3 ingredients, and rub on all sides of ribs. Arrange ribs over unlit side of grill.
GRILL, covered with grill lid, 2 to 2½ hours, basting with Grill Basting Sauce during the last 30 minutes. Turn once after basting. Serve with The Sauce.

Grill Basting Sauce:

MAKES 5 CUPS

Prep: 5 min., Cook: 1 hr.

    2¾ cups red wine vinegar
    1¾ cups water
    ¾ cup dry white wine
    ¾ cup ketchup
    ¼ cup firmly packed brown sugar
    ¼ cup prepared mustard
    ¼ cup Worcestershire sauce
    2 to 3 tablespoons salt
    2 tablespoons dried crushed red
        pepper
    2 tablespoons ground black pepper

COOK all ingredients in a large saucepan over medium heat, stirring occasionally, 1 hour.

NOTE: Grill Basting Sauce will keep in the refrigerator up to a week.

The Sauce:

MAKES 2½ CUPS

Prep: 5 min., Cook: 18 min.

    1 tablespoon butter or margarine
    1 medium onion, finely chopped
    4 garlic cloves, minced
    1 cup ketchup
    ½ cup white vinegar
    ¼ cup lemon juice
    ¼ cup steak seasoning
    2 tablespoons light brown sugar
    1 tablespoon Cajun seasoning
    2 tablespoons liquid smoke

MELT butter in a large skillet over medium-high heat; add onion, and sauté until tender.
ADD garlic and remaining ingredients; reduce heat, and simmer 15 minutes.

NOTE: For testing purposes only, we used Dale's steak seasoning and Luzianne Cajun seasoning.

25th Anniversary Bonus Section

CHICKEN-AND-SAUSAGE GUMBO

freezeable

MAKES 10 CUPS

Prep: 18 min.; Cook: 2 hrs., 30 min.

We give a tearful but heartfelt salute to former Foods Editor Dana Adkins Campbell, who passed away this year, for the Gumbo she shared in November 1990. Hailing from the Bayou State, Dana knew her gumbo and called it Cajun chicken soup. The trick to great gumbo is the roux. "It's an easy process, but not to be interrupted," Dana warned in her story that accompanied this recipe. "As long as you stir over medium heat for a half hour or so without stopping, you can get a rich, deep-brown roux without any burned mishaps."

- **1 pound hot smoked link sausage, cut into ¼-inch slices**
- **4 skinned chicken breast halves**
- **¼ to ⅓ cup vegetable oil**
- **¾ cup all-purpose flour**
- **1 cup chopped onion**
- **½ cup chopped green bell pepper**
- **½ cup sliced celery**
- **3 garlic cloves, minced**
- **2 quarts hot water**
- **2 teaspoons Creole seasoning**
- **1 tablespoon Worcestershire sauce**
- **½ teaspoon dried thyme**
- **½ to 1 teaspoon hot sauce**
- **2 bay leaves**
- **½ cup sliced green onions**
- **Salt to taste**
- **Hot cooked rice**
- **Gumbo filé (optional)**

COOK sausage in a Dutch oven over medium heat until browned. Remove sausage, reserving drippings in pan, and set sausage aside. Cook chicken in drippings until browned. Remove chicken, reserving drippings.

MEASURE drippings, adding enough oil to measure ½ cup. Add oil mixture to Dutch oven; place over medium heat until hot. Add flour, and cook, stirring constantly, until roux is chocolate-colored (about 30 minutes).

ADD chopped onion, green bell pepper, celery, and garlic to roux; cook until vegetables are tender, stirring often. Gradually stir

in hot water; bring to a boil. Add chicken, Creole seasoning, and next 4 ingredients to Dutch oven; reduce heat, and simmer, uncovered, 1 hour, stirring occasionally. **REMOVE** chicken from Dutch oven; set aside to cool. Add sausage and green onions to Dutch oven; cook, uncovered, 30 minutes. Bone chicken; coarsely shred. Add chicken to gumbo; cook until thoroughly heated. Add salt to taste. Remove and discard bay leaves. Serve gumbo over hot rice with gumbo filé, if desired.

HOT-WATER CORNBREAD

Find the recipe along with tips for cast-iron cooking on page 112.

Assistant Foods Editor Cynthia Ann Briscoe wrote about her childhood memory of making crisp, pancakelike Hot-Water Cornbread in the January 2001 issue. It left those of us voting this a 25-year winner feeling like we'd had a deprived childhood! The pones are especially handy to have on hand as you sit down to a bowl of greens. The secret to their golden crispness? Why, the cast-iron skillet, of course, to keep an even heat of the hot oil as you fry them.

BABY BLUE SALAD

Find the recipe on page 178.

Chef Franklin Biggs of Homewood, Alabama, has a way with salads, and we're eternally grateful that he shared Baby Blue Salad with us in our April 2000 issue. Our staff makes this in our homes all the time. You might have a little dressing left over, which is a real bonus because it's great as a marinade for chicken, fish, or steamed fresh veggies. And the spiced pecans used as croutons? You might want to double the recipe because it's hard to stop nibbling once you taste them.

KING RANCH CHICKEN

MAKES 6 TO 8 SERVINGS

Prep: 20 min., Cook: 10 min., Bake: 45 min.

King Ranch Chicken that we ran in February 1994 originated in King Ranch in Kingsville, Texas. We liked it so much that we developed this quicker and easier version that appeared in September 2002 to make for our families during the week. Instead of first boiling a chicken, this version starts with chopped cooked chicken that you might have leftover or you can buy in the freezer section; it also uses crushed tortilla chips instead of steaming and cutting corn tortillas. You can even enjoy this recipe if you're watching your fat intake; just substitute low-fat soups for the full-fat versions, and use baked tortilla chips.

- **2 tablespoons butter or margarine**
- **1 medium onion, chopped**
- **1 green bell pepper, chopped**
- **1 red bell pepper, chopped**
- **3 cups chopped cooked chicken**
- **1 (10¾-ounce) can cream of chicken soup**
- **1 (10¾-ounce) can cream of mushroom soup**
- **1 (10-ounce) can diced tomatoes and green chiles, undrained**
- **1 teaspoon chili powder**
- **1 teaspoon ground cumin**
- **2 cups coarsely crushed tortilla chips**
- **2 cups (8 ounces) shredded Cheddar cheese**
- **Garnish: chopped fresh cilantro**

MELT butter in a medium skillet over medium-high heat. Add chopped onion and bell peppers; sauté 8 minutes or until tender.

STIR in chicken and next 5 ingredients; cook, stirring occasionally, 2 minutes. Place half of crushed tortilla chips in a lightly greased 13- x 9-inch pan. Layer with half each of chicken mixture and shredded Cheddar cheese. Repeat layers, ending with cheese.

BAKE, uncovered, at 325° for 45 minutes or until mixture is thoroughly heated. Garnish, if desired.

Top 5 Quick & Easy Recipes

QUICK BUTTERMILK BISCUITS

fast fixin's

MAKES 8 BISCUITS

Prep: 5 min., Bake: 14 min.

We printed our favorite biscuit recipe in February 1988 and haven't found one since that tops it in terms of flavor, texture, or simplicity. It's the Southern-produced soft wheat flour that gives Quick Buttermilk Biscuits their light-as-a-feather interior. The three ingredients are a snap to stir together, and if you pat the dough instead of rolling it, you can have the South's best biscuits ready for the oven in 5 minutes flat.

⅓ cup butter or margarine
2 cups self-rising soft wheat flour
¾ cup buttermilk
Butter or margarine, melted

CUT ⅓ cup butter into flour with a pastry blender until mixture is crumbly; add buttermilk, stirring until dry ingredients are moistened.
TURN dough out onto a lightly floured surface; knead 3 or 4 times.
PAT or roll dough to ¾-inch thickness; cut with a 2½-inch round cutter, and place on a baking sheet.
BAKE at 425° for 12 to14 minutes. Brush with melted butter.

NOTE: For testing purposes only, we used White Lily Self-Rising Soft Wheat Flour.

SPICY-SWEET RIBS AND BEANS

make ahead

MAKES 8 SERVINGS

Prep: 15 min., Broil: 22 min., Cook: 6 hrs. (HIGH) or 10 hrs. (LOW)

There may be no better, or easier, way to make dinner than using our favorite slow-cooker recipe that ran in December 2002. Bottled hickory-flavored barbecue sauce and hot jalapeño jelly make preparation a breeze, and the long slow cooking makes the meaty ribs extra tender.

2 (16-ounce) cans pinto beans, drained
4 pounds country-style pork ribs, trimmed
1 teaspoon garlic powder
½ teaspoon salt
½ teaspoon pepper
1 medium onion, chopped
1 (18-ounce) bottle hickory-flavored barbecue sauce
1 (10.5-ounce) jar red jalapeño pepper jelly
1 teaspoon green hot sauce

PLACE beans in a 5-quart electric slow cooker; set aside.
CUT ribs into serving-size portions. Combine garlic powder, salt, and pepper. Sprinkle both sides of ribs with seasoning mixture. Place ribs on a lightly greased rack in a broiler pan.
BROIL 5½ inches from heat 10 to 11 minutes on each side or until browned. Add ribs to slow cooker, and sprinkle with onion.
WHILE ribs broil, combine barbecue sauce, jelly, and hot sauce in a large saucepan. Cook over medium heat 4 minutes or until smooth, stirring constantly. Pour over rib mixture; stir gently.
COVER and cook on HIGH 6 hours or LOW for 9 to 10 hours. Remove ribs. Drain bean mixture, reserving sauce. Skim fat from sauce. Arrange ribs over bean mixture; serve with sauce.

NOTE: For testing purposes only, we used Kraft Thick 'n' Spicy Hickory Smoke Barbecue Sauce and Tabasco Green Pepper Sauce.

SHRIMP DESTIN

fast fixin's

MAKES 4 SERVINGS

Prep: 22 min., Cook: 8 min.

Shrimp Destin from Frances Ponder of Destin, Florida, caught our eye when testing recipes for the February 1982 issue, and old-timers on our staff have made it in their homes ever since. No time to peel shrimp? Purchase 1½ pounds of shelled shrimp instead. Give them a quick sauté in their garlic butter bath and you'll be amazed how quickly you can make this memorable entrée. Put crusty rolls on to toast as you start the sauté, then drizzle the butter sauce along with the shrimp over the toast for serving.

2 pounds unpeeled, large fresh shrimp
¼ cup chopped green onions
2 teaspoons minced garlic
1 cup butter or margarine, melted
1 tablespoon dry white wine
1 teaspoon lemon juice
⅛ teaspoon salt
⅛ teaspoon coarsely ground pepper
1 teaspoon dried dillweed
1 teaspoon chopped fresh parsley
2 French rolls, split lengthwise and toasted

PEEL shrimp, and devein, if desired.
SAUTÉ green onions and garlic in butter until onions are tender. Add shrimp, wine, and next 3 ingredients; cook over medium heat 5 minutes, stirring occasionally. Stir in dillweed and parsley. Spoon shrimp mixture over toasted rolls, and serve immediately.

NOTE: Shrimp Destin can also be served over hot cooked rice instead of rolls, if desired.

PIMIENTO CHEESE

fast fixin's

MAKES ABOUT 4½ CUPS

Prep: 13 min.

Pimiento Cheese has to be one of the true Southern culinary icons, and this recipe is a definitive one. Recipe Development Director Mary Allen Perry drew upon childhood memories to develop the recipe for our August 2001 issue. Her secret? Using a regular shred for the sharp Cheddar and a fine shred for the extra-sharp Cheddar creates a pleasing texture variation.

- 1½ cups mayonnaise
- 1 (4-ounce) jar diced pimiento, drained
- 1 teaspoon Worcestershire sauce
- 1 teaspoon finely grated onion
- ¼ teaspoon ground red pepper
- 1 (8-ounce) block extra-sharp Cheddar cheese, finely shredded
- 1 (8-ounce) block sharp Cheddar cheese, shredded

STIR together first 5 ingredients in a large bowl; stir in cheeses. Cover and store in refrigerator up to 1 week.

JALAPEÑO PIMIENTO CHEESE: Add 2 seeded and minced jalapeño peppers.

CREAM CHEESE-AND-OLIVE PIMIENTO CHEESE: Reduce mayonnaise to ¾ cup. Stir together first 5 ingredients, 1 (8-ounce) package softened cream cheese, and 1 (5¾-ounce) jar drained sliced salad olives. Proceed with recipe as directed.

PECAN PIMIENTO CHEESE: Stir in ¾ cup toasted chopped pecans.

ROASTED PECAN CLUSTERS

MAKES 4 DOZEN

Prep: 12 min., Bake: 30 min.

In Hondo, Texas, Margaret Haegelin's love for homemade candy led to her creation of Roasted Pecan Clusters that we first printed in October 1985. The recipe is so simple, yet so yummy, that we honored it as one of our 25 All-Time Best Desserts in our December 1990 celebration of the 25th anniversary of *Southern Living*. Toasting the pecans really brings out their flavor and crunch.

- 3 tablespoons butter or margarine
- 3 cups pecan pieces
- 6 (2-ounce) squares chocolate bark coating

MELT butter in a 15- x 10-inch jellyroll pan while oven preheats to 300°. Spread pecans evenly in pan, tossing to coat with butter. Bake at 300° for 30 minutes, stirring every 10 minutes.
MELT chocolate bark squares in a heavy saucepan over low heat. Cool 2 minutes; add pecans, and stir until coated. Drop by rounded teaspoonfuls onto wax paper. Let cool. Peel from wax paper, and store in an airtight container.

Top 5 All-Time Best Desserts

HUMMINGBIRD CAKE

MAKES 12 SERVINGS

Prep: 36 min., Bake: 23 min.

Pineapple-laced Hummingbird Cake with its nutty cream cheese frosting first appeared in February 1978, before this book series began, and it garnered the top spot in our 25 All-Time Best Desserts story in December 1990.

Submitted by Mrs. L.H. Wiggins of Greensboro, North Carolina, it's known to have won numerous blue ribbons at county fairs. No one knows what hummingbirds have to do with it, but the cake is so moist and delicious, no one cares!

- 3 cups all-purpose flour
- 1 teaspoon baking soda
- ½ teaspoon salt
- 2 cups sugar
- 1 teaspoon ground cinnamon
- 3 large eggs, lightly beaten
- ¾ cup vegetable oil
- 1½ teaspoons vanilla extract
- 1 (8-ounce) can crushed pineapple, undrained
- 1 cup chopped pecans
- 1¾ cups mashed ripe banana (about 4 large)
- Cream Cheese Frosting

COMBINE first 5 ingredients in a large bowl; add eggs and oil, stirring just until dry ingredients are moistened. Add vanilla, pineapple, pecans, and banana, stirring just until combined.
POUR batter into 3 greased and floured 9-inch round cakepans.
BAKE at 350° for 23 minutes or until a wooden pick inserted in center comes out clean. Cool in pans 10 minutes; remove from pans, and cool completely on wire racks. Spread Cream Cheese Frosting between layers and on tops and sides of cake.

Cream Cheese Frosting:

MAKES 3¼ CUPS

Prep: 5 min.

- ½ cup butter or margarine, softened
- 1 (8-ounce) package cream cheese, softened
- 1 (16-ounce) package powdered sugar, sifted
- 1 teaspoon vanilla extract
- ½ cup chopped pecans

BEAT butter and cream cheese at medium speed with an electric mixer until creamy. Gradually add powdered sugar, beating at low speed until blended. Beat at high speed until smooth; stir in vanilla and pecans.

PECAN PIE CHEESECAKE

MAKES 16 SERVINGS

Prep: 15 min., Bake: 50 min., Stand: 1 hr., Chill: 8 hrs.

Pecan Pie Cheesecake We put last year's $100,000 grand-prize winning Cheesecake in our first annual Reader Recipe Cook-Off up against our most memorable dessert recipes, and it maneuvered the top tier. Ginnie Prater of Anniston, Alabama, started with a frozen pecan pie to keep it simple, and her deft hand stirring up cheesecake batter marries the two flavors in Southern bliss.

- 1 (2-pound, 4-ounce) package frozen pecan pie
- 2 cups graham cracker crumbs
- ½ cup sugar
- ½ cup butter, melted
- ¼ teaspoon ground cinnamon
- 2 (8-ounce) packages cream cheese, softened
- 2 large eggs
- ⅔ cup sour cream
- ½ cup half-and-half
- 1 teaspoon vanilla extract
- 1 cup powdered sugar
- 1 tablespoon all-purpose flour
- 16 pecan halves

THAW pecan pie according to package directions. Cut into 20 thin slices, keeping wedges intact; set aside. Stir together cracker crumbs and next 3 ingredients, and press onto bottom and 1½ inches up sides of a 10-inch springform pan.
ARRANGE 10 pecan pie wedges in a spoke design in prepared pan, placing 1 cut side of each wedge on crust with narrow end towards center of pan. Reserve remaining pie wedges for another use.
BEAT cream cheese until smooth; add eggs, 1 at a time, beating after each addition. Add sour cream, half-and-half, and vanilla; beat until blended.
FOLD in powdered sugar and flour. Carefully pour cream cheese mixture evenly over pecan pie wedges in pan, making sure wedges remain in place. Arrange pecan halves evenly around edge of cheesecake.

BAKE at 325° for 45 to 50 minutes. Turn off oven, and let cheesecake stand in oven 1 hour. Remove to a wire rack, and let cool completely. Chill at least 8 hours before serving.

NOTE: For testing purposes only, we used Mrs. Smith's Special Recipe Southern Pecan Pie, McCormick Gourmet Collection Saigon Cinnamon, Philadelphia Cream Cheese, and Domino sugars.

PECAN PIE CAKE

MAKES 12 SERVINGS

Prep: 35 min., Bake: 25 min.

It's no secret that we're partial to pecan pie, because the flavor essence makes an encore appearance on this spectacular dessert list in Pecan Pie Cake. *Southern Living* Editor John Floyd challenged Recipe Development Director Mary Allen Perry to create a stately cake based on the South's favorite pie for our October 1998 issue, and reader mail tells us you enjoyed it as much as we did. A creamy caramel filling is sandwiched between feathery cake layers encrusted with toasted pecans. It's pretty enough for a centerpiece and is worth every minute it takes to create.

- 3 cups finely chopped pecans, toasted and divided
- ½ cup butter or margarine, softened
- ½ cup shortening
- 2 cups sugar
- 5 large eggs, separated
- 1 tablespoon vanilla extract
- 2 cups all-purpose flour
- 1 teaspoon baking soda
- 1 cup buttermilk
- ¾ cup dark corn syrup
- Pecan Pie Filling
- Pastry Garnish (optional)

SPRINKLE 2 cups pecans evenly into 3 generously buttered 9-inch round cakepans; shake to coat bottoms and sides of pans.
BEAT butter and shortening at medium speed with an electric mixer until creamy; gradually add sugar, beating well. Add egg yolks, 1 at a time, beating just until blended after each addition; stir in vanilla.
COMBINE flour and baking soda. Add to butter mixture alternately with buttermilk, beginning and ending with flour mixture; beat at low speed just until blended after each addition. Stir in remaining 1 cup pecans.
BEAT egg whites at medium speed until stiff peaks form; fold one-third of egg whites into batter. Gently fold in remaining beaten egg whites just until blended. (Do not overmix.) Pour into prepared pans.
BAKE at 350° for 23 to 25 minutes or until a wooden pick inserted in center comes out clean. Cool in pans on wire racks 10 minutes. Invert layers onto wax paper-lined wire racks. Brush tops and sides of cake layers with corn syrup; cool completely.
SPREAD half of Pecan Pie Filling on 1 layer, pecan side up. Place second layer, pecan side up, on filling; spread with remaining filling. Top with remaining cake layer, pecan side up. Arrange Pastry Garnish on and around cake, if desired.

Pecan Pie Filling:

MAKES ABOUT 3 CUPS

Prep: 7 min., Cook: 7 min., Chill: 4 hrs.

- ½ cup firmly packed dark brown sugar
- ¾ cup dark corn syrup
- ⅓ cup cornstarch
- 4 egg yolks
- 1½ cups half-and-half
- ⅛ teaspoon salt
- 3 tablespoons butter or margarine
- 1 teaspoon vanilla extract

WHISK together first 6 ingredients in a heavy 3-quart saucepan until smooth. Bring mixture to a boil over medium heat, whisking constantly; boil 1 minute or until thickened. Remove from heat.
WHISK in butter and vanilla. Place a sheet of wax paper directly on surface of mixture to prevent a film from forming. Chill at least 4 hours.

NOTE: To chill filling quickly, pour filling into a bowl. Place bowl in a larger bowl filled with ice. Whisk constantly until cool (about 15 minutes).

Pastry Garnish:

MAKES 24 PASTRY LEAVES AND 12 PECAN
PASTRIES

Prep: 32 min., Bake: 18 min.

- 1 (15-ounce) package refrigerated
  piecrusts
- 1 large egg
- 1 tablespoon water
- 24 pecan halves

UNFOLD piecrusts, and press out fold
lines. Cut 12 leaves from each piecrust
with a 3-inch leaf-shaped cutter. Mark
leaf veins, using tip of a knife. Reserve
pastry trimmings. Whisk together egg
and water; brush on pastry leaves.
CRUMPLE 10 to 12 small aluminum foil
pieces into ½-inch balls. Coat with
cooking spray, and place on a lightly
greased baking sheet. Drape a pastry
leaf over each ball; place remaining pastry leaves on baking sheet.
BAKE at 425° for 6 to 8 minutes or until
golden. Cool on a wire rack 10 minutes.
Gently remove leaves from foil.
REDUCE oven temperature to 350°.
Pinch 12 pea-size pieces from reserved
pastry trimmings. Place between pecan
halves, forming sandwiches.
CUT remaining pastry into 2-inch
pieces; wrap around pecan sandwiches,
leaving jagged edges to resemble half-
shelled pecans. Brush with egg mixture,
and place on a lightly greased baking
sheet.
BAKE at 350° for 10 minutes or until
golden. Cool on a wire rack.

TART LEMON-CHEESE CAKE

MAKES 12 SERVINGS

Prep: 20 min., Bake: 20 min.

In January 1988, then-Assistant Foods Editor
Phyllis Cordell shared Tart Lemon-Cheese Cake,
a recipe from her late mother Elise Young, and
our staff awarded it our highest rating. This old-
fashioned layer cake contains no cheese, but is
justly named for its rich, cheeselike filling. Three
tender white layers give it an elegant presence,
and swirls of lemony white frosting make you
want to dive right in.

- Lemon-Cheese Filling
- 1 cup butter, softened
- 2 cups sugar
- ¾ cup water
- ¼ cup milk
- 3¼ cups sifted cake flour
- 2¾ teaspoons baking powder
- ½ teaspoon salt
- ½ teaspoon rum flavoring or
  1 teaspoon vanilla extract
- 6 egg whites
- Lemony White Frosting
- Garnishes: lemon slices, orange
  leaves

PREPARE Lemon-Cheese Filling. Cover
and set aside to cool.
BEAT butter at medium speed with an
electric mixer until creamy; gradually
add sugar, beating well.
COMBINE water and milk; set aside.
COMBINE flour, baking powder, and salt;
add to butter mixture alternately with
milk mixture, beginning and ending
with flour mixture. Stir in rum flavoring.
BEAT egg whites at high speed until soft
peaks form. Gently fold beaten egg
whites into batter. Pour batter into 3
greased and floured 9-inch round
cakepans.
BAKE at 350° for 20 minutes or until a
wooden pick inserted in center comes
out clean. Cool in pans 10 minutes;
remove from pans, and cool completely
on wire racks.
SPREAD Lemon-Cheese Filling between
layers and on top of cake. Spread
Lemony White Frosting on sides. Garnish, if desired.

Lemon-Cheese Filling:

MAKES 2 CUPS

Prep: 5 min., Cook: 10 min., Cool: 45 min.

- 1 cup sugar
- 3 tablespoons cornstarch
- ⅛ teaspoon salt
- 2 tablespoons grated lemon rind
- 1 cup fresh lemon juice
- 6 egg yolks, beaten
- ⅓ cup butter or margarine

COMBINE sugar, cornstarch, and salt in
a heavy saucepan; stir well with a wire
whisk. Whisk in lemon rind and juice;
cook over medium heat, whisking constantly, until mixture thickens and comes
to a boil. Boil 1 minute, whisking constantly. Remove from heat.
GRADUALLY stir about one-fourth of hot
mixture into yolks; add to remaining hot
mixture, whisking constantly. Cook over
low heat, whisking constantly, 3 minutes. Remove from heat. Add butter, stirring until butter melts; cool completely.

Lemony White Frosting:

MAKES 3 CUPS

Prep: 5 min., Cook: 15 min.

- 1 cup sugar
- ⅓ cup water
- 2 tablespoons light corn syrup
- 2 egg whites
- ¼ cup sifted powdered sugar
- ½ teaspoon lemon extract

COMBINE 1 cup sugar, water, and corn
syrup in a heavy saucepan. Cook over
medium heat, stirring constantly, until
mixture is clear. Cook, without stirring,
until mixture reaches soft ball stage or
candy thermometer registers 240°.
WHILE syrup cooks, beat egg whites at
high speed with an electric mixer until
soft peaks form; continue to beat egg
whites, adding hot syrup mixture in a
heavy stream. Add powdered sugar and
lemon extract to mixture; continue beating until stiff peaks form and frosting is
thick enough to spread.

GRAND MARNIER SOUFFLÉS

MAKES 6 SERVINGS

Prep: 22 min., Cook: 11 min., Bake: 35 min.

John Feagin, husband of former Assistant Test Kitchens Director Judy Feagin, proved there were two great cooks in that house with his Grand Marnier Soufflés that ran in our November 1989 issue. The airy orange liqueur-spiked soufflés mightily rise upon baking, but they don't rise out of the cups and they don't need a collar as you might think when you see how full they fill the cups. Ladle the liqueur-laced custard over the puffy pillows, and serve immediately after removing from the oven.

    Butter
    1 tablespoon sugar
    1 cup milk
    ¼ cup butter
    ¼ cup all-purpose flour
    4 egg yolks
    2 tablespoons Grand Marnier or other
        orange liqueur
    ¾ cup sugar
    2 tablespoons cornstarch
    5 egg whites
    1 tablespoon sugar
    Custard Sauce

LIGHTLY butter 6 (6-ounce) custard cups; coat bottom and sides of cups with 1 tablespoon sugar. Set aside.

HEAT milk in a heavy saucepan. Cover and set aside.

MELT ¼ cup butter in a large saucepan over medium heat; add flour, stirring until smooth. Cook, stirring constantly, 1 minute. Gradually stir in warm milk, and cook, stirring constantly, until mixture thickens and begins to leave sides of pan. Remove from heat.

BEAT egg yolks until thick and pale. Gradually stir about one-fourth of hot mixture into yolks; add to remaining hot mixture, stirring constantly. Stir in Grand Marnier; set aside.

COMBINE ¾ cup sugar and cornstarch, and set aside. Beat egg whites at high speed with an electric mixer until foamy. Slowly add sugar mixture; beat until stiff peaks form and sugar dissolves (4 to 5 minutes). Gradually stir about one-fourth of sauce mixture into egg whites; gently fold into remaining sauce mixture.

SPOON evenly into prepared custard cups. (Cups will be very full, but mixture will firm up during baking and will not overflow.) Sprinkle tops of custards with 1 tablespoon sugar. Place cups in a large shallow pan. Add hot water to pan to a depth of 1 inch. Bake at 400° for 10 minutes.

REDUCE oven temperature to 350°, and bake 20 to 25 more minutes or until tops are golden brown. Remove custard cups from water. Serve immediately with Custard Sauce.

Custard Sauce:

MAKES ABOUT 2½ CUPS

Prep: 1 min., Cook: 27 min., Cool: 45 min.

    ½ cup sugar
    2 tablespoons cornstarch
    4 egg yolks
    1 cup milk
    2 tablespoons Grand Marnier or other
        orange liqueur
    ½ cup half-and-half
    ½ cup whipping cream, whipped

COMBINE sugar and cornstarch in a medium saucepan; add egg yolks, and stir until smooth. Set aside.

HEAT milk in a heavy saucepan. Gradually stir hot milk into egg mixture, stirring until smooth. Cook over medium heat, stirring constantly, about 6 to 7 minutes or until mixture thickens and thermometer registers 160°. Remove from heat; let cool about 45 minutes.

STIR in Grand Marnier and half-and-half. Fold in whipped cream. Store in refrigerator until ready to serve.

Top 5 Chocolate Recipes

PERFECT CHOCOLATE CAKE

MAKES 12 SERVINGS

Prep: 23 min., Bake: 22 min.

Looks like Perfect Chocolate Cake was an appropriate name for the towering layers with a whipped cream filling and creamy chocolate frosting submitted by Dondee Gage Steves of San Antonio. Originally appearing in September 1977, it made an encore appearance within our pages as a winner in December 1990's All-Time Best Desserts feature.

    1 cup cocoa
    2 cups boiling water
    1 cup butter or margarine, softened
    2½ cups sugar
    4 large eggs
    2¾ cups all-purpose flour
    2 teaspoons baking soda
    ½ teaspoon baking powder
    ½ teaspoon salt
    1½ teaspoons vanilla extract
    Whipped Cream Filling
    Perfect Chocolate Frosting

COMBINE cocoa and boiling water, stirring until smooth; set aside.

BEAT butter at medium speed with an electric mixer about 2 minutes or until creamy. Gradually add sugar, beating 5 to 7 minutes. Add eggs, 1 at a time, beating just until yellow disappears.

COMBINE flour and next 3 ingredients in a medium bowl; add to butter mixture alternately with cocoa mixture, beginning and ending with flour mixture. Beat at low speed just until blended after each addition. Stir in vanilla. Do not overbeat.

POUR batter into 3 greased and floured 9-inch round cakepans.

BAKE at 350° for 22 minutes or until a wooden pick inserted in center comes out clean. Cool in pans on wire racks 10 minutes; remove from pans, and cool completely on wire racks.

SPREAD Whipped Cream Filling between layers; spread Perfect Chocolate Frosting on top and sides of cake. Chill until ready to serve.

Whipped Cream Filling:

MAKES ABOUT 2 CUPS
Prep: 4 min.

- 1 cup whipping cream
- 1 teaspoon vanilla extract
- ¼ cup sifted powdered sugar

BEAT whipping cream and vanilla until foamy; gradually add powdered sugar, beating until soft peaks form. Cover and chill.

Perfect Chocolate Frosting:

MAKES 2½ CUPS
Prep: 17 min., Cook: 5 min.

- 1 (6-ounce) package semisweet chocolate morsels
- ½ cup half-and-half
- ¾ cup butter or margarine
- 2½ cups sifted powdered sugar

COMBINE first 3 ingredients in a medium saucepan; cook over medium heat, stirring until chocolate melts. Remove from heat; add powdered sugar, mixing well.

PLACE saucepan in a large bowl of ice. Beat at low speed with an electric mixer until frosting holds its shape and loses its gloss. Add a few more drops of half-and-half, if needed, to make a good spreading consistency.

CHOCOLATE DECADENCE

MAKES 10 TO 12 SERVINGS

Prep: 25 min., Bake: 15 min., Cool: 30 min., Chill: 8 hrs.

Chocolate Decadence looks a little homely when you cut it, but set a wedge of the dense fudge, almost flourless, cake in a pool of ruby raspberry sauce, dollop it with whipped cream, sprinkle fresh raspberries on top, and it's enough to make a chef famous. That's actually what it did for its creator, Chef John Wagner formerly of the Flamingo Cafe in Destin, Florida.

- 2 (8-ounce) packages semisweet chocolate baking squares
- ⅔ cup butter or margarine
- 5 large eggs
- 2 tablespoons sugar
- 2 tablespoons all-purpose flour
- Raspberry Sauce
- Garnishes: whipped cream, fresh raspberries

LINE bottom of a 9-inch springform pan with parchment paper; set pan aside.

COOK chocolate and butter in a heavy saucepan over medium-low heat until melted, stirring occasionally. Beat eggs in a large mixing bowl until blended; gradually add chocolate mixture, beating at medium speed with an electric mixer 10 minutes. Fold in sugar and flour. Pour into prepared pan.

BAKE at 400° for 15 minutes. (Cake will not be set in center.) Cool 30 minutes. Cover loosely, and chill 8 hours.

SPOON about 2½ tablespoons Raspberry Sauce on each dessert plate; place wedge of chocolate dessert on sauce. Garnish, if desired.

Raspberry Sauce:

MAKES 1¾ CUPS
Prep: 2 min., Cook: 41 min.

- 2 cups fresh raspberries
- 2 cups water
- ¼ cup sugar
- 2 tablespoons cornstarch
- 2 tablespoons water

COMBINE raspberries, 2 cups water, and ¼ cup sugar in a large saucepan; bring to a boil. Reduce heat and simmer, uncovered, 30 minutes. Press raspberry mixture through a wire-mesh strainer, using the back of a spoon to squeeze out juice. Discard pulp and seeds. Return raspberry mixture to saucepan; set aside.

COMBINE cornstarch and 2 tablespoons water in a small bowl, stirring until smooth. Stir cornstarch mixture into raspberry mixture. Cook over medium heat, stirring constantly, until mixture comes to a boil. Cook 1 more minute, stirring constantly. Remove mixture from heat; cool completely.

SWEETHEART FUDGE PIE

MAKES 8 SERVINGS

Prep: 12 min., Bake: 25 min., Chill 8 hrs.

Peggy H. Amos of Martinsville, Virginia, originally made Sweetheart Fudge Pie as a valentine treat for family and friends, but we found this rich and fudgy pie delightful anytime of year, and printed it in December 1986. It's equally endearing almost 20 years later.

- ½ cup butter or margarine, softened
- ¾ cup firmly packed brown sugar
- 3 large eggs
- 1 (12-ounce) package semisweet chocolate morsels, melted
- 2 teaspoons instant coffee granules
- 1 teaspoon rum extract
- ½ cup all-purpose flour
- 1 cup coarsely chopped walnuts
- 1 unbaked 9-inch pastry shell
- Garnishes: whipped cream, chopped walnuts

BEAT butter at medium speed with an electric mixer until creamy; gradually add brown sugar, beating well. Add eggs, 1 at a time, beating until blended after each addition. Add melted chocolate, coffee granules, and rum extract; mix well. Stir in flour and 1 cup chopped walnuts. Pour into shell.

BAKE at 375° for 25 minutes; cool completely. Cover and chill 8 hours. Garnish, if desired.

25th Anniversary Bonus Section

WARM FUDGE-FILLED CHEESECAKE

MAKES 12 SERVINGS

Prep: 17 min.; Bake: 1 hr., 15 min.

Dessert doesn't get much better than Warm Fudge-Filled Cheesecake that hails from the January 1998 issue. Recipe Development Director Mary Allen Perry developed this recipe that reminded her of a cafe where she worked in the seventies. A full 2 cups of chocolate mini-morsels are sandwiched between vanilla cheesecake that sports a crunchy pistachio crust. Serving it warm is the key so the chocolate is soft. The cheesecake just melts in your mouth.

- ½ cup butter or margarine, softened
- ⅓ cup sugar
- 1 cup all-purpose flour
- 1 tablespoon vanilla extract, divided
- ⅔ cup chopped pistachios
- 4 (8-ounce) packages cream cheese, softened
- 1½ cups sugar
- 4 large eggs
- 1 (12-ounce) package semisweet chocolate mini-morsels
- Sweetened whipped cream (optional)
- Garnish: chocolate shavings

BEAT butter at medium speed with an electric mixer until creamy; add ⅓ cup sugar, beating well. Gradually add flour, beating at low speed until blended. Stir in 1 teaspoon vanilla and pistachios. Press into bottom and 1½ inches up sides of a 9-inch springform pan.
BAKE at 350° for 12 to 15 minutes or until golden. Cool on a wire rack.
BEAT cream cheese at medium speed with an electric mixer until light and fluffy; gradually add 1½ cups sugar, beating well.
ADD eggs, 1 at a time, beating just until yellow disappears. Stir in remaining 2 teaspoons vanilla. (Do not overbeat.)
POUR half of batter into prepared crust; sprinkle with chocolate morsels to within ¾ inch of edge. Pour in remaining batter, starting at outer edge and working toward center. Place cheesecake on a baking sheet.
BAKE at 350° for 1 hour or until set. Cool cheesecake on a wire rack 1 hour.

Serve slightly warm with sweetened whipped cream, if desired. Garnish, if desired.

CHOCOLATE MOUSSE CAKE

MAKES 10 TO 12 SERVINGS

Prep: 31 min., Bake: 35 min., Chill: 8 hrs.

Desserts from Holly Leiser of Dunwoody, Georgia, look as pretty as they taste, and Chocolate Mousse Cake is a grand example. The dense chocolate cake that appeared in November 1987 is a cross between a cheesecake and a mousse that's capped with a whipped cream topping. Holly crowns it with a doily and sprinkles cocoa over the top; once the doily's removed, the lacy chocolate design beckons chocolate lovers to take the plunge!

- 1 (8-ounce) package cream cheese, softened
- 1 (3-ounce) package cream cheese, softened
- ⅔ cup sugar
- 6 eggs
- ⅓ cup whipping cream
- 1 tablespoon plus 1 teaspoon vanilla extract
- 9 (1-ounce) squares semisweet chocolate, melted
- Chocolate Crust
- Whipped Cream Topping
- Cocoa

COMBINE first 3 ingredients in a large bowl; beat at medium speed with an electric mixer until light and fluffy. Add eggs, 1 at a time, beating after each addition. Add ⅓ cup whipping cream, vanilla, and melted chocolate; mix at low speed with an electric mixer just until blended. Pour into Chocolate Crust. Bake at 375° for 30 to 35 minutes or until edges are firm and lightly browned and center is still soft. Cool at room temperature; cover and chill 8 hours.
REMOVE chilled cake from pan. Spread cake with Whipped Cream Topping. Place paper doily on top, and sift cocoa over it. Carefully remove doily.

Chocolate Crust:

MAKES 1 (9-INCH) CRUST

Prep: 13 min., Bake: 8 min., Chill: 30 min.

- ⅓ cup butter or margarine
- 2 (1-ounce) squares semisweet chocolate
- 1⅓ cups fine, dry breadcrumbs
- ⅓ cup sugar

COMBINE butter and chocolate in a small, heavy saucepan; cook over low heat until chocolate melts, stirring occasionally. Remove from heat.
STIR breadcrumbs and sugar into chocolate mixture, blending well. Press into bottom and 2 inches up sides of a 9-inch springform pan.
BAKE at 350° for 8 minutes. Refrigerate until well chilled.

Whipped Cream Topping:

MAKES 3 CUPS

Prep: 8 min.

- 1½ cups whipping cream
- ¼ cup sifted powdered sugar
- ½ teaspoon vanilla extract

BEAT whipping cream until foamy; gradually add powdered sugar, beating until soft peaks form. Add vanilla, beating just until blended.

Southern Living 2003

Cook-Off 2003 Winners

The second annual Cook-Off showcased winning recipes and Southern hospitality.

After endless hours of pouring over entries and tasting thousands of recipes, it all came down to 15 finalists and a weekend competition. Here's a rundown of some great contest moments.

Thursday: The 15 finalists are greeted in the lobby of Nashville's Opryland Hotel by members of the Cook-Off team. At orientation, Foods Editor Scott Jones explains the rules. Finalists then tour the competition kitchens to check the supplies provided for them. Later, everyone gathers for a buffet dinner.

Friday: Contestants have 1½ hours to prepare their dishes. Each category will be served to the judges in 30-minute intervals. In the meantime, the finalists will rehearse on stage with *Southern Living* presenters for tomorrow's show.

Saturday: After their breakfast with the *Southern Living* Cook-Off staff, the finalists enjoy makeovers at the hotel's salon.

Show time begins at 2 p.m.; contest host, Al Roker, "Today Show" weatherman and creator of TV Food Network's "Roker on the Road," welcomes the crowd. He briefly interviews the three finalists in each category, who then prepare their winning dishes with the assistance of *Southern Living* food experts. At last, the five category winners are on stage, waiting to hear who will be the grand prize winner. Streamers, screams, and applause accompany the announcement, as a shaken Susan Rotter is awarded a gigantic $100,000 check.

Note: To enter the contest, you must use at least one sponsor's product.

TASTE OF THE SOUTH

GRAND PRIZE WINNER

TASTE OF THE SOUTH
Category Winner

SOUTHERN-FRIED STUFFED CHICKEN WITH ROASTED RED PEPPER-AND-VIDALIA ONION GRAVY

MAKES 4 SERVINGS

Prep: 25 min., Cook: 12 min. per batch

Susan Rotter created her $100,000 dish to try to prepare something better than her husband's grandmother's fried chicken. *(pictured on page 301)*

- 4 ounces PHILADELPHIA® Cream Cheese, softened
- 1 cup dry chicken-flavored stuffing mix
- ½ cup (2 ounces) finely shredded Romano cheese
- ½ cup chopped Vidalia onion
- ¼ cup minced fresh basil
- 4 large boned chicken breast halves with skin
- 4 OSCAR MAYER® Ready to Serve Bacon slices
- 1 large egg
- 1 cup milk
- 1 cup BISQUICK® Original All-Purpose Baking Mix
- 2 teaspoons Creole seasoning
- 1 teaspoon black pepper
- Canola oil
- Roasted Red Pepper-and-Vidalia Onion Gravy

STIR together first 5 ingredients in a medium bowl. Set aside.

PLACE chicken, skin side down, between 2 sheets of heavy-duty plastic wrap; flatten to ¼-inch thickness, using a meat mallet or rolling pin.

SPREAD one-fourth of cream cheese mixture on skinless side of each chicken breast half; top each with 1 piece of bacon. Roll up chicken, jellyroll fashion, lifting skin and tucking roll under skin.

WHISK together egg and milk in a bowl. Combine baking mix, Creole seasoning, and pepper in a shallow dish. Dip chicken rolls in egg mixture; dredge in baking mix mixture.

POUR oil to a depth of 2 inches in a large skillet; heat to 350°. Fry chicken rolls, in batches, 10 to 12 minutes or until dark brown and done, turning chicken rolls often. Drain on wire racks over paper towels.

SPOON ¼ cup Roasted Red Pepper-and-Vidalia Onion Gravy onto each of 4 individual serving plates; top each with 1 chicken roll. Drizzle with remaining gravy.

Roasted Red Pepper-and-Vidalia Onion Gravy:

MAKES 3 CUPS

Prep: 20 min., Broil: 10 min., Cook: 25 min., Stand: 10 min.

1 large Vidalia onion, halved vertically
1 large sweet red bell pepper, halved and seeded
REYNOLDS WRAP® Release® Non-Stick Foil
1 tablespoon olive oil
¼ teaspoon MORTON® Kosher Salt
3 tablespoons butter
3 tablespoons all-purpose flour
2 cups chicken broth
2 teaspoons Creole seasoning
2 tablespoons minced fresh basil
Black pepper to taste

DICE 1 onion half; set aside.

CUT remaining onion half into slices. Place onion slices and bell pepper, cut sides down, on a baking sheet lined with non-stick aluminum foil; drizzle with oil, and sprinkle with salt.

BROIL onion slices and bell pepper halves 5 inches from heat about 10 minutes or until bell pepper looks blistered. Place bell pepper halves in a zip-top freezer bag; seal and let stand 10 minutes to loosen skin. Peel bell pepper halves, and dice 1 half. Reserve diced bell pepper and remaining half. Dice roasted onion, and set aside.

MELT butter in a large skillet over medium-high heat. Add reserved diced raw onion, and sauté 10 minutes or until onion begins to brown. Stir in flour; cook, stirring constantly, 5 minutes or until flour mixture is caramel-colored. Stir in chicken broth and Creole seasoning. Reduce heat to medium, and cook, stirring constantly, until thickened.

PROCESS gravy mixture and reserved bell pepper half in a blender until smooth, stopping to scrape down sides. Combine gravy mixture, diced bell pepper, diced roasted onion, basil, and black pepper.

SUSAN ROTTER
NOLENSVILLE, TENNESSEE

SAUTÉED SMOKED GOUDA CHEESE GRITS WITH BLACK BEAN SALSA

MAKES ABOUT 6 SERVINGS

Prep: 10 min., Cook: 15 min., Chill: 3 hrs., Cook: 10 min. per batch

2 cups milk
¾ cup water
¾ cup grits
¾ cup chopped smoked Gouda cheese
½ teaspoon MORTON® Iodized Salt
2 tablespoons butter, divided
2 cups all-purpose flour
2 tablespoons MORTON® Iodized Salt
2 teaspoons black pepper
1 cup beer
Butter
Olive oil
Black Bean Salsa
½ cup sour cream
1 medium tomato, seeded and diced
2 tablespoons chopped fresh parsley
2 tablespoons chopped green onions
12 fresh chives, cut into 1-inch pieces

STIR together milk and ¾ cup water in a 1½-quart saucepan over medium-high heat; bring to a boil. Stir in grits, cheese, and ½ teaspoon salt; cook, stirring constantly, 9 minutes or until thickened. Stir in 2 tablespoons butter. Pour grits into a lightly greased 11- x 7-inch baking dish. Cover and chill 3 hours or until firm.

COMBINE flour, 2 tablespoons salt, and pepper in a shallow dish. Pour beer into a small bowl.

CUT grits into 2-inch squares. Dip grits squares into beer; dredge in flour mixture, repeating procedure twice.

MELT 1 tablespoon butter in a large skillet over medium heat; stir in 1 tablespoon oil. Cook grits squares, in batches, in hot butter mixture 5 minutes on each side or until golden, adding butter and oil as needed.

ARRANGE 3 grits squares in center of 6 individual serving plates.

SPOON Black Bean Salsa evenly over grits squares. Top evenly with sour cream. Sprinkle evenly with tomato, parsley, green onions, and chives.

Black Bean Salsa:

MAKES ABOUT 4½ CUPS

Prep: 15 min., Cook: 5 min.

2 tablespoons butter
1 medium onion, diced
2 garlic cloves, minced
2 (15-ounce) cans BUSH'S® Black Beans, drained
⅔ cup picante sauce
2 medium tomatoes, seeded and diced
2 teaspoons chili powder
1 teaspoon MORTON® Iodized Salt
½ teaspoon black pepper
¼ teaspoon ground cumin
3 tablespoons chopped fresh parsley
3 tablespoons chopped green onions

MELT butter in a medium saucepan over medium heat; add onion and garlic, and sauté until tender. Stir in beans and next 6 ingredients; cook, stirring occasionally, 3 minutes or until thoroughly heated. Stir in parsley and green onions.

JOHN AND GRETA BARBOUR MILLS
JACKSON, MISSISSIPPI

Judges' Notes

Southern Living Foods Editor Andria Scott Hurst, chief judge for the Cook-Off, offered some insight into the winning dishes. "Overall, I'm extremely pleased with every finalist's recipe," she says. "Choosing a winner was not an easy job, but it was a delicious one."

"The grand prize winner, Southern-Fried Stuffed Chicken With Roasted Red Pepper-and-Vidalia Onion Gravy, is a Southern icon turned into an elegant knife-and-fork food. All the category winners are tops, but this one does it all. It has great flavor and appearance and makes great use of sponsor products. I like that she leaves the skin on the chicken, making it crisp and wonderful."

DOWN-SOUTH CRAB CAKES WITH COLLARD GREENS AND ROASTED-GARLIC BEURRE BLANC

MAKES 5 SERVINGS

Prep: 30 min., Bake: 12 min.

- **2 cups cornbread crumbs**
- **¼ cup diced red bell pepper**
- **¼ cup chopped fresh chives**
- **¼ cup Creole mustard**
- **½ cup mayonnaise**
- **2 large eggs**
- **1 teaspoon chipotle pepper sauce**
- **1 teaspoon Worcestershire sauce**
- **¼ cup chopped OSCAR MAYER® Ready to Serve Bacon**
- **1 pound fresh jumbo lump crabmeat**
- **PAM® Cooking Spray**
- **Collard Greens**
- **Roasted-Garlic Beurre Blanc**
- **Garnishes: chopped fresh chives, diced red bell pepper**

PREHEAT oven to 375°.
COMBINE first 9 ingredients in a large bowl. Gently stir in crabmeat. Shape mixture into 10 (3- to 3½-inch) patties. Place on a baking sheet coated with cooking spray.
BAKE at 375° for 12 minutes.
SPOON Collard Greens onto individual serving plates, using a slotted spoon; top each serving with 2 crab cakes. Drizzle with Roasted-Garlic Beurre Blanc. Garnish, if desired.

Collard Greens:

MAKES 10 CUPS

Prep: 10 min., Cook: 55 min.

- **½ cup diced prosciutto**
- **3 tablespoons butter**
- **½ cup diced onion**
- **2 tablespoons minced garlic**
- **2 pounds fresh collard greens**
- **3 cups chicken broth**

HEAT a large Dutch oven over medium-high heat; add prosciutto, and sauté 2 minutes. Add butter, onion, and garlic; sauté until onion is tender. Add collard greens and chicken broth. Bring to a boil; reduce heat, and simmer 30 to 45 minutes or until greens are tender.

Roasted-Garlic Beurre Blanc:

MAKES 2 CUPS

Prep: 40 min., Bake: 25 min., Cook: 35 min.

- **6 garlic cloves**
- **Olive oil**
- **MORTON® Salt and black pepper to taste**
- **½ cup fresh SUNKIST® lemon juice (2 SUNKIST® lemons)**
- **½ cup dry white wine**
- **1 cup whipping cream**
- **¼ cup cold butter, cut into pieces**
- **1 teaspoon MORTON® Kosher Salt**
- **½ teaspoon ground red pepper**

PLACE garlic in center of an aluminum foil sheet. Drizzle garlic lightly with oil; sprinkle with salt and black pepper to taste.
BAKE at 350° for 20 to 25 minutes or until golden.
SQUEEZE out pulp from each garlic clove into a medium saucepan. Add lemon juice and white wine to garlic.
COOK, uncovered, over medium-high heat about 20 minutes or until reduced by three-fourths. Stir in whipping cream; reduce heat, and simmer, uncovered, 10 to 15 minutes or until reduced by half. Remove from heat; gradually whisk in butter, a few pieces at a time, until sauce is slightly thickened and smooth. Stir in salt and ground red pepper.

BENJAMIN CHAPIN
PUNTA GORDA, FLORIDA

ONE-DISH SUPPERS

SPICY TEX-MEX CHICKEN COBBLER

MAKES 4 TO 6 SERVINGS

Prep: 10 min., Cook: 22 min., Bake: 20 min.

Ruth Kendrick hoped the name 'cobbler' might catch the judges' attention. *(pictured on page 302)*

- **1 medium onion, sliced**
- **2 tablespoons vegetable oil**
- **1 (15-ounce) can BUSH'S® Black Beans, rinsed and drained**
- **1 (10-ounce) can ROTEL® Mexican Festival Diced Tomatoes With Lime Juice and Cilantro**
- **1 (10-ounce) can enchilada sauce**
- **2 cups cubed cooked chicken**
- **1 teaspoon MORTON® Iodized Salt**
- **½ teaspoon ground cumin**
- **½ teaspoon chili powder**
- **½ teaspoon dried oregano**
- **½ teaspoon ground pepper**
- **1½ cups BISQUICK® Original All-Purpose Baking Mix**
- **1 large egg**
- **⅔ cup milk**
- **1 cup (4 ounces) shredded extra-sharp Cheddar cheese, divided**
- **½ cup chopped fresh cilantro, divided**
- **2 avocados, sliced**
- **1 tablespoon lime juice**
- **Sour cream**

SAUTÉ onion in hot oil in a 10-inch cast-iron skillet over medium-high heat 3 to 4 minutes or until tender. Stir in beans and next 8 ingredients. Bring to a boil; reduce heat, and simmer, uncovered, 15 minutes.
COMBINE baking mix, egg, and milk in a medium bowl, stirring until smooth. Fold in ½ cup cheese and ¼ cup cilantro; pour over simmering chicken mixture.

BAKE at 400° for 20 minutes or until a wooden pick inserted in topping comes out clean. Sprinkle with remaining ½ cup cheese and remaining ¼ cup cilantro. Sprinkle avocado slices with lime juice, and arrange over cobbler. Serve with sour cream.

RUTH KENDRICK
OGDEN, UTAH

OSCAR MAYER BACON® *Brand Winner*

Tomato-Leek-Bacon Tart

MAKES 4 SERVINGS

Prep: 30 min., Cook: 5 min., Bake: 35 min.

PAM® Cooking Spray
½ (15-ounce) package refrigerated piecrusts
1 (8-ounce) package shredded Italian three-cheese blend, divided
3 medium leeks, sliced (about 1 cup)
2 tablespoons olive oil
8 plum tomatoes, sliced
1 cup loosely packed fresh basil leaves, coarsely chopped
3 garlic cloves, coarsely chopped
½ (2.1-ounce) package OSCAR MAYER® Ready to Serve Bacon, chopped
½ cup mayonnaise
¼ cup freshly grated Parmesan cheese
1 tablespoon fresh SUNKIST® lemon juice
½ teaspoon pepper
Garnish: fresh basil sprigs

COAT a 9-inch tart pan with cooking spray. Fit piecrust into pan according to package directions.
BAKE at 450° for 10 minutes or until golden. Remove crust from oven; sprinkle with 1 cup cheese blend.
SAUTÉ leeks in hot oil in a skillet over medium-high heat until tender; sprinkle over crust. Arrange tomatoes over leeks; sprinkle with basil and garlic.
STIR together remaining 1 cup cheese blend, bacon, and next 4 ingredients. Spoon over tart, spreading to edges.

Judges' Notes

Spicy Tex-Mex Chicken Cobbler really does define its category. It's truly a one-dish supper—the entire meal is in it. You can put this recipe together and bring it to the table in its baking dish. The contestant used a cast-iron skillet—perfect—definitely added to this very Southern dish. You get an entire meal in a scoop of cobbler. It has the texture of cobbler—moist with gravy on the inside with a crisp crust. It's the heads-up winner of the One-Dish Suppers category.

Ruth Kendrick was sure her cobbler would not win. "I had turned my head to congratulate another contestant—sure that she would win—when Al Roker called my name," she says. "I was shocked—it's just a little homely dish."
Ruth entered the Cook-Off at the last minute at the urging of a friend. "Several of us enter cook-offs as a hobby," she says. "When I told her I wasn't going to enter, she said, 'You're going to enter, because when everyone else is getting called, you're going to feel really bad!'"

BAKE at 375° for 25 minutes or until golden. Cut tart into 4 slices. Garnish, if desired.

NANCY FAZAKERLEY
MECHANICSBURG, PENNSYLVANIA

Quick-and-Spicy Chicken 'n' Dumplings

MAKES 4 SERVINGS

Prep: 25 min.; Cook: 1 hr., 5 min.

8 skinned and boned chicken thighs
4 cups BISQUICK® Original All-Purpose Baking Mix, divided
1 teaspoon paprika
1 teaspoon ground red pepper
½ teaspoon garlic powder
½ teaspoon onion powder
½ teaspoon poultry seasoning
¼ teaspoon freshly ground black pepper
Dash of MORTON® Iodized Salt
2 tablespoons vegetable oil, divided
3 (14.5-ounce) cans chicken broth, divided
¼ (1.41-ounce) box coriander and annatto seasoning (2 packets)
⅔ cup milk

RINSE chicken with cold water, and pat dry. Combine 2 cups baking mix, paprika, and next 6 ingredients in a large zip-top freezer bag. Add chicken thighs, 1 at a time; seal bag, and shake to coat chicken.
HEAT 1 tablespoon oil in a 6-quart Dutch oven over medium heat. Add half of chicken, and cook 5 minutes on each side or until golden brown; remove chicken. Repeat procedure with remaining oil and chicken.
ADD ½ cup chicken broth to drippings in pan, stirring to loosen browned bits from bottom.
RETURN chicken to pan; stir in remaining broth and 2 seasoning packets. Bring to a boil; cover, reduce heat, and simmer 25 minutes.
COMBINE milk and remaining 2 cups baking mix in a medium bowl, stirring just until moistened. Drop dough by tablespoonfuls onto simmering chicken mixture; cook, uncovered, 10 minutes. Cover, and cook 10 more minutes. Serve immediately.

NOTE: For testing purposes only, we used Sazón Goya seasoning.

KAREN PETERS
HAWTHORNE, NEW JERSEY

SIMPLE & SCRUMPTIOUS ENTRÉES

SIMPLE & SCRUMPTIOUS ENTRÉES
Category Winner

TROPICANA® *Brand Winner*

MELT-IN-YOUR-MOUTH BRAISED AND BARBECUED CHICKEN

MAKES 4 SERVINGS

Prep: 15 min., Cook: 50 min.

Carol Daggers created a main dish that would mimic Asian barbecue. *(pictured on page 303)*

  2 tablespoons vegetable oil
  8 bone-in chicken thighs, skinned
    (about 2 pounds)
  ½ cup TROPICANA® PURE PREMIUM
    Orange Juice
  ½ cup pineapple juice
  1 tablespoon cornstarch
  ⅓ cup soy sauce
  ⅓ cup firmly packed light brown sugar
  2 tablespoons minced fresh ginger
  3 tablespoons cider vinegar
  3 tablespoons ketchup
  ½ teaspoon dried crushed red pepper
  2 garlic cloves, minced
  2 regular-size bags SUCCESS® White
    Rice, uncooked
  ¼ cup chopped green onion tops

HEAT oil in a large skillet over medium-high heat. Add chicken, and sauté 6 minutes, turning once.
COMBINE fruit juices in a large bowl. Stir together cornstarch and 1 tablespoon juice mixture until smooth; set aside.
STIR soy sauce and next 6 ingredients into remaining juice mixture; pour over chicken. Bring to a boil; cover, reduce heat, and simmer 35 minutes, turning chicken after 20 minutes.

PREPARE rice according to package directions. Keep warm.
UNCOVER chicken, and stir in cornstarch mixture. Cook, stirring constantly, 5 minutes or until sauce thickens.
SPOON rice onto a serving platter; top with chicken and sauce. Sprinkle with green onion tops.

CAROL DAGGERS
WILMINGTON, DELAWARE

Judges' Notes

The flavors in Melt-In-Your-Mouth Braised and Barbecued Chicken are just fantastic. The ginger really comes through. The contestant uses an inexpensive cut of meat and very contemporary flavors for a really different combination. The recipe combines barbecue with the hands-off ease of braising for a great dish that could work for a weeknight supper or dinner for company. Who knew chicken thighs could be this wonderful?

GRILLED CHILE-RUBBED RIB EYES WITH HERB CHEESE AND ASPARAGUS BUNDLES

MAKES 4 SERVINGS

Prep: 30 min., Cook: 5 min., Grill: 18 min.

  4 tablespoons PHILADELPHIA®
    Cream Cheese, softened
  2 tablespoons minced shallots
  1 teaspoon fresh SUNKIST® lemon
    juice
  2 teaspoons minced fresh chives
  2 teaspoons minced fresh basil
  1½ tablespoons ancho chile powder
  1 tablespoon paprika
  1 teaspoon garlic salt
  ½ teaspoon ground red pepper
  2 tablespoons olive oil
  4 (12-ounce) rib-eye steaks (1 to 1½
    inches thick)
  1 tablespoon MORTON® Salt
  4½ quarts water
  20 fresh asparagus spears (about ½
    pound)
  4 slices prosciutto
  1 WEBER® GENESIS Gold B Gas Grill
  Garnishes: fresh basil sprigs,
    SUNKIST® lemon wedges

STIR together first 5 ingredients until blended. Shape into a 4-inch log; wrap in plastic wrap, and chill until firm.
COMBINE chile powder and next 3 ingredients. Stir in olive oil to form a paste. Rub chile mixture on both sides of steaks.
COMBINE salt and 4½ quarts water in a large Dutch oven. Bring water to a boil; add asparagus. Cook 2 minutes or until crisp-tender; drain. Plunge asparagus into ice water to stop the cooking process; drain.
GATHER 5 asparagus spears into a bundle; wrap with 1 slice of prosciutto. Repeat procedure with remaining asparagus and proscuitto. Set aside.
PREHEAT grill according to manufacturer's instructions.
PLACE steaks on grill rack over direct high heat; grill, 10 minutes, turning once. Turn off burners that are directly below

steaks. Reduce heat to medium; grill, covered with grill lid, 6 to 8 minutes or until done.

REMOVE steaks to serving plates; top each steak immediately with 1 tablespoon of herb cheese log. Serve asparagus bundles with steaks. Garnish, if desired.

NOTE: For testing purposes only, we used McCormick Ancho Chile Powder.

GLORIA BRADLEY
NAPERVILLE, ILLINOIS

SUCCESS/MAHATMA® *Brand Winner*

TEXAS PESTO SHRIMP OVER RICE

MAKES 4 SERVINGS
Prep: 15 min., Cook: 15 min.

- 1½ pounds unpeeled, large fresh shrimp
- 1 cup fresh cilantro leaves
- 3 green onions, cut into thirds
- ¼ cup freshly grated Parmesan cheese
- ½ small jalapeño pepper, unseeded
- ½ medium tomato
- 2 tablespoons pine nuts, toasted
- 3 tablespoons fresh SUNKIST® lemon juice (about 1 SUNKIST® lemon)
- 1 teaspoon minced garlic
- ½ teaspoon MORTON® Salt
- ½ teaspoon pepper
- ¼ cup olive oil, divided
- Hot cooked SUCCESS® White Rice

PEEL shrimp; devein, if desired. Set aside.

PROCESS cilantro, next 9 ingredients, and 3 tablespoons olive oil in a food processor until smooth.

SAUTÉ shrimp in remaining 1 tablespoon hot olive oil in a large skillet over medium-high heat 3 to 4 minutes or just until shrimp turn pink. Pour cilantro mixture over shrimp, stirring well. Serve shrimp mixture over hot cooked rice.

LYNNE MILLIRON
AUSTIN, TEXAS

KIDS LOVE IT!

KIDS LOVE IT!
Category Winner

TEX-MEX EGG ROLLS WITH CREAMY CILANTRO DIPPING SAUCE

MAKES 28 EGG ROLLS
Prep: 40 min., Fry: 3 min. per batch

As a high school Spanish teacher, Stacy Lamons has a good idea of the kinds of foods that appeal to teenagers. *(pictured on page 303)*

- 1 (5-ounce) package MAHATMA Authentic Spanish Rice Mix
- 1 teaspoon MORTON® Iodized Salt
- 1 pound JIMMY DEAN Premium Hot Pork Sausage
- 1 (15-ounce) can BUSH'S® Black Beans, rinsed and drained
- 6 green onions, finely chopped
- 1 (1.25-ounce) package taco seasoning
- 2 cups (8 ounces) shredded Monterey Jack cheese
- 1 (14.5-ounce) can HUNT'S® Petite Diced Tomatoes With Mild Green Chilies, undrained
- 28 egg roll wrappers
- 1 large egg, lightly beaten
- 4 cups peanut oil
- Creamy Cilantro Dipping Sauce
- Garnish: fresh cilantro sprigs

COOK rice according to package directions, using 1 teaspoon salt. Cool completely.

COOK sausage in a skillet over medium heat, stirring until it crumbles and is no longer pink; drain well. Let cool.

STIR together rice, sausage, black beans, and next 4 ingredients in a large bowl. Spoon about ⅓ cup rice mixture in center of each egg roll wrapper. Fold top corner of wrapper over filling, tucking tip of corner under filling; fold left and right corners over filling. Lightly brush remaining corner with egg; tightly roll

filled end toward the remaining corner, and gently press to seal.

POUR oil into a heavy Dutch oven; heat to 375°. Fry egg rolls, in batches, 2 to 3 minutes or until golden. Drain on a wire rack over paper towels. Serve with Creamy Cilantro Dipping Sauce. Garnish, if desired.

Creamy Cilantro Dipping Sauce:

MAKES 3 CUPS
Prep: 10 min.

- 1 (8-ounce) package PHILADELPHIA® Cream Cheese, softened
- 1 cup sour cream
- 3 garlic cloves, minced
- 2 (10-ounce) cans ROTEL® Mexican Festival Diced Tomatoes With Lime Juice and Cilantro
- 2 cups loosely packed fresh cilantro leaves (about 1 bunch)
- Garnish: finely chopped fresh cilantro

PROCESS first 5 ingredients in a food processor until smooth. Garnish, if desired.

NOTE: For a beautiful presentation, cut top from 1 large red bell pepper, reserving top; remove and discard seeds and membrane, leaving pepper intact. Arrange bell pepper on a serving plate, and fill with sauce.

STACY LAMONS
HOUSTON, TEXAS

Judges' Notes

Tex-Mex Egg Rolls are just what kids love—finger foods, and they also love dipping them in something. The recipe has all the great flavors that are so popular right now. Any age children, or any age adults for that matter, would love them—they have wide, wide appeal. They would make great appetizers for a party.

TEX-MEX CHICKEN CRUNCHIES

MAKES 8 TO 10 SERVINGS

Prep: 10 min., Chill: 30 min., Fry: 6 min. per batch

- ½ cup BISQUICK® Original All-Purpose Baking Mix
- 1 large egg
- ½ cup enchilada sauce
- 2 cups crushed spicy tortilla chips
- ¼ cup minced fresh cilantro
- 6 skinned and boned chicken breast halves, cut into 1½-inch pieces
- 1 cup vegetable oil
- Ranch dressing
- Barbecue sauce

PLACE baking mix in a shallow dish. Whisk together egg and enchilada sauce in a small bowl. Stir together tortilla crumbs and cilantro in a separate shallow dish.
DREDGE chicken pieces in baking mix; dip in egg mixture, and dredge in crumb mixture. Cover chicken, and chill 30 minutes.
POUR oil into a large skillet; heat to 375°. Fry chicken, in batches, 3 minutes on each side or until brown. Drain on wire racks over paper towels. Serve chicken with Ranch dressing or barbecue sauce.

FRANCES BENTHIN
SCIO, OREGON

CARAMEL-PECAN FRENCH TOAST

MAKES 8 SERVINGS

Prep: 25 min., Cook: 5 min., Bake: 40 min.

- 1 cup firmly packed light brown sugar
- ½ cup butter
- 2 tablespoons light corn syrup
- 12 slices SARA LEE Honey White Bread
- ¾ cup CALIFORNIA RAISINS
- 1 cup chopped pecans, toasted and divided
- 6 large eggs
- ½ cup milk
- 2 teaspoons grated SUNKIST® lemon rind
- 1 teaspoon vanilla extract
- ½ teaspoon ground cinnamon
- 1½ cups whipping cream, divided
- ¼ cup powdered sugar
- Maple syrup
- OSCAR MAYER® Ready to Serve Bacon (optional)

COMBINE first 3 ingredients in a small saucepan; cook, stirring constantly, over medium heat 3 to 5 minutes or until sugar dissolves.
POUR brown sugar mixture into an ungreased 13- x 9-inch baking dish. Arrange 6 bread slices in brown sugar mixture, cutting slices as necessary to fit in dish. Sprinkle raisins and ¾ cup pecans evenly over bread. Top with remaining bread slices.
WHISK together eggs, next 4 ingredients, and 1 cup cream. Pour egg mixture over bread slices in baking dish.
BAKE, uncovered, at 350° for 40 minutes or until a wooden pick inserted in center comes out clean.
BEAT remaining ½ cup whipping cream until foamy; gradually add powdered sugar, beating until soft peaks form.
DIVIDE French toast evenly among 8 individual serving plates. Top each serving with whipped cream; drizzle with maple syrup, and sprinkle with remaining ¼ cup pecans. Serve with bacon, if desired.

KATHY SPECHT
CAMBRIA, CALIFORNIA

SIGNATURE DESSERTS

SIGNATURE DESSERTS
Category Winner

PHILADELPHIA® *Brand Winner*

CREAM CHEESE FLAN

MAKES 6 TO 8 SERVINGS

Prep: 20 min.; Cook: 5 min.; Stand: 5 min.; Bake: 1 hr., 45 min.; Chill: 3 hrs.

Jo Gonzalez-Hastings attributes the inspiration for this silky flan to her Cuban mother who always made traditional flan. *(pictured on page 304)*

- 1½ cups sugar, divided
- 7 egg yolks
- 1 (14-ounce) can sweetened condensed milk
- 1 (12-ounce) can evaporated milk
- ¾ cup milk
- 1½ teaspoons vanilla extract
- ⅛ teaspoon MORTON® Salt
- 4 egg whites
- 1 (8-ounce) package PHILADELPHIA® Cream Cheese, softened

COOK 1 cup sugar in a medium-size saucepan over medium heat, stirring constantly, 5 minutes or until sugar melts and turns a light golden brown. Quickly pour into a 2-quart flan dish. Using oven mitts, tilt dish to evenly coat bottom and sides. Let stand 5 minutes. (Sugar will harden.)
WHISK together egg yolks and next 5 ingredients in a large bowl.
PROCESS egg whites, cream cheese, and remaining ½ cup sugar in a blender until smooth. Stir egg white mixture into egg yolk mixture. Pour mixture through a wire-mesh strainer into a large bowl; pour custard over caramelized sugar.
PLACE dish in a large shallow pan. Add hot water to pan to a depth of one-third up sides of dish.
BAKE at 350° for 1 hour and 45 minutes. Remove dish from water bath; cool

completely on a wire rack. Cover and chill at least 3 hours.

RUN a knife around edge of flan to loosen; invert onto a serving plate.

JO GONZALEZ-HASTINGS
GULFPORT, FLORIDA

SWEET POTATO CAKE WITH COCONUT FILLING AND CARAMEL FROSTING

MAKES 12 SERVINGS

Prep: 1 hr.; Bake: 25 min.; Cool: 10 min.;
Chill: 1 hr., 45 min.

    PAM® Cooking Spray
    All-purpose flour
    1 cup butter, softened
    3 cups sugar
    6 large eggs, separated
    1½ cups mashed cooked sweet
        potatoes
    1 cup sour cream
    1 tablespoon baking powder
    1 teaspoon vanilla extract
    ½ teaspoon ground cinnamon
    ½ teaspoon ground ginger
    ¼ teaspoon MORTON® Iodized Salt
    1 cup chopped pecans
    3 cups all-purpose flour
    Coconut Filling
    Caramel Frosting

COAT 3 (9-inch) round cakepans with cooking spray; dust lightly with flour.
BEAT butter and sugar at medium-high speed with an electric mixer until fluffy. Add egg yolks, 1 at a time, beating until blended after each addition. Beat in sweet potatoes and next 6 ingredients, adding each ingredient 1 at a time. Add pecans and 3 cups flour, beating just until blended.
BEAT egg whites in a separate bowl at high speed with an electric mixer until stiff peaks form; fold into batter. Spoon batter evenly into prepared pans.
BAKE at 350° for 25 minutes or until a wooden pick inserted in center comes out clean. Cool in pans on wire racks 10 minutes; remove and cool on wire racks.
SPREAD Coconut Filling between layers.

Gradually pour about ½ cup Caramel Frosting on cake, spreading over top and sides with a small spatula. Place cake in refrigerator. Chill remaining Caramel Frosting 45 minutes. Pour another ½ cup Caramel Frosting on cake, spreading over top and sides. Repeat with remaining frosting, using ½ cup frosting at a time and chilling every 15 minutes. Refrigerate cake.

Coconut Filling:

MAKES ABOUT 1 CUP
Prep: 10 min., Cook: 5 min., Chill: 1 hr.

    ¼ cup sugar
    2 tablespoons cornstarch
    ⅛ teaspoon MORTON® Iodized Salt
    1 cup milk
    1 large egg, lightly beaten
    ½ cup frozen grated coconut, thawed
    1 teaspoon vanilla extract

COMBINE first 3 ingredients in a heavy 2-quart saucepan; gradually stir in milk, and cook, stirring constantly, over medium heat 3 minutes or until thickened.
STIR about one-fourth of hot milk mixture gradually into egg; add egg mixture to remaining hot milk mixture, stirring constantly. Return to a boil; cook, stirring constantly, 1 minute or until thickened. Remove from heat; stir in coconut and vanilla. Place heavy-duty plastic wrap

directly on warm filling. Cool completely; chill 1 hour.

Caramel Frosting:

MAKES 3 CUPS
Prep: 10 min., Cook: 15 min., Cool: 10 min.

    2 (3-ounce) packages PHILADELPHIA®
        Cream Cheese, cut into cubes and
        softened
    ¾ cup whipping cream
    2¼ cups sugar
    ⅔ cup water
    9 tablespoons butter, cut into ½-inch
        cubes

WHISK together cream cheese and cream in a small bowl until smooth.
COOK sugar and ⅔ cup water in a heavy 3½-quart saucepan over medium-low heat, stirring constantly, 5 minutes or until sugar dissolves. Increase heat to high, and bring mixture to a boil without stirring. Using a pastry brush dipped in hot water, wash down any sugar crystals on sides of pan. Cook, without stirring, 10 minutes or just until syrup turns a deep amber color.
WHISK in butter gradually; gradually whisk in cream cheese mixture until smooth. Remove from heat; cool 10 minutes, whisking occasionally.

LYNDA SARKISIAN
SENECA, SOUTH CAROLINA

Judges' Notes

Cream Cheese Flan is one of the richest, smoothest, creamiest confections that we've ever tasted. It wasn't until the stage show that we learned why—the finalist strains the custard as she pours it into the baking dish, so no bits of cream cheese or egg get incorporated. This flan melts in your mouth, and the cream cheese gives it a silkiness that outshines any flan we've ever had.

Taste is what made it win, but its simplicity makes it that much more appealing.

Winner Jo Gonzalez-Hastings created the winning formula by adding cream cheese to some of her already delicious flans. She says, "Cream cheese is my favorite ingredient. Flan is so simple. We entertain a lot, and I serve it often—it's very popular."

SARA LEE® *Brand Winner*

LAYERED ALMOND-CREAM CHEESE BREAD PUDDING WITH AMARETTO CREAM SAUCE

MAKES 12 SERVINGS

Prep: 30 min., Chill: 30 min., Bake: 1 hr.

- PAM® Cooking Spray
- 1 (16-ounce) loaf SARA LEE Honey White Bread, sliced and divided
- 1 (8-ounce) package PHILADELPHIA® Cream Cheese, softened
- 9 large eggs
- ¼ cup sugar
- 3 teaspoons vanilla extract, divided
- 1¼ cups almond filling
- 1 cup butter, melted and divided
- 2½ cups half-and-half
- Dash of MORTON® Salt
- 2 tablespoons almond filling
- 2 tablespoons sugar
- 1 egg yolk
- ¼ cup slivered almonds
- Amaretto Cream Sauce

COAT a 13- x 9- x 3-inch pan with cooking spray. Arrange 4½ bread slices on bottom of prepared pan, cutting slices as necessary to fit pan.

BEAT cream cheese, 1 egg, ¼ cup sugar, and 1 teaspoon vanilla with an electric mixer until smooth. Spread half of cream cheese mixture over bread.

WHISK together 1¼ cups almond filling and ½ cup melted butter. Spread half of almond mixture over cream cheese mixture. Repeat layers once, using 4½ bread slices, remaining cream cheese mixture, and remaining almond mixture.

CUT remaining bread slices into 1-inch cubes, and sprinkle evenly over almond mixture.

WHISK together remaining 8 eggs, remaining 2 teaspoons vanilla, half-and-half, and salt; pour over bread cubes. Cover and chill 30 minutes or until most of egg mixture is absorbed.

WHISK together remaining ½ cup melted butter, 2 tablespoons almond filling, 2 tablespoons sugar, and egg yolk until blended. Drizzle evenly over bread pudding; sprinkle with almonds.

BAKE at 325° for 1 hour or until set. Serve warm or chilled with Amaretto Cream Sauce.

Amaretto Cream Sauce:

MAKES ABOUT 2½ CUPS

Prep: 5 min., Cook: 10 min.

- ½ cup amaretto liqueur
- 2 tablespoons cornstarch
- 1½ cups whipping cream
- ½ cup sugar

COMBINE amaretto and cornstarch, stirring until smooth.

COOK cream in a heavy saucepan over medium heat, stirring often, just until bubbles appear; gradually stir in amaretto mixture. Bring to a boil over medium heat, and boil, stirring constantly, 30 seconds. Remove from heat; stir in sugar, and let cool completely.

NOTE: For testing purposes only, we used Solo Almond Filling.

JEREMY BAZATA
PANAMA CITY, FLORIDA

BRAND WINNERS

These recipes won recognition for best use of a sponsor's product. To enter the contest, you must use at least one sponsor's product.

MILLSTONE® *Brand Winner*

BROWNIES DELUXE

MAKES 24 BROWNIES

Prep: 20 min., Cook: 5 min., Bake: 35 min.

- 1 cup butter
- 4 (1-ounce) squares unsweetened chocolate
- ¼ cup strong brewed MILLSTONE French Roast Coffee
- 4 large eggs
- 2 cups sugar
- 1 teaspoon vanilla extract
- 1 cup all-purpose flour
- 1 (12-ounce) package NESTLÉ® Toll House Morsels
- 1 cup chopped walnuts
- REYNOLDS WRAP® Release® Non-Stick Foil

STIR together butter, chocolate, and coffee in a heavy saucepan. Cook, stirring occasionally, over low heat until butter melts; cool slightly.

BEAT eggs at high speed with an electric mixer. Gradually add sugar and vanilla, beating 3 minutes or until thick and pale. Add chocolate mixture, beating until blended. Gradually add flour, beating at low speed just until blended. Stir in chocolate morsels and walnuts. Pour into a 13- x 9-inch pan lined with nonstick aluminum foil.

BAKE at 375° for 35 minutes or until set. Cool in pan on a wire rack. Lift foil with brownies out of pan. Cut into squares.

CINDY BROWN
WICHITA, KANSAS

MORE BRAND-WINNING RECIPES

- **Bisquick®:** Spicy Tex-Mex Chicken Cobbler, page 324
- **Oscar Mayer Bacon®:** Tomato-Leek-Bacon Tart, page 325
- **PAM®:** Down-South Crab Cakes With Collard Greens and Roasted-Garlic Beurre Blanc, page 324
- **Sara Lee:** Layered Almond-Cream Cheese Bread Pudding With Amaretto Cream Sauce, page 330
- **Philadelphia Cream Cheese®:** Cream Cheese Flan, page 328
- **Success/Mahatma®:** Texas Pesto Shrimp Over Rice, page 327
- **Tropicana®:** Melt-In-Your-Mouth Braised and Barbecued Chicken, page 326
- **Weber®:** Grilled Chile-Rubbed Rib Eyes With Herb Cheese and Asparagus Bundles, page 326

ROTEL® *Brand Winner*

POTATO-CRUSTED CATFISH WITH WARM PINTO BEAN-AND-BACON SALSA

MAKES 6 SERVINGS

Prep: 15 min., Stand: 5 min., Cook: 20 min.

½ cup milk
1½ teaspoons fresh SUNKIST® lemon juice
½ teaspoon MORTON® Kosher Salt
½ teaspoon garlic powder
4 (6-ounce) catfish fillets
1 cup instant potato flakes
1 tablespoon vegetable oil
1 tablespoon butter
Warm Pinto Bean-and-Bacon Salsa
Garnishes: fresh cilantro sprigs, SUNKIST® lemon wedges

COMBINE milk and lemon juice in a shallow bowl; let stand 5 minutes. Stir in salt and garlic powder. Dip fish in milk mixture; dredge in potato flakes.
HEAT oil and butter in a large nonstick skillet over medium-high heat until butter melts.
ADD fish; cook 3 to 4 minutes on each side or until golden. Arrange fish and Warm Pinto Bean-and-Bacon Salsa on a large platter. Garnish, if desired.

Warm Pinto Bean-and-Bacon Salsa:
MAKES 2 CUPS

Prep: 5 min., Cook: 10 min.

1 (16-ounce) can BUSH'S® Pinto Beans, rinsed and drained
1 (10-ounce) can ROTEL® Original Diced Tomatoes & Green Chilies
¼ cup minced fresh cilantro
4 slices OSCAR MAYER® Ready to Serve Bacon, cut crosswise into thin slices

COMBINE beans and tomatoes in a small saucepan. Cook over medium-low heat until thoroughly heated, stirring occasionally. Stir in cilantro and bacon. Serve warm.

MARY LOU COOK
WELCHES, OREGON

VELVEETA® CHEESY POTATOES *Brand Winner*

SUNDAY NIGHT SPICY CHEESY SAUSAGE-SPUD BAKE

MAKES 8 SERVINGS

Prep: 25 min., Cook: 12 min., Bake: 40 min., Stand: 5 min.

1 (16-ounce) package JIMMY DEAN Premium Pork Sausage
PAM® Cooking Spray
1 large shallot, finely chopped
1 garlic clove, minced
1 (10-ounce) can ROTEL® Diced Tomatoes and Green Chilies, undrained
1 (10.23-ounce) package Kraft VELVEETA® Cheesy Au Gratin Potatoes
¼ cup chopped fresh parsley, divided
3 cups milk
8 large eggs
2 tablespoons BISQUICK® Original All-Purpose Baking Mix
½ teaspoon MORTON® Iodized Salt
KENMORE ELITE® Cooking Range

COOK sausage in a skillet over medium-high heat, stirring until it crumbles and is no longer pink. Transfer sausage to a 13- x 9-inch baking dish coated with cooking spray, using a slotted spoon; reserve drippings in skillet.
SAUTÉ shallot and garlic in drippings over medium heat 2 minutes or until tender.
SPOON shallot mixture evenly over sausage. Pour tomatoes over sausage mixture. Set aside cheese mix packet from Au Gratin Potatoes. Spread potatoes over tomatoes.
WHISK together reserved cheese mix, 2 tablespoons parsley, milk, and next 3 ingredients; pour over sausage mixture, covering potatoes completely.
BAKE, uncovered, at 375° for 36 minutes or until a knife inserted in center comes out clean and top begins to brown. Remove from oven; let stand 5 minutes. Sprinkle with remaining 2 tablespoons parsley. Serve immediately.

ELLEN CAVALLARO
BERKELEY HEIGHTS, NEW JERSEY

NESTLÉ TOLL HOUSE® *Brand Winner*

SHORTBREAD FUDGE CAKE

MAKES 2 DOZEN

Prep: 25 min., Bake: 50 min.

1 cup butter, softened
2½ cups all-purpose flour, divided
1½ cups granulated sugar, divided
½ teaspoon MORTON® Iodized Salt
¾ cup coarsely chopped pecans
1 (12-ounce) package NESTLÉ® Toll House Semi-Sweet Chocolate Morsels
¾ cup butter
4 large eggs
2 teaspoons vanilla extract
Powdered sugar
Sweetened whipped cream or vanilla ice cream (optional)
Chocolate shavings (optional)

BEAT 1 cup softened butter in a large mixing bowl at medium speed with an electric mixer until creamy.
STIR together 2 cups flour, ½ cup granulated sugar, and salt. Add to butter mixture, beating until crumbly. Stir in pecans.
PRESS dough evenly into an ungreased 13- x 9-inch pan.
BAKE at 350° for 25 minutes or until golden.
MICROWAVE chocolate morsels and ¾ cup butter in a 2-quart glass bowl at HIGH 1½ minutes or until melted, stirring twice.
WHISK in eggs, vanilla, remaining 1 cup granulated sugar, and remaining ½ cup flour until smooth. Pour chocolate mixture over prepared crust.
BAKE at 350° for 25 minutes or until set. (Do not overbake.) Cool completely in pan on a wire rack. Cut into 24 bars. Transfer bars to wax paper; dust with powdered sugar. Store bars in an airtight container. If desired, serve with whipped cream or ice cream, and sprinkle with chocolate shavings.

AMY ZITTA
STARKVILLE, MISSISSIPPI

Cook-Off 2003 Bonus Section

DOLE® Brand Winner

PRALINE-FILLED CARROT CAKE

MAKES 12 SERVINGS

Prep: 1 hr., Cook: 30 min., Bake: 23 min., Cool: 10 min.

- 1 (16-ounce) bag baby carrots
- 3 cups all-purpose flour
- 2⅔ cups sugar
- 1½ teaspoons baking powder
- 1½ teaspoons baking soda
- 1 teaspoon MORTON® Iodized Salt
- 2 teaspoons ground cinnamon
- 1⅓ cups vegetable oil
- 6 large eggs
- 1 (11-ounce) can DOLE® Mandarin Oranges, drained
- 1 tablespoon vanilla extract
- ¾ cup chopped pecans
- ½ cup sweetened flaked coconut
- Cinnamon-Cream Cheese Frosting
- Praline Cream Filling
- Spiced Pecans

GREASE and flour 3 (9-inch) round cakepans; set aside.

COOK carrots in boiling water to cover 20 to 30 minutes or until tender. Drain carrots, and let cool slightly. Coarsely mash carrots, using a potato masher, in pan or in a food processor until smooth (you will need 1½ cups).

COMBINE 3 cups flour and next 5 ingredients. Make a well in center of mixture. Add oil and next 3 ingredients. Beat 1 minute at low speed with an electric mixer; increase speed to medium, and beat 30 seconds. Stir in mashed carrots, pecans, and coconut. Pour batter into prepared pans.

BAKE at 350° for 23 minutes or until a wooden pick inserted in center comes out clean. (Do not overbake.) Cool in pans on wire racks 10 minutes; remove and cool completely on wire racks.

SPOON 2 tablespoons Cinnamon-Cream Cheese Frosting in center of a cake plate; top with 1 cake layer. Pipe or spread a 1-inch-wide border of frosting around outside top edge of cake layer. Spread a 2-inch circle of frosting in center of cake layer. Spread about half of Praline Cream Filling around unfrosted portion on top of cake layer.

TOP with 1 cake layer, and repeat procedure on top of second cake layer with frosting and filling. Top with remaining cake layer, and spread remaining frosting on top and sides of cake. Garnish with Spiced Pecans. Store in refrigerator.

Cinnamon-Cream Cheese Frosting:

MAKES ABOUT 5 CUPS

Prep: 10 min.

- 1 (8-ounce) package PHILADELPHIA® Cream Cheese, softened
- ½ cup butter, softened
- 2 teaspoons ground cinnamon
- 1 teaspoon vanilla extract
- 4½ cups sifted powdered sugar

BEAT first 4 ingredients at medium speed with an electric mixer until fluffy. Gradually add sugar, beating to spreading consistency.

Praline Cream Filling:

MAKES ½ CUP

Prep: 5 min., Cook: 5 min.

- 6 tablespoons butter
- 6 tablespoons light brown sugar
- ¼ cup heavy whipping cream
- 1 teaspoon vanilla extract
- 1 teaspoon bourbon

MELT butter in a saucepan over medium heat. Stir in brown sugar and whipping cream; cook, stirring constantly, until mixture comes to a boil. Reduce heat, and boil gently, uncovered, 3 minutes, stirring occasionally. Remove from heat. **STIR** in vanilla and bourbon. Cool to spreading consistency, stirring occasionally.

Spiced Pecans:

MAKES ABOUT ½ CUP

Prep: 5 min., Bake: 12 min.

- ¼ cup firmly packed brown sugar
- 1 tablespoon TROPICANA® PURE PREMIUM Orange Juice
- 1 teaspoon ground cinnamon
- ½ cup pecan halves

WHISK together first 3 ingredients in a small bowl. Add pecans; toss to coat. **SPREAD** pecan in a lightly greased 8-inch square pan. Bake at 350° for 10 to 12 minutes or until pecans are toasted and syrup is bubbly, stirring once. **POUR** pecan mixture out onto a wire rack lined with aluminum foil. Gently separate pecans with a fork, and let cool.

JENNIFER OWEN
MARION, INDIANA

HUNT'S® Brand Winner

BAKED CHICKEN-AND-CHEESE ENCHILADAS

MAKES 5 SERVINGS

Prep: 20 min., Cook: 10 min., Bake: 20 min.

- 1 (8-ounce) package PHILADELPHIA® Cream Cheese, softened
- 2 cups chopped cooked chicken
- 1 (4-ounce) can diced green chiles
- ¼ cup chopped onion
- ½ teaspoon salt
- ½ teaspoon pepper
- 3 cups (12 ounces) shredded Monterey Jack cheese, divided
- 10 (6-inch) corn tortillas
- 1 (14.5-ounce) can HUNT'S® Petite Diced Tomatoes With Mild Green Chilies
- 1 (15-ounce) can tomato sauce
- ½ cup whipping cream
- Toppings: sour cream, shredded lettuce

STIR together first 6 ingredients and 1 cup cheese in a large bowl until blended. **WRAP** tortillas in heavy-duty plastic wrap; heat in microwave according to package directions. Spoon about ⅓ cup chicken mixture down center of each tortilla; roll up. Place in a lightly greased 13- x 9-inch baking dish.

COOK diced tomatoes, tomato sauce, and cream in a 2-quart saucepan over medium-high heat, stirring often, 10 minutes or until thoroughly heated. Pour tomato mixture evenly over tortillas, spreading to ends of tortillas; sprinkle with remaining 2 cups cheese.

BAKE at 350° for 20 minutes or until cheese melts and tomato mixture is bubbly. Top with sour cream and lettuce.

STEPHANIE WOOD
WOODSTOCK, GEORGIA

Metric Equivalents

The recipes that appear in this cookbook use the standard United States method for measuring liquid and dry or solid ingredients (teaspoons, tablespoons, and cups). The information on this chart is provided to help cooks outside the U.S. successfully use these recipes. All equivalents are approximate.

METRIC EQUIVALENTS FOR DIFFERENT TYPES OF INGREDIENTS

A standard cup measure of a dry or solid ingredient will vary in weight depending on the type of ingredient. A standard cup of liquid is the same volume for any type of liquid. Use the following chart when converting standard cup measures to grams (weight) or milliliters (volume).

Standard Cup	Fine Powder	Grain	Granular	Liquid Solids	Liquid
	(ex. flour)	(ex. rice)	(ex. sugar)	(ex. butter)	(ex. milk)
1	140 g	150 g	190 g	200 g	240 ml
¾	105 g	113 g	143 g	150 g	180 ml
⅔	93 g	100 g	125 g	133 g	160 ml
½	70 g	75 g	95 g	100 g	120 ml
⅓	47 g	50 g	63 g	67 g	80 ml
¼	35 g	38 g	48 g	50 g	60 ml
⅛	18 g	19 g	24 g	25 g	30 ml

USEFUL EQUIVALENTS FOR DRY INGREDIENTS BY WEIGHT

(To convert ounces to grams, multiply the number of ounces by 30.)

1 oz	=	¹⁄₁₆ lb	=	30 g
4 oz	=	¼ lb	=	120 g
8 oz	=	½ lb	=	240 g
12 oz	=	¾ lb	=	360 g
16 oz	=	1 lb	=	480 g

USEFUL EQUIVALENTS FOR LENGTH

(To convert inches to centimeters, multiply the number of inches by 2.5.)

1 in					=	2.5 cm		
6 in	=	½ ft	=		=	15 cm		
12 in	=	1 ft			=	30 cm		
36 in	=	3 ft	=	1 yd	=	90 cm		
40 in					=	100 cm	=	1 m

USEFUL EQUIVALENTS FOR LIQUID INGREDIENTS BY VOLUME

¼ tsp	=						1 ml
½ tsp	=						2 ml
1 tsp	=						5 ml
3 tsp	=	1 tbls			=	½ fl oz	=	15 ml
	=	2 tbls	=	⅛ cup	=	1 fl oz	=	30 ml
	=	4 tbls	=	¼ cup	=	2 fl oz	=	60 ml
	=	5⅓ tbls	=	⅓ cup	=	3 fl oz	=	80 ml
	=	8 tbls	=	½ cup	=	4 fl oz	=	120 ml
	=	10⅔ tbls	=	⅔ cup	=	5 fl oz	=	160 ml
	=	12 tbls	=	¾ cup	=	6 fl oz	=	180 ml
	=	16 tbls	=	1 cup	=	8 fl oz	=	240 ml
	=	1 pt	=	2 cups	=	16 fl oz	=	480 ml
	=	1 qt	=	4 cups	=	32 fl oz	=	960 ml
						33 fl oz	=	1000 ml = 1 l

USEFUL EQUIVALENTS FOR COOKING/OVEN TEMPERATURES

	Fahrenheit	Celsius	Gas Mark
Freeze Water	32° F	0° C	
Room Temperature	68° F	20° C	
Boil Water	212° F	100° C	
Bake	325° F	160° C	3
	350° F	180° C	4
	375° F	190° C	5
	400° F	200° C	6
	425° F	220° C	7
	450° F	230° C	8
Broil			Grill

Menu Index

This menu lists every menu by suggested occasion. Recipes in bold type are provided with the menu. Suggested accompaniments are in regular typeface.

MENUS FOR SPECIAL OCCASIONS

A New Year's Menu From South Carolina

Serves 8

page 16

Michelle's Baked Ham   Michelle's Black-Eyed Peas
Esau's Collard Greens   Esau's Hoppin' John
Bob's Squab
Cheese grits   Cornbread

A Texas Football Buffet

Serves 6 to 8

page 18

Gorditas With Turkey Mole
Chili Con Carne
Buzz's Pot of Beans
Tortilla chips, salsa, guacamole, margaritas
Texas Sheet Cake

Feast for the Fireworks

Serves 8

page 162

Shrimp Rolls
Sweet-and-Savory Burgers
Potato Salad   Fresh sliced tomatoes
Marinated Green Beans With Tomatoes, Olives, and Feta
Chewy Red, White, and Blue Cookies
Fresh Blackberry Pie   Berry Blue Fizz

Sunday Brunch

Serves 8 to 10

page 166

Bacon-and-Egg Casserole   Pigs in a Blanket
Quick Double-Cheese Grits   Sliced fresh tomatoes
Fresh Fruit Salad With Orange-Ginger Syrup
Peach Streusel Muffins
Coffee   Orange juice

Wrappin' Picnic

Serves 3

page 168

Garden Wrap, Turkey Wrap, or
Mediterranean Wrap
Chilled Watermelon Soup
Sticky Fingers
Apple Lemonade
Cayenne Lemonade

Game-Day Menu

Serves 6

page 197

Sweet 'n' Savory Snack Mix
Zesty Santa Fe Salsa with
red and blue tortilla chips
Pineapple-Turkey Melts
Double-Chip Oatmeal Cookies

Wedding Brunch

Serves 6 to 8

page 197

Curried Pineapple
Shrimp-and-Artichoke Quiche
Vinaigrette over gourmet mixed greens
Croissants
Orange juice, sparkling wine

Fall Brunch

Serves 6 to 8

page 204

Balsamic Pork Chops With Apples
Farmer's Oven-Baked Omelet
Cornbread Waffles
Jalapeño-Pecan-Mustard Butter

The Season's Best Menu

Serves 6
page 210
Hot Spiced Wine
Trick or Treat Popcorn
Assorted Cheddar cheeses and crackers
Flank Steak With Tomato-Olive Relish
Garlic Grits
Mixed green salad
Creamy Garlic Salad Dressing
Roasted Pumpkin Seeds
Crispy Sticks
Pumpkin Cake With Little Ghosts

Thanksgiving Menu

Serves 8
page 230
Roasted Butternut Squash Bisque With Marmalade Cream
Apple Brandy Turkey   Cornbread Dressing
Double Cranberry-Apple Sauce
Green Beans With Grape Tomatoes
Potato Casserole With Caramelized Onions
Buttery Herb-Cheese Muffins
Ginger-Pear Cobbler

Festive Feast

Serves 6 to 8
page 240
Extra-Creamy Dried Beef Dip
Marinated Beef Tenderloin
Sugar-and-Spice Acorn Squash
Italian Green Beans With Onion and Basil
Spinach-and-Strawberry Salad With
Tart Poppy Seed Dressing

Holiday Fiesta

Serves 8
page 242
Asparagus-and-Mushroom Tostadas With Goat Cheese
Pistachio-Crusted Lamb Rack With
Cranberry-Black Bean Relish
Ancho Mashers
Roasted Root Vegetables
Hazelnut-Chocolate Truffles
Fig-Walnut Pudding With Rum Sauce

Creole Christmas Dinner

Serves 8
page 250
Spicy-Sweet Smoked Turkey Breast
Cranberry Jezebel Sauce
Shrimp-and-Ham Stuffed Mirlitons
Louise's Cornbread Dressing
After-the-Dance Pralines

Celebration Supper

Serves 6
page 258
Whiskey Sours
Potato-and-Blue Cheese Pastries
Skillet Filets Mignons
Buttery Broccoli Medley
Beer-Parmesan Rolls
Lemon Chess Pie

Classic Holiday Menu

Serves 6 to 8
page 276
Butternut Squash Soup
Creamy Crawfish Pasta
Garlic-Orange Roast Pork
Suppertime Pancakes
Nana's Collard Greens
Cranberry Conserve
Mama's Fudge
Coconut Cake

Holiday Dinner

Serves 8
page 294
Baked Artichoke Dip
Rosemary Rib Roast
Creamy Lemon-Poppy Seed Mashed Potatoes
Bourbon Carrots
Asparagus Amandine
Lime-and-Macadamia Nut Tart
Winter Wassail

MENUS FOR THE FAMILY

Italian Family Feast
Serves 6
page 34
Spinach-Red Pepper Crostini
Mixed green salad with
Creamy Gorgonzola Dressing
White Spaghetti and Meatballs
Orange Cream Pie

Family Favorites Supper
Serves 4
page 72
Chicken-Fried Steak
Three-Cheese Mashed Potato Casserole
Iceberg Lettuce Wedges With
Blue Cheese Dressing
Iced tea

Light Mexican Menu
Serves 6 to 8
page 128
Beefy Taco Salad or
Pork Tacos With Pineapple Salsa
Smashed Pinto Beans   Tex-Mex Rice With Corn
Light beer

Casual Weeknight Supper
Serves 8
page 142
Meatball Lasagna
Roasted Onion Salad
Parmesan Crisps
Ice cream

Southern Supper
Serves 4
page 178
Our Best Southern Fried Chicken
Tee's Corn Pudding
Baby Blue Salad
Key Lime Pie

Weeknight Meatless Menu
Serves 6
page 197
Blue cheese dressing over gourmet mixed greens
Spanish-Style Lentils and Rice
Breadsticks
Choco Cupcakes

Southwestern Dinner
Serves 6
page 197
Zesty Santa Fe Salsa with
red and blue tortilla chips
Grilled steaks
Tomato Grits
Tex-Mex Layered Salad
Lime sherbet

A Simple Pasta Supper
Serves 6
page 279
Pasta With Sausage and Kale
Holiday Citrus and Greens
Toasted Pizza Crust Wedges

WHEN COMPANY IS COMING

Company Supper
Serves 6
page 98
**Grilled Lamb Chops With Chipotle
and Cilantro Oils**
Onion Risotto
**Asparagus, Roasted Beet, and
Goat Cheese Salad**
Ginger Pound Cake   Ice cream

Special Occasion Brunch
Serves 10 to 12
page 118
Champagne Punch   Iced tea
Sun-Dried Tomato Cheesecake
Molasses-Coffee Glazed Ham or **Turkey Breast**
Lemon-Marinated Asparagus
Grand Oranges and Strawberries
Grits   Biscuits
Blueberry Bread Pudding

Fuss-Free Dinner From the Grill
Serves 6
page 124
Citrus Party Olives
Rosemary Grilled Flank Steak or
Lamb Chops
Italian Eggplant Vinaigrette
Smoked Mozzarella Pasta Salad
Very Berry Sundaes

An Easy Backyard Cookout
Serves 8 to 10
page 138
Barbecue Bean Dip and chips
Barbara's Big Juicy Burgers   Flavored ketchups
Horseradish Spread   **Pimiento Cheese**
Marinated Green Tomatoes   **Grilled Red Onions**
Five-Bean Bake   **Potato Cobb Salad**
Over-the-Moon Banana Pudding
Homemade Orange Soda

South-of-the-Border Brunch
Serves 6 to 8
page 197
Southwestern Brunch Casserole
Tomato Grits
Mixed fruit salad
Pineapple-Coconut Coffee Cake

Casual Supper Club
Serves 6 to 8
page 197
Savory Tomato-Bacon Biscuit Bites
Chicken-and-Sausage Jambalaya,
Light Italian Casserole, or **Chicken-and-Pepper Pasta**
Tossed salad
French bread
Peanut Butter-Brownie Trifle

Elegant Supper Club
Serves 8
page 197
Savory Tomato-Bacon Biscuit Bites
Deli-roasted chickens
Pear-and-Cranberry Wild Rice Salad (double recipe)
Dinner rolls
Bakery cheesecake and fresh strawberries

Autumn Menu
Serves 4
page 217
Glazed Roasted Chicken
Sweet Onion Risotto   Snow peas
Lemon Chess Pie

Vegetarian Dinner
Serves 6
page 236
Butternut Squash-Lime Soup
Polenta Lasagna With Cream Sauce
Salad With Dijon Vinaigrette

Recipe Title Index

This index alphabetically lists every recipe by exact title.
All microwave recipe page numbers are preceded by an "M."

338

Month-by-Month Index

This index alphabetically lists every food article and accompanying recipes
by month. All microwave recipe page numbers are preceded by an "M."

General Recipe Index

*This index lists every recipe by food category and/or major ingredient.
All microwave recipe page numbers are preceded by an "M."*

Sausage *(continued)*

    Skillet Supper, Chicken-and-Sausage, 49
    Stew, Frogmore, 181
    Stuffing, Sausage, 255
SEAFOOD. *See also* **Crab, Crawfish, Fish, Oysters, Salmon, Shrimp.**
    Pizza, Seafood Alfredo, 236
SEASONINGS. *See also* **Marinades, Oils.**
    Barbecue Rub, 130
    Barbecue Rub, All-Purpose, 130
    Basil Puree, 208
    Marinade, Italian, 180
    Marinade, Zesty Chicken, 180
    Roux, 111
    Rub, Brisket, 188
    Rub, Mediterranean, 180
    Salt, Dragon, 236
    Spice Blend, Southwestern, 180
SHRIMP
    Appetizers
        Afterburners, 159
        Bundles With Chive Butter Sauce, Crispy Shrimp, 91
        Rolls With Sweet Soy Sauce, Jumbo Shrimp, 248
        Steamed Shrimp, 206
    Burgers, Shrimp, 110
    Casserole, Cheesy Shrimp-and-Grits, 28
    Chowder, Artichoke-Shrimp, 91
    Coconut-Pecan Shrimp With Orange Dipping Sauce, 212
    Creole, Shrimp, 109
    Destin, Shrimp, 314
    Eggs Benedict, Shrimp-and-Grits, 53
    Firecracker Shrimp, 144
    Fried Rice, Spicy Shrimp-and-Pineapple, 285
    Fried Shrimp, 109
    Garlic Shrimp and Grits, 246
    Grilled Shrimp With Smoky Sweet Sauce, Mexican-, 32
    Gumbo, Shrimp-Crab, 111
    Marinated Shrimp With Louis Sauce, Citrus-, 66
    Mirlitons, Shrimp-and-Ham Stuffed, 251
    Pesto Shrimp Over Rice, Texas, 327
    Quiche, Shrimp-and-Artichoke, 196
    Rémoulade, Shrimp, 146
    Rice, Shrimp With, 219
    Risotto With Shrimp and Asparagus, 86
    Roasted Red Pepper Cream, Shrimp With, 97
    Rolls, Shrimp, 162
    Sauce, Creamy Shrimp, 53
    Stew, Frogmore, 181
    Tarts, Shrimp 'n' Grits, 254
SLAWS
    Coleslaw, 252
    Creamy Sweet Coleslaw, 105
    Freezer Slaw, 106
SLOW COOKER
    Ribs and Beans, Spicy-Sweet, 314
    Ribs, Slow-Cooker Barbecue, 160

SOUFFLÉS
    Grand Marnier Soufflés, 318
SOUPS. *See also* **Chili, Chowders, Gumbos, Jambalayas, Stews.**
    Acorn Squash-and-Apple Soup, Curried, 221
    Black Bean Soup, 219
    Butternut Squash Bisque, Roasted, 230
    Butternut Squash-Lime Soup, 236
    Butternut Squash Soup, 276
    Carrot-and-Parsnip Soup, Gingered, 221
    Cheddar-Potato Soup, M283
    Chicken Soup, Mexican, 63
    Egg Drop Soup, Spinach, 65
    Plum Soup, Chilled, 161
    Pork Rind Soup, 33
    Potato Soup, Baked, 29
    Pumpkin Soup, Creamy Southwestern, 221
    She-Crab Soup, 137
    Turkey Soup With Cornbread Dressing Dumplings, 239
    Watermelon Soup, Chilled, 168
SPAGHETTI
    Carbonara, Spaghetti, 123
    Salad, Asian Peanut-and-Pasta, 127
    Sauce, Sicilian Spaghetti, 62
    Tetrazzini, Ham, 174
    Tetrazzini, Turkey, 257
    White Spaghetti and Meatballs, 34
SPINACH
    Baby Spinach With Pine Nuts, 64
    Crostini, Spinach-Red Pepper, 34
    Holiday Spinach With Red Pepper Ribbons, 260
    Omelet, Spinach, Cheddar, and Bacon, 204
    Penne With Spinach and Feta, 170
    Quesadillas, Greek, 61
    Quiche, Mushroom-Spinach-Swiss, 59
    Salad, Spinach, 246
    Salad With Tart Poppy Seed Dressing, Spinach-and-Strawberry, 241
    Soup, Spinach Egg Drop, 65
SPREADS
    Cheese
        Cream Cheese-and-Olive Pimiento Cheese, 315
        Horseradish Spread, 139
        Pesto Goat Cheese, 110
        Pesto-Goat Cheese Spread, 208
        Pimiento Cheese, 139, 315
        Pimiento Cheese, Jalapeño, 315
        Pimiento Cheese, Pecan, 315
    Honey-Nut Spread, 46
    Not-So-Secret Sauce, 139
SQUASH. *See also* **Zucchini.**
    Acorn Squash-and-Apple Soup, Curried, 221
    Acorn Squash, Sugar-and-Spice, 241
    Butternut
        Bisque, Roasted Butternut Squash, 230
        Soup, Butternut Squash, 276
        Soup, Butternut Squash-Lime, 236
    Casserole, Easy Squash-and- Corn, 69
    Casserole, Hearty Tex-Mex Squash-Chicken, 107

    Mirlitons, Shrimp-and-Ham Stuffed, 251
    Salad, Squash, M184
STEWS. *See also* **Chili, Chowders, Gumbos, Jambalayas, Soups.**
    Beef Stew, Hungarian, 35
    Brunswick Stew, 29
    Chicken Stew, Greek-Style, 219
    Chicken Stew, Speedy, 42
    Frogmore Stew, 181
STRAWBERRIES. *See also* **Salads.**
    Dip, Strawberries With Brown Sugar-and-Sour Cream, 93
    Dip, Strawberries With Fluffy Cream Cheese, 93
    Dip, Strawberries With Mint Yogurt, 93
    Dip, Strawberries With Vanilla Pudding, 93
    Jam, Strawberry-Port, 134
    Oranges and Strawberries, Grand, 119
    Pops, Strawberry-Orange, 179
    Salad, Strawberry-Pretzel, 290
    Sauce, Strawberry, 55
    Sorbet, Strawberry, 171
    Trifle, Strawberry-Sugar Biscuit, 84
STUFFING. *See also* **Dressings.**
    Sausage Stuffing, 255
SWEET POTATOES
    Cake With Coconut Filling and Caramel Frosting, Sweet Potato, 329
    Casserole, Sweet Potato, M24
    Mashed-Potato Bake, Swirled, 293
    Praline Sweet Potatoes and Apples, 260
SYRUPS
    Bourbon Syrup, 233
    Maple-Banana Syrup, 47
    Mint Simple Syrup, 129
    Mint Sugar Syrup, Fresh, 89
    Mocha Latte Syrup, 46
    Orange-Ginger Syrup, 167
    Sugar Syrup, 224

TACOS
    Pasta, Easy Taco, 124
    Pork Tacos With Pineapple Salsa, 128
    Salad, Beefy Taco, 128
    Wrapidos, Tacos, 172
TASTE OF THE SOUTH
    Bread, Sally Lunn, 27
    Brisket Rub, 188
    Butter, Blackberry, 27
    Cake, Express Pineapple Upside-Down, 65
    Cake, Skillet Pineapple Upside-Down, 65
    Eggs, Basic Deviled, 88
    Main Dishes
        Brisket, Traditional, 188
        Oysters Rockefeller, 272
        Oysters, Southwest Fried, 45
    Mint Julep, Classic, 129
    Sauce, Brisket Mopping, 188
    Sauce, Brisket Red, 188
    Soup, She-Crab, 137
    Stew, Frogmore, 181
    Syrup, Mint Simple, 129

Favorite Recipes Journal

Jot down your family's and your favorite recipes for quick and handy reference. And don't forget to include the dishes that drew rave reviews when company came for dinner.

RECIPE	SOURCE/PAGE	REMARKS